Funeral Customs The World Over

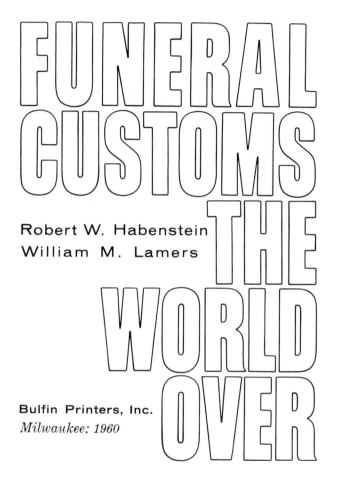

FUNERAL CUSTOMS THE WORLD OVER

Robert W. Habenstein
William M. Lamers

Bulfin Printers, Inc.
Milwaukee: 1960

First Edition

Preface

September 1, 1960

The intent of this book is to present a variety of profiles of funeral customs and procedures drawn from cultures, peoples, and nationality groups the world over. Inasmuch as such groupings number well into the thousands, no attempt is here made to provide a comprehensive, encyclopedic account of funerary behavior as it is found everywhere among all human groups.

Selections were made as judiciously as possible with an eye toward: giving adequate representation to the patterns of death beliefs and burial procedures defined by the major world religions, Christian, Hebrew, Buddhist, Hindu and Mohammedan; presenting a world-wide sampling of the funeral folkways in folk and tribal groups; and finally describing in some detail the European mortuary complex, in order to help make clearer the cultural roots of much American funerary behavior.

With respect to the latter, the reverse—American customs migrating to England and the Continent, among other places—is also at times indicated, though the process turns out for the most part as a piece-meal rather than as a wholesale incorporation.

The division of the chapters into sections follows closely but not identically the system used in the *Outline of World Cultures*, a handbook for the Human Relations Area Files, Yale University. The area designations of Asia, Middle East, Africa and Oceania, and the countries subsumed under them are followed, except that the western portion of Russia is included with Europe, and the Western Hemisphere is divided into two major cultural areas: Latin-American countries and Mexico; and Canada and the United States.

In keeping with the desires of the National Funeral Directors Association, the sponsors of this book, to add increments of professional knowledge to the literature of the field of funeral service, a compilation of brief histories of state funeral directors' associations is appended. These sketches were in most cases prepared by funeral directors themselves or through their auspices, and stand apart from the work of the authors. Editorial assistance for this section was provided by Robert A. Walczak. The second Appendix recapitulates valuable and interesting information on the rules and procedures of specific religious groups and fraternal organizations in the United States, regarding funeral services. Original research for this compilation was performed by John A. Meyers.

The research upon which the book rests has its bases in information secured from officers in the Foreign Service of the United States, from their counterparts in foreign diplomatic and consular agencies in this country, from scholars, competent observers and funeral service functionaries abroad, from the extensive materials in the Human Relations Area Files branch at the University of Chicago, from conventional library sources, and from funeral directors in America, several hundred of whom wrote careful accounts of patterns of funeral procedures in their sections of the country.

Recognition is elsewhere given to the many who have contributed time, effort and their good graces to the problem of securing reliable information. For those not otherwise mentioned or whose assistance may not have been adequately rewarded in the chapter notes, the thanks and gratitude of the authors are here tendered to Howard F. Barnard, Dr. Stephan and Suzanne de Borhegyi, George DeGrace, Charles D. Franz, Fred L. Hadley, James O'Hagan, Jr., Lindsey P. Henderson, Jr., Vernon Hill, Edward C. and Gail R. Johnson, Muriel Rae Kaufman, Joyce D. Kujawa, Dr. Charles Nichols, Dr. Donnell M. Pappenfort, Dr. Robert Sheldon, Dr. Robert F. G. Spier, and John W. Yopp, Jr.

Irene Zanoni typed much of the original draft, and Ann Milbank typed the final manuscript.

The manuscript was read, criticized, and improved by members of the Special Publications Committee of the National Funeral Directors Association: H. Fremont Alderson, Chairman, Harry J. Gilligan, and Jerry Spears. Helpful suggestions were also made by Arthur Taylor, currently President of the Association; and yeoman service in expediting the research, organization of materials and the production of the book was rendered by its Executive Secretary Howard C. Raether. Jane Habenstein lent her services to the editing of the book's copy, and assisted in much of the basic research. The aesthetic merit in the presentation of illustrative material derives from the talents of William F. Egner, Jr. Special assistance in research and writing of manuscripts was given by specialists in the funeral customs of various cultures: C. M. Austin de Silva, the Sinhalese; Sevil Erel, Turkey; Adrian Fochi, Rumania; Dr. Jane C. Goodale, Tiwi; Dr. Joseph T. Howard, Philippines; Paul R. Keenan, Canada; Howard C. Raether, United States; and Drs. Wilson D. and Ruth S. Wallis, Santee Sioux.

A few terms of reference frequently used in the book may need clarification. "Undertaker" in a general sense pertains to a functionary who undertakes to provide mortuary goods, funeral paraphernalia, and a minimum of personal services to the bereaved. In the United States the term has application to those functionaries of the nineteenth and early twentieth centuries prior to the advent of the funeral home. The term "undertaker" has been applied to persons in other cultures and nations who are more or less identifiable with the nineteenth century American funeral functionary. Or, if some group abroad preferred to designate itself by the name "undertaker," the authors accepted the self-designation.

The term "funeral director" is used in general to refer to funeral functionaries whose supplying of mortuary goods is considered in their eyes to be subordinate to the variety of personal services they offer the bereaved. Again, in a few cases where the self-designation of a group was "funeral director" but the services were perhaps less personal, the authors were content to accept the designated term rather than translate the term to "undertaker." The context of the term as used should make the meaning clear. The authors have termed the traditional wedge-shaped form of burial receptacle, which is usually of the simpler or less ornate type, "coffin." On the other hand, within the original sense of "casket" as a jewel box, a burial receptacle of the rectangular shape, adorned in an effort to add an aesthetic quality, has been referred to as a "casket." Although there may be more than a trace of ambiguity in their usage, the terms for the most part are expected to communicate differences of some significance, both to the lay reader and to those engaged in the field of funeral service.

In a work of this nature the authors must necessarily rely upon the accounts of ethnologists, anthropologists, interested observers, cultural relations specialists of various countries, religious officials, and a host of others whose eyes may not always have seen the same nor have their points of view led to the same interpretations. As far as possible the authors have attempted to maintain an objective and neutral position, holding the belief that nothing human, wherever found, is foreign to their concern.

ROBERT W. HABENSTEIN
University of Missouri
Columbia, Missouri

WILLIAM M. LAMERS
Milwaukee, Wisconsin

Contents

Funeral Customs The World Over

Part One

Stone elephants on approach to Ming
Tombs, Nanking, China

Asia

Religious philosophy mingled with
mysticism . . . ancestor worship a
dominant theme . . . geomancers and
diviners . . . happiness in death . . .
the grimness of air burials . . . hotels
for the dead . . . the noise and color
of funeral processions . . . burning
ghats and whirling prayer wheels . . .
Buddhist saffron and Shinto gold . . .
and the spirit tablet in the household
shrine

Milwaukee Public Museum

Funeral procession in Canton, China

Chapter 1

China

Death, Shen *and* Kwei

Chinese death beliefs and practices spring largely from their religion, which is a bewildering intermingling of Buddhism, Confucianism, Taoism, and Shamanism. Of particular significance is their belief in a duality of the soul. The principal soul, *shen,* represents an association with light, warmth, productivity, personality. The lesser soul, *kwei,* reflects darkness, cold, sterility, animal nature.[1] Both separate and leave the body at the moment of death. If interment is not properly carried out, or, if indeed the dead is not buried at all, it is possible for the animal soul (*kwei*) to re-enter the remains and walk around as a vampire. And, as the ghost possesses only an animal soul, it will not remember any of his old friends, but will attack any one it meets and try to do him harm or even kill him.[2] The Chinese, however, do believe strongly in an afterlife in which

1

Procession is led by women carrying
picture of deceased

Followed by men bearing favorite
sedan chair of master

there is close communion between the spirits of the dead and
the world of the living. In traditional Chinese religious thought,
the afterworld is divided into three planes. The highest, the
Upper Heaven, is governed by an emperor surrounded by a
court of many lesser gods. In the second, the Western Heaven,
Buddha rules, with another court of subordinate deities. In the
third, the Lower Spirit World, a place of entry, a ruler and ten
judges examine the records of the newly dead. If they have been
virtuous on earth, they may become gods in the two higher
heavens, or reincarnated to luxury or high position on earth.
If wicked, they are terribly punished by torture of confinement
or by loathesome reincarnation as rats and worms.

Ties between the world and afterworld are believed to be
very close. High office is judged to carry with it power over
lesser spirits, and good fortune in this world is thought to be a
reward from the spirit world, as disaster is a punishment.
"Thus," says anthropologist Hsu, "the spirit world and the hu-

P.I.P. Photo by J. Ph. Charbonnier

Musician precedes children of deceased clad
in special mourning regalia

P.I.P. Photo by J. Ph. Charbonnier

Six hired bearers carry massive coffin slung
between poles. Pall may be rented

man world are counterparts. . . . They exchange personnel.
They endorse the same virtues and condemn similar evils. . . .
In the popular mind the spiritual hierarchy is a part of the
social order just as much as the bureaucratic and political
hierarchy is. That is why it is irrelevant or even erroneous to
speak of different religions in China. . . . If two religions are
both true, they must find their place in the existing hierarchy."[3]

Ancestor Worship

Ancestor worship, set in the larger all-inclusive structure, is
the basic religion of China. The foundation of this worship is
father-son identification. Each is popularly judged according
to the other's deeds. This ancestor cult is based on three assumptions: the living owe everything to their departed ancestors, the spirit-world actions continue to affect the living, and
ancestors are interested only in their own descendants.[4]

The Chinese ethnologist, Fei, elaborates these assumptions

3

Widow, broken with grief,
is assisted in procession
by relatives

in his recent observation that: "The general view is that the spirits are partially dependent on the contributions of their descendants, which are made periodically by burning paper money, paper clothes, and paper articles. Therefore it is essential to have someone to look after one's well-being in the after-world."[5] Hence it is all-important for a man to marry and have children.

During imperial times, ancestor worship was practiced at two levels. The family worshiped its immediate ancestors, while the clan worshiped its remote ancestors. The Chinese considered as kinsmen those for whom they were required to wear mourning. Kinsmen included paternal relatives, maternal relatives, and relatives of the wife, extended to nine generations and five collateral grades. Kinsmen, all in all, included twenty-nine categories of relatives, and mourning prescriptions varied for each of these.[6]

Until recently ancestor worship seems to have been overwhelmingly and stubbornly the practice in China. Early Christian missionaries attempted to compel the native Chinese to abandon their ancestor worship, but without much success. Finally certain Protestant groups agreed to compromise the matter by allowing ancestor rites if the Chinese made it clear that these in no way replaced the true worship of God.[7] Also realizing that the worship of one God does not preclude the veneration of several generations of ancestors, the Catholic Church in China does not require her adherents to abstain from ancestor rites.[8]

With the decay of clan life in Central and North China has

Portion of a more elaborate funeral procession. Bands may play any type of music, including American jazz!

5

come a neglect of the clan shrines. Clans exist only in villages or small towns, seldom in cities. As a result, there are few clan temples in cities. Impoverished city workers know little about their clans. Most of the wage earners and lower-middle class people in Peiping a decade ago had no ancestor temples, no common clan graveyards, no clan heads. Only the more well-to-do have been clan conscious.[9]

When Death Comes

As soon as someone in a village dies, an elderly relative hurries to bring incense and food to the nearest temple to announce the event to the local god. His good will is important. He is the first major deity to be encountered by the spirit of the dead. While the people may have only vague ideas of what will happen in the next world, most agree that the spirit will have a difficult time before it reaches the Western Heaven, and that it needs friends.[10]

In most urban deaths, the diviner is called in immediately. His duties vary from practical to mystical. One of his duties is to present the police with a paper attesting the cause of death. If natural death is indicated, the police issue a passport which will enable the procession to carry the body past the guard at the city gate—Chinese cemeteries are always outside of cities. In cases of violent death, the police will not release the body for burial as long as it is needed in the solution of the crime.[11]

Another of the diviner's duties is to forecast the precise time at which the spirit in the visible form of vapor will leave the body, what its color and shape will be, what direction it will take. When the designated time comes, all leave the room. Because of the prevalent belief that to see an escaping spirit foreshadows an early death, the living must not wait in the spirit's line of departure. The diviner likewise designates an auspicious day and hour for the funeral.[12]

The world outside first learns of a death when the family hangs blue and white or blue and yellow lanterns at the front door and pastes white paper over the red good-luck strips.

6

In addition to this ceremony, it is customary in Peiping to station a drummer outside the front door, to the left of the entrance if a man has died, and to the right, if a woman. When visitors approach, he beats a tattoo. This warning gives the family a chance to drop whatever work they may be engaged in, and assume an appropriate posture of grief.[13]

As in any house in a crisis, many events take place simultaneously or nearly so. In the room where death occurred the assembled family weeps. The cries of a parent's daughters are supposed to be especially effective in opening the gates of heaven. A man who dies without daughters to bewail him is considered unfortunate.[14]

Bathing the body is the next step. In the well-to-do classes the servant who is sent to secure the water burns incense before an idol near the well, river, or lake, or burns paper money, or lights firecrackers. Thus he "buys" the water from its presiding deity. Water for bathing a body is usually heated before it is used. Although in Peiping no special ritual prescribes the manner of washing the body, in other places in China the front of the body must be bathed seven times and the back eight.

After bathing, the remains are wrapped in wadding and clothed. For the rich, the garments are silk; for the poor, cotton. Ties of the same material are used in place of buttons. In some parts of China the dead are dressed in old-fashioned garb, much like that worn by Buddhist priests. Officials are buried in their robes of office. The hair of a woman is dressed on the top of the head and adorned with ornaments of gold and jade. Gold leaf and pearls are placed in the mouth of the dead in some parts of China, and a ball of red paper mixed with incense ash is tucked between the lips.[15] After socks and shoes have been placed on the deceased, the feet are bound together with a hempen cord. This practice is rooted in a belief that if death has occurred at an unpropitious hour, evil spirits beat the body so that it jumps about. Tying the feet is therefore a precautionary measure.[16]

The washed and clothed body is now stretched out on the

Typical North-China style coffin; weight, approximately three hundred pounds

bed on the best bedding available, and it is left there while the coffin is being prepared. Friends may now view it. Over the body, but turned down from the face, a silken or cotton cloth is laid. In some places the face is masked with a sheet of paper; or, if infection has produced death, as a hygienic measure, with a book. While ordinarily a coffin is not purchased until death seems imminent, it may happen that a dutiful son will provide coffins for his parents while they still enjoy good health. Instead of alarming or depressing them, this provision pleases them because it gives assurance that they will be suitably buried. Pending their use, such coffins are stored in a coffin shop, a warehouse, or a temple.[17]

Coffins and Coffining

The Chinese coffin is both bulky and heavy—it sometimes weighs 350 pounds—and is usually made of white pine three to five inches thick, with each side, end, and the top wedged and glued together. The Chinese coffin is not rectangular like its American counterpart, but is deeper at the head end than at the foot. Generally it is lacquered black, or black and red, and highly polished by hand, although in Peiping the custom is to keep the wood unvarnished. Although the construction of the Chinese coffin is intended more for lasting qualities than for safeguarding health, its heavy construction and sealing tend

8

to preserve the body and to reduce the spread of diseases. Coffins may be bought from shops, where they are displayed and sold direct to the consumer, much like any other commodity. Better grade coffins are lined with calico or silk and padded with quilting, with a pillow for a headrest. Poor people and infants—if these are coffined at all—are buried in crudely made, thin wooden boxes.[18]

Hsu observes that: "Usually an aged person has a coffin made and stored in the clan temple long before death. The quality of the coffin is of as much importance as is the quality of a suit of clothes or a house. If the deceased or about to be deceased is a married woman, her parents' family may object if the quality of her coffin is in their estimation not fine enough. The same objection may come from a man's family if he is a married-in son-in-law."[19]

The making of coffins in China is a specialized trade. For centuries they have been fashioned of four half logs with square panels at each end. The Chinese stick tenaciously to this type of receptacle, even though the large logs, once plentiful, have long disappeared with the forests, and the wood most likely must be imported at considerable cost from southeast Asia. When heavy logs are not available, by skillfully fitting and varnishing smaller pieces, Chinese craftsmen manage to create the old solid appearance. Because of the cheapness of Chinese labor, the cost of the coffin depends largely on the cost of the wood. A poor family finds the coffin the most expensive item in a burial. To a wealthy family, however, this item is minor when compared to the total cost, which involves such items as the funeral festivities, feeding and lodging relatives and friends, hiring professional mourners, attendants, and coffin bearers, hiring and supplying equipment for the procession, and providing a grave monument or tomb.[20]

When the body is laid in the coffin, clothing of all kind is packed around it to keep it from sliding. Only furs are avoided because the Chinese fear that in its metamorphosis the spirit might enter into the animal which has yielded the pelt. Sometimes a woman's bridal garment is placed in the coffin. As

9

Overseas Chinese use European style casket; but follow custom practiced in parts of China of immediately removing dead from house in which death occurs

these sad duties are performed, the assembled relatives burst out into loud wails.[21]

In some places—but not in Peiping—bags of lime are next placed into the coffin, one for each year of the deceased's life. Poorer families do not package the lime, but sprinkle it over the body. When the packing is finished, the coffin, with the lid left slightly ajar, is placed on two stools, with the deceased's head pointing toward the door.

Mourning the Dead Body

Meanwhile many hands are busy arranging the interior of the house for the reception. On a table placed against the head of the coffin two vases are stood, holding blue and white paper flowers. Next to these stand candlesticks with candles, incense burner and incense sticks, and a pagoda-shaped oil lamp on a tall base. These objects are usually made of pewter, and are rented by a family of average means, although a wealthy family may own them. The lamp is used to illuminate the spirit tablet as long as the body remains in the house. However, the candles

10

The compound of a Buddhist temple, with funeral in progress. White arch denotes mourning

are lighted only at night. The spirit panel on which is printed the name of the deceased is the most important object in this collection because it visibly represents the spirit of the deceased. The table, likewise, has more than passing importance, since at each family meal, and when guests are fed during the funeral ceremonies, it is used to receive the food offerings to the dead.[22]

A visit of Taoist priests follows the completion of these preparations. If the deceased has led a virtuous life, the priests hang pictures of the gods near the coffin, and entreat them to admit the new candidate into the Western Heaven. If he has not lived a virtuous life, they implore the evil spirits to relinquish their hold upon him, lest his soul be lost. Simultaneously, but in a different part of the house or in a temple, Buddhist priests chant the office of the dead. This chanting may continue for three, five or seven days, or even beyond, and be repeated on successive seventh days for seven weeks, and on later anniversaries.[23]

If the deceased is a father or a mother, the sons, unmarried daughters, paternal nephews and nieces, and grandchildren re-

11

Entrance and
compound of
Shanghai's most
modern funeral home;
immediate post
World War II period

Front view of same
luxurious establishment

The main chapel; altar
in background

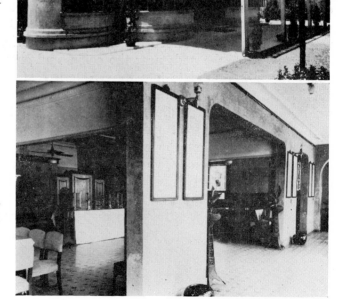

main in attendance during the day, and sometimes at night. Married daughters and their husbands are not expected to perform the duty.

While a portion of the household has been busy with certain of these tasks, the more distant members of the family and friends living nearby are personally invited to attend the funeral by sons or nephews of the deceased. Distant interested parties are sent obituary notices. For families of moderate means, these announcements are printed on large sheets of yellow paper and distributed in yellow envelopes, and on the front of each is pasted a strip of blue paper with a narrow strip of red paper pasted on the blue. The announcements provide facts concerning the dead person and the funeral.[24]

The notices sent by wealthy families are likely to be long, elaborate, fantastic, and costly. In addition to the usual necrological data, they set forth geneological and related items, long eulogies of the deceased person; his offices, achievements, good

Buddhist monks pausing while in funeral procession, North China

13

deeds, honors, virtues. Mixed with some facts will be certain fanciful incidents lifted from the classics. A repeated favorite tells how a dutiful son, desperately striving to find a remedy to cure an acutely sick parent, cuts off a portion of his flesh to throw into the medicinal brew. The age at death is generally exaggerated by five or six years. In China only the bad die young.[25]

When the beating of the drum in the courtyard tells the family that a guest is at hand, they kneel on both sides of the coffin in the order of precedence. While the guest kneels at the head, a brass wine cup is handed him into which a serving woman pours a little wine. The guest then pours the wine into a brass basin standing on the floor. Then all kowtow. When this ceremony has been performed three times, the guest weeps and the family does likewise. On days designated for their reception, guests are invited to join the family at either the noon or afternoon meal. Excellent food is served at tables in the mat-covered courtyard. After six men or six women have been placed at each table, a nephew of the deceased kowtows to each group of men, and the wife of a son or nephew to each group of women. It is considered imperative that the family should affect great humility and that they should appear indifferent to their own welfare and comfort. They must be entreated to eat.

It is customary for guests to bring gifts. Money is put into a yellow envelope with a pasted blue stripe on it. Among other gifts are satin banners and scrolls bearing the name of the giver and a motto, carts, horses and other objects all made of paper, cakes, candies, and sometimes a table of fine foods. The gift banners are carried in the procession, and the paper objects are burned. Incense is constantly burned on a table at the head of the coffin, and when the family eats food, food is also offered to the dead.[26]

The home by now has been transformed into a mood of deepest mourning. On the death of a parent, all signs of happiness are concealed. Weddings are postponed, rejoicings forbidden, and red, pink, or purple objects are either put away or

14

hidden beneath white, blue, or black material.[27] Sorrow is expressed in mourning dress, wailing and a total disregard of personal comfort and appearance.[28]

Chinese mourning customs are strictly observed. Both men and women are expected to wear an outer garment of coarse, unhemmed white calico, and the men, a cap of the same material. In some parts of China men bind this gown with a girdle of hempen rope, and both men and women wear white straw sandals. The period for wearing garments of this type extends in various places from sixty to a hundred days. While in Peiping, a man who has business is allowed to substitute a black gown with a white girdle, but he must resume his full mourning on his return home. During the sixty days he neither cuts, shaves, nor trims his hair or beard. Some Chinese wear variations of mourning clothes for as long as three years.[29]

Women are bound by much the same general mourning regulations as bind the men. For women, however, hair styling provides an additional means of expressing grief. Chinese women wind coarse black calico around their heads, and for sixty days do not wash their hair. Manchu women, on the other hand, put their traditional large Manchu hats aside, and make two braids of their hair. They use the positions of these —one may be knotted and fastened to the top of the head, while the other hangs—to indicate their relationship to the deceased.[30] Custom prohibits women from wearing silks and satin during the mourning period, and they must put aside their bracelets and other baubles, string thread through the ears in place of their earrings, and use a white bone instead of a golden hair bar. As mourning draws to a close, they may wear silver before gold. These regulations and numerous others vary with the relationship of the mourner to the deceased.[31]

Fung Shui, *The Geomantic Art*

While mourning rituals occupy the bereaved family, the geomancer is busy selecting the site of the grave. The geomantic art, *fung shui,* is practiced by special experts who by a method of computation seek favorable spots on which to build temples and tombs, or dig graves. This rite sometimes commands for whole generations the blessings of heaven and earth. De Groot notes "The fung shui of a grave, house, tomb, or temple is a fragile combination of imaginary influences of nature, fitting into one another and acting upon one another like the different parts of a machine, the slightest defect in which may bring the whole to a standstill."[32]

The length of time that a body is kept in the house before burial depends partly on the economic status of the family, partly on the age of the deceased, and partly on the diviner's ruling. For their elderly dead members, rich families observe the rule that the older and more venerable the deceased are, the longer their bodies are kept in the home. Unless grandparents are living, a son keeps the bodies of his parents longest there. Rich families bury their younger dead within three days. Poor families bury all their dead within this time. Divination is used to determine a suitable hour or day, or both. As long as the body remains in the house, incense is burned on a table near the head of the coffin, and at each family meal food is placed on the table, and paper money burned.[34]

However, the Chinese believe that to keep a body overlong in a house, even in an hermetically sealed coffin, will bring

Chinese funeral processions feature banners describing character of deceased

Photo Courtesy Vernon Hill

European Photo

16

Children carrying bamboo
shoot "flower trees"
march in the procession

White calico mourning
garments worn by
female mourners

down evil spirits. Therefore, while the fung shui professors quibble, the coffin is stored in a cottage, warehouse, or temple. The family pays rent for this occupancy. If the dead person leaves many children, it is not likely that the fung shui science will be able to provide equal benefits for all of them. This fact alone leads to quarreling and delay.[33]

The Glorious Funeral Procession

Meanwhile the family and friends of the deceased have been preparing paper gifts for the use of the spirit in the afterlife: houses, boxes of paper money, servants, carts, horses, even motor cars. It is believed that burning these will make them available in the spirit world; and so, on the eve of the funeral, they are taken to an open place and burned. The chants of Buddhist and Taoist priests rise as the flames mount, and a man with a pole beats the burning objects to keep off wandering mischievous spirits who might attempt to appropriate the gifts to their own use. As a further precaution, a watery, boiled rice is sprinkled over the flames, so that poor but beneficent spirits passing by may eat this food and leave the gifts to their rightful owner.[35]

When the relatives return from this ceremony, they find that the catafalque to be used in the funeral has been prepared. It is a heavy bamboo framework resting on thick poles. It is carried by bearers using smaller carrying poles. The body of the catafalque is covered with richly embroidered satin, and the poles are lacquered to match. Red or white are now the commonly used colors. The bodies of Chinese emperors and members of the royal family once were borne on catafalques of imperial yellow; in such cases the poles were likewise lacquered in the same color. [36]

Sometimes, where the home is large, three catafalques are used in a single funeral, the smallest to carry the body to the door of the courtyard; the middle, from the courtyard to the street; and the largest, to the place of burial. Generally, however, only one catafalque is used. This is made completely ready the night before and deposited on one of the wide streets

18

near the home. The satin coverings are then removed for the night.

On the morning of the funeral, while monks chant on, the person in charge performs the rites in the home, the family and friends remain in reverential attitude on the chairs and benches that have been placed around the room in which the sealed coffin stands. Meanwhile hired mourners wail loudly. If the service is long, the family and guests may visit, eat, sip tea, or walk about.[37] At the conclusion of the ceremony the mourners kowtow toward the coffin or the photograph of the deceased, and bearers raise the coffin and carry it, head first, from the house. This is the traditional Chinese funeral.

The procession now organizes itself. Many of the attendants at funerals are beggars, and in some places this prerogative is so firmly established as theirs that to attempt to deprive them of it might result in a riot.[38] Many of the mourners also serve as helpers at the funeral. Hsu found that death is a time of community reckoning, and that people refused to attend funerals of persons in families that had been unkind, so that the public esteem in which a family was held could be pretty well gauged by the length of its funeral processions.[39]

The sedan chair of the deceased, with his picture riding in it, is carried at the head of the procession. His cart, carriage, or automobile comes next, presumably bearing the soul, which is leading the body. Next come the male mourners. Then follows the catafalque, which is carried on the shoulders of hired bearers who are provided in multiples of eight. These vary in number according to size and weight of coffin and catafalque. The bearers wear green gowns with red designs printed on them. To keep the bearers in step a man walks beside them beating time with two pieces of wood.

After the catafalque, in strict order of precedence, follow the women mourners, in carts covered with white calico. Friends and acquaintances bring up the rear of the procession, which is colorful with satin umbrellas, banners, and many objects for burning at the grave, including flowers, plants in pots, and images of servants, all made of paper.[40] The condolence ban-

Funeral procession on Taipei. Note chief mourner carrying
spirit panel to be used in graveside ceremonies

ners brought by relatives, clan members, and friends are usually
inexpensively made of blue, black, or white silk. The inscriptions they bear praise the dead and assert that his spirit is
gone to the Western Heaven.[41]

The procession of a rich Chinese is many blocks long; and
if in a city, it winds its way slowly through the narrow streets.
Although wealthy Chinese are in a small minority, so that a
great procession cannot be said to be typical, a Shanghai report
of the 1940's showed that during a nine months' period, 1,636
funeral processions took place in one section of the city. An
estimated total of 33,000 persons marched in these processions,
an average of 200 persons each. Processions, of course, ranged
greatly in size and composition.[42]

The Chinese procession is not silent. Drums beat, horns
bray, cymbals tinkle, hired mourners and relatives wail. An
occasional evidence of Western influence may be seen in a
brass band, or in a paper funeral wreath patently based on an
Occidental original. At intervals during the procession firecrackers are fired off, and paper cut to resemble money is
scattered. The former are intended to frighten off homeless
ghosts; the latter, to bribe them.[43]

Although both men and women wail during the procession,
custom decrees that only women—usually the deceased's wife
and daughters-in-law—shall wail continuously while the coffin

20

is in the house and during the funeral procession. The closer
the kinship, the louder must be the wailing.[44] There is ample
time for it, for a procession moves slowly and sometimes is
held up altogether by important friends who halt the procession
along the way to offer sacrifices. Women mourners remain
with the marchers until the village boundary is reached, but
sons and grandsons continue to the grave.[45]

A Modern State Funeral

Lindsey P. Henderson, Jr., a funeral director in civilian life,
spent most of a decade in China and the Far East as an In-
fantry Captain. He was privileged to witness at close hand the
first state funeral authorized by the Nationalist government
after it was relocated in Formosa. His account, written expressly
for the authors follows:

> During our sojourn in Taipei, Taiwan, China, we had
> occasion to witness the funeral of one of General Chiang's
> most trusted advisers and oldest friends. This was the
> first State funeral since the Nationalist government had
> left the mainland. Because of his position in the govern-
> ment, the usual austerity ban was temporarily removed by
> presidential decree. The reader should keep in mind that
> in a Buddhist service, one or more monks or priests direct
> the proceedings from a religious standpoint. A member of
> the family and, in this case, the government, had rep-
> resentatives supervising various aspects of propriety and
> protocol. The funeral director, with the assistance of the
> above, planned and executed this intricate ancient burial
> rite. Aside from the sinful aspects of failure to observe
> the proprieties, it is a practical necessity with the Chinese
> to insure that these customs are followed. An ancient
> Chinese proverb states: "To serve those now dead as if
> they were living is the highest achievement of true filial
> piety." The following is an account of the proceedings as
> we saw them unfold.
>
> Shortly after our arrival in Taiwan, we had the occasion
> to meet a Lieutenant General who was a close friend and
> adviser to the Generalissimo. When he was stricken with

cancer and sent to the United States for treatment, we sent "get well" notes and when he died, we sent condolences to the family and flowers to the funeral home. Thus far we had followed American custom. However, the general was a Buddhist and we were interested in following the procedures incident to the funeral. Because of our social association with the family of the deceased, his friends gave us an account of what went on that we would not normally see or understand.

When the General died, the Buddhist Priests followed their basic religious rites over the deceased. Firecrackers were set off to chase away the devils, prayers were written on rice paper by relatives and friends and burned so that they could follow the spirit of the deceased, joss sticks were lighted, and other incense was burned; food, drink, tobacco, and money was placed conveniently near the deceased in order that the spirit might refresh itself when it wanted to.

The body was place in a heavy wooden casket that was magnificently carved and decorated with gold leaf. This was placed in a large state room at the funeral home. Because the Generalissimo had removed the austerity restrictions, and declared a State funeral, the deceased remained at the funeral home for forty-nine days of meditation of Siddhartha Gautama under the Badhi tree while he was seeking "enlightenment." During this time, the eldest son remained by the casket for six continuous days in mourning. On the seventh, the priests and the rest of the family would come and the eldest son was allowed to go home and bathe, change clothes, and sleep for the day. On the eighth day, the same procedure was started again. For the eldest son another six days of mourning continuing on to the forty-ninth day—needless to say, this was difficult on the funeral directors. During this time, funeral bands featuring weird sounding reeded flutes, drums, and crashing cymbals moaned, groaned, thumped and crashed their way around the clock. Long strings of "devil chasers" (firecrackers) were almost constantly being set off. Added to this was the din created by other funeral preparations in and around the establishment. Jangled nerves were "the order of the day."

Early on the morning of the forty-ninth day, crowds started forming along the march route from the funeral home past the Presidential Mansion and on to the cemetery, about five miles away. Thousands of troops lined the avenues as Guards of Honor. Special Honor Guard detachments from representative military units formed for the procession. Interspersed within all this were twenty-five full military bands, playing funeral marches. One would almost expect to hear them beat into "When The Saints Go Marching In"—a march traditional in some parts of the southern United States. All along the route long strings of "devil chasers" were strung on lamp posts, telephone poles, and even on trees. Thousands of little Buddhist shrines, called stupas or pagodas, were set up along the line of march where prayers and joss sticks were burned and offerings of food, drink and tobacco were placed on the altar tables. Mixed in with the marchers were beautiful floats of paper, gold leaf, and bamboo representative of all good things for a spirit to have in the next world. These consisted of palaces, ships, airplanes, servants, armies, etc. All of these were burned at the graveside rites in the cemetery.

This is based on the idea that a spirit wanders in purgatory for two years after death and must be assisted before it can enter heaven. These offerings indicate to the spirits that the deceased has been a good man, had a good life on earth and has all the material things necessary to carry on in the next world. Thus his soul should be sooner released from purgatory.

Some of the priests and monks rode in pedicabs and some walked in the procession. Many truck loads of flowers, real and imitation, followed behind. Most of the mourners carried paper lanterns to help light the spirit's way home. The coffin was carried part of the way by a very ornate hearse and the rest of the way by a team of pallbearers who changed off during the march. The mourners were dressed in "Sack-cloth" type hooded robes with ashes rubbed on the face and hands. The President, his staff, and the representatives of the diplomatic and foreign community rode in limousines.

It was an exhausting all day affair, but a magnificent example of the pomp and ceremony of an Oriental state funeral. However, we sincerely believe that the funeral directors were relieved to go back to the small one to five band, three to seven day funerals.

Burial and Last Rites

In rural China, burial of the wealthy has usually taken place in the clan burial plot. Cemeteries for collective burial such as we have in the United States are found in China only around large cities. The poor are buried on soil on which they labored. In most cases, if a grave is not dug, the coffin is placed on the earth, and over it is mounded straw, brick, concrete, or earth, whichever is most available. Sometimes a large mound is erected to cover several graves. Burial mounds are scattered so indiscriminately, and through the centuries have become so numerous, that China has been called "one vast cemetery." Erosion frequently uncovers both caskets and bones.[46]

At the grave the man who has kept the bearers in time beats his sticks together in order to gather the procession into a circle. Now to the music of drums and horns, all kowtow toward the grave, and wailing and weeping, take up a handful of earth, and cast it upon the coffin. The paper articles are burned, and then the mourners return home. In their absence workmen or members of the mutual aid group will have been busy removing all traces of funeral paraphernalia from the courtyard. Reaching home, the mourners find nothing remains outside to suggest a funeral had just occurred.[47]

The day calls for a last rite. A relative enters the bedroom of the deceased and there covers a brass tray thickly with incense ash. For three days the tray is left undisturbed and then examined. If the ash is judged to bear the imprint of a foot, the form tells whether the spirit has been reincarnated

24

as a man, bird, or beast. The lack of an imprint brings consternation. The spirit has not been reincarnated and must be hiding in the house. A person's beneficence in life does not automatically survive in his spirit in death.[48]

Death away from home poses difficult problems, particularly in a country in which travel and transportation are sometimes primitive. Even in such cases, however, great effort is made to return the body for burial in the ancestral graveyard. When such efforts prove unavailing, a rite begins in the home, the purpose of which is to call back the absent spirit. On an armchair just inside the gateway a suit of the dead man's clothes is placed for the spirit's use, together with a wash basin, comb and towel. On an offering table, among other gifts, is a yellow paper tablet telling that the clan, with incense, flowers, food, and scriptures, is inviting the spirit to return. Two rows of incense sticks serve to guide the spirit along the land which leads to the house from the main road. Priests pray for the dead and blow bugles and flutes. The wife, sons, and grandchildren of the deceased prostrate themselves, and wail until they are exhausted. At midnight, after paper money and a lotus lamp and spiritual banner have been burned, the chanting priests bear the spirit tablet of the dead across a symbolic bridge of benches to the family altar. There it is later burned.

If at some future date the body is brought home, the usual funeral takes place. On the return, a white cock chicken, called the "soul chicken," is carried upon the coffin. Its crowing is thought to be a command for the soul to accompany the body.[49]

Continued Worship of the Dead

On the third day following a funeral, the mourners return to the place where the body has been placed, to present food and burn money for the spirit. They take with them two cakes of white flour. They split these open so that they may roll into each a piece of lichen. Then they lay these divided cakes on each side of the head of the coffin, so that invisibly the wood there may likewise split, thus allowing egress to the spirit. They believe that a man has three souls, of which one goes to the future life; another remains at the grave; while a third enters the ancestral tablet. All must be freed.[50]

More ceremonies follow on the 21st, 35th, and 49th day after death, and on the 60th, a boat of paper over a light framework is burned with two paper bridges. On these, as on all special occasions, paper money is burned so that in the next world the spirit may pay its bills. "Everything possible is done to propitiate the dead, as, in China, it may be said that the dead rule the living in thought and custom, and by the fear and dread of calamity, if anything which should be done is omitted.[51]

Every morning and evening for a year after the death, a bowl of rice, flanked by meat and vegetables and topped by a pair of chopsticks, is placed before a tablet dedicated to the deceased. This tablet is set up in the living room next to the household gods. If a nephew lives in the home, he is assigned the task of offering the food to the spirit at mealtimes and inviting it to partake. Lacking a nephew, the family delegate the duty to some other member. The evening meal must be laid out for the spirit before dark, lest having been summoned forth it should be unable to see its way back, and becoming lost, injure the family.[52]

Three great festivals of the dead occur during the time when men labor in the fields. In spring the Festival of Ching Ming observes the renewal of life. This spring festival is normally the first excursion a family makes during the year.[53] In summer the Feast of the Hungry Ghosts provides opportunity to the generous to be charitable to the dead; and in addition to the usual family pilgrimages, the Society of Neglected Bodies visits graveyards and recommends essential repairs to relatives, and provides coffins and burials for the poor. Each member of the group contributes services and money to this good cause.[54] And in autumn, the Feast of the Tenth Month corresponds to All Souls' Day. At this time Chinese visit the burial places of their ancestors to make certain of their comfort during the dead winter season which lies ahead.[55] They bring with them a variety of rolls of paper representing bolts of cloth, together with money drawn on the Bank of Hell, all wrapped into a special parcel which is signed with the name of the deceased. They lay this gift on the altar, together with food and wine, and at nightfall they remove it and burn it. Out of the paper the spirit is expected to make warm clothing for itself.

All three great feasts are a restatement of the unity, solidarity, and continuity of the family. Yang says that in family celebrations there is to be found "one of the clearest indications of the family's exclusiveness, its conception of itself as a separate entity."[56] This sense of unity within the group and separation from those outside of it should not be taken to mean all members living and dead love one another, or would wreak no mutual harm. Like certain Europeans, the Chinese believe that there are special times at which unquiet spirits return to walk abroad. The first day of the 7th month is one of these. Such times strike terror, and children are cautioned not to stray after dark. Particularly to be feared are the spirits of those who have left no actual or adopted sons and nephews behind to minister to their needs after death.[57]

Departed family members have three places of residence: the graveyard, the family shrine, and the clan temple. The graveyard houses the body; the shrine and the temple, the spirits. While a proper graveyard is as much a matter of family pride as a decent house, few can afford this luxury. The graveyard of a wealthy family sometimes covers many acres. Although graveyards are seldom walled, they generally have entrance arches identifying the ownership. The location of burial places within a graveyard is prescribed, and follows in a general way a defined order based on descent, age, and sex, although violations seem to be common. Such disregard may be due to lack of space, superstition as preached by the geomancers, special honors which entitle a dead person to a higher position than he normally would have in the family, and the loss of fortune which makes a family less punctilious.[58]

A man who has provided his ancestors with a suitable graveyard—"good wind and water"—cannot feel clear in conscience until he has decorated the tombs. The tombs of the wealthy are massively built of granite blocks under a circular roof. In front of each stands a stone tablet which identifies the dead person, and names his achievements and his immediate ancestors and his descendants. To enhance his prestige, names of fictitious descendants are included. These tablets may occasionally be painted in color, and young people may oil their parents' and grandparents' tablets.[59]

The great clans maintain halls in which they keep the tablets of their ancestors. As each new generation is added to the family shrine, the tablets of ancestors of the fifth generation above are sent to the clan's ancestral hall. If a generation is figured at about 33 years this custom compels a family to keep in the family shrine the tablets of ancestors who may have died 130 or more years before. While this span is only a fragment in the extended history of Chinese culture, as judged by our Western practices it is a long period for a family to honor, memorialize, remember, and even know the names of its ancestral dead. In some cases the ancestral hall has a number of rooms, so that tablets may be classified. In the central hall is the tablet of the clan founder, and of the founders of its principal families; in another, of men whose piety was great; and in still another are the tablets of men who have made their marks in the world. Rooms are given to branches of the clan which have died out and the ancestors of these are honored, as well as those of living branches.[60]

Many conflicts within the clan arise from burial matters. Poorer families sometimes attempt to bury their dead too near the dead of more prosperous relatives. Necromancers may advise the digging of graves in inconvenient locations, a clan member may wish to sell off burial land, unrest and war may produce confusion and loss of records. The clan must guard against trespassers who by stealth place their coffins on top of the coffins legitimately there, and thus bury on its land; or against other clans which might encroach upon it. Though strangers may gain title to the land, the graves upon it cannot be removed or destroyed. When a clan moves, it may even carry the remains of its near ancestors to its new home.[61]

Some distinction is made between the housing of spirits given by the family shrine and that given by the clan temple. The family shrine, in theory at least, houses the descendants of common great-great grandparents; the clan temple houses all spirits of the common clan who are not given dwelling in the family shrine. Whatever its economic status, every household desires a family shrine. Generally it is set up on a specially built wooden platform in the middle of a second floor room which faces west. On it, beneath a silk pavilion, are placed tablets giving the name of the memorialized one. Next to the tablets stand images or tablets of Confucius, Buddha, and other Taoist gods. The offerings of food, incense, and flowers serve both the ancestors and deities.[62]

When a family can afford it, a person's tomb will be constructed during his lifetime and often under his personal supervision.[63] Hsu estimated the cost of a granite tomb in the summer of 1943 at a figure expensive by our standards. If a family cannot afford to make the entire expenditure at once, it builds the tomb bit by bit, much as one would build an estate. The completed empty tomb cannot be distinguished from the occupied tomb. When burial takes place, the back part of the vault is temporarily removed to receive the coffin. Parents take joy and pride in the fact that provision has been made for them.[64]

Many Chinese hold that certain days—sixteen or seventeen each lunar month—are "double death days." If death takes place on one of these, a second death will follow in the family unless precautions against it are taken. The bad luck is exorcised by hanging a cock by one leg in front of the corpse. While it is struggling to die, a small effigy is made of paper or wheat flour, and placed in a tiny reed or bamboo coffin. In the procession the dead cock lies on the head of the coffin while the effigy is carried by a helper. When a cross-road is reached, the cock is hung from a tree and the effigy in its coffin is buried beneath it.[65]

The belief in Life Stealing Ghosts who come and go, and levy goods and services from innocent families by being born as babies into them, produces some strange funeral practices.

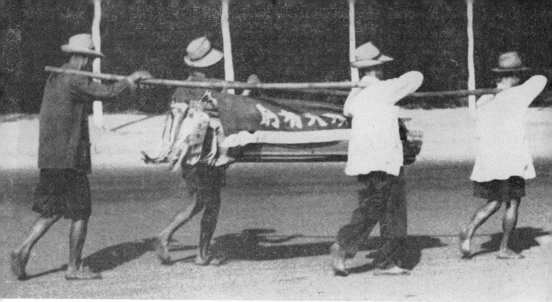

P.I.P. Photo

Burial in Red China: simplified funeral ceremonies and uncertainty as to place and method of interment

Families are certain that they are being haunted by one of these malevolent ones when two or three children die within a few years. To rid themselves of these ghosts, families do not give earth burial to the second infant, and all who may die in close succession after it. Instead they employ one of three rites of exorcism. Either they throw the infant body into a lake after having slapped its face with shoes, in the belief that the ghost that is drowned cannot again reincarnate itself; or if they prefer, they smear soot from the undersurface of a rice boiler on the baby's face, knowing that if the ghost returns it could be recognized; or they hang the infant body from a tree, in the belief that a spirit whose body does not touch the ground cannot be reincarnated. These rites are performed regardless of the sex of the infant.[66]

Economics of Chinese Funerals

The Chinese have a saying that a proper burial is the most important event in a man's life, indeed, a man's whole estate may be swallowed up in his funeral expense.[67] Fei and Chang describe the funeral ceremony of the father of a rural school

30

Coffined remains
in the "Dead Man's
Hotel," Hong Kong,
await propitious
moment for burial

teacher in which twice a day for six days the family provided meals for guests, for a total of 4,026 individual meals. When asked if this was not burdensome, the school teacher "argued vehemently" that only by spending as much as he was able could he pay honor to his deceased father. The authors point out that the conventional expenditure for funeral ceremonies is "more variable than that for marriages, since a marriage can be delayed and planned and accumulated for, while the time

Canton cemetery has bones exhumed as part of Red Chinese program to convert all available lands to agriculture. Mounds to be leveled

Largest modern
funeral home in
Hong Kong

Photo Courtesy E. C. and G. R. Johnson

for a funeral is determined by death alone." When a family
is extremely poor, it may have to borrow the money for a
coffin; and lacking even that much credit, it may deposit a body
at the side of a road. There it may remain for days until a
philanthropic organization picks it up and buries it.[68] At one
extreme the village funeral may represent a prosperous landowner spending a large sum of money for a great public ceremony. At the other, it may be a poor man begging money to
buy a coffin, and walking almost alone with it to a grave.[69]

A small but critical portion of a family's expenditures in
China is made up of the gifts which it makes to relatives who

32

Modern Hong Kong
funeral home. Person
at right wears mourning
regalia

are passing through crises. Such gifts are based on kinship
and friendship, and may be as low as 20¢ and as high as $5.
They average about $10 per year. Of course they are reciprocal,
in that all families sooner or later experience the types of
crises for which the gifts are made.[70]

In almost every district of China the traditional mutual aid
societies have flourished. These have served to provide funds
for meeting unavoidable heavy expenditures. One of their most

"Street of Coffin Makers," Hong Kong. Round type coffin popular in South China
is visible in picture at left, third shop; rectangular coffin, middle of right photo

33

Photos Courtesy E. C. and G. R. Johnson

Stylish Hong Kong funeral
hearse has body built
by local craftsmen

Typical Hong Kong hearse
outside funeral establishment
on "Street of Coffin Makers"

New and old style hearses,
Hong Kong

Hong Kong florist shop specializes in funeral wreaths

American style caskets being built to order on "Street of Coffin Makers"

important functions has been to make monies and labor available for the funeral. Until recently there was scarcely to be found in all of China a village which lacked a "Filial Mourning Headress Society"—a local funeral mutual aid group.

Social Change and Funeral Customs

Two kinds of recent changes are to be noted in Chinese funeral practices. The first is superficial and, at least up to the time of the Communist regime, was to be found in areas which had much exposure to Western culture. For example: In the old Treaty Ports, as well as in Hong Kong, the procession

35

Overseas Chinese
family grave,
Saigon, Vietnam

Photo Courtesy E. C. and G. R. Johnson

has been speeded up, paper automobiles are burned instead
of Peiping carts; brass bands playing Western music, appropriate and inappropriate, begin to replace the Taoist orchestras. In the large cities the motorized hearse has taken
the place of the satin-covered bamboo catafalques, and the
women follow not in sedan chairs, but in limousines.[71]

An American funeral director, Vernon Hill, reports that in his
extensive travels in China before World War II he saw only three
"better" funeral establishments.[72] Two were foreign firms in

36

Shanghai, one British and one American, and one was a firm in Tientsin. All served mainly the Western population. With Westerners now largely expelled from the country by the Communists, it is problematical whether those funeral establishments are still in operation.[73] Edward C. and Gail R. Johnson, from their early 1960 canvass of mortuary procedures in Hong Kong, report that the traditional modes of Chinese care for the dead persist, albeit somewhat streamlined and more closely under the surveillance and control of the local authorities than in the past. Funeral pro-

Hillside terraced cemetery outside Hong Kong

Photo Courtesy E. C. and G. R. Johnson

37

cessions, for example, are restricted to from 10:00 to 12:00 A.M. and from 2:00 to 5:00 P.M. Cemeteries are closed at 6:00 P.M. and indiscriminate burials outside cemeteries are prohibited. A few funeral homes are patterned after those in Western society, with numerous chapels, embalming facilities, some European and American style caskets, and up-to-date rolling stock.

By and large, however, Hong Kong Chinese are buried from their homes in much the traditional manner. Coffins, usually square or round-shaped, massive and heavy, are built in the coffin shops that cluster along one of Hong Kong's busy streets. Burial raiment, beautiful, colorful, expensive, is still used to cloak the dead; and simulated gold coins and currency still accompany the body in the coffin. Bodies and exhumed bones are stored in the "Dead Man's Hotel," a coffin dormitory operated by the Tung Wah hospital. Many bodies stored there are destined for burial on the mainland—when and if a more propitious time eventuates.[74]

The second kind of change is profound, extending to the very roots of Chinese society. Evidences were strong in 1949 of a degeneration of the traditional family structure and a transition to a new one. The traditional structure was rich in mutual reinforcements. The new lacks many of these. There is a change in the making, not only in the internal structure of the family, but in the total position of the family structure in the general structure of the society.[75] In the traditional family, an elaborate code of rituals governs every phase of family life, but especially those connected with birth, marriage, and death. Heaviest pressures are connected with the last. In all three events, both society and the individual are affected. In death, if abbreviation or mistake is made, the spirits of the dead are added as punishing agencies. Although the educated young people may still perform some of the rituals, there is evidence that they do so chiefly to please their elders. They have less understanding and respect for ancient rituals. The trend toward secularization is "spreading slowly from the modern urban intelligentsia to other segments of the population."[76] How extensive and far-reaching is this trend can only be a matter of conjecture.

Further evidence of change comes from the application by Red Chinese leaders of strictly rational and utilitarian concepts, as laid down in Chinese communist ideology. Revolutionary in character, the communist doctrines have found little common ground with the conservative, ancestor-deifying philosophies of the China of old. It has thus been a combination of philosophical necessity and political and economical expediency that has resulted in the all-out assault on traditional custom and usage. An excellent case in point is the matter of funerals and the burial of the dead, and illustrated here are the limits, perhaps, to which rapid social change may be effected.

When, after the Chinese People's Republic was established in 1949, land was distributed to the peasants in keeping with the Red Chinese promise of land reform, many Chinese immediately sold their holdings to pay for funeral debts incurred over the years—debts which could easily have been forgotten or renounced. Another Red Chinese program has been the projected complete simplification and rationalization of the burial of the dead. One feature, which to some extent has been effected, has been to exhume the bones from the thousands of beehive-like acres of burial grounds around the major cities and bulldoze the land flat enough for agricultural use. The bones were to be buried in a common grave—some reports have it, however, that they were in fact ground into fertilizer!

The second projected step was to erect crematories throughout the land and henceforth cremate all the dead. This plan was so strongly resisted that a compromise eventuated: all Chinese in the communes were to be given as one of their "16 Guarantees," free funerals and burials.[77] Burial was to be in the earth, but as an extension of the compromise the "deep burial" system was put into effect: the body is to be buried at least ten-feet deep so that the land which otherwise might be a graveyard can be used for orchards. Reports from refugees in Hong Kong, however, seem to indicate that once a body has been delivered to governmental authorities no accounting is given as to the actual method or place of burial.[78] The evidence, although scanty, indicates that while it may be true that funerals no longer are a dominant value in the minds of mainland Chinese, the disposition of the dead has not become equated with the disposal of refuse.

In a continent where great struggles are taking place for the control over the minds and destinies of hundreds of millions of people, venerable traditions may well be swept away in the tides of mass social movements. Or, as the case may be, some may simply be repressed, to spring back into use after a period of revolution and rapid social change. Funeral customs are not immutable. Their ceremonial value in traditional Chinese society has been paramount, but in the last analysis they served to restrict the actions of the living and to deify the memory of the dead. It is difficult to envision in present day or future China a resurgence of the traditional death customs, unchanged in character or saliency. Yet death is a phenomenon which is not readily understood, and which is almost impossible to explain away. In describing reactions to the crisis of death, "shock," "grief," "ceremonial," and "memorial" are terms of universal significance. It would be safe to venture that if since Communist domination these four features of death have not been rewoven into a distinct pattern of mortuary behavior, such pattern, however far off, is undoubtedly in the making.

Chapter 2

Japan

Buddhism and Shintoism

As is the case with most Asiatic countries, Japan is a land of multiple religious systems of beliefs and a variety of local and regional sacred folkways. For the Japanese, Buddhism is the most prevalent and in many ways the most influential religion. Nearly every family in Japan belongs to one sect or another.[1] The keeping of ancestor tablets in household shrines and daily offerings of food and drink are Buddhist household practices. All matters concerning the afterlife, such as funerals and memorial services for deceased relatives, are looked after by the local Buddhist priest.[2]

Shintoism is a more or less indigenously developed set of religious beliefs that revolve about a constellation of deities. Shintoism can be found in three forms: popular Shinto, sect Shinto, and official or state Shinto. In one form or another Shinto beliefs are held by all Japanese subjects regardless of their Buddhist affiliations.[3] Each village will have its local deity, and a shrine to house it. The practices revolving about such deity constitute popular Shinto. Sect Shinto organizes its adherents into named groups. Finally, state Shinto consists of a set of special sacred beliefs and practices associated with Japanese nationalism which are observed as part of the ritual of patriotism. As such, state Shinto is not a religion. By means of this distinction it is possible for Japan to have a constitutional guarantee of freedom of religion and still require Shinto observances of all her subjects regardless of whether they be Buddhist, Christian or agnostic.[4]

Japanese Village Funerals

Social and Religious Organizations

Dr. John Embree, an anthropologist who lived for eighteen months among the rural Japanese, studied the social organization of a Japanese village.[5] It was composed of small clusters of huts or flimsy houses presided over by a headman elected by the village members. All phases of the social and economic life of the village are characterized by a highly organized cooperative system. Although Shintoism is not without importance in the lives of the villagers the Buddhist temple exercises the most direct influence over their social affairs and the role of the Buddhist priest is crucial in most village funerals. Not only does the Buddhist priest generally preside at funerals and memorial services, but he derives the greater part of his income from them.

Response to Death

When a person falls sick, friends of the village visit his home to make social calls and to bring gifts of food to be eaten uncooked. If the sick man appears to be dying, the family gathers to keep the death watch. When he dies they telegraph the more distant relatives to invite them to the funeral—which usually

Japanese funeral hall entrance. Lantern, with coat of arms of deceased, serves as funeral announcement

Photo Courtesy Hidehisa Miyazaki

takes place the day following the death. A child is sent to notify the village headman.

Upon receiving notice of the event, the headman takes charge. As the family members remain more or less immobilized with grief the co-operative enterprise of preparing the dead and preparing for the funeral gets under way. Many tasks must be performed in a short span of time. Many hands are busied.

Preparation of the Dead

A coffin must first be procured. It can be purchased at a nearby town or it may be made in the village. The headman helps the family make decisions. Equipment and properties will be required, including paper flags containing prayers, paper processional lanterns, and a wooden candlestick. Men of the village gather in the yard to make these. Meanwhile the women set to work gathering and preparing the food required for the

43

Not all funerals in Japan are mechanized. Kobe funeral procession

feast which is given before the burial. One woman sews a white pilgrim's outfit with which to shroud the body. The pall-bearers spend most of the day digging a grave.

When the coffin is constructed or is purchased, the body, which lies behind an inverted screen, is disrobed by near relatives, thoroughly washed, shrouded, and coffined. So that the spirit may pay the ferryman for passage into eternity, a bag containing a few coins is hung from the dead person's waist, and meditation beads are entwined in his hand. Because it is considered indispensable to being fully clothed, a fan is laid in the coffin, together with some small, favorite object belonging to the deceased. Some days are considered

44

unlucky for funerals, and the body of one dying at such a time is thought likely to summon a living person to follow him quickly to the grave. To prevent so untoward an occurrence, a straw doll is placed in the coffin as a substitute. The dead are thought to listen, and so, as the relatives shroud the body, they describe aloud the tasks they are performing. To mask the odor of death, all who assist in coffining carry bunches of burning incense. On completing their task, they rush to bathe their hands in salt water.[6]

Meanwhile the priest waits in a neighbor's house until these arrangements are completed and the family summons him. At the feast, which begins shortly, and is considered a farewell meal with the dead, he sits in the seat of honor near the alcove in which is kept the Shinto god shelf. All participants in the funeral feast change to their most formal attire, and women

Floral wreaths, paper made, line the streets near where a wealthy Japanese died

wear a special funeral hair dress. Fish are banned from the menu of the funeral feast; and the cakes, although made of the same dry flour used for the cakes in the naming and wedding ceremonies, are dead white. While the family and the priest are thus solemnly employed within the house, the men of the community who have been assisting in the funeral preparations have gathered in the yard or barn to eat, drink, and enjoy themselves.[7]

The Funeral

When the ancient formulas have been recited by the priest, the men of the hamlet enter the house, carry out the coffin and bind it to poles which they raise and carry on their shoulders. The procession then forms in line, and the relatives march to the churchyard maintained by the hamlet. After the procession leaves the house, the women who have served remain behind to sweep the floor and eat their meal.[8]

At the cemetery the priest conducts a graveside service, and the body is lowered into the grave. When he concludes, he leaves. The relatives follow soon after. Talking and laughing, the pallbearers fill the grave and place the markers. Etiquette requires that the mourners do not remain with the family that night, but return to their respective homes.[9]

Additional Service

On the day following a funeral the relatives of the dead person again visit the house of the dead, and from there go to the cemetery. Before visiting the grave they wash their hands. The Buddhist priest also visits the family to collect for the funeral services and to make arrangements for seven memorial services, the first and seventh to take place at the home of the deceased, and the rest at the homes of relatives. While orthodox Buddhist rules require that these should be at seven day intervals, the practice is less strict, and the traditionally forty-nine day observance is sometimes telescoped into forty-two days or less. This short cut is made not from motives of impiety, but

46

because the villagers dislike having the period extend, by accident of the calendar, through parts of three months, or beyond the end of a year.

At each of these services the priest reads prayers before the dead man's portrait of *Amida*, the Savior. Relatives bearing gifts of rice attend these services, and, after visiting the grave, are entertained at a small party in the dead man's home. With the seventh observance, the mourning period closes, and food taboos are lifted. Prior to this time the bereaved family was forbidden to eat fish.[10]

The festival of Bon, which is similar to our New Year's, is celebrated from the thirteenth to the fifteenth day of the seventh month. On this great holiday the souls of dead ancestors are believed to return and to dwell in the *butsudan*, the Buddhist alcove with its scroll painting of Amida, the Savior. In this painting Amida is pictured with many golden rays emanating from him. The dead are believed to begin to arrive on the night of the thirteenth and to remain until the night of the sixteenth. At some time or other during this celebration it is customary in most villages for all members of the hamlet to pay a call at the home of a family which has lost a member by death during the preceding year. The visitors bring gifts: money, lanterns, rice, candles, rice beer, incense sticks, cakes, and noodles; and in return are feasted. Because this is a funeral ceremony, no fish is served. As a result of the campaign for economy in some hamlets, the visiting is dispensed with, and, instead, each family makes a small money contribution to the elected head of the clan, who passes it along to the bereaved family.[11]

Great preparations are made for the festival of Bon. Graves are cleaned up, so that the returning spirits will find them in good condition, and, on the thirteenth, containers of water and flowers in bamboo vases are placed on them. At the graves of the newly dead, relatives and other members of the hamlet sometimes offer flowers, or a mixture of rice and chopped eggplant or cucumber, or holy stones.[12]

Houses are also cleaned and decorated with flowers and

Making the lanterns which will line the streets on day of funeral

Floral funeral wreath used at altar

lanterns. The custom of bowing to ghosts as they enter the house on the thirteenth day, but not seeing them off as they leave on the sixteenth has passed. The path by which they go is lighted with candles, and the entrance to it, by torches. When the ghosts depart, the living accompany them, carrying candles and little pine torches. After bidding the ghosts goodby, the relatives return to the house for a drinking party.[13]

Urban Japanese Funerals

The Funeral Institutions

Great concentrations of population in Japanese metropolitan areas produce funeral practices and institutions quite different from those to be found in rural Japan. Among urban Japanese the funeral home, funeral hall, temple, crematory, and cemetery comprise the mortuary institutions which serve the needs of the masses who crowd into Japanese cities.

48

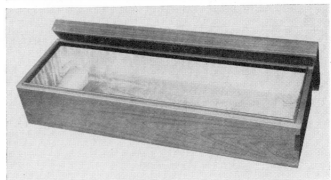

A quality
Japanese casket,
lined, with headrest
and small window
for viewing

Photos Courtesy E. C. and G. R. Johnson

Ownership, operation, and control of these institutions are divided among church, municipality, and private enterprise. Crematories and funeral halls tend to be municipally owned—as do some cemeteries. Temple grounds provide burial places for the ashes. The funeral home—which is not a "home" in the accepted American sense of the word—is a business establishment in which the paraphernalia of funerals is found but to which a dead body is never removed.

The Role of the Japanese Funeral Director

Because customarily the body is kept in the family home until the day of burial, the Japanese funeral director does not maintain a funeral parlor or similar facilities. Nor does he direct the funeral arrangements. His role is limited to providing

49

Altar set up by
funeral director.
Coffin behind altar
plays minor role
in funeral services

Deceased's family,
relatives and friends
at funeral service

Photos Courtesy Hidehisa Miyazaki

needed equipment, such as portable altars, curtains, coffin, and
hearse. His functions are therefore those of a funeral furnisher
rather than those of an undertaker or funeral director.

Funeral service in Otaru, a seaside Japanese city of two hundred thousand, is described by Mr. Hidehisa Miyazaki,[14] a
funeral director. Some twenty years ago, there were twenty
funeral undertakers in Otaru. They were united in a company
by means of "enterprise readjustment." At present three
branches of the Otaru Funeral Home serve the municipal area,
and handle approximately two thousand funerals a year. There

50

Buddhist priests conduct religious portion of funeral ceremonies

Master of ceremonies, a layman, addresses a farewell message to deceased

Photos Courtesy Hidehisa Miyazaki

is a municipal bureau which separately takes care of those who die in poverty or who are unknown. Mr. Miyazaki describes an average "death call":

As soon as a death call is brought into our office, usually by phone, a clerk is sent to the house. He talks with the family about price and place of funeral and other details. If death occurs during the night, he goes to the house the following morning at 9:00 o'clock.

The same kind of casket is used in every case. It is white and made of plain wood. The body with only a thin coat of white paint on its face is placed in the casket. (Dressing the body is not, apparently, a function of the Japanese funeral

51

Attendants stand as Shinto priest offers
prayers

Shinto priest prays as lay master of
ceremonies makes funeral offering

Municipal crematory at Otaru is
identified by figure at left

The interior of a luxury
class crematory

Storage drawers for cremated ashes of
the dead

Ordinary crematory interior. Lighted
lamps indicate cremations in process

52

director.) Seasonal flowers are put around the body. At night the death vigil is held for the family and public viewing. All services mentioned are done at the dead person's house. The funeral takes place the next day. Forty-eight per cent of our funerals are served at temples, forty-five per cent at houses, and seven per cent at (Christian) churches. This follows with cremation which has to be made between thirty-six and forty hours after death. The casket is put on a steel rack, pushed into a crematory and burned to ashes by coal. The bones are picked up from the ashes and put into an urn. This is taken home and a week after is placed in the charnel chamber of the temple. Burial is made by putting the urn in the family grave.

Last year in Otaru there were three Christian funerals. The bodies were embalmed by doctors, as there is no authorized embalmer, and burial was made in cemeteries attached to their churches.[15]

Care of the Dead

When death occurs, a Buddhist or Shinto priest, or a Christian clergyman, is called to the home, so that arrangements can be made for the funeral services. Frequently friends and relations of the bereaved family assume the responsibility of

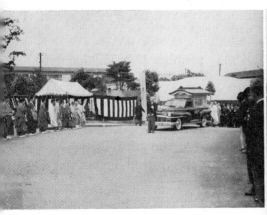

Funeral cortege enter approach to funeral hall. Musicians and priests conduct procession into hall

Photos Courtesy Hidehisa Miyazaki

Chapel
and altar at
municipal crematory
in Otaru

Photo Courtesy Hidehisa Miyazaki

making such arrangements. Family members seclude themselves as much as possible until the funeral.

Up to recent times Buddhist priests traditionally were called upon to be present with the dying. This practice was never the case with Shinto priests. Likewise, until a few decades ago, a Buddhist funeral called for the use of a barrel-shaped coffin into which the dead person was forced in a squatting position.

The care of the dead and the ritual to be followed by

54

mourning relatives have for centuries been most precisely defined and observed among the Japanese. Mourners must follow the injunction of self-control: "Do not burden others with your sorrow." Thus, in public the inner turmoil and heartbreak of the bereaved must not be displayed.[16] Friends are informed of the death by a small death announcement, *kichu*, which is displayed on the door.

The dead must be bathed and dressed. Traditionally the clothes are put on with the fold on the opposite side from the way the living fold their clothes. The hair is in part shaved off, the body clothed in white, and the head is covered with a ceremonial hat or a triangular piece of white paper tied on the forehead. These items and other funeral paraphernalia, if wanted, are supplied by the funeral director.

Kaiso *and the Funeral*

After the body is placed in the coffin some favorite object of the deceased is put in with it along with a protective charm or amulet. Imitation money may also be placed in the casket for the ferryman of the boat on the river *Sanzu*.

Not until the body is appropriately coffined will the family be ready for the *kaiso* or funeral reception. Friends and relatives call to offer condolences, give presents, and partake of refreshments or of a meal provided by the family. If the family can afford it, a funeral feast provides climax to the wake. This may come before or after cremation. Such factors as the schedule of the crematory, the convenience of the family, the length of time needed for the arrival of the guests, determine when the feast shall be held.

Buddhist and Christian funeral services are usually held in the home or in the temple or church, and Shintoist services in the home or some place other than the shrine. A pair of funeral services is traditional for Shintoists and Buddhists. In each case the first of these is private and is reserved for the immediate family, relatives and close friends. In the second or public service, which follows immediately, friends bid farewell to the departed, a Shinto, according to his custom, a

Funeral vehicles used by Japanese funeral directors. Bus in center carries passengers to crematory

Photos Courtesy Hidehisa Miyazaki

Buddhist, according to his. Christian services sometimes follow this double pattern which allows friends to be present and yet to spend only a brief time at the funeral.

The Funeral Procession

The traditional Japanese funeral procession is eloquently described by William Hugh Erskine:

56

The march from the house to the temple or crematory is a very unique funeral procession. First is a man carrying a white banner on which is written the name of the dead, giving in most cases both the real and the posthumous names, so that all can see whose funeral is passing by. Then come the flower bearers, the lighted candle bearers, the symbols of the denomination, animal heads for scaring away the evil spirits, the colored banners, the carriers of the paraphernalia of the priests and their assistants who follow, riding in palanquin or *jinrikisha*. The hired mourners come next with their weird noises. Then comes the casket, protected by a very large paper umbrella, and guided by the four lanterns, a relic of the night funeral. The casket is carried on a bier which rests on the shoulders of the six or eight carriers. It would take a book to describe the movements of the professional mourners, some of whom are acrobats, and perform all the way from the house to the crematory. Immediately following the body is the nearest relative who keeps the incense burning all the way to the grave. Then follow the rest of the mourners and friends. The women have their hair freshly dressed and tied with black string and no ornaments. The men all wear very coarse straw hats and all alike wear coarse sandals made especially for funerals.[17]

The funeral service in the home is conducted before the family altar. A screen surrounds the altar on three sides. The coffin is behind the screen and has little importance in the ceremonies. Lamps, incense burners, scrolls, memorial name tablets, sprays of flowers, bowls and cups for offerings, fruit, and gifts of visitors and relatives surround the altar. In the center above the altar table the picture of the deceased occupies a dominant position.

When the service is held at the temple or the funeral hall it tends to be more elaborate. Large funeral wreaths surround the rows of mourners seated before the altar. Incense is burned, prayers offered, and a farewell speech is given by the lay master of ceremonies. Priests chant antiphonally the *sutras* relating to the dead.

57

Typical Japanese
funeral coaches
for urban use

Photo Courtesy E. C. and G. R. Johnson

The service is not understood by the majority, for the Buddhist priests pronounce the words in an archaic manner which has long since been discarded by ordinary Japanese. Nevertheless there is a great charm in the mysterious and unknown, and the minds of the congregation are made solemn by the sights, sounds, and odors of the elaborate ritual of the dead. When the service is over the mourners advance one by one, and, taking their stand in front of the coffin, bow their heads in token of a last farewell to him who has gone before them into the unseen world. One by one they then file out of the temple.[18]

The temple rites complete the funeral ceremonies for most spectators. A final committal service is held at the crematorium where chapels are made available for what is usually a brief ceremony, attended by only a select few.

Erskine says: "Following the funeral is the consecration of the two *ihai* or tablets and the inscribing of the posthumous

58

Branch funeral
establishment

name, after which they are again consecrated. One is left at the temple, and the other is put on the Shinto god shelf or Buddhist family altar at home, with the proper ceremonies, and given the central position for one year, after which it is brought out on anniversaries only."[19]

Crematories and Cemeteries

Japanese crematories are large structures looking as one writer put it, "much like the waterworks of an American town of ten thousand inhabitants." A distinguishing feature is the tall smokestack towering over the building, sending thin spirals of smoke from its chimney.

On the day of, or the day after, cremation a family member goes to the crematory to perform the "honorable bone-gathering" duty. He receives the ashes in an urn, takes them home, and about a week later either deposits them in the temple or buries

Buddhist Japanese
family cemetery
plot, Otaru

Photo Courtesy Hidehisa Miyazaki

them in the family cemetery plot. In either case the act is done ceremoniously. The ashes are not buried in the family plot, however, until the grave has been properly prepared and an appropriate tombstone installed.

Japanese cemeteries are found in the center of large cities, in parks, on hilltops, and in ravines. Gravestones have been customary since the eighth century and tablets containing passages from Buddhist scripture written in Sanscrit have also been erected with the thought that they would be efficacious in expediting the passage of the spirit to its destination.[20] As a rule Japanese cemeteries are generally located near temples and are considered places appropriate for visiting, picnicking, and outings. Families as a group visit cemeteries to honor their dead. Incense is burned, tombstones are decorated with flowers, and before them are set bowls of rice and beans, and pieces of cooked fish. Also, little boxes for receiving the cards of the visitors are often found at the tombstone, along with bamboo vases that are kept replenished with freshly cut flowers.

A half comical, half pathetic sight in Japanese cemeteries is the stone image of Jizo, the Buddhist god of compassion. Mothers, grateful for the recovery of a sick child, often fasten baby bibs around the god's neck. Comments writer Frank G. Carpenter:

60

Another feature of Jizo's statue, whether in temple, in cemetery, or by the roadside, is the number of pebbles in its lap and piled about its base. According to the belief of many of the Japanese Buddhists, when children die their souls go to a place on the Sai-no-kawara, the Buddhist Styx. Here an old hag robs them of their clothes and sets them a task of piling up stones on the bank of the river. At night the devils come and scatter the piles, so that the work is all undone. Then the children in their discouragement run to Jizo, who hides them in the folds of his wide sleeves and comforts them. Whenever a worshipper on earth lays a pebble on the knees or at the feet of Jizo's image, he helps lighten the toil of one of these children.[21]

Japanese funerals have changed considerably in the direction of simplicity over the past several decades. Cremation, prohibited in 1875, now is virtually universal, despite the preference of the Shinto religion for earth burial. Expensive funeral feasts, once the highlight of many otherwise mundane lives,

Modern Japanese cemetery on outskirts of Otaru

Photo Courtesy Hidehisa Miyazaki

61

have been simplified. Elaborate gift-giving also has been reduced since each gift must be returned ceremoniously with one of approximately half the cost. The total cost of gift exchange was overwhelming to a society struggling against overpopulation and deficient natural resources, with its economy staggering under the costs of devastating overseas warfare.

Cremation, stringent sanitation laws, modern facilities, and the stepped-up tempo of the times all have militated against the once leisurely Japanese funeral in which days were spent visiting, offering condolences, sipping tea or *sake*, and talking about the life of the deceased, while Buddhist prayers and music of an orchestra provided a religious and aesthetic backdrop to an affair too important to be hurried. Even so, the basic core of sentiment, belief, and worship remains virtually intact and of continued significance to urban Japanese as well as to their rural brethren.

Chapter 3

Korea

Traditional Korean funeral beliefs and practices show the impress of Buddhism, Taoism, and Confucianism. Additional influences are shamanism—the acquisition and control of powers directly from the spirit world—and village folkways, built up over four thousand years of Korean history. Under the Yi dynasty (1390-1950) an intricate formality in funeral procedures was developed which, although varying as to class, social, or government position, pivoted on the proper maintenance of worshipful attitude and act toward one's ancestors.[1]

The hold of ancestor worship upon the Koreans is well illustrated in folk stories of sons who cut off their fingers to provide meat for soup for their aged parents, or who lay down in the beds of their parents before they went to rest so that vermin might satisfy themselves on them and not bother the parents. The faithfulness of a devoted son, who by prostrating himself in worship at his father's grave daily for ten years,

63

wore holes in the ground for his feet, knees, and head was much applauded.[2]

Ancestor worship is expressed in ceremonies and rituals performed in the presence of ancestor tablets which are kept in family dwellings. Many of the significant festivals and holidays of the year have as their basis the veneration or worship of ancestors. The most important celebration, the New Year, lasts fifteen days and begins with a feast to the ancestors.

The Moment of Death: Aigo, Aigo, Aigo

When a Korean is at the point of death, the family gathers round in silence and waits patiently until the end comes. Cotton or a piece of cloth may be placed over the mouth and nostrils of the stricken man. Death itself is not considered ugly, but beautiful. Koreans are fatalistic as to its coming, and respond aesthetically to its presence.

Once the person dies a chain reaction of varied responses occurs among the survivors. The loud wails of the women, *aigo, aigo, aigo* inform the village that someone has gone to his ancestors. A close male relative climbs to the roof and waves a garment of the deceased; he shouts his name, his highest rank, and news of his death. Rice may then be scattered across the roof or placed outside the door. The pronouncements are intended not only to advise the village of the event, but to "invite" the soul of the deceased to depart from the house. This is called the *Cho-Hon*, "Invitation to the Soul" ceremony.[3] In some villages a squash is broken and laid in front of the house, together with three pairs of new shoes and some rice. These are gifts for the three spirit messengers, the *Sajas*, who have been sent as escorts to bring the spirit of the deceased to King Yumua of the Buddhist underworld.[4]

Funeral Preparations

When news of the death reaches the neighborhood, all members of the mutual aid society gather at the home to help perform the funeral tasks. The oldest son is the chief mourner

64

and also directs the funeral arrangements. If he so desires he may delegate this duty to a friend or to someone in the neighborhood who has had practice in handling such matters.

A coffin, if it has not already been constructed, must be made. One Western observer reports that nothing gives a Korean greater peace of mind when he is lying on his deathbed than to hear his sons constructing his coffin. When it is ready, it is often brought into the room in which the dying man lies, so that he may feel happy looking at it. Relatives and friends come then to admire the coffin and to express their delight that it is so well made and so handsome.[5]

The rich will have a polished lacquered coffin prepared by skilled carpenters. The very poor, on the other hand, may be buried in a paper or rice straw sack bound to a plank. Coffins for the less well-off are usually of poplar or pine. Pine is preferred, for to Koreans it is symbolic of the life of man. Moreover, serpents do not frequent pine trees—a shamanistic belief.

Male relatives of the deceased keep constant attendance in the room in which the body lies, and one of them comes in and out of the room to consult about details with the person who is directing the funeral. Except in the larger cities there are no functionaries who make such work an occupation and who operate undertaking establishments.

The female relatives of the deceased fashion mourning garments out of hemp cloth and prepare the wine, rice cake, and other food. A man's mourning costume consists of a hempen mourning coat, a hempen hat, a belt and shoes of rice straw, and a cane. If the mother has died, the cane is made of wood; if the father, of bamboo. For a woman a mourning costume consists of a two-piece hempen mourning garment, rice straw shoes, and a mourning cane, again either of wood or bamboo.

On the day after death the face of the dead is washed with perfume and the body is clothed with hemp or silk garments and tied in seven places with ropes of hemp or silk. The tyings are correlated with the seven stars of the Constellation of the Bear, which Koreans consider lucky.[6] Thus prepared the body is laid in the coffin, the lid of which is fastened with

At Korean funerals the elaborate coffins are carried by bearers who keep in step by chanting "the river, the river flows only one way"

slanting wooden pegs. Relatives, friends, and members of the mutual aid society bring offerings—mainly hemp cloth, wine, incense, candles, and money—as gifts. A burial feast is then held in the presence of the dead with the immediate family of the deceased and his relatives and friends as sponsors.

66

Burial and Geomancy

Burial usually takes place on an odd-numbered day after death. During the first three months of the year, the third day after death is generally selected; during other months, the fifth day. For prominent people, however, burial may be delayed for as much as three months. In such case the family must bow to the coffin on the first and fifteenth of every month, and must offer fruit to it before they may eat any themselves.

The choice of an appropriate burial site calls for a fateful decision which traditionally has always been made with the aid of a geomancer, *i.e.,* one who divines by means of figures or lines.

When the geomancer has been guaranteed his pay, he will lay his "wheel picture" on the ground and discover the grave's proper direction. It must not point toward another visible grave. The geomancer next lays his "golden well," a frame in the shape of a parallelogram, to outline the grave.

In selecting the site, the first question to be asked is whether it has a "good advancing dragon." The "dragon" is considered to be an unbroken ridge sloping down toward the site. Such a ridge is hard to find. Even harder is the discovery of a grave site in which the ridges form an ascending chain, so that from the lowest one can see the highest eminence. When a man is buried at the foot of the bottom ridge, the Koreans believe he can look upon his line of ancestors.

The direction in which a grave lies is likewise important. While it may face east or west, it is preferable that it should look southward. A grave must never be dug facing north, away from the sun, and toward the shadows. Hills to the east and west are considered dragons, beneficent only when they are of equal length. If from the grave site a "spying peak" is visible, the effect will be baleful, because a baleful spirit crouching behind it will keep his evil eye on the grave, and the descendants of the man buried there will become robbers.

When the geomancer has indicated the depth to be dug, his official services are over, although the geomancy may continue for many years. If the deceased's descendants, for example, have

67

Native bearers in traditional Korean costume carry
canopy-covered *sanyu* in funeral procession

troubles for which no cause can be assigned, another geomancer
is likely to be summoned to see if the ancestral grave is at fault.
Usually some small defect is discovered and remedied. Sometimes the geomancer will suggest that the body has run away.
In such case he will agree to bring it back, usually within
twenty-four hours.[7]

Funeral equipment is supplied by the members of the burial
society. When not in use it is stored in an out-of-the-way enclosure. It consists of a covered wooden platform supported
by two parallel carrying poles, all painted in several colors,
together with decorations of red and blue cloth.[8] This carrier,

68

called the *sanyu,* may be specially made for the burial of an important person. From eight to forty bearers wearing coarse linen clothes and linen caps carry this gaudily painted equipage on their shoulders, steadying it with a network of ropes. Myriads of multi-colored paper flowers covering this device flutter as the bearers, chanting a weird song which enables them to keep in step, shoulder their burden without rest until the procession reaches the grave.

The Funeral Procession

The order of the funeral procession is fixed by tradition. First marches a man or boy carrying a red flag on which is painted in white the dead man's personal name and his clan names. Numerous lantern bearers march on either side. Next follow two men or boys carrying the spirit box or "box of soul." This is a small black painted box about twelve inches wide and eighteen inches long made especially to hold an unpainted strip of chestnut wood about ten inches long, two inches wide and three quarters of an inch thick, called a "spirit master." Also included in the box is a sheet of paper inscribed with the name and office of the deceased. In some obscure fashion the box is thought to hold the soul.

The bier leader is next in line, and is in turn followed directly by the carriers with the bier. Male mourners come next, led by the chief mourner; while relatives and friends, some carrying banners eulogizing the dead person, bring up the rear. In funerals of note, servants and professional mourners also are part of the procession, along with devil chasers under grotesque masks. In many funeral processions a second bier is carried on which a dummy coffin is placed to deceive any evil spirits that may have penetrated the screen of preventive precautions.[9]

With a view to distracting the evil spirits still further, a Korean sometimes stands up on the bier in front of the first coffin, strewing imitation paper money on the ground in front of it. It is hoped that evil spirits, who are believed to be as

Huge *palanquin* with over 200 bearers carrying body of former Korean emperor, Prince Yi, to mausoleum

covetous as human beings, will be so absorbed picking up the paper money that the real coffin with the body in it will be laid to rest in the ground without any of them being able to hurt the deceased.[10]

When the procession reaches the cemetery, the coffin is removed from the bier and, with the foot pointing downhill,

70

is lowered into the grave. After the grave is filled, the top is mounded with soil, and grass is sodded upon it. At its head a grave marker made of wood or stone, with the name of the deceased carved on it, is erected. Markers and graves are kept in good order, which corresponds to our perpetual care.

After the funeral the family returns home with the "box

71

of soul," which had been held open over the grave while the dead man's name was called out. It is thought that the spirit of the dead one would reside in the "box of soul" from that time on. Every morning and evening for a year, food offering is made for the soul. In the case of a father who dies before a mother, such offerings continue for a two-year period. When the period of food offering has expired, the "box of soul" is burned, and the soul ascends into heaven.

Memorialization

The Korean grave merits another glance. Hulbert thought the shape and appointments of the Korean grave the "most beautiful in the world." The gentle southern slope of a hill is dug into so as to form a wide flat space; the earth thus excavated is formed into a crescent-like bank all around the north, east, and west sides of the plot. In the center, between the arms of this crescent, the grave is dug, and when earth is piled upon it, the shape is that of an exact hemisphere. In front the ground is terraced down to the original slope of the hill. Back of the grave and on the two sides a thick grove of pine trees is planted. Nicely turfed and well taken care of, this grave is exquisite in its simplicity and neatness. These little groves of pines about the graves form bright spots in an otherwise rather forbidding landscape.[11] It must not be supposed that all graves are arranged so elaborately as this. Persons at the lower end of the economic spectrum are more likely to build up only a low mound of earth, susceptible to the forces of nature and vulnerable to the ravages of wild animals.

Monuments of the richer classes are of stone. Some resemble miniature houses or temples, some a ram's or horse's head. Two columns of masonry, "gazing headstones," sometimes flank the tomb to provide a comfortable perch for the soul, if it has been metamorphosed into a bird. A Korean burying ground tends to fill up with small obelisks, either painted at the top or surmounted by a carved head. When the grass grows tall, these latter monuments suggest spirits peering

72

Mound grave

Cemetery tomb

out of the brush.[12] At each grave a smoothly polished stone stands before the grave mound itself, to serve as a table for the annual offerings of sacrificial food.[13]

The conifer forest in which a clan commonly buries its members is considered clan property. Large and wealthy clans hire a grave guardian, who receives a plot of land near the graves as compensation, to serve as manager for them. For ten days in November, clan members in a group visit their ancestral graves. During a period of several days the grave guardian cooks for them and serves them. The clan controls the cutting of the conifer forest and uses the proceeds to support its poor families and to buy additional land. Korea has been recklessly overcut, and older trees are to be found chiefly in the neighborhood of tombs and cloisters.[14]

By venerable tradition the ground on which graves lie is held closed for eternity. When the Japanese established common cemeteries in an effort to prevent this scattered burial and improvident land use, they met with considerable opposition.[15] They took measures, nevertheless, that public burial grounds would be established on non-agricultural land on the higher hillsides, and that these would collectively serve a group of villages.[16]

73

Variation and Change

Dynastic Korea embraced ancestor worship as a way of life and a mode of organizing society. The system of class added variations in privilege, prestige, and rank. The two themes have long provided the underpinning for distinctive Korean funeral customs and manners.

The higher the rank the more elaborate the funeral. Preparations for the funeral of a king or queen might take three to six months, with costs up to the modern equivalent of a million

Manual of traditional Korean funeral procedures

dollars. On the other end of the social scale the expense of the peasant's funeral, carried out by the mutual aid society, would be shared by the community with negligible cost to the survivors. Status increased with age, parenthood, and grandparenthood, and was reflected in funeral obsequies. A child dying at birth might be disposed of without ceremony. Parents, on the other hand, would be buried with reverence and continued worship. Children were easy to come by, and came often; parents were irreplaceable.

The Korean funeral ceremonies served a variety of functions: The spirit world would be placated, ethical values reaffirmed, and social values reinforced. The emotional context for the Korean funeral has always been sensually exciting: feasts, wails, chants, bells, banners, signs, lanterns, contrasting dress, and a confusion of vivid color have been combined to make the burial of the dead a distinctive social and aesthetic experience.

But the sweep of Western influence and the pressures of an expanding population and economy have taken their toll on the static and leisurely oriental way of life of traditional Korea. In response to the need for arable land, cemeteries have been set aside for the dead, and the geomancer has withdrawn his practice to the hinterland. Christianity has made some inroads into the domestic and traditional religions. The shaman has been replaced by the minister in many areas. While in some quarters the disfavor of the spirits may no longer be feared, the wrath of the government remains to be avoided. The fast pace of industrialization, of collective and individual enterprise, and a rising nationalism dedicated to progress and change spell the eventual doom of traditional Korean social customs. Yet resistance survives. Funeral folkways form a strong residuum in Korean culture. *Aigo, aigo,* the wail of the widow, is still heard in the night, and by day funeral processions colorful, noisy, gay, clog up the streets of Seoul to halt the tram and auto traffic of a modern oriental metropolis.

Himalayan priest summons flesh-eating birds with horn made from human femur

Chapter 4

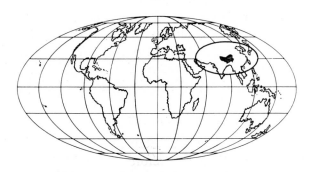

Tibet

Tibetans follow the Buddhist philosophy in dividing life
into four stages: birth, growth, decadence, and extinction.
While birth calls for no particular rejoicing, neither does
death call for an excess of sorrow.[1] Yet aging, demise, and
the departure from this world are soberly conceived:

> Now as life draws to its close,/ My slothfulness is past.
> Grant that steadfast I may live/As long as life shall last.
> Come thou down, most precious lama,/Thou my shelter be,
> From life's endless round, Chenresi,/Highest one, deliver me.

This fragment is from an old Tibetan funeral hymn[2] which
mentions death and the judgment of the dead, not as final
matters, but rather as links in the chain of Tibetan life. In
the Tibetan concept of the afterlife, as in many religious beliefs,
a journey awaits a dead person. The Tibetan must pass "Between the Two," through *bardo*, the state between death and
rebirth. It may be that he will have to enter a lower world,

even one of the hells, of which there are several, both hot and cold.[3] The hope of the ordinary Tibetan is eventually to return to this earth to follow a religious life. This return is contingent upon the goodness of his previous life and the prayers and religious observances of his relatives. "The Tibetan," says Bell, "cannot yet dare to hope for 'Sorrow Passed Away' "— the Tibetan term for *Nirvana*—"the heights of the Buddhas and Bodhesattvos far beyond his ken. Birth and death and birth again. For him the Wheel of Life goes on and on."[4]

The Moment of Death

When a Tibetan lies dying, the family calls in as many lamas as they can afford, to assist in the last rites. It is important that one of these should vigilantly watch the dying person in order that when death occurs he may immediately perform the "Passing Ceremony," by which the soul is allowed to escape from the body. This simple Buddhist rite is shared by many peoples and nations.

After excluding all onlookers, the lama seats himself at the head of the body, and plucks from its head a single hair, calling on the soul to leave the body through the tiny opening, which is thought to extend through the skull and into the brain. No one but a lama can perform this ceremony. If at death a lama is not available, a white cloth is thrown over the corpse to prevent the escape of the soul until the "Passing Ceremony" can be properly performed.[5] If because of accident or other reason the body of the deceased is not available for the soul liberating ceremony, the lama, in a state of deep meditation, performs the rite in spirit.[6] The lama who plucks the hair is well paid for his services, receiving a cow, yak, sheep, goat, or a sum of money, according to the wealth of the dead person. If the ceremony by which the spirit leaves the body through a hole in the skull is omitted, it is believed that it will exit by some other passage, and, as explained by the lamas, " . . . go in a state of damnation."[7]

Because the Tibetans believe that a soul does not immediately

78

have rebirth but hovers near the body, when death has occurred instructional passages are read to acquaint the newly released soul with the proper manner of conducting itself along the road to its rebirth. Meanwhile, an astrologer-lama casts a horoscope to determine such important matters as who may touch the body, what prayers should be said for the dead, what form of disposition shall be practiced, when the funeral shall take place, what god shall be made in effigy. Then a portrait of that holy person shall be painted on a religious banner. It is believed that at the judgment seat the god and the holy person will intercede to ask that the soul shall be reborn into a higher human state. Until these matters are settled, no one may touch the corpse.[8]

Once the horoscope has been rendered, a notice of the death is sent to all nearby relatives and friends. Within a few days these arrive to visit the living, and are given meals of rice and vegetables washed down with beer.[9] The Tibetan, however, does not regard death as an occasion for community festivities. Very few, say Shen and Liu, come to pay their last respects to the dead, and even fewer enter the room where the remains are kept. Those who wish to offer their condolences may present to the bereaved a silk scarf containing money; this will be used for defraying the cost of the services of a priest or for painting a portrait of the dead person's patron deity. The clothes and other goods of the deceased are given to the lamas as payment for their services.[10]

Preparation of the Dead Body

After the lama has spoken, those designated for the task strip the body, fold its arms over its chest, and conceal it in a squatting position in a corner behind a cloth partition. Tibetans feel that it merits little solicitude. In the belief that so it was born into the world, they place a five-cornered crown on its head. Generally it is kept in this manner for three days, although in winter the period may extend to fourteen.[11]

While the body remains in the squatting position in the

corner, butter lamps flicker and priests in relays chant day and night, praying that the soul may make speedy progress to the Western Paradise. During this period food is placed before the body in the amount that the dead person would have required in life.

On the day the body is borne from the house, a special feast, including pork and other delicacies and drinks of all kinds, is set before it. Presenting it with a long, silken "scarf of honor" a lama addresses it: "You now have received from your relatives all this good food and drink. Partake freely of its essence, as you shall not have any further opportunity of so doing. For you must understand that you have died and your spirit must be gone from here, and never again come back to trouble and injure your relatives. Come this way."[12] The priest then ties one end of the scarf to the body, and adjures the spirit of the dead to leave the house and, proceeding on the road to Paradise, never to turn back to vex the living.

The Funeral Procession

A three-man procession is then formed. First, marches a lama blowing a thigh-bone trumpet and ringing a bell or beating a skull-drum. Behind him comes the officiating lama, with the end of the silken scarf in his hand. And behind him struggles a *Ragyapa*, a disposer of the dead, bearing the corpse in his arms. Thus the body is borne to the place of disposition.[13]

In other instances variations in mode include the use of a coffin, and in still others, as Kawaguchi observes, "neither a coffin nor an urn is used in which to deposit the corpse." In such case the limbs are straightened and the body is laid on a rectangular frame made by tying four wooden poles together and filling the space with a rough network of ropes, covered with a cloth sheet. This bier is carried on the shoulders of two men, who stick their heads between the projecting ends of the longer poles.[14] The rank of the bearer of the dead depends on the social importance of the dead person. If he was a mem-

80

ber of the gentry, he is borne by a member of the *tom-den* class, low caste hereditary bearers of the dead. If of the lower or middle class, he is borne by a beggar-scavenger, of a caste so low as to be pariah. Relatives do not accompany the remains to the disposal ground. "They weep too much."[15]

Modes of Disposal

Four methods of disposing of the body are available to Tibetans: cremation; casting the body into a stream or lake; earth burial; and "air burial," by feeding it to vultures, eagles, crows, or dogs. The Tibetans conceive of the material universe as formed of four elements: fire, water, earth, and air. These methods of disposition insure the return of the body to one of the elements from which it was derived. Some writers consider embalming as a separate and therefore a fifth method of disposal. Inasmuch as the purpose of embalming is to preserve rather than destroy the body such classification is scarcely accurate.

Cremation is rare in Tibet because wood is scarce, particularly on the treeless plain, and cattle dung is not considered a good and proper material to use for burning the dead. Cremation is therefore reserved for high lamas. Several methods of burning are employed.

When the high lamas prescribe cremation, after the body is first burned in a closed oven, the ashes are scraped together and mixed with clay. The mixture is then molded into tiny pagodas which are dumped in heaps over the countryside.[16] Tagel saw another method in use in which the coffin is set in the middle of a funeral pyre about two meters high. In order to conceal the stench of burning flesh, pieces of butter, kernels of grain and incense, and redolent juniper twigs are constantly tossed into the flames. When this method is employed, after cremation the pieces of bone that may not have been consumed are gathered, together with the rest of the ashes, for later burial in a small grave.[17]

More common than cremation is water burial. The bodies

81

of the poor are sometimes thrown into rivers and streams, and bandits often use this method of disposing of those whom they have robbed and murdered. In eastern Tibet it is customary to provide water burial for beggars, lepers, and babies. In central Tibet, however, babies are placed in small boxes for earth burial. The better governed districts surrounding Lhasa prohibit water burial, partly to check the activities of robbers, but even more to prevent the pollution of streams from which many people drink.[18] A half century ago the body of a pregnant woman, or a barren one, or of a leper was stuffed into a leather bag and cast into the waters of the Tsang-po River.[19]

Water burial, too, has several variant forms. In most cases the body is cast into the water. Partly to make it sink, and particularly in cases of violence to prevent identification, a heavy stone may be attached to it. However, in other places, before a body is consigned to a large stream, it is thoroughly dismembered, and thrown into the water piece by piece, in the belief that if it were cast in whole, it would not speedily disappear from sight.[20]

Earth burial is rather infrequent in Tibet. In Kintschuan the dead are placed in a wooden coffin held together with wooden pegs. Iron, whether in nails, fittings, sheets or castings of all kinds, and stone are avoided by coffinmakers, because these are substances from which murder weapons could be fashioned. The space between the body and the sides of the coffin is filled with the finest dry clay mixed with cedar twigs. As the soothsayer rules, the coffin and its contents are either thrown into the river, or burned, or given earth burial.[21] If earth burial is decided upon, the family carries the coffin to the grave, which has been dug on a corner of the family plot. Graves are square and about one and one-half meters deep. To protect them from excessive dampness, they are lined either with masonry or planks.[22]

The Grimness of "Air Burial"

The commonest method of disposal in Tibet is air burial, *Ja-Tor*, in which the body is eaten by animals. When it is decided to give the body air burial, it is borne by members of the funeral caste to a desolate spot set aside near each village for this use. Shen and Liu observe that the spots used for air burial in Tibet are "innumerable." They describe one such spot: "We once ventured to one of these places. It was before sunrise when we arrived at a desolate rocky place that would make a perfect setting for a murder story. Two suspicious-looking men seated on a piece of rock were having their breakfast. A monk with a lantern sat a little distance off. We approached him and learned that it was a lama, his own spiritual teacher, that was going to be cut up for the birds. There was a white bundle lying on a huge boulder about fifty feet off. We walked some distance away in trepidation.

"The men started burning sandalwood, the aroma of which, as we learned later, aroused the birds high up among the rock caves. The men unbound the corpse and began the job, grinding the bones into bits and kneading them with barley. The birds swooped down in batches, about a hundred or so, walking and chattering noisily a good distance off. We retreated farther away."[23]

Kawaguchi describes the process of dressing the body with a broadsword: "The abdomen was first cut open and the entrails removed. Next, all the various members of the body were severed, after which some men, including a few priests, undertook the work of final 'dressing,' which consisted in separating the flesh and bones, just as the butchers do with slaughtered cattle."[24]

Shen and Liu continue their account: "The disciple looked on. Within a half hour everything was gone. Had anything been left behind, the disciple would certainly have deemed it a bad sign. Only the bodies of the condemned, it is believed, are shunned by the birds. But now he was satisfied. His master had given away everything. What else could be desired?"[25]

Kawaguchi was aghast to observe that certain Tibet gravediggers after cutting up a body and feeding the ground bones to the dogs did not wash their hands before preparing food or taking tea, ". . . the most they do being to clap their hands, so as to get rid of the coarser fragments. And thus they take a good deal of minced human flesh, bones, or brain, mixed with their tea or flour. When I suggested that they might wash their hands, they looked at me with an air of surprise, and observed that eating with unwashed hands added relish to food; besides the spirit of the dead man would be satisfied when he saw them take fragments of his mortal remains with their food without aversion."[26]

Distressing to western stomachs though air burial may be, Bell found that ". . . this method has much to recommend it in a country like Tibet. Burial is difficult, for the ground is frozen hard during the winter. Cremation is difficult, for there is no coal, and but little firewood. Casting into rivers pollutes the drinking supply."[27] "Barbaric as all this seems," says Heinrich Herrer, the German explorer who spent seven years with the Tibetans (1944-1951), "the ceremony draws its origin from deep religious motives. The Tibetans wish to leave no trace after death of their bodies, which, without souls, have no significance."[28]

Embalming an Uncommon Practice

The practice of embalming has ancient roots in Tibet. Early kings, venerated as reincarnations of Buddha, were embalmed and placed in tombs. Today embalming is reserved for two or three families that trace their descent for a thousand years, and for very high lamas. The embalmed bodies of persons of such high rank, like the bodies of cremated lamas, are placed inside silver covered clay vessels which are housed in mausolea. Embalming proclaims the divinity of such men, and they are considered worthy to receive the offerings of the sacred fire.[29]

According to one version, in the salting process of embalming the body is ". . . put in a big box and marsh salt is copiously sprinkled over it till it is thoroughly imbedded in this alkaline padding. The box is then kept in the temple for about three months, during which time offerings are made regularly, as when the deceased was yet alive, and his disciples keep vigil over it by turns. Before the coffin, lights are kept burning in several golden burners containing melted butter, while holy water is offered in seven silver vessels. By the time the three months have elapsed, all the watery portion of the corpse has been absorbed by the salt, and it has become hard and dry."[30]

Exorcism and the Cult of the Dead

Whatever disposition is being made of the body, while it is taking place, at the house of the deceased a ceremony is being performed to drive away the demon responsible for the death. Upon a plank, so that it may be carried, a foot-long model of a tiger has been constructed of mud and straw, with jaws and fangs of barley dough. Astride it is the barley dough image of the man-eating devil, whose belly holds a strip of paper containing the command: "Devouring devil, begone. Turn thy face toward the enemy." A bird-headed man fashioned of clay leads the tiger, and a monkey-headed clay model drives him.[31]

Their ceremony of exorcism begins at nightfall, when the officiating lama shouts a long incantation. Immediately the male mourners seize weapons—swords, agricultural instruments, and stones—and crying, "Begone, devil," attack an invisible opponent. The din goes on until a priest, whom the astrologer has designated for the purpose, takes up the plank with the models and carries it to a crossroads some distance from the house. Thus the evil spirit has been removed from the house where death has occurred. To prevent it from entering neighboring houses, priests draw a circle around them with magic barley powder.[32]

A final ritual remains to be performed. On the day the body is carried from the house an effigy of the dead man is drawn on a piece of paper on which his name is written, and the food which he would normally have eaten is placed before this portrait. Each evening in the presence of an astrologer the effigy is burned in the flame of a butter lamp, to be replaced next day by a copy, which is likewise symbolically fed. When the forty-eighth portrait has been fed and burned, it is believed that the spirit is freed to enter Paradise. To discover to which heaven it shall ascend, the astrologer watches carefully the drawings as they are being burned, and interprets the fate of the soul by the color of the flame and the form of the smoke. A brilliant whiteness indicates a perfection of soul that qualifies it for the highest heaven; a red flame that mushrooms like a lotus flower tells that the soul will reach the Paradise of Perfect Bliss; and a yellow and smoky flame, that it will reincarnate as one of the lower animals. The ashes of the pictures are mixed with clay and formed into small cones. One of these is kept in the family chapel, while the rest are distributed in caves or other out-of-the-way places.[33]

On the seventh day of the period of bardo—the forty-nine days between death and regeneration—other prayers are offered for the well-being of the deceased, and alms in tea, food, coin, silver and gold are distributed among men of religion. This observation takes place on each succeeding seventh day until the forty-ninth day is reached. Then rich people—and this is particularly true of Lhasa—give substantial alms to monasteries in place of subsidizing, as formerly, elaborate final ceremonies. Some give the clothes of the deceased persons to the professors or heads of the monasteries, while others bequeath their entire properties.[34]

Combs found that with the Tibetans mechanical prayer was an "obsession." Although such prayer is generally associated with the prayer wheel, it may take other forms. Thus when a father or near relative dies, a son or survivor feels compelled by filial piety to erect a *mani*, a stone or mud seat concealed under a pile of slabs inscribed with a formula and crowned with prayer flags. A mani may be cairn shaped, or wall shaped. In the latter case it may divide a road, so that by circumambulating it, devout persons may perform good deeds applicable to the dead.[35] A single mani flag may be attached to a small stake, so that whenever the breeze flutters the cloth, prayers that are written on it ascend to petition the gods to have mercy on the soul which they memorialize.

Chapter 5

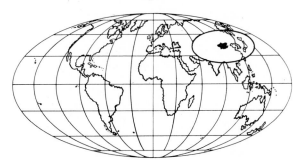

Mongolia

Sickness and Death

When a Mongol is injured or takes sick, he can expect little aid from modern medicine or surgery, but must rely on his natural strength of constitution. Common belief holds that all diseases are "originated by the activities of the evil spirits and the punishments of Buddha. . . . The greater part of the treatment is by incantations and prayers."[1] However, some simple medicines are prescribed. Among the stranger remedies used by the Mongols is the practice of attempting to lure illness from the dwelling of a sick person by means of a scapegoat. The lama, upon being summoned, fabricates a manikin, dresses it in the sick person's best clothes, and faces it in the direction that magic indicates will prove the best avenue of escape. Then real horses, cattle, and camels are tethered around the dummy, and

87

the lama prays that the afflicting spirit will join the mock flight. At the ceremony's end, the lama receives the animals as his fee.

Sometimes a man will accept the hazardous scapegoat assignment. Among the tribal leaders of the Mongolian steppes, such a one will array himself in his lord's best garments and ride long distances into the desert on his lord's familiar horse, in the hope of deceiving the evil spirits who afflict the great one with sickness or misfortune. The human scapegoat's rewards for risking desert and demons are the horse he rides and the clothes he wears.[2]

Even stranger is the practice of making a three-cornered ball, fashioned either of dough from ten centimeters to one meter thick, or of clay, if it is to be very large. The ball is left at a crossroads under a pagoda of willow sticks or silk cloth as the tribe moves on. Evil spirits are thought to be eager to enter this ball. Thus, they are enticed to abandon the ill. For his fee in fashioning this trap, the lama receives the silk cloth.[3]

When death appears imminent, the lama orders the sick person to be carried out of his tent and into the open, completely nude, so that the saying may be fulfilled: "The Mongol is born in a tent, but dies on the plain." Additionally, other considerations compel such action. Death is considered defiling, and the dwelling which has housed the dead is regarded as unfit for the living. Further, unless great precautions are taken, the spirit that death has liberated in a dwelling might find its familiar way back to afflict the living. For this reason if someone chances to die in a tent, the body is never carried through the regular door. Either a masking of straw is set up in front of the regular door, or an opening is made in the tent wall. When the body has been removed, the opening is closed, or the straw door burned.[4]

Departure of the Soul

To assist the soul in leaving the body, a prosperous family will retain the services of a lama, who remains until death comes. He sometimes carries out this function by continuously ringing his bell, pausing only once to pluck a hair from the brow of the dying person, thus opening an escape route through which the spirit can emerge. In other circumstances he sits cross legged in the presence of the ill person, so deep in silent prayer and meditation that his body seems to rise and float. His unspoken message to the emerging soul is that it has no further place in the body. It belongs elsewhere—and he names the place and the way thither, and thus assists the soul in freeing itself. His wordless, immobile absorption contrasts with the violent conduct of his assistants who chant, clash cymbals, ring bells, and blow trumpets. As the soul rises through the two great arteries of the neck and into the top of the skull where Mongols believe all the blood in the body meets and mingles, the meditating lama suddenly awakens from his trance and breathes heavily from the nose. By this act he assists the spirit, which has been rising through the body, in breaking through the fontanelle, that part of the top of the skull which in infancy is soft, but which later is closed with bone.[5]

When the *last* breath has been drawn, the lama sets the body up in a squatting position with the hands joined, and around its head he so wraps a blue scarf that the ends cover the face. Promiscuous handling of the corpse is avoided. A dead person is considered unclean, and to touch the body brings the need for purification by jumping over a fire in which incense smokes. Visiting relatives, who arrive bringing scarfs, tea, butter, and flour for the use of the dead on his journey into the afterlife, are careful not to approach the corpse.[6]

Modes of Disposal

Disposal takes place two or three days after death. Three methods are available to the Mongols: earth burial, cremation, or abandonment to scavengers. The chief lama decides which of these is to be used. In the interval before disposition, the lamas pray for the dead four times daily.

If earth burial is selected, before the grave is dug the precise location must be determined upon and the gods of the earth propitiated. To achieve these ends, the lama goes forth equipped with a white staff, a new rug, and the skin of a black goat. When he reaches a place, which he judges proper, he stops, traces a circle with his stick, throws the rug into the circle, and spreading the skin lays down. In this prone position he prays and mutters incantations. Suddenly he breaks off, leaps, and thrusts his staff through the goatskin to signify that the gods of the earth have given their consent. As fee for these services, he takes the rug and skin with him.

If cremation is selected, the lama goes through the same ritual for providing the site for burning as he would for burying, only now where he has thrust his staff, the members of the funeral party gather a sizable stack of faggots and lay the corpse upon it. Around these combustibles they build a wall of rocks, pierced through at the bottom to permit the fire to be lighted. Before the flame is applied, they anoint the brow of the corpse with a spoonful of butter and lay a yellow willow leaf 72 times upon the forehead. A person of nearly the same age as the deceased is selected to light the fire. When it is blazing, the lama thrusts his staff into the ground and attaches to it bits of cloth inscribed with prayers. While some wealthy Mongols may erect a tower over the place of cremation, others prefer to have their ashes gathered and sent to one of the several holy places or to a lamaserie.[7]

Among Mongolians, exposure or abandonment of the dead is the simplest and commonest method of disposal. It is generally effected by placing the body nude on the sands in the position in which it was tied at death. Again the lama plays an important role. It is customary to consult him with regard to the direction in which a body is cast away.[8] Two methods of exposure are practiced in Mongolia. The more common is to abandon the entire body to be consumed by wolves, eagles, or other scavengers. The less common is for lamas to strip the bones and feed the flesh to scavenger birds. This is the method commonly used by the Tibetans; less frequently by the Mongolians. Sometimes the body is placed on a cart and allowed to be jolted off and left behind as the springless cart is driven over rough ground. Such consideration, however, is accorded only to the remains of adults. When a Mongolian infant dies, the body is cast away with no ceremonies. The body of an older child, under ten years of age, receives little better treatment. At death it is stuffed into a sack and abandoned at a crossroads. The first Mongol thereafter to pass that way opens the sack so that the little spirit may wing its way to the afterlife.[9]

Exposure generally takes place on high pastures which lie so far from water that they are unsuited for summer camping and are so exposed in winter as to be too cold for winter quarters. In these lonely plains great herds of gazelles roam. Seeing them in the human bone yards, the Mongols get the erroneous impression that they eat the flesh of man. The Mongols do not, however, consider flesh eaters loathesome. On the contrary, they think it a good omen if scavengers make short work of the body. They permit not only wolves and foxes, but their own dogs to tear at the corpse.[10] And they repeat the folk saying common among the Chinese of central Asia that the eagle is the "nomad's coffin."[11]

Although exposure to scavenger birds and beasts may seem harsh to western sensitivities, Owen Lattimore found it "natural for grassland nomads, who have little use for spades and pick axes and little access to wood fuel, not to bury the dead or burn them as a common practice. Mongol feeling about the bodies of the dead," he continues, "is quite different from ours, as might be expected. If we think their feeling is callous, they think ours is morbid. The flesh, they say, is a burden and the life of the body a trial and full of sin." Lattimore speaks of a Mongol who could leave his children behind but not his mother. "She was old, and he must be there when she died. Then he would pick a fine place to leave her body, some lonely, clean, and noble place. Her spirit would be free and the body shed, the bones discarded. He spoke of this as tenderly and lovingly as people sometimes plan a beautiful and quiet tomb."[12] In this respect the Mongolian mode of disposal by exposure, as does the practice in Tibet, finds its rationale not in cruelty or inhumaneness, but in relation to the physical environment, and the means at hand to meet the universal problem of disposal of society's dead.

Mongol Mourning

During the forty-nine days of prescribed mourning, the widow and children of the deceased are not allowed to shave their heads, as they would normally be permitted to do, and the women do not wear their coral diadems. Instead they substitute a piece of blue cloth. Ordinarily, when two Mongols meet they salute each other verbally. During the mourning period they bow their heads and hold their silence.[13] Among some Mongol groups, for three years after a death no marriages are permitted in the family, festivities are reduced to a minimum, and the traditional redecorating of the shelter is eliminated.[14]

Chapter 6

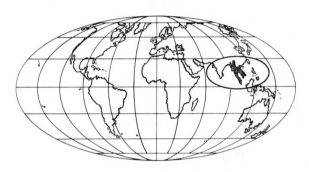

Southeast Asia

Laos

To a Westerner with a profound sense of the grave dignity of all matters connected with death, the gaiety of the typical funeral of a wealthy person in Laos sometimes seems surprising, more often shocking. And yet, the Laotian finds these funeral rites reasonable and fitting, in keeping with his whole life philosophy and in complete conformity with the teachings of Buddha.[1]

For a Laotian, death marks entrance into Nirvana, or as popular pronunciation has it "Nibanna," where begins a new and better life. Although Hindus may not agree as to the meaning of the word, and point out its etymological origins as indicating a place of eternal flame, Laotians generally think of Nirvana as a pleasant region, where their desires are satisfied.

93

The golden
casket in which
bodies of dead
Southeast Asian
Buddhist monks
are kept before
cremation

So enviable seems the lot of a dead person that a house in which
he is waked is called *heun di,* that is, the "happy house."
That death for Laotians who die of natural causes after a
good life is considered a happy event is well attested by their
funeral rites. Long ago these rites were fixed by royal edict
and written into law. The law makes a distinction between
those who die fortunately and must be cremated and those who
die less fortunately and must be buried. It also establishes six
categories of death: death from drowning, from being struck by
lightning, from falling out of a tree, from being killed by a
tiger, from hanging or being otherwise executed, and from
disease.

Among these modes of dying, natural death following disease
confers the right to the greatest burial privileges. Those who
have perished by violence must not be cremated, and must be
buried immediately. Many older prescriptions seem cruel today,
and are no longer strictly observed. Thus, under the old code,
a woman dying during pregnancy was not only refused the

94

Pyre and catafalque
being erected
for cremation of
a Buddhist monk

prayers of a Buddhist priest, but could not be cremated, or even buried in an ordinary cemetery. Many of the rules were and are obviously hygienic in intent.[2]

Happy then is the virtuous, prosperous, Laotian Buddhist who has lived well and who dies a natural death surrounded

Shrine in which
Buddhist monks
are cremated

95

Carved banana stalks are used to adorn
funeral pyre for dead Buddhist monk

by his kinsmen. His life and his manner of taking off entitle
him to the full rites. He has merited the blessed afterlife.

Preparation of the Body and the Wake

When such a Laotian dies, his relatives first close the eyes
and then wash the body in cool, perfumed water. They slide
a coin or a small piece of gold between the teeth. Thus they
symbolize the fact that earthly goods have so trifling value for
of all the deceased's possessions he takes only this little with
him into death. Similarly, the white cotton bands which encircle
the neck of the body and bind his wrists and ankles attest the
weakness of the ties which bind him to death: to his material
interests, his earthly love. After these services have been performed the body is covered with a white shroud and laid in a
coffin. This is constructed of six boards fastened together with
a small amount of *bong;* a sticky resin which a special messenger, sent by the dead man's relatives, has brought back from

the nearby forest. The coffin is then laid on a platform of banana logs. These, rather than hardwood, are chosen not only because their softness symbolizes the brevity of life, but because they teach the lesson that like a log, the man who lacks heart has no substance to his character.[3]

The prayers of the priests give further point to the message of the vanity of life, which forms the great lesson of death. With eyes lowered, they quote Buddha: "The body from which the soul has fled has no worth. Soon it will encumber the earth as a useless thing, like the trunk of a withered tree. Life lasts only for a moment. Birth and death follow one another in inescapable sequence. All that live must die. That man indeed is fortunate who achieves the nothingness of being. All animal creation is dying, or dead, or merits to be dead. All of us are dying. We cannot escape death."

For seven days and seven nights the "happy house" is the meeting place in which noisy ceremonies are held. No one publicly mourns death. The dead person must be considered well off. He must be envied. Only the priests pray: "O dead one,

Dragon boat carries ashes of cremated monks to be strewn into river

Janse Collection, Library of Congress

97

pursue your destiny. Flee to paradise. You will know rebirth into a better life. Do not linger to haunt those who remain here, and to share this life of invisible darkness which is the lot of the living. Those whom you leave behind reckon accurately your good fortune in your liberation. With happy impatience they await their own turn. You neither want nor need them, and they are happy without you. Now follow your destiny."

To attract the spirit of the dead and send it into the beyond so that it will be reborn quickly and to make certain that it will never return to haunt familiar places, the family, through the mediation of the priests, offers food and other gifts to it. These offerings are given to the priests and are repeated as long as the family feels that the spirit awaits rebirth or lacks necessities. A family is considered accursed which neglects to make these offerings. Without such gifts, the spirit wanders forever in the shadow of the nether regions.[4]

The Burning Bier

While priests pray and relatives keep vigil over the body, many hands build the catafalque and finish decorating the bier, so that the afterlife may continue joyful for the spirit. Young

Buddhist monk prays while neophytes look on

Cremation of casket follows ceremonies

P.I.P. Photos

98

"A tiger in the streets" of Burma. Casket held in tiger's mouth will be cremated along with huge animal effigy

girls roll cigarettes and prepare gifts. In the delight of a common task, those who make the funeral preparations feast heartily and play certain games. These games not only suggest that for the deceased death is the triumph of youth and life, but they reaffirm and illustrate the exhortations of the priests. Friends act out joyfully the life of the dead person. Even the members of the family take part in this common gaiety. Although they feel the normal sense of loss, they fear that if they yield to it, they risk holding back the spirit which is poised to take flight into the regions of the blessed. And so in a great feast of life the orchestra plays, laughter rings out, and the guests drink, dance, and give way to merriment. Life they hold is stronger than death because death is only the entry into a fuller life.

After seven days, the coffin is moved into a shelter built especially to house it, on a corner of the deceased's rice field. To this place each day the relatives make a pilgrimage, conversing with the spirit, bringing gifts of food, waiting on the body, killing the wood lice that threaten to destroy the coffin, and removing insects that would devour the body. Every

99

Giant effigy of former
Burmese dignitary
will be cremated at
final funeral ceremony

eighth and fifteenth day after the waxing and waning of the
moon, they invite Buddhist priests to join them at breakfast.
When the fourth month of the Laotian calendar ushers in the
dry season, and the days of rest from work in the rice fields
approach, all hearts rejoice. This is the month not only for
marriages but for the rites of cremation.

On the flat expanse of the dormant, dry rice paddy a great
pavilion is constructed. Beneath its roof workmen erect a
ceremonial canopy, a paper dome supported by four fragile

100

Effigies of Burmese dignitary and
wife on elephant effigy burned in
cremation ceremony in Rangoon

View of the scaffolding
used in building effigies

Body of Buddhist
archbishop hauled to
top of elephant effigy
before cremation

columns. This will be the last shelter or dwelling place of the body before it is reduced to ashes. The coffin now is trimmed in preparation for burning, the style of decoration varying according to region. In some places gilded paper leaves are glued to the wood, together with paper cut-outs representing flowers or divinities. The walls of the pavilion are likewise adorned with decorations that in some cases border on the obscene. The pavilion may be ready days before the funeral. In such event it becomes the scene of festivity, and young people gather beneath it to celebrate the feast of death through which in dance, song, and laughter they tell their joy of life. These festivities must last not less than six days and six nights. During this period processions and religious and other daytime ceremonies alternate with nighttime fireworks and games and feasts. All in the village participate.

Finally, on the sixth day the pavilion is partly opened, to allow men tugging at a white cotton rope to pull the catafalque inside until it rests under the paper dome where it is supported by two gigantic bird figures. When the catafalque is in place, wood is heaped beneath it and in the hollow bodies of the birds. The widow and children of the deceased are present for

Burial houses and spirit figures of Muong tribe of northern Vietnam

Malayan tribal
members smear grease
on memorial post
in cult of dead
ceremony

this ceremony. As a sign of mourning, their heads have been shaved, and they are clothed entirely in white.[5]

Cremation

Throughout the night preceding cremation, the vigil is kept by means of a feast of tremendous proportions. Finally, the supreme moment comes, and while the priests repeat their prayers, a torch is put to the funeral pyre. "The body which the soul has left is nothing. Life is a passing thing."—So reads the text. From the pyre a great flame swirls aloft as though it were the spirit of the dead rising heavenward. Throughout the remainder of the night and each night thereafter until the second waning of the moon, men guard the fire and rekindle it if it dies down. Meanwhile, the house of the deceased continues to welcome young men and women, who dine, drink, and dance until dawn.[6]

These joyous ceremonies finally come to an end on the second day after the waning of the moon, when once again the family

103

An Anamanite shrine
dedicated to the
worship of dead
whales

makes an offering on behalf of the deceased, and again invites
the priests to breakfast. Then, long before sunrise, the family,
relatives, and friends, accompanied by the priests, make a pilgrimage to the extinguished pyre to gather the scanty ashes
of the dead. These they place in a small jar to be deposited
in a pagoda until a monument suitable to the memory of a
virtuous man has been erected.

The *Rig Veda* contains a funeral chant which admonishes:
"Leave behind what is reprehensible and return to your real
home. Unite yourself to a glorified body. May your spirit flee
upon the wind." The rite of cremation is a response to this
last injunction. It provides liberation for the spirit. Beholding
it, each Buddhist may have a foretaste of the depths of joy
that sooner or later must be his. And yet he cannot fail to ask:
"What shall I become after death? With this single life shall I
have finished the cycle of my successive existence? Shall I go
hence with a carefree world into the company of blessed saints
to await the promised advent of a future Buddha? Or shall
I be forced once more to return to this world of travail, to
languish under the appearance of another body, and to repeat
this tedious cycle of birth and rebirth? No more than any
other man am I able to answer finally this question which
confronts all men."[7]

Thao Nhouy Abhay reflects on the seeming paradox of the

104

Laotian funeral. "There is a curious contradiction in all this: To die is difficult and sorrowful, yet above all things death produces a celebration, a feast, a spectacle, in which there is a discordant note of inhumanity and brutality. With many others, I deplore the public disrespect and indifference to the feelings of the suffering bereaved. And yet, while criticizing its excesses, I still admire the beauty of this tradition. It is not customary for us to lay bare our feelings at the moment when we lose those whom we love the most. We therefore abstain from a theatrical show of public sorrow. By becoming more dignified our grief becomes more selectively meaningful. In Laos we learn how to live in the presence of death."[8]

Lamet

Customs such as these which characterize the burial of a prosperous Buddhist in the Laotian centers of culture are not to be found among the hill peasants of Laos. The Lamets live in the midst of a large number of strange tribes in the north-west corner of Laos in the village of Mokala Panghay. They follow a kind of ancestor cult.

Death and Burial

The anthropologist Karl Gustav Izikowitz, in the course of a field study, had the opportunity to witness a Lametian funeral.[9] One night a terrible wailing that lasted for three days and three nights told the village that a ten year old girl had died. Although the cries blended into a monotonous melody in which most of the words were lost, the sentence, "She did not die, she was murdered," again and again was distinguishable. Her relatives apparently suspected that the child had been slain by black magic, and that her murderer was a man with whom her father had quarreled.

The next morning the relatives of the girl placed lances outside the door of the house in which she had lived. By this device they hoped to prevent the spirit of death from making an exit and roving at large through the village. As a double precaution, they lighted fires before the door and kept them burning until

105

Sitting coffin, Singapore, manufactured and sold by Buddhist monastery. Such coffins used only for cremation of Buddhist priests, nuns or very religious laymen

Photo Courtesy E. C. and G. R. Johnson

after the burial ceremony. Other relatives meanwhile had entered the forest, cut down a tree, and hollowed out the log for a coffin. They did not bring the coffin into the village, but left it standing next to the grave.[10]

The street and square bisect a Lamet village, and by custom death further divides it so that the portion containing the girl's home was closed to the other half of it, and the people living on the one side could have no dealings with their neighbors living on the other. This cleavage extended even to the community house, which has entrances on both sides. Temporarily, each group had to confine itself to the entrance nearer it, and use only that portion adjacent to that entrance. This isolation was rooted in the Lamets' belief that, although the spirit of death can cling to clothing and take possession of a living body, it cannot cross an open place alone. As a further precautionary measure, members of the family were not allowed to speak to other people, and except for attending the burial, for sixty days relatives of the dead were required to remain in the village. It was not difficult to identify these relatives. All were forbidden to wear headgear of any kind, and the men were required to shave their foreheads.[11]

On the day of the funeral, prior to the procession to the grave, two pigs were sacrificed amid prolonged incantations addressed to the spirit of death who was asked to leave the village and betake himself to the land of the dead. This mythical place is conceived to lie across the Mekong River, which mean-

106

ders down the peninsula into the South China Sea. The incantations describe the route into this land.

Men bearing the litter containing the girl's body headed the procession. Behind them walked the male relatives, supporting themselves with their lances. The parents, with their hair hanging loose, brought up the rear. On the march through the village, the men mumbled long incantations, the nature of which they refused to divulge.[12]

The Lametian Grave

Upon their return to the village the members of the family procession sought to drive out any spirits of death that might be lingering in the house where the girl had died. Boys and men ran through the house bearing torches. They jumped, screamed, stamped, wailed. They carried all the household tools and furniture into the yard. The commotion ended as suddenly as it began. The spirits had fled. The men could now remove their spears from before the doorway, and put out the fire.[13]

Because this was an unmarried child, the funeral ceremonies were far less formal and costly than they would have been for an older person, and particularly for an elderly man with living descendants. The burial of such a person is likely to involve one of the heavier expenses a Lamet family will ever be asked to meet: the greater the wealth of the deceased, the costlier will be his funeral.[14]

Although Izikowitz was not permitted to witness the burial, months later he found the child's grave. It lay in the woods, not far from a path leading to some barns. The Lamets believe that each person has two souls, the one dwelling in the head and the other in the knees. To fasten these souls to the earth, they place two stones over the corresponding positions in the grave. Because of their further belief that these two souls meet in the region of the navel, they stand up four stones in a kind of dolmen, or square box, in this third corresponding position. They use this box to hold erect a section of a small tree with the limbs chopped short so that the stumps serve as brackets.

On these hang some of the belongings of the dead person, and the skull of a sacrificed animal. Next to each of the single stones they drive a pole, on the top of which they place another skull of a sacrificial animal. On some graves a staff replaces a tree trunk, surmounted either by crossed sticks, or by a miniature model of a house. The grave itself is surrounded by a square bamboo fence, against the laterals of which sharpened bamboo stakes are leaned. Only two graves lay in the place where the girl was buried, although the Lamet have some larger burial plots. Over some of their graves they hang buffalo skins, which they allow to rot. Sometimes rich families set up large stones on their graves, and thereby gain prestige. Transporting heavy monoliths from a distance is costly.[15]

After the body is dressed in the deceased's best clothes, it is draped with a *sampot* of silk. When it is placed in the coffin, wooden knives are laid next to it. If the deceased possessed a gong or a bronze drum, but lacked male heirs, both instruments are pounded by relatives until the bronze shatters, and the pieces are then laid on the grave. The middle hole of a man's grave is decorated with his crossbow, wallet, baskets,

Decorated earthen burial mounds. Radhé tribes of northern Vietnam

Truck with flower-bedecked bier carries casket while veiled
Buddhist priests and family members follow

and rain coat. On a woman's grave an apparatus for distilling
rice wine, and a few broken bowls are stood. A man with male
heirs generally makes a verbal will in which he specifies the
inheritance which each of his sons is to receive. Custom
requires that elaborate feasts must be spread, and buffaloes
must be sacrificed. For obscure reasons—possibly the buffalo
is somehow conceived as being connected with the spirit of
death or with ancestral spirits—these beasts at burials are not
tied to the regular sacrifice poles that stand outside each
dwelling, but are slaughtered on the steps of the house.[16]

The Moi

The term "Moi" was coined by the Anamanite peoples of
Southeastern Asia to refer to the barbarous aborigines of the
territory which for many years was known as Indo-China and now
comprises the countries of Cambodia, Laos, and North and
South Vietnam. The Moi actually include some thirty identifiable highland Mon-Khmer-speaking tribes of Southeast Asia.
The burial customs of the Moi follow a pattern different from
the Buddhist pattern which dominates the funeral customs of
their Anamanite neighbors.

The Moi, as a rule, are extremely poor, and their funerals
tend to be simple affairs. The bodies are carried, completely
disrobed, to a "Soul House" which serves as a primitive

mausoleum.[17] The walls of this house, which is small, are decorated with sacred symbols, and before each house rather weird, carved wood, bird-like figures with long necks are placed. There are no cemeteries as such, and the sight of these figures sticking up through the weeds which overgrow the burial sites can indeed be startling.

The Panorama of Funerals From Mandalay to Singapore

The descriptions of the Laotian, Lametan and Moi funerals illustrate both the continuity and diversity of funeral customs in Southeastern Asia. The dominant pattern is Buddhism; from Burma to Malaya this religion interprets life and death to its millions of adherents and gives meaning to the specific funeral practices that have been developed in the various geographic regions.

Whether a death occurs in Burma, Thailand, Cambodia, Laos, Vietnam, or Malaya, for the followers of Buddha it calls forth a general pattern of activity: family lamentation, prayers by monks, swathing of the body, offerings to the dead, the preparation of a decorated bier or carrier, a noisy and usually

Cemetery in Saigon provides hearses and coffins for exhumed remains

Saigon funeral establishment, showing funeral vehicles and coffin display

Photos Courtesy of E. C. and G. R. Johnson

110

Photos Courtesy G. D. Webb

Modern funeral coach and casket used in Christian burials, Singapore

colorful funeral procession, cremation as the preferred mode of disposal, and ancestor worship in some form of cult of the dead. The services of monks, or lamas are everywhere sought. Around these central activities a host of various and sometimes competing practices develops. Inasmuch as Buddhism need not be embraced to the exclusion of other religious beliefs, Taoist, Confucianist, and Shintoist ceremonies often are intermingled in the totality of behavior toward the dead.

Southeast Asia, with many peoples from neighboring countries settled in specific areas or cities, presents a tremendously variegated picture of funeral customs and practices. People who call China, France, Britain, India, Persia, Japan or some other country homeland and who by religion are Taoist, Hindu, Christian, Moslem, Jew or of some other belief mix with, or dominate, or maintain minority status in the lands of the Mon-

Most modern
Singapore
funeral home

Photo Courtesy G. D. Webb

111

Khmer, Anam, Shan-Thai and Malayo-Polynesian peoples. Whatever the political destiny of this conglomerate of ethnic and racial and religious groups, their traditional death customs undoubtedly will persist tenaciously and remain long as a residuum in the cultures that have disappeared into mass societies.

Malaya

A case in point is Malaya, where still can be found jungle-dwelling Negrito tribes living on the "pre-civilized" level; where other native Malayan groups have caught the spirit of socio-economic and political progress and are busy developing a federation of new nations; and where in the large cities, Singapore the prime example, dominant or competing cultures are grafted onto the existing populace.

Within Singapore, and between this crown colony and the hinterland, can be found the most striking differences in death customs. A Malayan native tribe remembers its dead by building a rough scaffold about a crude memorial monument and then smearing it with grease from top to bottom. By contrast, in Singapore the Christian community memorializes its dead with monuments built by monumental masons who look to England for inspiration in craftsmanship and design, and with services that would readily be understood anywhere among English-speaking peoples.

In point of fact the Christian Community in Malaya buries the dead along lines similar in many ways to burial in England, and some Malayans have been trained by or have worked for British undertakers. The casket or coffin is selected at a casket works, or it may be built on the premises to suit. Most funerals take place in the home of the deceased. Embalming is the exception and when deemed necessary at all is generally performed in the home, also. Funeral homes have "chapels of rest" and a preparation room, but these facilities are not too often used. Bodies to be shipped will, of course, be embalmed in the preparation room of the funeral establishment. Cremation exists side by side with earth burial, although in either case the tendency is to bury within 48 hours after death.

112

Colorful procession of mourners with umbrellas leads Chinese funeral in Singapore, Malaya

Shrouds are available, but are used in only a minority of cases —most likely by Roman Catholics.

Funeral services in the Christian Community of Singapore are generally held at a church or the public cemetery or crematory chapels, rarely at hospital chapels or houses. Costs of funerals are lumped into one sum, as is usually the case in the United States, including: washing and dressing the body, the coffin or casket, pallbearers, hearse, religious artifacts, use of chapel, and, somewhat a novelty, the services of a private photographer and a set of photographs. Cemetery or crematory charges are not included in the single or "package" charge of the funeral director, nor, at this moment, is the charge for embalming the dead.[18]

113

The Taj Mahal, erected in 17th Century by Shah Jehan as a memorial to his favorite wife. Considered to be world's most beautiful architecture. Agra, India

Chapter 7

Hindu India

Hindu Religion

According to the 1951 Census of India, 85 per cent of its inhabitants were Hindus, ten per cent Moslems, a little more than two per cent Christians, and the remainder divided among the Sikhs, Jains, aboriginal tribes, Parsis, Buddhists, and Jews.[1] The focus of this section will consequently be upon Hindu burial customs and beliefs.

Hinduism may be regarded as a body of customs and beliefs suffused with religious significance. Hinduism differs from many world religions in that the term "Hindu" does not refer to the followers of a particular leader or creed. It is a way of life rather than a denomination.[2] Key terms of reference are *karma*, referring to the belief that the consequence of every action, good or bad, must be fully worked out, and *dharma*, the sum of prescriptions and ideals of a Hindu's life. Each person has his karma, the ethical consequence of all his acts, as

115

a rough equivalent to the idea of "fate" in Western beliefs. Another fundamental belief is that of the transmigration of souls, *sansara*. According to this doctrine the individual's station and lot in one life have been determined by his actions in a previous one, and his present behavior will shape his future fortune.[3] The ultimate goal of the soul is liberation from the wheel of rebirth, through reabsorption into or identity with the Oversoul, *Brahma*, the essence of the universe, immaterial, uncreated, limitless, timeless. Liberation may well be the happy fortune only for those whose karma has decreed it. However, only the bare outlines of one's fate have been sketched; many decisions and choices are left to each person to make. Death may bring liberation, or the soul may again transmigrate. In either case no terrors of finality and nothingness seem to exist for the Hindu. Although separation from the present sensible world of human associations is tragic and sorrowful for him, in the mind of the Hindu, death is release for a soul allowing it to journey down a path that must somewhere have an ending.

For the sake of his more immediate fortunes, the Hindu propitiates the gods and godlings that preside over various

Hindu funeral procession passes through native shop district of Agra

Hired female mourners weep as garland-bedecked body
of Hindu awaits cremation

facets of his life.[4] Further merit for his karma may be gained
by pilgrimages and almsgiving, and by the veneration of
Brahmins and holy men.[5] Beyond making such efforts, the
Hindu accepts life much as it comes. And, when death takes
place he regards it as a natural enough occurrence. Yet it is
one which he must deal with ceremoniously so that the spirit of
the dead, purified in all respects, may again be reborn.

Earth Burial and Cremation

A quatrain designed to be recited during disposition ceremonies gives significant evidence that in Vedic times—the pe-

117

riod from 1500 to 1000 B.C. when the *Vedas*, the most ancient literature of the Hindus, were written—the Aryans buried their dead in the earth:

Extend wide thine arms, O earth, to embrace the dead.
With tender pressure and with welcome sweet
Wrap him all tenderly, even as the mother
Wraps her soft robe about the beloved child.[6]

Cremation, which later was substituted for inhumation, persists to the present. The Indian Ministry of Scientific Research and Cultural Affairs reports that "ceremonies connected with death, cremation, and afterlife are very important to the Hindu. A mystic and pessimist by nature, in death he finds the full expression of his religion."

Hindus believe that before a man dies he should be loosed of his sins. To accomplish this end, old people who feel the finger of death upon them make long journeys to Benares or to some other holy city on the Ganges. There they may either wash away their sins on the banks, or die in the sacred waters. Relatives sometimes carry the dying into the stream, and hold them erect there so that they may breathe their last breath standing knee deep in the cleansing waters. At Benares the river banks have a sacred character equal to that of the river itself, and people of the neighborhood who are judged mortally ill are sheltered in huts at the river's edge, there to dwell until they die.

The same authority observes: "This method of absolving sins cannot, for obvious reasons, be practiced by all." On their death beds less fortunate individuals perform an atonement ceremony. The usual procedure is to invite a group of Brahmins to visit a sick person. After he has been propped into an upright or reclining position, the Brahmins ask him why they were invited. He tells them that from birth until that hour he has lived in sin. He prays for atonement, and distributes gifts of coins to the Brahmins. Having accepted these, they choose a representative from among the bystanders. This person steps forward and proclaims his willingness to have all the dying man's sins transferred to him except certain major

118

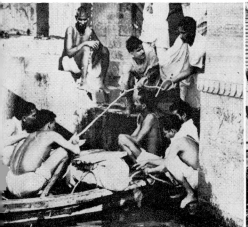

Body is ceremonially immersed in
sacred Ganges before cremation

Some arrive in boats to witness the
cremation ceremony

offenses, such as murder and adultery. After receiving a gift of
coins from the sick man the substitute leaves the house, loaded
with another's guilt. Thereafter the Brahmins take a purificatory bath to wash away any stain of sin from themselves.[7]

When it is clear that a man is close to death, he is laid on
a bed of Kusa grass in the open air, and his head is sprinkled
with water and smeared with mud, both brought from the
Ganges. Next, a *Salagrama,* a sacred ammonite or fossil shell
representing *Vishnu* "The Preserver," the second god of the
Hindu Triad is placed near him, and while the Vedas are
chanted, leaves of holy basil, a plant of the mint family, are
strewn over his head.

Preparation of the Body

Mr. C. J. Jayadev, Curator of the Anthropology Section,
Government Museum, Egmore, Madras, describes in some
detail contemporary Hindu procedure for disposal of the dead.[8]

The first step is to lay out the body, garland it, and place a
lamp at its head. Following this the navel is smeared with oil,
the nostrils are plugged with bats of cotton, the big toes are
tied together, the hands positioned across the chest, and the

119

eyelids closed. For those communities where burial is in the squatting posture "corresponding adjustments are made before the onset of *rigor mortis.*"

Preparation of the dead for ceremonial disposal calls for many diverse procedures, and requires a variety of personnel. Relatives must be informed, ceremonial materials needed for the disposal gathered, a bier constructed, arrangements made for carrying out the ceremonies of the funeral by the son or other close relative of the male line, and the body must be further prepared for the burial or cremation.

Meanwhile the women of the household have surrounded the dead and filled the air with their lamentations. Though a funeral is considered a celebration, members of the family, and especially the women, must mourn.[9] Any friend or stranger may enter the house to view the dead.

The next step is to prepare the body for the funeral and for final disposal. Preparation is carried out, Jayadev notes, by the men for a male, and the women for a female. The ritual consists of anointing the head of the body, first with oil, and then with soap nut powder and other preparations. Every participant in the preparations, beginning with the chief heirs, performs this rite. Both tradition and custom decree that whoever presides at this ceremony is the dead person's successor and inherits his property.

The presence of numerous relatives and friends is intended to establish the fact that death was the result of natural causes and not of suicide, murder or violence.

Because Hindus regard death as defiling they use the services of mortuary specialists. Included in this group is a grave digger, if the body is to be buried, and persons who conduct the ritual of burial.

Grave digging is carried out through the local town or municipal agencies. Certain charges are made, such as the cost of digging and filling the grave. In a cremation, a charge is made for the fuel for the pyres. Those who conduct funerals are recruited from one of five religious mendicant orders. Jayadev lists these as *Pandaram, Dasari, Panichavan,*

120

Vettiyan, Othuvan, according to the caste, creed, or community of the dead person.

The making of the bier, *Pallakku* or *Padai,* is the next step. In its simplest form the bier consists of two poles about seven feet long with seven short pieces of bamboo tied across at intervals of a foot or less. Over this framework is placed a freshly cut coconut frond, woven to form a mat. A pillow consists of a roll of straw. The bier may also be decorated with a canopy of flowers fastened to a bamboo framework.

The Procession

Meanwhile the dead body has been bathed, swathed in new linen, and adorned with sacred ashes and sandal paste or white clay. When dressed for burial the body of a married woman will display all the insignia of her wedded state: tumeric, vermillion, flowers, colored cloths, bangles, and jewelry. The procession is formed at the house of the dead. This custom is in keeping with the Indian tradition that all important rituals, especially marriage and funeral,—take place within the home. The procession is led by the chief mourner, who is usually the eldest son or a very near relative of the deceased. In his hand he carries a pot containing coals lighted from the consecrated fire maintained by the deceased. Behind him, and directly before the body, walk a handful of mourners chanting *Ram, Ram;* or *Ram Nam Sach Hai,* or "The Name of the Ram is truth itself." The uncoffined body is borne on its stretcher by the nearest relatives. In some places, musicians and drum players accompany the procession. The widow, however, always remains behind.

Cremation

A Hindu cremation presents a striking spectacle. The banks of the Ganges, India's most sacred river, are considered the most desirable place for it, and Benares, the holy city, has the greater part of its waterfront given over to burning *ghats, i. e.,* concrete or marble slabs at the river's edge upon which the funeral pyres are built.

121

Burning ghats at Benares.
Immersed bodies in fore-
ground, pyres above

P. Gendreau Photo

When the procession reaches the burning ghat the functionaries remove the body from the bier, immerse it in the
holy waters of the river and then place it on the pyre. One of
the priests stationed at the site performs a brief disposal
ceremony. In the Hindu caste system this occupation is considered very low, and upper class Brahmins will not engage in it.

The rite finished, the winding sheet is cut, the body is
smeared liberally with *ghi, i. e.,* clarified butter, and is laid on
the pyre. The chief mourner, usually the son, lights the pyre
with a flaming brand, ignited in his fire pot. For a man the
torch is applied to the head of the bier; for a woman, to the
foot. As the flames spread, the attendant priests recite an appropriate invocation: "Fire, you were lighted by him, so may he
be lighted from you, that he may gain the regions of celestial
bliss. May this offering prove auspicious."

Those who have come out to honor the dead march around
the pyre, but are forbidden to gaze into the flames. They are

122

expected, however, to see to it that the skull bursts in the burning. Hindus believe that at death the soul is trapped in the skull, and must be released. If fire does not split the skull, it is broken by blows from a cudgel.

After this, the mourners walk to the river, and having taken a purification bath, make offerings to the *manes*—that is, to the ancestral spirits of the deceased. Filling the joined palms of their hands with water they raise their arms and cry as they release it: "May this oblation reach you." When this rite

Cremation begins with
next of kin applying torch

P. Gendreau Photo by L. Green

Attendant insures completion
of cremation

Ewing Galloway Photo

has been performed, they recite elegiac verses, such as: "Vain is he who seeks to find the changeless in the human form, which is variable like the plantain trunk, and perishable like sea foam." "When the five element body, to receive the rewards done in its former person, reverts to its five components, what room is there for sorrow?" "Earth shall pass away, ocean and the gods themselves shall have an end. Mortal man, a bubble, should not he too die?" "All that is low must perish; all that is high must fall; all complex bodies must be dissolved; and life must terminate in death."

Post Funeral Rites

On the third day after cremation, a few close relatives of the deceased gather at the cremation spot for the bone-gathering ceremony. To assure his parents passage into heaven every Hindu piously hopes to cast their bones into the Ganges or into some other holy river. After a priest has read from the sacred texts and sprinkled holy water on the place of cremation, he gathers the calcined bones into a vase which he presents to the deceased's eldest son or nearest relative. The poor cast the bones into the nearest stream, confident that all flowing water ultimately is joined to the Ganges, the mother of all waters. Those who can afford to carry them later to the Ganges or to some distant sacred place, bury the vase containing the bones near the cremation spot. There it remains until the tenth day or the day of the Shraddha, when it will be dug up and given to the family.

It is believed that if a ten-day ritual is performed by the living the soul of the deceased will receive a complete, subtle, and tenuous body. It gets a head on the first day; a neck on the second; a heart on the third; a back on the fourth, a navel on the fifth; private parts on the sixth; thighs on the seventh; knees on the eighth; nothing on the ninth; and feet on the tenth. On the tenth day the subtle body is completed. If proper ceremonies are not performed, the soul either gets no body at all, or a partial one. In the latter event, it roams space as a misshapen, evil spirit.

124

To avoid such calamity, a Hindu prays fervently for a son who will perform his funeral rites.

During the ten-day ritual, the family of the deceased is considered unclean. On the first day after death, they may not cook in the house, and although they may eat food sent in by relatives, most persons prefer to fast. For the remaining nine days, they may cook and eat only certain kinds of food.

The Shraddha

Before the completed subtle body can journey to its celestial abode, it must receive nourishment. To provide this, the *Shraddha,* one of the most important and expensive of Hindu ceremonies, is performed, sometime between the tenth and the thirty-first day after cremation. Because it is believed that gifts which are made and feasts which are provided during this ceremony will reach the soul of the deceased, all Hindus are expected to give lavishly to the attendant priests.

The person who undertakes to have the Shraddha performed is expected to go barefooted to the house of his relatives and personally invite them to attend. The Shraddha requires a large number of metal vessels, silver for wealthy, brass for ordinary people. After the rites, these are given to the Brahmins. Musicians are hired to entertain the guests in the intervals between the various stages of the Shraddha. The ceremonies, which begin early in the morning, last until the afternoon, and are concluded by the distribution of gifts, the lion's share of which go to the *Guru* or religious teacher, and the *Purohita,* or officiating priest. The remainder are given to the other Brahmins, the first on the list ordinarily receiving about five rupees in cash, and a brass vessel worth about four or five rupees. Other Brahmins are rewarded in proportion to their status and importance in the ceremony. Poor people hold the funeral feast on the day of the funeral and thus terminate the mourning period. The wealthy defer and prolong the feast. On the second day they feed Brahmins, and on the third, the members of other castes. Although this first Shraddha ordinarily terminates the

125

formal mourning period, it does not by any means end the death observances. Like their human counterparts, the manes experience continuous hunger, and hence need more than one meal. For this reason Hindus perform as many later Shraddhas as they can afford: daily perhaps, or weekly, monthly, or yearly. These supplementary meals, however, usually are inexpensive, requiring the presence of only a single Brahmin and a few guests. It is customary in observing a Shraddha to make boiled rice balls—called *pinda*—and to throw these out of the house for the manes to feast upon.

The cycle of death observances concludes with the bone throwing ceremonies. When bones have been kept by the relatives, they must be cast into a sacred stream within the year following death. Persons living close to the Ganges usually perform this rite soon after cremation. Except for the very poor, however, those who live at a distance must bear the bones to the Ganges. Three cities, Haridwar, Benares, and Gaya, are considered most efficacious places for performing Shraddhas and throwing bones, and at each of them hundreds of professional priests daily line the river banks, performing the rites for thronging pilgrims. Another efficacious spot is near Bombay, at Nasik, where the Godavary River has its source. Middle class persons of Bombay, who cannot afford the trip to the Ganges, perform the bone throwing ceremony there.

Change and Continuity

Mortuary matters play a major role in the lives of the people of India. Next to marriage, funerals constitute the most important of Hindu ceremonies, and by the same token they exact a heavy financial toll. Although the burden of performing Shraddhas has impoverished many families, yet, as Jayadev points out, the loss of status and position is more feared in these matters than is impoverishment. Although the national government at Delhi in September, 1958, issued a "guest control" order stipulating that not more than 50 guests can be given food at wedding parties or funerals, it is questionable if fundamental changes in mortuary beliefs and practices can be seriously affected by governmental decree.

A case in point is the long outlawed (1829) custom of *suttee*, the self-immolation of the widow on her husband's funeral pyre. Scattered instances of the practice were noted until the 1860's. After this period it was considered to have fallen into complete disuse. Yet in 1954 in Jodhpur (population, 250,000), Sugan Kunwar, widow of Brigadier Jabar Singh, by her own act perished in the flames of her husband's pyre. "By the end of the week 100,000 people had visited the tramped-out fire," reported *Time*,[10] "some kneeling to scoop the dust, now sacred into their mouths. 'It was a great and noble act of suttee,' observed one of Sugan's relatives. 'Her name will long be remembered.'" That the act brought reverence from hundreds of thousands, and for months ballads and poems extolling her act were sold and in Jodhpur's homes "emotional wives worship before cheap lithographs showing a noble Sugan Kunwar, cradling the head of her dead husband in her lap as the flames consume both,"[11] may be merely an emanation of crowd behavior in a mass society. Yet, in a country where a mogul emperor put 20,000 skilled artisans to work for 17 years to build the most beautiful mausoleum in the world—the *Taj Mahal* —there is likely to continue this basic pattern of ceremonious funerals and the worship of the departed spirits of the dead.

Toda men bring in buffalo for sacrifice in funeral ceremony

Chapter 8

Tribal India and Ceylon

Tribal India

Cremation and Inhumation

In northern India the exceptions to the general rule that tribes who follow the Aryan tradition cremate their dead while menial groups among them bury theirs are to be found in the fringe lands. Thus the Naga tribes of Assam in northeastern India traditionally exposed their bodies on a platform. When the flesh had been plucked clean they gathered up the bones and stored them in an ossuary. Less frequently they buried their dead, and at the end of the ceremony, clad in full fighting regalia, with their weapons they beat the mound of stones which they had erected above the grave and shouted, "Where are you now? What spirit has killed our friend?" Then they cursed the evil one.[1]

The less civilized tribes of the fringe regions neither burned

129

nor buried the body, but flung it into a convenient ravine, and piled stones upon it to keep the spirit from "walking." Other primitives achieved the same results by burying the body face downward under layers of thorns. Perhaps the same purpose is at the root of the practice followed by some tribes of trussing up bodies with cords or burying them in a crouching position. It was feared that women dying in childbirth would turn into demons unless their bodies were kept close by, and their spirits propitiated. Hence, they were buried and not burned. High caste members of some Northern Indian tribes cremated their dead and cast the ashes into a river. The lower classes among them, who could not afford cremation, contented themselves with singeing the face before consigning the body to the water.[2]

Northern India

Moslem Tribes

Funeral rites among the Mohammedan tribes of northern India are relatively simple. When death seems certain, the chapter of the Koran that tells of the paradisal happiness of the true believer is read to the dying, and a few drops of honey are placed in his mouth. This food is to satisfy him so that in his agony he will not be tempted to take the sweetmeats offered by the evil one who lies in wait for his soul.

After death the eyes and mouth are closed. If death occurs during the daytime, after the body has been washed, perfumed, and shrouded, friends bear it, sometimes coffined, sometimes not, to the outer court of a mosque. There the members of the procession bathe, and recite funeral prayers. Repeating, "There is no God but Allah," they bear it thence to the cemetery where the grave awaits it. In this procession the face of the dead is turned toward Mecca. At the bottom of the grave, on the side toward Mecca, a recess is dug. Mohammedans lay the body on the right side with the head to the north. Before the grave is filled, a few clods of earth are cast upon the body to the recitation of the passage from the Koran: "We formed you of earth, to

130

earth we return you, and on the day of resurrection we will raise you up." If a man dies at night, after the body has been washed and shrouded, the procession and burial wait upon the coming of day.[3] These Mohammedans believe that two angels visit the grave to interrogate the dead concerning his beliefs and conduct. One angel is Munkar, "The Unknown"; the other, Nakir, "The Repudiator." During the interrogation the body sits on the side shelf. Lest in his fright he should forget the obvious answers, a stone tablet with the creed cut into it is placed in the grave.[4]

The Mohammedans of northern India have borrowed a few practices from the stricter mourning observances of their Hindu neighbors. The practice some families observe of giving the clothes of the deceased to the poor, together with food, most likely is of Hindu rather than Mohammedan derivation. So is the prohibition which forbids the family of the deceased from cooking in its home for two days after a death.

Of Mohammedan origin is the practice of holding a memorial service at a mosque. Friends and relatives attend. Passages from the Koran are read. A prayer is offered that the merit of the recitation may be applied to the soul of the departed. The death feast follows, and although orthodox Mohammedanism does not accept the concept that the soul must be fed material food, offerings are nonetheless made. Although similar feasts are prescribed for the fortieth day, and for the fourth, sixth, and ninth month, and on the last day of the year in which death occurred, only wealthy Mohammedans are able to complete this calendar.[5]

The period of public mourning is forty days. For the six months of family mourning no feast, music, or gaiety is allowed in the home. When a man dies, his widow takes off her nose ring and bracelets, and unless these are made of gold or silver, she breaks them and wears no such adornment until she marries again. However, her strict seclusion terminates after four months and ten days, and when she emerges, she is eligible to remarry.

Toda priests and
their abode

The Todas

The Todas are a small, pastoral tribe living on the undulating plateau of the Nilgiri Hills of southern India. The men are tall, bearded, straight-nosed, with light brown complexion. Men and women alike wear a coarse cotton mantle, much like the toga. Their material culture is meager. Their single source of livelihood comes from their buffalo herds and the attendant dairying industry. Some buffalos are considered sacred by the Todas, and are served by priest-dairymen. Women are not permitted to participate in dairying in any fashion. Inasmuch as Toda society revolves around buffalo herds, it is logical that the herds should figure prominently in the Toda funerals.

An additional feature of Toda society, intriguing to anthropologists, is their practice of polyandry—the mating of one

132

woman with several husbands, usually brothers. Of the thousands of known societies, the Todas are one of less than half a dozen in which polyandry is the preferred and dominant form of marriage. The custom has remained constant over the past several hundred years.

Funeral Places

The Todas observe a three-phase funeral ceremony, which on the whole, may extend over many months, as the periods between the first and second of these triple rites vary in length and are not prescribed by custom. In the first of these ceremonies the body is cremated; in the second, honor is paid to the remains; and in the third, which follows before daybreak on the day after the second phase, the residues of the first cremation are once more burned, and the ashes buried.[6]

Each Toda clan maintains at least two funeral places. One of these is reserved for the women, who are customarily buried on Thursdays and Saturdays; the other for the men, who as a general rule are buried on Sundays, Tuesdays and Thursdays. Some clans maintain one place for the first two ceremonies and another for the third, and some have a separate funeral place for boys who have not undergone the puberty initiation rite.[7] As a general rule, a special funeral hut is constructed within a stone circle at the funeral place. If the hut used at a man's funeral remains in good condition, it may be used for a second funeral. However, the hut constructed for a woman's funeral is always burned down after being used. Some clans have three-room dairying barns, one room of which may be set aside for the funerals of men. The only time a woman is allowed inside a dairy is at the funeral of a man—and even then her presence is restricted to the single funeral room. All Toda funeral rites are not only open to witnesses, but visitors are often given special invitations to attend them.[8]

While the body is being borne from the house, those who wish to witness the first phase of the ceremonies gather at the funeral place. When the body is set down at this spot, those in attendance approach the side of the bier, and, one by one, bow

133

G. G. Harrap Photos

Female servant of vassal Paniyan
tribe announces death of mistress

The sister of the dead woman
prepares a shroud

until their foreheads touch the body. Only persons older than
the dead are allowed by custom to make their obeisance at
the foot of the bier. After all have thus saluted, the body is
moved into the funeral house, where late comers are permitted
to salute the dead. Meanwhile the female relatives pair off,
and while wailing and weeping, in characteristic Todas fashion,
rub foreheads together.[9]

Preparation for Cremation

The men meanwhile proceed with preparations for the cremation. On a place which they clear in the woods they construct an oblong pyre, the top of which is about three feet
from the ground. Some of the wood they have brought with
them, the rest they gather in the vicinity.

When the pyre is completed a man digs up a little earth
at the entrance of the buffalo pen, for the "earth-we-throw"
ceremony. First a man asks, "Shall I throw earth?"—and
another answers, "Throw earth." After this interchange, in a

134

The senior members of the Todas do a solemn dance

Music is supplied by vassal Kotas

G. G. Harrap Photos

sequence determined by kinship, earth is dug and thrown. To perform this ceremony each man kneels with his back to the body, bows until his forehead touches the ground, meanwhile saying, "Swani." Then, covering his head with his cloak, he casts three handfuls of earth ahead of him into the pen, and three behind him, upon the body.[10] Sometimes the earth is cast into a small circle of stones constructed especially for this rite.

The buffalo slaughtering ceremony follows. For a man's funeral one buffalo must be a sacred animal. When a family does not possess such, it usually exchanges two ordinary buffalos for a sacred beast. Each kind of buffalo is assigned a special slaughtering place, marked sometimes by a stone and sometimes by a post. To prevent impoverishment, the

135

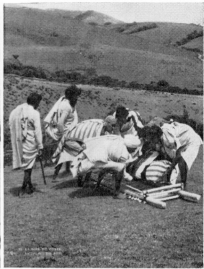

The male relatives prepare the bier   The body is tenderly laid upon it

government in the 1860's prohibited the slaughter of more than two buffalos at a Toda funeral. Since buffalo slaughter is a central part of the rites, this prohibition has reduced the elaborateness of the ceremonies. However, there are occasions when the government's restriction is ignored.[11]

The capture of the buffalos adds excitement to the rites. More buffalos are brought to the ceremony than are slain. Thus when two are to be slaughtered, four or five are led from the village and tethered out of sight. After the funeral preliminaries are completed the buffalos are driven forward by being lashed, and the spectators advance to meet them. Meanwhile several men, who wear capes and are selected for the service, run ahead to capture the infuriated animals. When the beasts appear, the men drop their capes and rush toward them. The method of capture is prescribed. A Toda must first seize the buffalo by the horns and then, grasping its neck, grab the sensitive cartilage of its nose. Meanwhile another man throws himself upon the buffalo's neck, and, heaving together, both men strive to throw the animal to the ground. This is rough business in which the men are sometimes severely gored.

136

A man who shows skill in such a capture may thereby acquire a great reputation.[12]

While the captors direct the animal toward the place of slaughter, other men urge it forward by beating it with sticks. Ordinarily the Todas treat their buffalos kindly, so that it appears that the vigor of the beating may have a ceremonial significance. Prior to slaughtering a buffalo, men hang a bell on its neck, and rub butter on its head, horns, and back.

Each buffalo is now led to its appointed slaughter stone or post, and killed by being struck on the head with the back of an axe. As the animal falls, the body of the dead person is carried forward and laid down next to its head. A hand of the dead man is uncovered and clasped around a horn; while the feet of a dead woman are placed near its mouth. After this rite the men advance to salute the beast by touching their foreheads to its horns and head. This gesture ushers in a spell of weeping, in which the mourners gather around the buffalo in pairs and, with foreheads touching, lament. Their words seem to indicate that the buffalo is somehow identified with the

Sacrifice of buffalos; a central part of funeral rites

G. G. Harrap

137

dead person, although the degree of identification is obscure.[13]

Meanwhile, an overlapping ceremony begins, in which a close relative of the deceased hands red cloths to men and women who have married into the family. These they lay on the face of the body. This is the last ceremony before the cremation. When it is completed, the body is returned to the bier and borne to the pyre. While the bier stands next to the pyre the deceased is given the last gifts needed in the afterlife: food, ornaments, and money. Some of these are tucked into a pocket in the folds of the shrouding cloak. Some, such as rings and other jewelry, are placed directly on the body.[14]

The pyre meanwhile has been lighted. At the funeral of a man, the fire is produced on the spot by friction. At a woman's funeral it is brought on a blazing rag from a fire already kindled. Before being laid on the pyre, the bier is raised and the body is thrice swung over the flames. The bier is then stood on the ground, to allow the attendants to remove all objects of value from it and from the body.

The sacrificial victims and the consecration of the funeral pyre

G.G. Harrop Photos

138

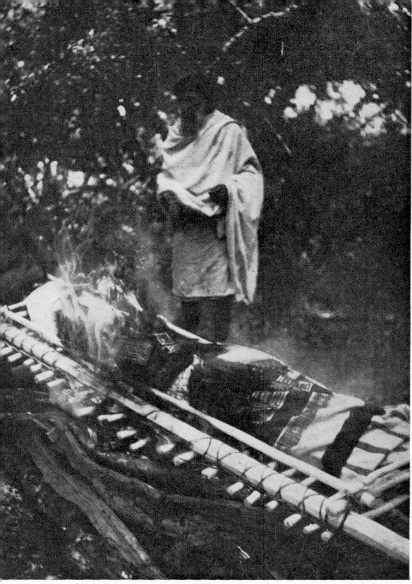

Priest attends blazing pyre

This swinging of the body over the fire represents a symbolic destruction of the body and the gifts, the latter may then be kept for the use of the living. As a final gesture a lock of hair is cut from the head of the body, to serve as a relic for the second phase of the funeral. The body is now ready to be burned, and is laid face upwards on the pyre.

Meanwhile Kotas—darker neighbors living in the midst of the Todas—have arrived and joined the crowd. Some of them are there to cut up the meat of the slaughtered buffalos—later they will eat it—and others to supply music, ordinarily on the clarinet and drum, sometimes also on the tambourine or on other horns. The cremation is a signal for them to play lustily. When the pyre is burned out, relatives poke among the ashes in search of a fragment of skull. With the lock of hair this is wrapped between two pieces of bark and kept for the second funeral. Wind and rain are allowed to disperse the remaining ashes.[15]

As soon as these relics are gathered, the relatives and other mourners return to their homes. Close relatives carry the relics with them, wrapped in a cloth which in turn is wrapped in a mantle. In one of its villages each clan generally maintains a small hut suitable to house relics prior to the second funeral ceremony. The chief village of the clan is never used for such purpose, nor may the relatives of the dead visit this chief village before the second funeral takes place. If they live there they must temporarily move elsewhere.[16]

The "Second Funeral"

The second of the Toda funeral ceremonies or the "second funeral," is held not earlier than a month and sometimes as late as a year after the first. The native name for it is the *Marvainkolder*. While the body was borne to the first funeral on a bier of wood, the small remains, wrapped in an embroidered mantle, are carried to the second funeral on a bier of bamboo At the burial ground they are placed in the hut, together with other objects to be burnt. This done, the women pair themselves, and, touching foreheads together, weep and lament.

The second funeral, like the first begins with an earth-throwing ceremony in which the relics are deposited at the entrance of the buffalo pen where the body was laid, and earth is thrown as before. The buffalo slaughtering ceremonies observed at this time are almost identical with those observed at the first funeral.[17]

140

At a man's second funeral, after the buffalo is killed, the men dance within the circular wall which encloses the funeral hut. They form a circle and move with a slow motion, one man crying out the name of the slaughtered buffalo, followed by the expletive, "Rhao, rho, rho!" while another echoes what he says. When the dancing ends, food is distributed to all present, and after eating, most of the bystanders disperse to their homes. However, the close kin of the dead remain at the hut, lamenting throughout the night and waiting for morning and the final rites, or "third funeral."

Activities leading into this concluding phase start next morning as early as 2:00 o'clock. At every place used for this final ceremony there has been erected a second circle of stones, smaller than that which encloses the hut. The entrance into this second circle generally faces east. Long before dawn a man digs a hole beside this entrance.

The various objects to be cremated together with fragments of the skull are now carried out of the hut and laid next to the wall. With their appearance, the wailing, which has lasted through the night, redoubles. Wood is stacked outside the stone wall, and lighted, and the flames are fed with butter. At a man's funeral one of his dairy vessels is burnt; and at a woman's, a buttermilk jar. At this time butter is rubbed on the pieces of skull and the lock of hair, and after the hair is fastened between the skull fragments, they are tied together with a string.

Now wood for a second fire is stacked up within the smaller circle of stones, and the relics are laid upon it. This pyre is lighted by taking three firebrands, one after another, from the first fire. As the flames spread, those present pick up burning sticks from the first fire and cover the relics with them. A man's gifts are placed on the pyre of a man: grain, money, sticks, a dancing pole, baskets, a bow, a knife, an umbrella, and other objects. The pyre of a woman is heaped with goods suitable for her use. When all contributions have been made, the people sort themselves into pairs, and, touching foreheads together, weep.[18]

This fire, not allowed to die to ashes, is quenched with water. When it is extinguished, the residue of wood and ashes is swept into the hole which was dug before the ceremony began. The hole is then filled with earth dug elsewhere, and a stone is laid to cover the spot. At a man's funeral, a man now marches thrice around the burial ground ringing a bell, behind him another man marches, with his hands firmly gripped about the bell-ringer's waist. When the pair has completed the triple circle, the bell-ringer raises an empty water pot over his head and smashes it on the covering stone. Then he kneels, makes obeisance until his head touches the stone, and rising, goes to the funeral hut without looking back. All the rest likewise bow before the stone and turn away. The bell-and-bowing ceremony at a woman's funeral is very similar to this, only the bell-ringer is her husband, or if she was widowed, her brother. Before saluting a mate's stone a married person draws up his or her cloak to cover the head, and does not drop it again until just before making obeisance.

Those who have attended the funeral have fasted through the night, and now partake of food. Each one cuts a lock of hair from his head, to signify mourning, and then returns home. When a woman has been buried, the woman who lighted the pyre has the duty, before she returns home, of setting fire to the funeral hut.[19]

Purification Ceremonies

Among the Todas the first new moon after the third and final funeral is the accepted time to perform purificatory rites. The ceremony is held on the Sunday following the new moon. On that day, whoever is designated as dairyman takes the bell used in the third funeral to the stream, and purifies it by rubbing it with pounded bark and water. Then using a new stick for a bracket he rehangs it in the empty dairy. Finally, new dairy vessels are purified and put in place.[20]

The Todas believe that their dead pass to a region to the west, which is lighted by the same sun as lights the world of the living. This place of the dead they call Amnodr. Day there and day here alternate, as the sun shines on Amnodr when it is night here, and vice-versa. This afterworld is conceived as lying below the level of the world of the living, and for this reason it formerly was customary to lay the body face downward on the funeral pyre. The netherworld is presided over by the god "On," and is peopled by beings called Amatol. Once the Todas journeyed freely between the two worlds, but now they go and cannot return.[21] In Amnodr the dead Todas lead a life much like their life on earth. They tend buffalos and dairies. The latter, however, are free from rats and other destructive animals. Curiously enough, in Amnodr, as they walk about, their legs gradually wear down, and when only knee-length stubs remain, they are reborn into the world as new individuals.[22]

Certain features of Toda funeral belief and practice seem to merit special consideration. One of these is their custom of killing buffalos. This slaughter takes place with but few exceptions at the funerals of men,[23] and it should be clear that the rite is designed not as a propitiary sacrifice, but to provide the dead with dairy cattle in the next world. A man's funeral among the Todas has a next world dairy orientation. Women have nothing to do with buffalos in this or in the next world. Another interesting feature is the earth-throwing ceremony. This rite would seem to be a relic of an earlier cultural stage in which the ancestors of the Todas gave earth burial to their dead.[24]

Ceylon

The Sinhalese and Buddhism

The traditional funeral customs of the people of Ceylon, the *Sinhalese*, are of venerable origin. Some of them certainly were derived from the Aryans of India, while others are rooted in the culture of the Dravidians, an ancient race forming the bulk of the population of Hindustan. While observance of these Ceylonese customs is general throughout the island conformity to them is particularly rigid in rural sections.[25] With the introduction of Buddhism to Ceylon, the older Sinhalese rites became associated with Buddhist beliefs and practices. Buddhism teaches that at the moment of death the dying person beholds signs which prefigure the nature of his rebirth. People who have lived the good life see visions of floral garlands and heavenly chariots, and thereby understand that they will have rebirth into the bright worlds of the gods. Evil persons who behold fragments of flesh know that they are consigned to be reborn into the world of mortals. To aid the dying to think holy thoughts so that he may be assured of a happy state in the next life, a Buddhist priest is invited to preach a short sermon to him.

Preparation of the Dead

When a Sinhalese dies, the body is bathed before it is dressed for lying in state. After being arrayed in suitable apparel and adorned with jewels, it is placed on a bed which has been draped with clean white sheets and, out of respect for the dead, hung with a white canopy. The head of the body always points westward, and for this reason no Sinhalese will sleep in a similar position. Next to the body and close to the head, a lighted, brass, coconut oil lamp with a trimmed wick is placed on a table, and kept burning during the whole period in which the corpse lies in state. The light is provided so that the spirit of the dead person may enter the regions of celestial light and bliss. Meanwhile, pictures on the wall of the drawing room and adjacent chambers have been reversed as a sign of mourning. This custom, found also among the Portuguese, is of more recent origin in Ceylon, and clearly traces back to the time of the Portuguese regime.

Mats have been spread on the ground about the body and when it is prepared for viewing, relatives and friends sit upon them as a mark of respect. Meanwhile, certain of the close relatives stand near it and wail loudly. Wailing is a duty performed chiefly by the women, who unbind their hair, weep copiously, and utter piteous lamentations. Such outward display of grief is considered particularly important by the rural Sinhalese, who believe that without it they do not show due respect and affection for the dead. In his work on Ceylon, Robert Knox, who visited the island in the seventeenth century, describes a funeral ceremony in which the women of the household surrounded the bier and with loud wails praised the deceased. This mourning continued for four days.

Ambivalence Toward the Dead

In spite of the reverence that is shown to the dead, the Sinhalese regard the body as unclean and refer to it as a *killa,* that is, a polluted thing. They believe that the pollution of a house remains with it for three months after death has occurred. During that period the household is subject to taboo. As long as the body is present, no fire may be kindled on the hearth, and no food prepared. Such cessation of domestic activity has further significance as an act of reverence for the dead. Meanwhile, neighboring households provide all meals for the bereaved family.

The body is usually removed from the house at some time in the afternoon, but before sunset. It is considered unlucky to remove it on Tuesday or Thursday, but if these days cannot be avoided, to counteract the bad luck an egg is placed in the coffin.

The Funeral

When the time for removal arrives, the closest relatives lay the body in a coffin, friends and the family asperge it with rosewater and other perfumes, and very close relatives take up the bier. Now the wailing women utter their loudest lamentations, and the beating of the funeral drums heralds the funeral procession.

Either before the removal of the body from the house, or at the grave, but before burial, the *Dunkhala* ceremony, an important Buddhist ritual, is performed. This rite requires the services of a number of monks. First, in the name of the dead person the relatives offer a piece of white cotton cloth or calico to the monks. Then a near relative pours water from

145

a jug into a large, empty bowl resting on a plate. Meanwhile one or two monks deliver funeral orations. This simple ceremony indicates the manner in which the merit accruing from good deeds can be applied to the advantage of the departed. If he lingers in a purgatorial existence, merits thus transmitted will enable him to achieve a higher, happier state.

The ceremony completed, the coffin with the body is placed on a funeral pyre for disposal by cremation. After thrice walking around it, two nephews of the deceased light the combustibles. When earth disposal is used, the closest relatives of the dead lower the coffin into the grave. On the day following a cremation, a few of the closest relatives come together at the pyre and collect into an urn or pot such human ashes and bone fragments as remain. These are then buried in a cemetery or some other suitable place.

Post-Funeral Activities

Immediately after the removal of the body, the house is swept clean and the floors are sprinkled with tumeric water. This liquid, made from the aromatic root of an East Indian herb, is considered a powerful disinfectant. At this time, a fire is again built on the hearth, and the women begin to prepare a meal for those who dwell in the house and the family and friends of the deceased. This meal, a memorial to the dead, is called *mala batha* or *mala dane*. The menu includes boiled rice, vegetable curries and cooked dry fish. All who desire to show respect for the dead participate in this meal, squatting on the mats on the floor.

When the meal has been eaten, some of the relatives gather to chant the *mala potha,* or book of the dead, a long poem set to a mournful tune. This recitation is designed to drive sadness and dullness out of the household of death. Further, to brighten the setting a coconut oil lamp is lighted in the death chamber and allowed to burn continuously for three days.

A mourning period lasting either three or six months is prescribed. During this time, to express their grief publicly, the close women relatives of the dead dress in simple white

Odd, streamer-bedecked Sinhalese graves

clothes, avoiding colored or otherwise elegant garments.

Seven days after death, Buddhist monks, in number at least five, and sometimes as many as twenty-five or even fifty, are invited to visit the funeral house, to participate in a *Sangika Dane,* or alms-giving ritual. When the gifts, consisting of food, cakes, sweets, and fruits, have been distributed, one of the monks delivers a sermon. In the concluding ceremony, water is poured into an empty bowl to indicate the fact that the merit of the good deeds has been transmitted to the deceased. The Sangika Dane ceremony is repeated during the third month after death and on the first anniversary.

Funeral Customs The World Over

Part Two

Semitic peoples perpetuate funeral customs
and rites of millennia gone by

The
Middle
East

Lamentation at death . . . family
and community involvement . . .
simplicity and dispatch . . . care in
washing and anointing the dead
. . . few if any paid functionaries . . .
a shrouded body on the bier . . . the
funeral procession on foot . . . tombs
and sepulchres . . . Moslem, Jewish,
Christian and folk variations . . .
the special case of the Parsis

P.I.P. Photos Top and Lower Right
U.P.I. Photo Lower Left

Brown Bros. Photo of Painting by Frank Dodd

Painting depicts early Turkish village funeral

Chapter 9

Turkey

Although in Turkey, as elsewhere, death may mean different things to different people according to their religious beliefs, the Turk who holds to the Koran takes his interpretations from it, and when death comes, accepts its teaching entirely and literally.[1] Devout Mohammedans believe implicitly that the soul of man neither dies nor degenerates into a lower level of existence, and that at death it returns to its eternal and proper homeland, leaving the outworn body to dissolve into its original elements. In the union of soul and body called "life," the body withholds the soul from the company of the souls. Sharers of this belief do not dread death. Rather, they look forward to it as a happy attainment of a much desired goal.

Although most Turks share these doctrines, a minority among them disbelieve in the afterlife. Others hold that at death they will live again on other planets. Still others believe that they will be reborn on earth in some other form. However, these exceptions to the prevailing viewpoint are not very numerous.

153

As the result of the almost universal acceptance of death as a transition into a better life, the Turk feels that it is not proper to greet the passing of a loved one with a great show of sorrow. The Moslem faith prescribes no period of mourning, and Turks are under no compulsion to wear black as a sign of death in a family, although it is customary for them to don dark colors.

In a biography of His Holiness Ismail Hakki, a fifteenth century sheik, the writer who was one of his followers, quotes the exact words which the sheik used to describe his father's death: "I was more than sad when my father died. I had to be prepared for the ceremony, to wash the body and perform the final rites. But I could not move. I felt as though I were frozen. My eyes were swollen with weeping, and a flood of tears remained unshed. My father's body lay stretched out on a bench. Again I sought through my tears to look upon it. And then suddenly I was struck with the fact that the face had changed expression. Quickly all worldly feelings faded, and I beheld a marvelous illumination. I cannot describe this light, for nothing on this earth can compare with it. My father, too, was staring at it. Then inspiration told me that this symbolized salvation for his soul. With that, all sorrow was purged from my heart. I even felt joyful, and I ran to my room, and put on my holiday clothes."

While the religious tenets of the Moslem Turks prescribe a high plane of conduct for the bereaved, in many cases the practice will be found to lag behind the precept. Some scream, or shriek, or wail over their dead. Some weep quietly, but not many are able to suppress all show of grief. Perhaps it is too much to expect that the loss of a member will make a family happy, and that the bereaved can find full consolation in the belief that the departed has achieved salvation. In Turkey, as elsewhere, the thought of death provokes anxiety and fear, and no one normally is eager to die or to have his loved ones die. Even belief in a better eternal life does not end the natural reluctance man has of facing death.

Upon investigation, Turkish funeral customs prove much

154

Photo by Tulgar Can

Istanbul funeral procession. Green pall has passages from Koran;
shawl on front indicates deceased a woman

the same as funeral customs elsewhere, with the exception of
some differences in the sequence of the death routines. Some
of these differences may have originated in local Turkish
customs; others are probably the result of superstition; and
the remainder probably represent logical reactions to the
Turkish concept of death.

It is worth noting that Turkish funeral customs exhibit little
regional or other variations. The mountain dweller performs
the same basic rites as the dweller on the plains; the peasant,
as the merchant. Such differences as do exist are so slight
as to be negligible. This standardization is largely due to
governmental intervention and to the Islamic Law of funeral
rites. In Turkey the government provides services for the dead.
The Turkish undertaker supplies coffin and hearse but plays
a minor role in the care of the dead or the funeral ceremonies.

155

Response to Death

When those attending the seriously ill conclude that death is near, they seek out one who is able to read the Koran, most probably a *hoca*, or holy man. While the reader reads in a tone just loud enough to be audible, the last drops of water are given to the dying person. This ceremony is regarded as highly important. It is a matter of common belief that when the death struggle parches the throat, Satan appears holding a glass of water in his hand. Thirst tortured, the dying one struggles to seize the glass. But Satan holds it out of reach, saying that he may drink only if he confesses a loss of faith in God (Allah). The ceremony of the final drops of water is designed to foil Satan's schemes, and to aid the dying.

Some hold that a few final tears start from the eyes of the dying. This concept is rooted in the belief that the eyes are the first of the bodily organs to die, and that these tears tell their death. After they have been shed, the dying person no longer can see this world, but looks upon eternity, and now if he speaks, he speaks with the voice of eternity.

When death comes, those in attendance close the eyes. Next, to prevent the jaw from dropping, they wrap a strip of fine batiste around the chin and knot it at the top of the head. They do not want to allow the mouth and eyes to remain open in the grave because they fear that insects or small snakes may enter the bodily openings and eat the dead body from within before it can decompose normally. They also see to it that the body is so arranged that it can be coffined, and so they stretch the hands along the sides and draw the feet together, binding them in the position by tying two toes on each foot with batiste. When these operations have been performed, the body is removed from the spring mattress of the death bed to a smooth bed made directly on the floor. In moving the body, care is taken not to disturb it, and it is raised by carefully lifting the four corners of the bed linen on which it lies. A pillow is not placed beneath the head after death. During these proceedings someone reads aloud from the Koran in a sad, musical voice. No restrictions are placed upon viewing the dead, and anyone may do so freely.

156

Meanwhile an announcement of the death has been made to the local authorities, and a physician arrives to examine the body and make certain that the death is from natural causes. When he has finished, he issues a burial permit.

Preparation for Burial

Burial preparations are made by a team—usually two men—employed by the government. The quality of the goods and services which the government supplies depends upon the money available in the dead person's estate. Three classes of funeral service are provided. If the dead person dies without funds, the government provides a free funeral.

Immediately after a death, someone notifies the relatives and close friends. An absent member of the family likewise receives notification, and if he is within reasonable distance, he will

Coffin being loaded in Turkish style funeral coach

Photo by Tulgar Can

attend the burial, which may be deferred for a day, or in special cases even two days, to accommodate him. In the meantime a black-handled knife is laid on the dead man's abdomen. This practice springs from the superstition that a knife of this kind will prevent bloating.

The most important task prior to the burial is the washing of the body. The Moslem religion prohibits embalming. Hospitals provide special facilities for these ablutions, and if death takes place in a hospital, the body is washed there. Some mosques contain facilities for body washing. When a body is washed in the house, a bench is stood near the door, and those in attendance raise the body from the bed by holding the corners of the bed linen on which it lies, carry it to the bench, and lay it upon it. All the necessities for the ablution, such as soap, wood to heat the water, a piece of cloth, and other items are newly purchased in the market place. Nothing is used from the stores in the house.

Turks believe that a body is very easily bruised and injured, and therefore must be gently handled. Accordingly, they cut away the death clothes with scissors, and gently pull them from under it. Next, someone pours warm water over the body while another carefully soaps it. A sponge made of fibers is used instead of a cloth, for washing. A second washing follows, the sequence of which is prescribed by the Moslem ritual: the nose is washed three times; the mouth, three times; the whole face, three times; the neck, once; each forearm, three times, with the right preceding the left; and in like precedence, each foot, three times. During this ceremony selections are read from the Koran.

When the body has been washed, it is dried with towels; and cotton plugs are inserted into the openings to prevent the escape of gases. After this, it is placed in the shroud. The shroud consists of a long rectangular piece of cloth, with a hole in the middle sufficiently large to allow the head to pass through. After the head has been inserted, the cloth is folded in such a manner that the two narrow sides overlap. These are left unsewed, while the long sides are sewed up. Because the

158

Funeral coach driver waits on *hoca,* holy man,
before transporting coffin to mosque

doubled cloth is longer than the body, the ends extending below
the feet are drawn together and tied with a rope. Then thyme
and spirits of camphor are placed on the shroud to drive away
insects that might be present in the grave, and the shroud is
sprinkled with rose water.

The Coffin

These steps complete the preparation of the body. The
coffin, meanwhile, has been made ready. It is very simple,
being constructed of wood that is unpolished and without
ornamentation. Some Turks remove the body from the coffin
before burial, and contribute the coffin to the mosque or to
the governmental funeral service, so that it may be used for

159

Photo by Tulgar Can

Sailors stand honor guard in court of mosque; funeral services
will be held in conjunction with regular divine services

the burial of poor who cannot afford to purchase a coffin of
their own. This custom is more commonly found in rural than
in urban areas.

Occasionally people wrap the body in a strip of matting,
and so bury it. Such procedure is designed to promote rapid
decay, because the Moslem believes that everything that originates in the earth should return to it. God has created the body
of man from the slime of the earth, and the body of man must
return to earth. For this reason embalming, which would delay
decomposition, is not practiced in Turkey.

The burial of Kemal Ataturk, founder of modern Turkey,
offers a good example of Turkish funeral customs. Ataturk died
November 10, 1938. A fitting monument had to be prepared
for him. For this reason his body was embalmed. After fifteen
years, when the mausoleum was finished, the coffin was
opened and the body buried in a simple shroud, in precisely

160

"Seven steps for the dead;" passers by join in carrying
coffin to the mosque

the same manner as all other bodies are consigned to earth.

Whether the coffin stands in the home of the deceased or
in a hospital, custom decrees that a piece of cloth embroidered
with verses from the Koran must be laid upon it. Within the
last twenty years another custom has been developing. When
a young man dies, it is likely that a Turkish flag will be laid in
his coffin. When a woman dies, a piece of green cloth—green
is associated with things holy to Moslems—covered with another
piece of hand-painted muslin is spread on the head end of the
coffin. The coffin of a young girl is draped with a scarf. Thus
is symbolized the fact that while she is wed to death, in the
next world she will satisfy all her desires. Prior to the revolution the practice obtained of placing a wadded turban on the
coffin of an *agha* or a *pasha,* and while the custom has fallen
into disuse, a vestige of it can be found in the helmets that
occasionally rest on the coffin of officers.

161

Services at the Mosque

When the time for the funeral arrives, the coffin is lifted and borne from the home or hospital on the shoulders of the pallbearers. On the journey to the mosque the members of the procession chant verses from the Koran. Traditionally Moslem women do not participate either in the funeral procession or the ceremonies at the mosque. In recent years, however, in the larger cities this prohibition has sometimes been partially disregarded, and women have joined the procession. But even now they are excluded from the rites at the mosque. As the body is borne from the home, the women of the household and the neighbors gather in the house of the bereaved and offer consolations to the near kin of the dead.

In the court of the mosque the bearers set the coffin down on a stone bier, *musalla*. Funeral rites are usually conducted after one of the five daily divine services. It is customary to delay the funeral so that the rites can be held after the second or noon service, or the third or mid-afternoon service. When funeral rites are combined with regular devotions, the number of persons present is increased. Moslems consider burying the dead a good deed, and worshippers leaving the mosque and seeing the coffin in the courtyard are likely to remain behind and to participate even though they have no acquaintance with the deceased.

The usual Moslem service of worship consists of two parts. In the first of these the *muezzin*—a Moslem crier of the hour of prayer—sings his *Ezan*—the announcement of the hour of prayer—from the outer gallery of the minaret. In the second, the worshippers assemble in the mosque, wash themselves, and perform the divine service.

The Moslem funeral service differs from the usual service of worship in that no muezzin cries over the rooftops from the minaret, nor are ablutions performed. These rites were supplied the dead person at his birth. For as soon as the newborn baby has been washed, the muezzin's announcement is cried into his ear. This cry is the Ezan for his funeral. The lesson that he is supposed to learn from this is the brevity of life.

162

Seven Steps for the Dead

When the service has been completed, the *hoca* asks the congregation to tell what manner of man they found the deceased. Everyone says, "goodhearted," even though he may not have been a good person. Prayers over, the bearers raise the coffin on their shoulders, and carry it from the court of the mosque. It is customary for every man in good health to carry the coffin on his shoulders for seven steps at least, and for passers-by to accompany the procession for at least seven steps. When a new bearer pushes under the coffin, another steps away so that eight or ten people are always under the load. These customs insure the fact that the remains will have an escort, even though the dead person may have no living relatives. At a prearranged spot, hearse and funeral cars await the procession. Only in small villages where distances are short is the body borne to the grave on foot.

Burial

At the cemetery the grave is ready, and when the procession nears it the lid of the coffin is raised and taken away. Only those men who are ineligible to marry her are allowed to place the body of a woman in the grave. Thus her father, brothers, uncles may render this service, but if she is married, not her husband. If she lacks close relatives, strangers are eligible for this last service.

When the body has been lowered in the grave, close friends and relatives cast handfuls of dirt upon it. After this, using a shovel, the sexton quickly fills the grave. During the whole of the burial, the hoca continues to read prayers. In some instances, and particularly if the deceased is a person of importance, after the grave has been filled and planted with flowers, a sermon is preached. Moslems do not leave cut flowers on the grave, but leave plants there, in the belief that every living plant utters the name of God. Care is taken that if a wreath is planted on a grave, the lattice supporting it is not constructed in the shape of a cross. It is also customary to sprinkle water over the fresh grave.

163

Moslem cemetery near Istanbul; pole-shaped monuments for men, board-shaped for women

Photo Courtesy E. C. and G. R. Johnson

Moslem cemeteries in the larger cities are commonly situated adjacent to mosques where funeral services are conducted. The monuments are not generally massive but are usually in the shape of a pole with an enlarged ball on top or are flat like a board.

Mourning the Dead

Belief has it that the newly released soul finds it difficult to adjust to the lack of a body and therefore usually returns to places it loved in life. For this reason a light is kept burning continuously day and night for forty days in the room in which death took place, and the arrangement of furniture is left unchanged so that the soul may wander without fear in familiar surroundings. These forty days are not actually a period of mourning, for there is no reason to mourn. However, out of respect for the deceased, the radio is not played in his house, and the members of his immediate family do not attend movies, the theatre, etc.

When forty days have passed, the bereaved chant the *Mevlut*, the Prophet's nativity hymn, in honor of their loved one. After this they distribute candy and rose water to all present. The Mevlut can be repeated, if desired, on every anniversary of a death.

164

Chapter 10

Iran

Iran, formerly Persia, is one of the largest of the Middle East *and Arab* countries. The funeral customs of this country are patterned after the Islamic laws dealing with the proper burial of the dead. But there are many deviations and local customs built around these laws. The emphasis in this chapter will be on the rich complex of customs and beliefs exhibited by the village and desert dwelling Iranians.[1]

Portents of Death

Among the Iranians certain signs of death are commonly recognized. A dog barks in the early morning because he sees *Azrael*, the angel of death. The householder, thus warned, places a shoe upside down before his door to prevent Azrael from entering the house. A weeping owl perched on a terrace or tree is another death portent. So that death may not ensue, someone bearing a mirror and a salt cellar tells the owl to become a good omen. Two deaths in sequence in the same

165

house are likely to induce a third, a disaster that can be averted only by sacrificing a black fowl and offering it to the poor. A dream in which the living is led away by the dead spells death for the dreamer. Such signs of death are counteracted by a sign of life. When several children of a couple die, their unspent expected years are added to their parents', and thus guarantee longer lives to their father and mother.[2]

When it appears that death is imminent, small lamps are lighted on the terrace of the house. These are a signal for the neighbors and passers-by to pray for one in his apparent last hours. Relatives meanwhile call upon mullahs or expounders of the law of Islam, to attend the dying.

Response to Death

As soon as a person enters his last agony, his face is turned towards Mecca, and special prayers are recited in his behalf. If he is a member of the Shi-ites sect—the Shi-ites consider Mohammed's son-in-law, Ali, as the Prophet's rightful successor—the *talqin*, the Shi-ite credo, is recited in an undertone in his ear. A small stone which has been prayed over before it is placed on the dying man's heart is believed efficacious in shortening a prolonged agony.

When the dying man can no longer speak, a mullah reads the Koran to him until death comes. At the moment of death a few drops of water mixed with dust from Karbala, a town southwest of Baghdad, are inserted in the dying person's mouth. After death the big toes are bound together, and the arms are straightened at the sides of the body. A band is placed around the head, closing the mouth, and the eyes are tightly closed as it is believed that if they are not shut the dead may return. Some Iranians place a carnelian—a reddish stone much used for seals—in the mouth. Inscribed on it are the names of the twelve prophets of Islam recognized by the Shi-ite sect.

If the features seem to be forming a smile, it is assumed that the spirit of the dead is enjoying paradisiacal bliss; if a frown, then it is expiating its sins. Persons dying after prolonged illness are believed to be transmitted directly to Paradise. So

166

are infants. When infants enter Paradise, they ask that their parents shall follow them, and angels promise this boon. Good infants are transformed into birds; wicked children, cursed by their parents, are damned, and become will-o'-the-wisps in cemeteries.[3]

The Iranians use euphemisms and circumlocution in speaking of death and related matters. If, for instance, they wish to announce a death, they do not say simply that "so-and-so died," but that "he has given his share of life to you." A death is considered bad news, which no one wishes to bear or transmit. Death notices are not sent to distant friends. A mullah announces the passing from the terrace of the house. This announcement is made once for a common person, but repeated twice for a man of prominence.

Death triggers strong family reaction. Relatives and servants scream, roll on the ground, rip their clothing from throat to waist, pluck out their hair, scratch their faces and chests, smear mud on their faces, and run through the city. The paroxysms of the women are more violent than those of the men. As a further sign of mourning, on the day of death members of the dead man's family daub mud on their hats and sleeves. Those who are unwilling to destroy their clothing make a token substitution. Sometimes they neglect to wash their faces, or to dye their hair. The men open their clothing, but do not tear it, and sift dust on their heads. The wearing of old clothing is a sign of mourning.[4]

Care of the Body

When death occurs during the day, the body is coffined as soon as possible; when it occurs at night, a copy of the Koran is laid on its chest, a candle is lighted at its head, and a reader keeps a vigil over it until dawn, lest the evil spirits take possession of it. A death in the house on Friday is considered unlucky.

Bathing the body is a major part of Iranian funeral ceremonies. If one meets a martyr's death the bloody signs of martyrdom must not be washed away. All other bodies must

167

be bathed. A body must be bathed three times—first with water mixed with lotus, then with water mixed with camphor, and then with pure water. Before pouring the last bowl of water on the head, the washer must blow on it. This act is called the "remission." Formerly the ablutions were made in the open, in a field or garden, and not inside the house. After washing with hot water, the body was anointed with perfume, and the head was shaved. Then the head was rinsed with much cold water.[5]

Although washing and burying the body were once family duties, in urban areas they have been taken over for the most part by the municipalities. When death occurs in such areas, permission must be obtained from the civil magistrate to employ the services of a washer of the dead. This functionary undresses the body, taking away the clothing with him, and he plugs the body openings with cotton. He washes common people in their own houses, and people of rank in the washing house. Next to the cemetery an enclosure has been erected in which a stream of water flows under a footbridge. The washer of the dead lays the body on the footbridge while he washes it. When the washing is completed, he stands the body erect and pours camphor water over the head, so that it trickles down over the whole surface of the body.

For fear of defilement, only those assigned to the task touch a body. Furthermore, even the water used is defiling. If someone malevolently sprinkled a neighbor's house with water that had been used for the ablution of the dead, such misdeed would cause the occupants to move out.[6]

After the ablution, the body is wrapped in a large seamless cotton cloth, which poor folk provide for themselves during their lifetime. Around the border of this cloth which has been carried around the Kaaba in Mecca or the sanctuary in Kerbela, are verses of the Koran printed in ink. These deal with death and resurrection. When the body has been shrouded, and the ends closed, the attending men stand before the body and recite the prayers of the dead. If the washing of the dead is performed in the home, burial is postponed until the following day.

In principle, the deceased must be buried as soon as possible, and in the nearest cemetery. If burial takes place on the day following death, the body is kept for the night either in the house or in the nearest mosque. In any event, two male readers take turns sitting next to the body until dawn and chanting the Koran over it. Meanwhile the bed is removed from the death chamber, and is replaced by a light.[7]

Death practices vary from place to place. Thus in some cities, among the Mohammedans incense is placed on a heated plate near the bed. When the clouds of smoke arise, several pages or more of the *Avesta,* the sacred book of the ancient Zoroastrian religion which once prevailed in these regions, are passed through the smoke. Even though no one present can read these pages or even knows what they are, the relic thus incensed is considered to be all-holy. The remainder of the funeral rites are carried out according to Mohammedan pre-scriptions.

Funeral Ceremony and the Funeral Procession

Traditionally a mullah brings the bier from the mosque. For a poor man the bier is a simple receptacle made of three rough and poorly jointed planks with a hinged lid—also made of a plank.[8] The shape of the bier follows in rough outline the shape of the body, being wide at the shoulders and tapering toward the feet. It is carried by means of four handles, and each bearer is expected to grasp one of these in rotation. In theory at least every passer-by has the holy duty of sharing the task for at least a few steps, saying the while, "There is no god but Allah." To assist in burying the dead is thought to be a great corporal work of mercy, and Mohammedans consider it highly meritorious for a man to assume the expenses of another's funeral.

For the funeral of a person of the middle class a departure from this ritual is made, and the bier is loaded into a black, completely sealed, man-carried hearse. The box of this hearse is surmounted by a dome which is topped in turn by a steel rod from which dangles a small metal ball. During the trip to the cemetery the hearse bearers run, meanwhile slowly repeating the words, *allah, allah.* Sometimes a reader rides on top of the hearse and chants continuously during the entire trip. The body of a child is borne in arms to the cemetery.

The hearse is not used in the procession of a great religious dignitary, but four men carry the body in a bier, or in a black, cloth-covered shrine. Beating their breasts the crowd which follows chants: "Our paragon of Islam has departed from this nether world." The custom formerly common among wealthy families of hiring musicians to lead the funeral procession has fallen into abeyance.[9]

The poor are not likely to form a procession to the grave. In the processions of the prosperous the nearest relatives walk behind the bier. To show their grief they unfold their turbans and wear mourning sashes which are crossed over the stomach. Processions are reported in which relatives and servants wearing only a skirt burn themselves and scratch their stomachs and arms until they draw blood. Although during the last century some Persians believed that to ride a horse in a funeral procession was a mark of disrespect to the angels who led it, in some processions half-naked horsemen dash hither and thither, wounding themselves as a gesture of mourning.

Separated by some distance, a crowd of women wearing black face veils and uttering plaintive cries brings up the rear of the procession. The mourners are surrounded by groups of spectators who march along with the funeral and who carry fruit, flowers, and branches of laurel and cypress.

In the funeral procession of a person of importance the mosque insignias are carried before the hearse. These are brass or copper lances, or crescents, and Arabic letters spelling out the names of Mohammed, his daughter Fatima, and his first 12 successors. All insignia are mounted on pikes, and are carried in groups of 14. Other pikes, tipped with brass or iron blades, have poles of such slenderness that they bend to the slightest motion. Full length streamers of taffeta are attached to the tips of these.

Behind this thicket of pikes four or five saddle horses parade,

170

bearing the turban and arms of the deceased. Next march thirty students, each bearing a section of the Koran and chanting from it. In the funeral procession of a woman of rank or wealth a canopy carried on four long poles is used to cover the bier. All these services are performed by neighbors or servants. There are no professional pallbearers. Community involvement is always a distinctive feature of Moslem burials.

Burial

At the grave, after reading a few verses from the Koran, the priest slightly elevates the head of the body. Before burial is made the bier is thrice set down and lifted up. It is hoped that by this device the deceased will learn to identify his tomb. Graves are not very deep, much less so than formerly. The body is removed from the bier and rolled into the excavation. While a masonry lining is not supplied for the grave, tiles are so placed on either side of the head that they meet to form a shelter and keep dirt from falling upon the face.

So that the occupant will receive remission of his sins, a chapter of the Koran is read and seven lines are drawn on the grave, which up to now has remained opened. After the recitation of the usual prayers, the two ends of the shroud are untied, and the grave is filled. When the burial is over, the mourners retreat seven paces from the grave and then return. Thus they signify that the dead person sees and recognizes them.[10]

Food is now placed near the grave for the use of the dead. Other food, in an amount in keeping with the wealth of the dead person, is distributed to the needy. During the evening of the week following a death, lighted lamps are placed on the grave.

The characteristic mourning food is *halva,* a mixture of wheat flour fried in butter, honey and spice, with saffron, sugar and rose-water added. For distribution, this paste is enclosed in loaves of bread. When an aged person dies, children are required to eat of the halva served at the funeral. It is believed that by so doing they partake of the deceased person's longevity.

171

Halva is distributed not only to the mourners within the home, but on the Thursday evening after the burial one or several persons stand outside and offer a plate containing halva, dates and figs to casual passers-by. Whoever accepts food from the plate recites a few verses from the Koran, to gain merit for the deceased.[11]

After the return from the cemetery food is served at the home of the deceased for those who have taken part in the funeral. When the head of a family has died, friends seek out the home of the heir to express their sorrow to him. The heir returns these courtesy calls a week later.

After the deceased has been removed from his room, a brick upon which a piece of meat has been placed is substituted in his stead. On the night following the burial, a glass of syrup, some halva and a light are placed in the room where the deceased had lain. In the morning the food is removed to the grave. Sometimes the meat is given to the poor.

The Post Funeral Ceremony of Hatm

On the day following death the ceremony of the *hatm,* or complete reading of the Koran, takes place in the home of the deceased. A separate hatm is made for the men in a large room of the men's apartments; and another for the women in their own quarters. The setting for both is identical.

Vases of flowers and an empty Chinese porcelain bowl, all ringed by small crystal flagons filled with rose-water, are placed on a cashmere shawl which has been spread on the middle of the floor. On a corner of the shawl stands a chest containing a Koran written in 30 separate books. These have been brought to the home from the local mosque. It is the custom in Iran for devout Mohammedans to give bound volumes of the Koran to their mosque.

Two or three chanters sit at the far end of the room and chant for hours at a time, placing each volume, as soon as it has been read, in a depository. The master of the house remains near the door to greet newcomers. As each arrives, a mullah standing in the rear of the room cries out *fatehe*

172

and pours rose-water on the visitor's hands. The visitor then rubs his hands over his face, accepts a cup of sugarless coffee and a volume. He reads from this in an undertone. Tea is served next. While all visitors are supposed to stay for lunch, which is laid in another room and has no traditional menu, actually as a general rule only relatives remain. Distinguished guests are allowed to leave so that they will not have to eat food offered in the name of the dead. The meal over, the reading is resumed and continues until nightfall.[12]

During the observance of the hatm the family of the deceased are required to remain in the house and to refrain from work. While the ceremony may be resumed early next morning, it never lasts beyond the second day. It concludes when a personage arrives and announces that the time for adjournment has come. When the reading stops, a preacher delivers the funeral oration, and after brief ceremonies all depart.

The women, meanwhile, are engrossed in the hatm ceremony in their own room set aside for this purpose. The lamenting women of the family take seats near the door. They uncover their heads, and as a sign of loss loosen their braids so that their hair hangs. As each woman visitor enters, the lamentation rises and then falls. Each newcomer joins the general grieving. As with the men, readers—in this case women—chant the Koran and distribute volumes. From time to time the introduction of an article of clothing or some possession of the deceased will result in increased lamentation. These ceremonies may continue for several days and are brought to an end by the appearance of a prominent woman, much as the ritual for the men's hatm was closed. Frequently in villages a banquet is served in the home following the hatm, with bouillon as the principal item on the menu.

The hatm of a great man is performed in the great mosque, and is concluded with a banquet provided at state expense. In such cases secondary hatms are sometimes held at lesser mosques.

Other Obligatory Ceremonies

While men and women observe the hatm in separate groups,

173

there are joint ceremonies the week after death, again after 40 days, and at the end of the year.

In the late afternoon of the eighth day after a death, friends and relatives bearing candles and dates march in procession to the cemetery and form a circle around the grave. One mourner takes two strides lengthwise across the bare grave, while others mark with two fire bricks the points of beginning and ending of the strides. Although the area which they designate may be less than that occupied by the body, it alone is considered sacrosanct and may not be trod upon. The tombstone is set between the bricks.

On the ninth day the mourners are led to the bath, and there washed, shaved, and freshly robed. Although this ritual terminates the public mourning, and the bereaved are permitted to make social calls, they lament for 40 days in the privacy of their homes on a progressively diminishing scale two or three times a week, and particularly at the hour at which death took place. Thereafter, they speak no more of the departed.

To entreat pardon for the sins of the deceased, halva, again prepared in the same manner, is distributed to beggars on the fifteenth evening following death. Three evenings later a light is left in the corridor leading to the room of the deceased. He is believed to return at this time.

Four days after death the mourners revisit the cemetery and spend an hour or two near the tomb. On the anniversary of a death, the women visit the cemetery to ask the permission of the departed to resume the wearing of colored garments. At all these obligatory ceremonies benediction prayers are recited.

Up until recent times persons of high rank or wealth generally provided that their bodies should be buried near the body of some holy person, or in a holy city or sanctuary. While awaiting transportation, the body was placed in a wooden coffin in a preservative mixture of lime, salt and perfume. The coffin in turn was placed in a masonry tomb, covered with an arch. For transporting, the bones were gathered and wrapped in a cloth, and carried without a bier to their final resting place. The bearers of remains such as these were

174

enjoined from passing through towns. The Persians have a saying that the dead must leave but may not enter.[13]

Memorialization

Tombstones may be extremely simple or quite elaborate. The grave of a poor person may be marked by two raised stones or even two bricks. Other tombstones not only become more elaborate but are protected from the elements. So that rain may not fall on the tombstone, persons of moderate means construct domes supported by four brick pillars, while the rich build chapels over their graves. The tombstone within such an edifice is surrounded by vases, lamps, flower pots, and related objects. Pictures of the deceased hang on the interior walls. Caretakers are paid to care for these chapels.

Occasionally tombs take other forms. Some are ornamented with cylindrical stones. Near the Caspian Sea tombs can be found which are constructed in the form of small mounds of earth with poles thrust in their tops. Sometimes a tomb will be found containing a likeness of the occupant. This may take the form of a relief plaque, a painting or a statue.

Tomb ornamentation is not uniform. A carved string of beads is used to indicate the piety of the tomb occupant. A carving of a razor indicates the burial place of a man. A comb or prayer brick may mark other tombs. The symbol of the dead man's trade may be engraved on his tomb. It is thought that the carved lion occasionally found to mark a Persian tomb may represent a survival in part of the former custom of adorning the tomb of a distinguished person with a scene from a lion hunt. Like the lion, the ram carved on a tomb may have been originally employed to symbolize the valor of the occupant. A tomb of a saint martyred by infidels was kept the color of blood.

Death Beliefs and Omens

The Persians believe that at death the soul does not depart immediately to the next world, but remains near the body. It follows the procession to the cemetery, hovering above

175

the grave. The dead is not separated by a single step from the living. First the dead person feels the crushing weight of the grave. Then eternal darkness settles about him. Then he is set apart from the living. Finally the angels of death arrive to ask his spirit: "Who is your God?" While he answers this and other questions, he leans on two sticks, one under each arm. These have been cut from a tree in his garden—preferably a fig or pomegranate. As he is being questioned, his head will strike the tombstone and he will sneeze and identify himself as a Mohammedan by saying: "Glory to *Allah*, lord of the universe." So that they may make this proper response after death it is wise for the living to rehearse it when they sneeze during life.[14]

Omens are sought to indicate the dead person's status in the afterlife. It is a very bad sign to have the shroud fall into the mouth of the deceased. A light bier that carries without jostling is a good omen. Precautions are also taken to deal properly with the returning spirit.

It is believed that on Thursday nights the dead are free to return to their earthly homes. So that they may find their way, lamps are lighted. During these hours care is taken to speak well of them. If one speaks ill, he adds immediately: "May the earth not apprise them of it."[15] Prayers for the dead are recited at this time. To add to their efficacy, villagers sometimes engage the services of a professional prayer reciter. This functionary has already prayed before an airtight goatskin or sheepskin, which he has blown into after each phrase. For a few pennies offered in behalf of the dead, he permits a little of his stored up sacred breath to escape. A belief in ghosts still persists in Iran. The ghost today is thought to be a half-shrouded skeleton who prowls only at night, and who returns either to avert disaster from the family or to seek revenge. It arises from the grave, enters the home stealthily, speaks in an almost inaudible voice, but attracts attention to itself by a creaking sound. Iranian black magic rites have formulas for evoking and rebuking ghosts who are injuring the living.

Social Change and Cultural Continuity

Modernization, reaching the countryside from the cities of Iran, has brought about the gradual disappearance of many popular death beliefs and burial customs. Now in cities the undertakers supply funeral paraphernalia and transportation for the body to the mosque and to the cemetery. Coffins made in the undertaker's coffin shops have become popular in metropolitan areas. A medical examiner must certify the cause and attendant circumstances of death. An agency of the Ministry of Health takes responsibility for many of the duties and services to the dead formerly discharged by family, friends, and lay experts. For those unable to afford the services of an undertaker in the cities, municipally operated mortuaries provide the essentials of the Moslem burial as provided by Islamic Law. Secularization undoubtedly has made headway in Iran, as it has in some degrees in all the countries of the Middle East. And in the villages and countryside the folkways of death have lost some of their saliency.

Arabian funeral procession crosses Kuta Bridge at Baghdad

Nevertheless there is a continuity in the broad outlines of the response to death and the care of the dead. Burial remains a simple, religious rite in which expedition in the disposition of the body is as paramount today, when preservative techniques are well-known, as it was a millenium ago. Washing, not embalming the body, remains the dominant physical action taken toward the body. The reading of the scriptures from the Koran is done with the same solemnity in the funeral ceremonies of the most urbanized Persian as it is for burials in the villages and remoter desert areas. The post-funeral ceremonies of the hatm, the week's mind, the forty-day's mind, and the year's end are felt by all Moslems to be an obligation and an unavoidable duty. There remains, in sum, a basic residuum and value, in part expressed in Islamic Law, which provides a substantial orientation for the funerary behavior of Moslems wherever they may be found—from Morocco to the Philippines.

Zoroastrians of Persia and India

Zoroastrianism was the common religion of the Persians prior to their conversion to Mohammedanism. It takes its name from its great prophet, Zoroaster, or Zarathustra. Zoroastrianism flourished in the first millenium B.C. Its sacred books, the *Zend-Avesta*, teach that Ormazd, or Ahura Mazda, lord of light and goodness, wages a ceaseless war, in which he will have final victory, against Ahriman and the hosts of darkness and evil. To aid him in the struggle, Ormazd created man. Today, a remnant of only about 5,000 Zoroastrians survive in former Persia, although over 100,000 of them can be found in India, mostly in Bombay, with isolated pockets in Aden, Lebanon, and Iraq. The Indian Zoroastrians are called Parsis or Parsees, from "Persian," and are descended from Persian refugees.[16]

Preparation of the Dead

When death occurs, among the Zoroastrians, the body is borne into the mortuary room in the home for the simple prep-

178

The Parsis, or Zoroastrians of Persia and India erect their "towers of silence" atop mountains or hills. Structures at left are for holding funeral ceremonies before the dead are left to the vultures in the huge, open topped tower

P.I.P. Photo

aration. In ancient times each community set aside a special building for funeral purposes, with separate sections for men, women, and children. Although the custom of the common mortuary still survives in India, it has been lost in Iran, where one room in the house is generally used for funeral purposes.[17]

There the body is washed, and dressed in a clean, white suit. A well-worn suit is preferred to a new one, as a suit used for a shroud is never worn again. After a member of the family girds the body with a sacred cord, it is laid on the ground or floor with a white sheet beneath it.

To provide a bridge across which the departing soul may enter the new life, two relatives, seated at either side, for several hours read sacred writings into the ears of the deceased.

Zoroastrian religious traditions and taboos designate the persons who may touch the body and the rules governing such contact. Any violations render the violator unclean, and compel him to undergo a nine day purification ritual, involving, among other matters, a washing of his person with cow urine.

Contamination is in part avoided by the Zoroastrians' delegating many funeral tasks to special funeral servants. Thus, when the two relatives finish their readings to the body, two

179

The Parsis do not want any outsider coming near their funeral towers. Guards like this one are in constant attendance to keep unbid visitors at a distance

such servants take over. These unfortunates are much despised, and generally considered unclean.

The Role of Exorcism

The funeral-servants cover the body, place it on a stone slab with the arms folded across the chest, and with a nail draw three circles around it, the outermost at a distance of three paces from it. No one except the bearers and funeral-servants is permitted within the circles, which are presumed to contain the malignant magnetic field given off by the body. The face of the dead may be turned in any direction except north. Out of the north the demons come.

The Zoroastrians fill their world with demons. Exorcism thus holds an important place in their funeral rites. Demons, they feel, may disguise themselves, and at death gather around the body in the form of flies. To kill them, while the priests chant prayers, a smudge of sandalwood and frankincense is kept burning. Wynn notes that the glance of a dog is believed to frighten away demons. In some communities, a 'four-eyed' dog

180

must be found, that is, one who has two spots above his eyes to make it appear he has four eyes. In other areas, any mongrel will do. Frequently a dog is led in the funeral procession. Sometimes bits of food are thrown around the body so that mongrels creep in and eat the food off the body itself.[18] Some hold that the dog would howl with terror if the body were not dead but merely in a state of suspended animation.

Today all Zoroastrian funerals take place within 24 hours after death, and always in the daylight so that the body may be exposed to the sun. When death occurs in the evening, the funeral takes place next morning; when in the morning, the funeral follows late the same afternoon.

When the time for the funeral arrives, the funeral-servants place the body on an iron bier. Wood is never used because the Zoroastrians believe that it can be contaminated by the remains. After relatives have entered the mortuary room for a final viewing, the bier is borne ceremoniously through a special door to begin the procession to the place of final exposure.

The Towers of Silence

The Zoroastrians believe that earth, fire, and water have a basic purity, which the burial, cremation, or putrefaction of a body would contaminate. To avoid this, they expose the dead to scavengers. In communities large enough to maintain them, exposure is made in huge, round "Towers of Silence." In the vicinity of Bombay the Parsis maintain seven of these towers. In smaller communities, bodies are left on a remote mountain or hill. This latter practice once was general, and seems to date from the sixth century B.C.

Among the Zoroastrians of Iran the funeral procession has a traditional order: it is led by a man bearing in his hands a vase containing the sacred fire, symbol of Ormazd, the Zoroastrian supreme deity. Next follow, in turn, the relatives, the bearers with the body, and the priests. If the Tower of Silence is nearby, the whole procession walks; if it is distant, it is likely that all except the priests will ride and that the body will be borne on a donkey. In Bombay the Parsis maintain a special aluminum

Hive-shaped funeral cabin where funeral rites for the dead are held. Save for the guards, and the young son of one of them, the scene is desolate

painted hearse to take the body to the Tower of Silence.

The procession halts at the entrance of the Tower for a brief ceremony, following which the funeral-servants alone carry the body into the great, round structure. The Tower is generally built of stone, with concentric beds or levels rising from the central pit or well. The unroofed interior is opened to the sky. This place the Zoroastrians consider the most impure on earth, so that only the unclean funeral-servants will enter it, and even they must wear special garments for the purpose.

Vultures look hungrily on while the funeral-servants remove the body from the bier, lay it on the stone bed, and strip it of the white garments. After these are thrown into the well, the bier

182

Interior view of a
"tower of silence"
shows what actually
remains of the bodies
after the vultures
have feasted upon
them. Parsis religious
beliefs prohibit
earth burial and
cremation

P.I.P. Photo

183

is borne from the Tower, and the vultures begin their meal. In the course of a few hours the bones are usually stripped bare. Formerly certain of the Zoroastrians gathered and preserved the bones, but the custom no longer is followed. Now at intervals the funeral-servants enter the Tower, gather the bones, and drop them in the central pit.

While the bearers are disposing of the body, the other members of the procession retire to a nearby chapel-like room for the reading of prayers.

Funeralization ends with purification ceremonies. The body-bearers enter a prolonged period of ritualistic cleansing. All who participated in the funeral procession wash their hands in cow urine, and on reaching home take a complete bath. Cow urine is used in the home to cleanse all places where the body was laid.

Wynn comments: "The entire funeral process is such a primitive ritual that it has become a source of embarrassment to modern Zoroastrians, some of whom are wealthy and highly respected citizens of places like Bombay and Aden. Enlightened Zoroastrians have long sought a substitute system for disposal of the dead which would appear less barbarous without offending the basic tenets of their religion."[19]

Festivals of the Parsis commemorate the phases of creation, Zoroaster's birth and death, the emigration of their ancestors to India and the guardian spirits of the dead. During this last festival, called *Farvardin* or *Muktad* ancestral spirits are thought to return to visit their descendants, and special welcoming ceremonies are held before the Towers of Silence. Although bodies are considered the ultimate of defilement, the spirits of ancestors do not share this odium, and rites to honor them are highly regarded.[20]

184

Chapter 11

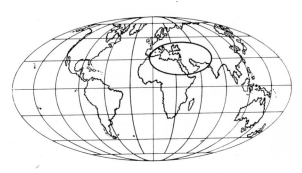

Lebanon

Moslem Funerals in Lebanon

The *Sunni* or orthodox Moslems form the largest religious
group in the Middle East, and the predominant group in
Lebanon. Their funeral rites are simple probably because
there is need for haste. Unembalmed bodies putrefy rapidly
in the torrid Middle Eastern climate. In addition, Mohammed
urged his followers not to delay burial. The righteous soul
should not be kept apart from its paradisiacal rewards, and a
wicked man should be quickly put away.[1]

Although theoretically the Arab Moslems have no priesthood, and all burial duties are assigned to the family, in
practice the sheik or holy man is called upon without fee to
render certain services. If the deceased is a man, the sheik
washes the body and wraps it in a simple linen shroud. A
woman's body, however, is washed by her relatives.

Burial takes place within twenty-four hours after death.
Mohammed taught that because angels walk before the bier, it

185

would not be fitting for men to ride. Accordingly, the entire funeral procession hurries forward on foot.

Because Moslems believe that attending a funeral is a meritorious act, they show respect for funerals of all faiths. It is even more meritorious to carry the dead, and the bier is borne by relays of four or five near relatives, aided sometimes by non-relatives. The body is enclosed in a plain pine box, built by specialized carpenters who otherwise have no connection with the funeral.

Local custom provides the order of the funeral procession. In keeping with the belief that angels walk ahead of the bier, in Lebanon it precedes the mourners; conversely, in Egypt it follows them. In some areas women are admitted to the procession, in others they are banned.

The ancient practice of employing professional mourners still persists in some areas, and is today defended on the ground that they assist the bereaved in securing emotional release, thus lessening their grief. Blind sheiks from the medieval University of Al Azhar in Cairo, who receive their food and lodging from religious endowments, secure money for their clothing and other necessities by serving as mourners for funerals of the rich. When several of them are so employed, they lead the procession, followed in turn by the male relatives and friends of the deceased, the bier, and the women mourners. Relatives in this last group provide themselves with a blue handkerchief which they wear about their shoulders or twirl above their heads.

Funeral services for an important person are always conducted in a mosque, for a lesser person they are held in a mosque or in an open space near the home of the deceased, but in either case, never in a graveyard. Unlike Christians, who hold them to be sacred ground, Moslems consider cemeteries unclean. Although in theory the recitation of the service of the dead is the responsibility of the nearest of kin, in practice it is customarily assigned to a sheik. The service itself is of ancient origin and among the Sunni Moslems exhibits no local variations. The Shi-ite (schismatic) Moslems believe that the dead will be questioned by angels for admission to Paradise. So that they may know the answers, it is customary at Shi-ite funerals to read the list of *Imams*, the twelve successors of Mohammed whom the Shi-ites recognize. The mountain villages of Lebanon lengthen the funeral rites with traditional dirges, which vary greatly from place to place.

After the rites are read, all sit for a while in silence. Then the friends and neighbors say to the relatives, "It is the will of God." And the chief mourner replies, "I am pleased with the will of God," and gives permission to the assemblage to leave the mosque. Some return to their homes; others follow the bier to the grave.

Lebanese graves are dug to a depth equal to the height of the breast of a middle-sized man, with a recess at the bottom to receive the body. At the grave the pine box is set aside, the shroud is loosened, and the uncoffined body is laid in the recess with its face turned toward Mecca.

Because of the Moslem tradition that the body feels pain, great care is used in handling it. After the recess is sealed with unburnt brick, the grave is filled with earth. Because Moslems believe that the dead body can suffer, they frown on cremation, even though the injunction of the Koran that the living shall not be burned is not extended to the dead. Burning is con-sidered to be God's, not man's, form of punishment.

Moslem cemeteries generally are situated on the outskirts of villages and cities. A village burial plot is allotted without charge to each family. Devout Moslems generally neglect their cemeteries in the belief that thereby they take a meritorious stand in avoiding idolatry. While tombs ordinarily are simple, an exceptionally wealthy or holy person may be honored by a showy sepulchre.

By and large, Moslem funerals are relatively inexpensive. Wynn comments that: "the cost is hard to estimate, but obvious-ly it can be held down to a minimum. The simple linen shroud in which the body is wrapped costs little, from one to ten dollars. The box in which the body is carried to the grave is a simple affair and very cheap. In Beirut, these simple pine boxes are built for around twenty Lebanese pounds, approximately six dollars." At the opposite extreme, at funerals of the very rich, "gaudy displays such as excessive numbers of mourners and distribution of gifts to the poor take place. These, however, are luxuries and do not form part of the funeral expense."

Occasionally the practice is followed by a family of employing readers to read the Koran for a fixed number of days after the burial. The cost of such services varies with the number of readers, the length and frequency of their readings, and the wealth of the bereaved family.

Christian Funerals in the Middle East

Middle East Christians are "divided into numerous small and intensely conservative sects," Associated Press Correspondent Wilton Wynn notes.[2] While each of these has its peculiar funeral customs, Christian funerals by and large are unlike Moslem funerals. A major feature of that unlikeness is the fact that Christian funerals are more elaborate.

Wynn finds the Maronites a fairly representative illustration of Christian funerals in the Middle East. This group of 400,000 Uniate Catholics—they acknowledge the Pope's primacy and agree with Rome in matters of faith, although maintaining their own liturgy and discipline—live in the Lebanese mountains. There since the seventh century they have maintained their identity.

As would be expected, older Maronite funeral practices are being modified today by Western influences, particularly in towns and cities, and funeral directors are beginning to establish themselves as a vocational group. In Beirut, in 1952, two funeral homes, each with a full-time director, offered all the usual funeral services except embalming. Even in the capital, however, a full shift to the Western practice of turning over the funeral tasks to the funeral director has not taken place, and families are likely to make a piecemeal use of his services.

When death occurs, after the attending physician has injected embalming fluid, the family washes the body, dresses it in the deceased's best clothes, and lays it upon a bed, with a crucifix beside it on the headpillow, and lighted candles at the head and feet. The clothes with which it is dressed after death usually serve as burial garments. Little restorative art is practiced, and the jaws are locked by a cloth tightly bound around the head and under the chin.

Burial follows within twenty-four hours after death, and ordinarily the body is kept in the home. During this time friends view the remains, and nuns from nearby Maronite convents sit with the body and read aloud the prayers for the dead.

Since the time between death and burial is brief, it is important that notices of death shall be sent immediately to all concerned. Although the funeral director now prints the time of death and place of death, and family and funeral details on black-edged folders, and provides for distribution of these, some member of the immediate family frequently spends an entire night addressing the envelopes. As a precaution against nondelivery, funeral notices are posted throughout the city, on church doors and in other prominent places.

The family receives condolences on the morning of the funeral. The men gather in one house in a great circle; the women, in another. Friends enter the room, shake hands with the mourners, and then sit quietly for a half hour before leaving.

Because many Maronites in Beirut have their family roots in mountain villages, and burials are made in ancestral ground, it is frequently necessary to arrange for transportation. Sometimes a hearse is hired; sometimes a family provides its own or another vehicle.

The body is not coffined until the time arrives to bear it to the funeral ceremonies. Although the funeral director stands ready to arrange for the purchase of the coffin, most Maronites prefer to make this purchase themselves. Coffins are bought from a carpenter who specializes in manufacturing them for all sects. The Marionites, on the whole, place more emphasis on the type and ornateness of caskets and coffins than do their Moslem neighbors.

The funeral procession always proceeds on foot. If the body has been transported, the vehicle bearing it is halted some distance from the church. There a group of mourners meet it, weeping loudly, and chanting strange dirges of mountain

189

origin. Maronite priests lead the procession, and family pride decrees that as many priests as possible, often ten to twenty, should be in attendance. Since the normal fee to a priest is one hundred Lebanese pounds (about $35), this item alone may involve heavy expense. Mourners follow the priests, and precede the coffin. Behind the coffin march male members of the family, and, in order, male friends, women relatives, and women friends.

As among the Moslems of the region, bearing the bier is considered particularly meritorious, and as many as can place their hands upon it carry it. The coffin of an old man or woman is borne on the shoulders; that of a young man is held at arm's length and as high as possible. In some mountain communities, when a young unmarried man dies the event is considered particularly mournful, and a mock wedding ceremony, with wedding dances to suggest that he was married, precedes the entrance of the procession into the church.

After the church services, the men, again on foot, accompany the body to the grave, while the women gather in the home of a friend for further exchange of condolences.

In the mountains Maronite tombs are vaults of huge stone slabs built large enough to accommodate very large families. After each burial, the tomb is completely covered with earth so that the entrance must be dug out for another use. Before the coffin is lowered into the entrance of the tomb, the lid is removed so that the mourners are permitted a final viewing of the body before it is laid to rest.

Chapter 12

Israel

The basic rites followed in Israel are substantially those followed everywhere by Judaism with slight modifications by force of local or communal traditions. Certain features mark these rites. Among them are reverence for the dead, simplicity, equality between rich and poor, rapid burial, the avoidance of cremation, keeping the body inviolate from embalmment, incisions and blood-letting, and the existence of burial societies.[1]

Burial Brotherhoods

In Israel there is no established occupational group of funeral directors operating private businesses. Instead, practically all the burial of the dead is carried out by 260 burial societies which operate mostly according to the tradition of the *Hevra Qadisha* (Holy Brotherhoods).[2] These are non-profit organizations of pious people who have assumed the responsibility for conducting funerals of Jews. A typical burial

191

brotherhood sets up four aims: (1) to acquire land in its town's administrative area and to fence and divide it, construct roadways through it, provide it with service buildings, and otherwise improve it so as to be a cemetery suitable for Jews; (2) to keep this cemetery in good condition; (3) to organize the members into an effective staff capable of caring for funerals and burials, and to engage in other good works; and (4) to co-operate with the authorities in any public enterprise initiated and sponsored by them, and to accept authoritative rabbinical guidance.

Any married Jew or Jewess is eligible for membership in a Hevra Qadisha as a volunteer worker on its rotation roster, if qualifying relative to the applicant's state of health, personal integrity, and religious observance. Admission is by vote of the brotherhood's central committee. The brotherhood derives its operating revenues from allocating burial plots, arranging funerals, and maintaining graves and markers. Money is expended for land purchase, preparation and maintenance of grounds, the construction of cemetery buildings, administrative and secretarial expenses, funerals and the funeral procession, and aid to enterprises initiated and sponsored by religious authorities.

Each brotherhood selects from its ranks "honest, pious people suited to the task of purification and funeral processing." After receiving instructions from supervisors these people are considered "professionals." All voluntary members are expected to visit the deceased's next of kin to try to care for them and "to try to lighten their grief in all possible ways."

Burial brotherhoods are organized on a local and communal basis. While the brotherhoods are prepared to supply all funeral necessities, a few Jews have kept their shrouds from the time of their marriage. For the most part, Jews are buried uncoffined, in their shrouds. This practice has its origins partly in the ancient laws looking to the rapid decomposition of the body and partly in custom. There are a few government-licensed burial societies that do not follow the Hevra Qadisha pattern but observe their own secular ritual; these are to be found with some collective rural settlements. Some hearses are found in Israel. These are owned by the burial brotherhoods; often a vehicle is owned in common by two or more such groups.

Rules for the Care of the Dead

The regulations of Judaism relating to death and burial are conveniently grouped into fifteen categories: (1) the care of a dying person and a dead body; (2) the tearing of a rent in the clothes; (3) the conduct of the next of kin; (4) the purification and the shrouds; (5) the removal of the body and the funeral; (6) the order of the funeral service and the interment; (7) concerning an Onain; (8) the meal of condolence; (9) the seven days of mourning; (10) the thirty days and twelve

Jews wearing orthodox garments make up funeral cortege on streets of Jerusalem

193

months; (11) timely and delayed news; (12) Kaddish and Yahrseit (death anniversary); (13) the unveiling of the tombstone; (14) the consecration of a new cemetery or fence; and (15) memorial services. Inasmuch as there is considerable detail to these regulations only the briefest summary of them can be made here.

Because a dying person still lives it is forbidden to lay hands on the body or to make preparations for a funeral. Touching the body may hasten death, thus involving the person who so acts in bloodshed. When death seems to have occurred a physician should be consulted. If none is available, a light feather held near the nostrils will suffice to detect breathing. Even today most Israelis die in their homes. Some deaths occur in hospitals. While a death certificate is issued by the Ministry of Health, the burial itself may be conducted only through the burial brotherhoods.

When the fact of death is clear the windows must be thrown open, mirrors covered, prayers recited, and garments rent. The eyes of the dead should be closed, by a son if the dead had sons, and by a first-born son if possible. The chin is bound and the face is covered. The body is left on the bed for an hour. At the end of that time it is removed to the floor, the feet pointing in the direction of the entrance to the room. The head is raised by placing a little stone beneath it, the limbs are straightened, and a sheet is spread over the body. A pair of lighted candles, one at the head and the other at the feet, are provided. Thereafter the body must never be left alone, and a constant watch is maintained to detect possible life. Food may not be eaten in the death chamber.

The tearing of the garments is governed by elaborate prescriptions. A brief listing will indicate the detailed nature of the regulations: The garment must be rent near the neck, in the front thereof and it must not be rent crosswise but lengthwise and in the cloth of the garment and not in the seam. In the case of the next of kin, the rent may be basted together after the seven days of mourning, and completely sewed up after thirty days of mourning, but in the case of

194

mourning for a father or a mother the rent may be basted together only after 30 days and never sewed up. A woman may baste it together at once.

The washing of the body waits upon the completion of the shrouds. The shrouds must be made without hem or knot. They may consist of three basic garments: a sheet, breeches, and an overgarment with a girdle. A white cap is put upon the head and white stockings are put upon the legs of the dead. The body of a man is wrapped in his fringed *Talith* (prayer shawl). In place of the Talith an additional overgarment is placed on a woman's body.

In washing a dead body the same respect must be shown to it as would be shown to a living body. Regulations governing this procedure are numerous and provide among other matters, that the conversation of the washers must avoid familiarity and must be limited to the matter of the funeral preparations, that the body must always be moved by two persons, lest the legs dangle, that during the cleansing it must be wrapped in a white sheet, and that it must never be placed with the face downward. The bodies of women are attended only by women, and the bodies of children must not be kissed.

While the law Deuteronomy 21, 23 provides that a body shall not remain unburied over night, when it is necessary for the purpose of honoring the dead to extend the time to procure a coffin or shrouds, or to await the arrival of relatives for the funeral, the burial may be delayed. When two burials are to be made, the one who has died first should be buried first. However, if one of the deceased was learned and the other ignorant, the remains of the learned person must be buried first, regardless of who died first.

It is meritorious to accompany the dead to the grave. For this reason anyone who sees a funeral procession should join it for a short distance. Relatives should bear the coffin. This is also a task for friends. The procession generally moves from the home or hospital to the cemetery. For over two millennia Jewish tradition requires utmost simplicity and democratic equality at burials. The mourners' procession follows the bier part of the way on foot. In Israel the body is generally borne on a stretcher, only wrapped in shrouds. When passing a synagogue, the procession halts and a prayer is recited. Eulogies are made at the home, on the way (near a synagogue or other suitable place), in the cemetery chapel, or at the graveside. Before placing the body in its final resting place, the burial society and friends ask the departed soul to forgive any slight or wrong and to depart in peace with the world. After the body has been lowered, relatives and close friends cast earth into the grave, and then earth is shoveled back into the grave until it is filled. Burial brotherhood members perform this task. As people leave the cemetery, they pluck some grass to cast over their shoulders saying, "He remembereth that we are dust."

The mourner's first meal on the first day of mourning is called the "Meal of Condolence." Neighbors supply the food for this first meal.

Mourning rites must be observed for seven classifications of next of kin: one's father, mother, son, daughter, brother, sister, wife or husband. No mourning is observed for an infant which did not live thirty days.

Mourning rites begin when the grave has been filled. They last seven days. During the first three of this no labor is permitted, even to the poor. On the fourth, to secure food if necessary the poor man may work privately in his home. These prohibitions, however, do not apply to a housewife. She may cook and bake.

Cohabitation is forbidden for the Onain during the seven days, as is the wearing of leather footwear, or washing, except for the face, hands and feet, and bathing except for health purposes. Laughter and rejoicing are likewise avoided. Prayer services are held twice daily at the mourners' home during this week.

This seven-day period of intense mourning ushers in a twenty-day period of less rigorous observance. During the whole of the mourning period the mourner must not cut his hair or trim his beard.

196

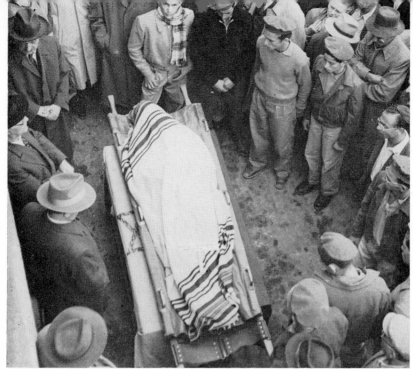

According to Jewish orthodox law, Jews who are buried in the Holy Land are not coffined, but are shrouded and carried to the cemetery on a simple wooden bier. Scene shows mourners crowded around bier of late president of Hebrew University

Although the law encourages children to say prayers for their parents it is more important that they walk in the right path. On the anniversary of the death of a parent, sons and daughters have a religious obligation to fast, attend synagogue services, and recite the prayer for the dead as a means of improving their conduct and of gaining grace for the parent. The Yahrseit is observed on the anniversary of the death.

Funeral Economics

The cost of a funeral varies with the financial standing of the deceased. The National Insurance Company, a governmental agency to which all Israelis must subscribe, contributes a sum equal to about half the expense of a normal funeral, and the family pays the rest. The rich people may make an offering several times as large as the normal figure with the understand-

197

Hearse belonging to the
burial society of Tel Aviv

Burial society members
carry shrouded body into
cemetery for burial

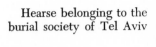

Gravedigger lines sides,
head, foot, but not bottom
of grave. Body will be
buried in shroud

Photos Courtesy George Goodstein

198

Son of recently deceased reads prayers while family members
and friends hold memorial service at the grave site

ing that whatever payment is in excess goes to charity. When
the decedent is indigent, without means to pay the family portion of the bill, the Ministry of Social Welfare and the National
Insurance Company jointly pay the whole cost.

Tombstones are generally ordered from a stonecutter through

the Burial Society. The poor use simple markers on the graves of their dead; the rich, more elaborate stones. Sculptured memorials are traditionally not used by Jews; markers, however, are inscribed. The setting up of a gravestone inscribed with the name of the deceased is encouraged because it keeps the dead in mind and encourages the living to pray for him. When this is done the relatives, friends, and rabbi gather at the cemetery and "unveil" the gravestone.

When a new cemetery is opened, an addition is made to an old one, or a new fence is placed around a cemetery, the brotherhood fasts at least until noon on the day that the ground or fence is consecrated. Those present at the consecration march seven times around the cemetery before listening to a sermon and reciting psalms.

It is customary in Israel to pray for the souls of the dead and to make contributions to charity in their memory. Such acts are deemed meritorious to the departed.[3]

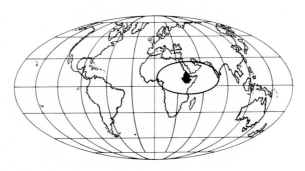

Chapter 13

Ethiopia

Ethiopia, an independent empire, lies at the foot of the Red Sea in northeastern Africa. Culturally it is bound to the semitic world, and for this reason is considered by ethnographers as part of the Middle East. Ethnologically, the Ethiopians are predominantly Caucasoid, with a subordinate Negroid strain. They speak a variant of the Hamitic language, and for the most part subscribe to the Coptic branch of Christianity which is centered in Egypt. Mohammedanism is professed by minority groups, especially those in the northern areas of the country. The funeral customs of most Ethiopians are an amalgam of Christian, traditional semitic, and indigenous native folkways, with Christian doctrines and practices predominant.

Response to Death

When an Ethiopian of the Tigre province becomes ill, his family and friends visit him as frequently as possible, and everyone who knows a remedy or method of healing offers advice and assistance. If these good offices prove unavailing,

201

and it becomes clear that the patient is dying, a message is sent to distant relatives advising them to come and "catch the last word." Even before death comes the neighbors congregate and begin to lament. The family greets all visitors by saying with false assurance: "He is all right. He will recover."

Separated from the rest by a curtain, in the same chamber where the dying man lies, or in an adjoining room, the elder relatives sit apart and weep. When death comes, they close his mouth and eyes, pinch his nostrils, and straighten the body. If he is a layman, they quickly arrange his upper arms along the sides of the body and cross his lower arms at his abdomen, holding them in place by tying his thumbs together with white string. For a person in religion, a monk, priest, or nun who had been married, the arms are folded crosswise over the chest. The arms of a celibate monk or virgin nun are folded so that the fingers rest on the mouth.[1]

While the body is being quickly arranged behind the curtain before *rigor mortis* sets in, the friends and relatives outside who have heard the news start "violent shaking, bitter weeping, merciless hair plucking, and fierce face scratching." Weeping at this time reaches its greatest intensity. In contrast to this abandon is the restraint of those who behind the curtain continue to prepare the body for burial. The deceased's confessor, or in his absence, a substitute, blesses a pot of water freshly brought from the river. The whole contents of the pot is used to bathe the body.

The dressing is begun by tying the big toes together and then the thumbs with a string drawn from the shroud. The arms of a priest are tied with a string pulled to the back, and the arms of a monk, who has kept his vow of celibacy, and virgin nuns, with a string around the back and over the chest and the arms.

Swathing and Coffining the Body

After the body has been bound, it is generally wrapped in a fresh sheet of calico or muslin. Nobles may use red or blue satin for the purpose. Although the shroud is generally purchased in anticipation of the death of a person who is seriously ill, when death occurs before this precaution is taken, the nearest neighbor who possesses a suitable piece of cloth must offer it. If this resource fails, then cloth must be bought in the market. Whatever its origin, the cloth must never have been worn or immersed in water. The shroud may be either cut and sewn, or left unsewn. In either case, it is bound to the body at the feet, ankles, knees, hips, breast, neck and forehead. At burial the knot which ties the string at the forehead is unloosed.

The shroud in turn is covered with a wrapping made of interwoven palm leaves, which is tied with white strings to the body. When the body is thus covered, the relatives surrender it to elderly men if the deceased is a man, or elderly women if a woman, and join the mourners. The whole group continues to lament and scratch their faces, and occasionally one will leap high and collapse into a faint.[2]

The body is now ready for the coffin. This is a bed, or bier, constructed of wood and leather, which is kept in the church solely for funeral use. Sometime during the night it is brought to the home. Empty, it is carried upside down. For use, it is inverted, the body is laid on it, and fastened into it with a long strap that is laced through holes in it. The loose ends of the strap are tied to the legs of the bier. A cloth of homemade cotton is draped over the body so that it fully covers the sides of the bier, and over this cloth is laid a multicolored drape provided by the church.[3]

Oai! Oai! Oai!

The elders, meanwhile, have sent invitations to villages in the immediate vicinity, and when the guests arrive, the younger men among them are paired off and instructed to equip themselves with metal rods in place of the wooden sticks which they generally carry. Each pair is then assigned the task of carrying the news of the death to a series of more distant villages, which must be close enough so that mourners attending the funeral can return home the same day. No

203

matter if it is night, the messengers set forth on foot, and at each of their destinations mount a nearby hill, and cry loudly: *Oai! Oai! Oai!* Then they name the dead, announce the date and place of the service, and beg for help in the burial. In Azebo and Raya, the messengers ride horseback and gallop from house to house shouting, "Life! Life!" Relatives who could not attend the funeral and return to their homes on the same day are summoned later.

Custom demands that those who receive invitations to the funeral must weep according to their degree of kinship with the deceased. Before they leave for the funeral, their fellow villagers gather around and briefly lament with them. Not only relatives are expected to come, but the friends of relatives, and the church must send at least two priests and three deacons. Many more go than are strictly required by convention to do so.

When a band of mourners draws near the house of death, they halt to give the women a chance to arrange their garments in folds that express mourning, and to afford the priests a few minutes to don their vestments and fasten the cross to a carrying pole. At this point the demonstrations of grief become violent, and friends are sometimes forced to restrain women relatives from plucking out their hair. Occasionally men rake their faces with their nails and throw themselves on the ground so violently that their companions seize them to prevent them from injuring themselves. When a band of weeping villagers reaches the weeping family, the interaction intensifies the mourning.

Meanwhile, throughout the night the village priests gathered around the bier have been chanting the office of the dead. For a layman or priest who has been married only once and spent a lifetime in faithful performance of his religious duties the ceremony is gayer than for those who have married more than once, and to the usual strictly religious prayers are added certain "memorials." The accompaniment for these is provided by a drum, *sistra*—the sistrum is an ancient framed rattling instrument shaped like a ping-pong racket—and dancing sticks.

204

For a child below seven years of age this ceremony in the home is omitted and the godfather takes the body in his arms and carries it directly to the church. A child seven or more years old receives the full rite, but invitations are not broadcast to neighboring villages, and only the men of the immediate family living in close proximity are in attendance. An unbaptized infant is buried in a special court outside the church precincts and only its mother or perhaps a sister weeps for it. A suicide is buried without religious ceremonies.[4]

Although an Ethiopian adage has it that if death occurs before sunset, burial must take place the same day, the bodies of those who die in the afternoon are generally not buried until the following morning, provided they can be kept inoffensive. This delay is made to allow mourners to assemble from points beyond the immediate village.

The Funeral Procession

The funeral ceremony begins at about nine in the morning. Four men raise the body with the bier and carry it feet foremost from the house. As they pass the door, a pot full of water is broken. At the gate before the house the bearers set their load down, and there a few minutes later the procession forms.

In its van are deacons bearing the cross, and a priest bearing the censer. Behind these march other priests, and behind the priests in turn march the pallbearers carrying the coffin. Men come next—members of the family carrying the deceased's rifle, shield, spear and headdress and then friends. The womenfolk follow in the same order, first the family and then friends. Sometimes junior deacons carrying wheat flour for making eucharistic bread lead the entire procession.

After walking a few paces, the bearers set the coffin down, and a woman designated as the "lamentator poet"—any person with a natural facility for making elegiac poems—begins to chant a lamentation. The mourners form a ring about her, and as she concludes a stanza of her song, they repeat the refrain. As they do so, they move rhythmically, each person

205

swaying above the waist. They have brought the handsomest of the deceased's apparel and goods with them, and they swing these objects about them as they dance. For a woman these include her tight purple, gold embroidered trousers, her double cotton sheet with a broad red band down the middle, and her fine cotton sheet with a middle band of variegated pattern. For a man these include a full suit of clothes and his weapons. So stormy is the manifestation of grief during this rite that each of the dancers is firmly held by a friend who uses restraint to prevent too much scratching of the face and falling down. For some women one attendant is not enough to control the paroxysm, and two or even three are needed.

However violent the demonstration may be, it comes to a halt at a signal from the presiding priest, and after a short prayer, a new set of bearers take up the bier. Since everyone considers it a privilege to carry the dead, it is likely that before the next halt is reached, several shifts of bearers may be made. The procession of a layman or a woman must halt seven times before it reaches the church; the procession of a priest, twenty-four times. In each case, the presiding priest indicates the place for halting, and in each case the rite is repeated.[5]

Burial Rites

If it has been decided to slaughter a bull at the church, the procession halts until the bull is slain. Then the coffin is carried across some sprinkled blood and into the courtyard, where it remains until the carcass has been butchered. The arrival of the coffin is a signal for the priests to begin a hurried saying of the Mass, or for friends to sing memorial songs. At the conclusion of one or the other of these ceremonies, the coffin is brought into the vestibule of the church if the deceased is a man, or to the door, if a woman; and the body is raised from the bier by means of the long strap, and carried into the sanctuary, laid prone, and made to worship by thrice inclining the head. The men then spread a garment over it and bear it to the grave.[6]

Graves may be single resting places, or sepulchres. The

206

single grave is dug sufficiently deep for the two men who stand in it to receive the body in their hands. The sepulchre, designed for multiple burial, is likely to be so deep that the body must be lowered with the aid of the strap. Both grave and sepulchre are rectangular with the long direction pointing east and west. The sepulchre flares from a very narrow mouth.

Before the body arrives, the priest has already blessed and incensed the final resting place. If a grave is used, the men who stand within it adjust the position of the body. Tomb burial is more complicated. The strap holds the body at the calves and the back, and the head is kept slightly higher than the feet. When the bottom is reached, the men in the tomb, having removed the strap, turn the body so that the head lies toward the east. Meanwhile guns are fired, bells are tolled, and the weeping is heavy. When the men emerge from the tomb, the opening is closed with a stone slab whose edges are cemented with mud. After this, the mourners, beginning with the closest male relative, deposit earth on the slab until a small mound marks the spot. Over this a slab of stone is stood. Because the sepulchre will receive other family burials, it is not filled, as is the single grave.[7]

The burial over, the priest signals for complete silence, opens the *Book of Shrouding,* and begins to read a passage which begs earth to receive the dead: "Dust he was and unto dust he has returned." Following this reading, the mourners leave the churchyard and enter the congregation meeting ground, an open field near the church. The women seek the shade of trees, while the men sit in the sun.

Here the bewailing continues until the lamentator poet again rises and begins to chant another short impromptu rhymed elegy in which she praises the dead person and eulogizes his ancestors. Although her verses are listened to in silence, the intervals between them are punctuated by outbursts of heavy weeping. Sometimes several lamentator poets in turn eulogize the dead. These amateurs are usually well rewarded for their services, although they perform without an actual fee.[8]

As midday brings the hot overhead sun, the elders advise an end to the ceremony, and the eldest priest from the deceased person's village arises, reads a passage from the *Book of Shrouding*, blesses the crowd, and especially the next of kin, and calls for the common recitation of the *Lord's Prayer*. When *Amen* has been said, the meat of the slaughtered bull is distributed to everyone, with a generous allotment for the clergy. It is expected that each person present will consume at least a small portion and then offer a prayer for the peaceful rest of the departed soul. At long last the immediate family and some of the elders separate themselves from the crowd, and sitting apart, receive the group condolences of the visitors from other villages in a simple ceremony. Bowing, the visitors say, "May God strengthen you." And the bereaved answer, "May he not tempt you to evil." This ceremony gives the local people a chance to count the crosses, to see which villages are represented, and what persons have come. When an expected delegation or person does not attend, such failure is considered a breach of etiquette, and provokes anger.

One by one the visitors leave, until at length only the mourning family and their neighbors remain. When they are quite alone, all rise and return to the village, the women leading and the men following at a distance. As they pass their homes, some of the women leave the party to boil coffee and roast grain to be brought to the house of mourning. Others continue with the family to the home, and either remain with them or return to their own homes. It is customary for the elders and most of the men to remain with the mourning group, lamenting, drinking coffee, and eating roasted grain.[9]

Mourning Behavior

Modification of dress is made as a sign of mourning. For a woman, various ways of arranging her shawl are prescribed in different villages. The man's upper garment serves him in a like capacity. Women who visit the house of mourning must bring coffee or other food. Although no such necessity exists for the men, in the towns they buy an alcoholic beverage to

208

bring with them. Unless one has been a member of the funeral party, he makes his gift only on his second visit to the home of the deceased.[10]

Custom prescribes that while all acquaintances of the bereaved family must either attend the funeral or pay a courtesy call within the week after death, only those who personally know the dead must weep. When the new guest enters, conversation ceases, the family begins to lament, and he remains silent for a few minutes, looking disconsolate. Then he bids them to cease their grieving. For seven days these visitors appear, and the villagers remain to comfort the bereaved family. Meanwhile the clergy read lessons which point out that death brings rest and is not to be feared, only the loss of life everlasting.

During the seven days of mourning, no food must be prepared in the house, and so each evening the neighbors bring in their own dinners, and something extra for the bereaved. While eating they tell jokes to distract the mourners, but seldom succeed in breaking their sorrowing mood.

At night the members of the family sleep on the floor, wearing the same clothes they have worn during the day. Custom prescribes that in the morning no one may rise before the next of kin to the dead has risen. He must begin to weep before it is dawn. In a short time the others join in the lamenting, and if a lamentator-poet is present, she is likely to provoke a fresh outburst of tears by her improvisations.[11]

On the whole, this is the normal routine. In a few exceptional cases the funeral ceremony is repeated. Such duplication takes place when the deceased is nobly born, when death has occurred away from home, or when for some reason or other, a hurried burial was made. For the nobility, the second ceremony provides an opportunity for bringing mourners from much greater distances, and for organizing more spectacular obsequies. Because it is considered fitting that once at least all close friends and relatives should gather for a person's funeral, the ceremony is duplicated for those who died at a distance. Sometimes persons must be hurriedly buried for sanitary reasons. Included in this group are women who have died in childbirth and all who die of dysentery. Victims of stabbing are likewise buried in a hurry. The second funeral provides an opportunity for bringing together at least once those who mourn for such as these. Generally this second ceremony takes place during mourning week, but it may be postponed because of bad weather or fear of contagion.

This second ceremony need not be performed within the church precincts; any convenient open area will serve. The center of attraction, resting on a rich carpet, is the bier, which is decorated as though it contained the body. In attendance are the priest, with the cross and the censer. While they may recite the ritual for the dead, it is more likely that theirs will be a silent role, because the church opposes the use of the ritual when the body is *in absentia*. At the head of the empty bier stands a servant bearing the dead man's gun, and next to him, a fellow-servant carrying his shield and spear, and at the foot, another servant holding a fly-whisk. In the front row of the audience are servants carrying pots, flasks, meats, knives, and straw work for the table—food and equipment symbolizing their late master's banquet arrangements. Behind them, servants hold the reins of their late master's horse and mule. The animals are arrayed in their best harness.[12]

Because the second funeralization permits the announcements to be sent to greater distances, the crowd of mourners is likely to be much larger than that gathered for a first ceremony. A procession now forms, and the male relatives and retainers of the deceased man shoulder their rifles and advancing, make low obeisances to the bier. Next the master of ceremonies orders silence, and the lamentator-poet, sometimes assisted by bards and pipers, begins to chant her elegiac improvisations. Meanwhile, the procession circles the bier, intermittently halting and resuming its march. Weeping alternates with the lamentator-poet's chanting until the ceremony ends. Again the family eyes the ranks of visitors to note who has breached etiquette by failing to attend.

In advance of this second ceremony, relatives have prepared pots of drink. They place these along the roads leading from the ceremonial ground so that returning mourners may be refreshed. Once the guests begin to drift away, the ceremony concludes, and the family and intimates return to the house of death to continue their mourning. Servants bring back the possessions of the deceased, and the casket is returned to the church.[13]

On the eighth day, all return to their homes, and the family is expected to resume its normal routines, and to eat and sleep as usual. While the men are likely to observe this custom, an occasional woman may persist in sleeping on the ground with a fleece for a mattress.

The termination of the week of formal mourning does not put an end to mourning itself, and the relatives respond with weeping to each fresh offer of sympathy, and among themselves, grieve quietly whenever they speak of the dead. Where the required dye is available, a man dyes his suit black and in the countryside, he uses tree bark to dye it yellow. Men of the upper classes don a white calico suit. Because this is the common apparel of country people, for a man of importance to wear it is deemed a sign of distress. Other customs describe how a cape must be worn to show grief. In towns, the more sophisticated indicate their bereavement by sewing a black patch on either the left arm or breast of their coat. Some who normally shave, let their beards grow to show their grief, and conversely some who normally wear beards, shave. Some shave their heads.[14]

Women in mourning dye their clothes, line their cloaks and capes with black, and eschew ornaments. They replace their black neck cord with a white string. They put aside their pendants, rings, crosses, earrings, finger-rings, and miscellaneous jewelry. Because they may already have pulled out much of their hair in their paroxysms of grief, they sometimes shave off the remainder, although a truly broken-hearted wife will not adopt this sanitary practice until the fortieth day of commemoration. Instead, as a symbol of her grief, she will neither wash, comb, nor put up her hair, but binds it in a rag and

211

welcomes dirt and lice. Nor will the faithful wife put butter on her hair until her husband has been dead for a year. When she begins to butter her hair, all know that she has ended her period of mourning. To encourage her to resume her normal life, the neighbors visit her and implore her to cease lamenting. Sometimes, when she is obdurate, the womenfolk will seize her and butter her hair themselves.[15]

Although certain Ethiopian funeral practices may seem violent to those who are indoctrinated into more reserved customs, the people of Tigre province remind one another in the house of mourning that when Cain slew Abel, Adam did not know how to express his grief, and so it grew intolerable, and his face became swollen with it, and his eyes reddened and bulged. Seeing Adam in this plight, the Lord sent angels to show him how to mourn by weeping and by scratching their faces. And Adam saw, and imitated what he saw, and thus his burden of grief was relieved.[16]

Funeral Customs The World Over

Part Three

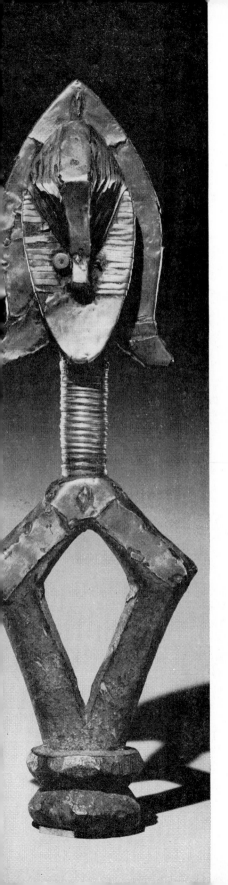

Left, Durban Funeral Chapel interior

Right, Ancestor figure from The Cameroons

Africa

Varied peoples, races and cultures, and a confusion of tongues . . . animism, a world of spirits . . . tribalism, exclusive . . . tribal man, a living personification of the ancestral dead . . . fantastically varied funeral folkways . . . the contravening forces of Christianity . . . and an archipelago of whites in a sea of blacks and coloured

Left, Dennis Cleaver Photo

Right, Chicago Natural History Museum

Native funeral procession in Ghana, formerly Gold Coast Colony

Chapter 14

Ashanti and Fanti of Ghana

The Ashanti

The Ashanti are a West African native group, numbering over 200,000 people, all speaking the Twi language. They live mostly in small scattered villages in the center of what was previously the Gold Coast area, but which is now the Republic of Ghana. Despite their earlier incorporation into a British Colonial system their native institutions have remained virtually intact for centuries. This is especially true in their ceremonial behavior, in which the funeral plays a most important role.[1]

The Moment of Death

When the illness of an Ashanti does not yield to the remedies provided by household magic, a doctor, who represents the Ashanti equivalent of either a general practitioner or a specialist, is called in. Disease is believed to originate in supernatural beings, and, although the physician may prescribe herbs, these are considered not so much natural remedies acting on natural causes, as supernatural upon supernatural. When it becomes clear, however, that the medicine man and witch doctor have failed to propitiate ancestral spirits and the gods, watchers wait for the moment of death so that they may put a little water into the dying person's throat.

This rite is important to the Ashanti, and he so fears that chance may deprive him of it that in his old age he seldom proceeds afar without a companion ready to administer it. This last drink is designed to assist the thirsting spirit to climb the steep hill that leads into eternity. As they render this service the watchers entreat the spirit not to permit evil to enter the house that he is leaving, and to allow the women of his family to bear children.[2]

The village chief is notified immediately of a death. To commence burial preparations without him is punishable by a heavy fine of money and a sheep. For washing the body with a new sponge and hot water and towel, the washers are paid in wine. Rum is poured down the throat to preserve the body, and on the ground to propitiate the spirit. Gold dust represents one form of wealth for these people, and it is sometimes sprinkled into the ears and a bag of it tied in the loincloth of the dead. The body is made to rest on the left side, so that the right arm and hand will be free to use in eating. The hands are generally folded against the right cheek. Sometimes a handkerchief is placed between the palms for wiping the sweat from them as the spirit climbs the hill into eternity. The fingers are sometimes placed in a pan containing gold dust and occasionally the head of the body is shaved, and painted with alternate colored bands so that if the dead becomes a ghost his identity may be established. Occasionally, too, the head is laid in a brass pan which is not removed at burial. When the head falls off the body, the pan holds it.

Mourning the Dead

When the body has thus been made ready, the wailing begins, and men fire guns. Mourners smear red clay on their foreheads and upper arms, or white clay over their entire bodies if they are of the family of a dead priest. All bind their heads with mourning bands which may enclose red peppers, and don russett colored mourning garments. Although they are now bound to fast, they are allowed to drink red wine.[3]

The next step is the offering of food to be eaten by the dead in his journey into the afterlife. A fowl, eggs, mashed yams and water are laid beside the body. In each case the formula is thrice repeated, "Here is a fowl — or an egg — for your soul." The wake now begins, and is continued day and night until the burial. Waking the dead consists of dancing, drumming, singing, firing of guns, and drinking and carousing, and most of the spectators grow very drunk. Meanwhile the widow remains with the body, while awake fanning flies from its head, and lying beside it when she sleeps. The superficial jollity of the funeral ceremonies must not conceal the fact that the grief of close relatives naturally may be very real and deep.

Rattray, the Ashanti authority, has collected songs sung at Ashanti funerals.[4] The nameless bards who created them clearly were poets of deep feeling and profound insight. The following is typical:

Solo: "O Amankwatia, son of Adu,
    Whom does death overlook?
    Mother hen do with your own chickens as you do with ours.
    You keep your own chicks behind you while you peck at ours.

Chorus: O Amankwatia, whom does death overlook?
    I am an orphan, and when I recall the death of my father water falls from my eyes upon me.
    When I recall the death of my mother, water from my eyes falls upon me.
    We walk, we walk, O Mother Tano,
    Until now we walk and it will soon be night.
    It is because of the sorrow of death that we walk."

The walk is to the burial ground. Amankwatia is a famous war chief. Mother Tano is the river. An elegy such as this will be known and sung, with local variations all over Ashanti land.

While some wail and others carouse, preparations continue to be made for the funeral. Relatives must be summoned, a generous supply of gunpowder purchased, and a final meal and gifts prepared for the body.

Funeral Preparations

Contributions to funeral expenses are so rigidly defined that they are now cited in courts of law as evidence of the relationship of a living person to the deceased in whose rites he had a part. Such contributions divide themselves into two groups. The first includes obligations for which the family of the deceased are primarily responsible. The second includes voluntary contributions made by non-relatives as acts of charity. These latter do not in any way make their donors responsible for the funeral debts, or for the debts of the deceased or his family, or give him a right to claim a portion of the estate as heir.

Custom rigidly prescribes the things that all members of the family must contribute: wives—gold dust to defray part of the funeral expenses, gold dust and charcoal to be placed with the body, a shroud and food; children — sheep, a cloth to be placed beside the body and gold dust; nephews — collectively a sheep, a cloth to be buried with the body and a sum of money; the deceased's grandchildren — a sum of money; and so forth.[5]

The deceased's blood family are expected to contribute: gunpowder — the family's wealth will be judged by the amount of gunpowder that is fired, and this item alone sometimes causes it to assume heavy debts; palm-wine or rum; food — chiefly sheep which are slaughtered, the mutton being fed to the young who are not bound to fast, or placed before the body for sustenance on its journey.

Rattray writes that the formal presentation of these gifts, especially those given directly to the dead, is an impressive sight.

The head of the family presents his group's gift of a sheep, addressing the body and saying: "May all your family have long life and health. May we get money to pay your funeral expenses. Do not let anyone die, or any cause of quarrel arise out of the

220

funeral." Frequently the gift sheep is slaughtered in the court-yard, in the presence of the body, and some of its blood is caught in a wooden bowl while the rest is allowed to spill upon the earth. The spouse presents her gift with the entreaty: "Let me bear children." As each gift is placed on a low table, it is de-scribed for the deceased, and he is entreated to use it.[6]

Burial

Burial takes place on the third day, and is no longer strictly a nighttime affair. Formerly the use of coffins was reserved for kings, but now it is becoming common for ordinary people, who otherwise are buried in a mat wrapping.

Before the coffin lid is nailed down, a sexton sits himself down upon the funeral mat, adds up the contributions and sets a value upon them, and declares the totals to the body. Rattray com-ments: "The firing of guns, the weeping and lamentations, the half-drunken jollity of the crowds, the songs, the dancing, the drumming, the nauseating stench of the body, the heat and the dust, all combine to drive away the European spectator from such scenes."[7]

When a member of the deceased's family has completed the enumeration of the services that were rendered to the dead and entreated the spirit not to allow any of the spectators to fall ill, but to aid them in gathering money for the funeral expenses and to allow the chief to beget children, the lid of the coffin is nailed down. As it is being carried outside through a hole especially made in a wall of the house, it is twice set down, probably to warn the earth goddess of its coming. When it is set down for the third time, the head man of the deceased's family steps forward, a branch in each hand. Touching the coffin alternately with these he declares that he thus separates the spirit of the dead from the living. He lays one branch on the coffin, to be buried with it; and keeps the other to adorn his own sleeping place.

At one time, if the king's permission was forthcoming, and the family could afford the expense, it was customary to sacrifice a slave. Even then, a sheep was sometimes substituted. Today, the sheep is left lying where it is killed, to be dragged away later to the grave. There one of its legs will be cut off and suspended on sticks.

In the procession to the burial grounds, which now gets under way, the spouse leads. On her head she carries a pot containing leaves and three stones. When a point is reached where the general mourners are supposed to halt and allow the immediate family to proceed alone to the grave, the pot will be tumbled backwards, breaking it and scattering its contents. Without a glance behind her the spouse will then run back to the town. As the sextons bear the body away, they twice make a token halt, touching the coffin to the ground in homage to the earth goddess.[8]

The Ashanti bury their dead in a burial ground, using an oblong trench for a grave. To one side of the trench, with its bottom higher than the bottom of the grave, they dig out a shelf. By the time the procession arrives, the grave has been prepared and the earth goddess has been propitiated with a libation. After the body has been placed in the shelf, frequently in the same position in which it was kept in the home, a mat is hung before the niche, and the remainder of the grave is filled with earth. In coffined burials it sometimes happens that a grave niche is not dug, so that the coffin is deposited directly on the floor of the pit. The uncoffined body is placed in the niche by persons standing in the grave; the coffined body lowered by ropes made of vines. When the grave has been filled, the wooden handles are knocked from the hoes and left behind, and the food that stood before the body in the house, and the sponge, towel, and water pots used in bathing it, are scattered. All present drink wine, and some of it is poured on the grave. Then all return to the village to bathe, and to begin a great celebration in which they drink, sing, and dance until exhausted.[9]

Post-Burial Ceremonies

Next morning, the fourth day after the death, the still-fasting family thanks all those who assisted at the funeral. On the fifth day the family ends its fast, and builds a crude hut on the village outskirts. The hut consists of a roof of sticks and branches supported by four uprights. Cooking utensils are placed beneath this shelter.

During the night of the fifth day a member of the family rises and all but dismantles this hut, and the next morning a sheep is killed before the remains of it, a libation of wine is poured on the ground, food is cooked in the utensils, and the family speaks the formula by which the funeral ceremonies are officially ended.

Blood relatives then proceed to shave their heads, placing the hair in a pot on the cover of which is a likeness of the deceased. After this all depart. But when the sun has set, a group of clanswomen pick up the pot, utensils, fragments of food, and the remainder of the hut, and without looking behind them bring their burdens to the burial ground to deposit them in a special area called the "place of the pots." As they return they put down a vine behind them, symbolizing the closing of their path. Meanwhile, seated on stools, the rest of the family awaits them in the village. When the women enter the family group, all push their stools forward slightly, thrice repeating this action. Thus the retreat of death and the advance of life is symbolized. After more ceremony the place in which the family group was seated is swept, and all return to their several homes. No outward show of grief is allowed during this ceremony, and regular clothes replace mourning clothes. Although this is the day on which it is believed that the deceased enters the spirit land, the rites are not terminated. On the eighth, fifteenth, fortieth and eightieth days, and on the first anniversary of the death, further celebrations take place in honor of the dead.[10]

The Fanti

Along with the Ashanti the Fanti tribe shares in membership in the great "Twi"-speaking native group of the Nigritic peoples, or true Negroes of West Africa. They, too, help comprise the modern west African republic of Ghana, formerly the Gold Coast Colony under British domination. In order to understand the complexity of their funeral customs it is necessary to relate them briefly to their rather unique social

223

system. The basis of this system lies in the full development in the tribe of a dual-descent kinship arrangement in which the matrilineal or "mother's line" of kin, called *abusua,* is emphasized as fully as is the patrilineal or "father's line."

James B. Christensen, an anthropologist who studied the Fanti intensively, remarks that the unity of the matrilineal system, or *abusua,* among the Fanti is best exemplified and publicly displayed when an adult member dies. Although such a one is always given a proper burial and funeral, whatever might be his relative merit, the "elaborateness of the rites performed at the death of an individual varies with his age and status, as does the responsibility for the cost of the burial."[11]

The body of a child who lives less than nine days is buried in a clay pot in a trash heap, and his parents undergo minimum purification. A person so inconsiderate as to forsake the world immediately is considered unworthy of much mourning! A pre-adolescent or adolescent traditionally receives greater attention, and is buried with fuller rites in a box made of packing crates. Today if such a child has embraced Christianity or is attending school he is likely to be buried in a coffin, with a regular service. Traditionally, up to the time a person marries, the father pays the burial expenses. After marriage the matrilineal system takes over.[12]

The belief persists among the Fanti tribe that the matrilineal clan "owns" its member. So strong is this belief that when a man dies, his matrilineal clan head ritually "notifies" his widow and children even though they may have been present at his death. Furthermore, the widow and children without the permission of the matrilineal clan may not participate in his funeral or even be present at it.

Mourning does not begin until the body has been quickly bathed, clothed and laid out on a bed in the house or courtyard. Then a gun is fired to announce the death and to usher in a night filled with lamentation, conversation, drinking and gun fire. The custom of requiring children, grandchildren, members of the deceased's extended family to shave their heads is no

224

longer mandatory; children in the matrilineal line paint red stripes on their foreheads and arms as a sign of mourning. Although some mourning by distant relatives may be formal and perfunctory, the grief of the intimate family circle is likely to be profound. The widow and daughters of the deceased and his close female relatives sit near the body, wail loudly, cry out the praises of the dead and rebuke him for forsaking them.[13]

Immediate Burial and the Delayed Funeral

Tropical heat promotes rapid decomposition thus making imperative the usual custom of burial within a day after death. The practice of burial under the floor of a dwelling hut was prohibited by the Gold Coast colonial government late last century and has been discontinued. Today the body is carried rapidly to a nearby graveyard of the matrilineal clan and there placed in a new grave, which is immediately filled. With the body are placed the personal effects, rings and other ornaments, which the deceased had indicated he wanted buried with him. Money will be needed for the spirit to "cross the river"—a theme common to many cultures, historic and modern. Formerly it was a common practice to include also a brass vessel containing butter and gold dust. Today a bit of currency suffices.[14] During the interment ceremonies relatives speak to the dead person as though he were setting out on an extended journey. Any time from a week to a year later following burial the members of the matrilineal clan meet to set the time at which the funeral begins. They base their decision on such considerations as the length of time it will take relatives to gather, and the status of the deceased. The greater the man the longer is the delay between his burial and funeral.

Funeral ceremonies get under way either on a Monday or a Friday night. A firing of guns summons friends and relatives to the house of the deceased. There throughout the night while close female relatives sit by a bed, on which some possessions of the dead person have been laid, and sporadically cry out in lamentation, the other guests sing, dance and tell

225

stories, their spirits lightened by the imbibing of palm wine, gin and beer. A hired brass band now generally replaces the professional singing groups of yesteryear.[15]

On the afternoon following the wake which ended at dawn the matrilineal clan and certain friends and fellow townsmen who have made gifts to it for the ceremony, gather for the libations, the last of the public funeral rites. With a glass of spirits in his hand the head of the matrilineal clan, in the presence of all assembled, addresses the dead person at length telling him that his relatives and friends have held his funeral and now turn him over to his ancestors. While he speaks the clan head spills the spirits on the ground for the spirit to drink.

Costs for the funeral and burial are not insignificant. For many families the coffin, cloths, drinks and other possible incidental expenses are too severe to be met *in toto*. Inasmuch as the abusua plays a dominant role in the burial and funeral procedures it is not unexpected that its members would share some of the costs. Actually, three sources of monies are usually available: Surviving relatives of the deceased will each make a contribution, small children excluded. Friends and others who have attended the funeral ceremonies, danced and imbibed, will have gifts to make, collected by the *abusua-panyin*—a responsible person in the matrilineal kin group. Finally, as already indicated, the abusua stands ready to help.

When all the costs have been totalled, usually the day following the funeral, if there are sufficient monies on hand they will be paid forthwith. If adequate funds are lacking some of the debts will be deferred until the abusua can collect, usually on a prorated basis, the necessary amount to cover them. The matrilineal kin slaughter a sheep and send the meat to kinsmen and friends who assisted in the funeral. Women parade through the town crying out thanks to those who made contributions. This thanksgiving ends the public rites. Six weeks later, and again at the end of the year, the members of the household gather to pour a libation to the deceased. "The respect for the dead is eternal," says Christensen.[16]

The funeral rites themselves indicate the Fanti believe that

226

the spirit of the dead person is in their midst. At the wake and at the graveside the mourners speak to the remains as to a familiar person. When returning from the cemetery no mourner looks behind him, lest the spirit follow him. For three months the widow, who is considered unclean, shuts herself in the room where her husband's body has lain. There she is attended by an old woman. At midnight on the day on which her isolation ends she carries a pot of embers to the sea. The old woman with her cries out a warning to keep out of the way. This is intended for the spirit of her husband who is thought to follow the widow, as well as for passers-by. To persuade the spirit to leave, the widow casts the vessel into the sea, and is herself thrice immersed. Only the sea, home of a great god, has sufficient power to cleanse.[17]

If a wife dies, the husband after remaining in seclusion for a week, bathes in the sea, shaves his body, and is thrice handed the tools of his trade by a kinsman. He thereupon is free to resume his normal mode of life.[18]

Ancestor figure, Cameroons area

Chapter 15

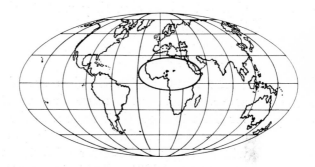

Nigerian Tribes

The Yoruba Tribe

Death Beliefs

The Yoruba people live in the western region of Nigeria, West Africa. Among the Yorubas the religious affiliation of the deceased determines the manner of burial. If he was an active member of the Egúngun cult—that is, a worshipper of the god of the dead—the cult members participate in the funeral, and sometimes take charge of it. If his affiliation with this cult is weak or non-existent, the family group, led by the chief landlord, exercises control. If he is a Christian—and the majority of the Yoruba people are now Christians—the Christian sect in which the dead man held membership conducts the ceremonies.[1]

The non-Christian Yorubas believe that the dead enter an afterlife of comfort or pain, their condition being dependent

229

on the life they have lived on earth. The offerings of clothes and food that are placed in the grave to be used in the life beyond bear witness to this belief. These are supplied for the journey into the hereafter, which the dead must make. Because the non-Christian Yorubas further believe that the dead have supernatural powers, they worship their ancestors and entreat their blessing and aid.

Burial Procedures

The non-Christian Yorubas consider the burial ceremonies as very important because they provide the final opportunity for them to show their respect to the dead. Moreover, they are convinced that if these ceremonies are slighted, the dead person will be angry and shower misfortunes upon the guilty person or persons. Additionally, it is a matter of public disgrace for children not to bury their parents in a manner deemed proper, or for relatives to fail other relatives in the matter. Such negligence indicts the whole family and all its members. Only when the dead person has been a public sinner or criminal is the neglect to give him a decent and proper burial condoned.

When a Yoruba dies, some member of the family quickly notifies the head of the compound, and the next of kin summons the immediate family and close relatives to a meeting. Next, if the deceased is a non-Christian, the next of kin informs the local head of the cult of the god of the dead. Only after these people have assembled does the preparation of the body begin.

After the body has been washed with hot water and shaved, it is dressed, stretched out on a mat, and completely covered with a fine cloth. When these preparations are completed, while the elders wail, the children of the deceased sing funeral songs over the body. These songs are traditional, and recount the adventures and brave deeds of the family's ancestors.

Interment

During the singing, gravediggers excavate a six-foot-deep grave in the piazza or square of the compound. A Christian is not buried in the piazza but in a cemetery. The use of cemeteries is a recent development, confined to Christian Yorubas.

When the grave has been dug, the body is laid in it, together with clothes that belonged to the dead person himself or have been contributed by his relatives. Popular belief has it that the clothes will be used by the dead in the afterlife. If the body is not buried in a receptacle, before it is interred, it is wrapped like a mummy in a piece of coarse fabric. Flat sticks or a piece of board are laid over the body before the grave is filled with earth or mud. Surplus earth from the grave is scattered over the nearest road. Small children are not buried in the compound. Their bodies are either flung into the nearest bush, or are partially buried by crumbling lumps of earth over them. Those so buried are called *Abiku,* or "ones who are born to die," and are thought to join the company of wandering demons.

The Annang Tribe

Death Beliefs

The Annang tribe dwells in southeastern Nigeria, in West Africa. To members of this tribe who have not accepted the Christian faith death is a gateway to the "outer world"—the country of the dead, the city of ghosts. It is a process of transmigration from the physical to the spiritual body. The dead travel to a land where rich remain rich, and poor, poor. Death is a kind of official command compelling the soul of a man to shed its bodily husk and become a participating citizen in the realm of the spiritual.[2]

The Annang tribe never think of the dead as "entirely dead." Their belief is that he still lives, sees, hears, remains around the grave, and travels back and forth between it and his old haunts. They are convinced that if they do not bury the remains with appropriate honors the dead will strike back and bring misfortune or death upon the neglectful family. For this reason, as well as for the affection they bear the deceased, the members of the Annang tribe spend time and money in making a decent and proper burial.

Burial Procedures

The Annang tribe organizes itself into a kind of hierarchy with a chain of authority which begins with the personal family and extends through groups of families, villages and clans to the whole tribe. At each level someone is recognized as head of the group.

When one of its members dies, the head of the hierarchical order to which he belongs assumes control of funeral matters. If the deceased was a poor commoner, his personal family assumes the responsibility through its head; if he was a well-to-do or important person such as a family head, several families cooperate by the joint action of their heads; if he was the head of a village clan the entire village joins in funeralizing him under the leadership of the chief; and if he was a clan head or tribal chieftain, the whole clan or tribe takes part under its leader.

In each case the responsible person cooperates closely with the various non-hierarchical organizations of which the deceased was a member. The latter are mutual aid groups and voluntary associations of various occupations. News of a death travels by a fixed route from the bottom to the top of the hierarchical order. Thus when a commoner dies the eldest son or daughter announces the death, first to the family head, then to the leaders of the various organizations in which he held membership, and then to other relatives and friends. In turn, the family head notifies the village head, who notifies the clan head. Again, the clan head informs the tribal chieftain from whom all family members, village clan heads, and other friendly chieftains receive the announcement.

While the women of the family sit around the body bending and stretching its joints to delay *rigor mortis,* the body is shaved, washed and given a change of clothing. In addition, it is constantly anointed with perfume. During these procedures grains of corn or, less frequently, aromatic leaves, are burned. The resultant smoke serves a dual purpose: to ward off the evil spirit and to cover or remove offensive odors. Meanwhile, the women continue speaking of the body as though it still contained the spark of life.

When these preparations have been completed, the body is laid in state. If the deceased was a first-born son, his right hand is raised and held up with a string tied to the ceiling. The body of a cock—probably because of the bird's fighting qualities—is suspended from the ceiling, as a mark of special homage for a warrior. Honorary captains of family units organized for defense are usually selected from first-born sons.

The Funeral

After lying in state, the body is removed from the house and arranged in a sitting position on a log bench placed between living trees which were specially planted in honor of the dead of the village. This bench is called the "seat of confidence." While the body is in this position, several live cattle are slaughtered before it, to honor the dead and to bid his spirit to begin its journey to the land of ghosts. Following this rite, strong men raise the body shoulder high and carry it off to the cemetery. The procession is led by the bugler, who plays constantly during the march. Behind him follow the warriors, brandishing weapons in mimic battle. Next parade the non-hierarchical organizations to which the deceased belonged. Their contribution to the colorful occasion consists of acrobatic displays. To their rear march the mourners. As the procession threads its way out of the village, a great talking drum, stationed at the home of the deceased, sends its reverberations far and wide with the message that this is the time for all persons within hearing to pay their last tribute to the dead.

Amid the booming of guns the funeral procession finally reaches the cemetery. This may belong either to the family or to the village, depending on the social status of the deceased. A wealthy family maintains its own cemetery.

To make the grave, a round hole—perhaps no larger in diameter than needed to pass the body through—is dug. As it grows deeper it is continuously widened until it is of considerable width at the usual depth of six feet. At the bottom, to one side, a large compartment, approximately six feet long and four feet wide, is excavated. In this recess the uncoffined body is laid to rest on floor mats. Buried with it are all kinds of paraphernalia, and a sum of money. A chief's body formerly was laid across the laps of condemned criminals, who were buried alive with him.

When the procession reaches the grave site, it halts; the veterans stage a mimic battle, and against the background of warlike drumming, the first-born of a chief's sons recounts the deeds of bravery that marked his father's life. The conclusion of each episode is punctuated with a thunderous roll of drums and an outburst of gunfire. Meanwhile the wife of the dead man continues to pray. As a sign of her final tribute, she bears on her head a new earthenware vase.

Mourning and Memorialization

The death of a member produces deep mourning in a family, and the closest of kin sequester themselves in their houses, and refrain from active work.

Not long after the burial, the family organizes what may be translated as the "Feast of Consecration," at which they feed and entertain numerous guests. This feast lasts from two to four weeks, and is terminated by a procession in which relatives, friends, and neighbors parade wearing sackcloth. Much pomp and circumstance and the firing of guns mark this ceremony. At its conclusion the property of the deceased is divided, with the first-born son receiving most, or—as trustee—all of it. A year or two later, the final memorial rites, the "Feast of Commemoration," takes place. To mark the grave, a furnished "memorial house" is built over it, or a tombstone is erected.

An Ibo Tribal Burial

While visiting Nigeria in 1959 Dr. Hans Müller, a Swiss physician, was privileged to see the funeral of a medicine man of the Ibo tribe. The locale was the vicinity of Otolopko, southern Nigeria. His account of the ceremonies preliminary

234

to the burial and the vivid photographs that accompany this account make a dramatic story. Dr. Müller writes:[3]

During a journey through the South Nigerian tropical forest on one of the back roads we came upon a procession in a small village. One of the medicine men had died. In return for promising to send snapshots we were given permission to photograph the scene.

The procession had gathered at a place near the dwelling of the dead man, and had formed a circle in the middle of which stood a basket containing the tools he had used at his job, and next to it a small ceremonial stool, the sign of status. A chicken had just been sacrificed, and the blood had been allowed to drop on the stool.

In the circle sat the musicians, next to them the professional colleagues of the dead man who were making ready their magic potions, the elders of the village and their chieftain. In front stood the relatives, painted white in order to keep away the spirits of death, and behind the circle the villagers who had followed the procession.

Now the chieftain, the medicine man and the relatives were dancing in turns around the circle to the monotonous rhythms of the drums and bells. At the end of the dancing the dead man, who was also painted white, was carried out of the hut so that we could photograph him. Unfortunately we were not able to wait for the actual burial which was to occur in the evening in the yard in front of the deceased man's hut. As soon as we were back home we kept our promise, sending back the pictures we had taken. In the way of thanks his sons wrote that we were assured of eternal friendship, and that their father was not dead any longer, but lived on with them in the picture.

At the suggestion of Dr. Müller the authors sent a letter to a young man of the tribe asking for verification of the physician's recollection as to the location and name of the native group whose funeral ceremonies he had observed. The youth, David Nwadiolu, a relative of the deceased, answered[4] that these facts were correctly reported, and that although the rites were "pagan"—he was attending missionary school and had, apparently, embraced Christianity—they would never-

theless fill the observer with "sympathy," even to the extent of making him "jealous." In the picture-story below the scenes depicting the funeral ceremonies take place before the family dwelling of this young Ibo correspondent.

The medicine men, colleagues of the deceased, brew their magic potion. They have marks painted above the eyes. They do not appear to take the death of one of their number too tragically. Medicinal and magical remedies are stored in the horns lying on the ground

P.I.P. Photo

The son of the deceased, painted white to keep away the spirits of death, stands shyly and without moving at the end of the circle. He views the ceremonies with a troubled look. In the background sit the village elders. The others who are standing are lookers-on

P.I.P. Photo

237

These are the musicians. To the left, three men beat small double drums—drums with two percussion surfaces—with the hands. The seated man to the right has a bell which he beats with a metal stick. The standing man at the extreme right shakes a stick which has several bells attached

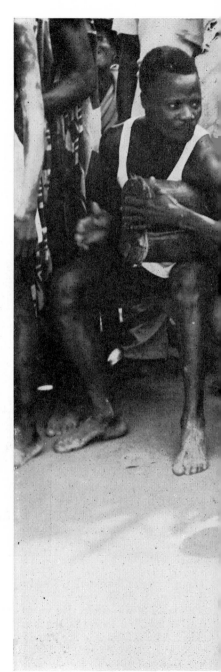

P.I.P. Photo

238

In the middle of the circle
stands the basket containing
the tools of the trade of
the deceased medicine man
and the small wooden stool
with a handle, the sign of his
status. The next of kin have
sacrificed a chicken and
allowed the blood to drop on
the stool as a symbol of death

The village chieftain dances
and waves the wooden bell of
the dead man, while in the
other hand he carries a fly
swatter, and on his head he
wears a red felt hat, both
signs of his status. Otherwise, he wears the toga-like
garment of the natives

240

The next of kin of the dead man — a sister and a daughter — begin
to dance. They also have their eyes, hands, and feet painted
white in order to frighten off the spirits of death

241

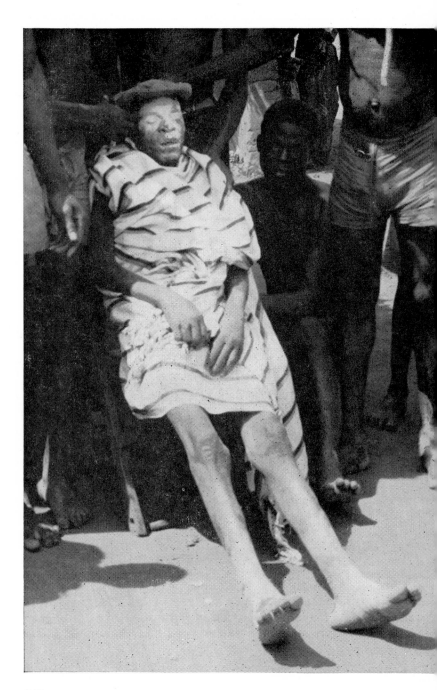

Dead persons are buried by the next of kin on their own
soil. This small roof marks a grave. Dead persons are
held in high esteem; the native religions largely involve
cults of ancestor worship

Finally, the dead person, who is also
painted white, is carried out of the hut and
sat upon a chair. In order to take this picture
Dr. Müller had to promise the next of kin to
send each a print of this picture for a keepsake

Funeral of a Fali Chief

Sharing the northeast tip of Nigeria and a corner of the Cameroons, the Fali tribe of the Lake Chad area has an interesting form of burial, which in some ways harkens back to the ancient Egyptian practice of the heavy swaddling of the dead. As particularly applied in the case of a dead chief the rites involve first the washing and rubbing of the body with aromatic herbs. Next, it is wrapped in cotton and strips of rawhide, and finally it is lowered into the grave in a sitting position—which by Fali custom is the position that in death befits the chief, as symbolic of his reigning in life from a throne or royal stool.

Preparing the dead Fali chief for burial with strips of rawhide and cotton. Note chief's hunting bow propped against shoulder

P.I.P. Photo

244

Members of the tribe, females included, lay hands on the chief's body as part of the ceremony attending preparation for burial

The chief's body completely wrapped and ready for burial

Body being lowered into the small entrance of tomb

Tomb is sealed with earthenware pot through the bottom of which a small hole permits the passage of the chief's soul

P.I.P. Photos

246

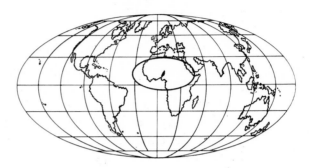

Chapter 16

Dahomeans of West Africa

Dahomey is a narrow strip of country, sandwiched between Ghana and Nigeria, stretching from the Guinea Coast of West Africa to about 120 miles inland into the interior of equatorial Africa. Once a powerful Negro kingdom, Dahomey for many years was a French colony and only recently has been granted the status of an independent republic in the French community of African republics. Noted historically for its heavy involvement in the slave trade, and at all times for its stuporous climate, Dahomey lies in the center of the Nigritic or true African Negro culture.

The funeral customs of the Dahomeans are varied, complex, and colorful. They have been painstakingly and minutely described by the anthropologist Melville Herskovitz, who with his wife lived and conducted field research in Dahomey. It is to this authority that we turn for reference in detailing the manner in which Dahomeans traditionally buried their dead, and the persistence of these customs into modern times.[1]

247

Ancestor Worship

The Dahomeans believe that long ago men lived poorly on earth, even before the sky god had divided the land among his children. To improve the condition of man and to give him tools, the sky god sent the god of metals and stone to them and the god of the sun. Later, supernatural beings appeared to establish family lines by mating with human women. Thence arose the blood families or, in anthropological terms, *sibs* which for the Dahomeans are composed of the dead in the next world and the living in this, related through a line of descent. Thus ancestor worship, which plays an important part in the culture, relates the dead to the living in a unity in which contacts and interchanges are frequent and close.[2]

In order that a sib may exist and be perpetuated, it is necessary that an elaborate ritual of ancestor worship be carried out. This worship is the focal point in the Dahomean religion, social organization, and funeral customs. The living must see to it not only that the souls of their dead are not lost to their sib, but that they are deified. The dead in turn can confer benefit or injury upon the living. Behind extremely costly and elaborate funeral rites is the urge of the living to assure security for themselves after death.[3]

To reach the solemn land of the dead the soul must cross three rivers and climb a mountain. At journey's end lies a valley where his ancestors dwell. Among these the newly arrived is given the lowliest place. Nor is he entitled to his full position until ceremonies have been conducted by the members of his sib to enshrine him among his sib gods. The ceremonies involved in such deification are long, elaborate, extremely costly, and can be accounted for only because, as Herskovitz points out, "the ancestral cult is paramount. In the life of every Dahomean, his ancestors stand between him and the gods who personify the forces of the universe that periodically threaten him with destruction."[4] It follows thus that in the main the prolonged and complicated Dahomean rituals of burial and mourning derive their significance from the cult of the ancestors.

248

The remainder of this section follows the death and burial incidents of an elderly, wealthy Dahomean farmer, the head of a compound, as described by Herskovitz.[5] The use of the "historical present" tense should be noted.

Response to Death

When the Dahomean appears to be seriously ill his wives hover about him, caring for him, and from time to time call upon the diviner to estimate his chances of recovery. Medicines are applied and administered, and charms displayed to placate the spirits. When these prove unavailing, the favorite friend and the children of the dying man are summoned, and with the wives, remain until death has occurred.

Ritualized wailing, joined in by all members of the compound, begins immediately and continues until it is gradually terminated by the favorite friend. After a time the dead man's family assemble in the house. Dahomeans organize themselves into groups for mutual assistance, "mutual aid societies." Now the relatives of the deceased watch the members of his mutual aid society wash the body from head to toe with soap and warm water. Ablutions finished, the eldest son shaves all hair from the body, and clips the nails, placing the trimmings in a cloth, to bury with the body. Next a death watch begins, lest anyone secure some charm from the body, a hair or a bit of cloth, or moisture from the mouth, and thus capture the soul of the deceased to use it in necromantic practices.[6]

The first clothes to be put on the body are the usual trunks. Next, a white cotton cloth is tied about the eyes and mouth, and stuffed into the ears and nostrils. The best friend supplies a large cloth which he wraps about the loins, with one end drawn between the legs. Ritualistic recitations accompany this binding. The eldest son supplies a similar cloth.

Finally the body is rolled into a large "cloth of the dead," and laid on its side on a mat. A lighted native lamp is stood next to it, and bottles of liquor, as well as cowrie shells are placed both at the head and at the feet; and as the first wife and an old woman begin the vigil, the family assemble

249

outside the door to wail. No cooking may now be done in the house. To feed the mourners each son-in-law sends prepared food and drink. The dead man's children sleep directly on the ground. An unfaithful wife must not approach the body. The chief, or brother of the dead man, now sends 41 cowrie shells to the grave digger, telling him to come; and notifies the relatives, using euphemisms for death. He asks the diviner to cast lots to determine proper times for the burials. He calls on the head of the dead man's mutual aid society to make funeral plans. He leads the council and important members of the family to the head of the dead man's sib, who is regarded as intermediary between the living and their dead ancestors. All kneel before this old man, who speaks not of death, but of the "great rain that has drenched you," and whose duty it is first to announce the burial dates. He is told these in a whisper, and feigns anger that they should have been set without consulting him.[7]

The party now returns to the hut where the death watch is kept, and where a pottery drum is played day and night. The dead must eat symbolically out of his own dishes and of food that continues to be prepared by the woman who last cooked for him. Each meal is handed to the old relative, who sets down three morsels and allows water to drip thrice near the body. She then tells the wife to remove the food. Tobacco is put into the dead man's pipe, and smoked by the watching wife and the old woman.

Preparation for Burial

On the night following death, or the second night thereafter if the succeeding day is one on which the digging of graves is not allowed, the grave digger appears, carrying his special hoe. As he works, the relatives of the dead man thrice approach him, each saluting him and presenting gifts. The first time they say, "Make a fine house for my father,"—or whatever the relationship may be. The grave digger sings at his work, the slap of his hoe beating out the rhythm of his song.[8]

Although the usual location for a grave is inside the com-

250

pound yard, a person may choose to be buried in his own house. In such event the grave opening is made outside, and the grave tunneled beneath the house. Although the digging is always completed in a single day, graves vary in depth. Because more gifts are buried with a person of prominence, his grave must be deeper.

Formerly, when uncoffined burial was provided for all but kings, a tunneled excavation was made, to shelter the body from falling earth. Coffined burial, introduced as a common practice through contact with Europeans, requires a simple rectangular excavation. The coffin is hexagonal, and covered with a cloth on which are embroidered four crosses emblematic of the sun god. Other designs reveal the dead man's membership in various clan and tribal groups.

With the third approach of the family to the grave, the eldest son then takes the hoe himself, and digs for a few minutes. Ascending, he gives the grave digger a pot, some fruit and a chicken. The grave is considered complete, and is covered with a mat to await the burial. Meanwhile each morning the children of the deceased enter the hut and throw themselves across the body and weep.[9]

"Partial" Burial

When the time for the partial burial arrives, the leader of the dead man's mutual aid society enters the hut of mourning, brings the body outside and rolls it in a large native cloth. The bundle is tied with cloth strips at the head, the waist, and the feet. If the family chooses to have the rite inside the hut, they must thereafter destroy the dwelling.

Two of the leader's assistants are assigned to carry the body. After they have raised it, they sing a dirge in which the sons and daughters are called upon to support the head. The children come forward in order of age, and chanting versicle and response, put money into the singer's mouth, and lay money and cloths on their father's body. Next, six members at a time of the father's society, three to a side, take the body on their interlocking arms, and with thudding feet dance vigorously with it. Sometimes a hundred men will press forward for the privilege of participating in this exhausting sequence. The old woman finally brings it to a conclusion by singing, "Bat, O bat, return to your home."[10]

At this injunction, the bearers run to the grave with the body. There the grave digger immediately takes the body and lays it on its side in the earth with its head toward the south and the arms and legs flexed. Halfway down in the grave planks are laid, and the earth is cast upon these. When the grave has been filled, the head of the family sends word to the relatives. They may now lie or sit on their mats and cook their food, although the widows must wear mourning bands on their abdomens, and the children must sift sand on their breasts and necks. Herskovitz distinguishes this "partial" or provisional burial from the "definitive" or final burial which "sends forth the soul of the dead on the path to the world of the dead."[11]

"Final" Burial

The final burial is held when the eldest son requests the village headman to open the ceremonies. To shelter these, two temporary mat houses, one for the mourning family to sit in, another for the headman, are constructed before the entrance of the dead man's compound. The ceremonies begin at night, in the flickering light of many native lamps. The family and friends contribute burial gifts; the eldest son, and the dead man's best friend each give a large mortuary cloth, a pair of breeches, a shirt, clay pipe, cap, mat, pot, soap, sponge, and water. The eldest daughter makes a similar presentation, adding a cloth believed to carry the dead across the river of death. Other children and friends come forward with gifts. Shouts and singing accompany the presentations. The final gifts are for all the male dead of the family, another for all the female dead, and a third for all the females who have married into the family. The dead man is asked to present these gifts when he is greeted in the world of the dead.

Elaborate ceremonies follow. The old woman of the family,

252

wrapping about herself the mortuary cloth provided by the eldest son, enters the house where the body lay, and kneels there for a while. Once it was customary to exhume the body, whatever its state of decomposition, for use in the ceremonies. Much perfume was required by those who approached it. Now a rolled cloth becomes a token body, and is wrapped in a mat.

By now midnight is long passed, and the members of the dead man's co-operative group, led by his best friend, march to the house of death, singing funeral songs to the accompaniment of gongs and rattles. With much ado the burial gift cloths are counted and sorted, and two men, little or not at all known to the dead, hold a mock argument concerning which of them was his best friend. A mock fight between them follows. It is believed that such goings-on provide the last amusement the dead will have.

After prolonged ceremonies the representation of the body is brought out, and boisterously danced with, again with three young men on each side. Sometimes the headman lies down beside the representation.

Suddenly the men of the co-operative seize the representation, and noisily escape with it through a narrow section of the compound wall, which has been torn down to provide exit for the dead. The "body" is taken everywhere, through the village, into the bush, to crossroads, to the homes of friends. The mourners follow, loudly begging for the return of the "body." Persons hearing the uproar shower money gifts on the bearers.[12]

At sunrise the "body" is returned to its house so that the family may pay respects, and make further gifts sufficient to enable the dead to live without shame in his new abode. Next, the diviner comes, to conduct a ritual to destroy the image of the guardian spirit and thus to separate it from the corrupting body.

When this has been accomplished, the headman orders the body or its representation to be borne to the grave. Young men run to the task, and at the grave, heavily perfumed to overcome the stench of the decay, the family have a final viewing, and amid much ritualized wailing, present their last gifts. If a rolled out mat has been used in the ceremonies, the body itself is now exposed, and wrapped in fresh cloths.

Final Ceremonies and Mourning

By nine in the morning the grave has been closed, and strong men from the co-operative begin to stamp it down, a little at a time with a slow, rhythmic tramping. The children of the dead man next take up the task, then the wives, and other relatives. After the ground is solidly stamped, the grave digger recites in minute detail the events leading up to the funeral and through it. Using their hoes for gongs, eight young men as a chorus accompany this recital, which continues well on toward noon, and is accompanied with further giving of gifts.

In the late afternoon the interrupted ceremony is resumed when the members of the societies present at the funeral sprinkle the compound with a medicine of crushed leaves and water, to disinfect it of the death producing evil. The distribution of the gifts of food that follows lasts until midnight, when the drums usher in the dance of the deceased's family. In ceremonies marked at every stage by the showering of substantial gifts of goods and money, the climax of giving is now reached. The head of the co-operative, who has received much, finally declares the ceremonies at an end, and returns home to divide his fees with his followers. While his departure marks the end of the definitive burial, it does not terminate the mourning period, and the family does not disperse, but sleeps in the compound, and rests the next day.[13]

That evening, the wake begins. To the throbbing of drums, young people come from nearby villages to receive gifts, listen to droll stories, and gamble. It is considered in bad taste to moralize concerning the dead. The merriment lasts most of the night and terminates with a ceremonial visit to the grave, where a long ritual takes place. At its conclusion the mourners are free to wash, shave the head, put on new mourning clothes, and begin a round of formal visits, sometimes in a procession. Three months later the family may discard mourning. The ceremonies for which are again prescribed and elaborate.[14]

254

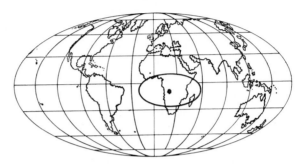

Chapter 17

Ovimbundu of Angola

The Ovimbundu are a Bantu-speaking group, numbering about one and one-third million, whose home is the Benguela Highland of Angola, Portuguese West Africa.[1] They are primarily an agricultural people. Although they have been in contact with Europeans for at least three centuries their social life, which revolves about a system of kinship and tribal organization—each tribe having its own chief—retains much of its traditional character. Their mortuary customs are a case in point.

Animism

The Ovimbundu recognize a Supreme Creator of all things. They believe that the human body is animated by the breath of life, and contains a soul or spirit. During daytime the soul clings as a shadow to man, but at night it wanders apart,

255

reporting adventures through dreams. At death it lingers near the body from which it has been separated and when the body is buried, it wanders as a ghost through the places it knew in life. It announces its intention to remain with some particular family by causing illness among its members. To eliminate this nuisance the householders consult an oracle who identifies the ghost and transforms it into a peaceful ancestral spirit with a home in the afterworld.[2]

The Ovimbundu also look with regard upon the much-honored spirit of the family founder, and they have a special fear of the spirits of stillborn babies, mental defectives, mistreated slaves, and persons killed by sorcery. The skill to use sorcery is thought to be inherited, and a family may be accused of being sorcerers for several generations.[3]

The local headman is the father of his villagers, the patriarch, and the village priest. His is the only compound with a "spirit hut," in which he prays to the village ancestors and holds communion with them. He serves as priest for the paternally related group forming the village. The chief's compound always contains a tomb for himself and his wives.

While his informant agreed that every human being had a spirit, the ethnologist Wilfrid Hambly could not learn whether the Ovimbundu, like some other Negro tribes, believe that a person had multiple souls. Their word for heart also designates that part of a man which dies. It is not likely that they believe that after death spirits will be segregated according to the rank they bore in life.[4]

The Ovimbundu believe in the existence of both good and bad spirits. The activities of bad spirits are one cause of sickness and death. The Ovimbundu fear death, and when the medicine man visits a home to foretell the future he brings along an image to which he puts questions. He himself answers for the image, using a falsetto voice which he modifies further by plugging his nostrils. The image suggests that an animal must be sacrificed. The medicine man then tells the good spirits that if this be done the family hopes that there will be no more deaths. The good medicine man makes useful divina-

256

tions, brings down rain, and heals the sick. The Ovimbundu conceives also of a wicked medicine man, a witch or wizard who operates in secret to injure people.[5]

Response to Death

When death occurs for a commoner, the Ovimbundu prepare the body for burial by extending it in a supine position. They tie thumb to thumb and palm against palm and stretch out the arms full length, binding them to the trunk with strips of bark. The large toes are similarly bound. Cloth also may be used for binding. The burial receptacle is a wooden box, tightly bound around with a blue and white checkered cloth.

The body is borne to the burial place in the receptacle which is slung from a pole resting on the shoulders of two bearers. As they walk, the burden sways and the movements of the coffin are taken to have meanings. When it swings forward it is understood to answer affirmatively any question put to it. When backward, to answer negatively—"Who ate you?"—that is, killed you—bystanders ask. "Was it so-and-so?" —And thus guilt or innocence is established. If by its movements the body gives no clear answer, divination is needed. Generally the guilty person is discovered within the kinship group.[6]

Funeral of an Ovimbundu Boy

Although they may not be exactly the same for an adult, the funeral rites of a twelve-year-old Ovimbundu boy as described by Hambly are instructive. In a secluded place in the tall grass he found a group of drummers holding drums of different lengths between their legs. Thirty-feet away a group of women clapped hands, first to set the rhythm for the drums, and then to accompany them. Hambly found more sociability than solemnity in a scene in which men sat on the ground, and a crowd of women walked about or were seated, both sexes meanwhile chatting and smoking pipes.[7] Along this line Childs, the British anthropologist, generalizes that most of the rites and ceremonies of the Ovimbundu are "very social," especially funerals and post-funeral rites inasmuch as these are "occasions which occupy the most time and attention and make for the greatest social cohesion. In this they surpass even the return from a trading expedition, and weddings."[8]

The boy's body had been placed in a receptacle which in turn was suspended from a pole resting across the shoulders of two bearers. These men remained motionless, except to transfer the pole from one shoulder to another, until the procession set forth to the grave. Meanwhile women emerged from the crowd singly or in two's and three's to spend several minutes dancing before the coffin. This performance lasted about two hours.

When the bearers finally moved off with their burden, some men followed on one side and some women on the other. They halted again when a woman holding a dish of corn meal moved close to the coffin and in a low tone asked the body if it had been murdered. She was the boy's aunt, his father's eldest sister. Her questions were interspersed with silent pauses, presumbly to give the ghost time to reply. In this instance Hambly could note no movement, but the consensus

Ovimbundu funeral gets under way with drumming and dancing of the men

Coffin being carried through brush to burial ground

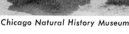

was that the coffin had swung backwards to indicate a negative answer. All present seemed relieved.

The wall of the Ovimbundu house is made of wattle and daub, and the roof of thatch. Most houses are circular, although an occasional rectangular house may be found. Burial huts are enclosed in strong, ten foot high wooden palisades. Pots and gourds are placed inside these enclosures, and a fire is lighted, with an attendant assigned to see that it does not go out. The wives of an important man are interred around him.

Special Rites

Diviners, medicine men, and kindred practitioners are buried with special rites. Another medicine man is summoned to take charge of a medicine man's funeral ceremonies. At death the body is tied in a seated position to a stool with the dead man's decorations attached to his robes, and his headdress of feathers, quills, or goat's hair held to his head by a band which passes beneath the chin.

ve you been murdered," asks old woman. Forward or backward movement of coffin supplies the answer

Ovimbundu chief's burial mound, enclosed by stockade

Chicago Natural History Museum

After three days in this position the body is borne to a grave which has been dug where paths meet. At the grave the same questions are put to a medicine man as to a commoner. When the body is placed in the earth the medicine men dance with wagging heads, and without pausing each tears to pieces and eats a living chicken which he has brought with him to the ceremony and carries in his arm. Others at the grave slaughter and eat a dog, a chicken and a goat. A mat is laid in the grave, along with horns filled with medicine and the skins which dangled from the medicine man's waist during his rituals. His rainmaking charms, on the other hand, are deposited outside the grave because to bury them would be to quench their rainmaking powers. The grave of a medicine man is likely to be looted of its bones and equipment. Other medicine men find these potent in making new medicines.[9]

Even though the traditional burial place of an Ovimbundu king seems to have been a cave, today he is buried in a small but sturdy hut with a strong wooden door in the village which he governed.

The burial position of a chief or king is the same as that of a medicine man. For a week after a king's burial his children wear oxhide strips on their left wrists as a sign of mourning. Meanwhile the village chiefs gather to select a new king, who usually is the eldest son of the favorite wife. However, if this choice seems poor, another may be selected. While the house of a king is not burned after his death, and the new king must use it until it collapses, the fence around it is replaced. When a king dies his heir sacrifices a whole herd of oxen so that his people may be regaled and the dead person propitiated.[10]

Mourning and the Levirate

During the mourning period a widow is not allowed to comb or dress her hair, and must wrap her body with a bark cloth from head to ankles. For three days she must fast and wail constantly and at night be with her husband's body with only a long stick separating her from the dead man.

Before burial takes place relatives raise the body and advance it toward the widow, while other relatives compel her to face it. Thus she says farewell to it. She does not attend the burial.

An Ovimbundu widow must wait a year before remarrying. Meanwhile she may live with her mother's brother or with her parents. If she remarries, her second husband will make a gift to those who have cared for her.

Among the Ovimbundu mourning and fasting lasts for a period of a month after the funeral. After a month the widow lies for a night on the place where her husband's body lay the night before burial. The next day at a drinking ceremony the medicine man guides her hand as she ladles out the beer. This ceremony ends the mourning.

Distribution of property follows the traditional prescription that "Movable property is inherited in the maternal line;

Ovimbundu
hunter's grave

land in the paternal line." Another practice termed the *levirate* is often followed. In this case the widow enters the household and marries her husband's eldest brother or one of her own mother's brothers. Sometimes, however, she returns to the village of her father. Wherever her disposition, her children go with her.[11]

An Ovimbundu woman must bring to the home the utensils of her daily work, pots, brushes, baskets and the like, and she is recognized as their owner. When she dies her husband receives certain of these and her own sisters are given the rest. When a husband dies his property passes to his mother's brother or his sister's sons. His own wife and children receive little. Women can inherit neither cattle nor the rights to land. The operation of the levirate, however, assures her of the continued security of a woman married.[12]

Chapter 18

Baganda of Uganda

In east central Africa, somewhat northwest of Lake Victoria
lies the Uganda Protectorate. The equator bisects it. It is inhabited by about a million natives, called "Baganda," or
sometimes simply "Ganda," who are members of the Bantu
branch of the Negro race. For many centuries it was an independent kingdom. The cruel and bizarre manner of burial of
royalty in Uganda made it one of the more written-about countries of Africa. Several serious ethnographic works are also
extant. Shortly before World War I the Reverend John Roscoe
wrote a highly detailed account of the manners, morals and
customs of the Baganda.[1] More recently Lucy P. Mair, a trained
anthropologist,[2] reported the results of her field researches
among them. Due to missionary influence and the acceptance
of Christianity by the natives there have been rather drastic
modifications in folkways. Likewise the policies of the colonial
administrators have brought their share of transformations
in the social, economic and political life of the Baganda. How-

ever, in many ways the present practices of burial represent an admixture or conglomerate of Christian and primitive practices in which no attempt is made to fit the individual acts into an articulate or comprehensive whole.

Death and Magic

To understand their burial rites one must remember that the Baganda, like many primitive people, believe that sickness and death result from magic rather than from natural causes, and that death follows when a ghost cannot be propitiated, or a god summons a spirit to leave the body. For example, the death of a king is usually to be attributed to ghosts, because no one would dare cast a spell on him, and is likely to be taken to indicate that he is being punished for a sacrilege, such as pilfering a temple.[3]

Because the spirit of a dead person is certain to be resentful if neglect were shown during his last illness, the Baganda lavish excessive attention and gifts on all the sick. At the same time they endeavor to meet magic with countermagic.[4] When a man takes sick, his wife summons the medicine man after an oracle has made a diagnosis of the illness and prescribed remedies. If the illness proves serious, she is expected to inform his clan by messenger, so that its members can assemble to nurse him. No wife wishes to assume the sole responsibility for nursing her husband lest he should die and she should be accused of having killed him by magic. Meanwhile the medicine man plies his craft, sometimes burning the patient with irons, sometimes administering herb remedies. A favorite treatment is to try to transfer the illness to some animal.[5]

When the patient is thought to be possessed by a ghost or spirit a fire is made of herbs alongside his bed or pallet so that he will be forced to inhale the smoke. While remedies work on the body, deeper causes for the illness are sought. For instance, the neglect of ancestral graves motivates angry ghosts to punish descendants with illness, and such vexed spirits must be placated before the natural remedies are able to work. A medicine man may even try to imprison an obnoxious ghost in a gourd,

264

and to drown it in a river. Sometimes sickness is thought of as punishment for violating taboos. In any event, the remedies seek to cure both the natural ailment and the more serious magic disorders underlying it. Fevers are treated with vapor baths.[6]

One fully trustworthy woman (a favorite wife or sister) is allowed to feed and nurse the sick man. When she discovers that he has stopped breathing, the wailing, which previously has been prohibited on the grounds that it hastens death, begins. Whether the dead person is king or commoner, Mair points out that the death of a person in a Baganda household gives rise to "three distinct necessities." The dead person must be mourned and the body disposed of in a manner satisfactory to the spirit; the place and authority of the dead person must be taken over; and disposition of his property must be made.[7]

After the women have washed and shaved the body, it is ready for public viewing. Once this was a two-day affair, but now by law burial takes place within twenty-four hours after death. The remains are displayed wrapped in a bark cloth with only the face showing. Friends come, bringing more bark cloth and sometimes muslin to wrap the body. It is important that it should be heavily swathed. The number of wrappings are a measure of a man's friends and therefore his importance. Before the face is covered for burial, each child formerly took farewell of it by streaking butter across it from forehead to chin. This custom has fallen into disuse.[8]

The former practice of delaying burial for several days was to make certain of death and to attempt to ascertain its cause. The chance always existed that the dead person might have been slain by poisoning or by one of two kinds of black magic. The first of these caused the nose to bleed and marks to appear on the neck. The second produced pimples. If a local person was accused of such murder, he was taken before the local chief and compelled to undergo trial by ordeal.[9]

Burial

The senior member of the clan present takes charge of the

burial, which usually is held in the morning. The body is lowered by means of bark strips into a grave about six feet deep, dug in a nearby banana grove. The chief and representatives of the senior clansman are in attendance. Dirt is thrown back into the grave and piled above it by hand, and then tramped upon or pounded down with poles. In places where stones are plentiful, the grave is mounded with them. Persons assisting at the funeral are given beer to drink, and if the family can afford the expense, the meat of a slaughtered cow. When the drinking ends the mourners return to their usual work routines.[10] Today, if the deceased is a Christian or members of his family are Christians, prayers may be said over the grave.

A chief formerly was buried in his own house, which thereafter ceased to be used as a dwelling. This custom, too, is dying out as well as is the custom of having the widows take turns in sleeping in a chief's burial house, and tending his grave. Nowadays it is likely that the chief will be buried under a concrete tombstone over which a small shelter is erected.

The spirits are believed to be much concerned with the manner in which the burial rites are conducted, and they are thought to observe critically the loudness of the wailing, the number of bark cloth gifts, and the manner in which the grave is tended. This belief lingers in a family so that it sometimes happens that long after a clan has wandered off, a member will reappear as a stranger in its old haunts, and weed a spot that has long since ceased to be identified as a grave. Not to mention the dead person by name is another method by which respect is shown to a dead relative.[11]

Death of a King

While the progress of sickness, death, and burial is in broad outlines the same for a king as for a commoner, variations are to be found in the complexity of the attendant rites. The serious illness of a king so provokes his wives to crowd around trying to help that the chiefs in charge forbid most of them to be present. Wives have been known to smother a sick king by lying on him, in the belief that he was already dead. The

266

inner court circle never admits that a king is ill, or dying, or dead, because even a brief period between kings produces disorders and anarchy. When the successor, a son of the dead king, has been determined, the symbolic fire that burns at the entrance of the royal enclosure is extinguished, and wailing accompanied by throbbing drums spreads the news of the royal death.[12]

The king's body is guarded by one of his sisters, who remains with it night and day, supervising the washing and covering of it, the placing of the hands across the breast, and the tying of the great toes. The king's wives exhibit wild grief, sometimes in solo and sometimes in chorus. They beat their breasts and smear them with wood ashes. As mourning spreads over the land, all work comes to a halt. Such abandonment probably is rooted in the fact that it once was customary to club to death the king's wives, his household officials, and hundreds of plain people, to provide companionship for him in the hereafter. On the possibility that some of the victims might have been merely stunned, the legs of all of them were broken, and the bodies were left unburied where they fell.[13] The sacrifice of wives and others ceased by edict of the British colonial administrators.

As soon as the new king is chosen he is allowed to look on his father's body, which then can be taken to the country to be embalmed. After covering his father's face, the new king leaves for his capital. When he has been crowned, drums tell the people to end their mourning.

Meanwhile arrangements are slowly being made for the burial of the body of the old king. Embalming is done by his former guards. After removing the intestines, they empty them, wash them several times in beer, spread them out to dry in the sun, and replace them in the belly cavity. Then the body is dried and squeezed, until no more liquid emerges from it. All body fluids and the beer used in washing the intestines and the body are carefully hoarded. They must be drunk by the widows and the chiefs of the guard who serve as embalmers. The royal widows meanwhile are heavily guarded, particularly those who have borne sons to the dead chief. The fear always exists that one of these widows may attempt to put her son on the throne. After three months the king's body is moved to another town for an additional two months of ceremony. Each time it is moved it is carried feet first. Now it is anointed with butter.[14]

The uncle-to-the-king is an important personage in this rite. At the time of the selection of the new king, his mother's brother severed the cord binding together the dead king's great toes. This ceremony gives him the office of Uncle-to-the-King. After this performance the uncle takes formal leave of the old king. First a bark cloth is smeared with butter and spread over the old king's body. Then the body is wrapped with more bark cloths. In the meantime a tomb is being constructed. When it is ready, a procession, led by a man holding a hoe, bears the body to it. In connection with his father's burial the new king formerly ordered his father's chief cook, chief herdsman, the supervisor of his will, the women in charge of his bier and bed chamber, and others, to be slain.[15]

A king's tomb is in the form of a well-built house with a single doorway, surrounded by a double palisade to keep out wild animals. Burial consists in placing the body on a kind of low couch in a shallow grave, and filling in the grave with bark cloths. Then the roof is collapsed on the interior, and the porch door jammed by loosening its canopy.

After five months the king's jawbone is removed so that an effigy can be made from it. The jawbone is cleaned of flesh by placing it in an anthill. The skull meanwhile is placed in another house, which is kept in repair while the burial house is permitted to fall into ruins. After the jawbone is cleaned, it is decorated, wrapped again and again until a large bundle results, and placed in a large temple, with the king's umbilical cord.[16]

Mourning the Dead

Mair remarks that among the Baganda the "customs of mourning have hardly changed from their traditional form." Mourning lasts until the heir is installed. The family marks

268

the period by suspending its usual activities. The dead man's gardens and field lie neglected, close relatives do not change the floor-rushes, nor shave their heads. Meanwhile other relatives and friends, bearing little gifts, make sympathy calls. Every relative-in-law brings a gourd of beer. Although the government protests against large gatherings of mourners and friends, alleging that such congregating produces idleness and drunkenness, and missionaries charge that the wailing is insincere, the customs remain basically unchanged.[17]

The Baganda cling even more tenaciously to the final rites by which mourning is terminated. This ceremony is called the "get rid of death" ceremony, and is reserved for persons who "have a place of their own" in the community—that is a position—status with duties which must be taken over by a successor. For a commoner, the person normally in command at this rite is the head of his sub-clan; and for a chief, the representative of the whole clan. In actual on-the-spot command is the eldest brother of the dead person.[18]

This ceremony attracts many more participants than the funeral rites themselves do. Husbands of the female line and their wives come from considerable distances. The drinking,

Rock tomb of hunter
in Ganda District

269

singing and dancing begin one afternoon and are carried on throughout the night, until early next morning. At this time the men gather on one side of the dead person's house, and the women on the other. Then the master of ceremonies shouts: "I have completed the mourning rites, my own and my children's."[19]

Installation of the New Heir

This announcement signals the beginning of shaving and washing activities which may last until noon. When all are shaved and washed, the heir is installed. This ceremony is conducted by the heir's mother or, in the event that she is dead, by the woman who has succeeded to her duties. Normally everyone designates his own heir, and only when the heir dies and the parent has neglected to provide a successor, or when the heir apparent proves totally unworthy, do the relatives select a substitute. At the actual installation a woman always accompanies the heir, on the apparent theory that the inheritance affects the whole household. Since only a member of his clan can participate with a man in matters wholly concerned with the clan, some woman is chosen from the clan to symbolize the wife. The actual ceremony of declaring the heir takes place after he has been given a knife, and his escort a gourd of beer, and the clan leader has called out "This is the heir."[20]

The heir is then enjoined to be religious and brave, and members of the clan approach him to make a small money gift and to announce their degree of kindred to him. A mock fight sometimes follows, and in the afternoon a meal of flesh of a goat belonging to the heir is served. When the meal is over, dancing and singing are resumed. Festivities last through the night and into the next day, terminating only when the grave is put in order and tramped down. After the dead man's property is distributed, most of the men return home. In modern times the arrangements made necessary by the dislocation of a household have changed greatly, due partly to the fact that land has replaced cattle as the most prized possession, and partly to the fact that polygamy has been curtailed.[21]

270

Chapter 19

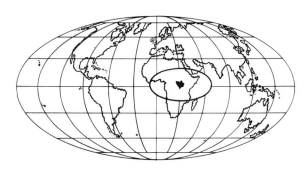

Azande of the Congo

Death Beliefs

The Azande of the central African Congo never regard death as a normal consequence. They concede that all men must die. But at each death they ask, "Why did it happen now, and in this way?" And the answer invariably is that the dead person was expiating a crime or someone wrought evil upon him. They incline toward the latter explanation. Accordingly when someone takes seriously ill his relatives consult both the oracle and the witch doctor, and if these agree and name the guilty person, demand is made that the evildoer "blow water." Thereupon he takes a mouthful of water and blows it upon the ground, and his wives do the same. All protest that they wish no evil for the sick person.

This procedure satisfies the relatives. If, however, the illness grows worse, they return to the oracle to ask if the

271

disease will prove fatal. If he answers yes, they leave the sick person where he is, and give him no more medicine. Instead they hurry to notify the relatives and friends on whom the cost of the funeral will fall.[1]

The Azande have little interest in a Supreme Being and seem bored when questioned on the subject. They recognize a god, *Mbori,* as the "big king of ghosts." While Mbori can help a person who directly petitions him, he is more likely to listen to the ghosts who surround him, and whose leader he is.[2]

To the Azande death means the separation of soul from body. Animals totemically share with men the possession of a shadow, soul, immaterial spirit. The spirit of a man is able to assume the form of an animal, or even the guise of a living man. A dead man can also appear in a dream to demand human sacrifices, and if an oracle approves the demand, some unfortunate person is likely to have his arms and legs broken, and to be dumped into the grave of the person appearing in the dream.[3]

Contrariwise, the dead are able to assist the living by being used as references to approve or disapprove the actions of the living. Thus the executor of his father's will speaks as though the father were still giving commands. The Azande believe that in dreams the living are able to see and speak with actual spirits of the dead who are thus able to report, praise, complain, or give orders. The noted British anthropologist, Evans Pritchard, points out that to the Azande a dream in which one sees another person on a bier foretells his own death, and if one meets that person he tells him of the dream and marks him on the arm with charcoal.[4]

A corporate body of priests is unknown to the Azande. The fact that each individual makes his own offering to the dead has militated against the establishment of a priesthood to serve the Azande.[5]

Recent ancestors are too well-known to be regarded with awe; distant ancestors too little known to be feared. Intermediate ancestors, however, are thought to be troublesome,

272

and to require worship. In addition, the Azande recognize several vague supreme beings. However, the Azande perform no real acts of worship toward these. Rather they address their sacrifices, rites and propitiations to the evil spirit whom they consider the active factor in disease, death, famine and mishap.[6]

The spirit of the dead can be moved by supplications and altar offerings to send rain. Some places appear to be more efficacious for securing favors than others. Success in hunting can be augmented by offering to the spirit the skulls of the game killed. Blacksmiths—the occupation is hereditary—offer food at the shrines of their smithies so that the spirits of their fathers will cause the iron to glow more quickly.[7]

Like the households of many ancient peoples—the Greek and Roman among occidental cultures, or the Chinese and Japanese among oriental—every Azande home has its ancestral cult. The ancestors, moreover, are part of a tribal cult. Their wills are still potent. They expect the execution of their orders, and if these are not obeyed, they invoke sanctions. They are not strangers in the household, or land. An earlier observer notes that ancestral spirits "continue in a way to take part in it. They haunt the living, appear in their thoughts, desire more and more attention, receive the first fruits of the harvest, take part always in the family affairs, having lost none of their authority."[8]

Among the Azande the king occupies a key religious as well as political position. His staff includes the sorcerer, royal physician, and the minister of the religious rites. The king is thought to control the weather. Death does not terminate his powers over the living, and hence his cult extends beyond the grave. As late as 1906 it was observed that the king's ministers were killed and buried beside his tomb, and his wife was interred with him. These, therefore, had good reason to look to his good health.[9]

Sickness is regarded as being caused by both witchcraft and disease, and hence the attack on it is made by a two-pronged program. Witchcraft is fought by magic, by consulting oracles, by public warnings to the witch whose identity is most likely concealed, and by the removal of the patient to the bush and out of the sphere of the witch's power. Disease is fought by the use of leeches and drugs. When disease proves serious, a witch doctor generally is summoned. Only in the case of sudden death is it necessary to wait the arrival of nearby relatives before proceeding with burial. Relatives are always notified when it becomes clear that a sick person seems likely to die, and they come immediately.[10]

Response to Death

Generally, though, the whole village gathers around the dying man, and when death comes, the women form in a circle around the body, and to the beating of a gong and a drum begin a plaintive chant. The men remain for the most part in an outer ring, whispering about the distressing event. While the villagers may watch and wail or comment, for the relatives death is a signal for great activity. All burial duties devolve upon the kinfolk of the dead. The husbands of the dead man's close female relatives immediately set out to dig the grave, sometimes within the homestead itself, more often apart from the village.[11]

Other relatives cut off a strip of bark cloth with which to wrap the limbs of the body. To make vengeance magic they add to this strip a cutting of a fingernail of the dead person, and sometimes a fragment of the first sod overturned in digging the grave.

The tropical climate results in rapid decomposition and makes early burial a necessity. Death in the morning means burial in the afternoon; death in the afternoon, burial the next morning. When a body remains unburied overnight an all-night vigil is observed.[12]

Burial Places

The usual Azande grave is a shaft six or seven feet deep, with a lateral chamber lined with wooden blocks upon which the body will rest. When the grave has been dug the grave diggers appear at the mortuary hut to call for the body, and

274

as payment for admission, they deposit at least one knife at the entrance. Without this payment they cannot enter. Without further ceremony they carry the body to the grave, uncovering the face so that the bereaved may have a last viewing. The body is generally borne on a kind of four-legged cot. Halfway to the grave they are stopped by the relatives of the deceased, and each of them must make payment of a knife, or he is not allowed to proceed. Again, at the grave, before the parents consent to the burial, the bearers are again taxed. These payment knives, and others contributed by the rich, are laid on the bier as a final gesture of sympathy.[13]

The bearers must descend into the grave to place the body in the niche. Of old the Azande buried the dead in a sitting position, chin on knees, with a roof of wood and grass just above and earth above the wood, then a pile of stones above the earth. Today Azande men are usually buried lying on their sides in a bent position, with crossed hands encircling the legs. The face of a man is turned toward the rising sun to indicate strength; the face of a woman, toward the setting sun, to indicate weakness.

A person is buried with those possessions he most needed in life: weapons, food, color for body painting, oil for anointing. All his goods are buried with a childless man. After these have been deposited the chamber is sealed with logs, and the shaft is filled with earth. The men who dug the grave make payment of spears for division among the kinsmen of the dead person, and on the next day a temporary shelter is raised on the grave, and magic objects are laid upon it. After the burial the bearers return to the house of death, and all present go to the river to bathe.

Mourners purchase their release from mourning. After the burial they give a trinket—a knife, or ring—for the first food and drink. In the same way they buy the right to sleep on the first night, and the next morning, the right to talk and to wash.

Before daylight on the morning after a burial the relatives of the deceased light their way to the tomb with straw torches. Arriving there they march around the tomb, so that by the flickering light the new spirit may discover a good resting place. The sons-in-law generally complete the tomb by raising a pyramid of superimposed clay rectangles, each smaller than the one beneath it. To shelter the pyramid they erect four posts, and surmount them with a roof.[14]

The top of an Azande grave may be protected in one of a number of ways. It may be covered by a small roof, or by a pyramid of stones, or by a shed taken from the roof of the deceased's hut. Sometimes a thatch of straw containing open panels may be used. Sometimes the whole problem is side-stepped by burying a man in his own hut. The funeral tombs of ordinary people are simpler than those of chiefs, and the funeral huts of certain of the Azande consist of no more than four stakes surmounted by a cone-shaped roof. These in size and shape resemble a sentry box.[15]

If burial has not taken place within it the house of the deceased is put to the torch, and the villagers may even abandon the village. The widow (first wife) cannot eat the fruits of his land, although his children and wives, if he has others, may do so. By custom the children and brothers of a dead man are entitled to take all his valuables which they can find in the village.

Secret Burial of a Chief

Seligman, noted anthropologist and authority on Africa, noted that when the poison oracle decreed that he had no hope of recovery a seriously ill chief is secretly removed at night to a place known only to his sons and a handful of courtiers. The eldest son keeps informed of his father's illness but does not attend him; and though his other sons may visit him, they appear at public ceremonies as though no crisis were taking place.

When the chief dies his burial in a forest on a river bank is kept as secret as his dying. His grave is a straight rectangle, the bottom of which is strewn with broken knives. Formerly several wives were buried beneath him, his body resting on their outstretched, broken legs. Mats are laid on top of his

276

body, and spears, sticks and more mats are used to take the pressure from the body. Once, earth was smoothed over a chief's grave so that it could not be identified. Now it is mounded, even though no one may visit it. Only when the burial is over do the dead chief's sons send couriers to announce the death to friend and foe alike. The bearers of the news always receive valuable gifts.[16]

Mourning

Only the chief wife is required to mourn, not his other wives or children; and only she is allowed by custom to betray outward signs of grief. When her husband dies she is expected to tear off her ornaments and clothes, and remain unadorned until his burial. For a year she wears her hair cut short. To eat of the flesh of certain animals is to invite death, and so she wears grass threads around her neck as charms lest she should partake of such meat inadvertently. Etiquette decrees that mourning women will not shake hands. Instead, the person greeting her holds out a small leaf or blade of grass. The widow then breaks off the projecting part with her thumb and right forefinger. A widower, too, is expected to mourn.

Although the Azande paint the body to indicate mourning they have not developed special designs for the purpose. Some women sprinkle their bodies with ashes and dirt, and put aside their public coverings as signs of mourning. Among the Makrakra, after mourning for three days a widower is bathed by the sisters of his dead wife.

Certain of the Azande men wear a mourning bracelet, the beads of which are interspersed with small, polished ivory squares. Each of these represents a dead wife. The bracelet is supposed to prevent the draining of a man's vitality by the loss of his women. Others wear mourning rings of copper and brass, or a tie around the neck made of native cord. All of these are first placed on the wife's dead body and then transferred to the husband's person.[17]

Even though the widower takes up a new residence with one of his other wives he must observe the usual mourning customs. He is required to shave his head, wear a plaited straw waistband, and trousers of new bark cloth. Other taboos forbid him to see visitors and compel him to eat food prepared only for him in a special pot. Mourning lasts only until the beginning of the next dry season, and is terminated with ceremonies followed by a great feast. When mourning has been concluded the son-in-law enters into negotiation with his late wife's father concerning total or partial return of the bride-price.

A widow passes through a similar period of mourning the termination of which is symbolized by her payment to the brother or eldest son of her late husband of a token fee with which they provide her. The widow's ceremony, like the widower's includes bathing, anointing with oil, and feasting.

Memorialization and Cult of the Dead

To prevent the ghosts of relatives from troubling their dreams or causing sickness as punishments for neglect by the living, the living organize a cult of ghosts. The intention behind this cult is entirely defensive: to keep the ghosts away rather than to entreat their aid. Ghosts can be appeased by offering them a portion of the first fruits of the chase and field. Accordingly the Azande builds a ghost altar in which to place his offerings.[18]

The commonest form of a memorial ancestral shrine consists of a stout stick one end of which is stuck in the ground. The other end is split a number of times, and the segments thus made are held apart by bamboo rings until they form a crude basket. A much less common form is a roofed-over, yard-square platform, supported on stakes and resembling a miniature hut. The liver of the first animal slain on a hunt, fowls, and the first fruits of the plantain are among the foods offered at the ancestral shrine. At most shrines no offerings are made unless real or impending calamity turns men's thoughts to their ancestors. The spirits are believed to consume the essence of the food while the material of it disintegrates.[19]

Frequently the Azande plant a euphorbia bush next to the

278

ghost altar. This bush provides the poison into which hunting spears are dipped. The proximity of the bush to the altar is thought to make the hunt successful.

Memorial huts contain relics of persons who died away from home, perhaps were killed in battle. Such a hut is nearly square with walls of clay matted on a wooden frame and a closed veranda. It is cared for by former servants of the person it honors. Large memorial huts are rare, being built only for important chiefs.

Formerly a son would watch his father's tomb closely in the belief that in three or four weeks he would either see the totemic animal or its tracks and would know whether his parent had been transformed into that animal. Strangely, while the Azande believe that the totemic animal will not wrong a member of the clan, they observe no elaborate totemic rites, and show their respect for the animal chiefly by abstaining from eating it.

The roof of the burial hut of a member of a leopard totem clan is carefully scrutinized for holes. The sudden presence of one is considered proof that the dead person has made his exit in leopard form, and so a witch doctor pours libations on the tomb to tame the young animal. If a young leopard is found it is chased with bells so that the dead person will maraud elsewhere.

Clans which recognize the lightning (atmospheric lightning) as their totem are safe from lightning, and when a man among them dies the storm that is certain to take place on the same day is noisy with thunder coming to greet him.

Beer Dances and Obscenity Songs

As part of the cycle of mourning, the Azande organize beer dances sometime after a year has elapsed following a death. They are required to raise a monumentary heap of stones over a grave. They generally begin preparations for the event about a year in advance. At a religio-economic ceremony women begin to thrash millet to use in brewing. Dances follow during the ensuing months, leading to the main dance.

While all who can come participate in the social fun of dancing, only the close relatives take part in the accompanying religious ceremonies.[20]

The Azande know certain traditional and extremely obscene songs which they consider wholly improper to sing on any but certain occasions. One of these is the feast at which a mound of stones is placed over the grave of a person some years after burial. In threshing the millet from which the beer is made for one of these feasts the women sing such a song. A year later, when they grind the malted grain to make beer, they sing another.[21]

Beating drums announce the main and culminating dance for the dead. Crowds stream toward the homestead of the man who has undertaken to sponsor the event. He is happy to see them; they bear public witness to the fact that he is fulfilling the rite and they will assist in carrying the stones.[22]

Mourning parties, reminiscent of Irish wakes, may be given by anyone possessing enough grain to make the beer. In return for their food and drink the guests provide the host with spears. For several days the men dance while the women sit wailing in the house. Parties may be given at random times for a year or more after a death.

Chapter 20

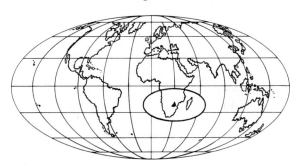

Ba Venda of Transvaal

The Ba Venda are a composite native people occupying approximately a third of the inhabited territory of the Zoutpensberg district in the northern Transvaal. Their funeral customs are described in great detail in the work of the anthropologist, Hugh A. Stayt, *The Ba Venda*.[1]

Spirit Worship

The Ba Venda recognize a mysterious supreme deity, called *Raluthimba,* who is in some way the creator of the universe and is supposed to dwell somewhere in the heavens. He is an oracle and rainmaker, who uses the stars as his instruments. His relations with the common people are slight and elusive;

281

they are likely to ascribe their day-to-day good luck or bad to their ancestors rather than to this astronomical deity.

In addition to this distant monotheistic deity, the country of the Ba Venda is dotted with places where, reputedly, spirits dwell. These spirits are supposed to be the ghosts of dead chieftains, some of whom have died lately and are remembered, and others, who have long since been forgotten.

Forests and mountains are regarded as favorite haunts of the spirits. At one time it was believed that a special mountain, grove, or forest was reserved for the ancestral spirits of each chief. Because burial places near a chief's *kraal* were abandoned for dwelling or agricultural use, the woods that grew upon them was likely to be considered a sacred place long after the presence of the grave was forgotten. Other spirits are thought to dwell in rivers and lakes.

Scattered throughout the country, small piles of stones or twigs are found. These represent the spots on which a burial party has rested its burden on its journey. Custom decrees that each passer-by must add a twig or a pebble to the pile. In addition to the spirits with known family attachments, woods and waters are considered inhabited by many other spirits who lack such connections.[2]

To the average Ba Venda these vague deities, and other dis-associated and transmigrated spirits, are distant and elusive compared with the direct relationship which he feels with his dead ancestors. This relationship is rooted in his concept of death and the afterlife. Death to many Ba Venda is the gate, the link between the two lives.

Beyond death, life has much the same problems as it had before death, only the dead are more prosperous. The dead marry, keep cattle, grind mealies. Ancestors lose none of their influence by dying. Quite the contrary, they gain influence and may become more difficult to please. If they are displeased, they take revenge by heaping troubles upon their descendants. The Ba Venda believe that most troubles that afflict people are caused by their irate ancestors. For this reason, ancestors are feared rather than loved.

282

Not all Ba Venda agree that the afterlife is busy and happy. Some hold that the individual spirit lurks for awhile about the grave, a combination of breath and shadow, seeking to create trouble for its descendants and yearning for a place to rest. Such a perturbed spirit will trouble the dreams of the living so that they will consult a diviner to discover its identity. Once they are able to identify the spirit they may avert disaster by propitiating it.[3]

Propitiation of Spirits

The Ba Venda attach great sentimental importance and value to heirlooms, no matter how intrinsically valueless they may be. They feel that old spears, axes, hoes, articles of wearing apparel are mediums through which the living may contact the dead. Even more, they believe that the dead may live in such objects in the same manner in which they possess certain animals and the river pebbles. When a spirit proves implacable, they may destroy its evil influence by destroying the spear which it inhabits.

The diviner is the indispensable intermediary between the living and their ancestral spirits. His dice tell not only what ghost is offended, but what the offense is, and how the angry one may be propitiated. Contact with the dead must be made through rigidly prescribed family channels.

The diviner designates a member of the family to take a mouthful of water from a wooden bowl and spray it over as large an area as he can. In this area a pinch of snuff is placed as well as the wooden bowl. Then by name the diviner summons the offended spirit, adding the names of all other ancestors who can be remembered. It is assumed that attracted by the snuff and by the water, which it finds cooling, the offended spirit lingers over the wet patch. Accordingly the bowl is set upside down to trap it.

If the diviner next concludes that the offended ancestral spirit is not satisfied with this ceremony, it may be necessary to sacrifice a goat at its grave. When the diviner finds that a spirit has become a menace that cannot be satisfied, its spear is tied around the neck of a black goat. The goat then is thrown into a deep pool. In this way the evil ancestor is forever destroyed.[4]

Only the very old are thought to die of natural causes; all others are murdered by angry or wicked ghosts, or necromancers. To discover the cause, a month or two after a death all the relatives, accompanied by a special messenger sent by the chief, visit the diviner. On their way, as they pass the grave, one of them removes a stone, so that the spirit may open the heart of the diviner, and thus enable him to tell the whole truth. Using his dice in a complicated ritual, the diviner identifies the culprit through his family. On their way back to the village, as the party again passes the grave, it restores the stone that was moved from it.

When they reach their village, all members of the party have their hair cut. Meanwhile the special messenger makes his report to the chief. The chief immediately points to the person accused, and there follows a rather complicated "buck-passing" procedure. Usually the accused brings his accusers to another diviner, in an effort to get the seers in disagreement. This process of appeal frequently ends in the physical and financial exhaustion of all concerned, except the chiefs and the diviners.

When the purses or patience of the relatives can stand no more, they ask the soothsayer to bring vengeance on the known or unknown guilty party. With a simple ritual the soothsayer then visits the grave and entreats the spirit of a tree whose shade is thought fatal to enter into the body of the guilty person, and kill him. This procedure is always efficacious. The next person in the village to die must have been the necromancer who slew the previous one. And so the case is closed.[5]

Response to Death

When hope of recovery expires for an ill person, his kinsmen are called to his kraal, or enclosure, to keep the death watch with him. It is dangerous to refuse this invitation, since such refusal is understood to indicate complicity in the death which

284

follows. The Ba Venda fear the contamination of death. To avoid it they frequently carry the dead into the bush. If death anticipates such removal, they burn down the hut or abandon it.

From birth the Ba Venda wear a *ludedi,* or belt of wild cotton. Later the boys are given a *tsindi,* or loincloth, and the girls a *shedu,* or apron. As soon as death occurs, a small piece is cut from the loincloth in the case of a man, or the apron in the case of a woman, and rolled in grass from the roof of the hut. The resultant small bundle is then placed in the trees outside until the propitious time for the mourners to refer it to a soothsayer. By examining it, the cause of death is ascertained.

Forms of Burial[6]

The body of a married man is bound with a tree fibre in a seated position, with the right side of the head resting upon the clasped hands. If *rigor mortis* interferes, the joints are cut with an axe. A rich man is folded in the hide of a black oxen; a poor man, in his blanket.

The place of the grave and the person first allowed to touch the body are settled by divination. Burial is usually made inside the dead man's cattle-kraal, or in the bushes just beyond it. Much care is taken to conceal the place of burial so that any enemy may not steal a piece of the body and put it to evil use. The brother of the dead person must be present at the digging, although anyone may dig the grave.

Burials are made between sundown and sunup. Male relatives carry the body—generally the brothers and eldest sons of the deceased. The eldest sister is permitted to help.

When the procession reaches the grave, the body is deposited next to it, until the eldest sister prepares a headrest of earth for it, so that it will lie on its right side with its head toward the northeast. When the body has been laid in the grave, the sister casts a handful of earth upon it, saying: "You must sleep in peace. You must not be angry with us, for we gave you all that you required, and wrapped you in the skin of one of your oxen."

When the grave has been filled in the presence of the rela-

285

tives, the eldest son stands a large flat stone at its head, and the other relatives stand smaller stones around it. A thorny branch is next placed so as to shelter the head of the grave, and the dead man's wooden plate, and sometimes his axe or spear, is laid on top of it. Whether the stones and branch originally were used to calm the restless spirit, can at this date be only a matter of conjecture.

The preliminaries for the burial of a married woman are much the same as those for a married man, except that her relatives see to it that the prescribed rites are carried out. The old women strip the body of ornaments, and having arranged it in the seated position, wrap it in a blanket, and never in a hide. When the graveside is reached, the woman's body is directly lowered, and this time the eldest son casts the first handful of earth, saying: "You can rest in peace, my mother. Do not trouble us. I will give you all that you require."

The remainder of the ceremony for a woman is identical with a man's, except that her personal possessions—stampers, pots, bracelets, and anklets—are broken by one of her female relatives and laid in her grave.

Small ceremony attends the burial of unmarried people. While parents may be present, they are not permitted to touch the body or to assist the old relatives who carry out the burial. A mother is not allowed to aid the old women of the village who bury her child. Such burials are all too frequent, some observers estimating that during the summer months infant mortality reaches 60 to 70 per cent. Some of this child slaughter is deliberate. Babies irregularly delivered or born deformed are killed by the midwives, who scald them with boiling water. Because twins are thought to bring misfortune upon the family or tribe, at one time the mother or the midwife killed them at birth by strangulation or scalding. More recently they have been permitted to die of neglect.

While a suicide is buried in the ordinary way, suicide is always regarded as a form of murder, and all the relatives are summoned to the chief's village to aid in identifying the culprit. If no one admits guilt, the chief confiscates the dead man's wives

286

and property to protect the rest of the family and to force the murderer to confess. If the diviner decides that a spirit is responsible, the property and wives are returned, except for two oxen, which the chief keeps as compensation for his services.

A person who dies away from home is buried in the bush some distance from the kraal. If he is known, his family is expected to dig up the body for burial at home. If transportation and reburial prove impossible, and the relatives judge from certain misadventures which they suffer that the spirit is angry, a mock funeral is arranged, at home, to quiet the ghost. A sheep is killed, and the severed head, which becomes the symbol of the absent body, is buried with the usual rites. Having thus received a grave, it is hoped that the spirit will rest.

Certain diseases call for special rites. The body of the leper is consumed by fire together with the isolated house in which he lived apart. A consumptive is not interred near the kraal, but in a damp place near the river. A pregnant woman is buried along the river bank with a diverted trickle of water over her grave. Generally the unborn child is buried apart.

Mourning Customs[7]

On their return to the kraal, the women and children burst out in a great wailing. Wives, especially, cast themselves about in paroxysms of weeping and are comforted by the men, who assure them that their husbands have gone home.

Like many other primitive peoples, the Ba Venda believe that the dead have much the same needs as the living. Accordingly, on returning from a funeral, a rich Ba Venda family will slaughter a goat and an ox, so that the deceased may own cattle in the afterlife. The stomach contents of these animals are placed on the grave, while the flesh is cooked and eaten.

To cleanse itself from the defilement of having associated with the body, the burial party must undergo purification rites. These begin with a bath in the river. Next they draw their hands and feet through a blazing heap of grass. In an alternate rite the medicine man makes small slits on the back of the thumbs of those who need purification.

Before the dead man's possessions can be touched, or his food or crops eaten, his relatives attend a ceremony in which all varieties of food seed are wet and stirred with powdered ostrich head. Each person rubs a portion of this mixture between the big and second toes of each foot, and on his knees, elbows, and wrists. He spits out another portion, which he has placed in his mouth. In this manner the seeds belonging to the dead are mixed with those of the living; and the spirit is discouraged from attempting to harm the crops, since he would thereby damage his own intermingled possessions.

After a funeral the dead man's relatives remain inside their huts. After three or four days of such seclusion, the medicine man visits the kraal and receives a goat. He ties the animal to a tree, and having prepared a purification potion, he summons the wives; "Come out of the mud plaster." On their emergence, he sprinkles them and the goat with his medicine, and leads them to the river. While the women bathe, he slaughters the goat and cooks its stomach contents, and mixes them with his medicine. When the wives emerge, he feeds this nauseous mess to them, and to the dead man's brothers who will inherit the wives.

The period of mourning, which begins with death, continues until the death has been revenged. Heads are twice shaved during this period, the first time, the day after burial, when the rite is informal and can be carried on anywhere; and the second, after a visit to the diviner, when the family is ceremoniously gathered together to be shaved by someone appointed. Because the thaha bird has a weird cry, a thaha nest is obtained, and the hair from the shaving is rolled into a ball, and placed in it. The nest then is buried in an anthill, to symbolize the fact that because the diviner has established the cause of death, an end might be put to lamentation and wailing.

Burial of a Chief[8]

Special rites and practices attend the death of a chief. News of his serious illness is suppressed by his court officials, who tell the inquisitive that a bad cold will keep him in his hut for some time. He is attended by his personal medicine man, and by his sister, and the husband of his wife's sister. His sister makes repeated pleas to the ancestral spirits to restore her brother's health. When the end is apparent, the medicine man withdraws, and after having announced his successor, the chief dies in the presence of a small group of close blood and affinal relatives.

While the death is kept a close secret, unlike the body of a commoner, the chief's body is not buried immediately, but is kept for several days.

The death witnesses and a few relatives who have been sworn to secrecy become the burial party. The counselors dig the grave, and line it with skins. The body is quietly borne by some of the chief's brothers, aided perhaps by a few of his sons. Commoners must be buried as though crouching; but the chief lies extended, his head resting upon an elephant's tooth and his body pointing toward the ancient city of Dzata. After lion or leopard skins are laid upon the body, the grave is filled, and the head of the chief's favorite ox is laid upon it.

It is difficult to imagine how the evidence of such an event can be concealed or overlooked, but apparently they are. Only after months do the people grow restless, and persistent, and they are then told that their chief has gone away. During this time his sister and his wife's sister's husband conduct public affairs, and it may be a year before the new hereditary chief is publicly given the vacant office.

When the family at large is told that the chief has died, before they can again partake of food, they must fill their mouths with meat from a specially roasted ox, and spit it out in all directions. The common people at the same time express mourning for the old chief and welcome for the new by shaving clean all their heads and beards. Thus they symbolize putting off the old order and putting on the new.

Not all chiefs of the Ba Venda are buried. Among the Phaphu-li, a division of the larger tribe, the dying chief is carried from the large hut where he lives to a smaller hut to die. When death occurs, the body is wrapped in an oxhide and the mortuary hut is sealed. Again the people are not told where the chief is or what has happened to him, although his heir is smuggled into the head village, and in due time assumes the chieftaincy.

Vhatavhatsinde chiefs are left in the death hut until the bones are bare. The skeletal remains are then revealed to the people and taken to a flat rock in the river. A hut is constructed over them, and hut and bones are consumed by fire. The residues are washed into the river.

Certain other chiefs are cremated on river banks. One family believes that its petty chieftains are one after another reincarnated into a ferocious lion which dwells in their forest. When a chief dies, his body is placed on a trestle, above a large clay dish. As putrefaction takes place, a worm emerges from the body and drops into the receptacle. The bones are then buried, while the worm is placed on the ground. When it reaches the forest, it is metamorphosed into a new lion. At the same time the old lion which incorporates the spirit of the previous chief disappears.

Chapter 21

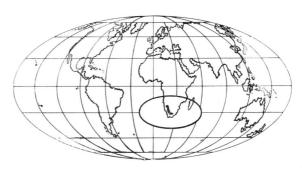

Hottentots of
South-West Africa

The Hottentots, one of the major tribes of the South African native groups, dwell mostly in the grassy and semi-arid veldt lands of the mandated Territory of South-West Africa.[1] They are for the most part nomadic herdsmen, possessing herds of cattle and flocks of sheep which they drive across the grasslands in a constant search for pasturage. A peculiarity of the Hottentots is their language, whose consonants are expressed in "clicking" sounds. The funeral customs of these itinerant natives are best described by Dr. I. Schapera, a student of South African ethnology, whose work *The Khoisan Peoples of South Africa: Bushmen and Hottentots*[2] provides the basic reference source for the present chapter.

Reaction to Death

The Hottentots attribute death to the work of the evil one, or to ghosts of the dead who waylay the living in dreams, or to wicked magicians. Death may likewise result from the failure to perform certain rites. Perhaps a person to whom water is forbidden has touched it. In such case no evil spirit or wicked human servant need be blamed for the calamity. Again, death may be recognized as originating in natural causes such as wounds, burns, falls, starvation. The Hottentot, however, is not given to splitting hairs in assigning the cause of death.

Among the Hottentots the custom formerly prevailed of friends and relatives gathering around the dying person to wail violently. Such writhing and screaming rose in crescendo, reaching its climax at the moment of death. Thereupon the body was seized firmly and before it cooled, the head was doubled between the legs, and the whole body was trussed in this position by the dead person's *kaross,* or upper garment. Burial was made as quickly as possible the following morning.

The grave was a deep hole, with a niche hollowed to one side to hold the body. It was dug at a place designated by a committee consisting of the head and several men of the kraal. If this group failed to find an acceptable site, or did not wish to excavate a grave, the body might be thrust into a convenient cleft in a rock or in some animal cave. The Hottentots do not set aside special burying grounds.

The trussed-up remains were kept in the dead man's hut until the grave was dug or selected. Then they were carried outside through a special opening made in the hut by removing a section of the mat covering the rear. No bier was used, but three or four men, selected by the head of the kraal or the family, bore the burden in their arms. Meanwhile all members of the kraal not making funeral preparations squatted at the regular entrance of the hut lamenting loudly, men in one group, women in another. When the body was borne from the hut, a procession formed behind it. At the place of burial, the body was lowered into the grave, and made to sit in the niche, or was thrust into the cleft or hole. The grave was then filled, and the mound, cleft, or hole covered with a pile of rocks to keep wild beasts from eating the body.

While Hottentots appear to lack definite ideas concerning the nature of the afterlife or of reincarnation, they seem pretty well agreed that the soul of the dead accompanies the body in the grave, and that it has the power of emerging either as a luminous, benevolent spirit, or as a malevolent ghost. Those who die "good deaths," that is tranquilly, live mild existences in the dreams of their survivors, while those who die "bad deaths," in great agony, or under evil influences, or remain unburied, or are devoured by beasts, are to be dreaded.[3]

Fear of Ghosts

Because the Hottentots believe that ghosts hover around the place of burial and may return to molest them, the members of a kraal refuse to live near a grave of one of their group. At a distance, they are safe from a malicious spirit as long as they do not take with them anything belonging to it to their new dwelling place. Although the Naman no longer move *en masse* from the grave area, they exhibit vestiges of the old belief when they visit former dwelling places, by using rites to propitiate the ghosts of ancestors and by the manifesting of great respect toward graves. They may not even point a finger at a grave, lest they disturb the dead and merit their revenge. Ghosts are blamed for most of the sickness and death among the Hottentots. Ghosts inflict these punishments directly, or with the assistance of magicians. Sometimes they appear in dreams to members of their family; at other times they give chase to a person who walks alone, and try to kill him. Again, on dark nights they may leave their graves, and making a rattling noise as if dragging skins over rocks, come to the kraal to whip people.

Among the less organized Hottentots dwelling south of the Orange River, for a few weeks after a burial the male relatives visit the grave each morning before sunrise. So that a ghost will not be able to grasp them by a garment, they discard their clothes. They speak to the grave, and beseech the ghost not to haunt them at night. After a month, they are satisfied that the ghost has abandoned the grave and taken possession

293

of an animal. This slinking creature prowls invisible at night, uttering a cry so loud that when sleepers hear it they draw up the covers, and when diners hear it, they cast food for it over their shoulders.[4]

On their return from the burial, the funeral party approaches the kraal, where in separate groups the men and women squat before the dead man's hut. After some ceremony, an old man enters the hut through the improvised opening in the rear, out of which the body was borne, and emerges bearing ashes, which he strews over the mourners, who rub them over their bodies. Some of the near relatives rub themselves with cowdung as well. When the group disperses to their homes, the family leaves with them. They fear to re-enter the house of death.

Next day, all the huts in the kraal, except that belonging to the dead man, are disassembled and the camp is moved to a new site. The abandoned hut contains all the dead person's possessions. Before leaving, his heir and each of his relatives who can afford to do so, slaughter a sheep, and the mourners feast. A portion of the stomach of the heir's sheep, strewn with aromatic leaves, is twisted into a necklace to be worn by him until it rots. Others slaughtering sheep make a similar use of the cauls. Relatives not so adorned as a sign of mourning shave ridges in their hair. It is not clear whether the Hottentots have special funeral ceremonies for chiefs, or whether mourning entails special prohibitions. It is clear that they observe some kind of mourning for a period lasting from several days to a week.[5]

Simplification of Ceremonies

Among the Cape Hottentots, one of the three major tribes of this native group, the death and burial rites have so disintegrated that the residues are now sometimes telescoped into a single day's performance. Immediately after death the body is prepared for burial. Formerly it was drawn together, with the head between the bent legs; and after being bound, was bundled in skins. Now, after the eyes are closed, it is washed by old women. Then, lying on its back with its arms

294

along the sides and the hands crossed over the bosom, it is sewn into skins whose hairy sides are turned inward. Only the face remains free, and that, too, is covered with a patch before burial. The skins are made aromatic with buchu leaves. Nowadays the Hottentots occasionally are known to substitute old bags for skins, and salt for buchu leaves. Whatever its shrouding, the body lies alone on the floor of the hut, while the mourners spend the night singing outside. Burial usually is made on the afternoon following the day of death.

The grave, which is about six-feet long and three-feet wide with a narrow niche on one side, is dug near the kraal. Relatives and friends remove the body through an opening especially made in the rear wall of the hut, and bear it to the grave. At the graveside, a woman selected for the task asks a relative if the dead person in life gave drink to the thirsty and was a man of virtue. Whatever the facts, the answer is always affirmative. When it is given, all the women present sprinkle buchu leaves on the grave. After the body has been lowered, two men enter the pit and push it into the niche. The traditional position in which the head faces east seems nowadays to be sometimes disregarded. The mouth of the niche and the floor of the grave are tightly packed with the branches of bushes, and these are so covered with flat stones that the body is sealed from falling dirt. All join in filling the grave by casting in handfuls of earth. Above the grave a mound of stones is erected, sometimes to a considerable height. To indicate the head, a foot-high stone or the gemsbok horn, which is used in digging the grave, is set on the ground. Again, all help, everyone adding at least a twig or stone. Next buchu leaves are strewn on the mound. Finally the grave is sprinkled with cold water, whether to "harden" it so that beasts could not ravage it or to cool the soul of the deceased is not clear.[6]

Purification Rites

A receptacle filled with water stands before the hut of the dead person, and upon returning everyone who has attended the burial, except the close relatives to whom water is taboo, washes his hands. The place where the body lies is also asperged. Hygienic considerations undoubtedly motivate these ablutions. Washing prevents the spread of contagion. Members of the bereaved family meanwhile borrow pots, and slaughter as many animals as they can afford. In one pot they place entrails; in another, blood; and in a third, meat. The blood is boiled until steam rises. When the food is considered ready, the pots are brought into the dead man's hut, and the close relatives gather around them, their heads covered so that they perspire. Then an old man not of the family takes pot-black and draws a line across the belly of each person, to prevent suffering from eating. At the feast which follows, the close relatives eat the flesh, and other kraal members eat the intestines. The boiled blood is reserved for the officiating man and other non-family elders.

Not being considered a member of the dead man's family, the widow is denied a part in these rites. She must, however, observe the restrictions imposed by mourning customs, and remains unclean until certain purificatory ceremonies are performed. These may take place immediately after the burial, or may be delayed for several days. In the meantime, lest she defile them, she must not touch uncooked meat or cold water, pass among the cattle, or touch her pots.

Her purificatory rites are conducted by another widow who is not related to her or to her late husband. This elderly person first thoroughly cleanses the whole body of the new widow with moist cowdung. After this she rubs her with a mixture of fat and powdered red mineral. She next crops her head, spitting on a tuft of it, and saying, "May your next husband be lucky, and may you get him quickly." Then she clothes her in a completely new set of garments.[7]

Meanwhile, within the hut a pot containing a bit of meat saved from the funeral feast boils over the fire. With potblack scraped from it, the attendant widow draws a line under each of the new widow's eyes, "so that people will be pleasant to her," and on her chest, "so that food will go down nicely." She then eats the meat in the pot, mixes the new widow's hair with the ashes, removes the latter from the hut, and kindles a fresh fire. The next morning the new widow scatters the contents of an animal's stomach over the cattle kraal so that the "milk supply may prove plentiful." Finally she milks a cow, fetches wood, and touches cold water. Now she is purified. The widower undergoes similar rites. When these have been completed, however, before he can leave the hut, two cuts must be made in his forehead with a quartz knife—a metal knife is frequently used nowadays—and astringent juice rubbed into the wounds. He, too, must visit the cattle kraals with an attendant, only he asperges the cattle with water in which tamarisk and acacia branches have soaked overnight.[8]

Various Hottentot ceremonies are directed toward protecting the living from ghosts. To become identified with local waters is conceived as one method of being considered a local resident, and thus immune to ghosts which prey on strangers. This belief is at the root of the practice of visiting an old waterhole, and smearing the body with clay from it, and of marking the forehead with wet clay and potblack when entering a strange kraal. Most of the graveside ceremonies are rooted in the Hottentot's desire to be secure from hostile spirits. Hottentots believe that the whirlwind "hides in its mass departed spirits which forebode ill for the living," and they therefore take precautions against it, and scatter cold water in its path. They regard all meteorological changes as produced by the dead. When stormy weather follows a week after a death, it is accepted as a sign that gall is leaving the body. In one instance cirrus clouds were believed to be sent by the ghost of a white man.[9]

The attitude of the Hottentots toward their dead manifests some ambivalence. On the one hand the living fear ghosts as the cause of sickness and death; on the other, they seek their friendly aid. The relations underlying this ambivalence are obscure. There is also some evidence of ancestor worship among the Hottentots, and praying at ancestral graves appears to be common practice. When wayfarers pass a grave close to a road they cast a stone on the mound that covers it, as a mark of honor to the dead who is buried there.

Memorial posts of Madagascar. Bara tribe left, southern Betsileo right

Chapter 22

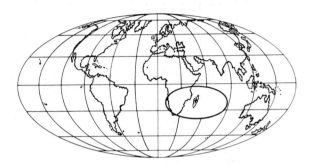

Tanala of Madagascar

The Tanala are a group of hill tribes spread across central Madagascar, now the Malagasy Republic. Their cultural backgrounds represent a mingling of Malay-Polynesian and Arabian influences. Following the ethnographical account of anthropologist Ralph Linton[1] the present chapter will describe the mortuary customs and manners of two of the principal divisions of the Tanala, the Menabe and the Ikongo.

Menabe

Death Beliefs

During the last century the Menabe tribesmen have acquired from their neighbors the belief that at death the souls of their kings pass into the bodies of large snakes. They also believe that each person has a soul which is a double for the body. They believe, too, in ghosts, some of human and some of non-human origin. They classify the spirits of the dead—which may or may not be ghosts—into two groups: (1) Near ancestors that remain in close contact with their descendants, who sacrifice to them and invoke their aid in religious rituals which are rooted in ancestor worship. The spirits, in turn, reward or punish the living. (2) Distant ancestors whose names and identities are hidden by the years, or who were the original inhabitants of the region, are included in the second group. They have little interest in the living, and no one invokes them or makes sacrifices to them unless he invades the lands on which they once dwelt or imputes to them an illness which he or his people suffer.[2]

Burial Rites

The burial customs of the Menabe derive additional interest from the fact that except for the expense of the funeral feast, they are the same for rich and poor. History lies at the root of this common ceremony. Once the Menabe were a casteless people, and even today when a poor person dies, his straitened relatives quietly carry the body into the forest. They will return to bury it after the rice has been harvested and their means are greater. Such cases are exceptional.

When death occurs, relatives of the same sex wash the body, arrange the hair, and wrap the body in a mantle of raffia, a palm fiber, leaving the face uncovered so that the spirit eyes may follow the road. When the body has thus been prepared, they deposit it, head pointing east, in the northern half of the house in which the dead person lived, to be kept there not more than two or three days, except for a king whose wake may extend for a week. There persons twenty years of age or more may visit it, and sing and dance.

On the day before the burial cattle are slaughtered for a great feast, and pounded rice is heaped on mats in the village square. There a man of the family of either the mother or father of the deceased rises, and in a speech acknowledges the small customary gifts of food made by friends and relatives. Some of the meat is cooked and eaten with rice on the

300

Native tomb,
Tananarine,
Madagascar

spot. In addition, uncooked meat is distributed to bystanders who eat it in their homes.

Next morning the body is borne directly from the house to the tomb. This task is assigned to certain designated persons, whose only qualification seems to be their willingness to handle the dead and enter the tomb. Each such person receives a chicken and 2.5 francs—a penny or so in American money—for his services. For ease in carrying, the bearers usually lash the body of an ordinary person to a pole; while they bear the body of a chief above their heads on their hands. On the way to the grave there is much singing and dancing in the procession. When they reach the tomb, one of the bearers makes a speech telling those who accompany the cortege that they must return home, and all except four or five of the closest relatives depart. The bearers then enter the tomb, pushing aside earlier remains to make room for the new arrival. After they have deposited the body, they place the skulls of the deceased's grandparents, which in some way they continue to identify, above it. When this task has been completed, they leave the tomb, and all relatives return to the house of death. After remaining in the vicinity of it for several days, they depart for their homes.[3]

301

Some northern members of the Tanala tribe apparently keep their unembalmed dead lying in state for as long as a month before burying them. Meanwhile they cover the liquid residues of decomposition with earth as they drip from cracks in the wooden coffin; and the surviving spouse sleeps in the house just as if the partner were still alive. Burial is made by conveying the coffin to a lonely spot in the forest and concealing it within a palisade of tree trunks.

Rites of Dead Chiefs

Certain groups among the Menabe preserve the eye teeth of their dead kings as memorials of the services which they have rendered their subjects. These human teeth, together with crocodile teeth, are kept in a small, finely woven basket on a small shelf above the eastern door of a house. In October or December the tooth collection is bathed. A procession comes to the house and a man enters, puts the tooth basket on his head, carries it out of the house, and respectfully places it on a mat. After this a noble person—man or woman—picks it up and carries it to the river and enters the water. Meanwhile the procession leads a bull to the bank and slaughters it, while the basket bearer swims with the relics. On the return of the swimmer, a feast begins, and when it is over, the basket is restored to its position of honor on the shelf.[4]

Chiefs of Arabian descent are placed in a coffin, the lid of which is shaped like a roof and surmounted with a pair of horns. Burial is made in a shed-like building which is reserved for the bodies of rulers, and which stands in a jungle thicket. For six weeks after the burial a likeness of the dead chief is displayed in his house, and is shown the usual courtesies of grief and mourning. When the six-week period is finished, the picture is ceremoniously thrown into a great river.

Mourning Customs

The Tanala observe public mourning by wearing old dirty clothes, neglecting to cut or trim their hair, and not bathing.

302

They are not given to violent displays of grief such as loud weeping or self-inflicted mutilation. The customary mourning period varies with the degree of kinship. Mourning for a spouse usually lasts for six months; for a child, for a year; for distant relatives, for a month or two. Mourning is terminated by close relatives in a ceremony at the house of the deceased. When all have gathered who attended the burial, an ox is slain, and a child sprinkles blood on the spot where the dead person lay. After this he uses a wooden bowl to mix the blood with rum, water, a white fungus, and certain chopped-up plants, and, carrying the mixture in a cupped leaf drops a little of it into the hands of everyone present. The mourning period formally ends when they wash their faces with it. After this they grease their hair, sing and dance, and finally make a feast.[5]

Tombs of the Menabe

While all Tanala use communal tombs, these show considerable variation from tribe to tribe, probably because of cultural intrusions from neighboring peoples. The Imerina and Betsileo who live west of the Tanala country use family vaults built in prominent places for burial. After a man has become rich enough to build one of these, it is used for three or four generations by his male descendants, until one of them decides to establish a new family by building a new tomb. No special tomb guardians are appointed, and no tomb sacrifices are made.

The tribes living east of the Tanala on the other hand used tombs established by the clan ancestor in a secluded place, and build no new tombs, so that, as the clan grows, several or more villages may use a single such tomb. These eastern neighbors of the Tanalas make their tombs the center of their religious life. The tomb guardian—the post is hereditary—is the religious head of the clan with a chief's authority. Sacrifices are offered and trials for sorcery are held at the clan tomb.

The northern Tanalas, the Menabe, sometimes maintain clan tombs which serve as many as twelve villages. Such a

Mahafaly tombs
and carvings,
Madagascar

burial place consists of burial houses each of which contains three stone-lined compartments, one for men, another for women, and the third for children. Among the rest of the Menabe it is customary for each village to maintain two or three tombs which are used in rotation. New tombs are provided when the old become overcrowded. Although these people prefer a cave tomb, when none is available, they will use a rock shelter instead. In such a shelter, under the overhang, they construct a covered box of planks, sometimes so large that it can hold a hundred bodies. If neither a cave nor a rock shelter is available, they dig a rectangular pit in a thicket which must lie at least a half-hour's march from their village. They line this excavation with stones, and they cover the opening with stone slabs or planks. Dirt is then mounded over this cellar, and a house is built above the mound.[6]

Burial is made by stacking the uncoffined bodies indiscriminately as to sex and age, with heads pointing east. Admission to the clan burial house is limited to the bodies of clan members. After interment elsewhere for a few years, the remains of those who die of contagious diseases may be admitted. The bodies of sorcerers and criminals are excluded, however, and left to be eaten by dogs. When the tomb is to be moved because a village is moving or a new site has been

304

found, the three leading villagers come to the tomb and so inform the dead. Next morning the remains are removed, bundled, and carried to the new tomb with much hilarity, and there deposited amidst singing and dancing.[7]

The Tanala Menabe do not consider the erection of a memorial stone as necessary for the peace of the spirit of a person dying away from his village, and as a consequence erect fewer stones. Menabe memorials are of two types: upright slabs, and irregular tables supported by three stones. Wherever possible, men are commemorated by upright slabs. Only if a family is extremely poor, or if a suitable slab cannot be found, is the table stone used for a man.

Ikongo

Burial Rites

When a member of the Ikongo tribe seems near death, the relatives gather at the house, and when the end comes, members of the same sex as the departed bathe the body, and braid and oil the hair. Then, having wrapped the body in mattings or a mantle, they bear it to the village assembly house where they stuff a piece of silver into the mouth and bedeck the neck and hair with beads. While messengers speed to distant relatives, able-bodied members of the immediate family select a tree, and hew a coffin out of the log, inserting pegs for feet. Meanwhile, several cattle are killed, and the meat is distributed throughout the village. The coffin finished, the builders joyfully set out to return to the village, and on the way are met by a crowd of rejoicing women and children, who turn back and accompany them. The coffin and body rest separately overnight on the east side of the assembly house. Next day, after the body has been placed in it, the coffin is covered with a lid of planks, bound with vines, and suspended in the meeting house. Ordinarily it hangs there two or three days. However, if the family is wealthy, it sometimes is not taken down for ten or fifteen days. In any event, the liquid by-products of decomposition which are likely to

305

ooze from the body are caught in a vessel and emptied outside of the village; meanwhile, fat is burned to hide the stench. In anticipation of a funeral feast the family kills cattle to feed the visitors.

Before the cortege leaves for the clan tomb, a chief tells the dead person that he is being carried to the house of his ancestors. There he must remain and he must not bring evil to his own household. If, however, he was murdered by witchcraft, he should quickly slay his assassin. People of all ages, singing and dancing, follow the burial party to the clan tomb. When the place is reached, the chief again speaks. Now he admonishes the spirits of relatives: "We are sending you one of our own. Accept him. Do not let him wander." Following the burial a feast of beef and rice is fed to all who assisted.

Of old it was customary to conceal the illness of an Ikongo king, and to bury him secretly at night. His relatives were not allowed to weep or wear mourning, and were supposed to answer inquiries regarding his health with the statement that he was well. Tribes that engage in constant warfare would not permit the announcement of the death of a king or allow public mourning for him until after his successor had been chosen. If a king makes a special request before his death that he should be publicly buried, his successor is selected without delay, and the body is placed in the village assembly house. There high caste women surround it, and a man lies down next to it and does not leave until it is casketed. When the men bring the coffin from the forest, the body is placed in it, and suspended from the roof. Early next morning the blare of conch-shell trumpets and the firing of muskets proclaim the death of the king, and summon his weeping subjects and even neighboring tribes to join the continuous feast at which great quantities of beef are served. The funeral feast of a king may be prolonged from fifteen to thirty days. Meanwhile, the coffin is taken down from time to time, to be drained of the liquid residues of decomposition. Decomposition is so rapid in the hot climate that often only a skeleton remains for burial.

306

Interment among the Ikongo is called "throwing away the body." If a grave is dug in the forest, nothing is left to indicate its presence except a notch cut in a nearby tree. A burial is neither solemn nor sad. The procession that bears the body over the forest road is noisy with much screaming and yelling, and now and then the bearers set the body down so that the spectators may pause to engage in wrestling matches and other games. The burial is accomplished with no great show of grief.[8]

However, a lost body provokes the relatives of the deceased to make great effort to discover and return it to the ancestral grave. When a person dies at a distance and is buried, on hearing of the event his male relatives wait until the flesh has decayed. Then they exhume the bones, and with the usual ceremonies deposit them in the clan burial house. To discover a body of a drowned person, a banana tree core encircled with a silver bracelet is cast on the water, in the belief that it will rest motionless over the spot where the drowned one lies. After this, if divers fail to bring up the body, the Ikongo conduct funeral services over the deceased's mat and pillow, which are then buried in lieu of his remains. Other groups of the Tanala observe the passing of an absent one with a feast, but bear nothing to the tomb. Still others use a banana trunk to represent the body of the dead person at burial ceremonies. The banana tree is reverenced thus because it is regarded as a symbol of the human family.[9]

Ikongo Tombs

While some Ikongo inter their dead others entomb them in caves. The cave selected will be far removed from the village in both distance and contacts, so that the dead will not disturb the living. Within the tomb bodies are heaped in layers, an exception being made only for a coffined king, who is laid on a shelf. The bodies of persons dying of contagion, or of infants under a month old, are not admitted to the tomb. Although the tomb guardian is only a simple chief, his regulations are obeyed. Among these is the prohibition that the forest in the vicinity of the tomb may not be cut down or burned over. Violation brings the heavy fine of a large ox. The tomb guardian has the duty of ordering the family to repair the tomb, or to provide a new one. During such operations, if the family is rich, the guardian may kill as many as twenty or thirty cattle to feed the workers.[10]

Erection of Memorial Stones

A second ceremony for the dead is always conducted during the months of January through April following the harvest of wet rice. At this time one or more stones are erected in the memory of the dead. The size of the monument varies according to the wealth of the deceased or the deceased's family. The stones, which are about three-feet wide, often tower ten times that high and may be of either of two types, menhirs (male stones) or tables consisting of a large irregular flat slab supported by three upright stones (female stones).

The need for this ceremony seems more necessary for the dead who have not been buried in the clan tomb. Preceding the performance, members of the family gather to discuss the preparations for the festival: the number of professional dancers and musicians to be invited; the number of oxen to be killed; and to pound the rice which will be given to the guests. This ritual takes place on Thursday, a lucky day, beginning at four or five o'clock in the afternoon. The women assemble in the wife's house while the new head of the family and the other men congregate to the east of the sacrifice post. Conch-shell trumpets and double-headed drums are sounded three times to convene the spirits that may be absent. The head of the family addresses the spirit of the deceased directly, asks for its favor and requests that it be received by the other ancestral souls. The trumpets sound, everyone weeps for awhile, then solemnity is discarded in favor of singing, dancing and other festivities lasting from three to fifteen days.[11]

308

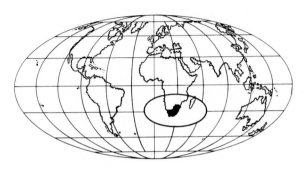

Chapter 23

South Africa

In a general geographical sense south or southern Africa refers to those countries in Africa lying below 15 degrees south of the equator. Included would be South-West Africa, southern Rhodesia, Bechuanaland, Mozambique, Basutoland, Swaziland, and the Union of South Africa. The Union of South Africa with an area about one sixth that of the United States is multi-racial. About 3,000,000 white people speak English and/or Afrikaans—a language derived from the Dutch. The remaining 10,000,000 inhabitants are of native and colored (Asiatic) stock. South Africa is divided into four provinces: Cape Province, Transvaal, Orange Free State, and Natal. While a central government governs that entire country, each province through its local assembly regulates such matters for itself as education, roads, and hospitals. The regulation of cemeteries and crematoria are among matters controlled by the provincial administrations.[1]

The first section of the present chapter will deal primarily

Photo Courtesy Oliver and Watson

South African funeral chapel. Chapels such as this are located apart from funeral establishments, generally in cemeteries

with the funeral customs and procedures of the English-speaking peoples of the Union of South Africa. The concluding portion will for the most part depict the mortuary complex among the Boer or Afrikaans-speaking peoples of South Africa and Rhodesia.

English-Speaking South Africans

There are many similarities between the funeral beliefs and practices of the English-speaking people of southern Africa and the beliefs and practices to be found in England and the United Kingdom. When death occurs among this group a member of the immediate family usually telephones the funeral

310

director who thus learns whether the remains are at the home, in a hospital, or at some other place, and when and where he should meet with the family to discuss the details of the funeral. He is prepared to interview them at their convenience in their home or at his office. After the time and the place of the funeral have been settled upon, the funeral director arranges to have the body removed to his preparation rooms.

Funeral Service Organization

In the Union of South Africa funeral establishments range from small owner-operated businesses in the rural areas to a great corporation having 150 branches with outlets in all the big cities and in many smaller towns and villages as well. This corporation maintains its own casket, hardware, and wreath manufacturing establishment in a central location. Larger centers having populations of 100,000 to 800,000 are served by an average of five funeral directors, whose annual volume of cases ranges from 250 to 1,800.[2] One East London, Cape Province, establishment and its associate handle a yearly average of 450 to 500 funerals. In Cape Town, the southernmost city of the same province, three white and several colored and native establishments serve a population of some 350,000. Most white establishments accept non-white

Another example of South African funeral chapels. Dutch architectural influence visible

patronage. Non-white funeral establishments, however, are increasingly providing funeral services exclusively for non-white clientele. A prominent South African funeral director observes that "the numerically superior but economically inferior non-white section of the community uses less expensive coffins. However, with the improving earning power of the urban non-white, funerals of a standard comparable with those of the whites are being increasingly provided."[3] The larger South African funeral establishments contain offices, showrooms and chapels. These last will probably seat some sixty persons apiece.

A notable upgrading in equipment has been evident among South African funeral directors during the past 30 years. Most funeral establishments now own their own premises, and provide chapels where services can be held. These may not be located in residential neighborhoods. Recorded music is generally used, although several funeral chapels are equipped with organs.

Funeral Procedures

In the interview with the family or their representatives, the funeral director secures the information needed to register the death according to the provisions of the amended Births, Marriages and Deaths Registration Act of 1926. Required are the full name, date of birth, age, sex, race, occupation, pension (if any), date of death, place of death, place of residence, place of burial, cause of death, and name of the medical practitioner in attendance during last illness.

With the family's wishes guiding him, the funeral director then makes arrangements for the burial. If earth burial is selected he ascertains the number of plots required in the cemetery. Only one private cemetery organization exists in the cities and towns of the Union of South Africa. The remainder are municipally controlled and maintained. If the deceased has a surviving spouse, the relatives usually wish to purchase two plots. Occasionally, depending upon family arrangements, a

312

family may wish to acquire three or even four plots.[4]

Cremation calls for another series of arrangements. The first South African crematorium was built about 30 years ago. Since that time the cremation movement has continued to gain popularity among the middle and upper class English-speaking group, to which it is largely confined, although earth burial remains the over-all favorite method of disposal.[5] In certain of the larger cities such as Johannesburg, Cape Town, Port Elizabeth, East London and Brakpan the municipalities provide crematoria. A privately owned crematorium has been established at Durban. Most municipal crematoria, however, are subsidized from the general tax fund.[6]

When these arrangements are settled upon, notices are placed in the local press and sent to newspapers in other parts of the country. Other items, meanwhile, are not forgotten, such as whether the family or the funeral director will supply the pallbearers and what arrangements the family wishes to have made for the digging of the grave. The major question is: What type of service do you want the funeral director to render and what type of casket is your choice? The funeral director's display room exhibits samples of the types of caskets commonly used in South Africa. Most of these are of the traditional English types, but if the family desires a casket of a kind not stocked it is usually possible in the alloted time to have such a casket especially manufactured.

Caskets and Embalmers

Metal caskets are not manufactured in South Africa and are scarcely ever imported from the United States and England for South African use. Wooden coffins, shaped to the form of the shoulders are favorites, along with locally made oblong-shaped wooden caskets. Prefabricated grave vaults are never used. If a vault is desired it is built at the grave site of bricks or concrete.

The coffin or casket provided is usually of a simple variety. Afrikaaners generally choose the type of caskets common in Europe having a canopied lid and straight sides. The need

313

Casket showroom in Natal funeral establishment. Variety in shapes, styles and prices

to carry three lines of stock—the English coffins, American-type caskets, and Afrikaaner coffins—adds to the cost of operation and hence of the individual funeral.[7]

Because the South African climate is warm even the smaller establishments have refrigeration facilities. Refrigeration is the method of preservation commonly used where distances are small between the places of death and burial.

South Africa has no embalming schools, nor are official examinations available for an embalming license, nor do government or municipal regulations set up embalming as a qualification to be met by those who engage in funeral service. Within the Union, however, there are a few embalmers certified by the British Institute of Embalmers. Most of them have qualified for this certification by studying in England and passing the requisite examination there. In 1938 an examiner was brought from England to conduct the British Institute of Embalming examinations in South Africa. Eight persons took the examinations. This was the only time such an event took place.[8]

Arterial and cavity embalming is used chiefly on bodies which are transported for considerable distances within the Union itself, and to countries overseas. Shipment of both kinds is fairly frequent. Because distances within the Union itself may be considerable, air transportation has greatly facilitated the funeral director's task in this regard. South African funeral directors make no effort to provide restorative treatment to mutilated bodies.

The Clergy

Once the questions involved in disposal have been settled, the matters of securing the services of a clergyman and of making provisions for church services come next in the discussion. It is likely that the services of a member of the Free Churches in South Africa will be held in the funeral director's chapel. Episcopalian services are seldom held there. If the cortege leaves from the chapel, services are conducted either at the grave or preferably in the church.

South African funeral directors provide funeral services for members of all religious denominations except those which maintain their own service organizations. The Jewish community buries its own dead in plain unadorned wooden caskets, and uses whatever profits accrue for welfare work among its members. Rich and poor are buried alike. Rich families, however, voluntarily pay higher fees for the services given their dead.[9]

Funerals and Funeral Economics

The funeral director provides transportation for the clergyman and the chief mourners. Because funeral establishments own their own fleet of vehicles there are no firms in South Africa specializing in the rental of funeral transportation to funeral directors. Today most South African hearses are locally converted from standard passenger cars. The favorite model for conversion has been the station wagon, the interior length of which makes conversion easy. However, a small number of American-made hearses and limousines have been imported from the United States.

Further, the funeral director directs the funeral operations, such as viewing, moving the casketed body to the church, transporting the floral wreaths to the church and thence to the cemetery. Only in exceptional instances does he order

315

wreaths for the immediate family. While the number of wreaths per funeral depends on many circumstances, and normally lies somewhere between 20 and 50, an exceptionally large funeral may bring as many as 300 wreaths. When the funeral is over the funeral director prepares memorial records for the relatives, in which he lists the wreaths, and encloses the press notices.[10]

In making preliminary estimates of the cost for submission at the initial conference with the family representatives the funeral director lists the following items: interment, interment fees, minister, church, transport, advertising, bearers, death certificate, embalming, purchase of grave and casket. The sum of these determines his charge.

South African funerals usually take place within two or three days after death. On the day of the funeral close relatives gather at the funeral chapel. It is not customary for more distant relatives and friends to attend a wake or a funeral. In this respect South African funeral practice resembles the British rather than the American.

At the burial the funeral director supplies grass grave linings, and, at the request of the relatives, a lowering device. The funeral chapels, hearses, ambulances, mortuaries, lowering devices, and other equipment used in Cape Town and probably in some other of the South African cities are up-to-date. Most of these, including artificial grass, grave sets, lowering devices and placers, church trucks, and removal stretchers, are imported from the United States.

After the funeral the funeral director pays the clergyman's stipend, the organist's and caretaker's fees, for the site purchased and the digging cost of the grave, or if the remains are cremated, the cremation fees.

Funeral costs range through six grades depending upon the wishes of the family and the status of the deceased. Payment is usually made from the estate of the deceased, and a delay of about six months between the burial and the closing of the account is normal. Sometimes the establishment waits two or three years for its money.[11]

316

South African funeral
establishment
incorporating offices,
chapel, shop and
living quarters

Photo Courtesy George H. Rogers

South African funeral;
funeral coach
American manufacture

Photo Courtesy Dove's Funeral Services

A very large number of South African funerals are provided for by funeral insurance, or as it is termed there, funeral "assurance." Many funeral directing firms have entered the business of providing such assurance, which is subject to careful government regulation. Some of them have formed their own companies, and one funeral assurance company reversed the process and entered the field of funeral service.[12]

Most of the larger funeral establishments hold membership in the National Funeral Directors Association of Southern Africa; and most of the larger insurance companies in the National Institute of Funeral Insurers. The former was organized ten years ago, the latter in the '40's. Both organizations hold annual conventions and the N.F.D.A.S.A. publishes a monthly journal.

Boer or Afrikaaner Funeral Customs and Procedures

The Afrikaaners are commonly associated with the areas encompassed by the Union of South Africa. Actually their pioneer forefathers, the Boers, settled far inland to extend their culture north as far as the Congo Basin. In many places in South Africa people of the two dominant white racial stocks live and work side by side and speak both English and Afrikaans. There are also many persons who speak English and not Afrikaans, and many others who speak Afrikaans but not English.

While some Afrikaaners born of Dutch stock long in South Africa have drifted away from their mother tongue, some of their traditional customs, and even occasionally from the religion of their forefathers, the great majority of them are still active members of the Dutch Reformed Church and adhere to its time-honored funeral customs.

Religion and Death

"The Afrikaaner takes death very seriously," comments C. Oelofsen, funeral director and embalmer of Kitwe in northern Rhodesia. Nor is this seriousness limited to his attitude regarding death. "He is a great believer in the Resurrection. He is very anti-cremation. He is not in favor of the crucifix being part of the coffin furniture or ornaments."[13] Both the clergy and laity of the Dutch Reformed Church have a horror of suicide, and in the past it was customary to set apart a "suicide section" in a cemetery. There suicides were buried without full funeral rites and contrary to custom with the head facing west, away from the rising sun. This viewpoint has been softened in recent years until now the clergy take the position that it is not theirs to judge a man, and they are willing to bury suicides in the normal section of the cemetery with full rites, and with the head toward the rising sun.[14]

Among the Afrikaaners the clergyman has a major role in the making of funeral arrangements. When death takes place, the bereaved immediately contact him. He comes to them as soon as possible, to express his sympathies, give them comfort,

318

and assist them with the funeral arrangements.[15] If death takes place in the hospital it is likely that the clergyman will be present.

Next the bereaved notify all relatives and friends. Afrikaaners like to have their families attend funerals, and when one of them dies, the survivors send notices of the death far and wide. Those living at a distance also attend the funeral if they can, arriving by plane or motor car.

Funeral Services

Afrikaaners are a self-reliant folk and in many cases, after arrangements have been made by the family and the clergyman, with friends assisting, some member of the family approaches the undertaker on the morning of the day when the funeral is to take place and requests that the funeral now take place, as every item has been attended to. This naturally comes as a surprise to the undertaker, as he generally has no information on the deceased. Moreover, he has to apply to the local council for a grave allocation, has to measure the deceased, and apply for a burial certificate. And, of course, the family expects a funeral notice to appear in the local press. "They don't seem to realize," says one exasperated funeral director, "that the undertaker has a lot to do and attend to if the funeral is to be conducted in a dignified manner."[16]

In places where such establishment is available it is becoming more and more customary to remove the remains to a funeral parlor. There they may or may not be embalmed as the relatives desire. The Afrikaaner is opposed neither to post-mortems nor embalming. For coffining, the dead are clothed in the usual white shroud.

Coffins and Caskets

The Afrikaaners very seldom use caskets. Oelofsen comments: "It may be because of the extra cost, but I personally feel that the general public, not only the Afrikaaners, prefer the coffin because it looks more like the proper thing to bury people in."[17] Ordinary coffins are fully lined with white calico and have the usual drapings. Better types are lined with embossed silk. Coffins are fitted with six metal handles and backplates. An engraved plate with the name, age, and date of death of the deceased is placed on top the coffin. An ornament (a metal strip) with the engraved word or words such as *Rest in Peace, At Rest, Mother, Father,* or some other appropriate title or legend is fastened at the head end of the coffin. At the foot end, an ornament—a metal bouquet of roses or a metal wreath—is placed. For all religions except the Roman Catholic this is standard coffin hardware. Catholic practice is to have a metal crucifix on the coffin.[18]

All children and youths up to 20 years of age are buried in a white coffin, the covering of which is made of embossed swansdown, a soft, thick cloth mixed with silk, rayon or cotton. If the deceased is tall and in the 16- to 20-year age group, the coffin has the usual six handles. Coffins for younger children have four handles. Stillborn children are buried in a white, handleless coffin.

Although the practice is dying out and is to be found only among old timers, the Afrikaaner in South Africa formerly kept his coffin in the loft of his farm house. Afrikaaners currently view the coffin only while the remains lie in state in the funeral parlor. However, they cling to the custom of making their own funeral wreaths out of fresh flowers. They are expected to bring these floral offerings to the funeral parlor about a half hour before the coffin is placed on the hearse, prior to setting out for the church services.

The Funeral Obsequies

The Afrikaaner likes a dignified if somewhat ostentatious funeral. For one thing he brings together a good audience of relatives and friends. Afrikaaner children of all ages are expected to attend funerals. Further he adds dignity to a funeral by carefully dressing for it. Among Afrikaaners black is the color on the day of the funeral. The women wear black, and the men wear black armbands. The undertaker wears a black

Memorial plaques
at crematorium

frockcoat that hangs just below the knee, a black waistcoat, black trousers, black shoes, black bowtie, and a white wing collar. During the hot season he wears gray striped morning trousers instead of black. He does not wear a "shiner" or top hat. His dress is almost identical with that worn by the minister of the Dutch Reformed Church.[19]

The other ethnic groups in Rhodesia—at least the English, Scotch, and Irish—even though they may have been in the country for years, dress informally for funerals. The men sometimes attend in short trousers, open-neck shirts, and short socks. Sometimes they arrive directly from work, wearing their work clothes. The women may wear white or even colored dresses with floral patterns.

Afrikaaners by and large insist that the remains must be brought to a church for services. For services the coffin is placed in front of the altar or in the church entrance, or it may remain outside in the hearse. No fixed rule is involved. When the members of the bereaved family enter, as a mark of sympathy the congregation rise in their seats. If the coffin is brought in, they rise again as a mark of respect.[20]

The services consist of a hymn or two, a prayer, the reading of a passage from the scriptures, and a sermon. Favorite themes for Dutch Reformed services are man's accountability

321

for his sins, and the inevitability of death. Services may last from 30 to 50 minutes. A funeral march is usually played on the organ when the mourners leave the church; sometimes the congregation remains standing during the march.

Friends attending an Afrikaaner funeral may skip the church and go directly to the cemetery where they await the cortege which forms at the church after the services. In the Union of South Africa it is very uncommon to have the funeral cortege originate at the residence of the deceased.

In the Afrikaaner funeral procession horse-drawn hearses were seldom used. Today hearses are motor vehicles, and in Rhodesia, generally of English make. The coffin is placed on the deck, and rests under the level of the doors where it cannot be seen. Although the undertaker has transportation available for funeral use, the bereaved usually prefer to drive their own cars. Upon arrival at the cemetery the pallbearers carry the coffin at arms-length by the six handles. Only in full-scale military funerals does the old practice persist of carrying the coffin on the shoulders of the bearers.

Interment

The verge of the grave is covered with artificial grass. During the graveside service the minister stands at the head of the grave and the undertaker at the foot. The committal services are simple. While the coffin is being lowered a hymn is sung. Following the hymn, the minister reads a short form: "It has pleased Almighty God, the Lord of life and death, to let the spirit of our beloved brother (or sister) return to God, who created it and Who has said: 'Dust thou art and to dust thou shalt return.' Therefore we now lay his (or her) body in the grave, until the day when all who are in the graves will hear the Voice of the Son of God and will come forth, those who have rendered good, to the resurrection of life, and those who have rendered evil, to the resurrection of judgment."[21]

After the reading of this form, a prayer is offered and a few words of thanks are spoken by the minister or some member

322

of the family. The minister then gives the benediction. At the conclusion of this ceremony the relatives and close friends may drop a handful of earth or a few flower petals into the grave. Occasionally some person associated with the deceased in his work or in some organization pays a short graveside tribute. Sometimes this tribute is paid in church after the sermon. Although the graveside service lasts about ten minutes it may be extended with additional preaching.

Many South Africans belong to an organization of veterans of both World Wars, called the "Memorable Order of Tin Hats" or "M.O.T.H." This non-political group which cuts across denominational lines has a clubhouse in most towns. When a member dies he is given a military-type funeral. His coffin is draped with the Union Jack, and a tin helmet and medals are laid upon it.

At the graveside, after the clergyman has performed all the usual rites except the final benediction, the M.O.T.H. bugler blows the Last Post and Reveille, and the local organization leader, known as "Old Bill," reads the M.O.T.H. prayer. Then the clergyman gives the final benediction. A similar organization of women veterans performs a similar ceremony for its members.[22]

Post-Funeral Observances

The custom, still to be found in England, of inviting friends and relatives home after the burial to partake of tea and

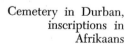

Cemetery in Durban, inscriptions in Afrikaans

snacks is observed in Rhodesia by a minority of families, including those newly arrived from England. It is likely that Rhodesians who keep this custom will in addition to tea offer their guests whiskey, beer, or other alcoholic beverages. Although the Afrikaaner does not follow this custom he usually is prepared to serve coffee and tea in the home after a burial.

W. L. Maree, Information Officer of the Dutch Reformed Church, comments that presently there are many variations as far as the rites are concerned. In olden days, and perhaps still to a certain extent in outlying districts, several customs were observed. A funeral notice was sent out, a special verger was appointed, a list of those present was read, and extensive use of crepe was made. As people had to travel long distances, a meal was served on the farm before they returned home. At the other end of the scale, many funerals in the cities are nowadays held in the parlors of undertakers. There the service is even shorter and simpler than the one described, although the essentials are the same. Hymns, for example, are often dispensed with. The proceedings at a cremation service follow more or less the same lines; sometimes the service is held in a church and sometimes at the crematorium.[23]

The custom of wearing mourning for a period after the funeral is still fairly widely observed, although in recent years the periods have tended to become shorter. Those observing mourning are expected to remain away from public entertainment, including movies. The ministers, elders, and deacons of the Dutch Reformed Church do everything in their power to assist families facing problems arising from a death.

In recent years the practice has grown more common among the Afrikaaners of Rhodesia of shipping the dead back to the Union of South Africa for burial in the family plot, preferably in the same grave in which the father and mother of the deceased are buried. Many English-speaking citizens of Rhodesia observe the same practice.

Funeral Customs The World Over

Part Four

Batak tomb near Balige, Sumatra

Oceania

A vast agglomeration of brown, white, and yellow peoples scattered across the Pacific . . . a continuum of islands from the tiny atoll to the continent . . . the gaiety of the burning biers of Bali . . . the solemnity of a funeral procession in Melbourne . . . bushmen dancing to appease the spirits . . . ancestor figures and elaborate festivals . . . and the gradual penetration into village and city of Western funeral folkways

Philip Gendreau Photo

Carved ancestor figure. Easter Island

Chapter 24

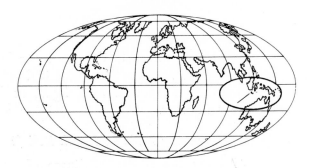

Bali

The Isle of Bali, which lies off Asia in the Southern Hemisphere, is sometimes called the "Last Paradise" or the "Paradise Isle" because of the unusual beauty of its natural scenery and gentle disposition of its handsome people. This island is the home also of strange and beautiful rituals. Not the least among these are the burial ceremonies.[1]

Primitive Balinese Burials

The modern Balinese are a mixture of pure Indonesian and Javenese, with traces of Polynesian, Melanesian, Chinese, and Papuan. The burial customs of the primitive Balinese prior to this admixture can be reconstructed by observing the rites in the few villages peopled by their unmixed survivors. These live in small clan communities ruled by priest elders, and dispose of their dead by earth burial or by placing them on a platform at the edge of a ravine, together with offerings to be

329

carried away by the spirits. If after three days the body is still present, it seems clear to them that the spirits have rejected it, and it is pushed into the ravine, to be eaten by wild beasts. The ancestors of this group probably went even farther than this, and themselves ate certain parts of the body in the belief that they thus would acquire magical powers. This belief seems to persist to the present and is performed symbolically by allowing water to drip over the body into a sheaf of un-husked rice. After the body is buried, the rice is husked, cooked, and made into the figure of a man, to be eaten at a funeral dinner.

Contemporary Balinese Death Beliefs

Among the modern Balinese of mixed cultural and racial background funeral customs are not grim. Quite the contrary. In contrast to Western attitudes toward death and disposal, where not even the cult of beauty can conceal the underlying sense of pain in loss, is the gayety that characterizes the final phases of the Balinese funeral rites. Anthropologist Miguel Covarrubias after much first-hand observation wrote that strangely enough the Balinese seem to find their greatest fun in their funeral ceremonies. The reason for this apparent contradiction is to be found in the Balinese beliefs concerning the nature of man and the afterlife.[2]

According to these beliefs, the soul, which is all-important, finds in the body only a temporary dwelling place, a container, as it were, and while the soul is everywhere within the body, it is concentrated in the head. Although in sleep the soul may wander from the body in dreams, complete detachment does not occur. Death comes only when the soul escapes through the mouth and refuses to return. When a dying person sinks into unconsciousness, his relatives visit the temple to entreat the gods to release and return the soul. Even after death, the soul remains near the body, hovering in the air or perched in a tree, until earth, water, or fire by destroying the body have severed the soul's last connection with earth. Cremation then is a means where the soul may be

330

Photos Courtesy Bernice Orr

Balinese men and women prepare offering prior to cremation

released to enter heaven for judgment, thence to be returned to earth and to be reincarnated in another human body. To neglect to cremate the body or to do so improperly would deny to the soul this release and rebirth, and consign it as a restless ghost to walk the earth and plague the neglectful descendants. But it is worth emphasizing: to the Balinese, only the soul has real importance. The body is an unclean incumbrance.

These beliefs and practices are deeply rooted in Balinese antiquity. Even prior to the thirteenth century, the Balinese believed that a man's spirit fluid was immortal, and that if his conduct was good he would be reborn into a higher caste, but that if bad, into a lower, and thus he would be delayed in his progress toward final perfection through successive reincarnations, which ultimately lead even the low-caste person to become a *Brahmana* who has been ordained a priest. Such achievement makes him godlike, and terminates the cycle. Not all reincarnation, however, is immediate. Between embodiments the soul may sojourn in *swarga,* a waiting place with both celestial and terrestrial advantages to recommend it, a sort of trouble free Bali.

To prepare for the elaborate cremation which he hopes to have, every Balinese attempts to accumulate enough money

331

Exquisitely fashioned flowers are added to offerings carried to temple

or goods—the latter to be sold or pawned at his death—to defray the heavy cost. With respect to the care of the dead there
are the fees of the priests, the expense of great quantities
of holy water, of coffins, offerings, elaborate and costly burial
towers. Expenses which involve the living include those for
food and entertainment for guests and assistants at the rites.
Although a Balinese may be parsimonious to the point of
penny-pinching for his personal needs, he will without hesi-
tation sacrifice all he owns—including his crops and lands—to
pay for a great public funeral for a loved one.

When the deceased's resources or the survivors' means are inadequate to provide complete cremation ceremonies, families
sometimes wait for years, accumulating the necessary funds.
Meanwhile they are haunted by the thought that they have not
properly dealt with their dead. Under these conditions a family
will sometimes bankrupt itself by sacrificing its crops and land.
Sometimes a compromise is made with the heavy expenses
through ceremonies involving multi-family cremations. In these
cases the poorer pay but a fraction of the costs, while those
more wealthy shoulder the brunt of the heavy financial burden.

The fees of the officiating priest are based on the ceremonies
required, and these in turn depend on the type of funeral.
Three types of cremation are available. These differ in the

332

power of the symbols and formulas, the types of holy water used, the qualifications assigned to the soul by the priest, and the degree of purification. Because it is deemed advantageous for a prince to enter the afterlife with a goodly retinue, it is customary to release the souls of commoners with his in a single cremation. Care is taken, however, that each of the dead receives only the rites proper to his caste.[3]

Response to Death

When a Balinese dies, his household spreads the news far and wide to his relatives. This must be done within three days so that the ghost of the deceased will not bring bad luck when they come together, bearing gifts for the immediate family. Death makes them all unclean, with an impurity that extends to the dwelling and even to the village; and until they have undergone purification rites, the family is excluded from the temples.

To announce the death to passers-by and to guide the wandering soul, a tall bamboo pole is erected outside the gate of the home. From it hangs a bird of white tissue paper stretched over a bamboo frame, and below the bird a lamp made of white paper over a bamboo frame is suspended. Each night as long as the house shelters the body, the lamp remains lighted. The body itself is kept within a pavilion of the house.

Not all bodies are buried or cremated before putrefaction sets in. The bodies of high priests and princes are mummified and kept within their houses until a time judged suitable for their cremation is at hand. In such cases an arrangement is set up so that the body fluids are drawn from the burial receptacle into a Chinese porcelain bowl, which the women of the household afterwards bury.

Purification Rites

For the rites of purification the body is placed on a stretcher in the courtyard of the house. There, two altars, the offerings

Cremation procession
led by Baris dancers

on which are renewed daily, have been dedicated respectively
to the sun and the diety who presides over the cremation.
When the ceremonies begin, the body is naked; the hand or
occasionally a small square cloth covers the sexual parts.
Prayers follow an asperging with holy water, the hair is
groomed and anointed, the teeth are filed down, and the
body is rubbed with mixtures of rice flour and tumeric, and
vinegar, and sandalwood powder. Next the toes and thumbs
are bound together with white yarn and the hands are folded
prayerfully. To symbolize the belief that in the afterworld
the dead will be reborn with powers perfected, mirror splinters
are laid on the eyelids, steel fragments on the teeth, and a gold
ring set with a ruby is placed in the mouth. Additionally
jasmine flowers are thrust into the nostrils, and iron nails
are laid on the arms and legs. The head is now covered with
a white cloth, and to signify the new purity of the body, an
egg is rolled all over it. Then the body is clothed by being
swaddled, first with white cloth, then with a straw mat,
then with a second white cloth, and finally with an outer

334

covering of split bamboo tied with rattan. In this condition it mummifies.

Earth Burial as a Preliminary

When earth burial rather than mummification is chosen as the method of temporal disposal, or a first step before cremation, singing relatives bearing gifts and holy water carry the body to the cemetery. The burial ground, a weed overgrown field marked by decaying altars and a temple of the dead, lies on the village outskirts. A prominent landmark in it is the mournful *kepuh* tree.[4] On reaching the grave, the burial party makes offerings to mother earth, prays for the dead, and casts rent money into the shallow trench. Then the body is lowered, with a bamboo tube in its mouth to permit the escape of the soul. After the grave has been filled, a shelter of white tissue paper over a bamboo frame is erected above it, and an altar is placed beside it. For twelve days daily offerings are made, and after a lapse an offering is again made on the forty-second day. By this time, it is believed, the soul has completely left the body.

Cremation Preparations

The date for the cremation must be far enough in the future to permit preparation for the rites. Furthermore, it must be propitious, and thus the advice of the high priest is sought in settling it. A few days prior to the date determined upon, the relatives dig up the remains. Even if these prove scanty, they are arranged so as to resemble a human body, wrapped in a white cloth, and returned to the home pavilion. Here they are richly shrouded with white cloths bearing cabalistic symbols, and covered with offerings and with accessories for the ritual. Among these is a symbolic skeleton, made with white yarn to represent the nerves, and black Chinese coins, the bones. In addition, the higher castes and prosperous folk use a skeleton made of silver plates and wires, or even of gold. This effigy becomes an heirloom and is not cremated, as

335

is the yarn and coin skeleton. Among the accessories are the soul's tickets to the afterlife, written by the priest on small pieces of paper. Offerings include food for the soul and its company on the journey, and presents for the soul to make on the road.[5]

The *adegan* is the effigy around which the cremation rites revolve. If no remains can be provided because they are lost, or totally destroyed, or unavailable because death took place at a distance, it is used as a substitute. The first part of the adegan is a stylized silhouette cut from a palm leaf; the second, a realistic drawing upon sandalwood. These are bound together and deposited in a silver vase which stands upon a silver platter. Inside this platter are placed objects designed to make the soul comfortable: betel nut and sirup leaves for his chewing, and even a golden image and other objects. Lest the soul thirst, daily drinks of holy water, brought from distant mountains in new clay pots decorated with the lotus symbol, are set before it.

earers carrying cremation
iimal pursue erratic
urse to confuse spirits

.P. Photo

Many men shoulder tower
to cremation ground

P.I.P. Photo

By now the body means little and the soul is all-important. To capture any straying souls of their departed members, families bring effigies to the burial grounds to receive them. There the kneeling company strew offerings upon their family graves, excavate a little earth on each, scatter coins to distract demons who might wish to take possession of the effigies, and call upon the sleeping souls to waken. In the returning procession the effigies are borne on the heads of girls, and are thought to contain the souls they represent. At the home shrine, after being purified by much the same rites as those used to purify the body, the effigy is set near the remains, with a vigil lamp to light it.

Cremation Towers and Effigies

Meanwhile, under the direction of master craftsmen, artists have been constructing the towers on which the bodies will be paraded to the place of burning, and the animal-shaped containers in which they will be burned.

Cremation towers express the Balinese conception of the universe. A turtle with two serpents coiled about it forms the broad base of the tower as of the Balinese world. Three receding towers resting on the turtle symbolize mountains. Above them, in an open space to portray the zone between heaven and earth, the body is fastened on a protruding platform. The entire structure is topped by pagoda-like roofs which represent heaven. To reach the upper platforms a bridge is provided. The back of the tower is concealed by a great winged mask of *Bhoma,* son of the Earth. Although it is constructed only of wood and bamboo tied with rattan, and the decorations are of tinsel and paper, the tower and the runway used to reach its upper levels are so heavy that as many as seventy-five men may be required to bear it.

The animal-shaped receptacles are no less elaborate and costly, being carefully hewn from a tree trunk, which is split, hollowed, and lidded. Although caste rules determine which animal may be represented, whatever the form employed the exterior is covered with felt or velvet and richly ornamented.

338

Low-caste Balinese are allowed to use a figure that combines an elephant and a fish. For noblemen the figure of a bull is used; for a noblewoman, the figure of a cow. A king or queen is eligible to have a coffin shaped like a winged lion; a soldier, like a deer. Until the morning of the cremation day the towers and the receptacles are hidden in an out-of-the-way place under palm-leaf screens.[6]

A splendid procession forms on the eve of the cremation rites to carry the bodies to the house of the high priest. It is led by massed orchestras and dancers, followed by squads of spear-carrying, banner-waving boys. Long lines of women bear gifts for the dead. Relatives clothe themselves in their richest garments for the march, and the youngest member of each family holds its effigy. Sometimes he is carried in a litter.

The priest's blessing is made in mystic formulas emphasized with symbolic hand gestures, and accompanied with the strewing of flowers and sprinkling of holy water. After halting for a last prayer at the family temple the procession returns to the home of the deceased, where at dusk begins the reading of a shadow play to entertain the guests, and war dances are held to frighten off demons.

The Burning Biers

Sunrise of cremation day brings an upsurge of excitement. The towers and containers are brought before the houses, where the relics of the dead repose. Guests arrive, final arrangements are looked to, and a feast is served. Then a bridge is set up over the walls of each house, or a hole poked through them, the body is taken out, and the village drum—a hollowed tree trunk—begins to throb. The procession forms outside each house, but before it sets forth, custom decrees that a rough and tumble sham battle must take place over the body to confuse it by twistings and maulings so that it cannot find its way back into the house. Finally the body is brought to the tower and is lashed to the platform. At this time the procession begins to move: orchestras, spear bearers, dancers, body-bearing men and effigy-bearing women, and the shouting

339

tower bearers and their burdens. Clowning still continues. The tower dips and tips crazily. Through barrages of fireworks the bearers deliberately tramp an erratic course, seeking out rough places and mud holes. Little reverence is shown the body.

At the cemetery the wooden containers are deposited on the cremation pavilions, and lines of men take their places along the bridge or runway which has been placed against the cremation tower. When the body reaches the ground, a free-for-all follows for its possession. When this fight ends, women attendants bring the body to this unlidded receptacle and place it inside. As watching relatives crowd around, some expose the body by cutting into the shrouds with a special knife. Now the din subsides, and the high priest begins to pray. He interrupts his prayers constantly to soak the body with holy water. As he empties each pot he smashes it by hurling it to the ground. After the burial accessories are placed on the body, the lid of the container is closed, masses of combustible offerings are stuffed beneath it, and the priest offers a final prayer and kindles the fire.

Immediately the din breaks out afresh and swells to a roar of screaming voices and throbbing musical instruments. Some spectators clamber over the towers and fight to snatch the fire threatened ornaments, while others heave tinder into the flames. Men assigned to stoke the bodies poke them with irreverent jest, and scold them because they burn too slowly. Piece by piece the flaming receptacles crumble so that sometimes they spill out their charred contents. Such unconsumed remains are mounded with burning debris from the collapsing towers, and no one takes offense at the gruesome sight. Meanwhile the high priest stands in a trance on a platform, with symbolic and magical gestures reciting for the last time the cabalistic funeral office. Only the wives and daughters of the dead are withdrawn in the background, and remain quiet.

Royal Suttee

At one time the wives of princes might not have maintained so inconspicuous a role. When the Dutch first arrived in the

Malay Archipelago they found prevalent the custom of burning the princess and certain of her female slaves. After being borne to the cemetery on flower decked bamboo towers and there fed, the princess and her attendants were led to troughs where they were killed by being stabbed, the princess being the last to die. In another type of widow-sacrifice the women, apparently partly hypnotized and drugged with wine sometimes to the point of not even crying out when meeting incandescent heat, jumped into the fire and were burned alive.

Strangely enough, the decision to burn or not to burn was left to the women themselves, although they had to make the decision before the eighth day after their husband's death. The compulsions were rooted in their beliefs. To die was to make a short-cut into the beauties of the afterlife. Upon reaching the decision to be cremated, the widows were treated as already dead and deified. Covarrubias notes that only the wives of princes were so sacrificed. Brahmanas did not believe that the salvation of the souls of their wives called for such a measure, and the common people would have none

Deceased's remains put in cremation animal

P.I.P. Photo

of the practice.[7] The costliness of this widow slaughter and the Dutch prohibition of it stamped out the custom.

Concluding Ceremonies

When the fires are no more than glowing embers, any unburned sticks are raked away and little boys are allowed to hunt for the keepings. Then at sunset the embers are quenched, and any charred bones and fragments are mounded, covered with palm-leaves, and placed in an urn fashioned from a coconut shell and covered with a white cloth, for carrying to the sea. When the procession reaches the shore, the priest enters the water, and after having begged it to bear the ashes safely away, scatters them on the waves. Finally all present bathe, and make their way home in the darkness.

All this costly ceremony, however, while it has rid the soul of the unclean body, has not consecrated it as an ancestral deity. To achieve this greater end, more ceremonies are required. Following cremation twelve days are given over to the latter task. An attempt is made to communicate with the dead through a medium, to learn how successful the cremation has been. Further offerings are dedicated to the soul. Its last earthly ties are severed by the symbolism of burning a string and breaking an egg. And all things not marked for destruction which have been rendered unclean by their contact with death are ritually cleaned.

The Mukur

Finally, forty-two days after the cremation, in a ceremony almost identical with the cremation itself, but with effigies cremated instead of bodies, the *mukur* is performed. Because the soul is still thought to be travelling into the afterlife these ceremonies are designed to assist it in reaching the highest heaven assigned to its caste, and to placate the supreme judges so that they will render generous judgment. Again the procession forms. But this time the priest enters a boat and scatters on the open sea any debris or relics of the tower burning ceremony that may have drifted to land and been gathered

The "burning biers of Bali"

in mounds. Now nothing is left to return to the shore. Covarrubias comments: "The crowd returns in the blazing midday sun—hot, exhausted, and considerably poorer than before, but in high spirits and happy to have accomplished their greatest duty to those to whom they owe their existence: the consecration of their dead so that they shall continue to guide them as deities in the same way in which, as ordinary human beings, they helped and protected them. All of this has been achieved by the triple purifying action of earth, fire, and water."[8]

343

Carved tomb in Philippine Moro cemetery

Chapter 25

Philippines

In reviewing the burial and funeral customs of the Philippines it is well to keep in mind that while many generalizations may apply there are also numerous peculiarities of funerary behavior arising in the various regions and sub-regions.[1] In the following chapter emphasis will be placed on the village folkways of the Visayans, a major ethnological grouping in the Central Philippines, and on the urbanized culture of the more cosmopolitan city dwellers of Manila.

Organization of Funeral Service

The Philippines' political system revolves around the municipality, which contains a town proper in which the mayor's office is located, and villages which are scattered throughout the municipality's legally defined area. All matters relating to burial are handled by the officers of the municipality, and burial must be made in places designated by it.[2]

345

In Manila funeral establishments vary considerably in size and kinds of services available. The situation is reflected in the four classes of licenses for funeral homes. Class "A" establishments will have an operating room, at least one licensed embalmer, chapel, casket display room, an office for the arranging of funerals, and adequate transportation facilities for the number of funerals performed. A class "B" establishment will not have chapel service to offer; class "C" will be without chapel or preparation room; and class "D" will be without chapel, operating room, and transportation facilities. The larger establishments will have a number of chapels which face out to the street and which are without doors. These are rented, much like hospital beds, with the charges increasing as a family seeks to reduce the number of bodies sharing the chapel they wish to rent. Sole occupancy naturally would cost the most.[3] In many ways the larger establishments are oriented in their operations to the American pattern. Beyond the Philippines, toward Asia, they will most likely be of a British, or possibly, French character.

In the central district of the Islands it is usual for a funeral director-embalmer to live in an incorporated city and maintain offices in the smaller towns. Such an office usually consists of a casket display room, with a casket-maker's shop attached to its side or rear. The workmanship of these hand-made caskets is likely to be excellent, particularly of the very ornate models. The branch office not only sells caskets but provides a convenient point of contact for persons who seek embalming service or wish to rent a hearse or other funeral equipment from the funeral director. Although some of these establishments have chapels, the use of this facility has not become widespread.[4]

Rural Sociologist Joseph T. Howard points out that one of these small funeral chapels may constitute in some instances the "ground of compromise in a family divided over religion. Where refusal to have a Catholic service is made, or there is objection to taking the body to a Protestant chapel, it can be agreed to have services in a funeral-parlor chapel. It is also a place where the body may lie in state when the family does not wish to have it in the home."[5]

346

Embalming

Embalming was practiced in the Philippines for generations before the Spanish-American War. The Spanish had embalmers in the larger cities and the natives themselves attempted various rudimentary embalming practices, with poor to fair results. Attention to embalming was also drawn by the activities of the Quartermaster Burial Corps of the United States Army during the Spanish-American War.[6]

Nevertheless today embalming is not widely practiced in the Philippines and the dead are generally buried on the day of death or, less frequently, within the next 24 or 48 hours. The only embalming school in the Philippines is in Manila, and the government issues a license to embalmers anywhere in the archipelago to those who pass a regular board examination. American observers tend to agree that the modern day embalming practices of licensed embalmers who operate in the larger cities is exceptionally good, although there is little use of cosmetics, and very few attempts at restorative art.[7]

Care of Body

When death occurs in Manila the family usually contracts the services of a funeral director who within 24 hours, if death occurred from a non-communicable cause, or within 12 hours, if from a communicable cause, presents the attending physician's certificate to the health department. This presentation must be made before a body can be embalmed. If no physician was in attendance the certificate is completed by the health department's medical officer, after he has satisfied himself concerning the cause of death. All cases of death from suspicious or undetermined causes are referred to the Police Department, which either clears the matter or orders an autopsy. If death is from a dangerously communicable disease the City Inspectors see that the remains are properly isolated until they have been embalmed, and sealed hermetically in a casket.[8]

When the death certificate has been registered and the remains have been inspected, the burial permit is issued. Unless applica-

347

tion is properly made for an extension of time, this permit automatically expires after 48 hours.

If the deceased is an indigent or pauper, the family (along with hospital authorities if death occurred in such a facility) file with the Health Department or the Mayor's office, a pauper burial request, supported by the death certificate. If the application is found worthy, it is approved and forwarded to the City Undertaker whose undertaking establishment is under an annual contract to the city government to supply pauper funerals. He in turn assumes charge of the body and takes it directly to the South Cemetery which is operated by the City of Manila and which contains a paupers' plot. Each pauper is given a casket and an individual grave.[9]

When the body has been made ready it is casketed, and the casket is placed in the *sala* or main room of the house. Cellophane-wrapped artificial wreaths, about a foot and a half in diameter, called "coronas," are grouped around the casket. A sign is mounted on the front of each wreath stating the name of the donor. Wreaths are sent by individuals, groups, and business concerns. They are made in homes, and their manufacture is considered a skilled occupation.

Although a poor person's death may prompt no contributions of artificial coronas the few natural wreaths or crosses that friends bring may be attractively made of banana stalks, covered with leaves from trees and vines, and entwined with tropical flowers. Natural wreaths are not exhibited until just before the procession begins, because the tropical heat wilts them rapidly. It is customary to carry wreaths to the cemetery with the procession, although the family may put aside a few of the artificial ones to keep as mementos. In electrically equipped homes electric candelabra furnished by the funeral director add their steady illumination to the flickering light of wax candles.

While these arrangements are being made in the interior of the house a wide strip of black cloth is being draped across the front of it, usually below the windows. It is put there on the day of death and may hang there for an indefinite period extending up to six months.[10]

348

Luxury class funeral
home in Manila

Volume-type funeral home
in Manila; each archway
fronts viewing room

Photos Courtesy E. C. and G. R. Johnson

It is customary in the Philippines to insert as large an announcement of death in the newspaper as the family can afford.
In place of the one-column death notice universally used in
the United States a Manila paper may sometimes carry a full-
page notice telling of the death and the time and place of
burial and requesting prayers for the repose of the soul of the
departed. An announcement of this kind obviously can be purchased only by the very wealthy. The "card of thanks" after the
funeral is also generally much larger than its American counterpart.

Funeral Processions

Burial processions in the Philippines "run all the way from
pitiful, the sight of four or five persons struggling under the
weight of a casket being carried by hand under the heat of the
tropical sun, to a full-scale dress parade, complete with band and
mechanized conveyances for the mourners."[11]

349

In towns in the interior, processions may occupy the whole road; in larger places, only one half of a provincial or national highway. However, the poor who cannot rent a hearse are likely to use the shoulder, while the more prosperous may even crowd the whole highway. To walk in a funeral procession in the Philippines is to pay higher honor to the dead than to ride. As a result, even though they are able to hire a vehicle, all able bodied persons prefer to walk to the cemetery. Only the infirm ride willingly.[12]

Although well-equipped urban funeral establishments in the Philippines have available the latest American-made automobile hearses, horse-drawn hearses are still used, and are considered to put a funeral in a higher social status than their motorized counterparts are able to do. A funeral of this kind is designed to show honor to an important person who need not be rich. Thus remains of priests are borne in horse-drawn hearses, as are the remains of bearers of eminent names even though they may have fallen into straitened circumstances. For such use the horses are entirely plumed with "shako" type plumes rising from their collars. As many as six horses may be used, in accordance with the accepted viewpoint that the greater the number of horses the higher the status of the funeral. Uniformed attendants march at the heads of the horses to keep them in order.[13]

Many Philippinos prefer the old-time, battleship gray, highly ornate, carved, high box-type hearse, which was popular in America decades ago. They feel this vehicle is much more in keeping with a funeral than is the modern, streamlined limousine. As a result the well-equipped funeral director is prepared to supply either type of hearse according to his customers' wishes.[14]

When a family cannot afford to hire a hearse it falls back upon one of several methods to transport the body to the grave. In some rural areas the casket is pushed in a small cart. Another method used frequently is transportation by the bamboo bier. This framework of poles is so arranged as to provide a platform to hold the casket, projecting handles for carrying and legs so that the bearers can set down the load to rest without having the casket touch the ground. It is sometimes necessary to carry a casket for several

350

Philippine naval officers stand honor guard before Manila military funeral home

miles with this device. In such case the male members of the procession, without ado or discussion, take turns at the task.[15]

The brass band is another commonly found feature at a Philippine funeral. The presence of a brass band in a funeral procession does not mean that the person being buried was either rich, prominent, or important — only that his family could afford the hire. The band marches at the rear of the procession. A favorite funeral selection is Chopin's "Funeral March."[16]

As a substitute for a band, funeral directors have recently begun to equip their hearses with record players for mechanical music during the procession.

Female mourners in the procession are marked by their black dresses and male mourners by their black armbands, or by the small black ribbons which are pinned to their shirt pockets. The length of time they continue to wear these signs of mourning after the funeral depends on their closeness to the deceased and their feelings toward him. Mourning attire is worn for a period of one month to a year, depending on the degree of relationship between the deceased and the wearer. Conservative-minded next of kin hold rigidly to the year. The ultra-conservative sometimes wear mourning for life.[17]

On the way to the cemetery the procession usually "passes the church."[18] In most cases for Catholics this means bringing the

351

Chapel in Manila
Old Paw cemetery,
established 1820

Photo Courtesy E. C. and G. R. Johnson

remains into the church for a funeral Mass, for others it means routing the funeral procession so that, as the phrase goes, it passes a church. Some processions omit this gesture. In the Philippines, as in many Catholic countries, older cemeteries are an extension of the churchyard, and a chaplain is assigned to say prayers at the graveside at funerals. When this procedure is followed it is customary to make an offering for the service rendered. If the parish priest goes to the cemetery, there may be an additional fee for him over and above the stipend given for the church services. Protestants generally hold three services, the first in the home, the second in the chapel, and the third at the grave.[19]

Interment

The fact that some towns in the Philippines have two cemeteries is rooted in history. During the period of Spanish occupation, which ended with the Spanish-American War, the Colonial government recognized only the Catholic religion, and freethinkers, Masons, the excommunicated, and heretics were buried outside the cemetery walls in unconsecrated ground. Crypts in these places remain today. Meanwhile in 1896, even before the

Spanish War broke out, a war of independence began in the Philippines, and with the rebels supporting a constitution granting religious freedom, a Philippine Independent Church was organized, the members of which are usually called "Aglipayans" after its founder, Bishop Aglipay. A town where this sect exists will have its own cemetery and, also, a municipally owned and maintained cemetery applying no religious test.[20]

In addition to these two cemeteries in almost all first-class towns and chartered cities there is a cemetery for the Chinese who form a small but economically important minority. In places which lack a Chinese cemetery the Chinese use the municipal cemetery. While they borrow much from Philippine funeral practice these Chinese yet retain much of their own in their funerals. They do not put the same emphasis on walking as Philippinos do, and use buses, trucks, and cars in the procession. They carry banners with Chinese inscriptions. Mourners wear black shirts and pants, and continue to do so for several months after a burial. And their bands are noisier, and play Chinese music.[21]

Photos Courtesy E. C. and G. R. Johnson

Old Paw cemetery circular wall has niches for mural burials. Used as a fortress during World War II, the wall today shows scars of cannonading

Typical older cemetery has mural burial space to rent to families on yearly basis

Barong clad Philippine funeral director helps carry casket from church

Photo Courtesy E. C. and G. R. Johnson

Burial is commonly made above ground in stone or concrete crypts. A family which possesses the means to do so usually erects its own crypts. The size and ornateness of the structure is taken to indicate the family's wealth and position. Families which cannot afford a private crypt rent a place in public crypts. The minimum rental period is three years. If when the lease expires it is not renewed, the cemetery removes the bones to a large stone or concrete bin provided as a common receptacle in an obscure part of the grounds. If death was due to non-communicable disease exhumation may be made after three years; if to communicable, after ten years. To exhume, proper application must be made to the Health Department and a small fee paid.[22]

The widespread use of hollow concrete blocks for crypt building in recent years has made it possible for many middle class families to move from the crypt rental to the owner group. A few cemeteries maintain sections in which below ground burial is allowed. The reason usually given for not permitting more burial of this type in the Philippines is that in many places the land lies so low that water is likely to fill a grave excavation.[23]

Graveside services are rarer in the Philippines than in the United States, because the priest seldom accompanies the procession to the cemetery. Among the small Protestant minority graveside services, including preaching, are customary. Customary

354

also is a pattern of behavior at the grave which allows women mourners to sob heavily, scream loudly, and beat the breast vigorously. In the midst of such unrestrained grief it is to be expected that some older and sometimes even younger women faint. Therefore, someone generally is at hand who knows by experience how to revive them. Protestants tend to discourage such abandon, which usually breaks out as the body is being placed in the crypt, or lowered into the grave. Philippinos are not so observant of the tradition of not stepping on graves as Americans are, and interested spectators at a burial will clamber over crypts to get a better view of proceedings.[24]

Post-burial Wake

Following burial, a wake, generally known as the "nine nights," takes place in the home of the deceased. This name is derived from the fact that it is customary to say special prayers for the repose of the soul of the dead for nine days after the burial. The "nine nights" wake is especially popular in rural areas.[25]

Profusion of flowers in Manila funeral chapel

When the family and guests have assembled, prayers for the dead are said followed by a round of singing, storytelling, and eating. If the family can afford it, it provides a water buffalo, or calf or several pigs for the feast. On this occasion children are not required to go to bed at the usual hour and are fed sweet rice cakes, which have been baked especially for them. Generally a storyteller can be found among the participants, to tell folk tales to the children. Meanwhile the grown-ups wash down their heavier food with coconut liquor.

As spirits liven, some person with a good voice begins to improvise words to a pre-Spanish Malayan melody. Although western music is well known in the Philippines, on this occasion alone the primitive tunes are preferred. The improvisation most likely deals with the life facts of the dead person. Sometimes singers compete in a kind of contest. Persons known to have this skill are very welcome, because they add to the success of the wake. Meanwhile table games are played. The lowest classes prefer a native card game; the others, *mah-yong*. If the moon is full, outdoor games are added to the program. For Protestants the observances are much the same, except that devotional messages by the pastor or layman take the place of the Catholic prayers for the dead.[26] Although the wake has a festive air, the parents and brothers and sisters, or children of the dead remain in the privacy of their bedrooms in attitudes of decent mourning. On the ninth day after the burial the closest relatives of the deceased have Mass said in the parish church, and afterwards in the home serve food to the guests.[27]

On All Saints' Day, November 1st, relatives bring gifts of flowers to the cemetery, which from the decorations and the candles takes on a jubilant air. Again the relatives conduct a vigil or wake, this time in the cemetery, which is crowded with people, many of whom remain throughout the night.[28]

Chapter 26

Tiwi of North Australia

About thirty miles due north of Darwin, Australia, lie two islands, Melville and Bathurst, containing together approximately 1,000 square miles and inhabited by a single tribe of aboriginal Australians, the *Tiwi*. Their funeral customs have been intensively studied by anthropologist Dr. Jane Goodale.[1]

The establishment of a mission on Bathurst Island in 1911 and a government settlement on Melville, just prior to the second world war, drew the Tiwi into two communities from their previously scattered and independent groups. Today the complete Tiwi funeral ceremonies are carried out only at the government settlement, while at the mission and among a small Tiwi group, living and working in Darwin, more simplified ceremonies are held for deceased Tiwi who are not converted to Christianity.

Life After Death

The pattern of life after death was set in the mythological past when a Tiwian hero, Purakapali, returned one day to his camp after a hunt to find his infant son dead, because his wife and the Moon had left him unattended while they made love in the bush. Tjapara, the moon, tried to placate the enraged father by promising that if the dead son were given to him, he would return with him alive in three days. But Purakapali would not listen, and killed the moon in a mighty battle. He then walked backwards with his son into the sea, proclaiming that, "As my son has died and will never return, so shall all men after me."

When a Tiwi stops breathing, he has ceased to live; and although his spirit rises from his body, it does not stray very far. This spirit, *mobuditi,* can never return to the world of the living, but lingers in the general area in which its body was buried. Usually there are other mobuditi about, and in swarms they hunt for food, and are the uninvited spectators at every important event which occurs among the living inhabitants. Often they perform rituals similar to those performed by the living. The living can do little to influence the behavior of a mobuditi, while a mobuditi may help the living more often he will injure them. The dead person may have borne as many as 20 names. All of these are tabooed immediately upon death, the mention of any one of them may attract the mobuditi. People who claim to have seen mobuditi describe them as being like glass, or being black by night and white by day. Those professing to have seen them rarely are able to identify them by name.

The Burial

Burial takes place within twenty-four hours after death. When the breath ceases the body is covered with a piece of cloth. In the past it was covered with paper-bark. Close relatives, their bodies daubed with ochres, charcoal or dirt, sit nearby and wail. Shortly, one of the relatives on the father's side

Funeral ceremony leader describes roles to be enacted dancers in Tiwi dance for the de

Photo Courtesy Jane C. Goodale

of the family—father, son or brother—will begin to sing, composing new words to a traditional funeral chant. Other men beat time, their hands slapping against their buttocks or thighs, and either the singer or another man dances to the beat. There are many dance styles—the one used most frequently at this stage of the burial is the imitative style where the dancer depicts the actions of certain animals. A father teaches these dances to his children. In performing them the dancers alternate. A boy may dance a solo and then dance for a moment with his sister. When these two retire, another couple takes their place and repeats their performance. The women meanwhile, as a group, perform a shuffling dance while the men, as a group, sing and clap hands. The widow or widows—the Tiwi are polygamists—or the widower dances a distinctive, slow dance and sings a special wailing chant. This performance is quite apart from the funeral dancing, although it is generally simultaneous with it.

Soon the *yempi*, the Tiwi equivalent of undertakers, are chosen by the relatives from community members who are most distantly related to the deceased. These men now carry the body to the area selected for the grave, usually some distance from the camp. Everyone follows the yempi, but the funeral procession itself is without ceremony. The yempi proceed to dig the grave and clear the ground of obstructions for the dancing which will follow. After laying long sticks on the bottom of the grave the yempi lower the body until it rests on the sticks. Next they lay shorter sticks cross-wise over the body, and then leafy branches. Finally, they fill the grave with earth and raise a low mound above it.

Once the actual burial is completed, more formalized dancing begins. The men alternately sing and dance, while the women either join their husbands or brothers in the imitative dances, or dance as a chorus. At this time the widower sings a special song in which he describes his dead wife and their marital life. Boys, eight years and up, who have mastered their inherited dance step perform at the graveside, and little girls, two years and up, are usually found in the female chorus line.

360

Ritual expressions of grief are most apparent at the graveside, and are exhibited by all but young children. In addition to wailing loudly, the mourners make a great show of self-mutilation. They cut their heads and scalps with a knife; they beat their bodies with sticks and clubs; they indulge in a variety of such unformalized acts as crawling around and sometimes into the grave, jumping into the air and falling flat, or eating grave dirt.

The dancing at the burial ceremony may last for an hour or two. When it concludes, young children and elderly people are carried or helped over the burial mound, and the new mobuditi is especially asked to leave these people alone in the coming months. Fires are lighted around the dance area, and one day's supply of food and water is left on the grave. In this way, it is hoped the spirit will be restrained from returning to the camp for at least a night.

The grave is now deserted and the area around it for as much as a mile in all directions is tabooed for any but the

Grave is filled by *yempi*, Tiwi funeral functionaries

yempi and other distant relatives until the holding of the final and most important mortuary ritual. This will take place in three to six months time.

Taboos

From the moment of death until the final moments of the last regular ritual certain of the relatives of the deceased are under a number of strict taboos. They must not touch water; thus they may not bathe, and a container of water must be raised to their lips by some friend or relative whenever they wish to drink. They must not touch the food they consume; and therefore must be fed by others. Usually they do not hunt or gather any food during this time, but if they should, they must give the food away, but not to children because for them it is considered dangerous to eat food which the tabooed have touched. Every day they paint their body and hair with red or yellow ochre and with white clay or charcoal. They encase their upper and lower arms in woven pandanus rings which they do not remove until the end of the ceremony.

Children and very elderly people are exempt from these restrictions, but except for these all members of the immediate family and, of course, the wife (or wives) or husband must put on the paint and the pandanus rings, and observe the taboos.

Preparation for the Final Ritual

While the eldest male relative of the deceased is assigned the nominal charge of the final rites, in practice the wife (or wives) or the husband and all close paternal or maternal relatives are given a voice in the arrangements. A date is set, usually three to six months away. Inasmuch as travel is difficult during the rainy season these rituals are usually held during the dry season. A messenger, bearing the news of the death and date for the final rites, is sent to all localities where relatives of the deceased reside.

A month or so before the announced date, members of the deceased's community appoint pole-cutters from among the eligible yempi. The number appointed and the number of poles they are instructed to prepare depend on the numerical strength of the deceased's kin-folk who must pay for them, and on the age and prestige of the deceased. Today, at least, there is no discernible difference in the number of poles provided for a man's or a woman's grave.

Funeral poles are a major artistic outlet for the Tiwi. Cut from blood-wood trees they may measure up to twenty feet in height and three feet in diameter. Today, using steel axes, the yempi carve and hollow out the poles in elaborate geometric shapes, each man designing his own pole and rarely producing two that are similar—even over a period of several funerals. The poles are smoked over a fire to blacken the background and rubbed with turtle egg or juice from orchid roots as a base for the ochre paint. Red and yellow ochre, charcoal, and white clay are applied to the poles with twig brushes in an infinite variety of geometric patterns and color combinations. It is important to note that pole-cutting is not a profession but a social duty.

Pole cutters carve and paint poles for final dance at grave

All Tiwi paint bodies for
final mortuary ritual

Photo Courtesy Jane C. Goodale

During the preparation of the poles, the yempi are fed by
the relatives of the deceased, and each evening the entire
community gathers for an *ilanea,* a song and dance ritual
similar in many respects to the ritual performed at the graveside. Beside certain inherited dance forms, at this time and
also later during the final ritual, dances are performed which
are traditional to certain kin groups in relation to the deceased. For example, brothers and sisters dance as if something were wrong with one of their legs, and mothers dance
holding their breasts. At this time or later during the final
ritual new songs may be composed and new dance steps may
be worked out for presentation. Many of these are story-telling
songs and are accompanied by interpretive dancing by groups
of men and/or women. Ilanea are also held each evening
by groups on their way to the final ritual. After arriving at

364

their destination, while waiting for all preparations to be completed, they repeat the performances. Although each independent community formerly held separate ilanea and as a group kept apart at the final ritual, individual Tiwi shifted from one group to another. Behind the individual shifting from group to group lay the fact that one is obligated to dance at least once with all of one's brothers and sisters, and this classification covers many who do not share the same parents and who may be widely scattered throughout the island. Today two groups keep apart; one crowd of the visitors; the other crowd of the local people.

The Final Mortuary Ritual

When the yempi announce that they have completed the poles and have set them up in rows in the prepared dance grounds, one for each group, the final ritual begins.

Everyone, including children, must now paint their bodies in extremely elaborate and individualistic designs. Feather beards, cockatoo feather headdresses, braided human hair belts, pandanus arm rings with attached feathers and feather pom-poms worn suspended from the neck complete the personal adornment. Nearly an entire day is needed to make this personal preparation.

The two groups march separately through the bush toward the grave, each led by the closest paternal relative of the deceased within the group. Near the grave, another very short ilanea is held, after which the groups one after another rush upon the grave itself, running through the lines of poles and throwing themselves on the bushes with which the yempi have covered the mound. After a period of slashing their scalps with knives, beating their bodies with clubs, and other ritual expressions of grief, each group retires to its own ground and poles, to dance well into the evening. During the night most of the crowd retire to their family fires to sleep, and the widow (or widows) or widower and several of the yempi take turns in singing widowers' songs to the deceased.

The following morning the formal dances begin again, and

Photo Courtesy Jane C. Goodale

Yempi enter dance area; items on pole are payment for their labors

about mid-morning the ritualized payment to the yempi for their services takes place. Each yempi is given payment for the poles he has cut—the amount varying according to the size of the pole. Payment consists today of western goods. Although every relative contributes to the cost of the funeral, the fact that an ordinary grave is decorated with 10 to 15 poles makes a heavy drain on the family's resources. In the old days, payment consisted of items of native manufacture, ochres and food. Now payments are made in money. If the yempi are satisfied they demonstrate their satisfaction with a dance, and then move their poles to the grave and set them up encircling the mound. A yempi who is not satisfied does not move his pole from the dance ground until adjustment is made. It is not always made. With the poles in place, the relatives who have been under the taboos may now wash the accumulation of paint off their bodies and remove their arm-bands. When they place them on the grave the taboo is lifted.

Again each group rushes upon the grave, and for the final time expresses its grief. Several groups may dance around the ring of poles. Then, as each individual chooses, he leaves the grave. The widow (or widows) or widower is usually the last to leave.

The grave area is now no longer tabooed. The poles are left to the mercy of time and weather, and unless some relative has been absent from the final ritual, no further ceremony is held there. When a relative is unable to attend the final ritual he must at his earliest convenience, hold a "memorial"

Dancer circles massed poles in finale of dance ceremony

service at the grave. During this service a pole purchased by him is added to those already in place.

Social Function of Funerals

Funeral ceremonies are the most important ritual in Tiwi life and bring families and tribes together more than any other event. During these ceremonies old social contacts are renewed and new contacts made. Through song and conversation, news is distributed, old tales are retold, and myths are kept alive. In the composition of original songs, the development of new dance steps, and the creation of abstract sculpture and painting to express their creative talents, those who give evidence of much ability receive high praise. Thus the funeral ceremonies represent an important opportunity for a Tiwi to gain prestige as an artist. At the same time they enable him to participate as a member of the tribe in a highly regarded act of public service.

Chapter 27

Australia

Like their English cousins Australians for the most part take a common sense attitude toward death, as in its presence there is no violent outward show of grief, and very little observance of public mourning. This attitude is reflected in their funeral customs and procedures which on the whole involve little ceremony apart from the usual church or lodge service.[1]

Funeral practices differ but little in the six states forming the Commonwealth of Australia. When death occurs in a private home the relatives contact the funeral director. In most cases the remains are brought to the mortuary. The funeral director assumes the responsibility of securing a medical certificate of death which must be filed before he can obtain a burial certificate. If the death occurred from natural causes and there was a physician in attendance, no difficulty is encountered in securing the medical certificate. If these circumstances do not prevail, the death becomes a matter for investigation by the coroner, who will have to issue the medical

Funeral procession for
five Australian
children, war casualties

P.I.P. Photo

certificate of death. When he has obtained the certificate the funeral director makes arrangements for the time of service, the opening of the grave or the use of the crematorium, the insertion of death notices in the newspapers, and the registration of the death at the proper government office. While funeral arrangements are generally made in the home, the family may prefer to make them in the funeral director's office.

When death occurs in a public hospital it is seldom that the remains will be released in less than eight hours. In most cases an autopsy is performed in the hospital mortuary. In a case requiring the service of the coroner, remains may be held for 24 hours or more.

For all but Catholic funerals—these normally take place in church—Australian funerals are held in funeral homes or parlors, although some use of the family home may still be found. In western Australia at least 90 per cent of the funerals originate in a funeral home.

The Australian funeral home is in a transitional state, moving in the direction of the American-type funeral establishment. The preparation facility generally is not so well designed or equipped as its American counterpart, and most funeral homes do not carry a stock of caskets nor do they have display rooms. Instead they maintain an office in which families are

370

quoted prices for goods and services. Because of increasing traffic, business establishments including funeral homes are being required by municipal authorities to establish off-street parking.

Nowhere in Australia today is there a state registration or licensing requirement for a funeral director or embalmer. However, a permit must be obtained from the Town and Country Planning Authority for specific buildings to be used by a funeral director or embalmer. These authorities therefore have the power to restrict the establishing of funeral homes and businesses and to require them to meet certain standards. In all urban areas funeral directing is a full-time operation. The annual case load varies from 30 or 40 to as high as 3,500 cases. Because there are fewer funeral establishments in proportion to the population than in England the average number of cases per funeral establishment in Australia is higher. In smaller towns funeral directing may be joined with the operation of a hardware store, a building trade, or a service station.

The Australian Funeral Directors Association is the national organization. In addition there are state organizations. There are few co-operative funeral homes in Australia.

It is customary in Australia to hold funeral services within 48 hours of death, so that the remains of a person who dies in the morning are buried or cremated the next day. This brief interval between death and burial is one of the principal reasons why embalming is not widely employed in Australia. A permit is needed to remove the remains from the place of

P.I.P. Photo

Solemn moment in church funeral, New South Wales

Typical Australian triple-lid coffin

Australian pall-bearers carry coffin on shoulders, following British custom

Photos Courtesy John Allison

death, and when a delay occurs in obtaining it, the funeral director may have time only to compose the features before the services begin. Although in most of the metropolitan areas of Australia capable embalmers can be found, only four or five funeral directing establishments are equipped to embalm. The remaining Australian funeral directors rely chiefly on refrigeration.

There is no state or Commonwealth law requiring embalming. Temporary embalming or preservation is being increasingly employed, particularly during the summer months. Complete embalming is carried out when the remains are to be shipped from one state to another or overseas, or when it is requested by the family.

It is not customary in Australia to dress the body in street clothing. Instead a "breasting" or shroud is used. In western Australia night attire or silk gowns are also employed.

The Australian coffin is made of wood. In perhaps 99 per cent of all Australian burials the body-shaped, or so-called "anthropoid," coffin is used. However, the American-type

372

casket is used in a minority of Australian funerals. The usual Australian coffin allows only the face of the dead to be seen. The liner comes up over the chest. In Victoria the coffin is borne on the shoulders of the pallbearers, and the handles therefore have only an ornamental use. In other states they are used in lifting, and must then be more firmly attached.

In most cases the funeral director manufacturers his own coffins. The staff of carpenters, polishers, and trimmers he employs for this operation creates a labor pool upon which he can draw for servicing funerals during busy periods.

Flowers form an important element in an Australian funeral. Floral tributes are always in the form of a wreath or sheath, and are rarely delivered to the family or funeral home more than an hour before the time appointed for the funeral. Australian hearses are likely to have flower racks on the top, and floral tributes are loaded there. Some hearses have additional spikes or hooks fastened along the sides to allow wreaths and bouquets to be attached. The typical Australian hearse is a locally produced, individually tailored hybrid. The funeral director needing a new hearse purchases a motorized chassis from a car dealer, and then arranges with an automotive engineer to extend the chassis, and finally with a body builder to complete the hearse body. From four to six months are required for the work. Australian hearses closely resemble American hearses.

Although the pattern of Australian cemetery ownership varies from state to state, the most common types are semi-government and municipal trust ownership. There are no cemeteries in Australia owned or operated by mortuaries. While there are a few lawn-type cemeteries in operation, the headstone and "kerbing" cemetery remains the general pattern.

Concrete or metal grave vaults, such as are found in the United States, are not used in Australia, and only rarely is a bricked grave or a private mausoleum to be found. Australia has no public mausoleums and few garden crypts. With few exceptions an eight by four foot grave is initially sunk. A grave of this size will take two or three burials.

Australian funeral home,
city type

Photo Courtesy W. H. Robinson

In western Australia 50 per cent of all dispositions are by cremation. Whether the body is interred or cremated the family follows the remains, in the one case to the cemetery, in the other to the chapel of the crematory. At Church of England burials in Australia it is customary only for the male members of the family to attend. Religious services are conducted according to the belief of the deceased at the crematorium or the graveside. Special Masonic services are conducted at the graveside. At the graveside services of members of the armed forces or war veterans the coffin is draped either with the Union Jack or with the blue flag of Australia. In Australia as elsewhere the Roman Catholic Church requires that its mem-

Funeral procession for
late Premier of
New South Wales;
music by police band

P.I.P. Photo

bers be interred rather than cremated. Orthodox Jews have the same regulation. However, liberal Jewish congregations allow cremation. The Jewish fraternity conduct and arrange their own burials. The funeral wake is not commonly found in Australia, except occasionally among families of Irish descent.

Certain major changes are to be noted in the funeral customs and practices in Australia today as compared to those of 50 years ago. The most important is the increase in the number of funeral homes and their much greater use. In western Australia approximately 90 per cent of all funerals are conducted from the parlors of funeral directors. The conservative formality and the traditional drabness of funeral appurtenances are disappearing. This is evidenced in a variety of ways: in the garb of the mourners and principals—the almost complete elimination of the frock coat and top hat and the use of white or colored dresses or coats by the women as opposed to the traditional black; the use of various hues instead of the traditional white flowers in funeral bouquets; and the increase in the number of private funerals attended only by the families and close relatives of the deceased.

Last Rites for an Australian Bushman

According to Australian Bushmen, some of the most primitive of all aborigines, nobody dies a natural death. Rather, death must be caused by an unnatural influence, some form of human magic.

The aborigine reasons further: since the spirit of the dead one is resentful of losing its body, it hovers around the vicinity, planning all sorts of mischief. The only way to placate the spirit is to mourn for it properly, or to avenge it. Since avenging it might get its friends in trouble with the white police, an elaborate ritual of mourning will usually suffice to rid the community of the spirit's presence. The following picture sequence shows the disposal of a dead warrior's bones in a hollow pole-coffin at Goulburn Island in the far north of Australia.

Bearing bones of dead warrior, tribesmen dance toward totemic pole-coffin

P.I.P. Photo

The bones, bleached
in the hot sun for several
months, are carefully
cleaned and painted
before being placed in
the hollow coffin

P.I.P. Photo

Gift of spears tied to
pole-coffin is for visiting
tribesmen who conduct
the ceremony. Kingfisher
totem symbols have
now been painted along
the pole, showing totemic
group of dead warrior

P.I.P. Photo

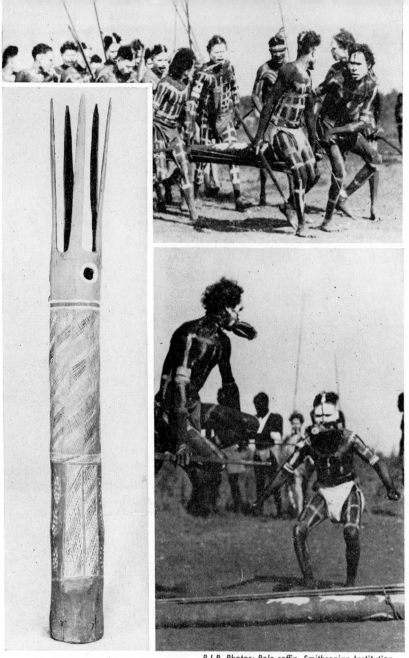

P.I.P. Photos; Pole-coffin, Smithsonian Institution

Upper: Bushman funeral procession. Tribesmen carry the pole-coffin, bones within, singing as they go to the burial ground. *Right:* Dance over the bones on the ritual ground. Mourners really suffer, and use biting-bags to soothe their emotions. Bags contain magic charms in whose potency wearers have implicit belief. *Left:* Another example of pole-coffin shows more finely detailed totemic designs

Pair of strenuously stomp-
ing mourners have been
spray-painted with paste
mixture of flour and water

Mourners sing
throughout as pole-
coffin is planted
upright in the ground

Covered with white clay and dressed in mourning regalia the father
of the dead man holds the sheaf of spears as ceremony concludes

380

Chapter 28

New Zealand

New Zealand has a population of some 2,000,000 people, including about 125,000 Maoris who are the native group. Its trade is largely confined to countries of the British Commonwealth, of which it is a self-governing member. Therefore, its funeral practices are much the same as those of other English-speaking countries.[1] G. W. Clark, editor of the *New Zealand Funeral Directors' Journal*, writes that: "New Zealand religious groups are the same as those of Great Britain, the Anglican, Roman Catholic, Jewish and non-conformist sections of the community each having their particular service, but not, I believe, differing to any degree from those of Western European countries. There is no category, in my opinion, that would come under that of 'special religious group.' The Maori people of our country belong to the above religious groups and conform to the traditional European way of burial."[2]

A. H. Marker, New Zealand funeral director, comments on his countrymen's attitude toward death: "As far as the family

381

is concerned, they appear to accept death with customary reserve, except in the case of sudden deaths, or the death of a younger person, when they take it to heart more." In most cases the average person attends a funeral as a mark of respect, and others as a duty. The meaning of death, or the attitude toward death is, as elsewhere, mainly governed by the religious or other beliefs of the individuals concerned. There is no particular "New Zealand" church or religion, and the teachings of the established churches of the old and new world are generally accepted. The average man accepts death as some thing that is inevitable, and gets on with the business of living out his life meanwhile.[3]

As in other newly settled countries with a scattered population, organized funeral services grew slowly. In the beginning anyone—carpenter or otherwise—with tools and skills to make a casket would be likely to be called upon to do so, and might also assist in other funeral arrangements. Even today in rural areas the carpenter is likely to include undertaking among his tasks. In the larger cities, on the other hand, funeral directing has become a full-time occupation which is gradually striving to grow in professionality. The battle at times has been uphill. As Marker, points out: "As a whole the people in this country are not funeral-minded as in your country."[4]

Funeral Service Operations

Funeral directing in New Zealand is practiced by some 150 firms operating within the framework of the Burial, Health and Cremation Regulations of the Dominion. Each of these firms is subject to annual inspection by the Health Department, and is licensed to operate for a twelve-month period. The funeral directors of New Zealand have their own professional organization, the New Zealand Federation of Funeral Directors Inc., which has its headquarters in Wellington. This national body serves as parent organization for a Provincial Funeral Directors' Association in each province.[5] While New Zealand funeral directors operate in many respects similar to

382

Modern Wellington crematory chapel in final stages of construction

their American counterparts their funeral homes are not so
commodious or well-equipped as American funeral homes are,
nor is their other equipment of the same quality. At the same
time, while the establishments are making a constant effort
to improve their goods and services, their clientele is less demanding.[6]

Care of the Dead

When death occurs in a home—and this is exceptional,
because in New Zealand today most deaths occur in public or
private hospitals—the custom practiced is to first call the
doctor who has been in attendance, and then the funeral director. While the latter call may be made any time during
the day and night, if the funeral director receives it between
8 A.M. and 10 P.M. he immediately visits the family or as soon
thereafter as possible. His first concern is to look to the registration of the death. After this he makes arrangements for the
funeral. Prior to his arrival a nurse, engaged by the family has
laid out the body. The funeral director has the responsibility
of arranging for the time and place of the funeral, the registration of the death, the collection of the death certificates, the
insertion of death announcements in newspapers, the provision
of transport, and the efficient and dignified conduct of the

383

Funeral service,
Wellington chapel

A fully draped casket
in the Cathedral Church
of St. Paul, Wellington

Photos Courtesy G. W. Clark

funeral. The family is responsible for securing the services of pallbearers—either four or six. Before announcements of the death are made or death notices are inserted in newspapers the clergyman is consulted.[7]

Meanwhile, when a person dies in a home, the family usually closes the blinds or draws the window drapes, and to the extent to which it is able goes quietly and respectably about its normal business. Mourning clothing is limited to black ties worn by the men.[8]

Embalming

The New Zealand funeral director is required by law to register with the Registrar of Deaths the fact of death, together

384

with a death certificate signed by a physician and a burial certificate signed by himself and the officiating minister. Arterial embalming is less frequently practiced than in the United States. Clark notes that except in special cases, the purpose of embalming "is more of a temporary nature." It is mandatory, of course, for bodies which are transported. Although New Zealand funeral directors are able to obtain an embalming course at a school established by the Federation of Funeral Directors, at most a few firms have qualified embalmers on their staffs.[9]

Another reason for the infrequency of embalming in New Zealand is the shortness of time elapsing between death and disposition. Normally a funeral follows death after a lapse of thirty-six to forty-eight hours. The custom is a hold-over from early pioneering days when prompt burial was a necessity and is still adhered to.[10]

Caskets

Metallic caskets are rarely used in New Zealand. "Wooden, casket-shaped (rectangular) containers are used almost without exception," Clark reports. "The timber used is very largely New Zealand grown *Rimu* or *Tawa*. Six burial handles are provided on the casket, and a breast plate carrying the name of the deceased. The exterior of the casket is stained and lacquered, then brought to a highly polished finish."[11] The casket most commonly used is made of polished New Zealand red-pine, with what New Zealand funeral directors call "simple, dignified casket linings, and silver plated handles."[12] The interior of the casket is waterproofed and lined with calico or swan's down. Pillows and side drapes of varying types of material, design and color are used. The side drapes completely cover the body from chest to feet.[13] Most New Zealand funeral directors manufacture their own caskets, and if there is a call for it, may produce an oblong American-type casket.[14] Today the majority of New Zealand funeral directors operate their own funeral chapels. They have borrowed this type of establishment from American practice.

Funerals and Burial

As in the United States about 75 per cent of all funerals leave for the place of burial or cremation from a funeral director's chapel or from a church. In the case of a funeral of a Roman Catholic the body is usually taken to the church the night before burial for the saying of the Rosary. The Requiem Mass is celebrated the next morning, at the present time usually at 9:00 A.M.[15]

New Zealand funeral transport is very similar to that used in America: hearses, mourners' cars, service cars. However, the rolling stock is likely to be kept in service for a longer period than is generally the case in this country. A special car for the officiating clergyman is included in the cortege.[16] New Zealand funeral establishments supply no ambulance service. This facility is municipally provided.

It is the usual custom in New Zealand for local bodies, that is City or County Councils, to own and operate all cemeteries and crematoria, except church burial grounds. Cemetery plots are purchased and a legal deed of ownership, giving title in perpetuity, is issued by the administering local body. Church burial grounds are rapidly becoming closed cemeteries.[17] Although it was long customary to cover burial plots in New Zealand with monuments surrounded by stone or concrete slabs, in recent years the lawn cemetery, with markers set flush to the sod, has become the almost universal development. Double burial—one on top of the other—is permitted in New Zealand.[18]

Paid pallbearers, as in the United States, are not part of the New Zealand funeral tradition. Close friends and relatives of the deceased consider it an honor to be asked to serve in that capacity. The body is lowered into the grave by a mechanical device. New Zealand does not follow the American custom of using an outer grave vault. When graveside services have been concluded, the mourners leave, and cemetery operatives fill the grave.

In spite of the fact that the first crematorium in New Zealand, located in Wellington, was built only a half century ago, cremation as a form of disposal is increasing particularly in the city areas.[19] Cremation services now account for approximately 50 per cent of all Protestant funerals in New Zealand. Nine crematoria, situated in the main cities and the larger provincial towns, presently operate in New Zealand. Eight of these are owned and operated by City or County Councils. New Zealand has its cremation society, the Cremation Society of Canterbury, with headquarters in the City of Christ Church.[20] Generally when a funeral leaves a chapel for the crematorium the only service held is at this facility.

Cremated remains are disposed of in several ways. Sometimes they are buried in the usual cemetery plot, or in a small ashes plot which can be purchased at any cemetery. At other times they are deposited in an ashes niche, purchased at a columbarium. The niche is marked with a bronze or marble plate inscribed with name, age, and date of death of the deceased. The more general practice, however, is to have the ashes scattered, usually by the sexton of the cemetery or crematorium.[21]

The Maori

An aborigine group in New Zealand, the *Maori*, deserve brief mention. The 125,000 members, about six per cent of the total populace, are of Polynesian stock. New Zealand law grants them full equality, and in some areas they preserve virtually intact many of their traditional customs. This is less true for their funeral customs which historically were so bizarre, even bloodthirsty—involving human sacrifice and cannibalism—that they could not be tolerated by the English who came to dominate the Maori tribes.

Contact with the white man's ways tends to modify these traditional beliefs and practices, and in the main the Maori have adopted European burial customs. Thus when a Maori dies in one of the native villages it is likely that his relatives will hurry to a nearby white town to purchase a shoulder casket. The local funeral director sees no more of them. They manage their own funeral and burial. Even today they bury their dead with many of their belongings, placing some of them in the grave, and some in the casket. To make room for such gifts they frequently purchase oversize caskets and dig oversize graves.[22] However, in their burials the Maori must conform to the regulations set down by the government authority, the New Zealand Health Department.

If a Maori dies in a hospital or institution, relatives secure the services of a white funeral director to bring the body to the native village. When the pick-up wagon arrives there, the women are waiting for it. They have decorated themselves with ferns, and are seated on the ground. After prolonged wailing, which is torrid and rather unmelodious, relatives bury the dead. Although many of the Maoris have become Christians the graveside services are always in their native tongue. Sometimes a white clergyman officiates, and sometimes a sermon in English is part of the ceremony. Most Maoris understand English and many speak it very well.[23]

Burial is followed—or may be preceded—by a great feast called a *tangi*. To prepare for it the Maoris gather food and drink for weeks. Anybody who so desires may attend the feast, and some participants come many miles to partake of it. Roast wild pigs, laid on the ground to be plucked at by the eaters are a favorite dish. Because people enjoy themselves at a tangi the Maori have been known to hold the casket and remains unburied during a feast, and later to transport them elsewhere, to hold a second feast.[24]

388

Oceania, *Passim*

Images of idols contain
skeletons of former New
Hebrides chiefs held
together with baked clay

New Guinea platform
burial

Melanesian native
burial ground

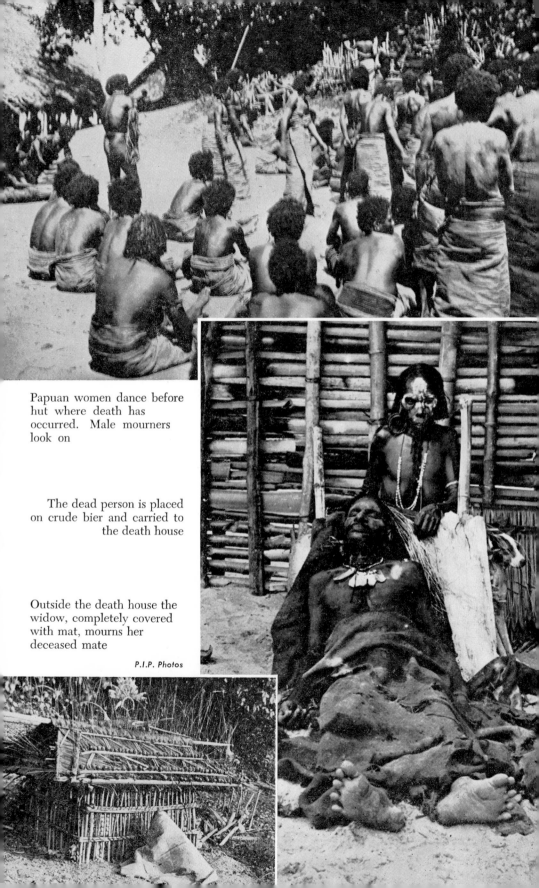

Papuan women dance before hut where death has occurred. Male mourners look on

The dead person is placed on crude bier and carried to the death house

Outside the death house the widow, completely covered with mat, mourns her deceased mate

P.I.P. Photos

Natives of Sumatra take mummified remains out for yearly airing in this hearse

Carved and painted boards
for ceremonies in honor
of the dead, New Ireland

Samosir Island burial vaults and skull urns

Funeral Customs The World Over

Part Five

"The Funeral of Stef Halacek,"
oil painting by Ivan Generalic

Europe

The dominance of Christian belief . . .
a heavy overlay of folk and regional
death customs . . . municipally operated, competing with private enterprise funeral services . . . the involvement of co-operatives . . . laying out
the dead in home and hospital . . .
embalming a rarity, except in Great
Britain . . . cemetery chapels and
magnificent, crowded cemeteries . . .
earth, crypt, mausoleum burial . . .
cremation.

Sledge funeral in northern Sweden

Chapter 29

Sweden

Organization of Funeral Service

In 1959 there were 480 funeral establishments, private and co-operative, in Sweden, and about 70,000 deaths, for an average of 146 deaths per establishment. On an average each establishment served about 15,000 people. In addition to the Association of Swedish Undertakers, Sweden has the Swedish Burial Association and the Swedish Cremation Association. Not including the personnel of the Cemetery Department, a government agency, from 800 to 900 persons are employed in funeral service in Stockholm alone.[1] Strict regulations cover procedures between death and disposal in Sweden.

In Stockholm, which may be taken as a rough index of the country, about 25 per cent of funerals today are provided by burial co-operatives, with the remainder divided among 36 private funeral establishments. The operators and owners of these have formed their own association, *Sveriges Begravning-*

sen treprenorers Forbund (The Association of Swedish Undertakers), in competition with the co-operatives to promote private enterprise.[2]

The establishment of a private funeral director in Stockholm usually consists of a small office, many times without a casket display room. In such event caskets are selected from catalogues ordered from one of the city's two large casket wholesalers and delivered from the warehouse directly to the place where the body lies. This practice of ordering from the catalogue is rather widespread in Sweden.[3] A larger private establishment may add goods and services. Thus one large Stockholm establishment, housed in a store front building, with a vase of flowers and a cremation urn in the windows to identify the nature of its business, maintains a large office staff working behind a battery of arrangements desks. A nearby building houses its casket display room. Available for selection are baroque-styled caskets, and state caskets made of oak, as well as a line of ordinary caskets. A special sewing department in the same building produces shrouds for men and women.[4]

Care of the Dead

Whether a private undertaker or the co-operative makes the arrangements, the procedures are complicated by a variety of forms which must be filled out before burial is allowed. In the words of one observer:

> It takes a well-trained staff to handle all the paperwork necessary before a Swedish burial may take place. In all about 30 forms are needed. A death certificate from the doctor has to be registered in the census office, and a permit for burial is then delivered, the first two forms to be obtained. A doctor's certificate is necessary for cremation, and it has to be countersigned by the police. The Township Real Estate Department has to deliver a special permit for burial in private grounds, and this is favored outside the city limits, usually on one of the islands in the Stockholm Archipelago in the case of the Swedish capitol. Only wealthy citizens request such permits.[5]

Free burial ground is provided if interment takes place in

the parish in which the deceased is registered. The Lutheran Church, which is the state church of Sweden, keeps the registry books. If a family wishes to bury its dead elsewhere it may do so at its own expense. In addition to securing the necessary permit the family must purchase a cemetery lot in a cemetery not owned by the parish.

The body is casketed as soon as possible after death, and removed from the home. Embalming is provided if the family so desires, although the practice, called "balsamering" is restricted at present to medical practitioners.[6]

Wooden caskets are commonly used in Sweden. The cheapest and most popular of these is made of pine, and painted to imitate oak, and as a separate item is used in both burials and cremations. The varnished beech model, costing about ten times as much, is the most expensive of the standard models.[7]

Although an occasional civil funeral service may be found, a clergyman officiates at most Swedish funerals. The choice in this matter is not limited to the local minister. Notice of the death must be given. Generally this is made by inserting a paid announcement in a daily newspaper. Sometimes the statement is added that "no other announcement will be

Formal mourning dress worn by nobility of Scandinavia at funeral of Prince Charles of Sweden. *Right,* Typical mourning dress: sombre clothing, veils and often a bouquet of flowers

P.I.P. Photos

399

made." For more formal announcement, cards are sent to friends, inviting them to be present at the cemetery or crematorium; and the closest among them, to lunch or dinner following the ceremony. For a small fee the funeral director mails out these cards. He also inserts the death notice in the local paper. When privacy is desired the notice is withheld until after the funeral. However, private funerals are rare in Sweden.[8]

If the family owns a cemetery lot it may choose to hold a religious service in a church prior to bearing the body to the cemetery. When disposal is by cremation the common practice is first to invite the mourners to the home of the deceased. There the minister gives a brief talk in which he calls the dead person to mind and urges his listeners to bear their grief with fortitude. When he concludes, a portion of consommé and a glass of sherry are customarily served. After this light lunch the funeral procession is organized, and the mourners in cars proceed to the crematorium. Each car is marked with a purple flag to warn motorists not to break into the cortege. This custom has been maintained for years by the two major funeral car renting agencies in Stockholm. The body is transported to the crematorium in advance and independent of the mourners.[9]

Mourning Behavior

Etiquette prescribes that as soon as her husband dies the widow dons a black hat to which is attached a long black veil which reaches to the bottom of the rear hem of her coat, and a short black veil which covers her face. She wears these veils until the funeral is over. They tell people that she is in mourning and must not be disturbed. The custom is of long standing. A special mourning garb characterizes those districts of Sweden in which traditional folk costumes are regularly worn. Also observed is the old custom of flying a flag at half-mast until the minister completes the reading of the committal prayers. It is also customary in hamlets that in sympathy with a neighbor's bereavement all flags will be flown half-mast by those whose houses have a flag mast.

400

Swedish church funeral, family on right, close friends in opposite wing, floral wreaths around casket

In some parts of rural Sweden pine branches are spread outside the house until the casket containing the body is carried from it. The old practice of closing the blinds until after the funeral services is falling into almost complete disuse.

Persons whose daily work brings them outside of the home cannot, of course, observe all the old rules made for persons not required to leave the home. Men in mourning, however, still make an effort to wear a black suit and white tie, and women in mourning change as soon as possible into black stockings and black dress. The widow's black hat has a white band descending into a point; and a daughter's black hat has a white ribbon that winds around the brim. A granddaughter's black hat is without trimming. Close women relatives of the deceased wear white collars which come to a point in front, and white aprons. Formal wear for men at funerals is a full-

401

dress suit with a black band on the left arm. Although office workers and others may find it difficult to observe these niceties of dress, their associates nevertheless recognize their mourning status and lower their voices in speaking to them.[10]

Flowers are an important accessory in Swedish funerals as gifts from friends. An average funeral will bring a minimum of 15 wreaths, while a funeral of a public figure may bring 100 or more. Wreaths are trimmed with two pennants. One of these is usually blue and the other yellow, the national colors of Sweden. However, other combinations are sometimes used. On the pennants hand-painted familiar phrases and quotations convey the sentiments of the donors. *Rest in Peace, A Last Greeting, A Last Thank You and Goodbye* are among the favorites. Stockholm has a company which specializes in the manufacture of floral decorations for caskets. The local florist also supplies these."

Committal service in cremation chapel, casket sinks to lower level for cremation at close of ceremony. *Right,* Clergyman sprinkles sand on caskets in mass burial of children killed in school bus accident

Eight pallbearers carry casket of Swedish film magnate down church steps to funeral coach. *Center,* Friends of deceased motor scooter enthusiast carry casket from church. *Right,* Wreath being placed on grave holding ashes of Swedish Nobel-prize winner Selma Lagerlof

Swedish Funerals

At the church services the family sits to the right of the aisle, while non-family members sit to the left. During the ceremonies the casket, with wreaths surrounding it, stands on a catafalque near the altar. After a hymn has been sung, the minister delivers a eulogy of the dead. A member of the family follows with a speech in which he thanks the minister for his many services. One Swedish observer reports: "There can sometimes be a lot of speeches. We are known in this country for our habit of making speeches whenever we have an opportunity."[12] This speechmaking is followed by another hymn. Then the body is borne from the church on the catafalque. The hearse leads the procession, followed in order by a flower car, the family, and the friends. Horses were last used in funeral service in Stockholm in 1950. Most motorized funeral equipment in Stockholm is now rented from one of two companies owning together about 40 vehicles. In country towns taxicabs and private cars are the major sources for transportation.[13]

When the procession reaches the graveside the minister

403

Cemetery employee
lists wreaths received;
pennant reads "Good-
bye, little mother"

Etienne J. Guerin Photo

says an Our Father, and then takes a shovel full of earth,
and thrice spilling portions of it on the casket, says each
time: "Dust thou art and unto dust thou shalt return. But
Jesus, the Almighty God, will waken you on the last day."
After repeating the Our Father, he reads the final blessings.
When he concludes, the relatives approach the open grave to
pay their last respects to the dead by casting flowers into it.[14]
   At the crematorium the casket is placed on a section of the
floor with an elevator beneath it, so that while organ music
is played the casket slowly sinks into the crypt. A few weeks
after the funeral in the crematory the urn containing the
ashes is taken to a cemetery or columbarium. The returning
mourners gather at the home of the deceased and there
they are served food or drink or both. Sometimes a lunch or
dinner is provided, and sometimes only coffee. Although
the general custom is for the family to provide a quiet meal
in which the sociability is limited to toasts offered for the
deceased, in some parts of Sweden, where distance and lack
of transportation prevent people from seeing one another frequently, the gathering occasionally becomes highly sociable,
festive and noisy.[15]

404

Newly dug grave in Stockholm cemetery

Finishing touches being applied to casket in cemetery chapel before burial ceremonies

Etienne J. Guerin Photos

The highest percentage—about 90 per cent—of cremations in Sweden is to be found in Lapland where earth burial is impossible during the nine to ten month period when the ground is frozen so that graves cannot be dug and uncremated bodies must be stored. In Stockholm a fair majority of the dead are cremated, but for the country as a whole the figure is about 25 per cent.[16] There are about 40 crematoria in Sweden.

In rural areas and for most parts of Sweden earth burial remains the preferred practice. Two principal cemeteries serve Stockholm. The oldest, in the heart of the city, contains separate sections for the burial of members of different religious groups. This cemetery has been overcrowded for several years. The

405

Cremation chapel,
casket, flowers
and candelabra

newer cemetery, located in a Stockholm suburb, Enskede, is
beautifully landscaped and is famous for its chapels designed by
the late famous Architect Gunnar Asplund.[17]

In order to allow the soil to settle before placing a heavy
weight upon it Swedish law requires a lapse of six months
between the filling of a grave and the erection of a gravestone.[18]
The Swedish Cemetery Department allows a casket to remain
in a grave for 25 years, or for double the original fee, "all
framitden" (the whole future). A family grave, purchasable
for a modest price, holds from two to four caskets. The use of
a family grave is becoming increasingly common.[19]

The Flower Fund

An interesting development in Sweden has been the *Blomster
Fonden* or Flower Fund, which was founded in Stockholm in
May, 1921. This fund accepts contributions as expressions of
sympathy and in memory of the deceased to build apartment
houses for old people in straitened circumstances. The Fund
has already built seven apartments in Stockholm on land
donated by the city.[20]

406

Chapter 30

Denmark

Organization of Funeral Service

There is no professional funeral directing group in Denmark today because there is no school or course in which professional training is offered. In Denmark the requirements for organizing a funeral business are simple, and any man or woman, without regard for education or training, can set up an establishment. Danish funeral establishments were first organized by cabinet-makers, who as a sideline manufactured coffins in their work-shops, and sold them in their furniture shops. Even today this is the customary method of funeral furnishing, particularly in small villages and towns in which funerals are infrequent. About a century ago, however, the first funeral establishments as such were set up in urban areas and particularly in Copen-hagen. These confined their activities to selling coffins and making funeral arrangements.[1]

The first undertakers in Denmark were usually cabinetmakers who saw business opportunities in specializing in mortuary serv-

Ceremony at grave;
clergyman throws three
spade-sticks of sand
on lowered casket

P.I.P. Photo

ice. In Copenhagen today, four or five funeral establishments manufacture their own caskets. The remaining forty or fifty purchase theirs from factories specializing in casket manufacturing.

Burial Procedures

The practice of embalming is not so common in Denmark as in America. Danish law requires that the remains of members of the royal family must be embalmed, as well as remains destined for vault burial or for overseas shipment. The number of persons embalmed in Denmark in any one year will hardly exceed fifty. Most of these are carried out by medical practitioners, and only a few by the two or three authorized embalmers serving in city hospitals. Restorative art has never been practiced in Denmark, and is not to be found there today.

The body is coffined for the funeral. The type commonly sold is constructed of fir—with a lining of paper, linen, or silk. Silk, of course, is used only in the more expensive coffins. Ash, teak, or walnut is also used in coffin manufacture. An outer box is never used. Steel outer vaults are not used in Denmark.

The Danish funeral director maintains no funeral home, and the funeral parlor as it is known in America nowhere exists in Denmark. The Danish funeral director's establishment consists of a one or two room office and a shop or store in which he exhibits caskets and urns.

When death occurs in a home, the body is coffined there

Upper left, Typical Danish church funeral service.
Upper right, White-painted casket, typical of Scandinavia, being carried.
Lower, Funeral procession from cemetery chapel to grave

before being transported to a church or to the crematory chapel in the cemetery chosen for the burial. More than half of the burial services are held in such chapels. Only those who are closely connected in some way with the church are given burial services in church.

For burial the body is usually clothed in either a shirt, night-shirt, pajamas, or collared white shirt. It is placed in the coffin between bed linens, with the head resting upon a pillow. When a young married woman dies she is occasionally buried in her wedding dress. Men are sometimes buried in their best suits. In rural areas young women commonly prepare the dresses in which they hope to be buried years later.

Little ceremony attaches to the removal of the body from the place of death, whether the home or hospital, to the chapel, crematorium, or church; only the nearest of kin and a few close friends follow it. It is customary after a church ceremony for almost all who have been in attendance to form a procession and follow the body to the cemetery or crematorium.

When the officer of a trade union is buried, union members follow the hearse on foot to the place of burial. If a large attendance is expected, the funeral service may be transferred to the union headquarters or the city hall. Horse-drawn hearses are no longer used in Denmark, being entirely replaced by motorized hearses.

Cremation

The percentage of disposals by cremation is high in urban areas, low in rural. There are 24 crematoria in Denmark. About 29 per cent of all funerals end in cremation.[2] In Copenhagen 66 per cent of all disposals are by cremation, in Alborg, Arhus, and Odense, 25 per cent are cremated. There has also been a sharp rise in the use of common graves, where the ashes are placed under the turf. In Copenhagen such inhumation of ashes accounts for 40 per cent of all cremation funerals.[3] In smaller towns and rural areas the percentage of cremation may be as low as 10 per cent. Crematoria are always owned by municipal governments. In each case virtually all the remaining disposals are given earth burial. Only a few bodies are entombed above ground in family vaults or in family mausolea. The casketed remains of members of the royal family are placed in Roskilde Cathedral Chapels and mausolea located near the castles on many large estates serve a similar function for the bodies of the nobility.

There is little observance of formal mourning in Denmark. Close relatives wear dark clothing for the funeral, and in Copenhagen after the burial they occasionally invite those who have been in attendance to drink a cup of coffee with them either at home or in some quiet restaurant. Outside of Copenhagen and in rural districts the custom of inviting those attending funerals to coffee at the community house is universally observed.

With exception of the use of cremation, no great differences are to be found in Denmark between urban and rural funeral practices, other than that in rural areas services are generally held in a church on the grounds where the cemetery is located. The ritual used is the same everywhere. The state church of Denmark is the Evangelical Lutheran. It is called the *Folkekirchen;* its ministers and other employees are paid by the state, and it holds churches and other church property in the name of the state. Also to be found in Denmark are some Mormon; Catholic; Methodist and other Protestant churches. These are not state owned or subsidized.

Upper, Boat funeral on canal at Spreewald near Berlin.
Lower, Miners, carrying miners' lamps, accompany casketed bodies of dead fellow workers

412

Chapter 31

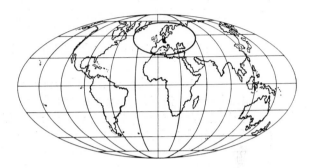

West Germany

West Germany covers an area just slightly smaller than the state of Oregon. The city of Bonn located about half way between the northern and southern borders is the capital. The country, with its nearly 54,000,000 population, is about equally divided between Catholics and Protestants.[1] In any consideration of the burial customs of the Germans several factors must be kept in mind: the pagan heritage of the Germanic peoples, its residual influences still apparent in some of the folk customs and in the art symbolism of the present-day Germans; the role of the Christian Church, differentiated along lines of Catholic and Protestant doctrines; the rationalist and materialist philosophies of the nineteenth century which have in part become expressed in the socialist movement; and, somewhat related to the latter, the municipalization of many social and some personal services to the public.

413

Organization of Funeral Service

In direct contrast to the practice in the United States, where only the most limited kind of public regulation of burial tasks is found, the general tendency in Europe is to regard the burial of the dead for the most part as a public utility which must be controlled and regulated to some degree at least by the state. West Germany provides an illustration of a country in which the funeralization of the dead is carried out partly by state and municipal authorities and partly by private enterprise.[2]

The rise of the undertaker as a more or less independent tradesman in Germany dates from about 1860, when the so-called "free trade laws" were passed. These permitted certain firms and individuals to engage in various lines of retail trade, undertaking among them. In Dresden there is record of a private undertaker in 1860; in Frankfort-am-Main in 1888; but in Berlin one firm claims continuous operation since 1830.[3]

A survey made in 1910 showed that in some German cities transportation of the body was municipally provided; in others, except for supplying coffins, burials were under full municipal control; and in others virtually all goods and services were municipally supplied. In 1928 Berlin was operating eighty municipally owned cemeteries, three crematoria, and three municipally controlled undertaking establishments, which provided funerals for 60 per cent of the deaths. Competing with these public institutions were a hundred private undertakers. After World War II West Germany saw a growing strength on the part of the private enterprise undertakers, and the growth of trade associations among them as an instrumentality for protecting their interests, for resisting the encroachments of the state, and to reduce monopolies held in many places by state funeralization. A case in point is the association of undertakers in Munich, especially dedicated to the promotion of individual enterprise in funeral directing, and to the elimination of all publicly operated establishments. It derives encouragement from the fact that under present leadership the Bonn government favors and encourages all types of private enterprise. Undertakers in all West Germany

414

Casket covered with flowers awaits committal service in crematorium chapel, West Berlin

Funeral chapel scene shows typical German wooden casket

Photos Courtesy Heinz Neff

are organized into an occupational association, the *Verband Deutscher Bestatter.*

The typical privately owned and operated funeral establishment in Munich occupies a store front building and contains an office in which services are arranged for and goods sold from a catalog. In addition it carries a selection of silk coverlets and pillows from which its clients may choose. In order to compete with the funeral provided by city welfare establishments, it sells comparable funerals for slightly less, makes very little profit on the service, but seeks to balance the scale by the profit on an occasional more expensive funeral.[4]

Another phase of the German funeralization complex is burial insurance sold by independent burial insurance firms who in turn contract with funeral establishments for specified services. Burial insurance with monthly premium payments is most popular. The size of such payments depends upon the type of funeral desired and the age and physical condition of the insured. The general practice in West Berlin is for an adult to carry a burial insurance paying at death sufficient monies to provide for specified funeral services from the pickup of the body at the home to its delivery at the grave.[5]

There is a tremendous variation on volume of business between small and very large funeral establishments. For example, the *Gemeinutzige Bestattungs-Gesellschaft* maintains branches in 20 cities and provides 6,000 funerals a year. Its Berlin office, with 43 employees, has a main entrance into the Western Zone and another into the Eastern Zone. This office operates a fleet of four funeral coaches and three limousines. The firm was founded in 1925 to service the burial insurance contracts, which were issued by a company, originally in the fire insurance field, that went into burial insurance as a side line. In 1945, the Berlin City Government ruled that the sale of both types of insurances could not be carried out by a single company.[6]

Another Berlin firm, Julius Grieneisen, with 145 employees operates 15 branches throughout West Berlin alone. Founded in 1830, it still remains in the possession of the founding family. In its own factory, built in 1910, this company manufac-

416

tures all its oak and pine caskets, as well as the pillow and lining sets with which the caskets are trimmed. Although it buys the cheap white paper shirts ready-made which serve as shrouds, its seamstresses make its own cotton and silk shirts, and add lace, frills and pleats to the luxury line. It uses power tools to carve casket decorations, and casts its own casket handles and metal trim.[7]

These are funeral giants. On the other hand most of the more than 100 funeral directors having establishments in West Berlin in 1959 were small businessmen who rented much of their equipment from a livery service.

In common with funeral establishments and municipal monopolies in many European cities, funeral directors in Berlin, Munich, Hamburg, and the like must be prepared to offer a variety of classes or types of funerals, running from the simplest and least involved to the expensive, sumptuous, luxury-type with its fine draperies, floral ornamentation, liveried attendants, bands, automobile procession, etc. Additional services, speeches, transportation, and other extras can, of course, make the figure considerably higher in any class of funeral.[8]

The nineteenth century witnessed the development of a casket industry in Germany. The joiner who once built a single wooden coffin on special order has been displaced by the casket factory whose commercially mass-produced products are sold to undertaking establishments. Some undertakers maintain their own factories, and manufacture a variety of models and colors of wood and metal caskets.

The Germans still favor their old-fashioned pine or oak caskets. These generally conform to a standard pattern. The bottom and the lid are separate pieces. The shape is octagonal, with the ends and sides receding, the base deeper than the top, with small wooden legs on the bottom. Such receptacles are usually painted black or brown. This style is reproduced with minor variations in the newer metal and plastic caskets. Caskets are available at a wide range of prices, depending on quality, with the differences to be found in the kinds of wood used, the type of finish, and the ornamentation. The customer pays extra for the lining, which may be

417

Baroque-style caskets displayed on wall

of paper or silk, and for a bed of moss or excelsior. A pillow is included for the head.[9] Metal caskets are increasingly popular although in some cities, notably Berlin, their use is prohibited inasmuch as burial space is at a minimum and cemeteries depend on the more rapid disintegration of wood to make space available for new burials. In such circumstances, when the ground has been rented, the reduced remains are transferred to a smaller grave. Outright permanent ownership is expensive.[10]

Both municipal funeral service agencies and independent undertakers with large scale operations maintain a variety of rolling stock. Hearses are constructed on various chassis, such as Opel, Mercedes, and Volkswagen. One unique vehicle found in Germany is a small, closed trailer unit for transporting over extended distances. This provides the most inexpensive method of transportation, inasmuch as transporting a dead body by train in Germany is quite expensive. Only casketed remains can occupy the baggage car, so the fee is equal to that for the use of the entire car. Thus the trailer is a necessary expedient.[11]

Berlin law forbids the family to ride in the same open compartment with the remains, and to conform, the funeral coach is so designed that the family is seated in a private compartment immediately to the rear of the driver, between him and the compartment in which the body is transported. After the war the scarcity of automotive equipment in Berlin led the city to permit a hearse to carry two caskets to the cemetery simul-

418

Window display of West German caskets

Photo Courtesy E. C. and G. R. Johnson

taneously. West Berlin funeral directors, however, are forbidden by law to offer ambulance service.

The custom, commonly found in predominantly Catholic countries, of supplying a special horse-drawn funeral hearse to transport the remains of infants and children has fallen into disuse in Berlin since the 1930's.

Whether the funeral services will be handled by a private undertaker or provided by the municipality at public expense, a doctor's certificate, establishing cause of death, must be obtained immediately after death.[12] Either the city's functionary or the undertaker will assume responsibility for the task of registering the death at the registrar's office. After the family has settled the general time of interment, the clerk of the cemetery must be requested to allot burial space and to confirm the time of burial. The next step is to provide for printing and sending out black-bordered letters announcing the death to members of the family and to friends.

Two forms of death notices are commonly used in the newspapers of a German city or town. The survivors themselves insert the first notice, which confines itself to the simple facts. In addition, when the deceased holds membership in a group, such as a fraternal organization, political party, sports or other club, his associates insert a second notice. This sketch, which may be in the same column as the family notice, covers the offices the deceased has held, speaks of his fine qualities, and expresses his friends' sense of loss.[13]

419

If the deceased belonged to a burial insurance society which pays a cash sum at death the member of the family making the arrangements secures a death certificate from the attending physician which he will present to the insurance office and receive the payment provided for. Most funeral arrangements in Germany are cash transactions.

The next visit is to the undertaker's establishment to select the casket. Funeral homes with caskets of the high baroque style displayed in the windows are sometimes seen on the main streets of West Germany. Other funeral establishments are situated in courtyards concealed from view. Some funeral establishments include a casket display room, others have only a catalog, and perhaps a few samples of silk pillows or linings from which the patrons may choose the casket interiors.[14] In larger cities the main business of the German undertaker is to "fabricate, display, and sell caskets, to dress and casket the deceased, and to transport the body from the home or morgue to the cemetery."[15]

When the casket has been selected the relatives arrange for the transportation of the body from the home or hospital to the cemetery. It is not unusual for a day to elapse between the time of death and the time that the undertaker's men call for the body. Usually a period of three days is allowed to elapse between death and burial. The length of time is considered sufficient to prevent the burial of an unembalmed living person suffering from catalepsy.[16]

The undertaker in the Provinces may be a female—the *Todenfrau.* Whether male or female, this person generally brings the casket, shroud, winding sheet, and cushion to the place where the body happens to be, *i.e.,* the hospital, home or police mortuary. On request, the undertaker's men (women are also available) wearing white coats, wash, if necessary shave, and casket the body in the home. The fee for this service is paid immediately and directly to them. Church volunteers sometimes perform this task as a corporal work of mercy. When the body has been prepared it is clothed in a sheet made of paper, silk, or other material, and placed in the casket. While the eyes are closed and the lower jaw is tied with a

420

Hearse for middle
class funerals,
West Berlin

Photo Courtesy Heinz Neff

Trailer for conveying
caskets on long trips

Photo Courtesy E. C. and G. R. Johnson

handkerchief which is removed after *rigor mortis* has set in, no cosmetics are used.[17] In the larger cities the procedure is generally the same, but the women serve mostly as assistants to the undertaker. Also, the body will be clothed in burial garments, as a rule.

After casketing, the body is generally removed to a reposing room at the cemetery chapel. Many churches have their own cemeteries and a familiar scene is the "death house," a small edifice at the edge of the cemetery where the dead bodies await funeral services and burials. However, in the large cities municipal cemetery chapels have refrigerated cubicles with clear glass windows through which the body may be viewed. Only the bodies of important men are kept in the home for a few days for viewing and only high officials are likely to be embalmed. In such cases the operation is performed by a physician, or by a technician in a university anatomy department.

Whether the casket is kept in the home or in the cemetery chapel, whether it is closed or left open so that the remains can be viewed, it is supported on a stand against a background of laurel bushes, and framed in floral arrangements. Flowers may be placed on the casket itself. Casket sprays are an exception in Germany. Floral offerings generally are made into wreaths. It is customary to send wreaths or sympathy cards to survivors. If the family is poor, gifts of money to be used in meeting the funeral expenses may be made to it.

In cities when the time for the funeral arrives most relatives and friends make their way to the cemetery by any means available. If they wish to view the body they arrive early because the lid of the casket is nailed or screwed down before the service starts and is not reopened.

The last half-century has seen the passing of ordinances eliminating funeral processions from cities and towns, so that it is only rural communities which carry on the old tradition in which funeral attendants dressed in black mourning suits and black top hats follow the hearse, drawn by horses which are draped in black.[18] The procession from the chapel to the grave is likely to be impressive. If the family is wealthy the procession may be headed by a brass band. The casket follows, carried by six professional pallbearers dressed in black and wearing high silk hats and white gloves.[19] Behind the pallbearers walk the close relatives. They wear the full black of mourning, except for some men who have black ribbons wrapped around their left arms. The widow is garbed wholly in black, with a black veil about her head. Many of the men wear tall black silk hats. During the procession the bell tolls. It is considered a mark of respect for the dead for friends and relatives to take part in the funeral procession, and when this is long, people comment that the deceased must have been a worthy person to merit such an honor. The type of service provided is determined by the religion of the deceased and in each case is very similar to the religious services performed in the United States. After the funeral the family sometimes holds a reception for the relatives of the deceased.[20]

German cemeteries, which usually are city or church owned,

Above, Rural church and cemetery with "death house" for body storage at right.

Right, Unusual grave marker in North Tyrol

provide perpetual care. The cemetery funeral chapel is a small building with a basement storeroom and is generally the only funeral chapel available. Cemeteries set the time for the burial, usually three to five days after death. If the deceased were a Protestant, the cemetery in consultation with the family arranges for the services of a minister to conduct the last rites; or if he professed no religion, for the services of a speaker. They may also provide music—a singer or an organist—and the tolling of bells. The family has the choice of dealing with the cemetery directly or through the undertaker.[21]

Within the cemetery row graves lie close to one another and are merely outlined, without borders or ornamentation. Individual graves are separated, bordered, frequently mounded, and may be marked with trees such as weeping birches or evergreens, or with hedges, or even iron fences. Paths around graves or burial areas are carefully laid out in finely pulverized white or black crushed stone. It sometimes happens that a square grave, made by joining in a single mound the burial places of a husband and wife, can be found in a German cemetery. In some localities because of an acute shortage of land, burial ground is available only in the case of actual death, and is usually leased, with allotment

423

being made by the city registrar for community cemeteries, and by the religious authorities concerned (Catholic, Protestant, or Jewish) for cemeteries under religious jurisdiction.[22]

West Berlin's 60 cemeteries are segregated according to religion into Catholic, Protestant and Jewish cemeteries. Grave space is leased, never sold. Three types of leases are available: for serial burying grounds (25 years); for family graves (30-60 years); for solidly constructed tombs (60 years).[23]

If the contract is not renewed at the expiration date the grave is flattened and the bones are reburied in the same cemetery, but below the normal grave level. At the expiration of the contracted period, if survivors so desire, the grave contract can be renewed at half the original fee for another similar period. This renewal charge is called "wine-buying," because formerly it was believed that the money was used by the church for the purchase of wine for the altar. If an individual grave is not demanded a row grave may be rented for a very nominal sum. Installment payments are available.[24]

Dirt from the excavation is mounded around the open grave, and boards are laid across this pit. When the procession reaches the grave the casket is placed on the boards and remains there while the clergyman reads the committal service. The pallbearers lower the casket by hand, using either ropes or straps, until it rests on the bottom. The clergyman ends the service by casting in three handfuls of dirt, and after the relatives have one by one performed the same ceremony, the gravediggers fill the excavation, using most of the surplus earth to form the casket-shaped mound which is characteristic of German cemeteries. Later, the relatives plant ivy and flowers on the top and sides of this mound.[25]

Enclosures are usually placed around graves, and sepulchral monuments commonly take the form of stone crosses or marble markers. Several varieties of grave markers are used in German cemeteries, many of them resembling the markers commonly used in the United States. A simple grave marker in Germany may cost little, but there is no limit, beyond the ability of a family to pay for it, set upon the cost of a memorial.[26]

424

German crematories have a chapel and a cemetery as part of their establishment. After the committal ceremony is read in the chapel, the body is lowered into a chamber for later cremation. With cremation there is, of course, no procession to the grave. There is no waiting by the family for the cremated ashes.

Costs of cremations at the municipal crematory in West Berlin are fixed by a charge which covers chapel services, cremation, and delivery of the urn to the cemetery. It is a common practice to inter the ashes in the family grave. While Berlin cremations total 40 per cent of all disposals, cremations in predominantly Protestant Hamburg reach 60 per cent.[27] Despite the slow growth of cremation and its increasing favor in the working classes of the urban centers the practice accounts for only a small percentage of all West German burials. In the total of 62 crematoria in West Germany and Berlin there were 58,463 cremations in 1956—9.9 per cent of all deaths; 61,744 cremations in 1957—10.06 per cent of all deaths; and in 1958 the 61,447 cremations accounted for 10.3 per cent of the deaths.[28] No statistics are presently available for East Germany.

Other areas of Germany have variant funeral customs. In Baden-Würtemberg, for instance, the control over burial of the dead is exercised in large cities by a municipal funeral office—called in Stuttgart the *Friedhofsamt*—while in small towns

Wrought iron filigree tombstone decorations, southern Germany

the local mayor has authority over burial matters. It should be emphasized that these public officials not only control the legal aspect of burial, but also bear the responsibility for making arrangements and of providing the burial goods and services. In contrast to northern and western Germany, Würtemberg has no private undertakers; the dead are again buried with the aid of public officials, or by officers of the labor union, *Gewerkschafft Offtenlicher Dienste, Transport* and *Verkehr.*[29] A staff officer of the municipal funeral office, the *Bestattungsordnic* or burial orderly is often a key figure in the making and carrying out of the funeral arrangements and procedures.

In still other places, an unusual person in many West German towns and villages is the aforementioned *Todenfrau*, or funeral arranger. This female is called in by the relatives when someone dies, to care for or to arrange for the care of the body, to inform other members of the family and relatives of the death and the funeral, and to carry out such other instructions as she may receive. If requested she will arrange for the digging of the grave, the purchase of the casket from a manufacturer, the rental of a hearse, and other arrangements for the burial service. She pays all funeral bills, and in turn collects from the family.[30]

To serve American personnel the American government operates a number of funeral homes in Germany of the type common in the United States today. This fact has created some interest in American funeral service, especially in its economic organization, and may well lead to an adoption of funeral standards in Germany more closely attuned to those in the United States.

Chapter 32

Russia

In the following presentation the authors will deal only with that part of Russia lying west of the Urals and north of the Caucasus, which for convenience in organization of materials will be considered a portion of the cultural area of Europe. The Baltic countries presently under Russian domination will not, however, be included; other countries and cultural groupings lying behind the "Iron Curtain" will in part be dealt with separately.

Pre-revolutionary Cults of the Dead

Both peasants and city dwellers in feudal and even in more recent times observed special days in remembrance of ancestors. Not even the Christian innovations with which these were fused could wholly conceal the pagan ancestor worship underlying these observances. Most of these days were in the spring. Among them were the eve of Shrovetide (Ancestor's Saturday), the Tuesday of the second week after Easter (Commemoration

427

Traditional Russian
peasant sledge burial

of the Dead), Demetrius' Saturday (Saturday before October 26), and the eve of Trinity (Undine's Saturday).

In public ceremonies in honor of the dead a combination could be found of funeral motifs, lamentations, wailings, and all other kinds of expression of grief for the deceased, with outbursts of unrestrained merriment, gluttony, drunkenness and debauchery.[1] Sokolov quotes a Russian description of such a ceremony on the eve of Trinity Sunday: "On Trinity Saturday, throughout the villages and throughout the church yards, men and women go out on mourning ceremonies and lament at the graves of the dead with a great crying. And when the buffoons begin to perform all kinds of demoniac games, then they cease from their weeping, and begin to leap and dance, and to clap their hands, and to sing satanic songs; at these same mourning ceremonies there are thieves and rogues."[2]

For many centuries throughout the southeast Russian

428

province of Saratov several days were annually set aside for remembering the dead. Believers began the observance on each of these by attending a memorial Mass, followed, in church, by a general office of the dead. While the prescribed prayers were being said, a bowl of porridge sweetened with honey was placed on the lectern, surrounded by pancakes brought by everyone. This food was placed in the church with the understanding that later it would be given to the priests and poor of the parish. Following the church ceremonies, the priests and a large number of people gathered at ancestral cemeteries and placed pancakes, pretzels, loaves of bread, and one or two decorated eggs on the graves. Sometimes they added a cup of meal or a bit of sweetened cereal. After the ceremony priests later gathered together the remaining food and took it home. Finally, the priests said the office of the dead. Weeping and wailing was left to the women, but grief did not prohibit the mourners from washing down their lunches with much tea and vodka.[3]

These observances bear much resemblance to an older, less Christianized version called "grandfather's ceremony" by the White Russians of the central western part of the country. In this version, again held in the spring and fall, it is apparent that the expressions were not limited to "veneration, attention, and concern for dead ancestors, but that the spirits were invoked (by means of prayer or magic) for the purpose of securing their aid in the everyday life of the family and tribe and in agricultural activities. So the cult of ancestors was closely interwoven with the agricultural cults." Further evidence of this point was to be found in the memorial feasts held by members of families living in close proximity. In each case at the general table the oldest man present would stick a spoon into the food, imploring: "Let it bear, let it grow, let it live,"— an obvious request to the departed for aid in the welfare and fertility of the household and harvest.[4]

Funerals in Czarist Times

In the larger cities, at least prior to World War I, during the days of the Czars, the custom of elaborate funerals was to

429

be found everywhere in Russia. So thoroughly did it permeate the whole social structure that many poor families almost bankrupted themselves in an effort to provide a stylish funeral for their dead. The rites occupied a greater part of a day, and became publicly conspicuous when a long procession passed through the streets.[5]

To make the procession more impressive a band of mutes (professional mourners) wearing cocked hats and black coats with silver pipings and trimmings was employed to lead the cortege. Their leader carried a large cross, while those that followed bore lighted candles, banners, icons, or, if the deceased belonged to the nobility, the insignia of his rank. If he had been the recipient of imperial decorations, these were borne in state on velvet cushions. The number of attendants was taken as indicative of the wealth of the family. The hearses used in first-class funerals were very elaborate. They were drawn by matched teams of six white or six black horses, with a groom holding the bit of each horse. Behind the hearse the procession straggled on foot. Everyone walked, although on occasions the priests would ride. When carriages were included, even though they followed the hearse, the family did not occupy them. Sometimes the funeral marchers chanted a weird dirge. As the procession moved slowly along, those whom it passed on the streets removed their hats respectfully.

The Orthodox church services were very long, and generally were conducted by more than one priest. At their conclusion the practice was rather general to carry the open coffin outside the church. There a photographer waited to take a picture of the coffin, the body with a crucifix in the hand, and the family grouped behind the remains.[6]

Funerals Following the Revolution

The Russian revolution made substantial changes in Russian social, political, economic, and, above all, religious beliefs; and naturally, these changes profoundly modified the pattern of Russian funerals. For one thing the Orthodox services gave way to a secular ceremony, or none. In their program to de-

430

molish or weaken the social institutions of the previous regime, leaders of the Russian revolution applied a strictly rational and utilitarian philosophy to the matter of the care and disposition of the dead. Animism, ancestor worship, cults of the dead, and formalized religious worship, they held, could play little or no part in the business of consolidating the revolution and building the "society of the future." The dead human body, a husk, had little value. Its presence was an embarrassment to those who must now bend all energies to remaking the world of the living. Logically, in view of the premises of the revolution and the materialist philosophy upon which they ultimately rested, the dead should be given minimum attention, and the least amount of energy expended in their care. Since grave space robs the land of productive uses, so the argument went, the better alternative is to cremate the dead because a few ashes waste less ground than a full-length body. Thus the crematorium in Moscow, the first in Russia, not only would inau-

Funeral of two children; early post-revolutionary period

P.I.P. Photo

Russian interment
scene, 1930

gurate cremation as an actual practice, but would symbolize the new program of a completely simplified, rational disposition of the dead.

It is difficult to assess the impact of this new program of disposal of the dead on the masses of Russians. Living on the thinnest edge of subsistence, with a country devastated by war, revolution, and counter-revolution, Russian people may have accepted some of its features as the right thing to do, others as the only thing left to do. In any event the immediate consequence was to reduce the care of the dead to an almost primitive level. Western reporters and writers were appalled at the lack of ceremony, the apparent callousness of those functionaries in charge of expediting the government's program, and what seemed a general degradation of what they felt should be a profound emotional and religious affair.

Examples of the rather unceremonious treatment of the dead are given by author Harry A. Franck, who, writing in the early thirties, describes a variety of funeral scenes in the Soviet Union: two old men carrying a box, with two old women following them; for a more prosperous family, a truck lurching

432

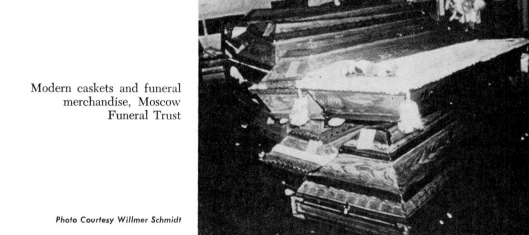

Modern caskets and funeral
merchandise, Moscow
Funeral Trust

down a cobble-stone street, "with a coffin bouncing in the box
and a corpse bouncing in the coffin"; a young couple chatting
easily as they tramped out to the cemetery or crematorium
with the body of their child, which the husband carried slung
from his shoulder in a little yellow coffin; a procession of four
children, a pair of boys and a pair of girls, the oldest not
more than thirteen, walking two miles to the cemetery with
their mother's corpse to bury it; mother and sister pulling a
child's body to a cemetery in a homemade express wagon in
the summer; in the winter, a couple dragging a body to the
cemetery on a child's sleigh.[7]

However, a return to a more formal and ceremonious funeral
is reported some fifteen years later. A revealing example comes
from an account by journalist William L. White of the last illness, death, and funeral of a factory worker.[8]

The man's illness was diagnosed as pneumonia, and both
the private and government doctors were called in to provide
treatment. When it grew apparent that their medication was to
no avail, the children were awakened to say goodbye to him.
They tiptoed into the room, which was lighted only by a tiny
lamp, placed near the bed.

The wife wanted a religious deathbed service; and although
he was not very religious himself, the husband would have
consented, had not one of their older sons been a member
of the Communist Party. The presence of a priest in the home
might have blighted the young man's career.

433

Death came at about six in the morning, and ushered in a round of family weeping. When the first rush of tears had subsided, the women washed the body and laid it out on the bed for viewing. During the day all members of the family came in, and workers from the factory. The family purchased a coffin which had to be carried to its flat three flights above the street.

On the next day, at five o'clock, the funeral was held. It was delayed until this late hour so that the factory workers could be present after work. The body was placed in the coffin, and the coffin carried downstairs and placed in the hearse. When the hearse was driven slowly away, the family followed in a carriage, and behind them walked a long procession of friends and relatives. Some carried floral wreaths, crowns and bouquets, the gifts of friends and of fellow workers at the factory. Some must have cost ten rubles.

The grave was ready when the procession reached the cemetery, which lay two miles beyond the limits of Moscow. As the body was lowered, the wife fainted, and had to be supported by friendly hands. All present wept.

The ceremonies that traditionally followed the old religious themes were replaced by political broadsides. The first volley was fired by the union boss, who commented that the deceased had been a faithful worker for the Soviet economy. It was too bad that he had died young. He was the kind of person that the revolution had saved from exploitation. The family refused to take these remarks seriously. The boss really had little acquaintance with the deceased.

The family listened, though, when the dead man's best friend told what the factory was like before he came, what a fine man he was, and how many friends he had who appreciated his kind and understanding heart. Here was a speaker who knew his subject.

When he was finished, a long and difficult pause followed. Although the wife was supposed to throw the first handful of dirt into the grave, she shied from the task. When finally she picked up the clod and cast it upon the coffin, each of

434

Sculptural figure, glass encased, in Moscow cemetery. Note crosses on domes

435

the children followed suit. After this, the family were helped into the carriage and were driven back to Moscow, while the rest of the procession made its return on foot. The flowers were left behind, heaped upon the grave.[9]

It is evident that earlier governmental plans, or the statements of revolutionary spokesmen about what these plans should be were not to be realized in the actuality of events in the decades following the revolution of 1918. Rational disposal became mixed with ceremonial activities, and there soon arose differences in the manner in which peasants, workers, and the rising group of bureaucrats were buried. Likewise, the tradition of state funerals and the glorious memorialization of the leaders of the land was continued. The permanent embalmment and continued display of Lenin's body is presumptive evidence that memorialization of leaders was never eclipsed in the "new" program to simplify funerals. Some thirty years after Lenin's tomb was first displaying the body of the intellectual leader of the Russian revolution, the body of Joseph Stalin was placed beside it. Thus, a cult of national heroes persists, and the opulence of state funerals in Russia today, the elaborate procedures, and the high degree of ceremonialism, present a picture of burial scarcely different from that in non-Communist countries of the Western world.

Funerals in Present-day European Russia

Although the picture may be hazy in a few details it is possible to present an up-to-date account of funeral procedures for working class members in the cities of European Russia, Moscow in particular. From this, one may draw certain inferences on the manner of burial for those in the middle and elite classes of Soviet citizenry. Contrariwise, little can be said for the care and disposition of the dead in the agricultural areas, and for all of the Soviet Republics which lie east of the Ural and the Caucasus mountain ranges.

Even so, local customs and usages, where they do not directly conflict with municipal regulations and religious procedures, where they are permitted to be followed, make gen-

436

eralizations on funeral customs hazardous. This has been variously pointed out by Soviet authorities in their correspondence with the authors. With this in mind the authors present the following information which was provided by D. Nosov, manager of the Moscow City Funeral Trust.[10]

In cities of the Soviet Union special state-controlled agencies provide all funeral arrangements. All of these agencies operate under the local, regional, or city Soviets of Working People's Deputies, and all funerary organizations are state financed. The Moscow City Funeral Trust, for example, makes these arrangements in Moscow. This trust controls the cemeteries, crematoria, shops providing funeral accessories, and other enterprises whose goods and services are required at funerals.[11]

When, for example, a worker dies, his or her relatives receive a free grant of 200 rubles from the Soviet government. This grant is designed to cover funeral expenses, and is paid the beneficiary at the institution at which the deceased was employed or in the case of a pensioner, at the Social Insurance Bureau of his place of residence. The 200 rubles are sufficient to provide for all necessary funeral furnishings, as well as for the cost of the ceremony.[12]

As indicated by the price list the principal items of expense for a worker's funeral are a casket—including transportation, 55 rubles; the digging and mounding of the grave, 50; the transportation by motor hearse, regardless of the distance and including the cost of carrying, setting up the casket to and from the house, 30 rubles. These major items total 135 rubles, leaving 65 rubles for minor items. These, says Nosov, although he does not specify them, are "inexpensive."[13]

Church and state are separated in Russia, but according to Nosov, "each citizen is free in the religious funerary rites. There are churches in the Danilovsky, Rogozhsky, Preobrazhensky and other city cemeteries in Moscow and the citizens freely use church rites during the funerals."[14]

Although Russian cemeteries make no denominational distinctions, there are several national cemeteries in Moscow (Armenian, Hebrew, Moslem) where people belonging to these groups may elect to be buried. At these national cemeteries there are "religious communities," which, at the wish of the relatives, perform national religious rites during the funeral.[15]

Relatives of the deceased take an active part in making the preparations for a funeral in Russia. At the shop for funeral accessories they order the coffin, and set the date and hour for the ceremony. The operator of the shop then transmits this information to the cemetery which makes ready the grave. If the relatives so desire an agent of the Funeral Trust is sent to the home of the deceased to assist in making arrangements.[16]

At the appointed hour the hearse arrives at the home of the deceased, and the funeral takes place. According to Russian custom all of the close relatives of a dead person take part in the funeral procession, including those who live in other cities. In addition, groups of employees or workers from the institution where the deceased worked are present, and "surround the bereaved family and the relatives with friendly care."[17]

The Soviet government has no special policy with respect to cremation regarding it as a matter to be left to the personal choice of the citizens. One crematory is maintained in Moscow, and all who so desire may use its services for the cremation of members of their families.

This is a bald outline, delineating the essentials of the services performed by the government functionaries. Reports of American funeral directors who visited state controlled funeral agencies seem to bear out the factual correctness of Nosov's outline.[18] There is evidence in sufficient amounts to indicate that far from having reduced burial to a matter of simple disposal of a meaningless dead body the Soviets have come to a position, perhaps grudgingly, where most of the conventions—as defined by Western European standards—will be met at least minimally by the government agency. Or if not by it, by other groups including family, relatives, fellow workers, and religious denominations. Of all the non-government groups the religious are no doubt the most restricted, or the least encouraged to play a role.

438

It would perhaps be a fair statement to say that if care and burial of the dead can be considered one of society's institutions, such institution was not permanently reduced to the level of simple, rational expediency in the Soviet Union. The situation has by no means become stabilized, but might best be viewed contemporarily as a tug-of-war between forces favoring the ceremonial and reverent care of the dead, with their roots reaching deep into the historical past of mother Russia; and of forces toward simplification and rationalization of burial represented by the materialist ideology of early twentieth century communist doctrine. As a measure of the strength of the former we note that from time to time there appear pronouncements against funeral ceremonial by watchdogs of party affairs. For example, in May, 1959, an Associated Press release from Moscow stated that in Soviet Georgia a regional Communist Party secretary reminded his followers to "cut out big funerals and weddings to avoid disrupting work; that

Widow in mourning decorates grave in military section of Moscow cemetery

such affairs were survivals of an ancient tradition and have no place in modern Soviet life."[19]

Projected plans for universal substitution of cremation for earth burial in Russia have been aground on the shoals of cultural resistance for the past 40 years, and this in face of an admitted grave space shortage in the larger cities. An Associated Press dispatch from Moscow, December 9, 1958, discloses that *Izvestia* itself reported "caretakers and grave-diggers at crowded Moscow cemeteries have been taking bribes to find space for the dead. The Government said two cemetery directors have been convicted, five others arrested, and twenty dismissed for demanding and accepting bribes."[20] On the face of the matter it would seem that in one administrative gesture the government might have established cremation by decree, raised crematoria by the score, and have had done with the matter. Evidently the "matter," as much of the above chapter suggests, is not conducive to such an expeditious solution. At the present writing there is still only one crematorium in Russia.

Not as a conclusion, but more as a commentary on the core of human sentiment that exists among peoples everywhere, the visit of the American writer Marshall MacDuffie to a Russian cemetery is described. In the cemetery he found a mixture of graves of Communist heroes and Christians. A Communist grave can be readily detected by its marble obelisk surmounted by a red star. The Christian graves are neither so rich nor so recent, and are generally marked with a double-barred Greek cross. A stone monument, Christian or Communist, was likely to contain a glass-covered portrait of the deceased. MacDuffie also found a newly made grave, "covered with mounds of artificial flowers bearing white paper streamers each printed with black messages: 'To the unforgettable Valentina Karovna from the Kvass factory . . . To beloved Valya from Katya, Tanya, Ala and Uncle and Aunt . . . To Valentina from House Number 11'."[21]

Chapter 33

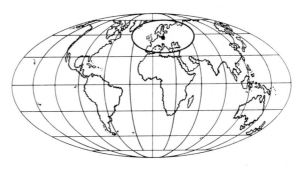

Village Poland

Peasant Poland

The Polish peasant is a Roman Catholic with a mystic's sense of the close interrelationship of this world with the next. Further, he is a poet who lives with a feeling of wonder about the universe which surrounds him. Louise L. Jarecka, a writer, speaks of the "song and ceremony" with which the rural year flies by: "Always there is the lurking sense of the marvelous, the supernatural; nymphs in the forests, voices in the whirlwind; vampires, phosphorescent, wandering flames in the swamps, fiery dragons, planet men that cause the wind and the rain. In the cycle of days there is always a festival close at hand to keep the heart alive. On All Saints' Day in the autumn the cemeteries are little cities of golden light, a candle flickering the night through beside each grave."[1]

441

Death in the Peasant Culture

In the cycle of the year, All Saints' Day, November 1st, is felt to usher in winter, the season of death and the dead. The eve of All Saints—Halloween—is not associated with festivities and pranks, as is the case elsewhere, but is observed with religious solemnity as befits the belief that on this night the dead return to visit their former homes. Thus, a feast must be prepared for them. All Saints' Day and the next day All Souls' Day, which follows it immediately, notes folklorist Sula Benet, are considered to be especially "dedicated to receiving, honoring, and above all, to speeding safely on their way the souls of those who have died."[2] On other feast days the return of the dead may be an incidental but happy event. On the eve of the second of these feasts, at the precise stroke of midnight, a great light is believed to fill each church, when all departed souls kneel before the great altar. After prayer, they disperse to their former homes, where doors and windows have been left open for them, and the hospitable living await to serve them.[3]

Among Polish peasants the Christmas Eve supper is regarded as an important occasion for divining one's personal fate. Straws of varying lengths are placed under the tablecloth, and a person's life span is estimated by the length of the straw which he draws. When the Christmas feast has been eaten, it is thought that the first to rise from the table will die before the next Christmas. It is believed that at certain periods of the year when the members of families draw close together, the family dead return to the familiar places. For this reason the custom of setting aside food for the dead at the beginning or end of a feast is almost universally practiced in Poland. Throughout the thirteen days from Christmas Eve through Epiphany the dead are believed to return to earth to dine with the living, and the man of the house will go to great lengths to do reverence to the spirits of his family. He will blow on a bench before he sits down, and walk carefully lest he should crush a spirit. After sunset he will not spin or twist anything, lest he should entangle one. His emotions,

442

of course, are a mixture of reverence and fear. An injured spirit might seek revenge. Benet comments: "The Christmas observances, like so many in Poland, reveal the assumption that a feast is not entirely over when the eating is done, and people are not permanently gone when they have been buried."[4]

As in all Catholic countries, Holy Week in Poland is observed with much religious ceremony. It is thought that these days of mourning leading to the Easter resurrection are a good time to die, not only because of the intense religious activity of the week, but because symbolically all graves are open, and with the earth lying lightly upon those dying at this time, they will rest in peace.[5]

Peasant death beliefs in Poland have much in common with peasant death beliefs elsewhere in Europe. The word for death in Polish is of feminine gender, as befits the fact that death is personified as a tall, white, emaciated woman. The Poles do not consider death to be an evil personage. On the contrary, she is God's benevolent servant, ordered by Him to carry out His will, sometimes against her inclinations. Nor is she all-wise or all-powerful. It is possible that she may be deceived, begged off, driven away, or that she may become the dupe of a sorcerer and used by him for his black ends. Her presence is made manifest by various portents. Floors creak under her unseen tread, and dogs growl even at her distant approach. Ravens and owls are her companions, and a crowing hen her mouthpiece. She may also leave her mark on one whom she has doomed. A white spot may blossom under the nail of the small finger of the victim's left hand. Yellow blotches may disfigure his hands. His dreams may tell of her impending triumph. He may fail to throw a shadow at the Christmas Eve feast. Divination practiced on festive occasions supplements such signs. For example, if smoke from the candle fails to rise on Christmas, New Year or Easter, it is certain that death will strike.

Although the Polish peasant may fear the dead, "death itself," says Benet, "he views with resigned fatalism." This attitude is based partly on a level view of life: a normal death

443

at the end of a long life is the awaited end of a normal cycle; and partly on the profoundly religious outlook of the Pole: he firmly believes that death is the entry into a certain after-life. The aged look toward death with equanimity. They ready themselves for it, make provisions for the distribution of their goods, and discuss their funeral garb. Benet points out that, "most old women make and cherish their own burial outfit, as fine as can be afforded."

Such calmness of acceptance, however, does not extend toward death that is premature, by violence, or accompanied by prolonged agonies. Sudden or unnatural death is particularly feared since it does not give the slain one an opportunity to be shriven and thus to make his final peace with God. Under such conditions, it is believed, he must be suffering the machinations of the evil one or the justice of the Lord. A bitter curse among the Poles is, "May sudden death befall you." And they repeat with much feeling the imploration of the major litany: "From a sudden and unprovided death, O Lord, deliver us."[6]

The Pole is more concerned that he should meet death with dignity, than that he should be funeralized with pomp. "His ideal," says Benet, "is to die composedly in bed, with one's family gathered about and with religious ceremonies administered fully and impressively. The funeral is nevertheless a matter of great moment. Contracts with tenant farmers, the landless *Komorniki*, sometimes stipulate that if the tenant dies the landlord is obliged to give him an honorable funeral."[7]

The Response to Death

When death threatens, the priest is called to administer the Sacrament of Extreme Unction. Before he arrives, the dying person is freshly clothed and given a candle blessed on Candlemas Day, and a prayer book; and the bed and room are put in order. During the anointing, the family kneels in prayer at the bedside. So that the dying one may have less difficulty in saying farewell to this life, they make great effort to restrain their show of grief.

444

If dying is difficult, the onlookers give aid. They may reverse the entire bed, so that the patient's feet interchange position with his head; or they may remove featherbed and pillows, so that he will not be tempted to linger in their comfort; or they may lay the dying person on straw or ground, so that he may be free from knots that might entangle his soul with his body. A child who struggles with death is sometimes removed from his crib and laid with his head extending from the door. In this position, it is believed, he is started on his journey to eternity.[8]

Wicked souls, particularly if they have bartered themselves to the devil, may try to escape from the bargain by refusing to leave the body, so that the evil one may be forced—and generally he is successful—to extract them with tongs. Even when the soul has relinquished the body, it hovers near it until the bell tolls for the funeral, the procession reaches the cemetery, or the priest chants *Requiescat in Pace*. A sudden increase in the weight of the body tells the pallbearers that the soul has departed heavenward.

Jarecka points out that, "when death enters a peasant dwelling, precaution is taken to open all the doors and windows at the moment of passing. Sometimes a part of the roof is removed in order to liberate the soul."[9] The Polish peasant finds it difficult to grasp the wholly spiritual nature of the soul: "It is pictured as the breath, or in a more condensed form, as a puff or fog; or it is imagined as a ghost or spirit. It is also identified with the shadow, and murderers, who have no soul, may be detected by their lack of shadow." During life, the soul resides somewhere vaguely near the heart. "Souls are seldom seen, but often heard. They have their chosen haunts, indoors and out, and the living must be careful not to offend them." There is even a formula for dealing with a soul. Hearing a spirit, one says, "All spirits praise the Lord." "I praise Him too," the spirit will respond. Then one must ask what must be done so that the spirit may have rest. Perhaps a wrong must be righted, an injury undone, a debt paid. If so, the wish must be carried out. If the spirit makes no request, the interrogator must at least pray for its repose.[10]

It is expected that at the moment of death the bereaved family will burst into weeping and wailing, and that the length and loudness of this response will provide a public measure for its grief. The reservation is made, however, that parents can overdo their lamentation for children. When the dying person has breathed his last, a member of the family places his hands over his heart, and closes his eyes with coins, so that he cannot cast a spell. So that the dying person may not tear his clothes with his teeth and thus turn into a vampire, or bite the onlookers, the lips are closed, and sometimes the jaw is tied. Mirrors in the house are covered, so that both the dead and the living may not see the reflection of the dead person or of death itself.[11]

The Polish Peasant Funeral

Notification of death must now be made. First to be told are the cattle and bees. The new master hastens to give these creatures the news, so that they will not blindly follow their old master in dying. Sometimes he makes a similar announcement to the farm buildings and the orchard. The notice to the neighbors, usually carried by a messenger bearing a stick or staff, starts clusters of people toward the house of death. They have no trouble in identifying it, because it is marked by a mourning flag at the gate, or by a wagon symbolically upturned at the entrance. Later, a pile of shavings from the coffin will serve as another marker. Because belief has it that even after it leaves the house and is buried the body for a time keeps sense and sensation, in preparing it for funeralization it is treated as if it were living. Polite requests are made of it: "Give me your hand or arm." It is exposed only when fully dressed.[12]

A funeral is considered an improper occasion for a family to prove itself niggardly. The body must be well clothed, so that it can appear unashamed in both worlds. If secondhand clothing is used, the dead may become a vampire and destroy the original wearer. In western Poland shoes are included to be worn on the difficult journey into eternity. In

446

Modern day Polish funeral procession; note priest preceding casket

other places the body is buried in linen hose, partly because boots are a symbol of earthly vanity, and partly because they might assist a mischievous spirit to wander about doing harm. As an added precaution, the feet, or the big toes or thumbs may be bound together. The body is laid out on a bench or on planks supported on chairs, with an extra chair for the soul to sit on. Next to the door a towel is hung for it to weep into. The room is lighted, and food and drink are provided for the spirit.[13]

Like most Europeans, the Poles "wake" their dead from the moment of death until the funeral. Their motives seem to be mixed; on the one hand, they wish to keep the dead from injury by malevolent powers, and on the other, to keep them from injuring their friends and family. At night, brothers, neighbors, friends, and old men and women hired for the purpose keep the vigil. Younger women do not participate. During the day the guard dwindles to a few old folks. Singing is continuous throughout the "empty night," because of the belief that it is antidote against evil spirits. The old people sing about the tribulations of the soul. When psalms are sung,

447

the singers stand. Were they to remain seated, the body itself might rise. While the somber proceedings are taking place, other activities less religious, elegiac and dignified are likely to occur, particularly during the night watch. Those who come to pray are served refreshments, and dragging hours may be filled with dancing, singing and other frivolities.[14]

Folk beliefs regulate details of family living in the presence of death. Benet mentions some local prohibitions: The family must not sew or pound for fear of pricking or bruising the soul. They must not whitewash their house for nine months after for fear of sealing up the soul inadvertently. They must not leave food in the same house with a body. It might spoil. In the presence of a dead person they must not plow or fertilize their fields. Such operations would produce no crops. Later to use a comb with which the hair of the dead has been arranged is to risk losing one's own hair. To step on coffin shavings is to court injury. A pinch of dirt placed in a drink will make it a fatal potion. And these by no means exhaust the list. Conversely, the great influence of death can be put to advantageous uses. Benet gives numerous illustrations, of which a few must suffice. Pouring water in which a body was washed on the corners of a house will destroy vermin; and burning a few coffin shavings on a field will keep birds from eating newly sewn seeds. Strangely, it is believed that to rub a watering trough with a piece of clothing of a man who has been hanged will make cattle wax fat.[15]

The British student of Polish culture John R. Rose makes references to certain localized death practices in the Sandomiers country: In one section, for instance, the body is laid in the barn, on a bed of pea vines or straw, with the eyes closed, so that the dead should not look upon living members of the family. Lest finery should attract evil spirits bent on plunder, the body is not arrayed in fine garments. Among peasants the shroud is made without seams which might provide space for hiding sins, and no pillow is placed in the coffin under the head, so that the soul may shorten its stay in purgatory. In another region, when the body is carried from church, a coin is placed under the head, so that the dead feels no need to rob the living. In the same region, pious tradition has it that the candles are set beside the casket to light the soul's way into eternity. Otherwise it would wander on earth until the echo of the tolling of the church bells dies in its ears. In the Duchy of Teschen, after the coffin has been removed from the house, a pail of water is thrown from the door to clear the air of evil influence.[16]

It is particularly important that one should not bargain about a coffin, or purchase a coffin in advance except for one's personal use. Nor should relatives place the body in the coffin, because the dead might interpret that act as indicating their desire to rid themselves of him. In rural Poland it is customary to place articles in the coffin for the use or pleasure of the dead. These may include objects which the dead particularly cherished, or food and clothing for the journey, and money. Money is included because it can pay the spirit's fee into heaven. Moreover it may represent someone's unpaid debt, or the token payment which heirs make for their inheritance.[17]

Polish funeral
procession

The family gather on the morning of the funeral for formal leavetaking. They kiss the body as if it were alive, embrace it, take it by the hand, and praise the virtues of the deceased. Finally, amid loud weeping, the lid of the coffin is closed and nailed down. To confuse the deceased, so that he cannot find his way back, the body is borne feet foremost from the home. Following an ancient custom of obscure origin and unknown meaning, the coffin is thrice touched on the inner and thrice on the outer step, each time with the imploration, "Eternal rest grant unto him, O Lord."

Outside the house a wagon waits for the dead. When the coffin has been hoisted into it, all outer windows and doors of the house and inner cupboards and chests are flung open, so that the dead spirit may take farewell of his home and possessions, and not be trapped by them. It is customary in some regions of Poland for the driver of the wagon to start and run the horses three times, to give a lingering spirit a chance to accompany the body.[18] "The beasts that draw the hearse," Jarecka points out, "are led by pedestrians and the funeral procession is never permitted to cross a plowed field, pregnant with life."[19] Normally there is a funeral mass before the body is borne in a final procession to the grave.

Priest and acolytes precede the wagon which carries the body. Behind it march the man who leads the singing, the next of kin, other relatives in order of kinship, and friends. When the first roadside shrine is reached, the procession halts while another eulogy is pronounced and more farewells are spoken. In some parts of Poland the procession breaks up at this point, near relatives return home while a handful of friends escorts of the body to the grave.

Digging the grave usually waits the arrival of the body, and is performed by grave diggers, or by friends or distant relatives. Mishaps are judged to have special meanings. The collapse of a wall is taken to show that the dead man was a miser, and water in the grave, that he was a drunkard. The coffin is lowered with the head toward the east. When it has come to rest, the priest, followed by all present, thrice casts a little earth upon it, singing: "May earth rest lightly upon him." As each mourner takes final leave of the grave, he looks upon it and says, "Remain with God," and turning, hurries away without looking back. Evil spirits might seek to follow him home, and a backward glance might cause another funeral within the week.

Mourning and Memorialization

The *stypa*, the funeral feast, usually held in the house of the deceased, follows the return from the cemetery. For this feast, as for the feast of All Souls', peas and noodles prepared with poppy seeds and honey are traditional foods. In addition, according to their means, the family makes every effort to provide a repast that will indicate both their economic status and their reverence for the deceased. During the meal the mourners speak only good of the dead. Instrumental music, singing, and dancing are not considered out of place on this occasion, and at some point during the feast, food will be given to beggars. Benet finds here a mixture of Christian and pre-Christian elements: Christian charity and the offerings for prayers mingling with pagan ideas of gifts of food to the dead.[20]

On the eighth day after the funeral, the estate is settled, sometimes with much argument, among the heirs, in spite of the fact that they believe the spirit of the dead is present and watching them. During the mourning period, which traditionally lasts a year, remarriage is considered in poor taste, although excuses will be made for a widower with small children. The fact that white is now being substituted by black as the conventional Polish mourning color is of little importance to the peasants, since as a rule they do not wear mourning clothes. For all, however, mourning is a time in which the family avoids dancing and other amusements. The Poles have a long memory of their beloved dead, and the funeral feast is repeated at intervals long after the period of mourning, and particularly on the anniversary of death. Moreover, the dead are in the minds of the living, and often they find their way into their prayers and conversation.

451

How long or well these peasant beliefs and practices will survive persecution and Westernization is not easy to predict. Benet may have the answer: "The history of Poland has been one of basic consistency and but superficial change. Throughout the centuries, her boundaries and her rulers have changed, but always the Polish people have felt an essential core that has remained untouched. This has been true of all Poland and especially of the peasants who form so large a part of her population . . . the strength of peasant convictions concerning human dignity and human rights may be expected to oppose even the most inexorable attempts to destroy them."[21]

Urban Poland

In the urban and metropolitan areas of Poland, especially since World War II, funeral customs and procedures have undergone substantial change. The occupation and continued domination or attempted domination of Poland by the Soviet Union has produced a pattern of funerals combining family-neighborhood-church care on the one hand and state or municipality owned and operated services on the other. The undertaker is a petty bureaucrat without stature in the community.[22]

In Warsaw, for example, many aspects of funeral service are provided or made available through undertaking agencies which are part of a state bureau. These agencies issue permits to bury, provide transportation, sell caskets and coffins, and make available undertaking personnel to assist with the proceedings.

Upon death the body is first cared for in the traditional Polish fashion. A priest will have been called to administer last rites, and the family members summoned. Should the death take place in a hospital, a permit must be obtained to remove the body to the home. There is no embalming available except by medical pathologists who perform this service in case a body is to be shipped a considerable distance. A casket

452

will be procured from the undertaking agency and the body will be laid out in the home. The wake will then be held on through the second night after death, with the casket lid open. A wreath or basket of flowers placed outside the entrance to the home announces the presence of the body within.

On the third day, generally, the funeral is held. The procession will either move on foot or in automobile. Although the Polish prefer to follow the tradition of walking in the funeral procession, the distance to the cemetery sometimes makes this prohibitive. When on foot the pallbearers carry the casket on their shoulders, and, led by the priest, walk in measured treads to the cemetery. Following the casket will be the bereaved relatives, friends, and members of the community, men in their Sunday best, women always in black. In the case of a motor procession, there is no funeral coach of the type familiar to Americans. Rather, the agency provides a plain black panel body truck to deliver the casketed body to the cemetery at the appointed hour.

When the casket is brought to the cemetery it is placed on a special two-wheeled cart. No motor cars are permitted on the grounds. The casket is then wheeled to the cemetery chapel for religious services—almost always Catholic. The cemetery maintains its own staff of uniformed attendants who give physical assistance whenever needed. After the Mass service in the chapel the casket is wheeled to the grave, and placed on canvas strips where after the priest has completed the committal service, it is lowered into the grave. As the casket is lowered, wailing breaks out among the mourning family and flowers are thrown into the grave.

The newer cemeteries in and about Warsaw are partitioned into a variety of sections, the poor, the well-off, the war heroes, soldiers, and nurses and doctors, who served during World War II, all have their own cemetery areas. Those who died in the Warsaw uprising are buried along with the soldiers. On weekends the cemeteries in Poland are dotted with people who come to take care of the graves. Cemeteries remain a rather enduring testament to resistance to rapid social change. The inscriptions have not varied in any measure in the last century:

> Here rests in the Grace of the Lord
> My dearest husband and
> Our loved father and grandfather.
> In memory of Albert _____,
> Born 1872, died 1949. Hail Mary.

Chapter 34

Hungary

In religion today, Hungary is about 65% Roman Catholic; 20% Calvinist; 5% Lutheran; 5% Jewish, with the remaining 5% scattered among Unitarians, Greek Catholics, and other groups. No one faith is identified exclusively with any ethnic group in Hungary, and the distribution indicated above is rather evenly maintained throughout the country, although the percentage of Protestants is slightly higher in the east. Whatever his present church adherence may be, the Magyar peasant still retains some of the common, traditional religious beliefs and practices of his forebears.[1]

A comparison of old Hungarian records and cultural and archaeological remains with funeral practices in Hungary today shows clearly that although considerable effort has been made to modify or root out old funeral beliefs, many traditional customs still persist strongly, particularly among the inhabitants of out-of-the-way villages. Although such persistence is less likely to

455

be found in metropolitan areas, everywhere in Hungary, according to Hungarian traditions that are centuries old, the dead are buried with great pageantry. Hungarian customs, rooted partly in fear of dissolution and partly in love of family, offer no exception to the rule that the mystery of the afterlife in all places and among all peoples surrounds death with strange beliefs and practices.[2]

Signs of and Reaction to Death

When the condition of a sick man becomes critical, the church bell is tolled, the people of the village begin to pray for him, and relatives, neighbors and friends start for the house in which he is dying. Already certain portents will have foreshadowed his death. Physical changes characterizing dissolution will have, of course, been noted. Also the voices of domestic animals or the cries of birds, especially the hooting of an owl, will have spoken his doom; and the movements of celestial bodies will have had a morbid construction.

In the meantime the dying person makes his will, and if he is a Catholic, Extreme Unction is administered to him. If the dying one lingers, and the priest has left the house relatives and women pray and speak. During these ceremonies a "sleeping place" is being prepared beneath the main beam of the room. There a mat is laid lengthwise on the floor. The belief is prevalent that those who were borne out of mother earth find rest in no other place. The dying person must lie with his feet toward the door, and the pillow under his head must not be stuffed with chicken feathers. Children, however, are exempt from this practice. The dying child is laid not upon the earth itself, but on a table and is covered with a fancy shawl which was a wedding present to the mother; and the mother's bridal wreath is placed on the child's head.

So that the soul may escape from the house easily, all windows and doors are left open. Wardrobes, however, are closed so that the emerging soul may find no hiding place within them. The dying person is fanned, the onlookers pray for him, his temples are bathed in holy water, a burning candle is twice carried around him, and its smoke blown on him. As life ebbs,

456

Hungarian woman in white mourning, a hand-embroidered death cloth hangs by her side

Kankovsky Photo from Viski, Hungarian Peasant Customs

a sieve is placed on his head to purify his soul and speed its exit. He is forbidden to weep for the tears might cause the departing spirit to look back to life instead of forward to eternity. Thus, he might find dying more difficult and he might resist death.[3]

All the necessary activities associated with the preparation of the dead body are performed by women. When death occurs, they close the eyes of the dead. In some places it is customary to use two round crocks, and in others two coins to hold the lids. Next, the women tie up the chin, place money in the dead person's hands, and bind the toes so that they are straight. Once more the knell is tolled in a way which indicates the age of the person who has died. For a grown man the tolling is slower than for a woman or a child. In the house of death lighted candles are placed in the window, and mirrors and pictures are covered so that the soul may not see its reflection in them. Clocks are stopped, all sleeping persons are awakened, and the news is announced even to the animals in the stable and the bees in the hive.

Care and Casketing of the Dead

Relatives now make up the bed of the deceased person, and the women take over the preparation of the body. The clothes for the dead are the best they knew in life and may have been carefully kept for years. Brides sometimes keep their wedding dresses a half century or more so that they may be shrouded in them. When they reach forty, some widows begin to embroider their winding sheet so that they may enter eternity suitably arrayed. Unmarried girls and spinsters often are buried in bridal clothes, with a bride's wreath on their head, and in some regions, a young man who has not as yet married is given a mock bride, a young woman in wedding garments who accompanies him to the grave, and, like a dutiful wife, mourns for him. Even more strange, she and her family reckon themselves as relatives of the deceased.[4] It is well said that "customs connected with marriage show surprising parallelisms with burial customs."[5]

When the remains have been clothed, they are placed in the casket. The Magyars' love of color is apparent even in their casket. While today these are mostly black, especially for the aged, caskets painted pale or dark blue, red, green, or white, are not unusual. Nor is it unusual for an old man to carve caskets, headstones and crosses for himself and his wife.[6]

The Hungarians observe a venerable custom of placing in the casket goods which the traveler into eternity will need for the long journey. An Hungarian chieftain in ancient times was buried with his horses, bows and quivers. Later the horse was decapitated and the head was interred with the dead warrior. Nowadays her sickle and comb are placed in a country woman's casket. Toys are tucked in with a child. Next to the body of an unbaptized infant, a shirt and swaddling clothes are laid, and sometimes a needle and thread. Food and drink—a bottle of wine—and a dead man's pipe may be included. The pious are given a bible and psalm. If the dead person is a Catholic,

458

as in many Catholic countries the rosary is laced through the lifeless hands.[7]

The Wake

After the body has been placed in the casket, a three-course feast is held in its presence. This is called the "last supper," because it is actually the last meal eaten in the presence of the dead.

The death vigil is kept by relatives and neighbors, and the body is not left unattended, even for a moment. Such attendance is called "keeping the vigil" or "mourning." The news of the death brings crowds of sympathizers, some from considerable distances. The house of mourning is well marked, by a black flag which flies in front of it; the lid of the casket which hangs on the wall facing the street; and candles burning in its windows. As long as the body is present, the house remains unswept and without a fire. It is feared that to sweep or build a fire might induce the spirit to return. Mirrors are covered so that if the spirit does return, it will not be able to see its reflection in a glass, and thus set off a chain of evil.

No one receives an invitation to participate in the wake, but all come voluntarily, and everybody, including personal enemies, is welcome. Liquor is served to all visitors. The vigil continues through the night, and from sunset to dawn the watchers mourn and pray continuously. When casual visitors arrive, they do not greet the family, but press one of the toes of the dead body, so that at night the dead person may not arise and frighten them. Having praised the dead man's virtues, and wished him everlasting peace and happiness, they leave, again without greeting the family.

Next morning, the grieving breaks out afresh. The lament, chanted to an ancient melody, probably will be constructed out of emotional language devoid of regularity, rhyme and stanzaic. Nonetheless, it may be deeply moving because of its intense sincerity. The Magyars believe that without proper mourning the dead is, as it were, orphaned. For this reason, up to very recent times, when the family felt that its demonstrations of

459

Hungarian "Kopja-fa," traditional grave markers of carved wood

grief fell short of what was meet, it hired professional female mourners to wake for it. These women were well equipped with laments to fit most situations.

The Funeral Procession

On the day of the funeral, the bier is carried on two poles to the cemetery. When the casket is borne from the house it is customary to touch the doorstep with it three times, and three times to push the door with it. In some places custom demands that the casket be carried head foremost through the door because popular belief holds that a man must make his exit from the world in the same fashion as his entrance. Sometimes a man's most precious possessions, his horse and oxen, accompany this procession. As the marchers walk in a row to the cemetery, they sing vigorously, carrying hoes in their hands. Until recently, it was customary for marching mourners to bear pikes with banners on the poles, white pikes for young men, and black pikes for old. An ornamental pike holder stood on each grave.

460

While the earth was being shovelled on the casket, the pikes were deposited in the holder. During the ceremony, the favorite songs of the deceased were played, lively tunes as well as sad. Great numbers of grave decorations of this kind are to be found in the Protestant cemeteries in Transylvania and the Great Plain. Pikes and pike holders are among the finest examples of Hungarian wood carving. To the German poet, Count Alexander of Wurtemberg, the vertical pikes of a graveyard looked like the masts of ghost fleets.[8]

The grave is dug by friends, and faces east. Although digging always begins at dawn, it must not be completed by night, so that the evil one may not appropriate the excavation for a hiding place. When the casket has been lowered, the grave is covered with a cloth to indicate that it is a bridge to the afterlife. Those in attendance generally cast earth upon the casket so that the dead may not return to haunt their dreams.

The Hungarian Funeral Feast

On their return from the cemetery, the procession takes a route other than the one by which they reached it. Arriving at the doorway through which the body was carried, the men throw their hats at the portal, and thrice pound the eaves with their fists to ward off the soul of the newly dead. The filling of the grave ended the prohibition against work, and allowed preparations to be begun for the funeral feast.

Anyone may partake of this feast who participated in the burial. The atmosphere is festive. Even though it takes place on the day of the funeral, gypsies play and dancers swirl and stamp. Although the place at table normally occupied by the dead person is left empty, a singing woman puts food on the plate and fills the glass with wine. It is believed that before morning the dead return to eat food that is left for them on the banquet tables.

In some places burial feasts are held in churchyards. There the serving of cakes and wine is followed by a brief period of dancing. At its conclusion the women retire to the house of the dead person while the men hold a feast in an inn. As

461

Hungarian funeral procession lad by banner-carrying women

part of the ceremonies, beans and peas and flour and fat are passed out to beggars—a group now become extinct. In addition, all the clothes of the dead man, and some of his personal effects of small value are given to them.

The burial feast ushers in a period of mourning and fasting in honor of the dead. Near relatives, at least, avoid places of amusement for six months. In many places the bereaved fast on the deceased's birthday, the eve of his death day, and on the death day itself.

According to venerable religious traditions, certain persons who die under unusual circumstances receive a special type of burial. Thus unchristened children are encased in a pot or box which is borne to the churchyard and buried without religious services in a burial trench. The same trench is also used for the burial of suicides and murderers. When passers-by see such a grave they remove their hats and scatter green leaves upon it. The custom is passing, due in part to the influence of modern education.

462

Urbanization and Change

A word must be appended in reference to modern-day funeral practices in the metropolitan areas of Hungary. As is common in European cities, and the prevailing practice in countries within the orbit of Russian influence, a municipal agency directs and provides most of the paraphernalia for funerals. A medical examiner must certify the natural cause of death and grant permission for burial. At his discretion he may order an autopsy. The undertaker is an employee of the city burial agency. He assists the family in ordering a casket, arranges for transportation, and helps in the making of other necessary funeral arrangements.

If the dead person is a Catholic, a priest officiates. Most funeral ceremonies begin in the home and end at the cemetery chapel and the graveside. Simplification of ceremonies and a state encouraged campaign against folk-beliefs are taking their toll on traditional funeral customs. One cannot completely discount, however, the deepness of sentiment that death has always aroused in Magyar peoples, expressed in laments, elegies, folk-beliefs, and ceremonies. And it is this spirit, whatever practices are substituted for those of yesteryear, which is likely to be most characteristic of Hungarians in their care for the dead.

Trees planted at foot of Rumanian graves have previously
been carried in ceremonial processions

Chapter 35

Peasant Rumania

Rumanian peasant funeral practices[1] originally were developed to fulfill two purposes: to prevent the dead from returning from the afterlife, and to keep them from hurting the living. Although nowadays these functions are largely lost sight of, the practices nevertheless persist. In their grief, peasants take comfort in old rituals and time-honored traditions. The abandonment of some of the superstitious beliefs in which these practices were rooted is due chiefly to the improved educational opportunities for the peasant class.

It is still believed, however, that coming death is announced by signs and portents such as the hoot of an owl near a house, the howling of dogs in the yard, a rooster crowing like a hen, or the mysterious breaking of household articles.

If an ill person suffers long and painful agonies, it is customary for those who attend him to lift him from the bed and set him upon the earthen floor, facing the east. In some localities he is given an oxen yoke for a headrest. Meanwhile, in anticipation of his impending death, one of his relatives holds a lighted candle at his side. In a variant of this process a lighted candle is sometimes placed in the hand of the dying.

Response to Death

When death comes, the eyes of the dead are closed, and the windows and doors of the house are opened. Water jugs are covered. Then one of the relatives washes the body. The water used in this ablution is carefully cast away in a place so secluded that neither man nor animal is likely to set foot upon it. The nails of the body are trimmed and the cuttings are laid upon the bosom of the body. Next, if the deceased is a man, his face is shaved, and if a woman, her hair is combed. Toilet articles used in preparing the dead are either thrown into a body of water or placed in the casket for burial. In either event, they are never used again.

When the body has been thus prepared, it is robed in a death shirt, especially made for this use, or in the shirt worn by the deceased as a bride or a bridegroom. The dead person's best clothes are used for burial purposes; never the clothes worn at the time of death. The feet of the body are frequently tied together with a kerchief, called the *fetter*. Sometimes a second kerchief is bound around the head and chin to keep the mouth closed.

The washed and robed body is stretched out either on a table in the middle of the house, or on a bench near a window. Whatever the location, the feet are invariably pointed toward the door. The hands are laid across the breast, with a candle, a small icon, and a coin between them. The last is to provide a fare for the soul. Finally, all mirrors in the house are reversed so that they face the wall.

Lamentation

Only now is the news of the death made known to the civil and religious authorities and to the village at large. Public announcement is usually made by tolling the bells of the

466

Death is announced to Rumanian countryfolk by alpenhorn.
Right, Folk dirges or laments are first chanted at side of coffin

village church. Variations in the rate of tolling or the pitch
of bells used are sometimes employed to indicate the age and
sex of the deceased. In some sections of Rumania an alpenhorn or pipe is used instead of bells. This public announcement is a signal for the beginning of the period of formal
lamentation. In most parts of Rumania this rite is carried
out by members of the family, and especially by the women,
who wail three times a day, as long as the body remains in the
house. An exception is to be found in certain parts of Transylvania, where the services of professional wailers, who are not
family members, are secured. Such services are rewarded not
with money, but with gifts.

Formal lamentation is a universal custom in Rumania. Two
types of lament are to be distinguished. The first includes a
series of dirges which express the spontaneous grief of the
mourning kinfolk and which disregard fixed patterns of verse
and music. The second are ritual chants, formal age-old elegiac
songs. Some of these are designed to be sung when the deceased
is a child. Others are intended as laments for the aged. Some
express the grief of a brother or sister, or a father, a son, a
daughter, or mother. In addition to certain fixed traditional
laments, they give the singer an opportunity of making special
improvisations describing his relationship with the deceased.
These ritual chants represent perhaps the oldest productions

467

Dirges are also chanted outside house. *Right,* Arranging "pom"
or fruit tree in preparation for funeral ceremony

in Rumanian folk literature, and through the sifting of the
centuries have acquired such literary quality that they are
rightfully considered material for anthologies. They are sung
in a tone of voice called "griefless."

Three of these ritual songs are universally recognized as
most important. The first, titled "The Great Song" (Centecul
cel mare), is most common in southern Transylvania. One
version of this ritual hymn is called "The Rooster."

"The Dawn" (Zorile), the second of these ritual songs,
is commonest in the region of the Banat. It is so named
because it is sung as an invocation to the morning. The third,
"The Song of the Fir Tree," which is found in a limited area
extended over the western end of the southern Carpathian Mountains, is sung only at the burial of unmarried youths.

Rumanian Dirges

Rumanian dirges may be roughly classified into three groups.
The first group contains completely improvised songs. These
are commonly found in the area comprising Walachia, the
southern portion of Moldavia, and Dobrudja. The second group
comprises improvised verses in alternate lines of five feet and
six feet. This form characterizes the dirges sung in Ottenia
and in a small adjacent portion of the Banat. The third con-

Photo Courtesy Adrian Fochi

Vigil starts with family; later villagers join and play
variety of ritual games

tains certain traditional formulas which can be adapted to
meet various needs. This group is to be found in Transylvania.
In northern Moldavia the traditional patterns allow for very
little adaptation. The wailing voices here are commonly accompanied by a musical instrument, usually a large shepherd's pipe.

Whether in whole or major or minor part these dirges are
improvised, their recital cannot be other than deeply moving
to the listener. They tell plain feelings in plain language. They
are not subtle, learned, self-conscious, literary; they speak
eloquently the "short and simple annals of the poor." The
whole family shares grief, and finds an outlet in the lamentation.

Wailing or chanting for the dead is carried out in five distinct
places: at the bedside, at the casket, inside and outside of the
house, in the funeral procession, and at the cemetery.

Funeral Arrangements

As soon as the formal lamentations begin in the home and
the death is announced, members of the family provide a
coffin, probably of local manufacture. The color of the coffin
may have a symbolical meaning. To determine how large it
must be made, the body is measured with a reed called the "dead
man's measurement." This is later laid in the coffin next to the
body. The coffin's sides are pierced with small openings called

469

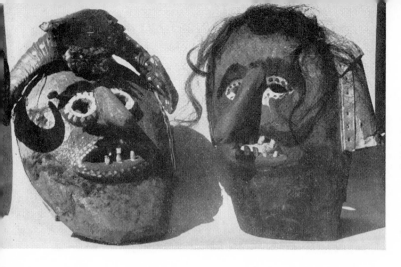

Grotesque masks
used by Rumanian
peasants in games
played at wakes

Photo Courtesy Adrian Fochi

"windows," and it is lined with a shroud or winding sheet (*giul-giu*) which is wrapped around the body before the lid is fastened down.

The family also makes a candle of the same length as the body. Called a "staff" (*toiag*), it is twisted into a spiral and laid on the chest of the dead person. Belief has it that it will guide the spirit on its journey to the afterlife. It is lighted during the funeral service.

These and other arrangements keep the family busy. The "fruit tree" (*pom*) must be prepared. This is a cleaned branch which is decorated with various fruits and sweetmeats. Related to it is a ritual dish (*coliva*) compounded of stewed wheat grains sweetened with sugar and honey and ornamented with various confections. The good things of both the fruit tree and the ritual dish will be distributed as alms at the cemetery. In addition to these, the family busies itself in baking small ring-shaped loaves of bread (*colaci*). While the Rumanians serve small loaves on other occasions, the funeral bread has a unique and unmistakable size and shape.

Nor does the family's labors end even with this. Objects to be given away as alms in the farmyard or at the grave must be provided. But the great task is the preparation for the funeral feast that follows the burial. This event may involve the whole county. Invitations may be sent not only to close relatives and kinsfolk, but to neighbors. In addition to various groups of these, it is not unusual for an entire village to be invited as guests.

470

While the body lies in the house, it is customary to watch it constantly lest it should turn into an evil power which threatens the living. It is especially important that this vigil or wake (*privigiu*) shall be kept on the first three nights. All the inhabitants of the village participate in watching the dead. Meanwhile, they play games. The intent of these is not only to make the long night hours pass more quickly and pleasantly, but to distract the bereaved family. The watchers tell tales or jokes, and play cards. Sometimes they find release in certain other games, which, owing to the fact that they are found only at wakes, may be considered as ritualistic. Thus in certain sections of Rumania where archaic customs most persist, grotesquely masked persons participate in the waking of the dead, and dancing takes place in the presence of the body, to the accompaniment of a shepherd's flute. Explanation is made that such festivities constitute a farewell party for the deceased. In any event, it is worth emphasizing the fact that all participants try to have fun according to their age and sex, and that the resultant hilarity sometimes gets out of hand.

Burial Ceremonies

Burial usually takes place on the third day after death. Interment is the common method of disposal in Rumania,

Priest in wagon holds Holy Sacrament, friends carry banners in peasant Rumanian funeral procession

Various objects are passed across grave as it is being filled by gravedigger

cremation being used in rare instances by urban dwellers. After the body has been placed in the coffin, the coffin is carried through the door, feet foremost, and placed either on a cart or sledge, or on a "stretcher" (*nasalie*). While it rests in the farmyard, various farm objects—sometimes even animals —are given away as alms. The funeral procession then forms. Some of the marchers bear crosses, candlesticks, and religious banners. The ritual fruit tree and the *coliva* are carried in advance of the coffin. The family follows the coffin. Villagers follow the family.

On its way to the church, the procession makes a series of ritual halts (*stari*), usually twelve, at various types of locations along the route. Bridges, crossings, curves—natural or artificial features with an element of hazard to the pedestrian— are selected. At each spot the family of the deceased spread a towel on the ground. These towels—so placed—are considered symbols of the toll gates through which the soul of the dead person must pass in the afterlife, and are left as offerings for the priest and the pallbearers.

When the coffin has been carried into the church, the priest performs the service for the dead, and at its conclusion the

472

Ring-shaped bread and candles are given to mourners at funeral feast.
Right, On certain days following funeral, food and drink are
distributed to villagers as alms

procession moves to the grave. At every major point in the
last journey the wailers have chanted texts, appropriate to the
sad occasion and suiting each circumstance. They sing one
dirge when the body is borne from the house, another when
it is carried away from the homestead, another when it arrives
at the church, etc. The last lament breaks out at the graveside.

In each community persons are to be found who specialize in
digging graves for a fee, and only in rare instances is the task
performed by members of the family and not by them. The
grave is dug before the procession reaches it. When the coffin
is set down next to it, the wailers grow silent, the body is
lowered with the help of ropes, and the religious commitment
services begin. At the conclusion of the reading, a close relative
casts a few coins into the grave. The dead pays for the earth
which has become his new dwelling. Before the grave is filled,
the priest "seals the tomb." While repeating a traditional
prayer, with a shovel he marks a cross on each of the four
sides of the coffin. After this, all present scoop up a handful
of soil and cast it into the grave, expressing the wish that
the earth will rest lightly upon the dead. Even before this
ceremony is concluded, the grave digger begins to shovel earth
upon the coffin. Meanwhile a second ceremony has begun.
A near relative of the deceased passes a black hen, a jug of
water, a towel, a ring-shaped loaf of bread, a candle, and a

473

Food and fire are
left for dead
who are thought
to revisit homesteads
on Thursday
before Easter

During regular
mourning period
a jug of water is
placed at crossroads
to pay the dead's
water alms

Photos Courtesy Adrian Fochi

lump of salt over the grave. These will be left behind as
gifts for the gravedigger.

When the grave is filled, the gravedigger places a wooden
cross at its head, with the name and age of the deceased
written upon it. Later, prosperous families decorate the grave,
either by planting flowers on it, or by covering it with a stone
slab with a stone cross at the head. On their return from a
burial those who have participated in any way in the ceremonies always wash their hands.

Funeral Feasts and Mourning

Some of the mourners do not return to their own homes, but
join the bereaved family at the home of the deceased. The

feast that follows a burial is called *prasnic* or *comindare*. Convention neither prescribes nor limits the number and variety of the dishes that may be served. The only restriction placed upon the menu is that during one of the four annual periods of fasting, it must provide only fasting dishes. It is customary in some parts of Rumania to limit the food to the deceased's favorites. Each person attending the burial feast receives a small ring-shaped loaf of bread and a candle, as memorials of the dead person. In some parts of the country the funeral feast is repeated on the third, ninth, and forty-second day after death, and on the first, third, seventh, ninth, and twelfth anniversary. On an early one of these occasions alms are distributed in the name of the deceased, or gifts are made. The latter may include animals, such as hens or sheep. More often they consist of articles of clothing.

In addition to these individual death observances, Rumanian families set aside certain days of the year, called "ancestors," to commemorate all their dead members. On these days small ring-shaped loaves, candles, *coliva*, etc., are distributed through the village as alms, being given to neighbors, children, and the poor. It is believed that on the morning of Maundy Thursday —the Thursday of Holy Week—the spirits of the dead are permitted to return to their former homes. To provide for their

Decoration of a fir tree to be planted at foot of grave

The lonely widow
chants over the
grave of her
beloved husband

needs, offerings of food, particularly bread and water, are set out; and fires are built here and there in the farmyard so that the ghosts can warm themselves. Although this custom once was widespread, it is gradually falling into disuse. In certain parts of Rumania, however, the custom is still observed of women returning to the cemetery at appointed times to incense the graves.

The Rumanians practice other interesting mourning customs. In Wallachia, for instance, to gain merit for the soul of the deceased, relatives of the deceased arrange to have a girl carry water to people's homes. These deliveries are made for six weeks after a death, two pails a day, except for holidays, until the tally shows that eighty pails have been carried. Count is kept at the well from which the water is drawn, by cutting notches in a wooden tally board, and is double-checked in the village. In other regions, as an alms offering, for forty days a filled water jug is placed at a crossroads so that a thirsty traveller may drink.

The alms dance, once a rather universal custom in Rumania, but now only rarely observed, merits mention. Sometimes all those present at the cemetery after the burial began to dance around the grave. At other times this rite was postponed to become part of the usual village dance. Sometimes it was performed in connection with a wedding. In this event, the family

476

of the deceased requested the musicians present to play any dance tune in honor of the dead. For a fee they received money and gifts of various objects made as alms. All those present entered the dance and were handed a lighted candle that was kept burning until the dance was done. This custom affords another proof of the profane character of some of the burial customs of the Rumanian peasants.

The length of the period during which mourning is worn is determined by the closeness of a person's family ties with the deceased. When a parent dies, sons and daughters may wear mourning for as long as a year. During the mourning period women and girls put aside jewelry and other personal ornaments, and men go bareheaded. If possible, the mourners dress entirely in black; otherwise, they make an effort to wear at least some black articles of clothing. Sometimes men allow their beards to grow as a sign of grief. It is a traditional practice for girls in mourning to abstain from participating in the village dance. The length of the period during which they forego this pleasure varies according to the closeness of their relationship with the deceased.

Customs No Longer Observed

In olden days it was customary to disinter the dead at certain appointed times: three years after death, for a child; five years, for a youth; and seven years, for the aged. A definite ceremony accompanied this rite. The bones were dug up, washed with wine and water, put into a small linen bag, and taken to church. There a religious service was held for them. At its conclusion the bones were returned to the cemetery and reburied with the same rites used in the original burial. Nowadays this custom is rarely to be found.

Another custom of ancient origin provided that suicides should not be laid to rest in the village cemetery, but should be buried outside of it, in a corner called *sniamen*. The bodies of persons who died violently as a result of accidents were similarly excluded, but were interred within the village boundaries. In each case a cross was erected at the spot where

477

the fatal accident occurred, in an effort to destroy the evil power of the place. These customs long ago fell into disuse. Still observed, however, in some parts of Rumania, is the custom of token burial. When a person dies and has been buried elsewhere, a second symbolic burial is made in the cemetery of his birthplace. A grave is prepared for him, a cross is erected at its head, and clothes are draped on the cross. At the conclusion of the burial ceremony, these are given away as alms.

The Rumanians, like certain other European peoples, have developed special funeral observances for unmarried youths of marriageable age. These practices include a series of nuptial rites which suggest a marriage ceremony within the framework of the funeral rites. Thus in some places certain mourners assume the roles of members of a wedding party. When a young man is being buried, a young woman dresses as a bride; and when a young woman is being buried, a young man is attired as a groom. Even more common is the practice of having bridesmaids and groomsmen march in the funeral procession. In all such cases the deceased and all others who carry out mock-wedding roles are dressed for the parts they are supposed to play. Bride and bridegroom wear proper, traditional wedding garb with nuptial cockades, and bear wreaths. These may be specially purchased in town, or the metal crowns used in the wedding service may be borrowed from the church.

The custom of mock nuptials is not widely observed today, the practice in most cases being reduced to dressing a dead maiden in bride's clothes. In regions in which it is customary to prepare a special banner for a wedding, this custom has also been transferred into the burial rites with one difference; the wedding banner is white, while the funeral banner is black. In southern Transylvania the funeral banner is set up on the grave and left there.

Even more interesting, though much more obscure in its origins, is the widespread Rumanian practice of decorating a fir tree for use in both wedding and funeral rites. Some clue to

478

the tree's symbolism in the wedding rites probably is yielded by the fact that a fir tree is placed on the roof of a newly built house at the time of the house-warming celebration. The mountainous sections of Rumania contain extensive fir forests. In such areas it is usual to decorate a fir tree in much the same manner as for a wedding, and to carry it to the cemetery where it is stood at the head of the grave of an unmarried youth, next to the cross. Although this custom is to be found today in Nasaud, Vrancea, Gorj, Hunedorara, and some parts of Banat, only in Hunedorara and Gorj is the wedding rite within the burial ceremony linked to a specific ritual chant called the "Song of the Fir Tree." This chant, in its poetic conception, diction, and melody, is of very ancient origin, and clearly stands as a high-water mark of Rumanian folk-culture.

The complex fir tree ritual of the Gorj-Hunedorara district merits further consideration. The tree is felled in the forest by an odd-numbered group of young men, each of whom is allowed one stroke of the axe. Not any fir tree will do. The tree sought should be about thirty feet tall and possess an excep-

A ritual or "second" grave is erected at the birthplace of Rumanian peasants who die away from home

tionally fine crown. When it has been felled, and the lower branches have been removed, it is carried, butt foremost, to the village. At the outskirts a crowd of girls and women meet it. They begin to chant the fir tree song, and continue until the procession and its burden reach the farmyard of the deceased. There the tree is so placed that no part of it touches the ground. Later, an odd-numbered group of girls decorate it with ribbons and kerchiefs, meanwhile singing the fir tree song. On the way to the cemetery, when the religious music lapses between the halts, the fir tree song is repeated. At the cemetery the fir tree is planted at the head of the grave and left there to rot. In some regions of Rumania the fir tree is considered to be the bride or groom of the deceased.

Rumanian peasant burial rites resemble those of neighboring peoples, and are common to the whole of southeastern Europe. Many of them have origins in pre-Christian ages. Some are clearly indigenous, and date back to Geto-Dacian times. Others give evidence of being brought into Rumania from the Mediterranean zone with the Roman and Balkan penetrations; still others, infiltrating from the northeast, bear the marks of Slavic and Germanic influence. It is difficult if not impossible at this point to make full and final assignment of these customs to their several places and cultures of origin. However, it should be added that in spite of their confused sources, the elements which constitute Rumanian peasant burial rites have fused into a basically single core which is common over the whole area in which the Rumanians dwell.

Variations, however, are not wanting. Through the centuries, political, economic, and social forces have operated to produce local modifications of this basic national and racial pattern, so that today only a few regions can be found where Rumanian funeral rites retain all the traditional elements without change. Reference is made, of course, only to the ceremonial practices of the village community, which are rooted in the age-old folk tradition. The rites of the Orthodox church, with which most Rumanians are buried today, manifest no such variations.[2]

480

Chapter 36

Yugoslavia

This people's republic, formerly the kingdom of the Serbs, Croats and Slovenes, or the South Slavs, was created after World War I from Serbia and parts of the former Austro-Hungarian empire, chiefly Bosnia and Herzegovina. The most popular religions are the Serbian Orthodox and the Roman Catholic.[1]

Certain beliefs and customs connected with the funeralization of the dead have great antiquity among the South Slavs, and while in some places they are slowly being modified, in most others they can be found either in their original or in slightly amended form.

Preparations for Death

The practice is everywhere common of providing or preparing everything needed for burial before death occurs. Included are such items as fine clothes, a cover for the body, wax candles,

Funeral procession
in Serbian village

a casket, the burial place, food and drink for quieting the departing spirit, and the death-stipend—the fee which is given to the priest who performs the ceremony.

Ancient beliefs prescribe deathbed ceremonies. It is thought, for example, that if a person is so unfortunate as to die without lighted candles he will become a vampire. The ceremony of forgiveness is one of the most beautiful of South Slav customs. A sick person calls together his acquaintances, friends, and relatives, says farewell, and begs their forgiveness for any wrongs he may have done them. In addition, just before dying he makes his final confession to the priest.

Oddly enough, long and intense suffering is interpreted as a mark of sinfulness in the dying. The South Slavs believe that anyone whose last suffering is brief, must be sinless, while anyone whose final sufferings are prolonged, must be sinful. Very sinful persons are thought to suffer particularly acute death agonies, and even before death, to start to corrupt. The national folk songs describe how while they live, the grass begins to grow up through their bones, and snakes squirm in their rotting, dying bodies. Certain sins are considered particularly grievous. Among these are theft from a church, sacrilege, incest, the murder of a pregnant woman, injury to best-men and godparents, maltreatment of parents, body-snatching, and hatred for brothers and sisters. It is thought proper that a dying person should breathe his last in the arms of the nearest of kin.

When death occurs, it is customary to shut the eyes of the body. It is believed that the dead have the power to cause death in others, and if the eyes are allowed to remain open they might cause some living person to die. Because the eyes of the dead are evil, no pregnant woman should approach the body lest the face of her child become shrivelled and yellow. As soon as death occurs, all windows are thrown open, to permit the released soul to fly from the house.

The body is then washed, and the custom is widespread of immediately crossing the hands over the chest, with the right hand uppermost. To close the mouth a handkerchief is pulled around the head and tied under the chin. After the body has been dressed in the best clothing available, the body is either left on the deathbed, or placed on the floor, on a table, or laid across benches. Whatever the bier, the body is covered with a fine cover.

Funeral hearse and mourners, Belgrade

Death Wails

Death among the South Slavs is first proclaimed by the wailing and moaning of women—rarely joined by the men. The people seem "ready to shed tears and inclined to go to extremes in their sorrow." From a hundred yards off the death wail was compulsive in its intensity, "a terrible rhythmic chant" that set the mountains re-echoing. For some it is scarcely an expression of personal grief—hearing others wailing, they inquire the name of the dead man before they join in the lament. The wail is a panting sob, a "convulsion of diaphragm." It is accompanied by streaming tears that soak their clothes, a clawing of the face, a rhythmic swaying of the body, a fearful frenzy, in which the mourners seem to enter upon a trance as they drum loudly with closed fists upon breast and temple, and dance wildly, leaping a yard or more into the air.[2]

Wailing waits upon death, because if the dying person heard it he "could be cut in two," as the saying goes in the Valley of the Aleksinac. Immediately after the wailing begins, the bell of the village church tolls, twice for a woman and thrice for a man. For an adult the bass bell is tolled; for a child, the treble. On hearing the announcement, the nearest acquaintances, friends and relatives proceed to the house of death, and there light candles. In some parts of Yugoslavia it is customary for these visitors to greet the members of the family and extend their sympathies. In others they merely approach the body, light the candles, and leave in silence. In some districts the visitors give money to the dead, "in case they should need it in the next world." While the candles are being lighted, the women in most cases wail. Their purpose in so doing is to ask the dead man to convey their wishes to other dead members of the family.

Because the belief obtains that the body is unclean, if it is clothed at the time of death, the clothes are subsequently burned although on occasions, which are infrequent, they are cleaned and given away. Even the house and room in which death occurs are considered unclean, and to remove the uncleanness the priest passes through the entire house saying a

484

prayer, sprinkling holy water, and burning incense in every room, and particularly in the room of death.

Mourning Customs

Mourning customs are observed by the immediate family, and in some cases by the whole brotherhood or village, or in former times by the whole clan. Black is the usual color of mourning. Women are clothed in black, while men wear a black armband or a black lapel ribbon. Local exceptions are to be found to these customs. Thus among the Roman Catholics of Bosnia and the Orthodox in the Valley of Aleksinac, women in mourning dress in white. The period of mourning usually lasts a year. During this time no member of the family of the

Service for the dead in Zagreb funeral

Photo Courtesy Service d'information Yugoslavie

dead person sings, dances, makes merry, or in any way expresses happiness. Mourning is sometimes terminated prematurely if the widow or widower desires to remarry before the end of the normal period, or if young people of the group marry, or if a newly born child is to be christened.

In former times local customs prescribed that mourners should express the grief in their persons as well as in their raiment and conduct. Thus when the wearing of beards was general it was customary to cut the hair and shave and scratch

the face until it bled, as signs of mourning. Even today disfigurements can be observed in some districts near Svetozarevo and Zagorje in Herzegovina, and in some places in Montenegro. To show the deepest mourning, women shave their heads and go without head covers for as long as a year and a half. Others—men and women—do not cut their hair, and men who ordinarily go beardless do not shave, so that they look like savages. Girls and women who usually braid their hair, leave it unbraided.

Priests lead funeral procession from church to cemetery, Zagreb

Photo Courtesy Service d'information Yugoslavie

487

Burial occurs 24 hours after death. Most burials are casketed, the caskets being made of wood, sheet metal, or stone. Some uncasketed bodies are still to be found. Bodies are borne to the grave on a bier, in a hearse, or by some other mode of transportation. Only the bodies of small children are carried in the arms. The relatives or nearest friends generally serve as pallbearers. Before it is taken from the house, the body is blessed by the priest, who then accompanies it to the graveyard. The removal of a body from the home is surrounded by many customs, the meaning of which is obscure. Thus great care is taken not to touch the threshold with the bier, some object is taken and broken so that the spirit will not return, and all doors and windows are left open.

The South Slavs consider the burial ground a sacred place. Cattle are not permitted to trample it, and nothing can be removed from it. Each religious group maintains its own graveyards. In the old days people were wont to bury their dead in certain particularly well-loved spots. Archives reveal that those who died of contagious disease were not buried in the common graveyards. Even today stillborn and unbaptized children are not buried in the common graveyard, but are given resting places under a tree, in a deeper than usual grave, lest they be accidently dug up. Many adults are today buried near the place where they died rather than in the common graveyard.

The funeral songs of the simple Yugoslavian peasants stress the fact that the deceased was wise, quiet, provident, and so kindly that he injured no one, "not even a tiny little ant." The living express concern, however, that they may have offended the deceased.

Procession and Burial

Among members of the Serbian Orthodox Church a bearer with a wooden cross leads the funeral procession. He is followed by another carrying a platter of wheat, and—where the custom decrees that the caskets shall be borne open—by still another, bearing the casket cover. Next march a group of hymn-singing laymen. Then, in turn, comes the priest, and perhaps the village teacher. The nearest relatives follow the bier, and after them troop the other mourners.

Among Roman Catholics the cross is followed by acolytes with candles and by the bearers of the censer and incense boat. The priest wearing a burial cape follows. Next in line is the casket followed by the relatives and other mourners. The body is first taken to church, in communities where there is one, to be blessed or for the Funeral Mass. Elsewhere the blessing occurs in the home or cemetery chapel. Bells toll as the body is carried to the graveyard, and at nearly every crossroad the procession halts so that the priest may pray. When the grave is reached, the priest concludes the prayers, makes the sign of the cross, and moves away. Then while the women prostrate themselves around the casket and begin to wail, the relatives kiss the body for the last time before the casket is lowered into the grave with the feet of the dead turned eastward.

The actual burial is surrounded with customs, the meaning of which is not always clear. In many places great care is taken that no knots shall be present on the clothing of the dead or on the casket. Before the body is lowered, the grave must be swept. All present throw a handful of soil into the grave, saying, "May the soil be light above you." In some regions in

Photo Courtesy Service d'information Yugoslavie

Moment of prayer
at graveside

south and southwest Yugoslavia the custom of double burial is found. The body, once buried, after a short lapse of time, is exhumed, sprinkled with wine, and reburied.

Memorialization

In a Christian funeral, a wooden cross is stuck into the soil at the head of the grave. Generally this cross is replaced by a headstone. Moslems place the stone marker at the foot of the grave. Markers have a variety of shapes and ornamentation. They frequently contain designs which depict symbolically the occupation of the departed. The text upon the stones likewise shows considerable variety. It may consist of a brief biography of the deceased, or a short elegiac poem.

In some districts, when a boy or girl dies, a pear, apple, or peach tree which is just ready to bear fruit is dug up and its branches are festooned with ribbons or red threads. So decorated it is carried before the dead body to the cemetery and there planted at the head of the grave.

Each day for the first six days after the burial, the nearest of kin visit the grave, and again on the fortieth day, the half-year observance, the funeral anniversary, and All Souls' day. On these occasions they bring quantities of food, and arrange it on the grave as for a banquet, leaving it there lest the dead in the next world should suffer the pangs of hunger.

Wealthy families of Yugoslavia traditionally buried their dead in the costliest of mausoleums. Lovett F. Edwards describes a mausoleum in Supetar in which are buried members of the Petrinovic family. He calls this edifice "one of the most beautiful works of art in the world." It stands next to the sea in a cypress planted graveyard. Every part "of this marvellous tomb is a work of art filled with piety and poetic truth." The white stone building is surmounted by a mourning bronze angel "with wings folded over bent back and bowed head." The bronze gates tell the story of the triumphant struggle of angels over devils for the soul of the dead. A bronze St. Michael at the gate calls the spirits within to the glory of resurrection.[3]

In Sarajevo, Edwards found Moslem graves in the "most

unlikely places"—in the public park, next to the main motion picture theatre, and in the center of one of the principal streets. Moslem graveyards were frequently small and grass-grown, consisting of five or six anonymous graves, with the religion of the buried persons indicated on turbaned headstones on which were engraved a text from the Koran and perhaps a sword. The latter device identifies the man who sleeps beneath it as a janissary. The impression created by a Moslem cemetery is likely to be one of great abandonment and desolation; so much so that the Yugoslavians have a saying "as dreary as a Turkish graveyard."[4]

Actors of players' guild carry body of brother actor
in Vienna funeral procession

Chapter 37

Austria

Government and Funerals

In major Austrian cities funeral agencies are municipally operated. In small towns private undertaking establishments are found, and in some rural areas the practice of neighbors burying neighbors still persists. When neighbors bury neighbors, the church (mainly the Roman Catholic Church, inasmuch as Austria is predominantly Roman Catholic) provides the facilities. The Federal government controls the establishment and maintenance of cemeteries; and municipal governments regulate all other matters pertaining to burials.[1]

Municipal funeral services in Vienna developed as a result of a conflict beginning in the 1880's. Then two very large establishments held a mutual monopoly on all funeral business. The fashionable Viennese funeral of the time conducted by the so-called *Enterprise des pompes funèbres,* was as suggested by the name of the directing company, pompous.

Uniformed paraders, each group properly identified by distinctive costumes, bedecked horses, highly decorated hearses, ornamented carriages, banners, wreaths, and robes, all combined to make a truly gala affair. The German term *Prachtleiche* (splendid burial) is quite explanatory.

The French name for the funeral service company had a twofold purpose. Basically, being in a foreign language, the connotation of death and bereavement was minimized. Also, because what was considered as "fine" by the Viennese was connected with French terms, such a name as *Enterprise des pompes funèbres* suggested the ultimate in the final rites for the departed.

Under this arrangement the wealthy received pompous funerals, which they could afford, at high costs, but the working classes could afford only funerals of the kind ordinarily given to paupers. These were described as being "carried out in a singularly brutal and revolting manner." In 1889 a prolonged, bitter controversy arose, concerning the charges made by these two establishments; and popular demand was heard for the public control of the funeral business. In 1906, in addition to the two large establishments, 80 small undertaking businesses were operating in Vienna. Then on June 21, 1907, the Act of the Community of Vienna was passed, organizing funeral services as a community function and establishing municipal funeral offices. Since 1907 the development of funeral service as a responsibility of the community has been a matter of steady growth.

In 1928 there were still seven private funeral establishments in Vienna, operating under municipal licenses and charging prices approved by the city authorities. At that time the Manager of the Municipal Burial office predicted that in view of the fact that no further private firms would be licensed, in a "measurable space of time" such establishments would disappear, leaving the municipal establishment without competition. Today funerals in Vienna are entirely on a city operated basis, with 25 arrangement offices and two establishments where caskets are manufactured and displayed.[2]

Funeral Procedures

When a person dies in Austria the official physician of the district in which the death occurs examines the body, and if he is satisfied that death resulted from natural causes he prepares a report, on the basis of which the local registrar subsequently issues the official death certificate.[3]

If death occurred in a hospital it is likely that an autopsy will be performed. Since the reign of the Empress Maria Theresa (1717-1780) when a decree was issued providing that an autopsy must be conducted on the body of a person dying in a hospital within 24 hours after death, the practice of conducting autopsies in the city of Vienna has been very general, and today the percentage is among the highest in the world.

After the visit of the official physician, members of the family or of the undertaker's staff dress the hair and clothe the body at the place of death. Meanwhile representatives of the family visit the arrangement office. In Vienna, such an office is likely to be located in an office building, fronting on a narrow street. The quarters consist of a large room, containing about a dozen arrangement desks, and several smaller offices for private conferences. In all instances the necessary arrangements are made in circumstances in which the arranging parties are at ease.

On each desk a looseleaf arrangement folder, describing various goods and services, is available.[4] If a need arises for a "state" funeral, the municipal authority is prepared to supply all uniforms, equipment and accessories. A trade license, issued by the Federal authorities, is required to engage in the practice of undertaking. However, all embalming in Vienna is done by physicians. These procedures are common throughout Austria. What happens next varies somewhat. In urban areas, as soon as the casket is delivered, the body is placed in it and removed immediately to the cemetery for storage in the cemetery chapel until the disposal rites begin. The Vienna municipal monopoly uses an American station wagon for removal, and American glass-side casket coaches for funerals. Everywhere in urban sections the horse-drawn hearse has gone, to be replaced by the automobile. Hearses are of American manufacture and

Coffins being
delivered to
Vienna's municipal
mortuary, 1945

Modern funeral
coach

Photos Courtesy Hans Jerusalem

conform in simplicity and lines to those used in this country.
There are actually very few funerals which can be identified
as processions. At the cemetery, the remains are placed in a
storage room in the chapel where they are kept until the day
of the funeral, which normally follows death by three days to a
week.[5]

In addition to cemeteries owned by religious bodies, in
1928 the city of Vienna itself owned 28 cemeteries and one
crematory. In this municipal burial ground a variety of grave
leases are available. The rental charges depend on location,
and length of time. Highest charge is "for the duration of the
cemetery." Up to recent times at least, the city of Vienna buried
paupers in trenches or pits.

496

Funeral Rites

On the day of the funeral the closed casket is taken from the storage room and placed in state in a visiting room, against a background of floral arrangements, potted plants, and candles. The usual Vienna cemetery chapel maintains a large number of visiting rooms where bodies lie in state prior to interment, and as many as 30 to 40 bodies may be in these rooms in a single chapel at one time. Such a chapel is likely to have a service every 30 minutes throughout the day.[6]

For the majority of funerals religious services are held in these chapels. The coffin is opened only if requested by the family. Relatives and friends gather to pay their last respects.

An eyewitness gives a vivid description of the ceremonies held at a Viennese cemetery chapel:

> On the day of the burial, the mourners gathered at the cemetery in a small chapel reserved just for this purpose.

Collection of outmoded rolling stock formerly used in municipal mortuary

Portion of business offices of Vienna's "Städtische Bestattung"

The coffin lies in this small room and is surrounded with bouquets and wreaths of flowers and evergreens sent by friends. The most moving impression of this room is its darkness and silence. There are no windows and the thick walls are hung with a heavy black cloth. Six candles flicker on each side of the coffin. Although it is February the doors to the chapel are wide open and there is no heat in the room. Mourners gather inside this small room; they do not speak a word. For half an hour we stand there in the dark, cold silence, contemplating the death of our friend, our death, and life and resurrection. Occasionally friends of the dead woman enter and lay bouquets of flowers on the floor beside the coffin. No one speaks.[7]

The funeral rites in the chapel are performed according to

498

the religion of the deceased. At their conclusion employees of the undertaker, dressed in long black robes and medieval black hats, place the coffin on a wooden platform, spread a heavy black cloth over it, and bank wreaths around it. Then they carry the coffin on their shoulders to the grave, followed in order by the immediate family, all the remaining men in one group, and all the remaining women in another. Meanwhile the chapel bell is vigorously tolled. Vaults are seldom used in Austria, and because of a shortage of cemetery space one burial may be made on top of another.

When the body has been lowered, the family and friends step up to the grave and, using a little shovel furnished by the undertaker, scatter earth on the casket as they pass it. Then friends step up and express sympathy to the family. A few days later a Requiem Mass is said for the deceased, usually at his parish church.[8]

In rural areas, after the body is casketed it is laid out in state in the home, usually for a day or two. During this period a wake is held which is attended by relatives, friends and neighbors. When the time for the funeral arrives a horse-drawn hearse carries the body to the church. There a low Mass is said or a high Mass sung. Family and friends follow the body to the cemetery.

The typical Austrian family visits the graves of its dead with great regularity. Special days for visiting are the birthday of the deceased, the feastday, Christmas, Easter, All Souls' Day, and the anniversary of the death. At the time of the visit the living care for the grave, place lighted candles on it, and pray for the dead. Such practices, kept up for a half century or more after someone has died, lead one observer to comment that: "In Austria I feel a greater sense of community between the living and the dead because the dead are still very much a part of the way of life. I know more than one Austrian who will make it a point to visit the grave of a parent at least three times a month."[9]

Because a large percentage of the people of Austria are Roman Catholics the cremation movement has made less head-

Body of
Austrian lies
in state

way there than in certain of the Protestant countries of Europe. As in Germany and Switzerland the cremation movement in Austria has been primarily a movement among the working classes. There are six crematoria in Austria, situated at Graz, Linz, Salzburg, Steyr, Vienna, and Villach.[10] About eight per cent of the dead in major cities are cremated. The procedures followed prior to cremation are about the same as those followed for earth burial, except that the body to be cremated is borne to the cremation hall instead of the grave.

In Austrian cities, during the last 25 to 50 years, a marked movement has been evident away from the elaborate and toward the simpler funeral. Pomp has been reduced, the uniforms of the professional bearers have grown less ornate, the practice of laying out bodies in state in apartments or churches has become more infrequent, and that of transferring the entire funeral ceremony to the cemetery, almost universal.[11] Funeral customs and practices in the rural areas of Austria exhibit no major changes during the last half century.[12]

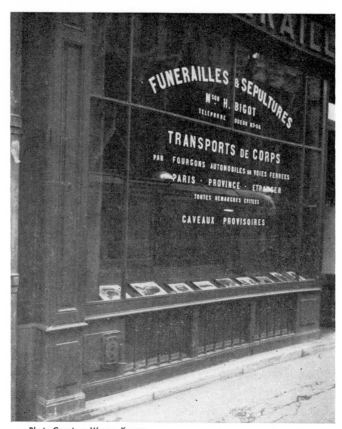

Typical French store-front undertaking establishment, Paris

Chapter 38

France

Funerals and the Community

Life in France has always been centered around the village or town. Farmers for the most part live in villages and go out from their homes to till their fields, so it is quite natural that funeral arrangements have historically been a community affair. Under the Napoleonic regime burial was an ecclesiastical function, with the church officials subletting the privilege in each Commune. This arrangement continued for a century, but in 1904 legislation was enacted which transferred the control of burial procedures from the Roman Catholic Church to local civic authorities. The law makes a distinction between exterior and interior service. Exterior service which covers the transportation of the human remains as well as the transportation of mourners, the furnishing of caskets and other burial supplies, and the exterior decoration of the home or place of service was legally placed under the direct control of the Commune. Interior service

503

which includes the decoration of the interior of the home and the place of the religious service is left to the family or its appointed representatives.[1]

In 1904 when the Paris Commune took over the exterior servicing of funerals, it granted a monopoly to a private corporation known as *Pompes Funèbres*. For the three years of this corporation, it provided "all the paraphernalia of funeral and interment services under an elaborate tariff of fees, graded to fit the several classes of funerals of persons of varying social and financial conditions."[2] The corporation also functioned as a supplier of mortuary goods to independent undertakers. At the beginning of 1908, the municipality assumed these functions and dealt directly with the undertakers, who obtained coffins of various classes, funeral vehicles, pallbearers and draperies (decorations) from the municipal bureau at legally fixed prices.[3]

The municipal funeral operation thus established has operated at an annual deficit for many years, partly because of the unclaimed dead who receive free burials,[4] and partly because of the disinclination of the French to make a profit on a municipal service.

While the account which follows deals almost entirely with Paris, other large French cities follow almost identical procedures, while smaller villages and towns sublet the tasks to a concessionnaire on a contract basis. In any event, the monopolistic pattern is maintained.

Response to Death

A death in France sets in motion certain administrative routines. These are performed by a member of the immediate family or a representative who may be an undertaker employed for that purpose.[5] Even though the engaging of an undertaker involves additional costs it is customary for all but the poorest classes. While technically the undertaker "represents" the family to the various authorities, he also in part serves as a supplier of funeral paraphernalia, some of which, drapes for example, he may own.

The family can deal directly with the municipality which will deliver the furnishings ordered, supply the hearse and limou-

504

A solemn moment as French parents go to funeral services for children lost in sinking ship

European Photo

sines and pallbearers; however, the agency will not provide personnel to conduct the funeral. And so if the family wishes to have professional direction of the funeral, it enlists the services of an undertaker, or on occasion the family may simply buy the casket and the members conduct the funeral themselves.[6]

For 24 hours after death a dead body may not be embalmed or removed from the place of death. During this period the death must be registered at the city or town hall. A certificate from the attending physician must accompany the request for registration. The next step is for the city doctor to inspect the remains. If he is satisfied that the death was due to natural causes he issues a death certificate. If the decedent had not been attended by a physician, the city doctor orders the body brought to the city mortuary for an autopsy. Since autopsies are performed only by the police surgeon, and the number of autopsies performed daily are limited, this may result in a delay of several days to a week before burial.[7]

Among factors which tend to prevent changes in funeral practices in France are an innate kind of conservation and an adherence to the tenets of the Napoleonic Code, drafted over one hundred fifty years ago. Many of the regulations of the Code still persist. For instance, the remains must be prepared for burial

505

at the place of death. This, plus the time provision against moving the remains, discourages the use of funeral homes or chapels and the practice of embalming. Bodies consequently are seldom embalmed, and when they are it nearly always is at the place of death.[8]

Embalming

If embalming is desired the undertaker must first obtain three certificates—one from the attending physician, one from the city health officer and a third from a police doctor. These are taken to the prefect of police who alone has the authority to authorize embalming. If he grants permission a witness, appointed by him, must be present, and the embalming must be completed in a single operation.[9]

Because of the legal difficulties and red tape involved, embalming is as a rule limited to the bodies of prominent people which are to lie in state, or to be interred at distant points. The shipment of a dead human body demands the completion of additional forms, and compliance with additional regulations, which will be touched on later. Shipments to America today are most generally by air, and the charges will approximate $1,200. The

European Photo

Drum and bugle corps and representatives of occupational groups lead funeral procession for dead French syndicalist leader

Five hearses carry bodies of persons killed in political mob action

minimum charge for embalming in such instances is in the neighborhood of $100. Embalming is generally done by medical practitioners. In the whole of France in 1953 there was but one funeral director who was also a licensed embalmer.[10] The fear of being buried alive bothers a few of the French, and such persons ordinarily specify in their last will and testament that their bodies be embalmed. Dry ice is sometimes used as a preservative, though not too effective a one.

Because there is little viewing of the dead, the clothing used is likely to be of an informal nature, in many cases a shirt or pajama is considered sufficient.[11]

Caskets

In Paris, the undertaker orders the casket from the municipal monopoly,[12] specifying the time and place of delivery. In most instances the body is placed in the casket at the location where death occurred.

507

Catafalque used in
luxury class
French funeral

Wooden caskets are used and follow a general pattern. Although oak is the wood most often used, caskets are made of mahogany, other fine cabinet woods, pine or poplar and are supplied by the French Communities or by their licensees. The Paris monopoly operates its own casket factory with a daily production of about 150 units and endeavors to maintain an inventory sufficient for the needs of the next 30 days.[13]

When a funeral director procures a casket from the Paris municipal monopoly, a duplicate copy of the order is sent to the family or legal representative of the decedent and there can be no additional charge made. A violation of this provision subjects the violator to a fine.[14]

The casket used in France is shoulder-shaped and usually covered with a pall of black for an adult; of white for children. The pall is put in place as soon as the body is placed in the casket and is not removed until the burial.

In Paris the municipal monopoly specifies six classes of funerals. Thirty years ago there were ten. Each class of funeral calls for a type of casket falling within a certain price range. The casket in the first-class funeral is made of ebony, mahogany, or finely panelled oak; in the second class, of polished oak; in the third

508

class, of unpolished oak; in the fourth class, of a poorer grade of oak; in the fifth class, of thinner oak boards; in the sixth or lowest class, of pine. Poplar is also used in the lower classes of funerals.[15]

If a family in Paris wishes a casket that the monopoly cannot furnish, such as an American-styled metallic casket, the monopoly must still be paid for a casket of the first class, so two receptacles must be purchased although only one will be used. The same rule applies to other materials or funeral personnel.

Elaborate draping is the vogue in French families who can afford it. If the death occurs at home the walls of the room where the body lies before and after casketing are covered with black draperies from floor to ceiling. Both catafalque and casket are heavily draped. The church, too, is heavily decorated. Black carpets are laid down; black covers are placed on the chairs; the high altar and the walls are draped with black. On the front of the church, black drapes are used, often with shields containing the initials of the deceased. This device is used to identify the burial for mourners who wish to attend. The pall and other draperies are rented from the undertaker. A source of income to the church accrues from its share of the drapery rental used there.[16]

Burial

After casketing, remains must be buried within 48 hours, even when embalmed. If it is desired to keep a body unburied for a

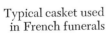

Typical casket used
in French funerals

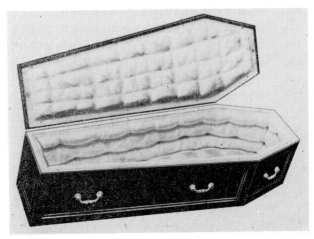

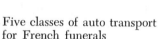

Five classes of auto transport
for French funerals

longer period, transport it to a distance of more than 125 miles,
or to place it in a vault for 48 hours, it must be put inside an
airtight metal lining inside the casket.

If this procedure is followed, interment may be delayed for
months. The French do not observe the custom of viewing casketed remains. When the body has been placed in the casket,
the lid is screwed down, and may not be reopened. If the body
is to be transported for burial at a distant point or to be placed
in a vault, pending final disposal, the police seal the casket at both
ends. Metal bands are also used to reinforce the casket to prevent tampering with it. The role of the police in keeping informed as to the whereabouts of the body and insisting that

Corbillard hippomobile - 1ᵉʳᵉ Classe.

Corbillard hippomobile - 2ᵉᵐᵉ Classe.

Corbillard hippomobile - 3ᵉᵐᵉ Classe

Corbillard hippomobile - 4ᵉᵐᵉ Classe.

Corbillard hippomobile - 5ᵉᵐᵉ Classe.

Corbillard hippomobile - 6ᵉᵐᵉ Classe.

Traditional horse-drawn hearses still available, in six classes, to the French

P.I.P. Photo

French floral car;
hearses also have
flower racks on roof

Women in mourning,
a familiar sight
in French cemeteries

proper measures are taken to protect the public health is important. Fees are assessed to cover the costs of these services.

The monopoly also arranges to supply uniformed pallbearers, who handle the casket. If burial is to take place in a Paris cemetery, the monopoly supplies the hearse and funeral cars. If the funeral is outside the city, the undertaker can use his own equipment. Automobile hearses are now universally used in Paris, although horse-drawn hearses can still be seen in the Paris suburbs and in the provinces. The class of funeral determines the type of hearse and the degree of elaborateness of adornment and livery. It also determines the number of cars for the mourners and a variety of items incidental to the funeral. The old practice of the mourners marching behind the hearse to the church and less frequently from the church to the cemetery was still in vogue only a few years ago. Many Frenchmen then still felt that using motorized equipment was "rushing the remains to the cemetery."

Though the monopoly provides a small stipend for a church service it has been common for families to arrange for a more impressive ceremony.

512

Cemeteries

The city of Paris also has a monopoly on the operation of cemeteries. Family vaults in Paris cemeteries are usually constructed with a capacity for 20 caskets. When the vault has been filled, after a lapse of ten years, it is permissible to exhume the remains and place them in a single casket. Thus 19 additional places are provided.

Graves may be rented in a Paris cemetery for a minimal rental period of five years. The next longer period is thirty years, and the cost difference between the five and thirty-year periods is not great. Moreover, at the expiration of the contractual period, the family has the option of renewal. Graves can also be rented for a period of one hundred years or in perpetuity. If the rental period expires and is not renewed, the city of Paris—owner and operator of the cemeteries—exhumes the remains and reburies them in a common grave. Approximately 65 per cent of all five-year rentals are not renewed, and non-renewal of thirty years is frequent. This releases additional grave space annually and makes it unlikely that cemetery space will be exhausted.[17]

Elaborate monuments, mausolea, and wall crypts
at Campo Di Staglieno, Genoa

Chapter 39

Italy

Italy is predominantly a Catholic country, and, apart from the relatively small Jewish, Protestant, non-Roman Catholic minorities, standard Catholic burial practices, from the liturgical point of view, prevail. The influence and control over funerary matters, however, as is the case in most European countries, is shared with municipal governments. Italy has no national law affecting funerals and interments, as does France and Switzerland. Consequently the pattern of municipal rules and regulations varies.[1]

Organization of Funeral Service

In general most Italian municipalities control the "exterior" aspects of the burial of the dead, such as hearse and carriage transportation and earth or mausoleum burial. Private undertaking firms may be engaged by families to assist in the "interior" arrangements, such as the making of reports and the

515

Horse-drawn hearse is still used in some upper-class Italian funerals. *Upper right*, Child's hearse. *Lower*, Funeral passenger coach

securing of necessary forms and permits, the decoration of the inside of the home, the furnishing of candles, and the arranging of numerous personal and religious ceremonies. Some cities, such as Rome, will extend to a private undertaking concern what amounts to a municipal monopoly on funeral services to be provided at standard rates. The classification of funerals is standard procedure in most of Europe, with the major items that differentiate the classes usually consisting of type of casket, type of hearse and funeral carriages, and the type and place of interment.

In Italy it is customary to send for a priest when someone is thought to be in danger of death. The person who takes it upon himself to summon the priest may not be aware of the religious beliefs of the dying one, and yet so acts because of his or her own religious conviction. When death occurs the body is immediately washed, and clothed in the deceased's best garments, although shoes are not put on. If death occurred in the home, the windows are generally blacked out, and candles are lighted in the room in which the body lies in state. The majority of hospitals in Italy are served by members of religious orders, and they convene at the bedside of a dying

Italian funeral procession and modern funeral coach

person, and keep the death watch. When death occurs they pray for the repose of the soul of the dead.[2]

Embalming is seldom practiced in Italy today. Its use is reserved for the remains of important personages, which must lie in state for public viewing, and must, therefore, be preserved from rapid decomposition. All embalming is done by doctors who embalm the body arterially. There is usually a room set aside for embalming in the cemetery chapels. Italian medical practitioners have been also known to use oils and bandages to effect an embalmment through osmosis. Results, as indicated in the use of this method in the preservation of the late Pope Pius XII, have been unsatisfactory and dis-

Metal-cased tapered coffin for mausoleum interment

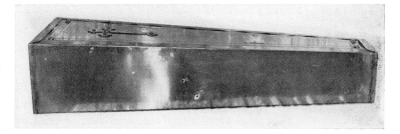

517

appointing.[3] Restorative art of any sort is virtually unheard of in Italy.[4]

In the period before the dead are casketed, they may be viewed, although viewing seems to be less a practice in Italy than in America. The minimum period of keeping the body uncasketed is twenty-four hours. In the case of violent death the law provides that this period must be extended to a minimum of forty-eight hours. The casket is closed as soon as the body is laid in it. The ceremony generally takes place the night before the funeral, or at the latest, an hour or two before.[5] For earth burial, bodies are placed in wooden caskets. For entombment above ground, or in wall niches, metal inner liners which are sealed and placed in the outer casket of wood are used.

Funeral Ceremonies

In Italy there are still some private chapels in homes or palaces, and permission may be granted to have a Mass celebrated in one of these before placing the body in the casket. Such practice is of course highly exceptional. Only the family or closest friends could attend such a private Mass.[6]

The common practice is for relatives and friends to gather for the funeral at the house of the deceased if death took place there, or at the hospital, if there. The funeral generally begins at one or the other of these places. A priest accompanies the body to the church. Catholic funerals in Italy, as is always the case, take place in the morning, and a funeral Mass in the presence of the closed casket is the high point of the religious ceremony. Italians consider funerals important events, and make much of them.[7]

The Funeral Procession

After the Mass has been said, the procession forms. Whenever distance permits—and one or two miles are not considered excessive—the procession walks from the church to the graveyard. The procession is led by wreath bearers. Children march next. The priests follow. Then come the bearers with the casket, then the close relatives, and finally friends and acquaintances.

518

Two views of horse-drawn funeral coach in funeral procession, Pizza

It is customary for four people to act as bearers and to hold a tassel hanging from the four corners of the casket or wheeled conveyance. If the deceased were a man, four men act as bearers; if a woman, four women.[8]

When distance makes walking prohibitive the procession proceeds either by horse-drawn or motorized transportation. Most Italians still consider the horse-drawn hearse and carriage with their uniformed attendants as the ultimate of stylishness in funerals. Motor hearses in the large cities are nevertheless replacing their slower, if more majestic, counterparts. Some

519

Above, water-borne
funeral, Venice

Workmen load metal-clad
coffin to be placed
in mausoleum

municipalities and private undertakers own or operate a
variety of motor hearses and limousines. Among them may
be seen the all-white child's hearse, a common type of funeral
vehicle in America in the late nineteenth century.

In the provinces of Belluno, Balzano, Padova, Rovigo, Tren-
to, Treviso, Venice, Verona, and Vicensa funeral transportation
vehicles are not owned by undertaking establishments, but by
the municipal governments. As a result undertakers must
use such transportation facilities as are made available to them.
Frequently this means outmoded equipment. There is much
discontent with this arrangement. About the only defense that
can be made for it is that it limits competition by supplying
equally poor equipment to everybody.[9]

520

Burial and Cemeteries

At the cemetery, the casket is either carried to the cemetery church, or directly to the grave site. When the procession arrives at the cemetery, it may be met by monks, who accompany it. After the usual short graveside ceremony, including the final benediction, the body is buried. When burial takes place above ground, or in a wall niche, the casket is slid lengthwise into the opening, which is then sealed with a cemented stone or marble slab.

Cemetery space may be purchased for a limited period of ownership or in perpetuity. If a body is given "common ground" burial, it remains buried for a period varying from eighteen months to ten years. After this time, the grave is opened, the remains exhumed, and the bones are either burned or placed in a small wall niche, as the family desires. A metropolitan cemetery may contain a section reserved for the burial of Protestants, and another for Jews.

The regulations of the Catholic Church, which require that its members in good standing must be buried in consecrated ground, make cremation a rarity in Italy. Under these circumstances cremation in Italy is confined to small numbers of the minority groups.

There are presently twenty Italian municipalities, mostly in Northern Italy, in which crematoria may be found.[10] Paradoxically, it might be noted that in the nineteenth century Italy was the founding homeland of the modern cremation movement.[11]

Burial and mourning customs vary from region to region. These have been described by many Italian folklore writers, such as Giuseppe Pitre who deals with Sicily, and by fiction writers, such as Giuseppe Marotta who specializes in local backgrounds. Marotta writes of Naples, and in his book, *Salute a noi,* uses a funeral director as his mouthpiece who tells stories about his "clients." In another of his works, *Gold of Naples,* Marotta describes a colorful scene of mourning. This story has been filmed under the same title.

In certain villages in the Umbrian region—Umbria lies in

521

central Italy—older houses have a special door called the "door of the dead man" (*la Porta del morte*) which normally is walled up, and is unsealed only to allow a body to be carried through it on its way to the cemetery. Because the remains have in a most literal sense not left through the common doors of the house, folk belief has it that the dead person has not left his home, but remains forever with his dear ones.[12]

Italy is rich in local funeral beliefs and customs of many kinds. To cite but one instance, there are the burial activities

Special hearse
carries body of
Pope Pius XII in
procession through
streets of Rome

Photo by Il Popolo

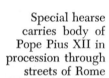

522

of the *Arciconfraternita Misericordia*—the Archconfraternity of Mercy—of Florence, the oldest existing charity organization of Italy, with roots that extend to the thirteenth century.

This venerable organization owes its beginnings to an old Florentine weakness for blaspheming God and His Saints. In the thirteenth century no group was more addicted to this evil habit than the *facchini*—porters who carried cloth and other merchandise from the workshops of Florence to the market, warehouses, or customers. Between loads these men loitered

Photo by Mauro

Left, the floral wreath is a commonplace of Italian funerals

Beautiful cemetery near Rome was damaged by allied bombings, now is restored

Photo Courtesy E. C. and G. R. Johnson

around the Piazza San Giovanni, and there in 1240 an older porter, known for his piety, suggested that as a penance each of his fellow workmen should voluntarily contribute a *soldo* to a common fund each time he curses. The fund grew rapidly, and was used to build wheeled stretchers for transporting the poorer sick of the city to the hospital, a task ordinarily performed by the porters. From this charitable deed grew the *Fratelli* or Brotherhood of Mercy.

All conditions and ranks of citizens later were admitted to membership, and through the centuries, other corporal works of mercy, including burying the dead, were added to transporting the sick. To make the doers of these good deeds unrecognizable, a costume, consisting of a hooded cape with concealment for the face, was adopted as the official garb of the archconfraternity. Today Florentines still contribute penance money, and tinkling motor ambulances—and sometimes even the antique hand-pushed stretcher carts—are a familiar sight on the streets of Florence. Whenever an accident occurs, words come naturally into the mouths of Florentines: "Call the Mis-

524

ericordia." Many members of the families of the old nobility of Florence serve in the ranks of the organization, but always behind the faceless anonymity of the hooded robes.

It has been eloquently written that "by tradition, funerals in Florence are held at dusk. If the deceased belonged to La Misericordia, the brothers generally turn up in their capes. As the cortege winds through the narrow streets followed by the gray-caped figures carrying lighted tapers, a gust straight from the Middle Ages seems to blow under the shadowy eaves of Florence. Not one among those brothers, no doubt, but has sometime indulged in a rip-roaring Florentine oath. Now they are accompanying a 'brother,' hoping that his good works will speak for him up there where blasphemies are recorded, and that theirs will speak for them when the day comes."[13]

Venice provides several interesting funeral variants. Of necessity, funerals there are in the main water borne, either in row boats or in special motor boats. San Michele, the Venice cemetery, is an island.

Venice, too, has a local private burial organization, the *Arciconfraternita di S. Cristofore Compagnia della Misericordia.* Annual membership dues in this organization are 80 cents

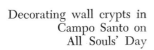

Decorating wall crypts in
Campo Santo on
All Souls' Day

European Photo

and convey to all members, rich or poor, the right to the same type of funeral. When a member is buried, other members in attendance wear black gowns and hoods, and violet girdles. The fraternity is allowed to operate its own motorboat, and owns its own piece of fenced-off land in the cemetery.

Chapter 40

Spain and Portugal

Spain

Spaniards for the most part react to death as do other Christians. Some accept it with resignation as the will of God, and, hoping for reunion with the dead, pray for the repose of the souls of their loved ones. Others welcome death as an end to suffering. Still others have little concern for what may happen after death. Then there are some who feel small need for ceremonies honoring the dead, but that good deeds for the living are more important.[1]

While there is a common core of religious ceremony underlying funerals everywhere in Spain, each of the 15 regions and 50 provinces exhibit some variation from the general pattern.

Funeral Establishments and Their Control

One of the most interesting aspects of Spanish funeralization today is the competition that exists between municipally oper-

Examples of luxury-type Spanish caskets. Upper casket has lock on side

Photos Courtesy John Plank, and American Funeral Director

ated mortuary services and private enterprise funeral establishments. Spanish funerals until 1944 were almost entirely conducted by private funeral enterprise except in larger cities, where municipally operated funeral enterprises existed. In that year there appeared on the scene burial insurance companies similar to those which operate in some of the states in the southern United States. These Spanish insurance companies issued a policy which designated the type of funeral merchandise and the amount of service that would be provided to a policyholder at the time of death, stipulating further that the merchandise and services must be procured from a funeral establishment designated by the insurance company.

Since 1957, as a means of meeting this competition, some funeral directors have started their own individual companies, in each case designating themselves as the official firm supplying the guaranteed goods and services. When a private funeral establishment operates its own insurance company, the death payments are made directly to the family and not to an intermediary. The family then is free to purchase the class of funeral it desires. Such arrangement, it is claimed, removes the funeral

528

director from the control of the great burial insurance companies. Naturally the latter oppose this plan.[2]

In over thirty cities, including the larger cities of Madrid and Barcelona, no private funeral homes exist, but instead a municipally licensed monopoly conducts all funeral services for the city. Because Spain is officially a Catholic country, burial is made jointly by the municipal authorities and the authorities of the Catholic Church. In Barcelona, for example, the Municipal Undertaking Service *(Servicio Municipal de Pompas Fúnebres)* has the exclusive rights of burial, and provides all necessary goods and non-religious services, while the individual parish churches attend to the religious services for the dead, both at the time of burial and later.[3]

Madrid, with a population of 1,750,000, has a single funeral establishment, *Pompas Fúnebres* (Funeral Pomp), which handles approximately 151,000 funerals a year. This establishment maintains a fleet of 50 funeral coaches and 50 limousines. Unlike its American counterpart, which renews its transportation facilities periodically, the Spanish undertaking establishment considers age a virtue, and *Pompas Fúnebres* still uses an 1880 hearse body, elaborately carved from black and brown hardwoods. When equipment was motorized, this body was removed from the horse-drawn vehicle and placed on an automobile chassis.[4] *Pompas Fúnebres* is a privately managed organization which operates under a municipal contract. Although the rates it charges are established by the municipality of Madrid, it offers funeral goods and services in several classes.

Outside the cities mentioned, one finds private funeral establishments operating much as they operate in other parts of Europe. Caskets are made at the funeral homes and delivered to the place of death, home or hospital, where the body is casketed, and funeral services are arranged. The Spanish funeral director may own his own rolling stock and manufacture his own caskets. He may also sell caskets made by others.

Arranging the Funeral

In a large city when the family reports the death of a member to the municipal funeral organization, a representative visits the home to make all arrangements for the burial. These include a notification to the Municipal Court. The court registers the death and issues a death certificate, after a coroner has certified the cause of death. If death has resulted from other than natural causes — from homicide or accident — or if grounds exist for suspecting foul play, the body is sent to the official mortuary for an autopsy, which when the legal time arrives is performed by the coroner on duty. No autopsies are permitted by law until at least twenty-four hours after death. In the case of an autopsy, registration of death at the civil registry is not made until it has been authorized by a judge, who takes no action until he has received the coroner's report.[5]

The representative of the municipal funeral service, on behalf of the family, arranges for the rental or purchase of a burial niche. If the family already owns a niche, mausoleum, or plot in any cemetery, the representative arranges for the re-opening and burial. A second burial may be made in a grave or niche only after two years have elapsed since a prior burial following a normal death; or six years, after a death from contagious disease.[6] The representative also provides the casket, hearse, and attendants. If requested, he arranges for floral bouquets and wreaths.

If, on the other hand, the family wishes to employ the services of a private funeral director, when death has occurred in the

Types of hearses used in Spain vary from traditional horse-drawn to latest motor coaches. Hearse at left considered most ornate in Madrid

Left Photo Courtesy John Plank, and American Funeral Director. Right Photos Courtesy Alcañiz

A casket being loaded
for delivery at
deceased's place
of residence

home, they leave the body on the death bed, and summon him. When he arrives, he confers with them and unless a funeral is to be supplied by contract with an insurance company, they select the casket, the type of hearse, and the floral wreaths; and make known their wishes concerning the funeral services. The bill for these goods and services is agreed upon at this point, and the funeral director follows through by contacting the church and municipal authorities. He sees to the filling out of all required forms and during the actual funeral ceremonies he remains with the family. A few days after the funeral he submits his bill.[7]

Burial Procedures

Except to shave and wash it, no preparation is made of the body.[8] The features are not arranged and cosmetic work is not performed. Embalming, expensive in Spain, is performed by physicians, who in the absence of standard or fixed rates for the operation charge what they will. An embalming may cost $200, or as much as $1,000. In view of the high charges, private physicians ordinarily embalm the bodies of the wealthy, persons of prominence for public viewing, and foreigners shipped abroad. Unembalmed bodies may be transported to any part of Spain, provided they are moved within a 24- to 72-hour period after death.[9] Funeral directors are not licensed as embalmers, but the municipal funeral service handles all paper formalities involved in transporting a body. It also provides the necessary caskets,

531

cases and outside boxes. For foreign shipment it makes sure that all customs regulations are complied with. To ship a body out of Spain costs approximately $1,000. Included are the embalming and preparation fees, and the charges for the casket, packing cases, freight, and documentation.[10] If a private funeral director is employed, he carries out all these functions except the embalming. The body of a person dying of a contagious disease must be buried in the location where death occurred, and it may not be exhumed until six years have elapsed after death.[11]

The dead are usually dressed in their ordinary clothing, although many people prefer to have their relatives buried in a sheet or a religious robe. The remains lie in state in the home until the time for burial arrives, when they are transported to the church for religious services, and then to the cemetery.

Funeral Processions

In cities, at the hour appointed for the funeral, the family gathers at the home of the deceased. The procession forms there, the hearse leads, and the passenger cars with the mourners follow. The casketed remains are taken to the cemetery church chapel, accompanied only by male relatives. The casket is blessed by the priest, but is not taken into the church. The funeral party enters the church for a brief prayer, while the hearse and casket proceed to a waiting point in the cemetery. After the prayers, the funeral party proceeds to the waiting point to rejoin the hearse and follows it to the place of burial or entombment. After the burial, all return to their homes. This is the common core procedure. Local variations are to be found.[12]

Thus, up to 1954, horse-drawn hearses were still used exclusively in Manresa, with the mourners following on foot. Of late years, at least one funeral establishment there provides a motorized hearse, and transports the mourners in limousines. The practice of stopping at the church en route to the cemetery is not followed as universally today as it was in the past. When such halt is omitted two or three days later the family provide for a public Requiem Mass. Friends attend this ceremony, to pray for the dead and to offer condolences to the family. This arrangement is gaining acceptance elsewhere in Spain.[13]

Rural patterns adjust to a wide variety of local conditions. In mountain villages, for example, where earth burial is the practice and motor-driven equipment is not available, neighbors of the dead person, in shifts of six, carry the body to the place of burial. Sometimes it is necessary for them to bear this burden up a stairway to a cemetery which lies on a mountain-side. Every hundred yards or so the body is transferred to another group of bearers, to give those who have borne the load a chance to rest. After the burial the returning relatives and friends gather for a great feast. Burial in rural Spain is a community rather than an individual or family affair. In some places the returning relatives and friends meet at a convenient bar, there to speak highly of the deceased and to deaden their sorrow with strong drink.[14]

Cemeteries and Mausolea

Since Spanish cemeteries in the larger cities are municipal prop-

Ornate Spanish catafalque with candelabra

erty, the sextons and gravediggers who bury the body are municipal employees. At the cemetery, the funeral director turns the body over to them together with the papers designating the place of burial. This is his final function. In larger cities in Spain, as in some other parts of Europe, cemeteries seem appalling. "Most Spanish graveyards," notes one report, "are places of desolation and decay, presided over by gravediggers so thieving and callous that relatives often slash the clothes of the dead to keep their bodies from being stripped."[15] A burial in one of these cemeteries is described as "dumping a box into a hole."

In Manresa, a city of 50,000, in the province of Barcelona, annually some 600 people die. Most of them are buried in compartments, called "niches," which each family owns in the local cemetery. After a burial has been made three years must elapse before the compartment can be used for another burial. In addition to such niches, the cemetery contains a common grave in which paupers are given earth burial, and marble tombs in which the wealthy bury their dead.[16]

Catholic interments in Barcelona, even those which are made underground, are made in niches which may be rented or purchased. Some families own their own burial plots and erect mausolea on them. Special sections are reserved in cemeteries for Jewish and Protestant burials. Only in these sections is earth burial, as distinguished from niche burial, to be found.

When burial is made in a niche above ground, the usual gravemarker in Barcelona is a marble plaque containing the name, date of birth, and date of death of the deceased. When the niche is below ground, the marker is customarily placed on the surface. It may be a simple stone, or even a large marble monument. Some families have special dedications incised into their marble mausolea or plaques.[17] The municipal funeral service in large cities provides a special free service for the poor, with burial in a common grave.[18]

Each year, on All Saints' Day (November 1st) and All Souls' Day (November 2nd) it is customary for members of a family to visit the cemeteries and decorate the niches and mausolea with flowers.

534

Mausolea in Spain and Portugal often have crypts above; platforms are raised for those wishing to decorate them

Photos Courtesy E. C. and G. R. Johnson

Portugal

Portugal, like its sister country, Spain, is predominantly Catholic. The principal difference between burial practices in the large cities of Spain and of Portugal seems to lie in the fact that municipal enterprise tends to dominate the former; individual enterprise, the latter. Not that large-scale operations are lacking among the privately owned establishments of Portugal. Lisbon, for instance, has some 40 funeral establishments. One of them, the *Agencia Barata,* in 1957 handled over 1,200 funerals. Because Portugal is at a geographic crossroads, Lisbon funeral directors carry on an extensive business in handling the remains of nationals of other European, South and North American and Asiatic countries.[19]

Unlike Spanish law, which requires burial within twenty-four hours, Portuguese law forbids burial within this time span, unless the approval of the family doctor of the deceased is obtained. As in Spain, embalming is rarely performed, being reserved for the bodies of prominent or wealthy persons, or for remains which are to be shipped long distances.[20]

Lisbon has six cemeteries, beautiful and well-kept, but crowd-

535

Set of deluxe
candelabra used in
Spanish funeral
ceremonies

ed. As a result, after five years bodies are disinterred and the
reduced remains reburied in two-foot-long permanent caskets,
in niches along the cemetery walls. Disinterred remains which
are unclaimed are placed in a common burial pit. Many well-to-
do families in Lisbon build private mausolea in public cemeteries for the burial of family dead. It is customary for the
cemetery authorities to require the creation of a fund sufficient
to maintain the care and upkeep of the mausolea. A structure
of this kind may contain space for 50 or more caskets, some above
and more below ground, and may be equipped with a small
altar.[21]

The Portuguese funeral maintains a tradition of ornate elegance.
At one funeral home the highest-priced funerals include the use
of an elaborate gold altar, supported by four carved lions on
which the casket is set; and gold encrusted drapes. Caskets are
draped in black or purple velvet casket covers, embroidered with
gold or silver thread, and decorated with yellow or purple inserts.
The Egyptian mummy case type of coffin—called an "urn" in
Portugal—is rapidly losing popularity, as the larger, American-
styled casket gains favor.[22]

Portuguese urns, coffins or caskets, display an elegance comparable to all other funeral furnishings, and are likely to be made
by the funeral director who sells them. Thus the *Magno* funeral
establishment in Lisbon operates its own casket factory. Portu-

536

guese caskets are made of wood: mahogany, oak, or pine, depending on the cost of the funeral. A fine casket of intricately carved Brazilian wood may require a month's labor by a skilled craftsman, and cost the equivalent of $350. Funeral homes often engage in the sale of religious articles such as rosaries, prayer books, religious pictures, or statuary.[23] The making of funeral draperies is another substantial part of the business. The altars at the church and the cemetery chapel are draped for funerals; and cloth-covered caskets are likely to have decorations—festoons and the like—made of gold embroidery sewed to them. Most caskets used in Lisbon are lined with lead. The cost depends on the kind of wood used, the amount and quality of the carving, and the quality of the hardware.[24]

To the foreigner perhaps the most distinctive element in the Portuguese funeral is the coach. Most coaches used by Portuguese funeral directors were originally built for noblemen who used them for their personal transportation. Earlier, very ornate coaches of this type were so heavy as to require eight horses to draw them. Later coaches were built lighter so as to be less cumbersome and to permit speedier travel. Lisbon funeral directors began to purchase such coaches about 1900, and by 1914 one of the largest establishments owned 41 of them. In 1930 these magnificent coaches began to be converted from horse to

Two examples of Portuguese funeral hearses. Hearse on left for children

Portuguese cemetery monument has carved replicas of artisan's tools-of-trade

Photo Courtesy E. C. and G. R. Johnson

motor power, by transferring the body to an automobile chassis. For a special occasion, however, a funeral director—if he is fortunate enough to own one—may use a sixteenth century coach drawn by eight horses. Or he may use an eighteenth century carriage to carry the priest to the funeral services. Few of these very beautiful coaches have been withdrawn from active service, and one large Lisbon establishment today is able to give its clients the choice of 23 such equipages. The same establishment's newest hearse has accommodations in a single compartment for 12 persons and the casket.[25]

Another modern Portuguese funeral coach is streamlined, with the cab over the engine to allow easier movement through the ancient, narrow, winding streets of Lisbon. Three seats are fixed on either side of the casket. The coach is surmounted by a white illuminated cross. The usual Portuguese funeral coach is black, ornamented with gold. White coaches, also gold ornamented, are used for infants, unmarried young people up to the age of 20, and, if requested, for spinsters.[26]

538

Chapter 41

Netherlands, Belgium and Switzerland

The Netherlands

Funeral practices in The Netherlands today do not vary greatly from those of mid-west United States. When a person dies, the reactions range from stoic acceptance to weeping. A doctor is summoned to make certain that death has occurred. Bodies are seldom embalmed, but are laid out by a nurse or undertaker.[1]

Organization of Funeral Service

The undertaker is responsible for dressing and casketing the dead, taking care of such legal formalities as obtaining death certificates and making contractual arrangements for services to the bereaved family, and placing death announcements in the newspapers. He also arranges for the services of the *aanzegger*, the announcer who in black formal attire visits the neighbors to inform them of the death. Additionally, the undertaker makes provisions for a "slumber room" where the body may remain and be viewed during the three days that usually lapse between death and burial or cremation. This slumber room may be either in a hospital where preparation of the body frequently takes place, in the home, or in the undertaker's establishment.[2]

The ceremonial observance of death begins when the family closes the curtains or hangs sheets over the front windows of the house in which death has occurred. The *aanzegger* then begins to make his rounds, telling the news to the neighbors.[3]

Funeral service in The Netherlands is available on the one hand through private funeral undertakers, and non-commercial mutual or co-operative funeral organizations on the other. The private funeral undertakers are organized into three associations: the Roman Catholic, the Protestant, and a non-sectarian association. These three co-operate to form The Netherlands Central Bureau for Funeral Service, with headquarters in The Hague.[4]

Although co-operative or mutual funeral associations generally are organized on a local or regional basis, a few national funeral co-operatives do exist. The local and regional co-operatives, in turn, belong to one of three national organizations: the Central Association of Organizations for Funeral Service, The Netherlands Association of Funeral Organizations (these are associations formed by co-operatives, not by the memberships of individuals and they do not directly serve persons as the co-operatives do), or the Federation of Mutual Funeral Organizations of and for Roman Catholics in The Netherlands. The first of these, the Central Association, comprises co-operative cost-price organizations; and the second, the Federation, "natura" organizations—groups dealing in insurance to cover funeral costs; the organization basis of the third group is religion.[5]

Distinctive Features of Funeral

Funeral services in The Netherlands are very similar to those commonly held for Catholics and Protestants in the United States, with the exception that a church or chapel service is perhaps less infrequent. And yet The Netherlands' funeral keeps

540

a distinctive character. Horse-drawn carriages are common—the procession is not completely mechanized as in the United States—and as the cortege proceeds to the cemetery, if necessary, it makes a detour so that it will pass the house of the dead person. When it has passed by, in front rooms of the houses along the streets the curtains are opened, the sheets removed, the shades rolled up.[6]

Graveside oratory is another Netherlands custom. Sometimes four or five persons deliver brief funeral orations at the grave. Not all people, however, anticipate such speechmaking over their remains with equanimity, and some even specify in their wills that it be omitted entirely, or that it be limited to a single speech or specified speaker. Graves are marked with headstones. These contain the name, birth and death dates of the deceased, and frequently a legend such as "Rest in Peace."[7]

The observance of public mourning is more conspicuous and more unusual in The Netherlands than in the United States, with considerable local variation in form, intensity and duration. Personal taste also enters into the matter of mourning observance.

Changes in Procedures

The last decades have seen important changes in connection with the burial of the dead. Chief among these, perhaps, is the replacement in rural districts of the old-established neighbor's help (*buren-hulp*) with more organized funeral services. A second is the gradual replacement of horse-drawn by motorized equipment. The development in larger towns of co-operatives which provide a uniform type of funeral for all members is another.[8]

Another development has been the increasing use of cremation. Cremation has been legally recognized as a legitimate form of disposal in The Netherlands only during the past few years. Prior to then, it was occasionally practiced and for decades the crematorium at Westerveld was the only one of its kind in the country. At present there are two, and more are being planned.

Those who wish to qualify for a Diploma in Funeral Undertaking, which enables them to serve as a professional funeral at-

541

tendant, may do so by successfully completing a correspondence course organized and directed by the Association of Professional Examinations for the Funeral Service. Headquarters of this Association are in The Hague. The disposal of the dead is regulated by the "Act Dealing with the Disposal of the Dead." This Act is now being revised with regard to cremation.[9]

Belgium

Organization of Funeral Service

In Belgium a death must be reported immediately to the local bureau of vital statistics. The marriage book, or, if the deceased is an alien, the passport must be submitted with the report. The fact of death is then verified either by the burgomaster, the bureau of vital statistics, or a doctor appointed by the municipality. After this formality, a death certificate is issued and authorization is granted for the transportation and burial of the remains.[10]

Remains are rarely embalmed in Belgium, even though facilities exist for both arterial and "surface embalming"—a process in which the body is wrapped in a winding sheet which is saturated with diluted formaldehyde. Licensed embalmers are not to be found in Belgium as a distinct occupational group. When relatives desire to have a body embalmed, or when it is to be shipped to a foreign country whose customs regulations require embalming, the services of certain medical doctors, licensed by the government as embalmers, are used. Embalming in Belgium is solely for preservation from decay or dehydration. No effort is made to reconstruct the features or to improve the appearance by the use of restorative procedures.

Burial Procedures

Shrouding is done by relatives, friends, nurses, or members of religious sisterhoods. Relatives select the garments to be used: suits for the men, dresses for the women. White clothing is sometimes used. Burial usually takes place two to four days after death, the length of the interval depending on the cause

542

of death and the condition of the remains. On the day before the funeral, the remains are generally put into a casket for viewing, although they sometimes are displayed on the bed.

During the period between death and the funeral, the house of the deceased is usually kept closed, as a sign of mourning. It is customary in small villages to stand a crucifix before the house. Since the greater majority of Belgians are Catholics, most Belgian funerals are conducted according to Catholic rites. On the day of the funeral a hearse brings the body to a church for religious services, and from the church to the cemetery.

Any resident of a community is entitled to a burial place as designated by the municipal authorities. If it so desires a family may purchase a plot for one or several of its members, and for the duration of the existence of the cemetery.

Remains may be cremated in Belgium itself only when the deceased has so provided in his will. If no such testamentary provision has been made, and the relatives wish to have the body cremated, it must be sent to Germany or France.

Funeralization, including the preparation, transportation and burial of remains, and the making of arrangements for religious services, are handled by undertakers who operate in the context of private enterprise. Belgian undertakers belong to a professional organization.

In recent years the most significant change in Belgian funeral customs has been the substitution of motor-driven for horse-drawn hearses. Only in very small villages can the latter be found.

Switzerland

Each Swiss community provides burial as an official service, except Berne and the French cantons. In these places undertaking exists as a commercial enterprise, which, for a fee, takes charge of all burial formalities.[11]

Switzerland has no funeral homes in the American sense of the term, and the casketed body is generally kept for three days after death in the best room of the residence. If the deceased died in a hospital, it is likely that the body will be sent directly to be laid out in a special chapel at the cemetery. Normally the body is not embalmed or prepared. Embalming is reserved for cases in which shipment to another country must be made, and the remains preserved for a later funeral.

There is no class of embalmers as such in Switzerland. When embalming is desired, the services of a physician or medical professor are sought, and the operation is expensive. The dead are generally clothed in fancy white shirt with lace. Inexpensive caskets are lined with cotton; the costlier grades with silk or velvet. A special white pillow is provided for the head. In Zurich and Basle the community furnishes the casket and the family provides the other funeral necessities. Floral gifts are made by friends.

Details of the Community Service

In most places in Switzerland, when a family wishes to take advantage of the community funeral service, it notifies the local authorities concerning the death of one of its members. These then provide a simple funeral, free of charge. Included are the dressing of the body, a casket, and a plain grave in a row. In Zurich and most of German Switzerland the community furnishes a free casket to those who cannot afford to pay for one, or who are satisfied with the simplest burial. It also provides trained people for laying out the body, and the use of a hearse. The family makes all funeral arrangements.

If the family does not own or wish to purchase a cemetery plot, it may apply for a burial space at public expense. Such space, however, is not for permanent burial. In Berne, for example, public graves have a twenty-year use. A family plot with fifty-year use and the option of renewal is available for a fixed charge. This is for interment of remains and not for burials of ashes. Urns may later be added.

Chapter 42

Ireland

The Republic of Ireland

In Catholic countries such as Italy or Ireland—the Republic of Ireland is 93 per cent Catholic—people have been trained to send for the priest when it is believed that an ill person is in danger of death. In such circumstances, if he has not done so already the priest administers Extreme Unction—the last sacrament of the Catholic Church. If the patient does not die but lingers the priest may be sent for again—or come without being sent for. If he finds the sick person in *arteculo mortis,* he will not administer the last rites or sacraments a second time. Instead he will recite the "prayers for the dying" or some other kind of common prayer.

Burial Procedures

When someone dies in the Republic of Ireland, one of the

first duties to be performed—frequently by the family, some-times by others—is to place a small white card edged in black announcing a death on the front door of the residence. This card is left there until after the funeral.[1]

The body is laid out in the home by a nurse, in a habit supplied by the funeral undertaker. Embalming is very rare, and the practice of restorative art is unknown. The casket is also supplied by the undertaker. It is made of native chestnut, or of Japanese or American elm, or of oak. The use of metal caskets, or of an outer wooden box in which the body is placed for below ground burial is very rare, and are used only by very wealthy families or for bodies prepared for shipment out of the country. For the latter use, an inner-liner sealed by lead is enclosed in an outer casket of oak.

Within at most 24 to 36 hours after death, the body is re-moved from the home to the church, usually the deceased's parish church. When removal takes place in the evening, the men of the family sometimes walk in procession behind the hearse, while the women of the family follow the marching men in the first car. Whether or not this custom of going afoot is followed nowadays depends a great deal on the distance between the home and the church, and on the economic status of the people involved. The more prosperous are not in the habit of walking, and prefer to use their cars. In the poorer sections of the city a wake is generally held. The practice is common for friends to send fresh flowers or porcelain wreaths to the family of the deceased. Catholics prefer to have Masses said for the repose of the departed soul.

On the morning following the removal to church, Catholic funeral services are held and burial takes place immediately thereafter. Thus the body is not kept unburied very long. For example, if a man dies at 6 A.M. on Tuesday, his body is re-moved to church the same day at 5 P.M., and the following morn-ing the funeral takes place.

The funeral procession is organized in a definite pattern. The family car, which directly follows the hearse carries the im-mediate relatives. Succeeding cars carry the remainder of the

546

family and friends. A clergyman usually attends each funeral, and it is customary to provide him with a car for his personal use. Most funeral equipage is of American manufacture.

The ritual of the Catholic Church prescribes prayers that traditionally are to be said in Latin; there is, however, a movement afoot to permit many prayers to be said in the vernacular. The priest says these prayers many times in both languages, as many Catholics are fairly familiar with them in both languages. Following the recitation of these prayers it is customary to say jointly a certain number of prayers in the vernacular. In Ireland the Rosary is frequently recited at the graveside.

Cemeteries in Dublin are located within the city and on the outskirts. Graves must be dug to a depth which will permit three feet of gound to be placed on the casket below the ground surface. Public authorities check and inspect to see that this regulation is complied with. Perpetual care is looked upon as a luxury and needless expense, and few graves are so provided for. Grave markers are similar to those used in the United States.

Some ten days after burial, acknowledgment notices are inserted in the local newspapers. Typical of these is the following:

> O'Connell—The wife and family of the late Sergeant O'Connell, Kelcock, wish to thank most sincerely all those who sympathized with them in their recent sad bereavement by sending Mass cards, telegrams, and letters of sympathy; those who called personally and attended the removal of the remains to Church, Mass and funeral; a special word of thanks to the priests in attendance, and doctors, sisters, and nursing staff of the Richmond Hospital. Trusting that this will be accepted by all as a token of our deep appreciation, the Holy Sacrifice of the Mass will be offered for their intentions. (*Irish Independent*, Wednesday, Nov. 5, 1958)

After the funeral the family enters upon a period of mourning which may last up to six months. During that time, women generally wear black, and men wear black ties, and all family members avoid the theatre and dances.

The functions of the Irish undertaker correspond much more closely to those of the traditional British funeral furnisher and undertaker than to those of the American funeral director.

547

Undertaking in Eire

J. Kirwan, an Eire undertaker, describes the bundle of tasks of the metropolitan undertaker: His function is "to make all the arrangements concerning the execution of the funeral, including the supplying of a casket, hearse, cars, arranging for the opening of the grave, inserting obituary notices in newspapers, supplying habit for remains and a nurse to lay out the body. Necessary arrangements with the local clergy are usually made by the relatives of the deceased, as it is considered bad form for them to appoint a third party such as an undertaker to make the arrangements for the church service." "Embalming," Kirwan observes, "is very rare in Southern Ireland, as is also any type of restorative art. Cremation is not practiced at all. It is, of course, against the Roman Catholic faith." There is no crematorium in either Southern or Northern Ireland. Those who wish to have their dead cremated must ship the bodies to England. The nearest crematorium is in Liverpool.

According to Kirwan, "Legal qualifications for admission into the occupation (of undertaking) are nil." Except in Dublin where the trade unions demand the employment of union casket makers, drivers and polishers, and restrict each group to its own narrow function, so that a casket maker is prohibited by the casket makers' union from polishing a casket or from driving a hearse or a funeral car, the undertaker needs only to own a hearse and to be able to provide a casket to be in business.

While undertaking establishments vary from small to large, most undertakers maintain a small office, a garage for their hearses and cars, a casket manufacturing shop, and, where deemed necessary, a casket display room.

Local funeral undertakers' associations exist only in Dublin and in Cork. There is no national undertakers' association.

Northern Ireland

Burial Procedures

When a person dies in Northern Ireland, which is predominantly Protestant, the relatives contact the funeral director, by either telephone or personal call. The funeral director then ascertains the clients' wishes as to "where and when they wish to bury the remains, what type of casket is required, how many following cars will be needed, which newspapers they wish to insert notices in, what sort of floral tributes are desired." Also to be settled is the matter of attire: Are the remains to be dressed in "day clothes, night attire, or a night dress to be supplied by the firm?"[2]

At this conference the funeral director makes arrangements for his staff to prepare the remains. When the funeral takes place in the home, the remains may be laid out on a bed, or more commonly, they are casketed. In all other circumstances, they are casketed.

Preparation consists of washing and shaving, taking the normal precautions against purging, dressing and setting the features in a normal state with the aid of surgical and other devices. For export purposes, the remains are always embalmed or hermetically sealed. When burial is not expected to take place for three or four days after death, it is usual to embalm.

Meanwhile, in case of sudden death, a coroner's inquest is generally held. In such case, his permission must be obtained before a funeral can be held. For the shipment of a body, two certificates are needed. The medical practitioner attests that the body is free from infectious diseases, and the coroner grants authority to transport. An embalmed body can be shipped by either sea or air, provided it is packed in a strong outer cover or case. An unembalmed body requires a hermetically sealed casket. A body to be cremated must be accompanied by two forms. On the one, the relatives must state their reasons for desiring cremation. On the other, two medical practitioners certify the cause of death. In the extremely rare case in which burial at sea is desired, the coroner must be notified. Funeral directors are authorized to deal with all forms affecting their business except the death registration.

Although the percentage of funerals taking place from funeral directors' chapels shows a constant annual increase, whether the ceremonies are held in these establishments or in the homes, the form is much the same. On the day of burial, the mourners

549

gather wherever the body is laid out. Viewing is not a universal practice in Northern Ireland as it is in America. In "quite a number of cases nowadays," notes N. Lancaster, Jr., American Consul General in Belfast, "the casket is closed immediately, especially in burial from the home. In mortuary chapel funerals the opposite is true, and the casket is likely to be left open for viewing and closed just before the service begins."

When the service is concluded, the casket is brought outside and either carried a short distance before it is placed in the hearse, or is put directly into the hearse. In either event there is a token procession in which the mourners follow the casket on foot. After proceeding for a short distance, those who wish to attend the burial—and this group consists almost entirely of men—enter waiting automobiles and ride to the cemetery. Some cars are supplied by the funeral director; some relatives and friends drive their own.

At the cemetery, after the funeral director has removed the casket from the hearse, and placed it over the grave, a religious committal service is held. The mourners usually remain while the body is being lowered and the grave is being filled. They leave only when the floral tributes have been placed above the grave.

A funeral in a consecrated church or chapel is somewhat more complicated. In such cases a brief service is generally held in the home; then the main service is held in the church in the presence of friends and relatives. After this, the casket is placed in the hearse, and as many as care to, follow it to the cemetery.

There is no crematorium and no cremation in Northern Ireland. To be cremated, a body is shipped to England or Scotland, and the ashes are returned. Before the remains are sent away, a short service is generally held in the director's chapel, and after the ashes have been brought back, a graveside committal service is read.

Changes in Funeral Service

In the last quarter-century considerable change is apparent in Northern Ireland in the whole matter of funeralizing the

550

dead. Embalming and cremation are steadily on the increase. Motor driven equipment has entirely replaced the old horse-drawn carriages and hearses. At the same time the estimate of the occupational status of the funeral director has increased in the public mind.

This new and higher image is based on many considerations. Among the most important of these is the fact that the amount of capital needed nowadays to set up a funeral establishment is "very considerable." Even more important is the new bundle of expert tasks now being assigned to the funeral director. The successful performance of these requires much more training and skill than were involved in supplying furnishings and routing the procession.

While families can determine how much they want to pay for a funeral, they do not always have a full understanding of these matters. "There is no public relations between the funeral directing profession and the public and as a result most people are ignorant of requirements and affairs of the profession." So writes an observer.

The National Association of Funeral Directors serves both the United Kingdom and Northern Ireland. In the latter country, about half of the funeral directors are members. Through its programs the Association strives to raise the ethical standards and practices of the profession, to promote mutual aid among the membership, and to develop better relationships with governmental agencies. It represents the profession in dealing with legislative bodies. While the head office of the Association is located in London, offices for Northern Ireland are maintained in Belfast.

Girl pipers play lament in English funeral procession

Chapter 43

England

With English as a common language, and with many Americans regarding England as our mother country, it is but natural that the practices and customs of our English "cousins" should be of interest to those who share in its great cultural heritage.[1] Differences in point of view between the people of both countries are reflected in the willingness to accept social innovation. The traditional conservatism of the average Englishman is regarded as an evidence of an unprogressive attitude by most Americans. On the other hand, the American willingness to adopt and accept new ideas and programs is regarded by the English as an evidence of brashness and immaturity. In nothing is this contrast more striking than in the attitudes toward funeral and burial customs.[2] It is interesting to note, however, that in both countries among a minority of funeral directors, and in segments of the public at large, there are those who favor "foreign" rather than national practices and programs for the care of the dead. Paradoxically, it

553

is the English who at the moment seem to be the most receptive to innovation and change.

First Steps in the Care of the Dead

The answer to the first question arising after death—shall the body be buried or cremated—determines to a large degree the procedure that must be followed. If there has been a physician in attendance who will certify that the death has been due to natural causes, the funeral director may assume charge and remove the body from the place of death, providing that earth burial is to be made. If there has been no attending physician or if there is doubt that the person may have died of natural causes, the body may not be disturbed until the Coroner's officer—a policeman assigned to the Coroner's staff —has viewed the body and questioned those who discovered it. If further inquiry is necessary, the Coroner has the authority to order an autopsy and to conduct the hearing. If, however, the Coroner's officer is satisfied that death resulted from natural causes, he may authorize the removal of the body without further viewing of it.[3] As will be discussed later the procedure varies if the body is to be cremated.

Unlike its American counterpart the office of Coroner in England is not elective, and hence not political. To qualify for the position hereafter, the law requires that a candidate must hold a degree either in medicine or law, and some coroners now hold degrees in both fields. English law has long excluded funeral directors and all others associated with the trade, even indirectly, from seeking to become coroners. One British funeral director comments that "the power of the coroner is virtually limitless. Lawyers have no standing in his court inasmuch as they appear and question witnesses only through his courtesy. Hearsay is admissible."[4]

When the body is to remain in the home it is customary for the funeral director to consult with the family there during usual office hours, unless requested otherwise by the family. Families may request "Last Offices" or "First Offices." "Last Offices" are rendered by a qualified nurse who stands ready

554

Coffin in funeral director's chapel; pall indicates body will not be viewed

to go out at any hour to close the eyes, tie up the jaw, wash the body, plug the orifices, shave the men, and dress the women's hair. She strips and remakes the bed, puts a diaper on the body, and redresses it in night attire. These services are commonly requested in urban areas and particularly in London. When the funeral director carries them out they are called "First Offices." The clue to this interesting distinction in title can be found in the person performing the function. The nurse carries out the last services for the living; the funeral director, the first services for the dead.[5]

Funeral Arrangements

Two sets of factors, one economic and the other social, operate to influence the making of arrangements for the funeral.[6] The first has to do with the elaborateness and size of the funeral establishments, which may vary from a back street workshop where the proprietor may fill in his time with ordinary upholstery and carpentry business, to the adapted

555

Left, Typical English funeral establishment will have its own coffinmakers and monumental masons. *Right*, Chapel will be a separate building

country manor house in which all the appointments of the modern American funeral home will be found, and in which a staff of specialists will operate within the context of a large-scale business enterprise. The second dimension is reflected in the varying regional customs and practices. These exist for the northern, midland, and southern counties. The contrast between north and south is exemplified in the matter of what is done following the graveside ceremonies. In the South the funeral finishes at the graveside with the mourners being motored back to the home of the deceased, whereas in the North, the graveside or crematorium service is followed by a high tea arranged for the mourners by the funeral director at a restaurant or café to which the funeral party is driven in seven-seater Rolls, Daimlers or Humbers.[7]

Coffin or Casket Selection

If death took place during the night, on the following morning the funeral director meets with the family, either in the home or at his office. One of the tasks to be faced is the selection of a burial receptacle. In this regard English practice differs considerably from that in the United States. Many if not most English undertakers and funeral directors make

556

or assemble and trim their own wooden coffins, some using "prepared coffin sets" of elm, oak, agba and chestnut, which are supplied by wholesale manufacturers. Within the past decade or so the beginning of a trend toward the use of factory-made coffins has developed. But the typical undertaking establishment will have its coffin workshop and its contingent of woodworkers who both make and assemble burial receptacles. Also in a minority are the establishments with display rooms, though these too are increasing, if slowly, and gaining acceptance by the English public. Metal caskets have been accorded a mixed reception in England. They are most likely to be found in those establishments which have display rooms. Although a metal casket company was founded in England in the early 1900's, there has been no growth of such industry and in 1954 it was still the only company of its kind in the United Kingdom.[8]

English undertakers and funeral directors distinguish "coffins" from "caskets." The former are of the traditional tapering, kite-shaped, eight-sided type, not too unlike those in which American colonists buried their dead. "Caskets" are burial receptacles similar to modern American rectangular cases and known by the same term. The English casket styles are most frequently of the full-couch, hinged-panel variety, although an occasional half-couch design may be noted. The hardware and trimming for either type may be of wood or metal. Wooden hardware, *i.e.*, handles, corners and other trim, is most likely to be found on coffins and caskets used for cremation, although the more expensive caskets may feature metal hardware, guaranteed to be combustible in English crematoria.

Coffin interiors are likely to be less elaborate with thinner lining than is found in caskets, often without counter-lining or pillow. Coffins may be of polished wood but for some a cloth covering, with studs of various decorative designs, is substituted for the finished wooden exterior. Many burial receptacles contain nameplates with the date of birth and burial inscribed. The use of the pall to cover coffin or casket while the body rests in the home or the chapel is a regular feature of English care of the dead. The choice of a burial receptacle will be made from pictures unless the funeral home maintains a casket display room. However, selection of coffin or casket is, as in America, only one of a variety of arrangements to be made. Other things to be decided will include where the body will be kept—at home or in the funeral director's "chapel of rest," the time and place of the funeral, the obsequies to be observed, the amount and type of transportation needed, and, of course, the price. The funeral director is under legal obligation to mention the "simple funeral," *i.e.,* a minimum service in which the essentials will be provided for a fee equivalent to the sum given survivors under the National Service Health Act. The English are not likely to let the matter rest at the minimum figure. "A death, like a birth or a marriage," notes the British Journal, *The Economist,* "is one of the most important events in British life, especially the working classes. It provides an occasion for a family to meet and show its solidarity and, as such, is a time when it is felt that no expense should reasonably be spared."

Forms and Certificates

Meanwhile the family will have notified the physician and have learned from him when the death certificate will be ready at his office. Inasmuch as office hours normally extend from 9:00 to 11:00 A.M., and 5:30 to 7:30 P.M., and the physician is away on calls during the remainder of the day, it is not unusual for the issuance of this certificate to be delayed eight to ten hours after death.

The physician in England is not allowed to charge for death certificates, as reports, *per se.* However, the Minister of Health does not regard as "reports" the two statutory certificates demanded for a cremation, and for this reason medical practitioners may charge what fee they will for completing them.

The next of kin takes the medical certificate to the local Registrar of Births, Marriages, and Deaths, which officer alone can issue the disposal certificate. While this officer and

Modern English hearse

his staff keep long and arduous hours, they are available for registration only for a portion of the time: in large towns on Monday through Saturday between 10:00 A.M. and noon, and on Monday through Friday, from 2:00 P.M. to 4:00 P.M. In rural communities the opportunity to register a death is even more limited by the fact that when a registrar serves a considerable territory he may be able to sit only a half day in each district each week.[9]

In exchange for the medical certificate the Registrar issues the Certificate of Disposal. The next of kin turns this certificate over to the funeral director, who when necessary uses it to secure a body from the hospital, and to dispose of it. For earth burial the certificate is given to the cemetery superintendent at the time of burial. If there is to be a cremation the superintendent of a crematorium must have the certificate at least twenty-four hours in advance thereof.

The task of the Registrar is not only to register a death but to check the medical certificate to see if it resulted from natural causes, and to take appropriate action if there is doubt in the matter. Under such circumstances he will impound the medical certificate and immediately notify the coroner who in practically all such cases orders an autopsy.[10]

Embalming

The family turns over the disposal certificate to the funeral director, and only now—and if the family so desires—will he embalm the body. A British funeral director who has supplied much of this information comments: "Either he does embalm the body which will be treated to 'hold up' until the day of the funeral—temporary preservation it is termed—or else nothing

559

will be done at all."[11] Another commentator points out that in lieu of embalming, cavity aspiration is often performed, and the orifices are plugged with cotton.

Somewhere between seven and ten per cent of all bodies are given temporary preservation, most of them in private homes and on the bed on which they died. There are few preparation rooms in Britain of the type everywhere to be found in the United States.

Although Charles A. Renouard conducted the first class in arterial embalming in England in 1900, sixty years later only 1,000 members of the British Institute of Embalmers, including registered students and 34 members residing outside the area of Great Britain, serve a population of well over 50,000,000 people.[12]

In explanation of the fact that the British public are not entirely "embalming conscious" the British Institute of Embalming suggests three reasons: (1) Customs die hard in Great Britain, and in no case harder than in funerals. (2) The traditional British undertaker has been loth to introduce a service involving a field of knowledge which he did not possess. (3) Up to the present there has been little government support or recognition of the science of embalming. With exceptions, the medical profession ignore it.[13]

As late as 1954 no licensing of embalmers was required, and a certificate of embalming was demanded only for bodies which were to be shipped abroad. In spite of these adverse circumstances, however, embalming in England is being practiced (1960) "far more than at any time in the past."[14] Many large funeral establishments employ full-time embalmers, and some of these establishments embalm every body which they handle. The number of firms of trade embalmers is increasing. These supply embalming services to smaller funeral establishments or to large establishments, which for one or another reason do not wish to add embalming to their staff duties. In addition hundreds of funeral directors are also qualified embalmers.[15]

Even where a body is embalmed and lies in state the British

560

do not look with favor upon the routine use of cosmetics in preparing the body for viewing, and resort to such expedient only in exceptional circumstances. However, they do make "judicious" use of stain in their arterial fluids.[16]

Obituary Notices

Normally the obituary notice appearing in an English newspaper contains thirteen points, and while some of these may be omitted the order is invariable. These points tell (1) the time; (2) the manner; (3) the place; (4) the person; (5) the position or titles; (6) the residence; (7) the list of relatives; (8) the age; (9) the time and place of the funeral service; (10) the burial arrangements; (11) whether letters of mourning are desired; (12) whether flowers are desired; and (13) whether there will be memorial services. In the

English cremation coffin, all wood including oak ring handles

Modern English polished oak casket

majority of cases paid death notices do not appear in English newspapers. Families use the columns of local newspapers for making acknowledgment of services, and of flowers and other gifts.[17]

For such as wish them the British newspapers carry the briefest death notices in the classified advertising section under the title "Deaths." Following these are "Acknowledgments and thanks" and "In Memoriam." The "Acknowledgments and thanks" are brief. Typical is the following: "Mrs. Baker, son and daughter wish to thank friends and neighbors for the sympathy and floral tributes in their sad bereavement." The "In Memoriam" items are more personal. For instance: "O'Neill, Nancy. In precious and treasured memory, also remembering her birthday, loved, remembered, mourned for always, dearest mother—Your grateful Sheila," or "Plowman. Fondest memories of my brother Eddy. He lived bravely and died bravely." Some memorial items are put into verse.

Viewing the Body

Viewing customs in Britain likewise exhibit variance from the American pattern. For instance, it is customary in Britain to bring the coffin into the family home on the same day in which the funeral arrangements are made. When the body gives evidence of decomposition it is placed untreated in the coffin together with dry ice and a packing of some kind of absorbent material, such as sawdust, and the lid is screwed down. At the funeral director's suggestion a body in such condition is generally removed to his premises. The funeral director, too, largely determines the manner in which an embalmed body is viewed. In most places in England the lid of the casket is so segmented that only the face is displayed. A notable exception to this practice may be found in Lancashire, where the opened portion of the lid allows the hands to be likewise uncovered. While it is usual for the body to be coffined for viewing, some funeral directors either leave it on the bed for showing at home, or have it on a bed in their establishments.

562

A British authority on embalming, A. C. A. Hall, feels that the fact that there is little public viewing prevents people from comparing the work of embalmers, and that this lack of comparison keeps families from shifting from one funeral director to another to secure more competent embalming and cosmetic services.[18] Except possibly in Yorkshire wakes are not part of the British funeral pattern.

By and large it is not likely that in England a body will be taken to a funeral home for lying in state and for the service, as is common in the United States. However, signs indicate the possibility of shifting in this matter in Britain. Indicative of this is the fact that certain English funeral directors, after visiting America, pioneered the introduction of funeral homes —including private chapels and rest rooms—in England, and as of 1960 several such homes are being built.[19] About two dozen were in operation. It may be expected that in the future there will be more extensive use of funeral home facilities by the families of the dead.

Funeral director and assistants carry wreaths into churchyard cemetery

The Funeral

If the body has been kept in the deceased's home the hearse and such additional transportation as may be needed are brought there on the day of the funeral. Sometimes wearing tall hats and tails, the bearers, who are employees of the funeral director, walk with the funeral director in front of the procession, while the family follow in cars. The funeral director now appears in the characteristic attire of his occupation. Most English funeral directors wear black dress, with an occasional concession for striped trousers. In the north of England the common dress is frock coat, or sometimes, a tail-coat with striped trousers. The wearing of a black jacket is highly exceptional. Hall reports meeting only one funeral director who wore a blue business suit while conducting a funeral, and he was so garbed only because the family, which abhorred mourning, had requested this dress. Winter or summer the English funeral director wears a silk top hat, and in the winter he wears a black overcoat. He carries an umbrella in wet weather.[20]

The bereaved family, too, gives some thought to proper clothing for the occasion. The matter of mourning dress is one of economics as well as style. Among the poorer and less educated classes the custom of wearing black at funerals is fast dying out, and nowadays any subdued color is approved. Among the well-to-do, black is still used universally, not because it is the color of mourning so much as because formal morning attire in England is black, even on joyful occasions. Hall observes that if a funeral director were presented at court he would be properly dressed if he wore his usual business clothes. A person who does not wear black at a funeral will often wear a black armband, two or three inches wide, and with few exceptions all men must wear black ties.[21]

After a family has put off all other signs of mourning the members will frequently continue to wear black armbands and black ties. When the royal court is in session an officer in active military service wears a black armband about five inches wide. The custom is observed everywhere in England of closing all the curtains in a house on the day a person dies there, and of keeping them drawn until the family returns from service. On the day of the funeral all near neighbors also keep their curtains drawn until the cortege has left the street. The English do not put crepe on the door, or candles in the window as a sign that death is in the house.[22]

On the appointed schedule the members of the funeral director's staff close the coffin and place the floral gifts of the nearest of kin on the lid. Pallbearers bear the coffin from the house to the hearse on their shoulders. The family occupy the cars following the hearse, without much regard for precedence. If the funeral director maintains a funeral home the funeral services may be held there and the cortege originates there. Most generally, though, the procession moves from the residence to the local church or, more likely, to a building set aside for services at the cemetery or crematorium.

Except in the case of public personages, owners of large estates, and other distinguished persons, attendance at funeral services in England is limited to members of the immediate family, and seldom are there more than twenty people present. The number of friends and neighbors who call to pay their respects is likewise limited. Hall explains that "most families just would not understand if they (friends) wished to do so. My own attitude is probably typical, and I should consider the attendance of someone not of my immediate family at a funeral to be an impertinence, an intolerable intrusion into what is a private matter."[23] This feeling that funerals are private greatly reduces the number of "visitors" at the funeral establishment. Thus when a past president of the British Institute of Embalmers died recently, a nationally known figure in and out of his profession, a public benefactor and a prominent fraternalist, less than 100 persons attended the church services. Hall adds that: "It is unlikely that the number of mourners would exceed eighteen and more usually there would be a maximum of twelve. The pallbearers are members of the funeral director's staff. Sympathy is expressed through the medium of floral offerings, and the expenditure

565

for this purpose may exceed the cost of the funeral itself."[24]

At an Anglican funeral the minister comes to the church door or hearse door and leads the processional into the church. As he does so he begins the ritualistic prayer, "I am the Resurrection and the Life." While certain prayers have been designated and set aside for just such occasions, there is no obligation that the service be restricted to their recitation, and other scriptural passages may be chosen at the option of the officiating clergyman, and sometimes the suggestions of the family may be sought and followed.

Although usually there is no singing in a Church of England service, when the casket is in position before the altar and all the mourners are in their places, the choir and the congregation sometimes sing Psalm 23 or others selected by the clergyman and the service proceeds in the manner set out. The lessons are often left to the bereaved to choose. After the service the body is again placed in the hearse, and the procession moves to the grave. The minister and the funeral director lead on foot; the hearse follows, and the family ride behind the hearse.

Cemeteries and Interment

Meanwhile if disposal is to be by interment, the grave has been dug in the cemetery. Old cemeteries in England are much venerated places, and are very well kept. In rural England many of them are still used for burials for the ordinary families of the parish. The nobility are more likely to be buried in vaults under the floors of the parish churches. While Westminster and other great cathedrals may make tombs available to the great—whether churchmen, statesmen, soldiers, prelates or writers—the families of such illustrious persons or the individuals themselves, by written or oral instructions, frequently choose burial with their kin on their family burial plot or in their family vaults.

The old problem of the difficulties of securing sufficient cemetery space grows more aggravated as time goes on. Despite constantly increasing prices many cemeteries are operating

Funeral of a Battersea street-trader. Horse-drawn hearses now a rarity in England

at a loss, and it is estimated that a deficit of as much as £5 ($14.10) is incurred in some municipally operated cemeteries for each burial.[25] Cemeteries and crematoria are largely municipally owned, and while privately owned crematoria compare favorably with their public counterparts privately owned cemeteries are likely to be less well kept.[26]

Many reports comment on the lack of burial space in a densely populated island, and on the serious overcrowding of British cemeteries with burials made one on top of another in a single grave. Equally difficult, too, is the problem of thickets of headstones and markers in many crowded English cemeteries. It is noted, however, that the sale of markers has decreased somewhat in proportion to the rise in cremation.

At the cemetery gate the cortege halts while the funeral director enters the office to hand the superintendent the disposal certificate. After this it proceeds to the cemetery chapel for the services. The coffin is brought into the church, but is not opened.

Many English funeral directors supply paper-bound booklets containing the Service of the Dead which carry on the front

567

Greengrocer's horse and wagon used as hearse in unusual English funeral procession

cover the name of the deceased and the place and date of burial. Booklets of this type are used in a church, or cemetery, or crematorium chapel when no music is available or used. The attending clergyman normally extracts selections from such a booklet, and announces them as he reads them. When hymns are to be sung a white broadsheet is passed out instead of the grey booklets. The cover of this broadsheet also contains the name of the deceased and the place and date of burial.

The dirt that has been removed from the excavation is temporarily heaped around the grave to a depth of perhaps three or even four feet. Boards are laid across this earth to give the pallbearers and family access to the grave. Although some funeral directors line the excavated earth and the excavation itself with mats of imitation grass, many make no effort to conceal or disguise the freshly dug soil. Mechanical lowering devices, tents, seating accommodations are not used at English funerals. The typical English cemetery with its cramped space provides no room for these. "Indeed," says Hall, "in most cemeteries the graves are set so closely together that it is only with difficulty that the casket is shouldered from the hearse, between the line of markers, and up on the mound

568

surrounding the grave."[27] The height of the mounded earth is another result of the crowding of the grave space.

The minister takes leave of the members of the family after the committal, and the funeral director escorts him home. Except in Yorkshire, he then bids them farewell and leaves them. In Yorkshire it is customary to follow the committal service with a "funeral tea" at a public restaurant. Because it is the practice to serve ham on this occasion the phrase "being buried with ham" has gained popular acceptance. Elsewhere in England it is customary for relatives returning from the funeral to gather at the home of one of them and there partake of light refreshments. When the meal is held outside of the home, the funeral director makes the arrangements for it.

Funeral Economics

Rarely are funerals paid for in advance, and since the disbursement for the cost of the grave, the doctor's fees—if there is cremation the services of two doctors are involved—must be paid in advance, the funeral director is called upon to advance these sums, which many times exceed the charges for his own services and merchandise. As a consequence it is not unusual to present a bill and receive payment at the completion of the service.

This love of solemn splendor—and conversely the stigma of a pauper's grave—have been a foundation stone in the British funeral director's business. During the nineteenth century it led to the building up of an elaborate system of burial insurance, the weekly premiums on which often started the moment a child was born. These might have been expected to fall away when, under the National Health Service, a death grant of £20 (recently raised to £25) was made by the state to cover funeral expenses—and when the limit for private burial insurance, which can only be taken out on the lives of parents or grandparents, was fixed at £120; nevertheless burial insurance continues to be bought today by large numbers of people. Every year about 5 per cent, or 280,000 of the five and one-half million new industrial insurance policies, are taken out explicitly to cover funeral expenses, and indications are that in England today between five and one-half and six million people collectively hold funeral policies with an assured value of £100 million.[28]

Cremation

Before cremation may take place two medical certificates, as noted above, are required. The first must be signed by the doctor who attended the dead person. The second, a confirming certificate, must be signed by another doctor who is not a partner of the first and who has practiced medicine for at least five years. The usual charge for signing these certificates is £4.4.0 ($11.88), half the weekly wage of the average worker. Some doctors charge double this fee. Before cremation is permitted, the next of kin must file a declaration that the deceased never objected to cremation. It is illegal, under penalty of imprisonment, to cremate any one whose known wish, no matter when it was made, was in opposition to having his body cremated. Even where all the required forms have been filled out and sent to the crematorium to be inspected by the Medical Referee, if he is dissatisfied with the two medical reports, he may still order an autopsy.[29]

The crematoria refuse to cremate if any non-combustible metal is attached to the casket, and object to embalming to the extent that there is afoot in England today a movement to prohibit by law the embalming of a body that is to be cremated. There are some legal objections to cremation on the basis that it may be a method used to conceal criminal acts. Much of the regulatory procedure set up about it is designed to circumvent such concealment. However, the regulation that bodies which are to be cremated must be held for longer than a week makes the reasons for the objection to embalming difficult to understand. Although cremation is little practiced in the rural areas of Britain it is becoming increasingly common in large towns, and there 60 per cent or more of all disposals may be cremation.[30] Figures for 1958 indicate that Great Britain leads Europe not only in the number of cremations (180,075) but in the number of crematoria (120) and the percentage of cremations (30.58 per cent of all deaths). Denmark, with 24 crematoria and 11,436 cremations is a close second in the percentage column with 28.6 per cent of all disposals made by cremation.[31]

The greater scarcity of land in England weighed powerfully in promoting the cremation movement in the early days. Added impetus came from its support by the medical profession, and from its espousal by wealthier Britons to whom it has become fashionable. Others favor it because of the added expense involved in earth burials.

The cremated remains are usually scattered on a lawn, or at the foot of a tree or bush, or, less frequently buried in the family grave, or placed in a niche in a columbarium.

However, the popularity of cremation in urban areas brings with it its own set of special problems. One of these is scheduling. The demand in England for Saturday cremations is double that for cremations on any other day, and the time available on Saturday is less than half. As a result, clients who cannot be accommodated on the first Saturday after the death of a relative, sometimes wait for the next Saturday.

British and American Funeral Services Compared

British and American funeral directors naturally have many common duties, some differences or specialization, and some common and some unique problems. For instance, the British funeral director shares with his American counterpart a close personal relationship with his clients. As Ivor Leverton pointed out to the British Cremation Society: "Although a funeral director starts as a stranger to many of his clients, he must in a short time be accepted in the same category as an old family friend, with a mixture of the trust confided in their solicitor, doctor and clergyman, all in one."[32]

Perhaps one of the most important differences between funeral directors in America and funeral directors in Great Britain is the fact as expressed by a British mortician, "that you (in America) are licensed, and we are not."[33] It is still

571

true that in Great Britain any person can set up a business as a funeral director. He need have no qualifications to his name and is answerable to no one. Another notable difference stems from the fact that the British operate within the framework of the welfare state.

In Britain as in America a considerable percentage of funeral service personnel are people born to the occupation. Family firms constitute the core of the business and may run as far back as seven generations. Training, which is by an informal, voluntary apprenticeship lasting one to two years, begins in the workshop and garage and moves into the preparation room and office. No examination must be taken and no license is required. The National Association of Funeral Directors with 3,400 members represents the occupation.

Burial of Royalty

The monarchy is an institution that is dear to the hearts of most Englishmen. The cry "For God and Country" is no more appealing to them than is the cry for "King and Country," or for "Queen and Country." At no time do the English pour forth their affection and respect for a reigning monarch than at the time of his death. His obsequies are clothed with all the traditional regal and medieval pomp, and pageantry. The most recent royal funeral—that of King George VI in 1952—is still well remembered.

For the greater part of that time the body lay in medieval Westminster Abbey, on a high catafalque, flanked by "guardsmen in gleaming cuirasses and Tudor-clad Beefeaters from the Tower of London" and attended by certain officers of the Court. Outside the great queue waited for a last look at the dead monarch, and serpentine columns of persons came to pay their last respects "formed and reformed, doubled, branched and coiled back again along London's streets and across chilly Thames bridges." The "endless line" in all brought 305,806 people before the bier. Members of the family came at intervals. On the third night after his death, his mother, Queen Mary and the Duke of Windsor stood for twenty minutes be-

572

fore the casket. The next evening brought the new queen, Elizabeth II, and the widowed Queen. A reporter for the weekly magazine, *Time*, concluded that Londoners "felt a strong sense of history and a deep compulsion to share it."

Members of the royal families of Europe and special representatives of friendly governments hurried to London to attend the final services, and to convey personally the assurances of sympathy and grief from their nations. The United States was represented by Dean Acheson, the Secretary of State, and General Dwight Eisenhower, the Commander in Chief of NATO forces.

On the morning of the funeral the vast cortege was assembled to escort the casket through the streets of London to Paddington Station and the special funeral train that would carry the body of the late King to Windsor Castle where it was to be entombed in the Chapel of St. George. At this juncture the common people packed the curbs and hung from rented windows to see the procession.

Mid the tolling of church bells, and with muffled drums and crepe-draped bugles, the line slowly moved forward. First came soldiers from the far-flung colonies, then the personal regiments of the Royal family, and sailors and marines followed by England's top commanders and greatest living heroes. The casket containing the body of the King lay on a gun carriage which was hauled by lines of enlisted men in blue from the Royal Navy.

In the red and gilt state coach behind them the Queen and the Queen Mother rode and behind them walked the Royal Dukes of Edinburgh, Gloucester, Windsor and Kent. Then with strict adherence to protocol marched relatives, members of the nobility, government representatives, and distinguished personages.

As the procession trouped by Marlborough House all the blinds were drawn, except in one window, where the Dowager Queen sat; and as the bier approached, Queen Mary rose and stood, and the veiled women in the carriage bowed and the Royal Dukes saluted—then the blind was drawn. At

Piano monument erected over grave of musical genius who died early in career

Paddington Station, as the bagpipers of the Cameron Highlanders skirled out a dismal threnody, the body was placed on the funeral train.

Another procession formed at Winchester to escort the bier to Windsor Castle's Chapel of St. George for the last rites. There the Archbishop of Canterbury read the words of the Book of Common Prayer; "For as much as it hath pleased Almighty God of His great mercy to take unto Himself the soul of our dear brother here departed, we therefore commit his body to the ground; earth to earth, ashes to ashes, and dust to dust."

A vault had been opened to receive the body, and as it was slowly lowered, Elizabeth took a handful of earth from a silver bowl and dropped it onto the casket.

Throughout the length and breadth of England at an appointed hour, to honor the dead King, men and women paused in silence for two minutes. Buses came to a halt, "miners stopped work at coal faces; occupants in British planes stood up and Englishmen everywhere bowed their heads in sorrow."

574

Funeral Customs The World Over

Part Six

Left, Wall crypts, Santiago, Chile
Lower right, Scene in Columbus cemetery, Havana
Lower left, Flowers at funeral in Buenos Aires

Latin America

Racial amalgam and cultural division . . . cosmopolitan urbanity cut across by Latin emotionality . . . Indian naïvete and the love of color . . . variation in death customs set off by unifying religious services to the dead . . . grinning cake skulls, fiestas, and fireworks . . . sociability at the wake . . . dispatch in burying the dead . . . the bizarre funeral folkways of the remote jungle people

Tom Hollyman Photo for P.R.I., upper
Ph. Gendreau Photo, lower left
P.I.P. Photo, lower right

Funeral procession in rural Mexico

The undertaker's assistant delivers
a casket in Mexico City

Grave with rough stone marker.
A typical scene in Mexican
village cemeteries

Chapter 44

Mexico

Burial in Urban Areas

Government Control

Burial of the dead in Mexico is regulated by federal law, which provides that no interment may be made until 24 hours have elapsed from time of death, but interment must take place prior to the expiration of the next 24 hours unless the remains have been embalmed, or the Department of Public Health has ordered the preservation of the body, or judicial investigations indicate that burial shall be delayed. However, in spite of the law, burial in most cases is made within 24 hours, and unembalmed remains are practically never kept for the full legally allowed 48 hours. Interment of embalmed bodies, conserved under the regulations and supervision of the Department of Public Health, may be deferred for extended periods.[1]

When contagious disease is established as the cause of death, burial must take place within the 24 hour limit. The various types of diseases considered contagious are enumerated in the sanitary code. Families are not permitted to bring into the home for viewing the body of someone who died of a contagious disease.

Preparation of Dead for Burial

Ordinarily the dead are dressed in clean, light clothing and wrapped in a clean sheet.[2] If the relatives so desire, the dead may be buried in their best clothes, a rich gentleman in his dress suit; a rich lady, in her finest gown. Until the turn of the century some families clung to the ancient custom of dressing the women as nuns for burial, and the men as monks or friars.[3]

Today, the remains are kept in the deceased's home for viewing by friends and relatives for a period which may extend to 24 hours. However, chapels in which the body may be in state are available in many Mexican funeral homes. While most Mexican funerals are still conducted from the family home, in Monterrey and Mexico City a good number are now conducted from the funeral home, whence they move to the church and to the cemetery.[4]

Although many women do not attend funerals, nearly all pay visits of condolence and wear mourning clothes. When friends are unable to call upon a family immediately after a death they customarily send cards or letters of regret.[5] In urban areas an announcement of a death is made through newspaper notices and announcement cards.

At the present time federal regulations provide that "embalming can only be conducted by a medical doctor." A movement is afoot to change this law, so that a group of licensed, professional embalmers can be developed, apart from the medical profession. Although modern arterial embalming is practiced in all cities along the United States border and in Monterrey, elsewhere in Mexico, including Mexico City, there is little appreciation of the value of embalming, and except for those consigned for shipment, bodies are usually not embalmed.[6] The law provides that to be shipped the embalmed body must be enclosed in a metal liner which is sealed by welding. The liner is placed in a casket, which in turn is sometimes packed into a wooden box. However, few bodies are shipped within Mexico; most of those shipped are destined to the United States.

Caskets used in urban areas in Mexico are similar in shape to those used in the United States. They are grouped according to cost into four classes, and are selected by families according to their economic circumstances. Caskets for babies are frequently painted light blue.

Undertakers furnish the catafalque or bier on which the body is placed, and all the needed appurtenances, including the crucifix and statues of the saints. Four candelabra are stood next to the casket, one to a side. They remain there until the body is borne from the home. Loose flowers are laid on top of the casket, particularly on the casket of a dead child or woman.[7]

Role of the Catholic Church in Funerals

In most places in Mexico, since the population is overwhelmingly Catholic, the body is taken to the church for a church ceremony. Permits are sometimes obtained from the Mexican authorities to allow priests to conduct funeral services at cemeteries.

The usual funeral cortege in an urban area of Mexico consists of automobiles following a modern automotive hearse. In Mexico City, because the traffic is heavy and the cemeteries are few and therefore distant from many sections, buses are substituted for mourners' cars. A few horse-drawn hearses are still in use in Guadalajara, the second city of Mexico. Some Mexican automotive hearses are of American manufacture; many others have been locally converted from panel trucks.[9]

The conversion of a great number of panel trucks or station wagons for use as hearses is due to the heavy duty—100 per cent of price, with a minimum duty of $3200 (American)— which the Mexican government places on imported hearses, new or used.[10]

Ewing Galloway Photo

Photo Courtesy Robert Sheldon

Photo Courtesy Kay Habenstein

Upper left, The Zocolo
flower market,
Mexico City

Above, Elaborate, glass
front monument-chapel
in Acapulco

Left, Wreaths and flowers
still cover monuments
two months after
All Souls' Day

There are four types or grades of hearses, and the number
of hired automobiles in the procession indicates the financial
standing and social position of the deceased. Another index
is the number of floral wreaths sent by relatives, friends
and business acquaintances. Flower cars transport these offerings to the cemetery.

582

At one time in Mexico City the use of funeral cars, at first horse-drawn and later electrically operated, was general. In Mexico City as late as 1907 the streetcar company enjoyed the exclusive right of conveying all dead bodies and accompanying mourners to the cemetery. Before the electrification of the street railways the poor were granted the free use of a funeral car and one coach.[11]

The electrically operated funeral car contained at the center a raised platform on which the casket was placed. Such a car had open sides and was surmounted by a canopy. The elaborateness of its decoration and draperies varied according to the means of the bereaved family. Some of the higher priced cars were trimmed with black silk, or for the burial of infants or children, with white satin. Behind this hearse a car with good appointments and draperies was provided for the mourners. The car used by the poor lacked such luxurious appointments, and was closed on the front and sides, with doors at the back, and was so arranged that it could provide transport for several or more funerals at one time, the interior being lined with shelves upon which coffins could be stacked. The accompanying mourners' car was painted black, and was wholly without decoration or drapes.[12] Within the last quarter century the use of the street railways for carrying the remains and the mourners to the cemetery has entirely died out.

In Mexico, according to Benito Flores, a spokesman for Mexican funeral directors, the populace can be divided into three classes, the rich, middle, and poor. Women of the first and third groups customarily attend funerals; middle class women do not.[13] To provide for this last group a brief service is read at the home of the deceased; and another, attended only by men, at the cemetery. Whether they attend the burial or not, Mexican women do play an important role in funeralizing the dead. At the family home during the wake they serve coffee, soft drinks, and food to those present, and for several months after a death they observe mourning by wearing black clothing and veils, and by keeping to their homes.[14]

Burial Places

In urban areas the poor are buried in the earth; the middle class, in walled masonry crypts; and the wealthy, in expensive mausolea. Burial in churches has been prohibited since sometime before 1920.[15] Ordinarily, grave sites may be purchased or leased. When the rental time has expired, if the remains have not already been taken up by the family, the funeral authorities remove and burn them. When the family itself has them exhumed, they are placed in a metal container and kept in a small plot purchased by the family and located in another part of the cemetery.[16] Such arrangements are found in the better cemeteries. In rural areas, also, graves are usually leased for a term of one to seven years. If at the expiration the lease is not renewed, the grave is emptied and the bones cast into a charnal house. The comparatively limited area assigned for cemetery uses is one factor leading to the leasing of graves for a limited period of time. In general sanitary experts criticize Mexican cemeteries because of the grave rental system and because many of them have menaced the health of their communities. In the past they were frequently located on hillsides and within urban boundaries, so that they drained into the water supplies of the district which they served.[17]

The practice of constantly reusing a small area of ground for burial in the soil or in niches sometimes produces a spectacular graveyard. A case in point is the cemetery of Guanajuato which lies on a high point overlooking the city, and covers an area of perhaps three acres. It is surrounded by eight-foot thick walls, honeycombed with thousands of burial recesses. Many of these spaces are rented for a five-year period and each may be occupied by a single body or the bodies of a family. Even the low rates charged are usually beyond the purses of the poor who consequently are given earth burial, in graves two feet wide, seven feet long, and eight feet deep. Such a grave is used for multiple simultaneous burials. As each body arrives it is taken from the rented casket, laid in the grave with its head on a cushion of leaves, and covered with six inches of dirt. The grave is then ready to receive another body.[18]

584

On All Souls' Day Mexican bake shops specialize in bread and cakes for the dead — to be consumed by the living

P.I.P. Photo

When the rent has expired the bodies are dug up or taken from the wall recesses and placed in a stone tunnel twelve feet high, six feet wide, and over a thousand feet long. This tunnel runs beneath the entire periphery of the cemetery. In addition to loose bones it contains many bodies which have been mummified in the dry air.

In urban areas persons who die in hospitals, and whose bodies are unclaimed, are given an inexpensive burial at state expense, with the cheapest kind of coffins, and transportation to the cemetery supplied by a hospital cart. In rural areas it is not uncommon for the unclaimed dead to be carried on a rude bier to the cemetery and buried without ceremony.[19]

Cremation is very uncommon in Mexico, and up to now has been largely confined to the bodies of a few Americans whose remains were returned home by air express. An American consular officer notes that in the Peninsula of Yucatan "since there is no crematorium, the procedure of burning bodies is very rudimentary."[20]

The custom of photographing the body of a dead person with the family surrounding it is passing in Mexico. However, it still happens on occasion, and when flashlight equipment is not available long exposure, using lamps or candles, is substituted. Such pictures are becoming collectors' items.

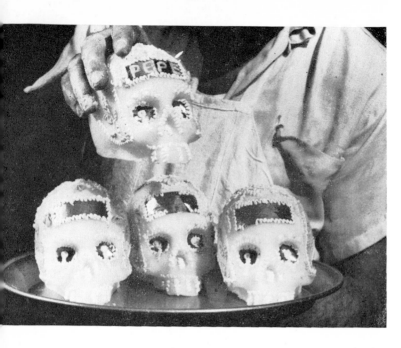

Grinning skull cakes,
monogramed, are sent
to friends on
All Souls' Day

P.I.P. Photo

Mourning Behavior: The Day of the Dead

The wearing of mourning clothing is still common in Mexico. Although their mourning periods are short, Mexicans are likely to wear black even for intimate friends and distant relatives, so that a lady is likely to have a black dress as a standard part of her wardrobe.

In general Mexican mourning customs follow Catholic tradition. In families with strong religious beliefs prayers are said at the home of the deceased, in the evening, for nine consecutive nights. Thereafter, the services take place once a month, and then once a year. In the case of yearly services, dinners are served. In Mexico, as in other Catholic countries, All Saints' Day (November 1) and All Souls' Day (November 2) are days of special prayer and religious observance. At this time the poor set tables with fruit and even entire meals in their homes in the belief that the dead will return to eat the foods they most loved during their lifetime.

All Souls' Day is the official day for visiting the cemeteries. Since All Saints' Day is the eve of All Souls' Day, it is natural that the visitations start on that day. At this time relatives and friends in great numbers bring floral wreaths, crosses, and bouquets to decorate the graves of their dead. On this day, too, they may set up tables near the graves, and load them with cakes and candies in the form of skulls and other reminders of mortality. In the midst of these sweetmeats they place a real skull and a bowl of holy water.[21]

Mexicans look forward to All Saints' Day and All Souls' Day as Americans look forward to Memorial Day. The whole nation dons black. During these two days pottery dishes finished with a black glaze, including plates, cups, bowls and candelabra are used. These are on sale only in late October. The center-piece is a late-blooming flower, golden in color, called the "Flower of the Dead." So that they may never again be used, when the observance is passed the black dishes are broken. Excepting their presence, the spirit at the meals is not solemn.

Carefully made hard candy skulls, ranging from a few inches across to life size, are everywhere sold to children at this time. Some have a child's name written across the forehead, and a mother of a dead child will purchase one of these containing her child's name, for use as a table decoration. The more expensive skulls have red candy inserts in the eye sockets. While normally these skulls are eaten as candy, they are sometimes put aside as mementos, and last for years. The same shops that sell candy skulls also vend candy skeletons, chocolate caskets, and sugar-coated tombstones.[22]

In describing these feast days a traveller speaks of the "gleaming gay skulls, sugary-white and with splendid gold trimmings," and of a "whole city being given over to death," with "feasting in the cemeteries." Everywhere, he observes, there are dancing skeletons, and pastry and candy take the shape of skeletons as naturally as our gingerbread takes the shape of Santa Claus at Christmas. One cannot even open the newspaper without seeing skulls. Famous men from the President down are pictured with fleshless grins, and someone writes very nasty epitaphs of them. These are days, not only for pious religious observances, but "for morbid joys and gruesome delights, for death casts its juggling ribaldry over everything."[23]

In urban areas at least, the present century has seen a substantial raising of the level of funeralization in Mexico. In 1900 John W. Wagner, an American funeral director, wrote:

> Undertaking in the Republic of Mexico is in the primitive state. The conditions in the City of Mexico are passable, but in the provinces they are in the crudest state possible. In cities of 200,000 the carpenter makes the casket, of which he usually keeps two or three on hand for contingencies. The remains are laid in the receptacle, and then covered with a blanket. Although a simple casket sold for $3.00 even this low price was prohibitive for many poor people, who were forced to rent a casket for about 50¢, to be carried to the cemetery on someone's head, or across someone's saddle.[24]

Changes have been marked in the past half century. Among the more noted are the increased use of the funeral home for waking the dead, the higher percentage of bodies being embalmed, and the general improvement in sanitary practices.[25] In some Mexican cities Protestantism has obtained a foothold, thus introducing a new funeral pattern into a culture in which, since the Spanish conquest, burials were conducted according to Catholic rites.[26] Also, the separation of church and state has brought a diminution in the religious influence over funeral procedures.

Mexican funeral directors are organized into a number of state associations, such as the Funeral Directors Association of the North, which has headquarters in Monterrey. The National Association of Proprietors of Funeral Establishments, also with headquarters in Monterrey, covers a more extensive territory. It was organized in 1955.[27] In the State of Yucatan in 1959, however, one finds "no agencies or groups, secular or spiritual, exercising control over, or participating in, the burial of the dead," although, "in a very few instances, since most of the population is Catholic, the parents or relatives pay priests to have funeral orations delivered in churches or at the cemeteries right before the body is interred." In the ritual of the Catholic church there are special Masses

588

which are said or sung on the death of a person, on the day of burial, on the seventh day, on the thirtieth day after death, and on the anniversary of the death.[28]

Burial in Rural Areas

Chan Kom Funerals

In the Mexican hinterland one sometimes finds early Indian beliefs and practices modified by Christian teachings. Thus in their study of *Chan Kom,* a Mayan village, anthropologists Redfield and Villa[29] point out that the natives believe that when a good man dies his soul goes to *Gloria,* whose gate is guarded by St. Peter. Other less clean souls go to Purgatory, to be burned white so that they may enter Gloria. The souls of the wicked do not enter Gloria at all, but are consigned to a region below the earth, called *Metnal,* to keep company with demons. It is recommended that suicides, who are destined for Metnal, be buried face downward so as to be headed in the proper direction. Certain wicked souls, which are changed into animals, may someday gain release and be admitted to Gloria. Sooner or later all souls return to earth to be reincarnated as little babies. God does not have enough souls to repopulate the earth indefinitely. Certain physical signs such as an abundance of hair or unusually bright eyes mark the new born infant with the reincarnated soul. Sometimes a soul is hindered from reaching Gloria, by the struggle between the forces of good and evil made at the moment of death. In such cases, first it wanders near the scene of death and causes dogs to howl and horses to snort.[30]

Response to Death

When death seems certain the *maestro cantor* is called to recite the prayers for the dying. The purpose or object of the recital of these is to release the soul from the body and confound the demons who cluster around the house waiting to seize the soul. Sometimes the dying man sees the demons. Sometimes

589

he watches them wilt at the hearing of prayers. Because belief has it that the soul of a dying person briefly leaves the body to see Gloria and Purgatory, and then returns, the dying are thought to possess a special wisdom.[31]

Those at the bedside do not weep as death approaches. For them to weep might be to stay the departing soul, or, as the phrase goes, "wet the road to Gloria." It is especially important that parents should not bewail the loss of a child. A child in Gloria may be their promise of salvation, which they might lose if their tears called it back. To liberate a soul reluctant to depart, bystanders sometimes beat the body with a rope, although how much of the beating is symbolic and how much is real is not clear. When death seems imminent, all seeds are removed from the house so that they may not become infertile when their hearts die.[32]

A hole is made in the thatch of the roof for the soul to mount through after it leaves the body. At one end of a masonry house a small window near the roof serves the same purpose. Death is announced to the village by the tolling of bells in the chapel.

Care of the Body

At the family's request friends shroud the body in a sheet. To show that a dead child has become an angel they wrap aound its shoulders a cape with wings attached; on its head they place a crown, and in its folded hands a stick with colored paper attachments. From an adult's girdle they hang a rope with fifty knots, to be used in heaven to whip the spirit for the sins it committed on earth.

After the body is stretched out on a table, shrouded but otherwise uncovered, with lighted candles at the head and feet, the wake begins, and friends and neighbors come with gifts of food, coffee, and candles. While the young deport themselves in card games, dances, and drinking, the old people make solemn conversation or offer prayers.[33]

Twenty-four hours after death, while the chapel bells toll, the last clothing worn by the deceased not used to clothe the

590

body—is laid on the bier together with his rosary and the last cup from which he drank. Then, as a final kindness from him his relatives scatter corn to the barnyard fouls and bread to the dogs. Now they place the body in a casket, red for a child and black for an adult, and holding lighted candles, and chanting, they carry the body to the cemetery. It is noted, incidentally, that the custom observed by many Mexican Indians of placing corn and other edibles in the casket so that the strength of the dead may be sustained on the long journey into the land of the spirits is an inheritance from their Aztec forbears.[34]

While the grave is being dug the casket is placed in a thatched hut. There the maestro cantor recites more prayers for the dead. Interment is made without ceremony, although holy water may be sprinkled into the grave, and a candle lighted. A small wooden cross is set at the head of the grave.[35]

Mourning Behavior After the Burial

A novena, or nine-days' prayer, to assure the repose of the soul and its detachment from the living, begins on the day following burial. Although the dead are commemorated at fixed intervals after death, there is little actual mourning. Women may occasionally vary their costumes slightly to show grief; men never do so. As most elsewhere in Mexico the souls of the dead are thought to return for an annual visit on the eve of All Souls' Day and on the feast itself; and on these occasions food is provided for them, each family looking to the needs of its own departed. Flowers are gathered to decorate the tables and to hang on the door as an invitation to the spirits to enter. The quantity of food and the number of candles vary according to the means of the household. At the family meal the maestro cantor recites prayers for the dead. Later that day a dinner is held to honor the dead. The fowl served always consists of cooked hens. A bowl of water is provided so that the dead may wash their hands. On All Saints' Day the "dinner of the big souls" is given in honor of the adult dead.[36]

Elsewhere in Rural Mexico

In Mexico everywhere the Day of the Dead celebrations combine a curious admixture of ancient Indian and Catholic beliefs and practices. For example, shortly before midnight, thousands of Tarascan Indians gather at Pátzcuaro, Michoacán, to hold their *Dia de los Muertos* ceremony on the little island of Janitzio, to which they bring offerings of food and drink for their dead. An observer has commented that the "magnificent spectacles of thousands of glowing torches and candles, lighting up the tiny island like a Christmas tree in the middle of the lake, lasts until dawn."[37]

In Oaxaca, ceremonies are held in the graveyard and in the city. In many houses shrines honoring the dead are erected, and in the markets small caskets, skulls and skeletons made of sugar or baked clay are sold. While the living, to the accompaniment of music and firecrackers, eat a steer and drink in a two-day ceremony, gifts of cooked fruit are placed on the church altars so the souls of the dead, too, may hold their feast. At the same time, Yecapixtea, Mexico, at its most important annual market day features in its stalls *Dia de los Muertos* art and food.[38]

Rural Funeral Processions Described

A procession with the father carrying the tiny white casket of his child, followed by the barefooted mother and their other children, slowly winding their way through the streets to the cemetery, is a common scene in Mexico.

In his colorful account of life in Mexico author Arthemise Goertz[39] gives a description of a weird funeral procession in a Mexican village. "Six men carried the casket—on their shoulders, so that the polished silver handles would be sure to show." The "solemn black suits and laced shoes of the leading pallbearers lent a certain splendid style to the long cortege of worn *huaraches* and white *pantaloons*." The mourners—all men, since women seldom go to funerals in Mexico—marched slowly and silently behind the body, in a thick column

592

more than a block long. All the fathers and brothers and husbands and sons of the *barrio* of Cocolapam must have been there, "together with many of the dead man's midnight friends from around the *plaza* and the market place, too. They walked with bowed, bare heads. Their eyes fixed on the wet cobblestones of the street. Those who could afford it carried candles, which smoked and sputtered in the grey mist."[40]

As the funeral passed, the men on the sidewalk stood still and took off their hats, and the women crossed themselves and muttered a prayer for the repose of the soul of the dead man. Prisoners, pressed against cell windows, likewise prayed. In the home of a friend "everyone including the servants of children, knelt down on the damp floor and mumbled their *Aves* and *Paters* in fast, frightened whispers."[41]

Coffin is carried home from market place in Chichicastenango

Chapter 45

Guatemala and El Salvador

Guatemala

Organization of Funeral Service

In urban areas of Guatemala funeral customs and practices for the most part resemble those found in the United States. However, several points of difference can be noted. For one thing, embalming is expensive—the charge is $300 upwards—and it is generally not practiced. For another, no effort is made to improve the appearance of the remains by the use of the cosmetic arts. A major point of difference is to be found in the fact that Guatemalans, unlike their North American brothers, favor music in their funeral processions. A marimba band is the common choice, and it accompanies the cortege in much the same fashion as the jazz band once made a New Orleans funeral lively. Strangely enough all hearses in Guatemala are government owned.[1]

There has never been an organization of funeral directors in Guatemala, although in 1959 there were reports that an attempt was being made to form such an organization. Presently all matters concerning burial in Guatemala are legally regulated and administered by the Ministry of Public Health.[2]

Among changes to be found in Guatemalan funerals during the last half century are the elimination of horse-drawn hearses, and a gradual replacement of them by deluxe ambulance-type vehicles. Sentiment is growing strong to allow private funeral establishments to own their own hearses.[3]

Funerals in Rural Guatemala

More distinctive and therefore more interesting are the funeral practices found in rural Guatemala. The American anthropologist Charles Wagley describes such practices in the village of Santiago Chimaltenango.[4] These are characteristic of village practices to be found generally in Guatemala.[5]

Response to Death

When death seems certain, women kneel beside the dying person and begin to wail so loudly that the sound can be heard throughout the village. Men meanwhile maintain a stoic silence. Says one of Wagley's informants: "It is only the women who cry. God does not like too much sadness. It is best for the dead person not to be too sad, because God might not accept the spirit."[6] In keeping with this viewpoint the male relatives stolidly prepare for the wake, which takes place during the night on the day of death and for the funeral, which follows on the morrow. Meanwhile the tolling bell tells the sex of the deceased: three strokes for a man; two, for a woman. One stroke of the bell signifies the death of a child.

Immediately after death the body, dressed in the deceased person's best clothes, is stretched out full length on a blanket-covered bench. In anticipation of her shrouding, an old woman may have woven an elaborate funeral *huipil* or blouse for herself which she has never worn during life. It is to be used only for her burial. Candles are stood near the head, and flowers

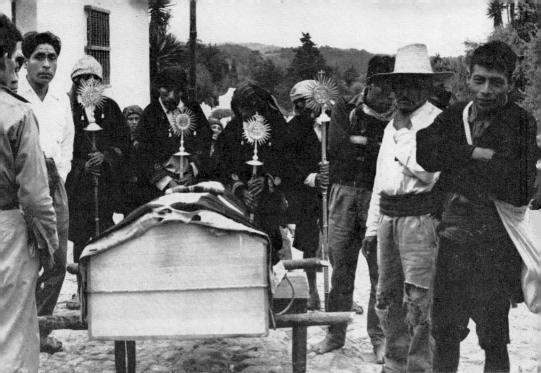

Mourners in special robes ready to
lead Guatemalan funeral procession

Draped coffin is carried in
procession to church service

and small postcards picturing saints are laid on the chest.[7] In
some areas the body is dressed in the clothing worn at the time
of death.

Close friends and relatives attend the wake, the size of the
crowd being partly determined by the importance of the deceased, and by the amount of *aguardiente*, a distilled liquor
made from corn or sugar cane, that they anticipate will be
served. Music proves another attraction, a marimba band playing during part of the evening.[8]

During the wake the body lies in state inside the house, attended throughout the night by the relatives and companions of the deceased. These watchers are served coffee and rolls. From time to time as less close relatives or friends and acquaintances arrive, they enter the house quickly to pay their respects, and as quickly leave. Even a long glance at the body is thought to absorb contagion and thus produce illness.

Meanwhile the band plays on the porch, and liquor is freely distributed to everybody, including the players. As the liquor takes effect on the musicians and the crowd, the music becomes more lively and the people begin to dance. Eventually the music stops and the crowd disperses to their homes, leaving the group within the house to their quiet, all night vigil.

Early the next morning the male relatives and friends of the deceased leave the watching group, and while some of them take turns digging the grave near other family graves in the village cemetery, others construct a rough coffin out of planks. Most graves in Guatemala are so dug that the head lies toward the west, why, no one seems to know. These tasks consume the whole morning. When they are finished the workers rejoin their wives in the house of the deceased.[9]

Their arrival there is a signal for the organization of the funeral procession. Singers and marimba players have already marched to the house through the village street. The marimba players, playing dignified slow measures, lead the procession. Bearers follow them with the body, using the bench as a bier. Next march the chanters, their singing consisting of slow responses to the music of the marimbas. Two by two the mourners follow; first the near relatives, and then the more distant relatives and friends. As the procession moves gravely through the village to the cemetery by the most direct route, it stops momentarily at halting places selected by the chanters, and occasionally a woman, possibly the deceased's wife, breaks from the ranks and runs forward, to walk alongside the body and weep.[10]

Only rarely does the marimba band play at the graveside. There the singers lead the ceremonies. After the bench with the body upon it is stood at the margin of the grave, the chanters, refreshed by an occasional drink of liquor, intone their litanies in Latin, sometimes for several hours, to the accompaniment of a violin or guitar. The music of these instruments is considered better suited to so mournful a place. The male relatives stand near the singers and share the bottle with them.

Meanwhile the women of the immediate family seat themselves on the ground near the body and wail with increasing loudness. Women less closely related, and the intimate friends of the deceased form another group, who seat themselves some distance apart, and make solemn small talk. Other groups, comprised of neighbors and lookers-on gather some distance away. Coffee and sweetbread are served to the persons in the first two groups, and occasionally to some persons from the third group who come forward to ask for them.[11] The chanting and drinking continue throughout the afternoon, and if, as usually happens, the singers become drunk, intoxication is considered to add to the excellence of the performance.[12]

Toward dusk a straw mat is placed over the body, and with the aid of two long cloths the body in its wrapping is lowered into the grave into which the male relatives have previously put the coffin, rough box, or sometimes simply a lining of boards. After the body has been lowered, flowers and some personal possessions are cast into the grave and only then do the male relatives and intimate friends of the deceased begin to shovel earth upon it. As the dirt falls the wailing of the women rises to a new climax. When the grave has been filled those who have attended the burial struggle back to the village, friendly women supporting the women of the family who have exhausted themselves by the frenzy of their grief.[13]

Both the elaborateness and cost of a funeral vary greatly, and are used as yardsticks to measure social prestige. Items to be bought are a straw mat to cover the body, boards for the grave lining or coffin, the coffee and rolls for the mourners, and the liquor. The singers are paid for their services at the wake and for their chanting at the grave. These fees are inconsiderable in comparison with the obligation of plying them with all the liquor they want or can hold.

If the family can afford the additional fee it hires a chanter to return to the grave the day after the funeral, to continue his chant; and it employs him again on the twentieth day. At this time, belief has it, chanting will assure the safe passage of the deceased into the hereafter. Newly departed spirits are believed to suffer a loneliness so intense that by their pining they are able to bring about the death of other survivors, and thus provide company for themselves. To prevent such a catastrophe many families hire a chanter to visit a grave every five days during the first month after burial.[14]

A son is expected to bury his parents; or a brother, to bury a brother; or a father, his younger sons. Parents are concerned that their children shall not be derelict in this obligation toward them, and continuously remind them to save their money for their funeral expenses.

The simple rural folk of Guatemala are not given to prolonged mourning, and in a month or so at most they are resigned to their loss, and return to their normal pursuits, saying of children, for example, "They are with God." After this they no longer visit the newly filled graves. Spouses, if they wish, are then eligible to take new partners.

Only on All Saints Day, November 1, are the dead again publicly brought to mind. At this feast bouquets of marigolds are fastened to the door of every house where a recent death has occurred. Now all return to the cemetery to place food and "flowers for the dead" upon both the old and the new family graves. And all that night, as at the wake, in each house where a recent death has occurred, liquor flows and marimba music once more can be heard.[15]

El Salvador

In common with most of its Central American neighbors, El Salvador, the smallest American republic, is indigenously an Indian country.[16] Since the Spanish Conquest of the early sixteenth century as a colony of Spain it has been part of the captain-generalcy of Guatemala, and later of the vice-royalty of Mexico.[17] Since gaining its independence in 1821, El Salvador has progressed toward a truly republican form of government. In consequence of these historical developments, the Salvadorian culture reflects Indian, Spanish, modern Latin-American, and to some extent North American influences. The orientation of El Salvador to the United States has venerable historical roots. In 1822 it proclaimed a desire to be annexed to the United States, and since that time in matters of political, judicial, economic, and educational organization has looked to this country for inspiration and example.

In the matter of Salvadorian funeral customs and procedures a variety of usages and conventions exist. For the most part the disposition of the dead in rural areas follows a pattern not too different from that described in Guatemala. Emphasis in the following pages will be on the care of the dead in San Salvador, the urban center and capital of the republic.

Funerals in Urban El Salvador

In San Salvador the care of the dead is primarily a family matter. However, if the deceased is without a family, close personal friends assume the responsibilities. If a person dies without family or friends, a relatively rare event, government employees remove the body directly to a special section of the general cemetery and bury it with a minimum of ceremony.

As soon as a person dies it is the general practice for the family to turn to the local *funeraria* for the purchase of the casket, and the rental of other funeral items, but not for personal services. In mid-1960 El Salvador had one funeral home of the type common in the United States, and very few people made use of its chapel.[18]

The greater part of the funeral business of San Salvador is in the hands of the owner of the funeraria, a funeral supplier or furnisher. His establishment occupies store-front quarters, with caskets on display. He usually is by trade a cabinet-maker or carpenter, who makes or employs others to make

601

Photos Courtesy Oscar Reyes Duran

Above, Modern funeral coach and uniformed attendants, San Salvador.
Lower left, Variety of coffins and caskets reflects prevailing Latin American styles. *Right*, A 1928 hearse still in use in San Salvador

wooden caskets. The wood he uses ranges in quality from the cheapest pine to the most expensive mahogany. The funeraria also rents hearses. For the most part these are of the decorative kind widely used in Europe, although a newer type, made by converting a panel truck, is becoming available. Occasionally an open pick-up truck is used to bring the casket to the home. The funeraria also supplies chairs, candleholders, black decorations and drapes on a rental basis. All of these are for use in the home where the body lies in state. Likewise, the funeraria makes catering arrangements. Such services are needed because it is usual for the family to provide a light lunch for those who come to view the body and to keep the twelve-hour vigil.

The eldest male survivor in the immediate family usually picks out the casket. If it is a wooden casket or coffin it will be of local manufacture; if a metal casket, it will be imported, generally from the United States. American-style caskets made without a glass panel are now beginning to supplant the older type, glass-paneled caskets. The funeraria delivers the casket to the home. Meanwhile the family prepares, washes and dresses the body. When the casket arrives the family lays the body in it.

Up to now embalming has been practiced in San Salvador only to preserve the remains until some relative has arrived from a considerable distance, or to transport them for burial elsewhere. Municipal Health Department regulations do not allow a wake to be held if the body remains unembalmed for more than twenty-four hours following death.

The failure for the practice of embalming to make much headway in San Salvador has been due in part to the fact that it is not customary, and in part to the lack of a corps of trained embalmers. These two causes interrelate. A third reason for the infrequent practice of what traditionally has been called "hypodermic injection" lies in the fact that embalming until recently has been the prerogative of physicians who charged between two and three hundred dollars for performing the service. Few families could afford to pay this fee.

The casketed body is placed on a stand in the largest room of the house—usually the living room. A lighted candle is stood at each side of it, and as friends and relatives arrive with floral offerings these are grouped around the casket. Unless they have been embalmed the remains are kept for one full night, and buried within twenty-four hours after death. The wake lasts throughout the night. Relatives and friends gather, some of them from a considerable distance. Some remain for the entire night. At intervals the assembled mourners say prayers

603

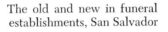

The old and new in funeral
establishments, San Salvador

in common. It is customary for a priest to visit the home and
to offer the usual prayers for the dead.

For the procession the funeraria furnishes the chauffeur as
well as the hearse. Almost universally the funeral services begin
in the home. Rarely are services conducted in the church. The
priest blesses the casket either in the home or at the cemetery.

When, however, the body is taken to the church for a
Requiem Mass, the priest usually accompanies the procession
to the cemetery, and there blesses the casket and the grave. If
Mass is not celebrated, the priest generally joins the procession
at the home, and accompanies it to the cemetery.

In rural areas, where hearses are not available, the funeral
procession proceeds on foot with the pallbearers carrying the
casket on their shoulders. In urban areas the pallbearers,
selected by the family, carry the casket to the graveside and
cemetery employees lower it into the grave.

For earth burial a grave about six feet deep is dug, and
the casketed body is lowered by ropes. After the gravediggers

604

have filled the grave, the mourners place wreaths and bouquets of flowers over the mound. Some families prefer to remain at the grave until it has been entirely filled. Others leave while the casket is being lowered.

The cemeteries of San Salvador closely resemble those of Mexico, Cuba and other Spanish-American countries. They are municipally owned. Burial space may be purchased outright or rented, and the seven-year lease is common. Interment may be made in the ground, in crypts, or in mausolea. Lots for earth burial may be purchased individually or by families. A lot usually consists of a burial place for three. Earth burials are made in layers instead of in separate graves.

It is usually a matter of several months or a year before memorialization is completed through the erection of a mausoleum or monument if the body has not been given crypt burial. Many monuments in the cemeteries of San Salvador are large and ornate. Unless the casket has been of the most expensive variety the cost of the monument will ordinarily be the largest item of funeral expense. When a mausoleum is erected the cost usually exceeds that of all other material items of the funeral combined.

Mourning dresses are worn by women for a period of three months to a year. For the most part the men resort to the black arm badge to indicate their bereavement. If the deceased was Catholic it is common for a novena to be said. This nine-day sequence of prayer is observed by friends and relatives who gather at the church each day at a specific hour. Also, in keeping with the common pattern in Latin America, All Saints' Day and All Souls' Day are observed in church services and with visits to the cemeteries to decorate the graves of the dead.

Wall crypts in Panama cemetery for Chinese whose bones eventually
will be returned to China for permanent burial

Chapter 46

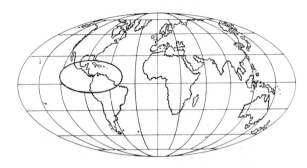

Panama and the San Blas Cuna

Rural Panama

The Panamanian farmer and his woman "live a life of hard work and simple pleasures with few comforts or luxuries."[1] Sickness, old age, and death come early to the subsistence farmer. Sanitary facilities and practices are little known to him and medical care is poor.

When a Panamanian farmer is critically ill the neighbors gather and discuss death and disease freely and pessimistically. Often they wail, and while some of this is genuine grief, some is purely conventional. However, they accept death, and when the little bell tinkles to tell that the priest is making a visit to a home to administer Extreme Unction, they follow along out of curiosity.[2] As news of a death spreads quickly by word of mouth, friends and relatives flock to the home of the deceased to observe an all-night wake.

With a crucifix at the head and four lighted candles set

607

about it—two at the head and two at the feet—the body lies on a hide on the floor, or on a sheet on the table. Everyone, except the few who are most deeply concerned, enjoy a most pleasant social affair. Food is cooked and served to all comers by the women. Cigarettes are passed around; coffee and liquor freely distributed. While clusters of men play checkers or dominoes on the patio, women talk. Occasionally one will suspend conversation to wail. This custom is a carry-over from Spanish colonial days when professional women mourners were hired to raise a commotion and extoll the virtues of the dead. In the midst of this enjoyment the serious business at hand is not neglected, and the family is given comfort and sympathy.[3]

These rural Panamanians fear that the souls of those whose bodies lie in unconsecrated ground cannot enter heaven, and they regard with peculiar horror the tragedy of one who dies alone and in the open, and whose body is eaten by buzzards. When someone drowns, every effort is made to recover the body, and when usual measures fail, a candle and a statue of St. Anthony are placed in a small boat which is allowed to drift freely. St. Anthony is one of the auxiliary saints, *i.e.*, saints called upon in special needs. He is the finder of lost objects. He is thought to point out the location of the body by halting the boat over the place where it lies, and that is where men dive for it.

Although the rural Panamanian, for whatever reason, may have attended church irregularly or not at all during his lifetime, he wants to be buried from a church. To transport him thither, if the family lives on or near a road leading to a village with a church, the family makes a crude coffin, which is placed in the grave. If the body must be carried through roadless woods or thickets or mountainous country, it is wrapped in a white cloth, and tied, and carried in a bamboo litter. The latter is not buried with the body. The women do not attend the actual burial as that is considered a task for the men.[4]

In rural Panama, mourning ceremonies continue in the

home for nine days after a death. White sheets are hung on the walls of the front room. On a table, draped in white, stand statues of saints, lighted candles, and a primitive lamp made by inserting a wick in a glass of oil. Below the table a glass of water with a sprig of sweet basil is placed, so that the spirit, which returns each of the nine nights, may quench its thirst. A bench stands before the table for the use of the hired prayer leader. Each evening the house fills up with friends and family members, and after the prayer leader has led in the praying, with responses by the assembled group, those who are not too overcome with grief enjoy themselves by singing, talking, eating, and drinking. Two similar ceremonies are held; the first a month after a death, and the second on the first anniversary.[5]

Urban Panama

Panamanians generally have strong family feelings, and children and other relatives take the old into their homes when they are no longer able to work. Among the urban poor, when someone young or old dies, a black-bordered notice stating that fact and the time of services and burial is tacked up on walls and bulletin boards, which persons concerned are likely to pass, while friends are told by word of mouth. The simple funerals of the poor require only simple arrangements, and the time of burial.[6] Moreover, in a warm climate a lack of embalming makes a delay of several days undesirable. As a result, when death occurs in the morning, burial is likely to be made on the same evening; and if death takes place at night, burial follows the next morning.

In urban Panama the use of the funeral director's services mark one of the major differences between the burial of city and country folk. The duties of the funeral director revolve around making arrangements for the families of the dead with various authorities, of providing caskets or coffins, and arranging transportation for the dead, the bereaved, and the mourners. Usually he will assist in securing the death certificate, to be signed by the attending physician, and he will almost always obtain a permit from the Department of Health to carry out the burial. Other duties, specifically, include making arrangements with church and cemetery officials for the funeral ceremonial and the interment of the body.[7]

The body of a poor person is placed in a simple casket and kept for a brief viewing in the front room of the home. The floral offerings of friends are grouped around it. A white sheet is commonly suspended on one wall, and against it are hung a crucifix and holy pictures, and all of the furniture, except a semi-circle of chairs fronting the remains, is removed. As in the rural areas, an all-night wake is kept, at which refreshments are served, prayers said, and much talk indulged in. Men drink rum and play dominoes.[8]

For those of modest or better means the deceased may be permitted to lie in state in the chapel of the funeral home, the *salon de velacion*, literally the "wake room." Although this facility is not at present used to any great extent, Panamanians are showing increasing acceptance of the idea that it is the proper place to wake the dead. Embalming, as noted, is very seldom practiced, and cremation, in view of the restriction placed upon it by the Catholic Church, is non-existent.[9]

Before the body is removed from the home or chapel, the rosary is said. The funeral director's hearse carries the body to the church for simple burial ceremony. For some a Mass is provided; for others only the brief blessings and prayers. When the church services have been completed, the women return home to console the bereaved, while the men accompany the body to the cemetery. As each returning woman enters the house, the chief mourners greet her by sobbing afresh, "Did God see no one but my baby?"—or husband, father, son, daughter, as the case may be.

When a prominent person is being buried, his friends and associates, wearing white linen suits with black armbands, form in lines behind the hearse and march to the cemetery. On such occasions as many as twenty or more taxicabs, their roofs loaded with wreaths and other floral offerings, may form a colorful part of the procession.[10]

610

Sixty years ago Dr. Wolfred Nelson described a Panama cemetery:

> Facing the highway was a stone fence and an old time arched gateway of stone. Entering it, one had a full view of what was within. It was a quadrangle of niches of *bovedas*. Picture to yourself four sides of a square having three tiers of openings in them, one below, one between, and one on top, each opening being large enough to receive the coffin of an adult, and the whole whitewashed and backed by a substantial stone wall. Within the enclosure were monuments to several people who had been buried permanently. These niches are rented for the space of eighteen months. The coffin is placed within and the end is closed either with brick work or with a marble slab having a suitable inscription. At the end of eighteen months, failing a prompt renewal of the rent, the coffin and contents are evicted.[11]

Eviction meant dumping the contents out behind the cemetery "unceremoniously . . . without regard for the possible spread of disease or the aesthetic effect." Vaults such as these are still rented out in the same manner with eviction for non-payment of rent. In addition, in urban areas, Panamanians have available to them small burial plots for children, and family mausolea. A structure of this type has room for several above-ground burials. When it is filled, the greatly reduced remains of an earlier burial are removed from the casket and placed in a smaller concrete box, thus allowing for another full burial. A member of the family is always present at such a transfer to see to it that no bones are stolen. Panamanians regard human bones as good luck charms. Burial places are decorated with wreaths and other flower arrangements (real or artificial), urns, crosses, and photographs of the dead.[12]

At the cemetery, the body is pushed into a deep niche in the burial wall, or in the family mausoleum. A priest may or may not be present to conduct ceremonies at the grave. Humble people are interred with little said about their virtues or achievements. A prominent person receives much mortuary eulogy.[13]

Burial over, the men mourners join the women at the home for more talk. Again, as in the country, an organized nine-day period of mourning is observed, and each evening during this time the rosary is said. The final day of this period they attend an early Mass, and return to the home for coffee.

Although Panamanians continue for some time to write Q.E.P.D. (May He Rest in Peace) after the name of a deceased person, they actually are less dedicated to the prolonged mourning of the dead than some of their Latin-American neighbors, and are growing even less so. A half-century ago deepest mourning was observed. "They turned pictures to the wall or draped them in black, drew the shades, and ceased all social appearances."[14]

Today it is no longer the custom in Panama, as in some Latin-American countries, for close women relatives of the dead to clothe themselves from head to foot in black, and to wear this mourning for years. Except for a husband or mother, few Panamanian women wear unrelieved black, and not all daughters and wives do so. While some token of mourning may be worn for years, relatives less closely connected with the dead, if they wear mourning at all, may soon dress partly or wholly in white. Mourning customs for the men consist of black ties and armbands. During the period of mourning, relatives curtail their social engagements and amusements. The period of mourning observed by men is shorter than that observed by women.[15]

On the anniversary of the day of death, it is customary for relatives to have a Requiem Mass said for the departed. But it is nevertheless apparent that there is less intensity to the "cult of the dead" in Panama than in many other Central American countries. For example, November 1, All Saints' Day, now shares honors with the Day of the Founding Fathers of Panama.[16]

The Native Cunas of Panama

The Cunas, popularly called the San Blas Indians, live on

a string of islands off the eastern coast of Panama.[17] Although these Indians comprise less than ten per cent of Panama's population they are an independent group preferring isolation to social contact, and are content to perpetuate a way of life relatively unchanged in many centuries. There is a thin veneer of Spanish culture but for the most part it has been incorporated into the host Indian social fabric in a fashion that exhibits no particular rhyme or reason. Especially tenacious is the hold of these Central American aborigines on traditional customs associated with the burial of the dead.

Spirit Beliefs

The Cuna Indians' word *purba* represents a complicated concept, inadequately rendered by our word "soul." "Shade" or "shadow" probably are more accurate renderings.[18] The Cunas believe that after death they will find God just as invisible, just as unapproachable as they found Him in life. They believe that after a long and difficult journey the departed soul reaches the land of the spirits. But it will not have the beatific vision.[19]

Although the Cunas do not identify the spirits of the departed with the spirits of evil, they believe that when evil spirits are molested they lash out against their molesters, and sometimes against a mere passer-by. Evil spirits possess the power of making a person sick by casting a spell upon him; they may enter a body and dwell therein. When the soul cannot shake itself free from a possessing spirit, or when it is too long away from the body, as it may wander when the body sleeps, the body dies. A fever is a sign that a spirit has taken possession of a soul.[20] So greatly do the Cunas fear the spirits of their dead that they never mention the name of a dead person. To make such mention even to a friend or relative is to violate the death taboo.[21] This prohibition indicates the Cunas' belief in a continuous close association between the living and the dead. To name someone, they argue, is to summon him, it may be from the nether regions. This belief seems inconsistent with another belief of theirs, that the soul of the departed lives in the grave. However, belief does not always yield to logic.

Response to Death

When it seems that a Cuna Indian is dying, a medicine man is summoned. His treatment consists in fumigating the patient from head to foot with fumes from burning the cocoa bean, peppers, and other materials. While he carries out this purification he chants a sacred incantation in a monotone.[22]

As soon as the man dies the men of his family wash the body in warm water, dress it in his best clothes, and place it in his hammock. There it lies during a full day and night of mourning. Women perform similar functions for a woman. The hammocks in which the Cunas bury their dead are finely woven out of cotton wool.[23]

While the body lies in the hammock before being buried, relatives, friends, and even strangers pay the dead a social visit. The spirit is given messages to bear to the land of the spirits. Sometimes it is assigned duties to perform. Thus a mother of a dead child may press a bauble into the hand of the body of another so that its spirit may present the gift to the spirit of her baby.[24]

The principal mourning observance of the Cunas consists of chanting, which recounts the character and deeds of the deceased, together with comments concerning the joys and punishments of the hereafter. Often a death chanter is paid to sing of the soul's journey through the underworld into heaven. The Cunas select their chanters because of their ability to sing well. Most of their songs are happy, phrased in the present, and have happy endings. The only exception is the death chant, which apparently is sung for the consolation of the bereaved. The chanter sings not in his own person but as though he were the dying man, or the spirit taking the journey. The singer carries a Cuna picture-writing book containing the chant to be sung on the way to the grave. The pictures aid his memory.[25]

The title of the death chant is "The Guardian Spirits Who

614

Know the Way." It has the character of an epic poem, and is the high mark of the Cunas' imaginative conception. The intoning of the lengthy chant is a tremendous test of memory, voice and stamina, the full rendition requiring eighteen to twenty hours.[26]

The chanter paints his face for the ceremony and brings assistants with him. When he tires, one or the other of these continues while he rests. The journey described by the chanter has been compared to that described in *Pilgrim's Progress*. The chanter links his own soul to that of the dead man or woman and through his chanting hopes to gather a band of good spirits who will serve as companions for the dead person's journey into the afterlife. The belief of the Indians regarding a place of expiation for sins has some resemblance to the Catholic doctrine of purgatory. The wayfaring soul must pass through a snake world, a crocodile world, a tar pit. He must escape the giant scissors by which liars are sundered, and the mammoth sugar cane press in which the careless are caught. The hazards and their sequence never vary. Each phase of the chant entreats assistance for the traveller. By the time the rite ends it is thought that the soul of the deceased has reached heaven. Now the souls of the chanter and his assistants must hasten to return to earth. They have disturbed the spirit world, and if they tarry, they court death. The chanter therefore puts his painted sticks in the hammock with the body, and the body is placed in a large canoe for the trip to the mainland cemetery.[27]

Because the souls of children are thought to escape the journey through the underworld and pass directly into heaven, the services of the professional chanter are not utilized for a child's funeral.[28]

Burial Procedures

Cemeteries are located on the banks of rivers and at some distance from settlements. Access is by canoe. Each of the Cuna families living on the coral island of the San Blas Archipelago has built a funeral hut in a cemetery on the mainland.

On the second morning after death two body bearers, who will later serve as grave diggers, lash the body within the hammock, and carry the bundle suspended from a pole, to the canoe in which it will be borne to the grave.[29] These regular grave diggers are summoned by the family at about the same time that the chanter begins his chant. The canoe also serves to transport the dead person's nearest of kin. The procession of canoes for a funeral follows no particular order. During the whole of the journey from the house of death to their burying ground the mourners utter cries of lamentation.[30]

After the procession has reached the cemetery the body bearers now assume their duties as grave diggers. Among the San Blas Tule the grave is dug to a depth of five or six feet. The usual position of the grave conforms to the general pattern of the cemetery and is not determined by points of the compass. If a change in the prevailing direction must be made, the new grave is dug at right angles to the graves preceding it. In some places there is evidence that graves are oriented toward the rising sun.[31]

The grave is dug in a small plot belonging to the family. It must be deep enough to cover two hammock posts. Burial takes place toward nightfall. The hammock containing the body is placed in the grave and the ends are fastened to the posts. The upright hammock posts which are driven into the bottom of the grave are so set that when the grave is filled their tops will project a few inches above the levelled ground. The body is buried lying on its back in the hammock. A platform of sticks strong enough to sustain the pressure of the earth is erected over it. The hammock is suspended high enough so that it will not touch the ground. As a result, when the grave is filled the hammock, protected by the platform, swings freely.

The Cunas make a limited use of symbols in their funeral rites. Sticks—not less than four and perhaps more—are stuck upright under the head of the body-bearing hammock. These represent guardian spirits. To the top of each stick three yellow feathers are fastened. Implements and weapons of the deceased are arranged in rows between them.

616

In some ways the cemetery takes on the appearance of a Cuna village. Over each grave, or in some cases, over groups of graves belonging to one family, a hut without walls but with a thatched roof is constructed from the long spike wood of the sago palm. These huts look much like Cuna houses. However, they lack gable ends. The larger grave shelters may be ten or fifteen feet high at the ridge. The family keeps its burial huts in good repair as long as it makes active use of its cemetery plot.

The final service of the body bearers is to tie a miniature canoe containing paddles to the opposite river bank, and to attach a string to it leading to a protruding hammock stake. This string therefore crosses the river. Custom demands that the first person coming upon it in either direction by water must sever it, so that the soul of the newly dead may pass to the hereafter, riding in the canoe with the spirit of the string.[32] It has been suggested too, that the string serves to lead evil spirits from the grave to the river. To cut it renders them temporarily impotent. An Indian who passed beneath the cord without cutting it would become a victim of these spirits.[33]

Post-Burial Activities

The group of intimate mourners do not witness these last services. They have already returned to the village. To frighten off evil spirits who may be loitering in the vicinity of the cemetery, guns are fired by other spectators before and after the burial.

A kerosene lamp is left burning on the grave for several days after the interment. The family return to replenish it, or to bring food offerings. The relatives examine the food on their return the next day. If they find it as they left it, they rejoice because they read this as a sign that the soul has happily set forth. They are dejected and bow their heads if it has been disturbed because it is an indication to them that demons must have tried to seize the departing soul.[34]

A variant custom is the bringing of a lighted lantern and a

617

fire pot with fire to the grave. The lantern is intended to aid the family ancestors to find their way to the grave so that they may aid the spirit of the newly dead to leave. The fire in the fire pot is used for burning cocoa-bean incense.[35]

The Cuna do not shun graves as do many other people. On the contrary, they have been known to use their grave houses for drying crops. Children will play and people will eat in a cemetery, and if Indians find that they cannot reach home by nightfall, they may sleep among the dead.[36]

For a year the widow visits the funeral hut of her husband to sweep it out and to bring fresh food for him. The anthropologist Marshall quotes a wife as singing, "My husband is dead. He led a good life on earth. He kept me well supplied with plantain. He struck many tarpon for me. Now God has called him. My husband has gone to heaven. What shall I do?"[37]

Except as noted above Cuna Indians wish to forget their dead as soon as possible, and to assist in this process, they quickly dispose of their possessions. Some of these they bury with the body. Generally, only the great canoe of the dead man remains of his possessions. They either sell this or dispose of it quickly, so that the family will not have to keep it.[38]

While the Catholic missionaries have made little attempt to modify the Cunas native burial customs, an increasing number of graves in the Nargana cemetery are marked with crosses and concrete grave slabs. These sometimes are inscribed with the dead person's name in English or Spanish, but never in Indian, and probably are an imitation of practices found in a nearby mission cemetery.[39]

618

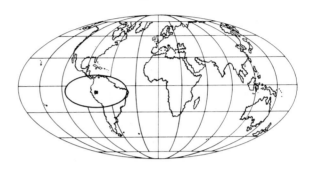

Chapter 47

Jivaro of the
Eastern Andes

The Jivaros are a linguistic and cultural entity of about
20,000 persons inhabiting the eastern slopes of the Andes in
the region belonging to Ecuador and Peru. They are well known
for their bellicosity and for their custom of shrinking and pre-
serving human heads. So warlike are they that there is almost
constant warfare among the four divisions of the tribe, although
when outsiders approach they may suspend their intratribal
feuds and join together to attack the common enemy.[1]

Conception of Death

To Jivaros there is no such thing as a natural death. While
they may realize that death is a separation of body and spirit,
they cannot seem to understand the general relation of natural
causes to it. Each death to them is "unintelligible, unnatural
and accidental," and "due to the machinations either of another
man or of a supernatural being." Even the death of an aged

619

man is ascribed to witchcraft. Since every death is presumably a murder, great excitement results. This is evidenced by the beating of the signal drum, summoning neighbors and tribesmen. The alarm is always sounded by a series of short, quick strokes, each group of which begins fortissimo and gradually diminishes. The Jivaros use the drum only when death occurs or when an enemy attacks a house. They put both emergencies in the same category.[2]

Because natural death is regarded as murder, it can lead to endless feuds. The relatives of the dead person search for clues to his potential murderer, so that they may wreak vengeance on him. A death necessarily causes a great deal of discussion. Every misfortune must be assigned to "some demon working under the direction of a personal agency." When the dead person has no known enemies in the district in which he lives, his death must have been caused by a stranger.[3]

Reaction to Death

The reaction of the warlike Jivaro to death is naturally violent. The kinsmen of the deceased shake their fists, curse and swear vengeance on their unknown enemy. By custom wailing is the duty of the nearest women relatives of the deceased. While some wailing has a formal or ceremonial character, much of it is personal and sincere. The Jivaro wife, for instance, will call her dead husband by pet names, praise his virtues, speak of the joys they shared and of her loneliness in his loss. The wailing widow will move about the body throughout the night addressing it in piteous language. However, in the midst of much tender talk she will suddenly burst out in violent denunciation of the supposed murderer.[4]

The Jivaro woman wails, sighs, and sobs more or less simultaneously. The wail begins in a high and strong falsetto with diminishing pitch and volume until it ends in a low murmur. Visitors at a hut where someone has died are greeted with a wail.

The Canelos are a related preliterate tribe living in the same area occupied by the Jivaros. They have, however, been

620

more receptive to Christianity; but in many ways their burial customs parallel those of their more savage neighbors. The usual plaint of the Canelos woman for her husband is:

> "My little gold
> My dead little man,
> Why have you abandoned me?
> What will become of me?"[5]

The Jivaros know only one musical motif and they use this for such different situations as the witch doctor's chant when he tends the sick, and the family's lament when it bewails its loss.[6] The outbursts of wailing reach a climax immediately after a death and at the time of the funeral. Thereafter for a long period a bereaved woman will wail when she is reminded of her loss.

Because the Jivaros believe that on the first night after death the soul remains in the house near the body, the survivors are expected to maintain an all-night wake. To sleep on this occasion is considered so serious an affront to a departed parent that the Canelos Indians believe that the spirit of the dead will disturb the sleeper, and cause him to die the next morning. After this first night the spirit is free to journey to the heavens, mountains, or forests. He enters upon the first stage of this journey in a canoe.[7]

The Gaming Wake

When the dying person has breathed his last, an invitation is sent to the neighbors to come to the wake, and play dice. They arrive at nightfall. Meanwhile the relatives have dressed the dead man in his best clothes and laid him on a bier which has legs so that it can stand in the house, next to a wall. Much food is provided for the dead; manioc, plantain, chickens, eggs, and chicha being the principal items. The food has been placed in gourds of various sizes, and stands everywhere. A plentiful supply of manioc-beer awaits the guests.[8]

On the night after a death of the head of the family or the housewife, as part of the vigil the Canelos Indians play cere-

621

monial games. The most important of these is a dice game, played with a canoe-shaped die. Entertainment is only a subordinate purpose for this sport. A more important purpose is to distribute by lot the belongings of the dead person among his survivors. The game removes the taboo from the property. Another important purpose is to protect them from the death-demon. In some groups only men may play this game, and then only if invited guests. If a near relative takes part, the spirit of the deceased will drag him into the afterlife, and he will soon die.[9]

For the dice game, the men are arranged in two rows of equal number, and paired off. The winner in each case is the member of the pair who casts the die, so that it remains upright, resembling in that position an upright canoe. Each successful cast is rewarded with an item of food. It may be a hen, a head of plantain, manioc, chicha. If one casts the die so that the side marked with three holes is upright, he receives three maize grains; if he casts it so the opposite side, marked with ten holes, is upright, he receives ten. In addition to his winnings, the winner gains the right to punish the loser by slapping his hand or patting his forehead.

This game continues through most of the night, until toward morning, when the hens, which have been won, are killed and cooked, and served to all present with manioc and plantain. At the end of the game, the maize grains are counted. The Indians believe that while the hand of the player may cast the die, the hovering spirit of the dead determines its fall, and in this way indicates the degree of its pleasure or displeasure with its former neighbors. He who wins few grains is out of favor with the newly dead, while he who wins the most is the favorite and is rewarded with many gifts of food.

Relatives neglect to provide a dice game at the risk of seriously offending the dead. A spirit so deprived will shower misfortunes upon his neglectful family, and will see to it that when they die, their survivors will similarly refuse to honor them. The possible harm wrought by the ill-will of neglected relatives terrorizes the Jivaros, as much as do the revengeful deeds of enemy ghosts. Jivaro fathers instruct their

622

sons to take such revenge as they can on family enemies on the grounds that thereby they will please dead relatives. For this they will be rewarded by good luck and plentiful crops.[10]

When the dice game ends, the bier is moved into the center of the room and a board is laid across the stomach of the body. The men then arrange themselves about the board, on which is placed a small cotton ball. The ball is set afire and the men blow it back and forth across the board. As quickly as the ball lands before a player he puffs and sends it back across the board. For the Jivaros this game is an extremely important precautionary measure. It nullifies the contagion in the dead body, and prevents the disease-demon from striking other members of the family.[11]

Underlying the watching and games of this first night are a few simple religious concepts. Foremost, is the desire of the bereaved to accompany the spirit of the dead on its last journey, and thus do honor to it. They further honor this spirit in the dice games, by allowing it personally to decide the throw, and thus dispose of the domestic animals. These generally constitute his most valuable possessions. These good deeds have a request attached. The bereaved would like to have the dead person assist them. His new supernatural state gives him great power to ward off the disease-demon for them. Indians regard the meal served on the morning after the wake as a gift by which the deceased rewards them for their offerings of food and their attendance upon him on his last journey.[12]

Burial Procedures

Burial takes place in the early morning of the day following a death. The Jivaros most commonly employ earth burials and platform burials, although they occasionally use all other kinds except cremation. Before the father of a family dies, he specifies which mode of burial he desires, with the reservation that by custom he must be buried within his house. His wishes are closely followed. The Jivaros fear that disobedience may convert a spirit into a revengeful ghost. Such house

623

burial, of course, necessitates the abandonment of the place as living quarters.

Several forms of house burial are practiced. In one of them the dead father of the family is seated on a small bench, with his head in his hands. Bench and body are then buried in a pit dug next to the central pillar of the house. Food and beer—renewed each day for a week—and a lance, basket, and other objects to be used in the afterlife are then stood on the level ground above the grave.[13]

Relatives put a lance into the hand of the dead Jivaro when he is tied to the house pillars "so that he can defend himself from other souls, human or animal, who will come to trouble his sleep." The women put around him many piningas of chicha, pots full of an infusion of guayusa, plates full of manioc and bananas; then the doors of the house are closed and fastened solidly and the family goes to live on some place far away.[14]

Platform burial, in which the remains in a receptacle are placed on a high framework in the middle of the house, is another kind of Jivaro house burial. The ends of the hollowed tree trunk, which forms the receptacle, are closed by pieces of bark. Once the father of the family has been so buried, the remains of other members of the family, similarly encased, are placed next to his. When house, bodies and receptacles disintegrate, relatives pick up the bones, and without ceremony give them earth burial. Presumably family members who have died before the father have been interred.

Sometimes the body is fastened to the principal log of the house in a seated position with a fire, that is periodically watched, at its feet. In some cases of this kind mummification results, and the body lasts as long as the shelter. When the shelter collapses, dampness hastens the putrefaction process.[15] As long as re-entry is needed the house cannot be entirely barricaded or abandoned.

Paul Rivet noted that in 1907 the prevailing mode of burial was to seat the dead person on a little platform in a shelter erected either in the forest or at a corner of the field, which surrounds his house. From the outside the shelter looked like

624

"an embankment surrounded by a strong palisade covered with living plants." A second palisade stood with the first, and inside of it the body sat on a backed chair. It was dressed in its best garments, surrounded by its personal ornaments, and hands and feet crossed. The second palisade, which tapers upward, surrounded the body so tightly as to keep it from toppling over. The small opening at the top of this palisade is plugged with a circular wooden disc, which in turn is kept in place by a large rock. Food, and drink in gourds, for the use of the dead, are stored in the space between the two palisades.[16]

Father Panchiri, a missionary, found the body of a prominent Jivaro buried within the inner of two palisades. The first of these was so strong that it had to be broken with a machete. The second, of cylindrical construction, was so solidly covered inside and out with large leaves, that not even mice could penetrate it.[17]

Because one death is likely to be followed by a second, the Jivaro believe that the murdering demon may be seeking fresh victims among the kinsmen of the dead. Children are considered particularly vulnerable targets for the "disease-demon." When the signal drums sound the death alert, a father wets the crown of each of his children with water from a gourd. Such baptism is thought to protect the children from the disease-demon.[18]

The Indians fear the death taboo, and take precautions to avoid it. Thus a widow is purified by smoke from a burning termite's nest. Further, she cuts her hair short immediately after her husband's death, and is not permitted to remarry until it has grown long again. Other female relatives may likewise be required to crop their hair, without being forbidden to marry.

Burial of Women and Children

The burial of a woman usually does not differ essentially from burial of a man, except that a woman's domestic utensils replace a man's weapons. The Jivaros believe that children who die before puberty are changed into small birds. When a child dies, the mother in her paroxysms of grief shrieks and tries to pull out her hair. Frequently a child's body is placed in a big clay pot used for storing manioc-beer. The opening is closed with a smaller, flatter clay pot. The top vessels are sealed together with wet clay. This urn is set on a tripod close to the house pillar, and kept there for a long time before it is buried. Mothers retain keepsakes or mementoes of their dead children, which they cherish tenderly.

Women and children are frequently buried in the earth, inside or outside the house. When burial is inside, the body is laid prone in the grave, and the floor above it levelled. Strangely, the family does not move from the house, as it would do if a man were buried there. Nor does it place food or drink on the grave. Apparently the Jivaros do not fear the spirits of women and children as much as they fear the spirits of men, and particularly of old men. The grave of a woman buried outside the house is covered with a simple thatch shelter supported on four poles.[19]

Miscellaneous Practices

The Jivaros living along the Yaupe place the body, together with his hunting and fishing equipment, in a hollowed-out log, a small canoe, or a split bamboo box. In each case a cover is provided, bark for the log, bark and leaves for the canoe, and split bamboo for the box. An ordinary warrior is suspended horizontally from the ridge pole of his house; a chief, upright. Women mourn before the body for six days, and then place food before it, thereafter it is abandoned except for a monthly replenishment of the food.[20]

The Jivaro lance "inspires not only living men but even the spirits and demons with fear." When a Jivaro has been slain with a lance, his spirit immediately flees from the body, and relatives bury it where it falls. They shun the place and put no food on the grave.[21]

The bodies of enemies slain in war, and even friends whose heads have been cut off by enemies, are allowed to remain unburied. The Jivaros bury the body for the sake of the soul, which they believe lives in the head. When the head is borne

626

off, the soul goes with it. Hence, no need exists to bury the headless body.[22]

Earlier, the Jivaros, like certain Colombian tribes, mummified their dead. The body of a chief was placed on a wicker framework and slowly dried over a low fire. In making such mummies, the Jivaro replaced the viscera with certain preservative herbs. The body of a common person was decapitated, and the head kept. The skull was removed, and the skin carefully dried and remolded, so that a mummified head, a sixth of its original size, remained.[23]

The practice of mummifying heads does not seem to have died out entirely. Among the Jivaros, in addition to its use as a trophy of war or a symbol of vengeance, the shrunken and mummified head has a religious significance, as the rites and ceremonies connected with its making prove. The possession of the largest number of such trophies in a band gains great honor for a warrior. The hair of those whose heads have been mummified is made into the captor's cincture. He wears this in war and at fiestas, and is buried with it. It is never kept by others as a remembrance.

The possessions of a dead man are disposed of in various ways. On the one hand those with which he had close contact during his last illness, for example, the clothes in which he died and the gourd from which he drank are buried with him or destroyed, because they carry the sickness and death taboo. On the other hand, articles with which he had little deathbed contact, such as his best loincloth, or his blow gun and lances, are kept for distribution among his sons. All of a woman's possessions, except those buried with her, are distributed among her daughters, or destroyed.[24]

A widow usually goes to live in the house of her brother-in-law; often she becomes his wife—polygyny is common among the Jivaros. She takes up this new residence as early as one or two weeks after her husband dies.

There is no need for a man to make a will. "He leaves few things on this earth, and all of them are of slight importance. The earth belongs to all; the house is subject to rapid deterioration; the gardens belong to the women; the sons will each one of them think for himself; the women will be carried away by the most immediate relatives who adduce inalienable rights over them. It is not unusual for fights and wars to arise over a widow. No one talks of the dead in conversation with strangers."[25]

During the usual six days of mourning which accompany house burial the women wail and tend the body, and the men usually go into the bush. Wailing, however, is not confined to the period immediately following a death. A woman may wail whenever something reminds her of her dead husband. She may even suddenly interrupt her work to break out into a combination of sobs and songs.[26]

Amazon Indian woman places body of husband, prepared for burial, into hammock as daughters look on

Chapter 48

Andeans of Ecuador

Among the native population of Ecuador, as in other South American countries where vestiges of high, pre-Conquest Indian culture still remain, fragments of native practices are mixed and fused with the predominant Catholic practices until they seem almost of one piece.

Burial Preparations

In Otavalo, a white Andean town about 70 miles from Quito, Ecuador—and "white" is used to refer to the predominant European culture and not to race—death takes place on one day and burial on the next, with the intervening night given over to the wake. In haciendas in the area it is common practice to observe a three-night wake. If the deceased has been married, the services of a master prayer-maker are sought. While the dead is being waked, the mourners eat and drink, and not infrequently become drunk.[1]

629

On the day of death, members of the family go to the street of the coffin maker in Otavalo and purchase a coffin and a cross for the grave. The coffin is of wood, painted white for a child and orange or magenta for an adult.

After the remains have been washed, they are rubbed with rosemary and carnation, and a sprig of rosemary is tucked under each arm. The body is then shrouded in white cotton, and thus prepared is placed in the coffin. Bread and fruits wrapped in cloth or packed into a food gourd are laid near the head, and flowers and rosemary sprigs—probably the same as were used to brush the body—are strewn over the lower members. The grave cross is temporarily displayed lying on top of the body.

When a child of fifteen years of age or less—locally called a "little angel baby"—is waked, its godparents dance to the accompaniment of a violin. Imitating the early Spanish manner, some mothers dance but do not cry; others cry but do not dance. The family provides the coffin for a child, and its godmother, the shroud and a gold paper crown. The godmother's obligation to make such contribution ends when her godchild marries. The Andean Indians believe that an infant—or, for that matter anyone—who dies unbaptized, becomes a night-wandering spirit. Consequently, the unbaptized are buried in a section of unsanctified ground in the cemetery.

Funeral Procedures

Sometime in the forenoon funerals pass through Otavalo. While the straggling procession sometimes stops at church for a service, more often it by-passes the church and heads directly for the graveyard. A child's casket is carried on a man's shoulder; an adult's casket is borne on a bier. The violinist to whose music the godparents have danced leads the child's procession, but does not play as it winds down the road.[2]

The cemetery is divided by a high wall into a white and Indian section. When the procession reaches the tall dominant central cross, the casket is set down at its foot, and the lid is removed, so that the shrouded body and the half-covered face are exposed. After candle wax has been dripped on the left upper edge of the casket so that a lighted candle can be affixed there, the women gather around, and several older women begin to lament: "We were companions. We shared experiences. The life we lived together was good." During this ceremony only the middle portion of the face of the dead is visible. The mouth is covered by the top of the shroud; the eyes, by the head cloth.

For an hour or more the wailing rises and falls. Not all women participate. Some carry on casual conversation. Some laugh. When the wailing stops altogether, the casket lid is pounded down with a stone and the casket is picked up and borne to the grave. At a child's funeral the violinist strikes up a tune only when he arrives at the head of the lane leading directly to the place of burial. At one funeral, when lowering ropes were lacking, the women present loaned their belts to be used as substitutes. When the casket rests at the bottom, someone may pass holy water to the cemetery keeper to be asperged on the grave with prayers. Such ceremony will be accompanied by renewed wailing. After the grave has been partially filled, the gravediggers leap into it to trample down the soil.[3]

Graves of these Andeans are dug on a north and south axis, with the head pointing south. They are extremely narrow —just wide enough to receive the narrow casket. The height of the grave mound is a matter of concern. A properly built mound should be about a foot high. When the earth available for its building proves to be the right amount, that fact is taken to mean that the dead person died at his or her appointed time. Concrete vaults are available in the local cemetery. Unlike the graves, which are orientated north and south, the vaults are orientated east and west, with the head to the west.[4]

Interment

When the grave mound has been built up, a cross is stuck into it with the name of the deceased and the date of death written on it by the cemetery keeper—sometimes on the spot. For the prayers and this service he is paid a small fee which is

Altar is made and relics honored with offerings of food and
drink on All Souls' Day

arrived at by bargaining—also sometimes on the spot. Finally a
cloth full of cooked food (potatoes, corn), is laid upon the
grave. This is the "lunch of the dead." It is a payment made
to the gravediggers for their services.[5]

At this point in the ceremony the women and all outsiders
withdraw to allow the men to form a circle around the grave,

632

so that they may listen to an elder among them deliver a long prayer. When he has concluded, the chief woman mourner steps over the grave mound, circles clockwise to the other side and steps over it again. This rite is carried out no matter what the age of the deceased may be. The people who practice it do not attach a meaning or interpretation to it. Elsewhere a small child is handed across a grave to tell the mourners to forget and to moderate their grief.

On All Souls' Day, which is an important Catholic feast day in Ecuador as everywhere, all over Quecha-speaking Ecuador, food is taken to the cemetery to be eaten there. On this day godmothers bake lambs or "little horses of the dead" to give to their godchildren.

A Case Report

The anthropologist Elsie Clew Parsons includes an interesting report of an Indian burial at nearby San Rafael.[6] The body of a father of a family had been laid out—eyes open so that the spirit might see the road ahead—on a ladder which in turn was placed across a table in the patio or yard. Surrounding the body was a sample of many things the dead man had enjoyed during life, including food and drink; other food and drink for the road, and a gourd cup. A pair of candles and a match in the hand were provided to give him light, and a pair of sandals to protect his feet on the thorny, rough road to the hereafter. A red flag on either side were symbols of purgatory, which all must pass through. Two sprigs of rosemary were placed next to the body. Rosemary can be used as a weapon in the hereafter. Before the body was moved from the patio two Indians passed four children, one at a time, thrice across the body. This rite was designed to cause the deceased's sons to forget. For the same purpose the hair of the dead man was cut, and burned, and the ashes were pulverized and placed in eggs, which were sucked, and on other food, which was eaten.

In the funeral procession four elderly men carried the body

and everything stacked on it, using the ladder for a bier. In this procession Indians played musical instruments so that the soul might depart happily.

The first halt was at the irrigation ditch. There the bearers gently propped up the body into a sitting position before a table, and having lighted two candles, began to pray aloud, and after an interval, without interrupting the prayer which an old man continued to lead, they undressed the body, and bathed it, using water generously. After once more clothing the remains, they brought them back to the home and placed them on a table.

Then the neighbors brought in all manner of food and offered it to the family to eat in the name of the deceased. The dead person shares this meal with the family. Before it begins, an old man leads all present in prayer for the deceased.

Variations in Customs: Cayambe

Funeral customs at Cayambe, another Ecuadorian town, show some variation from the foregoing. For instance, the body is immediately placed on a table and covered with a white sheet surmounted by a crucifix. Throughout the second night, simply to amuse themselves, those keeping the watch play various games appropriate to wakes. As the games are lightheaded, so are the forfeits paid by the losers. It may be that a man must kiss all the pretty unmarried women present, or make a noise like a bird or an animal.[7]

On the day of the burial the room of death is swept to remove illness, and to remove badness and the rubbish thrown into the street.

These Indians believe that while God appoints the hour of death, some persons die prematurely. Thus if in digging a grave the diggers come upon an unrotted casket they know that the person to be buried died before his time. Likewise if much earth is left over after a grave is filled, it is clear that death has been premature.

They believe further that to throw oneself into the grave of a loved one in the abandonment of grief is to sign one's

634

warrant for an early death. Hence those present at a funeral are on the alert to restrain members of the family and principally the wife, from attempting to throw themselves into the grave.[8]

Because the soul of the deceased suffers if the clothes he left behind remain dirty, on the day following burial, family and near neighbors take them to the irrigation ditch and wash them. Rum and food are served, and tricks are played. The commonest of these is to trip a person so that he falls into the ditch.

Only the family sheds tears when a child dies, and even the family dance with others who dance. An altar is prepared in honor of a dead child. Sinless, it has entered heaven, and there entreats God to bless its family on earth. The child's face is uncovered, its head is crowned, and its shroud is an angel's robe. A child is buried with music and dancing.

Cult of the Dead

In Otavalo the Indians celebrate Holy Week in a most elaborate fashion, the high point marked by a great communal feast in the local cemetery Thursday and Friday mornings. Indian women, all with small packs on their backs, stream down the road to the cemetery on Holy Thursday morning. The booths set out before the stores offer for sale among the bread rolls, little orange and magenta grave crosses. Parsons' field notes describe the scene:

> As one passes with the stream of Indian men, women, and children up the lane and through the large stone portal, what a sight is the slope-set cemetery! A mass of figures in blue or red ponchos, in white or crimson backcloths or headcloths, passing in and out between the tall eucalyptus trees, the cedars, and the little peach trees, or sitting in small groups around or on the uninclosed grave mounds of which many are planted to geraniums.[9]

This is the ceremony in which the Ecuadorian Indians give food to the poor and to beggars, in return for prayers for the family dead. Such prayers may be for individuals; others are for all members of a family. By noon the women still carry full or half full packs, but the beggars have their fill, and the cemetery is empty. Next day, Good Friday, the same procedure is repeated, only by noon the packs of the women are emptied. On this day more burials are made, and so popular is the occasion that a wake may be shortened or omitted altogether to allow a funeral to be held on Good Friday, when the cemetery is crowded.[10]

On the holy days the Indians drift to and from the churches not so frequently to hear Mass as to kiss the feet on a crucifix or a statue, or to sit on the floor with their backs against the wall.

Chapter 49

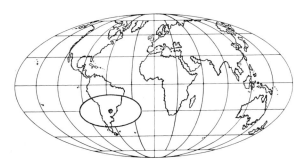

Kaingang of Brazil

The Kaingáng Indian tribes, now few in number, are scattered across the highlands of southeastern South America from Sao Paulo, Brazil, to Argentina.[1] Dr. Jules Henry, anthropologist authority on the Kaingáng, indicates that theirs is almost the classical example of the simplest kind of human culture: devoid of permanent shelter, agriculture, and boats. A hunting and food-gathering economy provides them with the barest subsistence. The continued existence of the Kaingáng has come to be doubtful inasmuch as the tribes, or large families—the basic social unit—have engaged in incessant massacres and bloody feuds which have literally decimated their members. They present a picture of social tragedy, in the words of one observer, "victims of an inadequate social order."[2]

The key to the variety and complexity of funeral customs among the Kaingáng is found in what would seem to us their pathological fear of both natural and supernatural spirits. They people their supernatural world with hideous beings whose bloodthirsty ferocity is detailed in awesome myths. In addition they believe that other spirits occupy all of nature: the winds, clouds, storms, and stars of heaven. These spirits dwell in the inanimate world of rocks, rivers, and cliffs; and populate the animate world of trees, birds, beasts, insects. Sometimes they take possession of the bodies of men. All spirits are potentially dangerous. Only through complex ritual and propitiatory ceremonies can the Kaingáng effect some sort of tenuous co-existence with these teeming animate and inanimate spirits.

Death as Disruptive Force

Among the Kaingáng death is conceived as the "perpetual threat," and when one of them dies they believe such powerful "forces of destruction" have been released that all their emotional resources must be mobilized to meet them. The great threat becomes momentarily actualized in the spirit of the departed, the "ghost-soul," and the most elaborate rituals this primitive people have developed are performed to eliminate the threat offered to the close relatives and the whole community.[3]

While the Kaingáng do not consider the dead unclean they believe that the ghost-soul craves a companion from among the living whom it has left. Such companionship means death to the living. While the ghost-soul's choice may fall on anyone, the person most likely to be chosen is the surviving spouse be it a wife or husband. The spouse therefore is a threat to the group, and the rites through which a husband must pass are intended not only to protect him from the ghost-soul, but to protect the group from him.[4] The same rites are provided for a wife.

When it seems that a Kaingáng is likely to die, a member of the family calls together the relatives and friends. Ghost-souls threaten the living, and so the living band together for mutual protection. They say they live "piled up."

Meanwhile, the close relatives keen, their voices rising into a rhythmic wail. Sometimes the mourner loses control of him-

638

self. No matter who the dead or dying person may be—child, husband, wife, sister, grandparent, another relative, it matters not—tradition requires that a stock complaint be made, "I long to see my father who always gave me food. I have been forgetting my mother. Will I see her again?"[5]

Absence of Spouse at Funeral

If the wife dies, even before her bones are buried the frightened husband leaves camp alone, remaining close enough to it to be safe from marauding enemies and to allow a woman to come out each evening and make a sleeping-place for him. He sleeps alone with two stems of a large fern in his arms, just as he used to hold his wife. The ghost-soul fears these. The widower takes with him his bow and arrows, an axe and a blanket, but no pot. Until the purificatory rites are completed he is not allowed to eat cooked food, because of the danger that it would roast his insides and thus destroy him. While he may kill a game animal, he is limited to slitting its belly and smearing its blood over his body. In this manner he is thought to "wipe away" the hunting he did with his wife. Meanwhile he eats raw vegetables and honey, and as the days pass, he grows thinner and thinner.[6]

During this mourning period, widows remain closer to camp than do widowers, and take their nursing infants with them. Like the man's sleeping-place, a woman's is prepared by another woman, who sometimes spends the night in the embrace of the widow, thus shielding her from her husband's ghost-soul.[7]

Burial Procedures

Cremation followed by burial of the bones has for many years been the preferred mode of disposition of the dead by the Kaingáng. The procedure is described by Jules Henry.

Prior to cremation the body is placed on a blanket, with the head toward the west and the feet toward the east, the direction in which the ghost-soul must travel into the afterlife. This position gives it a view of the road ahead. Bow and

639

arrows are laid beside the body. The bow has been chopped in half, and the bowstring has been cut, and is used to tie the arrows together in a bundle and to fasten them to the bow.

The pyre has been built waist-high of wood and surrounded by posts sunk on all sides in the ground, to prevent its collapse. After the body has been laid upon it, the mourners put wax, which is the symbol of honey, and meat into the dead man's hands, saying: "Take it and go and leave me. You go the many." Then they pound the chest of the body, crying: "Leave your animals to me and go. I'll shoot and eat them when I'm hungry. Leave your people and go. Leave the honey for me."

If the dead person has had many children, they implore: "Leave your children and things to me and go. When they are hungry they will kill and eat them. Now the things I have given you to be your own are in your hands. Take them and go." They speak in much the same fashion to a woman.

Blazing Pyre

After trying to persuade the dead to leave his possessions, they entreat him to speak well of them, and not to threaten them with death, because the living and the dead have been fellow sufferers. This is a prelude to the cremation, and they now kindle the pyre with flaming bamboo torches. They throw these away after using them at a cremation, and then quench the old fire, and start a new one with a fire drill. The old fire warmed the dead person while he lived. It is his fire. To lie beside it would be to die. As the flames lick through the stacked wood, the spectators sing. No special chant is assigned to these rites. Then all tramp back to the village to sleep, while the fire burns.[8]

After a long interval, the mourners rise and return to inspect the pyre. Standing near its head each speaks to the ghost-soul: "Do not threaten me with death. I have suffered much with you." Next they draw close to the remains of the fire. If combustion has been slow, it is likely that the body remains uncremated and in such event that the wood shifted so that the body has fallen and rests against the uprights. All

640

those whose bodies remain unburned are considered supernaturally dangerous, except children. When this misadventure occurs, the mourners build a second fire. Those who are exposed to the smoke in either case rub their bodies with leaves for five days to cleanse them.[9]

When the body is consumed, the mourners pick the bones from the ashes, gather them into a large basket lined with leaves and ferns, and carry them to the burial place. Meanwhile, if they are few in number, they chant a song which tells that they are carrying the excrement of the sun. If they are many, they do not sing. Dr. Henry is at a loss to explain the meaning of this song, but suggests that it probably has to do with the Kaingáng fear of death.

The procession next marches to a place other than that in which the dead person died. Along the way they cut down ferns constantly casting some of them aside, in a ceremony that may symbolize the fact that they are severing their connections with the dead. The remainder of the ferns they keep. Later they will pound these to a pulp and use the sap to wash away the perspiration produced by carrying the basket of remains.

On reaching the place selected for the burial, they clear the ground, dig a grave, and line it with ferns, and place therein the basket and bones. When the men have filled the hole, the women construct a little house over the grave.

Kaingang Keening

The keening of the Kaingáng is unrestrained, loud, and continued for long periods at frequent intervals. Keening for a dead person naturally begins immediately after his death when the mourners gather. It consists of a "rhythmic chant heavily interspersed with sobbing and snuffling." Such demonstrations do not end, as might be expected, with the burial. Kaingáng custom allows anyone to keen at any time and in any place, whenever he thinks about his dead relatives and the urge to mourn lays hold of him. While the Kaingáng do not seek out crowds as audiences, neither do they lower their voices, and their lamentations may ring out a quarter of a mile away. Morning and evening, before supper, when duties are light, are favorite times for keening.

Henry gives a number of instances of a woman's keening. One of them is Kuka's:

> I am remembering my mother. I want to call her mother. I am remembering my mother. I am the one who called her mother, but now it is all over. I am remembering my mother. When my mother would look at me she would remember that my father had seen me and she would weep—now that is all over. I am remembering my mother. I and my children used to call my mother mother—that is all over. I am remembering my mother. I want to see my mother. When my father would return after leaving me he would think of how I suffered, and he would weep. Grandmother, whose name I bear, would think of my sickness and suffering.[10]

Purification Rites

Although up to recent times a spouse dwelt apart until a special feast was held, today no fixed purification period is observed. Whatever the duration, before a man can emerge, he must submit to having his hair and fingernails cut by the people who go to fetch him. By this rite he is presumed to be cleaned of his wife's polluting influence. A woman must have her nails cut because while she cooked for her husband she got particles of meat under them. While the hair is being trimmed, the cutter holds it with a bit of medicine to protect himself from it; and when the barbering is over, he pounds the nails, hair, and certain leaves in a mortar, and throws the resulting pulp into the water. Meanwhile, the attendants chant to frighten away the ghost-soul. Finally the man is cleansed by being thoroughly rubbed with the raw food which the tapir eats.

Although it is hoped that the new cut of the hair will so modify a man's appearance as to make him unrecognizable to the ghost-spirit of his dead wife, as a further precaution his head is covered with feathers or feathered cloth. Beer meanwhile has been brewed to be drunk at the ceremony by which the widower is to be reintroduced into his group. The

642

cleansed man now sets out with his attendants for the camp or village. One of them walks before him, scattering herbs in his path to frighten away the ghost-spirit; the party moves, timidly, singing loudly. They still fear the ghost-spirit. When they near the camp, those who wait there raise their voices and whirl gourd rattles. They too are fearful of the ghost-spirit and wish to drive it off. When the parties come together, all drink beer until the supply is exhausted. Then they go to a nearby stream and wash their mouths out with muddy water, and rub themselves with sand and stones. To the Kaingáng water in general symbolizes life, since their ancestors emerged from the water. And stones and sand symbolize immortality because they do not rot.[11]

On returning to the camp the bereft spouse changes body symbols with the opposite sex as a further means of concealment from the ghost-spirit. Life routines, too, are shifted from man to woman. Thus, because as a married woman a mother rose early in the morning to take care of her husband and children she now lies abed until her children have arisen, as though they were to take care of her. The return alone does not remove the taboo on cooked food, but another rite, performed in a few days, is required. A tapir is killed, and cooked with leaves in a clay pot in which the water has been brought to a boil with hot stones. Having drunk this water, the spouse again can eat cooked food.[12]

In most recent times the pattern of burial has changed somewhat. The body is no longer cremated, but with the knees flexed is buried, along with the funeral deposit, in a deep chamber in the center of a large mound or tumuli. The villagers at once desert the settlement and hastily construct new dwellings in the woods and for three days eat only palm shoots and maize. The grave is visited periodically to renew the mound and to hold memorial services. At these there is lamentation, dancing, chanting, and drinking.[13] It is still customary for the relatives at dawn and dusk to cry out their mournful funeral laments.

War-like Umutina Indians
of Brazil's Mato Grosso
hold weird death cult
ceremonies. Dances and
rituals call for costumes
of skins, feathers,
reeds and straws

P.I.P. Photos

Chapter 50

Brazil and Paraguay

Brazil

Brazil has few funeral functionaries, and it is lacking in funeral establishments to which the remains are brought for preparation, viewing, and services.[1] Matters concerned with burial in Brazil are under the jurisdiction of the local municipality, and in some places the local charity hospital is assigned a monopoly over funeral services. This arrangement not only assists the hospital in meeting its budget, but gives it sufficient income to provide funeralization for destitute cases.

The care of the body after death—the cleansing and dressing —are tasks performed by friends and neighbors, usually women, who through experience have become deft and accustomed to this procedure. These women are given no special title or name, receive no special training, and are not paid for their labors. This service to the dead is a traditional responsibility of women, and is accepted by all without question.

645

Whoever undertakes to prepare the remains, washes and dresses the body. The body of a man is dressed in a dark suit, black socks, and sometimes black shoes; the body of a woman is clothed in a dress of somber hue, but not necessarily a black garment. No cosmetics are used, and no restorative art is applied. Bodies in Brazil are not embalmed except for shipment overseas, in which case a hospital physician performs the embalming operation. After the body has been washed and dressed it is placed in a coffin. Coffins are purchased from establishments who make and sell them, and who supply no other goods or services.

Customarily Brazilians place the dead in wooden coffins, and for the most part these are made of oak or some other native hardwood. Brazilian coffins have a one-piece lid; those with glass panels in the lid or with divided lids, popular in some Latin-American countries, are not used. Metal caskets are seldom employed inasmuch as they tend to be quite expensive. For shipping, or in disaster cases, the Brazilians use receptacles with zinc liners.

Although Brazilians recognize three classes of funerals according to the expensiveness of the burial receptacle and the amount of transportation supplied, the lines of demarcation between the classes are not rigidly drawn. And, despite the fact that there is only a relatively short period between death and burial, the funeral is a very social affair. Private funerals are a rarity in Brazil.

In rural areas when a suitable coffin for the body is not on hand nor immediately available through the services of a local carpenter, it is customary to wrap the body in a shroud and place it in the grave without further protection. This type of uncoffined disposal is especially common in the poorer communities of north and northeastern Brazil. Those who die one day are usually buried the next.

In urban areas, too, burial normally takes place within 24 hours after death, and while a regular obituary notice is published in the local newspapers, the family notifies by other means those who are expected to attend the funeral service.

Funeral of popular wagoner whose fellow workers banded together to take coffined remains and mourners to cemetery

People who are thus called upon make every effort to attend the services, and family members in particular make an effort to be on hand, even though such attendance requires traveling a considerable distance.

The body lies in state in the family home, with friends and relatives waking it throughout the night. Usually no group prayers are said during the wake. The hours are spent in talking, and in sipping coffee from demitasse cups served them by the family. While no effort is made to put a curb on public demonstrations of grief, and it is customary for Brazilians to mourn openly, they do not wail.

Because Brazil is 93 per cent Catholic, the religious rites predominantly performed are naturally those of the Catholic Church, and the body is taken to a church for services. Transportation for both the body and the mourners for middle and upper class urban funerals is furnished by a livery company. In the larger cities motorized hearses are used, but in smaller towns it is not uncommon even today to see a hearse drawn by four horses. Large, ornate hearses, covered with carvings and horse-drawn are also used in the ultra-luxury style funeral. In any funeral procession the hearse, adorned with wreaths—a favorite Brazilian offering of condolence—leads the way. Only the very poor walk in funeral processions.

647

A state funeral in Brazil is much the same as a state funeral elsewhere. When a member of a legislative body dies the remains lie in state in the legislative chamber, and later are borne in procession on a caisson drawn by soldiers. While the procession forms a part of every Brazilian funeral, it is particularly important in state funerals.

No restrictions are placed on attendance at a Brazilian funeral, except that children do not attend. Custom further does not permit a school teacher to send his students to a funeral nor to attend a funeral with them as a group.[2] The funeral nevertheless brings together many categories of people: friends, relatives, men, women, onlookers. The women in the funeral party wear black, and the men wear dark suits, or at least black armbands and mourning ribbons on their lapels. Those who observe public mourning dress in this manner for approximately a year.

In rural areas of Brazil funerals are one among a number of occasions on which country people converge upon the rural center. Everyone is expected to be present at the funeral rites of a neighbor. If the deceased was a tenant farmer, the landowner is expected to provide refreshments after the services for all comers at the center nearest the cemetery. Because such an occasion is conceived of as being part of a traditional rite, even those who normally abstain partake of whatever alcoholic beverage is served. Although Brazilians are light drinkers, on these occasions the drinking may become so heavy that some mourners will be forced to sleep off the effects of the alcohol before they set off for home.[3]

Since there are few cemetery chapels in Brazil, and the funeral Requiem Mass is usually said in the parish church of the deceased, at the conclusion of the service the parish priest accompanies the procession from the church to the cemetery and there reads the Catholic committal ceremony. In rural areas each parish maintains its own cemetery, and if the parish includes a town, the cemetery is likely to be outside the town limits. When there is a convent nearby the procession is likely to halt there, because a convent generally has a resident

Brazilian cemetery; in background Mt. Corcovado surmounted by a huge statue of Christ

chaplain who will give the blessing in case a parish priest is not available. If no priest is in attendance the burial takes place without the usual blessing. On All Saints' Day, however, wherever possible, priests visit the cemeteries and bless all the dead.[4] On All Souls' Day, November 2, Brazilians flock to the cemeteries to pay their respects to their dead, and at this time they usually decorate the graves with wreaths and bouquets of flowers.

Family plots are available for purchase in either urban or rural Brazilian cemeteries. The wealthy tend to bury their dead in family-owned mausolea. In municipal cemeteries, lots may be purchased outright, or they may be leased for a period of five years. At the end of this time the lease may be renewed. If it is not renewed, either the family purchases a niche in the ossuarium for receiving the bones, or the cemetery administration disposes of the remains.

As in many old-world, Mediterranean country, cemeteries those in the major cities of Brazil have been conceived of as "cities of the dead" in which monuments and statuary ornate, often magnificent, predominate. Mausolea are usually of white marble construction with carved angels, massive walls, and glass doors protected by ornamental ironwork. Usually the

649

doors are locked but on Holy Days they are opened to relatives who, many clad in mourning dress, may spend most of the day in communion with their departed loved ones.

Paraguay

One of the smaller republics in South America, Paraguay, is for the most part, a country of lowlands, swampy plains, and delta areas. The majority of its nearly two million population bear traces of the indigenous Indian racial stock (Guarani), but the racial and cultural patterns of the Paraguayans today are more heavily derived from the early Spanish than from the native peoples they conquered. One distinctive feature of Paraguayan culture, the fiesta, is found among all socio-economic classes. This form of celebration is interwoven with and to some extent expresses the predominating religion of Paraguay —"a folk-level form of Catholicism in which the cult of the saint predominates."[5] Fiestas also serve as an indicator of social prestige; all members of a community of whatever class or social standing are welcome to attend and to participate.

Funerals of the Paraguayans, by the same token, tend to become a means for the display or enhancement of social

Photo Courtesy Francisco Chichigno

Paraguayan funeral director seals metal casket with solder for mausoleum burial

Casketed body lies in state in Paraguayan funeral home

status in the community. Upon analysis, these funerals reveal: (1) predominantly the traditional funeral customs of Mediterranean countries; (2) some of the native love for colorful, sensuous display; and, (3) more recently, some of the *Yanqui* funeral procedures that are part of what American funeral directors refer to as their "program" of funeral service. These aspects will become identified more specifically in the following description of the manner in which the dead are cared for and buried in urban Paraguay.[6]

When a death occurs in an urban area of Paraguay the family notifies the funeral director, and, either in the family home or his establishment, selects the type of funeral which best conforms to its tastes and budget. The funeral director then sends to the home all the necessary equipment and supplies for laying out the body, including the casket.

When the dead lie in state, the funeral director supplies a large crucifix and candelabra as accessories. These latter provide the illumination. Either wax candles, torches, or electric light types are available.

651

Photos Courtesy Francisco Chichigno

Mourners gather around
casket decorated with
cruciform floral piece

Floral offerings are put
in and on funeral coach

Relative pallbearers carrying
casketed remains

Funeral bus
used in Asuncion

Photo Courtesy Francisco Chichigno

During the 24 hours that normally elapse between death and burial the funeral director takes care of the usual legal routines. He secures a death certificate from the physician in attendance which he takes to the municipal office building and there records it with the public health and civil registry authorities. When these formalities are completed, he makes arrangements with the cemetery authorities for the opening of the grave and the burial, and with the church authorities for the funeral services.

The typical Paraguayan cemetery contains burial chapels owned by rich families. In some of these the caskets are grouped and not placed in crypts or niches. In other family chapels, the caskets are placed in wall niches. Less pretentious burial is made in a niche in an open wall. The municipality rents this type of facility for specified periods of time. When a lease expires the family either renews it, or has the remains gathered into an urn, which is put into a smaller niche, or takes no action. In the latter case the remains are deposited in a common grave.

At the appointed time the procession leaves the home for the church with the mourners following the hearse in cars or

Above, A funeral
hearse for children
pulled by Asuncion
street car to
the cemetery

Typical Paraguayan-
style funeral hearse
leading funeral
procession

Photos Courtesy Francisco Chichigno

in buses. When the funeral has been concluded, the officiating
priest or minister joins the procession and at the graveside
reads the committal service.

The bodies of the poor are not placed in monuments or
niches above the ground, but are buried in the earth in wooden
coffins. Furthermore if the poor use transportation it is likely
that they will use a bus rather than motor cars. A streetcar
hearse still is used in Asunción to transport the dead to the
cemetery. Once it was customary in Paraguay for the pallbearers to carry in procession the coffin, holding it by handles
from the home to the church, and the church to the cemetery.
In such case the mourners followed very slowly on foot.

It is likely that Paraguayans of German, Russian, and Jew-
ish descent will use earth burial, while those of Spanish and
Slavic descent will bury their dead in niches and pantheons.
The Italians divide in their practice.

There are no crematoria in Paraguay, but for the very small
per cent of Paraguayan families who wish to use this method
of disposal, arrangements are made for cremation in Buenos
Aires in adjoining Argentina.

654

Latin America, *Passim*

A magnificent, ornately
carved funeral coach
arrives at the "City
of the Dead,"
Buenos Aires

Modern Buenos Aires
funeral coach retains
traditional sedan style

P.I.P. Photos

Above, Pallbearers
carry casket from
flower-laden coach
into El Bosque,
Santiago

Interior of
El Bosque

Tom Hollyman
Photos for P.R.I.

656

Right, Children carry casket in funeral procession of infant. *Below,* Coffin on head, Haitian strides through the streets of Port-au-Prince

Wall crypts in Santiago on day after All Souls' Day

Old couple polishing their coffins, Saba, Dutch West Indies

Beautiful statuary in Recoleta Cemetery, Buenos Aires

Priest and altar boys lead funeral procession in Youco, Puerto Rico.
Right, Children in Puerto Rican funeral procession

659

Flowers being
carried into
"City of the Dead,"
Buenos Aires

P.I.P. Photo

Woman mourns in
Dominican Republic
cemetery, note candles

Philip Gendreau Photo

Casket is brought into
Santiago cemetery for burial

Photo Courtesy American Cemetery

Funeral Customs The World Over

Part Seven

Interment ceremony for the Unknowns
of World War II and the Korean conflict
at Arlington National cemetery, 1958.
Standing at right foreground is
President Eisenhower, to his left is
Vice President Nixon

Canada and the United States

Cultural homogeneity across half a
hemisphere . . . universality of funeral home use and embalming . . .
professionality of funeral functionaries . . . aesthetics of casketry and
floral display . . . spiritual, social, and
utilitarian features of the funeral . . .
dominance of earth burial . . . sect,
folk, and aborigine groups . . . the
trend toward a common life-style

Department of the Army Photo

End view, totemic designs on British Columbia Indian cedar coffin

Chapter 51

Copper Eskimos

Death Beliefs

The Copper Eskimos of Victoria Island, north of the Arctic Circle, believe that once there was no death. Then one year at the end of a bitterly cold winter, so the myth goes, a family of four, father, mother and two sons, without food wandered starving from place to place. First, the mother died, then the boys and finally the father. All four were transformed into hills—and thus death came to the Copper Eskimos.[1]

Adult members of the tribe, although they apparently do not live in their memories or talk of the dead, look at death very matter-of-factly. It is commonplace for them to say in making plans for a summer hunt, "If we are still alive"; or to comment on the frequency of death in their communities. This realization of the inevitability of death does not prevent them from often discussing it in a lighter vein. "The foxes have eaten so-and-so" is a typical jesting remark.

It seems that Copper Eskimos have no clear idea of what happens to the soul or spirit after death. They accept the thought that it is freed from the body, and the fact that they leave offerings for the dead person at the grave indicates their belief that the spirit exists and needs material aids.

They do not, therefore, look to the spirits of their dead for help. On the contrary, they regard them as generally malignant, and strive to placate and appease them. Spirits of people who have led good lives may prove harmless; other spirits are transformed into demons and are associated with other evil spirits who never experienced human existence, although they possess the power to assume human form. It is these latter spirits that haunt Eskimos and strive to harm them. They exercise control over the weather and the supply of game. To counteract their malevolent influence, which causes sickness and ruins hunting, the services of the medicine men are most frequently sought.

Appeasement of the spirits by the Eskimos is achieved by offerings of food and drink. Thus when a caribou is killed, scraps of its liver or kidneys or the intestines are set aside for the spirits to eat. Likewise when a seal is caught, blubber scraps are left on the ice. At meals, the Copper Eskimos break off small portions of the food, and sprinkle a few drops of drink for the spirits.

Eskimos traveling alone shun graves, even those of relatives who were known to have died natural deaths. A still wider berth is given the graves of those who met violent deaths. It is their belief that the spirits of the slain linger near their graves and strive to do vengeance on passers-by.

Responses to Death

A form of deathwatch is set up in the tent of a person dying from natural causes. Eskimos who keep this vigil are described as "those who are afraid," and they remain until the end, relatives weeping and lamenting, and being comforted and consoled by neighbors and friends. When it seems apparent that a small child will die, the mother sometimes is

666

required to take the child beyond the village limits, so that the villagers will escape the death taboo; or she may be required to remain in her home, holding the child in her arms, for the same reason.

The apparent inability of Eskimos to distinguish unconsciousness from real death leads to many tales of the dead returning from the grave. There are authenticated stories of Eskimos left for dead, returning after several days to their villages. These apparently miraculous recoveries necessitated the services of the medicine man to remove all the taboo that had been created.

Care of the Body and Taboos

The Copper Eskimos prepare a body for burial by clothing it in its underdress and encasing the feet in shoes with soles of caribou skin. They then lace it up in the used platform skin of the dead, or if the deceased was a noted hunter, in a new skin.

When a woman dies, the body must lie in the house three days—a man, four days—before it is removed. During this time certain rules or taboos are followed. To violate these is to risk the transformation of the soul of the deceased into an evil spirit. During this period, those who are taboo may hunt; but if they catch a seal they may not use the skin for clothing. They may eat the meat and feed the skin to their dogs, and they may bring the seal into the house for these purposes. The women of the household may do no work of any kind, even sewing, during this period. At night, the occupants of the house sleep with their knives beside them. During this period no member of the family may comb his or her hair.

The loss of a stillborn or newly born child—many children are unwanted and strangled at birth—does not create many death taboos. Even for somewhat older children, there are few ceremonies or tribal procedures. However, a mother may not sew until her husband catches a seal or a caribou, and she must not leave her house without wearing a hood. For her to appear hoodless in the open would place a curse on the hunt-

667

ing. She may freely eat raw meat and intestines provided by other hunters.

When the days of the taboo have passed, the body is taken outdoors. Those who handle the body are required to cover their faces with the flap of their coats. So that they may see and breathe, they cut eye, nose and mouth openings in it.

Burial

The burial as well as the living customs of the Eskimos are directly affected by the weather. If death occurs when they are living in tents, the body is not carried through the door, but through an opening made in the rear of the tent. It is then carried to the place of burial on a skin. The grave will be located some distance from the village, in order that the dogs will not find and molest the body. The grave is formed by building a ring of stones, in the center of which the body is placed with the face of the body turned towards the rising sun. After the body has been placed in position, the thongs that bound it to the skin in which it was wrapped and carried are cut, so that the spirit of the departed may be free to leave, and an opening above the head is made to permit the soul to emerge. The body is then covered with stones. When snow is on the ground so that stones cannot be gathered, the body is brought to the burial ground on a sledge, and covered with a small snow house, with an opening above the head to allow the soul to emerge. When the Copper Eskimos do not build such a burial igloo, they most likely will surround the body with a windbreak constructed of snow blocks, pending a chance to transport it to the nearest beach where they will cover it with stones. Under such circumstances the relatives observe a day of mourning in their tents before they resume their usual activities. Whether the body is immediately buried under stones, or placed in a snow house or protected by a windbreak, the head is pointed to the rising sun.

The attendants—those who have dressed and carried the body to the place of burial—on their return to the house or tent immediately drink water to quench the thirst of the dead

668

man's soul. Special taboos apply to these people, generally two men.

After the burial they are not allowed to eat meat cooked in another's pot until they have first themselves caught a seal. As soon as they do so, they carry the seal from house to house and at each one they cut off and leave small pieces of blubber, which is used in lamps.

Post-burial Procedures

While a portion of a dead man's property is placed in his grave, the main part is distributed among his relatives. This division seems to be effected without discord. Although, the dead man should traditionally be buried with the tools and weapons essential to him in life, it is the practice to substitute less costly for valuable objects, and sometimes miniatures or replicas instead of such valued possessions as waterboots and bows and arrows. The Eskimos rationalize this procedure by believing that the dead have the power to enlarge miniatures to full size, and when the genuine articles are placed in the grave, they often return and reclaim them some time after death. It is customary to divide a dead man's property equally among his children without regard to age.

The explorer Rasmussen observed that the "deceased's clothing and the sleeping skins that have belonged to him thrown away, and likewise a tent in which there has been a death is discarded. If it is a snow hut, it must be alone immediately after the body has been taken to the stone circle." The people then move to a new hunting place keep the clothing of their dead child only as long remain at the place where he died. When they move it upon the child's grave.

Canadian sled hearse

Chapter 52

Canadian Panorama

Although there is much similarity between the funeral practices of the United States and those of Canada, sufficient variations exist to warrant consideration. Canada and the United
States have much in common, including 3,986 miles of unde-
fended border, and many similar interests.[1] Citizens of both
countries have much the same racial origins, and social-eco-
nomic and religious beliefs, and face similar problems in the
development of their respective countries. And many a Canadian
feels that the title "American" belongs as much to him as to a
resident of the United States.

The differences lie partly in the more conservative outlook
of the Canadian. At the time of the American Revolution,
citizens of the thirteen separating colonies who remained loyal
to England migrated to Canada to retain a familiar pattern
of life much influenced by old world ties. Their United States
counterparts, on the other hand, sought to break such ties,
and so moved more rapidly to a liberal viewpoint in managing

671

their affairs. Since then, however, the conservatism of the Canadian has been modified by economic influences largely originating in the United States. A common monetary system developed, imports and exports became a common meeting ground, and as a result the conservatism of the Canadian of British descent has been abridged until today he is likely to seek a middle ground between his British ancestors and his neighbors to the south.

Politically, Canada is divided into ten provinces, each with its own parliament, in addition to two territories—the Yukon and Northwest Territories, which are governed by commissioners and councils. Almost three quarters of the population occupies a narrow belt along the Canadian-United States border. Ontario has the greatest population, with Quebec a close second.

About half the population is made up of persons of English, Scotch and Irish origin. Approximately one third is of French descent. While the majority of these reside in Quebec, they spill over into Ontario, Manitoba, Saskatchewan and Alberta, and in smaller numbers into the Maritimes and British Columbia. The balance of the population is composed chiefly of people of Dutch, German, Ukrainian, Russian, Polish or Scandinavian descent. In more recent years immigration has brought other Europeans into Canada. These latest arrivals have tended to be absorbed into metropolitan areas.

Funeral Customs in General

A basic pattern of funeral practices is almost universally followed throughout Canada. Following a death, the family selects and notifies a funeral director, and he removes the body from the place of death to the funeral home. There he prepares it, using arterial and cavity embalming. If necessary he applies restorative art and uses cosmetics. Then he dresses and caskets the remains. Arrangements for the funeral are completed in the funeral home, as are the legal documents required by law.

As a general rule, the body lies in state in the funeral home. Since World War II this practice has rapidly increased, par-

E. Fred Miller Photo

Mourners in Newfoundland walking in procession to cemetery.
Women do not usually participate

ticularly in metropolitan areas. But even here some vestiges of the practice of conducting funerals in private homes still remain. In less populated areas, where the personal preferences or the convenience of the survivors may be better served by keeping the remains in the home, the facilities of the funeral parlor are less frequently used. The usual period for lying in state is from two to three days. However, this time may vary depending on circumstances.

The majority of Protestant funerals are conducted in the chapels of funeral homes rather than in churches. Two factors are mainly responsible for this trend. The first is a change in the pattern of funeral attendance during the last quarter century. In urban areas especially, friends either visit the family during the lying-in-state period or attend the funeral and committal services. They seldom do both. The result is a much smaller attendance at the funeral service itself. Consequently, survivors prefer to use a smaller facility for the service. In addition, the cost of heating a large church for a special short

673

service in a country which has cold weather during a large part of the year, may be heavy. Accordingly, there is a tendency to avoid this additional expenditure. Although some members of the Protestant clergy make a concerted effort to induce their parishioners to have church funerals, unless this practice becomes a tenet of their faith, the present trend toward services in funeral homes is likely to persist.

The funeral procession continues to be a part of the Canadian tradition, although processions seem to be becoming shorter. The cortege forms at the place where the body has been lying in state, and proceeds to the church, if the service is to be held there, and then to the cemetery or crematorium where the final committal service is held.

Cemeteries are usually owned and operated by churches or municipalities. However, there are many privately owned cemeteries in Canada. Cemeteries are closely controlled by law in most areas, due principally to a fear of exploitation of the public. The fear was produced by the promoters of certain privately owned cemeteries during the past decade. Many "family cemeteries" of the kind that can be found in a corner of a farmstead are still in use, but modern practice tends to the use of established cemeteries. In most areas, cemeteries are separately established for use by Catholics, Protestants and Jews, although some cemeteries admit all three groups, but set aside or reserve separate sections for each group.

Cemetery space may be purchased for single grave, or for several or many graves in a single lot or plot. Perpetual care charges are being included in the sale price in an increasing number of cemeteries, and, conversely, the number of non-perpetual care cemeteries is growing smaller. The majority of funerals use earth burial. This preference though does not rule out burial in a public mausoleum or in a crypt, vault or mausoleum that has been privately built for personal or family use.

Winter burials constitute a major problem over most of the country. The frost line, even in the most moderate areas is estimated at four feet, six inches. In areas where the weather is more severe, the frost depth is greater, and the condition of

674

the ground prohibits the opening of graves. Consequently, provision is made for temporary custody of the body within special chapels in the cemeteries in these areas. With the coming of spring, these bodies are interred under the supervision of the funeral director.

The practice of cremation is growing somewhat in popularity in Canada. In the main, crematoria follow the patterns of cemetery operation being municipally, or privately owned. No Canadian funeral home owns its own crematory. The distances over which bodies must be transported for cremation tend to restrict its use. In some areas of Canada, it is more expedient to ship remains to a nearby crematorium in the United States than to a distant crematorium within Canada itself. Among Catholics, in Canada as elsewhere, cremation is forbidden.

In most areas the law requires that cremation may not be carried out within forty-eight hours of death, and a coroner's certificate must be obtained, giving his permission to cremate. In addition, each crematorium makes its own rules.

Some variations in this pattern will be found in the funerals of Jews and Catholics. In Jewish funerals, burial practices depend on the adherence of the individual to Orthodox, Conservative or Reform Judaism. Some Jews favor embalming; others oppose it. Many Jews belong to a burial association which takes charge of funerals. The number of Jewish funeral

Funeral cortege
for wife of
Quebec resident

French Canadian funeral; note formal attire and arm badges of pallbearers

Philip Gendreau Photo

directors in Canada is small and these are found mainly in metropolitan areas. However, in areas lacking a Jewish funeral director, it is customary for the burial association to designate a non-Jewish funeral director to carry out the tasks. The dead are transported to his establishment for the religious rites. The procession continues to play an important part in Jewish burials, and it is customary for those attending a funeral to walk part of the way to the cemetery. They are prevented from walking the entire way by distance, and by the heavy traffic of the urban areas in which the Jewish population is concentrated. Jewish cemeteries are controlled, maintained and operated by the burial associations.

The practice of having a Requiem Mass as the central religious function of a Catholic funeral is followed throughout Canada.

When death occurs because of a communicable disease some modifications of the usual funeral pattern results. Regulations are made by the provincial departments of health and are administered at the local level by the Medical Officer of Health who is usually an employee of a municipality or of a regional health unit. Generally in such cases the funeral service must be held at the place of death, and the body must be taken directly to the place of burial. The funeral service must be held and interment follow within 24 hours after death, and attendance must be limited to members of the immediate family.

Various governmental units have legal authority to assist in defraying funeral expenses in certain instances. The National government is empowered to assist members of the armed services, war veterans, and Indians who are wards. Provincial governments may assist persons who are eligible for benefits under the Workmen's Compensation Act and inmates of mental institutions and tuberculosis sanitariums. Indigent and welfare cases are provided for by the local governments.

Monuments or Grave Markers

Grave markers in Canada may take the form of a private mausoleum erected within a cemetery, a pylon shaped column, or the more familiar and customary forms. Markers are made of natural stone, although in more recent years, some composition stone has been used. Usually markers bear an inscription showing the names of those buried, and the dates of birth and death. An epitaph is also commonly included. Soldiers' graves are marked with a simple cross.

Some ethnic groups prefer elaborate memorials. These often include more ornate carving than is usually found. Ornamentation differs too among Catholic, Protestant and Jewish cemeteries, due to the desire to include the symbols of faith of each of these groups. At least most cemeteries provide sections where only markers that are flush with the ground are permitted. In some cemeteries, no other type is allowed.

Funeral Merchandise and Supplies

Most Canadian funeral merchandise is manufactured in Canada. Main imports from the United States include special-order caskets and sundries. However, many of the latter are available through Canadian firms. Funeral supplies are manufactured by firms which range from a small plant operation, to those which spread from coast to coast.

Canadian manufacturers make many kinds and qualities of caskets. Different regions of Canada have distinct preferences for specific types. For example, wooden caskets are preferred in areas where the main industry works with wood. Conversely in areas where the metal industry predominates, metal caskets are more popular.

Burial vaults are mainly of two basic types, steel and concrete, and are manufactured in air-seal, top-seal and open-end styles, although the latter type is less popular than it formerly was. In some cases, changed cemetery regulations result in the use of a concrete grave liner in all burials. However, where this is not so, and where the family does not require a vault, the use of a painted pine outer box is still to be found.

Embalming chemicals are locally manufactured and distributed. Some United States chemical firms have formed subsidiaries or branches in Canada, and these companies distribute products which parallel those used in the United States. It might be observed that the same basic chemicals are available in both countries. Dry ice has also been used where normal embalming procedures cannot be applied. Hearses are frequently imported from the United States, although there are some which are locally made.

Canadian Royal Mounted Police serve as pallbearers in funeral of late Canadian Prime Minister

Modern Canadian
funeral establishment

Transportation

The country is served by two main railroads, the Canadian National Railway (government owned) and the Canadian Pacific, and by two air lines, the Trans-Canada Airlines (government owned) and Canadian Pacific.

Domestic transportation services are vital to the funeral director. Bodies may be transported by rail, subject to Provincial Health Department and Railway Regulations.

In the more remote areas of the country, railroads serve funerals chiefly in two regards. Frequently, the railroad is the only means by which a funeral director can get to the place of death if roads are impassable or non-existent. In these instances, he loads a casket and his equipment on a train, and remains at the location until the funeral has been completed. Again the railroad is sometimes indispensable in bringing a dead body from a remote area to a funeral director, in order that it may be properly handled.

Long distance and overseas transportation of the dead is more frequently completed by air. Funeral directors and the public are accepting this practice with increasing regularity, due principally to its speed and convenience.

Associations

In addition to various municipal, district and provincial associations, the Funeral Directors Association of Canada in recent years has represented the profession on a national basis. This Association is an executive organization, which has not grown as yet to the point where it can hold open conventions. Its members are the provincial associations, and these are represented by appointed delegates who are empowered to vote on behalf of the provincial groups. Expenses are met by a per capita assessment on the provincial associations. Also a considerable number of Canadian funeral directors are members of United States associations.

In recent years area conventions have become popular. The funeral directors of the Maritime Provinces as well as those in Ontario have found such an activity to be highly successful. The Western Canada Funeral Directors Association has held two biennial conventions, and interest has spread from the initiating provinces of Alberta and Saskatchewan to British Columbia and Manitoba.

Regional Customs

Variations in Canadian funeral service customs by geographical areas can be noted. In Newfoundland, for example, it is not customary to use a funeral home for lying in state. Especially in the larger centers, where embalming facilities are available, the body is removed to a mortuary where it is embalmed by cavity embalming. It is then dressed and casketed and returned to the residence where it lies in state until the third day. Also in Newfoundland the horse-drawn funeral vehicle is rapidly being replaced by motorized equipment.

In Nova Scotia, although some embalming is practiced in the home of the deceased, this custom is waning, and in most instances, bodies are taken to funeral homes for preparation. Funeral homes are rapidly achieving popular acceptance and the public is more inclined to use them for funeral services.

New Brunswick claims the only crematorium east of Mon-

Pallbearers carry casket from funeral home in Quebec

treal. Due to its geographic location and the cold weather of the northern portions, winter burials are not held in these regions.

Quebec's population is estimated to be about 93 per cent French in origin, and as a result, there is some variation from the funeral patterns found in the provinces in which the origins are largely English. In Quebec itself funeral customs vary considerably between the large urban centers, the rural areas, and the extreme northern areas which approach Arctic regions.

In the urban centers of Quebec, funeral patterns in general conform to the funeral patterns of urban centers elsewhere. However, the French Canadian tends to adhere strongly to certain of his old world traditions, and these can be found in evidence in many areas of Quebec. An outsider attending a funeral in a French Canadian Catholic church is reminded of the origin of the word "hearse," which came to us from the Old French *herce* meaning "a harrow." This device originally was as a "framework with prickets," which resembled a harrow turned upside down and used as a candelabrum over a coffin in church. A modified version of this old device may still be found in some Quebec churches, where the casket

681

is placed on an ornate, elevated, carved platform, painted in black with candles surrounding it according to Catholic custom. Catholic funerals are customarily held during the early morning hours, and hearses frequently are ornamented with crucifixes. Protestant funerals are usually held during the afternoon.

Cremation is not popular in Quebec, due to the large Catholic population. However, there is a crematorium located in Montreal.

Chapter 53

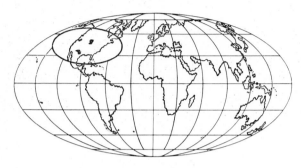

United States:
the First Americans

The Santee Sioux of Eastern Dakota

The Santee Sioux are the most eastern branch of the Dakota, who in turn form the second most numerous tribe of American Indians. Today the Santee Sioux live on American reservations in the Dakotas, Nebraska, and Montana, and on Canadian[1] reservations in southern Manitoba and Saskatchewan. Only a few remain in Minnesota, their home of pre-white days. The settlement of members of this tribe in Canada dates from 1862, when, after a disastrous uprising against the whites, thousands crossed into Manitoba. Although from the 1830's on Christian missionaries had sought to convert the Santee Sioux, the first thirty years of their labors had been crowned with small success, and when the Santee scattered they clung to their traditional beliefs, and performed their old rites as faithfully as the white authorities allowed. Even today, nearly a century after their expulsion from Minnesota a great deal of primitive culture is mixed in with their Christianity.

683

Sioux tree burial

Religious Background of Funeral Practices

The traditional behavior of the Santee Sioux at the time of a death followed their belief that each person possessed four souls, two of which were to be served by the old Sioux funeral rites. One soul, they believed, would never leave the dead body or the vicinity in which death occurred. Another soul set out at the moment of death on a four-day journey to the land of the spirits. These two souls possessed a ghost-like nature, and required propitiation. If the mourners failed to appease them by sacrifices, feasts, gifts and respectful conduct, the soul of the body would haunt the family and the tribe, and the travelling soul would not set out on its journey but remain behind to become a nuisance. Angry ghosts were believed to have the power to frighten fish and game, and to entice children to follow them into the hereafter. The Dakotas thought of the next life as very similar to this, only in the world to come work was reduced and pleasure increased, and the old became young again. They did not believe in an hereafter of punishment. Whatever retribution sin produced fell inevitably and heavily upon the living.

It would not be accurate, however, to ascribe the fear of ghosts as the great motivating impulse behind the traditional Dakota rites. They bore great affection for their kin, and their manifestations of grief were essentially sincere and genuine.

684

The Moment of Death

When a Dakota lay dying one of his tribe who possessed second sight would be likely to declare that he had a premonitory vision indicating death. For instance, a mother attending her sick child might see dim figures of women approaching, and might take note of their old-fashioned shawls, and even recognize her own dead mother among the group who had come to take possession of the child. Such a vision would proclaim that four days later the child would die. Men, and women, too, felt trembling in their limbs, and knew that soon they would be called upon to inflict gashes in them as a sign of grief. Or when their heads trembled they understood that in the near future they would tear out their hair. The dying person sometimes saw his father's spirit approaching, and asked that a seat be provided for it.

As the dying person appeared to sink lower and lower, friends and relatives crowded around his lodge, and when the announcement was made that he had died they broke into loud wailing and bitter complaint, and they tore off their garments and mutilated themselves. A common form of mutilation was to chop a joint from a finger. Men and women both were likely to run knives along their thighs and forearms, or to gash their limbs until blood covered them. A woman mourning for her child or her husband also gashed her shoulders and breasts. As a sign of grief the Dakotas hacked off their hair at shoulder or eartip length, and refused to comb it. Normally they took much pride in their hair. Chief mourners among the men painted their faces black and refused to wash themselves until they killed an enemy or gave a feast in honor of the dead relative. In the throes of wild grief mourners sometimes became violent. One man for instance, would feel compelled to make a daring, solitary raid into hostile country, while another would commit suicide so that his spirit might join that of his child on the hard journey into the afterlife. When a father died of loss of blood from his self-inflicted gashing, his relatives were likely to console themselves with the thought that he had relieved the loneliness of his helpless children.

If the person died while these manifestations of exceeding grief were being made, a man waiting outside the tent, gun in hand, fired a single blast into the air. The Dakotas believed that this shot would not only extinguish one of the four souls, but would announce the conclusion of the dead man's life drama.

Mourning signs were not confined to human beings. The manes and tails of the dead man's horses were cropped, and the hair was gathered, and mixed with the cuttings of the family's to be placed beneath the platform on which the body was temporarily laid. Although a dead man's horses were given away to his relatives and close friends, his continuing partial ownership in them was always acknowledged. In mentioning them recipients never failed to say that, "This is Black Eagle's horse."

Children were not allowed to linger around a place where death had occurred and to become a part of the proceedings or view the body, even a parent's body. To protect a child who had been close to a dead person the elders tied a bundle of calamus root to its wrist. This root, called "muskrat food" by the Dakotas, was believed to have great spiritual powers and its odor was used to counteract the contamination, physical and spiritual, produced by inhaling the stench of human decay.

Funeral Preparations

Women were assigned the task of preparing the body for burial. They painted the face red, sometimes even before death came. This painting was done partly to decorate the body, partly to serve as a preservative for the face. A hand, with the thumb reaching one side of the mouth and the spread fingers covering the other, was drawn in black on the face of a great warrior. The women clipped hair from a warrior's scalp-lock or the left side of a woman's head, to be wrapped and saved by the family at the interment a year or more after death. A bundle of a warrior's hair was sometimes carried into the tribal enemy's territory in the expectation that there it would be transformed into a roving malicious spirit which would spread disease and death.

686

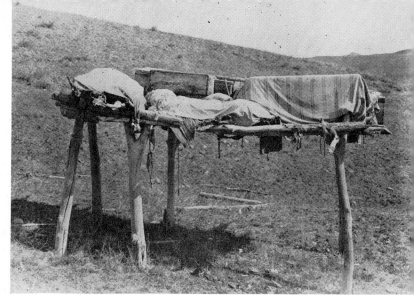

Plains Indian
scaffold burial

The body of the deceased was robed in its best clothing. Thus arrayed it once was sewed into a buffalo hide or deer skin, but later, as a result of trading with the white man, it was wrapped in a blanket. When the skin was used the seam ran along the top of the body from head to foot, and thongs were used to bind the skin tight at the neck, waist and feet. Unlike the skin the folded blanket produces pouches into which articles belonging to the dead person could be tucked. A dead warrior or a chief was likely to receive more elaborate treatment. Fellow warriors threw blankets and other gifts on his body. If he had been killed in a raid the body sometimes was placed in a sitting position with the face turned toward the country of the enemy. Confronting it the scalped head of a decapitated Cree or Chippewa Indian might be hung. Such a head, stuck in a cooking pot, was thought to be pleasing to the dead warrior.

While the women prepared the body the men constructed a platform on which to place it for temporary burial. Dakota burial was in two stages. The body suitably wrapped was for a year or more exposed to the open air laid across the branches of a tree or on a high platform. At the end of this period of air burial it was given earth burial.

The commonest kind of air burial was platform burial. The

usual platform for this purpose consisted of a bed of poles placed horizontally and laid close together. This bed in turn was supported about eight feet above the ground by six uprights, three at either end. To give stability these uprights were lashed together and fanned out at the bottom. The burial platform—or "scaffold" as it is sometimes called—was generally set on a hill or slight eminence near a Dakota camp. When it was ready the men carried the body from the camp and placed it on the scaffold. A century ago this was the universal manner of burial among this people, and can be found today. Contact with the white man sometimes caused the Dakotas to place the body in a box before giving it air burial. After the body was in position pots of food were set around it, and other offerings were tied to the uprights.

The Four-Day Rites

Next followed four days when the soul was believed to be close to the body, a period of supernatural danger to the settlement and especially to relatives. All who had addressed the deceased by a kinship term would mourn. During the first day they sat around the scaffold. One of the family would set up a doleful wail, others would join, and this would continue for a time. There followed a rest period when tears were dried and ritual pipes smoked. Then another cry would arise, and the pattern would be continued until a night and day had passed. All then would return to their dwellings. The food on the scaffold would be eaten by designated people in village or camp of the same age as the deceased. All possessions of the dead not laid with him or suitable for giving to others were burned.

The conduct of all kindred during the next three days would be sober and quiet. No one might visit outside his home. Hunting and household tasks were considered the only proper occupations, and the involvement in these was not to be extreme; for what one did at this time it was felt he would always want to do. Nor should one sleep too much lest this, also, become compulsive for the rest of his life. All food to

688

be eaten by mourners was first passed through purifying cedar smoke.

The Season of Mourning

The Dakotas assumed that by the end of the four-day period the traveling soul had reached a safe distance from the living, and never thereafter would they mention the dead person's name. Although members of the immediate family were now allowed to resume their normal mode of living, they still did not comb their hair, nor wholly terminate their mourning. The proper length of the mourning period differed with the age of the deceased and the condition under which the family was living. A child was mourned "for a season," that is, for three or four months; an adult, for about a year. During this time when the camp or village was semi-permanent the nearest relatives returned often to the platform where the body rested, to wail and to leave offerings of game. Before the Mandan Sioux left Minnesota it was their custom to bring gifts of the first fruits, and of maple syrup and wild rice, and a kettle of cooked corn, for the dead. Sometimes they placed the gifts on the platform that held the body of a child. On the other hand, if someone died on a distant and protracted hunting or trading expedition his relatives made great efforts to bring home at least a part of his body.

Tree burial,
Crow Indian

Memorialization

As has been indicated platform burial was only an intermediate and secondary stage in the full cycle of Sioux burial.
The final stage, earth burial, was more important and was
deferred until the family had gathered the means to conduct
one in such manner that it would conform to the tribal custom,
reflect favorably on the family pride, and be consistent with
their respect and affection for the dead person, and the fear
which they had for his spirits.

About a year after a person died his body was taken down
from the scaffold and placed in a shallow grave dug nearby.
The scaffold was then removed, and earth was carried up to
the hilltop and heaped upon the body. Because the Dakotas
for generations used favorite hilltops for their burials great
bare community mounds, with layers of graves lying beneath
the surface, were gradually built up. When a new grave was
filled and mounded a fence was placed about it to keep wolves
and dogs from rifling it. At the head of the grave of a noted
warrior or medicine man a stone, which had been given supernatural powers by being painted red and by being held in
smoke, was placed. A small flag, once of skin but later of cloth,
was flown over the grave of an important person. On a warrior's
gravepost human figures were carved to represent the member and sex of those he killed, or captured in battle: headless
if slain; hands tied if captured; and shirted if a woman. Objects of value were seldom placed on a grave, because the
soul which most was feared was by now believed to have departed, and the soul which always was part of the body was
sufficiently placated.

Continuity and Change

The first of the Santee Dakota funeral customs to be discarded in Manitoba was exposure on the scaffold and secondary
burial. Christian missionary influence, government pressure,
better digging tools, and free pine boxes supplied by the
Indian agent ended these practices. On the reserve at Gris-

690

wold a ridge above the Assiniboine River overlooks fields, flat to the far horizon. There the Santee Dakota lie buried, and there today are the white crosses of the two cemeteries, Anglican and Catholic. On the graves stand a few paper flowers, and a few planted iris and columbine that have survived a wind which sweeps the soil away. To this place the coffin is carried on a cart hauled by horses or a tractor, and here Christian prayers are read by a White missionary or a Dakota catechist. After a funeral the family will return to the house where neighbors have brought party food.

And yet something remains of the aboriginal Dakota funeral customs. From the moment someone dies until the end of the first year there is no relative nor friend who does not keep at least one of the distinctive beliefs in mind, and there are many who in modified form follow the whole range of old customs. Incidents of premonitory vision of ancestors coming for the dying, and the dying's own vision of their arrival, were reported in 1952. At the moment of death some families still wail in the old way, and although none gash themselves with knives nor sever fingers, men and women complain they suffer pains in the limbs and joints that formerly would have been cut. The hair of mourning women is not hacked off or unbraided and matted; instead, if it is long enough it is braided in the old Indian fashion. However, young women with short hair and permanents may remain well-groomed. Hair is still clipped from the dead and, by a few Santee at least, offered an occasional cup of tea. Horses also are clipped, particularly by old people.

Today the body is dressed in good clothing and wrapped in a quilt or a blanket, and certain personal possessions of the deceased are tucked within the folds. For an adult woman these always include her bundle of sewing equipment; for a man or boy, his cap, gloves, or shoes; for a young girl, her comb; for a child, a toy. When in recent years the resident Sub-Agent, a government functionary, forbade a poor couple to bury their son wrapped in new Hudson's Bay blankets, they gave them instead to a boy of the son's age.

691

During the four days after a death the relatives, who do not like hovering ghosts any better than did their ancestors, know that they can avoid such a visitation by refraining from alcohol, obscene talk, and an overemphasis on work. If one must leave the reservation he brings back a present for the deceased and lays it at his former place at the table. Someone later will receive the gift. At least one horse belonging to a dead person must be given away. This rule includes a colt which was owned by a dead child.

The ceremony ending the period of mourning is now held under various forms. In 1952 two of the four families at Griswold, Manitoba, having graveyards carried out their Dakota-Christian rites in different ways. The first family, poorer, less educated, honored the death of a great-grandmother and of an infant grandchild by a feast at which everyone who brought a plate was served meat, beans, home-made bread, cakes, and saskatoon berries. They laid material for a dress, and shoes, stockings, and a blanket on the great grandmother's grave; and they presented a corresponding outfit at the child's grave. Later they gave these gifts to an old woman and to a needy child.

At the service of the second family, dignified and thrifty, the grave of the dead father was covered with a new, home-made quilt. Only sons and daughters were present, together with an old man who gave a funeral oration and read prayers. Food was served and the old man, a life-long friend of the deceased, received the quilt. Both of these families it might be noted are leaders in the Anglican mission church.

For the majority of the hundred families the old rites have been forced into a foreign pattern. The ridge on which the Dakota buried their dead, from the early days of settlement on the reserve, is now consecrated to Christian usage. Wooden crosses mark and whitewashed stones outline the graves. Despite the Christian burial service and the conventional Christian appearance of the graveyard there are residual practices that indicate the assimilation of the new religion and its usages has not been complete. A case in point is the annual Flower Day. Although it comes on different dates for

692

the Roman Catholic and the Anglican Churches there is repeated the traditional pattern of laying gifts of food and cloth
on the graves, followed by a dinner outside the graveyard. To
the Santee a memorial service is, obviously, incomplete without
a give-away. In the Minnesota Santee communities at Prairie
Island and Morton the tradition of a family ceremony at the
end of the first year after death is still kept. Usually the family
holds a dinner in the community hall, with an oration, songs,
special attention to old people, and give-aways, such as food
and dollar bills. Whether the deceased Dakota is considered
as a lost loved one or fearful ghost, he is at rest only after
kinsfolk have performed the final rites.

The Salish Indians of Northwest United States

The Salish Indians, collectively the Salishan group, consist
of some 40 tribes in the northwest states of Oregon, Washington, Idaho, and Montana, and 15 Canadian tribes mostly located
in British Columbia. Once the most numerous of the American
Indians, and still one of the country's larger aborigine groups,
the Salish today live on reservations and practice agriculture,
fishing, and hunting as community enterprises. "Most Salishan
tribes," notes Harry E. Stafford, student of American ethnology,
"retain their original culture and community and religious
ceremonies, although they live to a great extent like their
neighbors of European extraction."[1]

The most popularly known ceremony of the Salish is the
potlatch, a formalized show of hospitality in which gift-giving
is turned into a competition for status, with the one giving
the most receiving the highest esteem. Their burial practices,
less publicized, show a variety of interesting facets worthy
of description. Although on the surface of the matter, adoption
of such modern practices as the use of coffins or caskets, and
burial at normal depth in cemeteries indicates some cultural
change, the basic ceremonies and the meaning they carry
continue relatively unchanged. Selected for emphasis in the
general discussion of the Salishan group will be the Coeur

d'Alene, Flathead (Salish proper), Thompson, and the Sanpoil tribes—all of the western and central plateau areas of the
northwestern United States.

Cosmology

Those of the Coeur d'Alene who hold to their native beliefs
have vague and sometimes conflicting ideas of the size, shape
and character and origin of the earth. For instance, some believe that it is round and surrounded on two sides by water,
while others hold that it is oblong with water on all sides.
Some consider that the earth is animate, a transformed woman.
In mythological times the culture hero, Coyote, gave the earth
its present form, destroyed the monsters that plagued the few
Indians then alive, and did much to improve the Indians'
lot.[2] The Flathead traditionally held that there are three
worlds lying in tiers, of which the upper is a sort of heaven,
ruled over by a good chief; the middle, the earth; and the
lower, a sort of hell, ruled by a bad chief. The Flathead pray to
the good chief, but not to the bad. They believe that the dead
go north to reach the good chief's country. Their spirit hero,
Coyote, was sent into the world by the good chief to make
matters more pleasant for man.[3]

In general the belief is widespread among the Salish that a
person has a spirit-ghost as well as a soul-ghost. The Salish
are sometimes confused in thinking and speaking about these
two which are very similar in form, but very different in
character. However, the Salish do not manifest the Navaho's
morbid fear of death and the dead, and suicides are not
unknown among them.[4]

The Moment of Death

A dying person is left alone with an aged man who neither
receives pay nor is expected to have special qualifications
for the task. To this person the one near death must confess
his misdeeds, inasmuch as the Salish believe that if these are
left unconfessed the ghost will roam the places it knew in life.
Such punishment may be eternal. If, however, misdeeds are

694

confessed the ghost will be able to reach the land of the dead, and will no longer be impelled to annoy or injure the living. These death confessions are held in the strongest secrecy. Convulsions or delirium were once considered signs that something had been unrevealed by the dying. A ghost so burdened would haunt the place of death.[5]

At the moment of death the body is rushed from the house and carried into a nearby thicket or woods. There it is laid across the limbs of a tree or placed in the midst of an impenetrable thicket, so that animals cannot molest it. To leave it in the house would provide an opportunity for its spirit or spirits to enter some person and make them ill. If the body cannot be buried before nightfall someone must keep a vigil in the home so that the spirit or spirits cannot re-enter there. When death occurs a messenger speeds to close relatives and friends to invite them to the funeral. Burial always takes place within twenty-four hours. Death during the night or morning is followed by burial in the afternoon. Remains kept over night are buried at sunrise.[6]

Burial Procedures

The Sanpoil Salish are buried in the clothes in which they died. After the body has been doubled so that the knees

A graveyard of the Salish Indians

touch the chin it is wrapped in a deer hide which has not been dehaired, and again in matting made of bulrushes. The hide is omitted for a poor person. The wrappings are lashed tightly with rope. To carry a body a pole is laid under the wrapping.[7] Among the Coeur d'Alene when a person dies the body is buried without having been washed or painted. For a wrapping poor people use a simple robe; others provide a robe in keeping with their wealth.

Generally among the Salish the family selects the pall-bearers, the choice not being confined to relatives. The family also appoints two or three men to dig the grave. These precede the cortege and try to finish their work before the body arrives.

Among the Coeur d'Alene to show sympathy and to assist the family, neighbors attending a funeral make small gifts, including food to the bereaved family. The food is used to entertain guests. Some neighbors also volunteer their services to prepare and serve the funeral feast. In former times the relatives of the deceased made no effort to reward kindly neighbors for their services in arranging the body and trans-porting it to the grave. Among the Salish such services are always performed by volunteers. There is no occupational group among them to which these tasks are delegated.[8]

Each village normally maintains two cemeteries, and the Salish use whichever is closer to the house of death. The Salish do not bury in family lots. Their cemeteries usually are in rocky sections, or at the rock-strewn foot of a cliff, or on sandy banks. To form a grave a shallow round depression is made by removing stones to a depth of three or four feet; or a shallow hole is dug in the sand. Bodies are never cremated or cast into the water.[9]

Among most Salish tribes the common method of disposal has been some form of earth burial. After being sewed up or tied up in robes, matting or skins, the body is removed from the home, and, while awaiting burial, is placed on a scaffold or in the branches of a tree. When mourners come together it is carried to the grave on a pole which is thrust through the lashings.[10]

696

Carved totemic animal decorates Katchikan grave

Rock slide burials are made in a variety of ways. Sometimes a place for the body is cleared at the bottom of a rock slide; and, after depositing it in a shallow depression, the stones are pulled down on it. If a camp is close to a small bluff containing a rock slide, rocks are moved to make level tiers and burials are made in these. Bodies are generally buried lying on their sides. When no slide rock is available, earth burial is used. In either event, a grave is shallow—not more than three or four feet in depth.[11]

The Sanpoil Salish traditionally buried their dead in sandy places. When they buried them in rock slides they heaped rocks over the shallow graves, and made a circle of rocks around a deeper grave. For a grave marker they sometimes used a pole, or less frequently a canoe. The use of grave effigies for grave markers is even less common. No grave tents or houses can be found. A fence around a grave or a cross surmounting it is a sign of white influences.

Whatever its form, the same burial is provided for everybody—ordinary person, chief, medicine man, child, suicides. Sometimes a baby is buried in or with its cradle. If the distance is too great or conditions make it too difficult to return a person who dies away from his own camp back to his own abode, the body is given the usual burial, and once buried the remains are not likely to be disturbed by the relatives.

697

The body of a hunter who dies on an expedition is returned home. Some years after burial the Thompson Indians dig up and rewrap the bones. The Coeur d'Alene Indians do not observe this custom. However, when bones are exposed, the finder is likely to put them in a tree or rebury them.[12]

In the past, when tribes were warring and burial was made in a strange or hostile land, pains were taken to obliterate all trace of the grave, either by riding over the grave with horses, or by building a fire over it so that it was indistinguishable from the sites of other camp fires. Graves were thus concealed so that an enemy could not find and scalp the remains.[13]

Funeral Ceremonies

Normally the funeral procession is led by the pallbearers, carrying the body on the pole. Behind them walk the relatives and friends. At least one medicine man marches with the mourners. No funeral can be properly conducted without him. He receives no compensation for this task and comes without invitation. When the procession reaches the grave the bearers deposit the body next to it, and stay for the ceremony.

An old man, usually a relative of the deceased, takes charge of the burial. His first duty is to call someone to step forward, to speak concerning the inevitability of death and in praise of the deceased. Next he calls on the Shaman to rid the grave of spirits by sweeping it out, and by sweeping off the body with rosebush sprays. Rosebush is selected because its thorns are thought to prick spirits and thus ward them off. When he finishes this task, he steps aside, and the pallbearers place the body in a sitting or lying position in the grave. With it are quickly placed certain of the deceased's belongings—keepsakes, ornaments and fetishes. The grave is then immediately covered. Haste prevents the spirits from re-entering it. The body is covered first with large rocks, and then with smaller stones, and finally with gravel and sand. Sometimes a topping brush is laid upon it. When the grave is filled, before the mourners return to the village, someone who has not previously spoken may deliver a speech of sympathy.

To prevent a woman's spirit from visiting the root and berry patches, and spoiling the crops and frightening the harvesters, roots and berries—fresh whenever possible—are placed on a woman's grave. Sometimes the deceased's horses are killed and their skins or hoofs hung on the grave. Canoes, too, are sometimes laid on the grave. Some of the articles placed with the dead—necklaces, or pipes,—are hung from the grave pole. Some are laid in the grave itself. Grave-poles are peeled of their bark, and in whole or in part painted red. Sometimes three poles, set up in the manner of a tent framework, are used to mark a grave. The present custom of coffined burial in a deep grave is thought by some to militate against the proper cleansing away of spirits. The presence of the latter is attested by the protests thought to be heard when a coffin is lowered.[14]

Before and after the funeral most of the mourners sing plaintive songs with improvised words set to a single melody. The women present among the spectator group usually join in. The Coeur d'Alene orphans follow the same practice observed among the Thompson Indians of jumping over the body of their dead parent; they are lifted over it when they are too young to jump.[15]

Post-funeral Activities

The post-funeral gathering at the home of the deceased is a solemn affair without gambling or other diversions. An abundance of food, generally more than the guests can possibly eat, is supplied by the deceased's family and cooked by the young women. Children are not allowed to participate. The feasting begins at noon if the burial has been in the forenoon; if not, on the succeeding day. In the afternoon the property of the dead person is distributed, with the father or one of the brothers making the distribution and the deceased's family becoming the principal beneficiaries. Clothing is not distributed, and a few days later is disposed of by being buried by an old woman. Property not useful to another person is burned. Horses are generally assigned to a brother.

699

If sufficient food is not at hand the funeral feast may sometimes be postponed for a year while supplies for it are being accumulated. Relatives divide the goods of the deceased as they see fit, some going to friends, partly to allay their grief, and partly to reward them for their good offices. Persons inheriting property wrap it in rosebush branches and put it aside for a month without using it. Thus they hope to drive out evil spirits from it, and avoid contamination. If the deceased dies in a temporary dwelling, it is burned; if in a winter house, it is torn down the following spring. Meanwhile it is fumigated with the smoke of green fir boughs and rosebush stalks. Because the log cabins in which the Salish now live are too valuable for burning, they are fumigated, and continue to be lived in. Home burning is therefore dying out.[16]

The Coeur d'Alene suspend strings of deer hoofs across the lodge, and shake them from time to time to frighten the ghost away. While their general practices in destroying or cleansing the house of death agree with those of the other Salish, the Coeur d'Alene fumigate such a house, move it to another spot, and fumigate there, before reoccupying it.[17]

Cleansing and Mourning

Not only are the goods and property of the deceased cleansed of spirits but the chief mourners and all who touched the body are rigidly purified chiefly by bathing and sweating in the sweat house. For the pallbearers and others who incidentally touched the remains a visit to the sweat house several times a day for a week is judged enough. For the chief mourners this is only a beginning. Sometimes they betook themselves to the woods for a month or two, swimming each morning, sweating during the day, and swimming again at night. After each swim or sweat they beat themselves with a fresh supply of fir twigs. Each morning and night, sometimes for a year, they drink a potion made with rosebush root or red ants. They sleep on fir boughs which they change frequently, instead of on regular bedding. They dispense with all covers. If a widower does not refrain from hunting or fishing for a year after his wife's death, his associates fear that all game will flee the country. They are equally certain that if a man fails to sleep on pine boughs, on resuming his hunting and fishing, he would find his weapons and tackle useless. It is also believed that a man who ate from a dead person's dishes would contract consumption unless he drank the rose and red ant mixture. In the wake of death night noises are interpreted as coming from the newly made ghost, and children and youths are afraid to venture out in the dark.[18]

A longer mourning period was once observed. For a spouse this might have lasted two, or even three or four years. During this time remarrying was forbidden. For persons in relationship other than that of a spouse a lesser period satisfied. This might be one year for a parent who had lost a child.

Mourning customs prescribe that a widow should trim her hair straight above the shoulder line and not remarry until it has grown "long." Men in mourning allow their unbraided hair to hang down their backs. All persons in mourning wear their oldest clothes without changing them, and avoid ornaments. During mourning faces remain unpainted, and widows wear quarter-inch buckskin bands around their necks and wrists. They do not remove these until they fall off. A person in mourning refrains from singing, and some—and this pattern generally is true of widows—avoid all work. Wailing is not prescribed as part of the mourning observance, nor are definite patterns of ceremony followed. A widow's mourning period ends whenever her parents-in-law tell her that she may resume ordinary dress and remarry. If such announcement is slow in coming the mourning spouse—widower or widow— may suggest to his or her own parents that they should ask the parents-in-law for the release. If the mourning period has about run its normal course a refusal is rare. As part of the mourning observance, for about a year the dead and living spouse are described by title rather than by name.[19]

Among the Coeur d'Alene, when a father, mother, son, daughter, husband or wife dies the relatives cut the close survivors' hair straight across the neck, and burn the hair

701

which is cut off. The length of the remaining hair indicates the relationship of the living to the dead. A surviving spouse wears the hair shortest. The trim is closer for adults than for children. When a man dies the tails of his horses are docked.

The widows among Coeur d'Alene Indians do not wear bands of deer hide around their necks and wrists. However, they wear rose twigs in their garments, much as the Thompson Indians wear fir twigs. Among the Coeur d'Alene both widows and widowers sleep on brush beds containing branches of the wildrose, and bathe in water in which rose branches have been boiled. For four days after a funeral they abstain from eating meat, and during the entire mourning period, they eat sparingly, avoiding delicacies. The period of mourning and purification observed by the Coeur d'Alene is shorter than that observed by the Thompson Indians, and exhibits some variations in length from person to person.[20]

Navaho of Southwestern United States

The Navahos are a segment of the southwestern branch of the great Athabascan Indian group whose ethnographical boundaries extend from northwestern Mexico to the shores of the Arctic Ocean, and from the shore of Hudson Bay to the Pacific Ocean.[1] Numbering about 65,000, the Navahos are the most populous of all present American Indian tribes; and, far from dying out, are actually growing through natural increase twice as fast as the people of the United States as a whole.[2] With their extensive shepherding activities, agriculture playing only a minor role, they have also become perhaps the best-off economically of the modern American aboriginies; nevertheless many of their members, far from being affluent, live on the barest edge of subsistence.

The immense reservation of the Navaho, located on the Colorado Plateau, covers an area approximately the size of the State of West Virginia and spreads across the adjoining corners of Arizona, New Mexico, Utah, and Colorado. Their dwelling is the *hogan,* a conical affair, built of heavy sticks

702

"And They Moved Without Him," by Blackbear Bosin.
"Raised above earth, toward Heaven, the plains Indian buried his dead.
The spirit of his horse, and food and clothing for the unknown
journey was left with their loved one. But the others, families and friends,
had to move on across the earth in loneliness."

Text by Bill Burchardt. From the permanent collection
of the Philbrook Art Center, Tulsa, Oklahoma

covered with a thick layer of earth which serves to keep off rain and insulates its inhabitants against the extreme daytime heat.

Socially the Navaho, like the Todas of India, are notable for their dignity and a philosophy of life based on the principle of submission. Their intense ceremonialism, and a system of beliefs in which death, ghosts, omens, and taboos play a central part provide the anthropologist with a key to a distinctive and complex culture.

Death Beliefs

The mind of the Navaho is filled with dreams, omens, and portents relating to death and the dead. Having no belief in a glorious immortality for the soul, holding rather vague conceptions of the afterlife as an ephemeral and shadowy existence, the Navaho holds death to mean only the end of everything good.[3] Death is to be staved off as long as possible:

703

religious and mystical formulas are repeated; a singer will be brought to the sick person to sing curative songs over him; a stargazer will attempt to predict the progress and outcome of the disease; and sometimes the patient is made to sit on a medicine man's sand painting.

Ghost fears abound among the Navaho, so much so that a body of "Ghost Way" rituals has been created to deal with the malevolent ghosts of dead relatives or tribesmen. Ghosts are conceived of as the witches of the world of the dead who can return to this world and plague the living with sickness, headaches, weakness, disturbing dreams, localized pains, and other ailments.[4] The dead, consequently, are always a potential threat to the living, and thus there has developed the body of omens, taboos, and prescriptions for dealing with the ghosts of the dead: homes of the dead are considered haunted, as well as ruins of earlier peoples; it is perilous to look upon the bodies of dead persons, or even animals not used for food; one may not whistle after dark, for whistling always announces the presence of ghosts; never wish another person death, for the wish may be actualized; never step across a grave—these are but a few examples of the hundreds which abound in Navaho culture. It is not an overstatement to say that the preoccupation with the dead amounts to a phobia, and that much of the ceremonialism of the tribe is based on concern for keeping at a safe distance the ghosts of the afterworld.

Care of the Dead

More energies are directed toward staving off death than are expended in the treatment and care of the dead body. A seriously ill person is sometimes borne from his own hogan to a nearby shelter, so that in case of death the dwelling need not be torn down or abandoned. At this time no matter how great his distress he will be clothed in his best clothing and jewelry. A cluster of family members and medicine men remain with him until it becomes apparent that death is certain. Then all but one or two depart. Only a few—perhaps

704

four relatives who are willing to expose themselves to the evil effects of death—remain to carry out the tasks.[5] They will serve primarily as the bearers of the dead.

When it is clear that death has occurred the Navaho, although their grief for their dead is deep, guard against too violent an expression of it for fear that by such action they might provoke ghosts to appear. When a Navaho dies the co-operation of friends and neighbors who have joined the family in caring for the sick and performing household tasks ceases abruptly.

All, or nearly all, return to their own hogans and stay there—they want no part in the burial, not even to witness it lest they bring misfortune upon themselves and their families. Close kin accept the responsibility of washing and dressing the dying or the dead, but there is nothing about the tasks which they consider a privilege to perform. Rather, they would gladly accept the services of volunteers. Strangers, or even white men under such circumstances would be preferred in this case to obviate exposure of relatives to the dangers involved in caring for a dead body.

Burial of the Dead

Bodies are buried as quickly as is possible. Usually the day following the death two body bearers appear at the deceased's hogan, if he has been allowed to die there, and entering remove the possessions they have decided to bury with the body. Customarily such possessions may include a saddle, blankets, tools, weapons, and other personal possessions which are loaded onto the favorite horse of the deceased. Then they close the entrance which faces east and cut a new entrance into the north side of the hogan. Having carried out the body through this, after placing a trail of ashes across the path from the hogan to the grave, they burn, dismantle or abandon the hogan. If the hogan is abandoned, as is sometimes the case, it is never reused. Usually ashes are also strewn between the abandoned hogan and the new camp to the south. Only the fire poker is saved and taken to the new hogan. Ghosts are as much afraid of it as of the ashes.

The Navaho use a number of knots for tying cords and thongs for ceremonial purposes. One of these is the death-knot, used to tie the rope that holds the blankets in which a body is wrapped for burial, or to fasten the door of a hogan in which one or more people are buried. A death-knot is never untied. If it must be unloosed, the binding itself is cut and the knife is thrown away.

Meanwhile other relatives, occasionally with a volunteer who out of intense friendship is willing to face the hazards of helping care for the dead, have dug a grave, usually within walking distance of the dead man's hogan, or have selected a sheltered crevice in a canyon wall into which the body may be placed.

With the few participants caught up in an atmosphere of dread, the funeral procession is silent and mournful. To help avoid contamination men have removed all clothing but a breech-cloth, and women wear only a skirt. Both leave their hair flowing, the women's hair hangs down to cover their breasts. All cover themselves with ashes and a line of red ochre and tallow is painted across the nose and cheekbones of each mourning relative. One of the mourners leads the horse deliberately toward the grave, followed by the two body bearers carrying the body on their shoulders. It has also been customary to put the body on the horse, with the body bearers supporting it from each side. A fourth mourner warns travelers to change their routes. All who have anything to do with the funeral and mourning keep strict silence.[6]

Although the Navaho mark various life crises with ceremonies, they hold ceremony at death to a minimum. Thus the body is buried with little or no ceremony. The members of the burial party either cover the body with earth, or with stones, brush, and dirt. Such possessions as were decided upon earlier are interred with the body, usually in one or two bundles. Until recently the horse was led to the graveside, faced north, shot and left beside the grave of its master. After interment shovels and other tools are broken and left on the grave, and all footprints are obliterated. In addition to keeping silence the mourners may not spit, nor turn over a stone, but on the return home are required to skip and hop and when possible take a circuitous route back to the family hogan so that no evil spirit would catch up with them.

When mourners return they must bathe carefully, and those who have seen the body or helped in any way in the care of the dead must have in the meantime fasted. Even infants may not be nursed until the burial party returns. As soon as they return and have bathed, the family may eat and drink sparingly.[7] However, the members of the burial party must eat separately, may not leave anything in the dish and for the next day they must observe so many taboos and restrictions on activity as to make them virtually a group apart from their community.

Post-burial Activities

Most important of the post-burial observances are the purification rites. Frequent washings for the mourners and for the clothes they wear is necessary, and if during the four-day mourning period, and for the next four days, if any of them is troubled by dreams of death or ghosts, a precautionary tribal ceremony, "Blessing Way," is performed to invoke positive blessings of the Navaho deities. If ghosts are actually seen by the mourners, or certain portents of their presence observed, more drastic preventive or curative ceremonies, the "Evil Way" for native ghosts or "Enemy Way" for alien ghosts, are called for.[8] At the end of the final four-day period a singer is employed for a one-night sing, also as a precautionary measure to avert illness from the family of the deceased.

The distribution of such of the dead man's property as was not buried with him calls for more ceremonial action. Within a month after the death a singer is hired, this time to sing over all the property, horses, sheep, and jewelry as a purificatory measure so that the recipients might be freed of ghostly worries, and as a preventive measure to keep the stock from falling sick and the jewelry from getting lost.[9]

Yet for the most part ceremonialism is intended to profit or protect the living from the dead, and not to propitiate or

707

enhance the spirits in the afterworld. The depositing of some of the body's property is, as the anthropologist Kluckhohn notes, "no spontaneous gesture of affection nor a disinterested desire to promote well-being in the afterworld. Navaho lore teaches that any stinginess on the part of the living will bring swift and terrible retaliation."[10] Thus the survivors must take care to equip the spirit with the possessions he cherished when alive. When it is clear from the absence of apparitions, portents, dreams of the dead and their ghosts, and other fearful signs that the spirits of the dead have been properly cared for, or neutralized, the major business at hand, that of wrestling with the rather grim and unyielding physical environment and of attempting to maintain the verity of the old ways in face of encroaching peoples and ideologies, goes forward. Yet there is no guaranteed surcease from the ghosts of the dead; only as time goes by and the dead move back further in the long procession of departed ancestors is the danger of their return lessened. It is not clear in Navaho thought whether this is because the souls gradually cease to exist, or because there is less motivation for ghosts to return when they have been joined by those who were their immediate relatives in the world of the living.[11]

Chapter 54

United States:
Folk and Sect Variations

The Amish

The Amish are one of the twenty or so branches of the Mennonites. In this larger group there is wide variety of tradition and practice. Amish-born and reared John A. Hostetler, now a sociologist, notes that:

> Some dress in "plain" clothes, but others embellish the traditional styles or disregard them altogether. The strict Amish offshoot of the Mennonite body bans automobiles, radios, and fancy clothing. Their tradition demands bonnets, braids, and beards. On the other hand, there are Mennonite groups whose members wear jewelry and make-up, who attend movies, and whose women patronize beauty parlors. Between the strict and liberal extremes there are many shades of practice.[1]

All Mennonites share the idea of Bible-centeredness and live by the formula of obedience, simplicity, and love. They derive their name from the reforming founder Menno Simons and

709

were originally called "Anabaptists" because of their practice of adult baptism. All Mennonites stem back to two main groups in Europe: The Dutch Mennonites of The Netherlands and the Swiss Brethren. The Amish belong to the latter branch.[2]

The three great values cherished by the Amish are a "devout religion, an agrarian way of life, and a cohesive family and community. The highest value and ultimate goal is eternal life." While the Amish believe in the supremacy of the Bible, they also believe that to attain eternal life they must be "separate from the world." They hold that baptism should follow not precede a confession of faith, that church and state should be separate, that absolute freedom in religious affairs is necessary, and that the believer must neither bear arms nor swear oaths, but follow Christ's peaceful example. They believe also that the highest wisdom is to despise the world and love God. They scorn riches, position, titles, fame, and power as worldliness. The Amish are traditionalists and conservatives who hold the customs and beliefs of their forefathers so sacred that they cling to their manner of dress, styles of worship, and ways of life. Hence they avoid using automobiles, tractors, telephones, electric lights, plumbing, radios, and many other modern devices. The Amish have completely disappeared in Europe.[3]

When the Amish were persecuted in Europe for their refusal to bear arms and their separateness they immigrated to Pennsylvania in the 1700's. Since then they have spread to Ohio, Indiana, Missouri, Kansas, and many other states, and even into Mexico and Canada. Their practice of living in colonies has sometimes made land acquisition difficult, and their migrations generally have come about because they were searching for large parcels of reasonably priced land, and because they wished to avoid compulsory school laws requiring more schooling for their children than they considered proper.

The Amish church is divided into two branches. The older branch, the "House Amish," hold their services in homes and select their clergy by lot without regard for requirements of formal training. Usually from 15 to 35 families living close to-

Left, Plain coffin is symbolic of the simple Amish life-style.
Right, Funeral director assists Amish pallbearers in loading coffin
into horse-drawn hearse

gether constitute a "House Amish" district. Such a unit, containing about 75 baptized members, includes a bishop, several
assisting preachers, and a deacon, all of whom are chosen for
life, and serve without salary.[4]

The younger branch, the "Church Amish," have regular
churches and regular preachers. This group separated from
the parent church in 1890.[5]

The Amish speak a German dialect, called Pennsylvania
"Dutch," in their homes, but they employ High German in
their services. When the children attend school they learn
English.

Basically the Amish dress as did their European forefathers
during the seventeenth century. All adult male members
must wear beards, but are not allowed moustaches. Men wear
"barn-door britches," trousers with drop-fly fronts. Although
they may use buttons on their shirts, underwear, and pants,
they must use hooks and eyes on their coats. For services
they don a "split tail coat."[6]

The dress of the women is generally black. In addition they
wear the *Kapp,* a prayer cap made of gauzy white material

711

ending in loose bows which are pinned to their dresses. In the winter they wear black bonnets over the Kapp. Men wear black hats in a variety of brim and crown styles.

When death comes, in compliance to state law in states in which no exceptions on the grounds of religious beliefs and practices are made, the body is turned over to a non-Amish funeral director for embalming. Formerly embalming was considered a denial of God's will, as an attempt to postpone the normal dissolution of the body according to the scriptural injunction, "Dust thou art and unto dust thou shalt return." Embalming is carried on in the funeral director's preparation room. Meanwhile close neighbors are notified regarding the death by means of personal calls—the Amish do not use telephones. In addition a death notice is inserted in the local newspaper.[7]

The Amish believe in the neighborly principle of taking care of each other, and because the Amish community is, in effect, one large kinship group, it is really like saying that blood relatives should take care of their "own."[8] Mutual aid provides the Amish with their own form of social security from birth to death.

As word of the death is spread from family to family the whole system of mutual aid goes into operation. The bishop and his assistant hurry to the home; the carpenter offers his

Mennonite funeral
procession en route
from home to cemetery

John Collier Photo Library of Congress

712

Amish funeral procession draws into cemetery

services; women begin preparations for the funeral dinner; and neighbors join in performing farm and other chores for the bereaved family.

The home must be prepared for a funeral in much the same manner in which it is cleared for a meeting. The family cleans the stables and yards, moves the furniture, and hauls and puts into place the backless benches. They open the panel doors which separate the rooms in the houses to make it into a large clear space. Although the funeral director has been called upon to supply the professional services required by law, traditionally Amish families themselves handle most of the details of their funerals. The dead like the living are simply clothed. The body of a man may be clothed in a white shroud;

and that of a woman, for the first time since her wedding ceremony, garmented in white. Frequently a man is buried in underwear and a clean white shirt.[9]

The Amish traditionally are buried in the old-fashioned coffin; a plain wooden box narrow at the head and feet and widening at the shoulders. Formerly a stick was used to measure the body, the length of the stick indicating the length of the body; the distance from one end to a notch, the width of the shoulders. Sometimes two pieces of string were used instead of a stick. These measurements were brought to the carpenter and every coffin was custom built. Today the body is measured with a ruler, but otherwise coffin construction remains much the same. Amish coffins are either made by a local Amish cabinetmaker or carpenter or on occasion are bought from a local funeral director.[10]

Usually the Amish coffin is made of hardwood, although in Wisconsin the small Amish settlement buries its dead in pine boxes. The coffin sometimes is left unvarnished and unpainted; sometimes it is finished with a walnut stain. The more conservative Amish insist that the interior be bare, although they allow a cushion made of a thin strip of cotton batting to be placed on the bottom. The less conservative Amish drape interiors of their coffins with plain white cotton material—colored or patterned cloth is not allowed. The lid of the Amish coffin is made in one piece and may be slid down to shoulder level for viewing, or it may have a split hinged top. In any event the coffin is plain and small, and during the ceremonies it remains half-open.[11] It has no fancy lining, no tufting, no pillows, no handles, no decorations. It rests on a pair of wooden sawhorses or turned stands resembling them.

The embalmed body is returned to the farm home for viewing and funeral services. At the wake, which follows the return of the body to the home, the room is lighted by two oil-burning chimney lamps. Friends and relatives come to express sympathy and to view the remains. Finally the family goes to bed, leaving six men on straight-backed chairs sitting about the coffin, keeping watch throughout the night.

714

Everything is very plain and simple. No flowers are used at Amish funeral services.

The number in attendance at a funeral varies according to the age of the dead person. Because the Amish marry early and inter-marry, and have large families that are likely to remain in the neighborhood, most Amish have many relatives living close at hand. Relatives are expected to be present at a funeral; even a six-weeks-old baby must attend, and the funeral of a matriarch or patriarch may bring together as many as 1,000 people.[12] Normally the funeral is held in the house, but even though many Amish houses are roomy if the dwelling proves too small to provide space for a large family, the funeral services may be moved to the barn.

On the morning of the funeral of a "House Amish," the yard and driveway fill up with buggies and wagons. As the friends and relatives alight the viewer is struck with the somberness that characterizes an Amish funeral service. The men wear their best black suits, and broad brimmed black hats. Services are held in the morning and at the appointed

Milwaukee Journal Photo   *Charles S. Rice Photo*

Above left, View of Amish graves showing head and foot stones. *Above right,* Amish grave is covered preparatory to burial. *Below,* Burial scene in an Amish cemetery

Charles S. Rice Photo

time the mourners seat themselves on plain wooden benches to listen to two and one-half hours of prayers and Scriptural reading delivered in German in a high-pitched uninflected voice.[13]

The Amish still use the *Ausbund*, the world's oldest Protestant hymnal, which contains words but no notes. The traditional hymns, sung in unison, sound almost like a chant. The *Vorsanger* (song leader) sings the first syllable of each line as a solo, and the others join in for the remainder of the line. A hymn is sung so slowly—a minute sometimes to a line—that it may require one-half hour's singing time.[14]

When the home services are completed some of the friends and relatives climb into their buggies and return to their homes. Most of them remain, however, to eat the funeral dinner which is an important part of the traditional Amish funeral. Much of the food is supplied by friends and neighbors, and for two days women relatives labor to provide a repast worthy of the reputation of the deceased. In good weather the dinner is spread at outdoor tables. If the crowd is very large—and it may reach 500—it is probable that cold meats will be served; if smaller, and it is practical to cook the meat, hot meat, probably fried ham, will be on the menu. Food is simple but plentiful: cold sliced beef, cheese, peas, pickled beets, hard-boiled eggs, several kinds of relishes, pies, and cakes. Raisin pie is a staple item at Pennsylvania Amish funeral feasts, hence the name "funeral pie." Quiet pervades the dinner, even the small children being silent. When all have been served and the women in charge of the dinner have been given an opportunity to pay their respects to the dead, the funeral gets under way.[15]

The body is placed in the hearse, which differs from the usual Amish market wagon only in being slightly larger and having wooden instead of canvas sides. Sometimes, instead of a hearse one of the larger horse-drawn wagons is used, a relative generally drives the hearse. The procession forms slowly. The hearse leads, followed by buggies and wagons carrying the mourners with a carriage length between them. The line may consist of several hundred or more two-seated buggies interspersed with plain farm wagons.

If the local cemetery is at a great distance from the home, the funeral director may transport the body in his hearse in advance of and apart from the cortege. In such event, the long procession of mourners comes later.

The typical Amish cemetery is a plot of ground on a farm, donated by the farmer for burial purposes. Men of the Amish faith always dig and close an Amish grave—the service usually being performed by relatives of the deceased.[16] On reaching the cemetery the four pallbearers place the coffin on wooden trestles, and it is again opened for a final viewing. Another short, simple ceremony follows. The Amish are plain people in death as in life. They use no artifical grass mats to conceal the mounded soil, no roughbox, no mechanical lowering device.[17] At the grave relatives screw down the lid of the coffin and lower it into the grave themselves. The custom once prevalent for Amish men to wear their hats throughout the funeral services no longer is strictly observed. However, they do wear their hats while the coffin is being lowered.[18]

Wooden sticks are temporarily placed at the extremities of the grave to mark its position. Later a white marker, giving the name and dates of birth and death of the deceased, will be placed there. Amish cemeteries are different from most others in that at the end of each grave a small "foot stone" is placed opposite the conventional headstone.

The Amish still maintain the old-fashioned social aspect of the funeral, and after the burial service many of the mourners stand around and chat. A recent observer has noted that: "Members of the Amish community have shown considerable stamina in that their way of life should persist into the mid-twentieth century and rather than dying out, display many signs that it is expanding. Temperance and frugality are outstanding attributes of the Amish. None is idle; none is on relief. The Amish faith stresses simplicity, hard work, and deep seated pacifism. The Amish lead lives of peace, serenity and contentment, seeking only to be allowed to pursue their own way of life."[19]

Latter-Day Saints[1]

When a member of the Church of Jesus Christ of Latter-day Saints (commonly called Mormons) is ill, the elders of the church are called in and one will anoint the sick person with "consecrated" oil which is poured upon the crown of the head. This anointing is then "sealed" by two or more of the elders who are present.

When a member of the church dies the funeral director is called upon to perform the usual service of preparing the body for burial. He learns the wishes of the family and carries them out. The Mormon people bury their dead in white clothing which fully covers the body, and the funeral services are usually arranged by the bishop of the ward in accordance with the wishes of the family.

The family has considerable voice in deciding what shall be included in the services. The office of the bishop, however, offers suggestions concerning the musical numbers. These would be appropriate and in harmony with church beliefs and not of the "popular" variety. Funerals are usually simple but impressive. At the mortuary, before leaving for the service, a prayer is offered with the family alone surrounding the casket. Usually the services are held in the ward meeting-houses, but at times are conducted at the mortuary, the home, or the graveside. On the day of the funeral, the bishop usually goes to the home of the deceased and before the cortege leaves the home, someone will offer prayer. Sunday funerals are discouraged.

The funeral director ordinarily takes charge of the casketed body as it is transported from the family home or funeral home to the place of service, and thence to the cemetery.

The bishop opens the service by expressing the family's appreciation to friends and relatives for their attendance, kindnesses, and floral gifts. If the bishop has been invited to speak he does so at this point, particularly if a member of the General Authorities—the body of Mormon High Church officials—is present.

Funeral directors who serve Mormons frequently have printed a program which not only indicates the sequence of the various services but contains a list of the principals who perform them, and other matters, briefly noted, which are pertinent to the particular funeral. Some of the latter include name and date of birth and death of the deceased, place and time of services, and place of interment. When the service is concluded the Bishop accompanies the procession to the cemetery. *The Handbook of Instructions* provides that the graveside prayer should be a simple and earnest one: "There is no set form and the person appointed to offer it may ask for such blessings as the Spirit of the Lord directs. Usually in such a prayer, expressions are used seeking the protection of the body from molestation until the time of the resurrection when it will again be re-animated by the immortal spirit and come forth in glorious resurrection to associate with relatives and friends in the life that never ends. The person appointed to offer the prayer should be a worthy brother holding the Melchizedek Priesthood."

The Church has always taken the stand that nothing should be done to destroy the body. It considers consignment to earth and the operation of natural causes the proper means of disposal. However, the wishes of the deceased are honored if he has expressed a desire for cremation.

Among the Mormons, and among their non-Mormon neighbors as well, it is customary for the women's groups of the various churches or lodges to assume the responsibility for arranging and caring for the flowers when they are moved from the home or the funeral home to the church or other place of service, and thence to the cemetery. To render this service the women use their own cars.

The funeral director furnishes service folders, a memorial record book, acknowledgment cards, envelopes for floral cards, and a folder on which the family can list food or refreshments brought to the home during the mourning period. This folder notes the kind of container used so that the family may identify and return it.

In keeping with a practice found almost universally in rural societies, on the day of the funeral neighbors and friends generally prepare and serve lunch in the home of the deceased.

The Mormons are generous in making their facilities available to non-Mormons. "It would be an act of kindness and true Christian friendship," says the *Handbook of Instructions,* "to offer the use of meeting-houses for the funeral service of respected non-members of the Church who may have no direct religious affiliation, or are inactive members of denominational churches." Families who wish to take advantage of this privilege may conduct services according to the church of their choice. However, this provision does not apply to the rituals of secret, oath-bound organizations.

American Gypsies

Two main groups, the nomad coppersmith and the "Boyasch" comprise most of the gypsies in the United States. The latter group are fewer in number, although in it are included numerous family groupings and a number of tribes. During the last half century the members of the Boyasch have become sedentary in their habits, dwelling mostly in the large cities of the East and Midwest. Many of them have given up the traditional gypsy garb, although the women tend to keep some of the clothing that has made gypsies distinctive among all peoples.[1]

When most persons think of or write about gypsies in the United States they have the more numerous, more visible, nomad coppersmiths in mind. The term "coppersmith" is something of a misnomer, inasmuch as the tinkering and coppersmithing vocational pursuits of this group over the past three or four decades have almost disappeared. Their nomadism, however, has not diminished, and one can usually find them working in carnivals and circuses, the women especially noticeable in their mode of dress as they ply their fortune-telling trade from tents along the circus or carnival midways.

The characteristic costume of the women includes a head

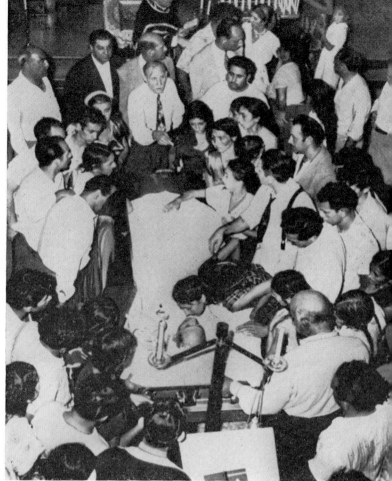

Mourner kisses
dead Gypsy
chieftain good-by
at services in
Serbian Eastern
Orthodox Church

scarf, a loose, low-cut blouse, and a long, full, highly colored skirt. The scarves are made of the brightest colored cloth obtainable. The women make their own skirts, frequently using expensive material. For dress-up occasions they are likely to add a heavily fringed Spanish shawl, with an over-all pattern of red or cabbage roses.[2] Their most distinctive article of apparel is jewelry—gypsy jewelry—in profusion, some cheap, some valuable. They make gold coins into earrings, bracelets, and necklaces. The coins are usually Mexican fifty-peso gold pieces, which they not only wear openly as jewelry but are also likely to hoard in their clothing.

In the United States, while the nomad coppersmiths are a

721

rather homogeneous group, looking alike, speaking much the same language, and following pretty much the same customs, they have nevertheless divided themselves into eight tribes: the Russians, Serbians, Kalderash, Argentines, Argentinos, Mexicans, Machwaya, and Greeks. The names are likely to be misleading. Thus the Argentines are Serbian and Russian nomads who came to the United States by way of Spain and South America, while the Argentinos are Serbians who came to the United States by way of Brazil. While the Mexicans, too, are of Russian and Serbian origin, they are given their present name because their wanderings carry them back and forth between the United States and Mexico—and so on.[3]

The majority of gypsies of the Russian-Serbian-Rumanian strain are members of the Russian and Serbian Orthodox Churches. Although the degree to which they conform to the beliefs and practices of the religion of their choice varies from person to person, it is likely that at their funerals those who in life were at least nominal members of an Orthodox church will have Orthodox ceremonies at the grave.[4]

The gypsies may be happy-go-lucky on the road, but in the cities they are likely to be characteristically unhappy, complaining. They have their share of the superstitions that afflict their numbers. They set great store on the interpretation of dreams, and are terrorized when one of them dreams of death or sickness or trouble. Many are hypochondriacs. A familiar sight in the rubble left behind by gypsies when they move on is a heap of empty patent medicine bottles.[5]

When a gypsy dies it is usually a funeral director who has had some previous experience with gypsy burial procedures who is called. On occasions, however, nomadic gypsies will bury their dead where they die, and in such instances the funeral director called may well never have had the experience of arranging a gypsy funeral. The consequences are likely to be surprising. In most instances, the dead gypsy body will be shipped to a large city and buried in one of the cemeteries long favored by the tribe or group.[6]

Except for the period when the body is undergoing physical

preparation by the embalmer or funeral director, it is henceforth never left alone. Once casketed, the deceased will have some close relatives at all times in attendance, and many others will be on hand to share in the wake.

The funeral arrangements will usually be made by the head of the family. Since a gypsy family may comprise a father with married children and their children as well, all living and travelling together as an extended family unit, the head of the family is likely to be a patriarch, with many relatives over whom he has authority. As already intimated, gypsy social organization does not end with the family unit, but includes tribes, made up of several or many families. The tribes in turn are identified with one or the other of the two major gypsy groups. Most tribes are ruled by a king who heads a royal family, or the ranking survivor, his word is final in the making of funeral arrangements and his control over the

Gypsy fiddlers play dirges at funerals of tribal members. Sister of dead Gypsy queen pours wine into grave to climax colorful burial ceremonies

Wide World Photo

Wide World Photo

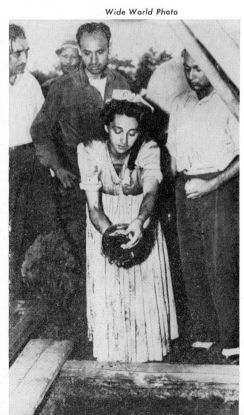

U.P.I. Photo

mourners is complete. Inasmuch as the funeral of a dead member is an occasion of great importance to the gypsies, funeral arrangements are likely to be rather elaborate. Expenses will of course vary with the rank and status of the deceased, but the gypsy funeral will usually be an average or above average priced service and include a vault, cemetery space in a preferred section, and, eventually, an inscribed memorial or plaque. Around these mundane considerations will be a host of colorful, if not bizarre, death customs.

However, the first task for those responsible for helping arrange the funeral will be to contact other members of family, tribe, or group. Naturally all members of a tribe would want to attend the funeral of a king or member of nobility. On the other hand, the funeral of a "commoner" might be attended by only those related to the deceased. Because caravans and isolated families or persons are likely to be out of direct telephone contact, most calls will be made to the police departments in places in which it is known that relatives are living or have set up *ofisas, i.e.* fortunetelling headquarters. The police then deliver the message. With long distance calls outgoing and incoming and funeral home telephones are busy day and night.

Everyone in the summoned group is expected to attend and participate in the wake. This expectation extends to children, babes in arms, the elderly—everyone. Soon the environs of the funeral will be taken up with parked gypsy autos, out-of-state licenses indicating the many areas from which the mourners have come. It is not unusual for several hundred gypsies to attend the funeral of one of their own tribal members; for the burial of a member of gypsy royalty the figure may be much higher.

Many gypsies will stay on the premises until the funeral is over. Others will come to the funeral home, participate in the wake for a few hours or a night, and then depart. It is likely that the funeral home will be completely taken over by the mourners for three or four days. The lobby, hallways, and even portions of the chapel area will be cleared and used for standing room for the visitors during the days and for sleeping space during the nights. All furniture, even some chapel pews will have been removed by the funeral director to make every inch of floor space available. Still some gypsies will sleep outside in their cars, and others may actually camp on the premises.

The wake will continue for three days, the open casket occupying the center of dramatic prominence with the deceased dressed in the traditional garb of his tribe, or if a member of nobility, in royal purple velvet. The burial robe for a female will be made by other female members of the tribe. Interestingly, the material will be obtained through an intermediary, inasmuch as gypsies believe that it is bad luck to purchase it directly. Another belief is that the dead will return again, and in light of such belief a complete change of clothing is put into the casket. For the women, gypsies thoughtfully include a spool of thread and a needle. Such clothes as are not put inside the casket are either burned or disposed of in some other way. Also, a silver chain may be hung across the open casket. The report occasionally met with that gypsies fill the casket with gold and then bury the treasure with the body has small foundation in fact and undoubtedly originates in the custom of putting a variety of coins as *tokens* into the casket.

Gypsy emotions are likely to be released uninhibitedly before the casket. Mourners in the funeral home weep loudly as they view the body, kiss the forehead or knuckles of the deceased, and mill around the chapel. The noise is likely to be startling to one used to the comparative quiet and solemnity of the usual American funeral.

One of the features of the wake is the funeral feast, which is set up in the same room in which the body lies. The gypsies bring in the food for the feast, so much that it covers the long table provided for it. Fish is one of the principal items on this occasion. At the funeral of a gypsy princess held the day before the burial in a North Dakota town, pork chops were the main dish. The gypsies did not use knives and forks but preferred to eat with their fingers.[7]

725

Gypsy funeral processions are likely to be colorful, even impressive in the emotionality expressed by the mourners. Flowers will have literally inundated the funeral home, and in the procession as many flowers as can be transported will be carried out to the cemetery. Music, so integral a part of the life of gypsies plays a continuing role in their death: a band, a group of violinists, some type of musical aggregation will lead the funeral procession. On the way from the funeral home to the church for the Funeral Mass a uniformed brass band played Chopin's *Funeral March* in the reported funeral of the above mentioned gypsy princess. For the funeral of a famous gypsy violinist-composer in Chicago his violinist colleagues marched in the funeral procession, playing some of the tunes he had composed or made famous.[8]

To the outside observer it would seem that the high pitch of emotional intensity is struck at the graveside ceremonies. The casket is opened at the grave and all crowd about it for the parting look, crying out in Romany their sorrows, moaning and wailing. Some of the women so overcome by the moment are unable to control themselves. "The women sometimes go to such an extent it's pitiful," notes an expert on gypsy affairs. "I've seen them run over and fall on their knees and butt their heads against tombstones, and when they stood up they'd be so dazed they'd walk around in circles and stumble into each other."[9]

Coins are again dropped into the open casket, and after the committal services the gypsies stay on to watch the filling of the grave. As dirt is being shoveled more coins are tossed in, and libations of wine are poured. Meanwhile all the mourners continue wailing and moaning until the grave is filled.

For some gypsies it is customary after the grave is filled to spread a cloth on the ground nearby and hold a feast. A prosperous family will provide quantities of cold turkey, legs of lamb and hams, while a less prosperous family will limit itself to cold cuts. In bad weather this funeral feast will be held under a tent.[10]

When the funeral is over the gypsies themselves clean up

726

the funeral home. In spite of the extensive round-the-clock use to which the premises have been put funeral directors report little damage and no loss by disappearance of property.

Mourning customs show variations. For instance among one group of gypsies during a six-week mourning period the mourners are permitted to listen only to funeral music. They are not even allowed to turn on the radio. For those who open ofisas in storefront buildings a crude shrine is often erected in one of the rooms partitioned off by blankets. Upon an orange crate they will stand a framed, colored or tinted photograph of the last member of the family to die. Generally the person is shown in his or her casket. Photographers customarily are hired to come to the funeral home to take this kind of picture. This portrait in death is flanked by a pair of pictures of the saints and in front of it they stand a stump of heavy candle, the bottom of which is pared down so that it can be stuffed into the open end of a quart milk bottle. On certain days of the year, in commemoration of special events in the life of the deceased, the candle is lit and a few prayers are offered for the repose of the soul of the dead.

"And all the air a solemn stillness holds . . ."

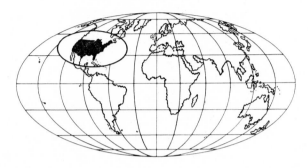

Chapter 55

United States:
Dominant Profile

The roots of American funeral customs and procedures extend back through Western civilization into early Judaeo-Christian beliefs concerning the nature of God, man, and the hereafter. An underlying pattern of conviction holds that the sacred quality of man exists in the soul or spirit, and that the body, as a chamber or hall for the spirit during life, deserves decent and respectful treatment, and is not an object to be disposed of without due ceremony.[1]

It is further felt that the ceremonial care of the dead is basically a religious matter, or, at least that participation by the clergy is essential in the services rendered to the dead and the bereaved. Around these beliefs and values a set of social usages or amenities has evolved together with the body of vocational tasks performed by lay persons (funeral directors) who arrange for and direct the sequence of events beginning with the removal of the body from the place of death and ending some days later with burial.

729

Response to Death

Unlike certain other cultural groups, including Latin Americans, most people in the United States do not regard death fatalistically.[2] High development in the health arts and rapid advances in medicine place such emphasis on health and well-being that death appears as the failure of man to insure and prolong life. Consequently, for an American the shock of death, universally felt because of the sundering of personal attachments, is accompanied by a sense of frustration.

Another factor in the American response to death is the aversion felt toward it. What with mobility of population and a breakdown of community attachments, death has become an event in which fewer people are directly affected or highly involved. In contrast to Colonial times, when all members of a community were somewhere involved in the death of a member and when death was a common event openly faced up to, death in contemporary America is subject to avoidance in thought and in action.[3]

Slightly more than half of all deaths occur in hospitals. For the remainder who die at home their removal to a funeral home takes place with an expedition unheard of in most other countries. Removals from hospitals are likewise rapid. In both cases the funeral director's desire to embalm and otherwise prepare the body as soon as possible constitutes another factor making for minimum delay.

On the whole the pattern of response to death tends to be: *personal* for the bereaved; *religious* as to the deceased's beliefs, and the clergyman's functions and duties; and *expediential*, inasmuch as the majority of details having to do with the physical dead body are entrusted to the funeral director.[4] No general set of death customs seems to prevail at this juncture. Some special usages may be noted. Among Russian Orthodox it is reported by funeral directors that the body can never be removed until the priest comes and says prayers. Likewise Orthodox Jews have an anointing ritual. As a perpetuation of certain inherited European customs, in some homes mirrors are covered when death occurs. Again, to close the mouth some

730

families tie a handkerchief around the head and chin of the deceased; and in other instances a member of the family closes the eyes. A custom which once was common to many people of various nationalities is the placing of coins on the eyelids after closing the eyes. This practice still exists, but is found primarily among persons of Spanish descent. Death sometimes produces shrieks, loud cries and lamentations from people of all nationalities and all walks of life. Then a quietness sets in, with a cessation of most household, social and everyday activities; and there may be utter abandonment into grief. But such release is not part of a consistent cultural pattern.

The First Call

A member or a representative of the family of the deceased, or a neighbor, a friend, the attending physician, a nurse or a member of the hospital staff notifies the selected funeral director of a death. Since it helps him to inaugurate the funeral arrangements to obtain certain vital data as soon as possible, this initial contact is important. If he lacks information he must consult early with members of the immediate family. Only then can he carry out his tasks.

Funeral directors are governed not only by state laws and regulations but also by ordinances of local government. Many counties and cities have ordinances regulating the manner of dealing with dead bodies or of reporting information about them. Some cities require a permit before a funeral director can remove a body from the place of death. To do this, many times a death certificate signed by an attending physician, coroner, or a medical examiner is required.

In all deaths, a death certificate must be signed by the doctor and in most instances the funeral director secures this signature. In instances in which no physician was in attendance or in which accident, violence or questionable circumstances are involved, laws and ordinances require that the death certificate must be signed by the coroner or medical examiner.

A permit is required for a burial. Special regulations govern cremation. In some areas permission must be obtained before

731

a body which is to be cremated can be embalmed. Today ten per cent of Americans are buried in a place other than that in which they die. To ship a body across state lines, a transit permit is required. Some states even require a temporary removal permit for shipping a body within a state but out of the registration district in which the death occurred.

Funeral Arrangements

Arrangements are seldom made by a single person. Generally the surviving spouse, parents, children, brothers, sisters, and other relatives, are on hand to discuss a host of details.

One of the first and perhaps the most urgent of these is the place for the service: church, residence, or funeral home. The time of the service must not only conform to the wishes and convenience of the family, but to the schedule of the officiating clergyman. Moreover, particularly in larger cities, the need for notification in advance of interment or cremation and the regulations governing the time of interments are growing more stringent and must be observed. The place of interment, too, many times involves important decisions. If a family plot is not available, those having the responsibility must purchase grave space. If a family lot can be used they must choose the exact location on it. In addition, they must settle details of transportation if the interment is to take place at a site distant from the place of death, the selection of suitable clothing, the casket, and the outside receptacle.

This list by no means covers all the decisions to be made. Among others are such matters as the wording of the obituary or death notices; the selection of family flowers; the holding of services by lodges or fraternal organizations; the utilization of family pallbearers (friends, business associates and neighbors) or professional bearers; and the method of providing transportation for those expected in the funeral cortege.

While these are matters in which the funeral director consults the family, there are others in which he proceeds without consultation, calling upon his professional experience to furnish the correct answers.

732

Protestant funeral service. *Below,* committal ceremony at cemetery

Life insurance policies for more than five hundred billion dollars are in force in the United States. When a policy holder dies, certain procedures must be followed before policy benefits will be paid. While variations in forms exist from one company to another, basically all companies require a statement by the claimant and another by the attending physician. These statements set forth pertinent data about the deceased which the company requires for its records. They may be supplemented by statements of the attending clergyman, the funeral director and a disinterested acquaintance. To provide the required in-

733

Catholic funeral Mass

formation it may be necessary to secure copies of birth records, death records of predeceased beneficiaries, and marriage certificates. Much of this task is assumed by the funeral director as a service to his clients. His experience makes him adept in handling these matters.

Burial insurance plans have been operating in some southern states for many years. During the depression of the thirties they became more prevalent. The policies provide for the payment of benefits in funeral services and merchandise rather than in cash. This type of insurance is prohibited by the insurance laws of many states.

Some insurance companies sell special "funeral" policies. Companies of this type operate according to the laws regulating legal reserve life insurance companies with the distinguishing feature that the proceeds of the funeral policies are earmarked for the payment of funeral bills. Insurance of this type pays cash to a named beneficiary. Policies naming the funeral director as beneficiary are legal only in a few states. In other states funeral directors are prohibited by law from becoming involved in any way in an insurance operation.

Besides the proceeds of insurance policies a variety of death

734

Traditional Jewish
service for the dead

benefits are derived from other sources, among them the Social
Security Administration, the Veterans' Administration, the
Armed Forces, and other governmental agencies, as well as
from fraternal groups and labor organizations. Again the advice
of the funeral director may be sought on filling in the necessary
forms or completing the required procedures so that the survivors may benefit.

Casket Selection

Funeral service pricing is predicated upon several factors:
(1) the expenses involved in providing the facilities of the
funeral establishment, (2) the staff services, (3) other opera-
tional costs and expenses, as well as (4) the value of the casket
merchandise.

As a practical matter the funeral director usually prices a
funeral based on a standard service which will include items
as listed on a card or in a brochure generally placed on or
in the caskets in the selection or display room. Therefore the
choosing of the casket is important in the making of funeral arrangements.

Although many people have a definite idea of what they want
to spend for a funeral, others are less certain. Their uncertainty
arises from the fact that it is not simple to judge what constitutes reasonable funeral expense as there are as many
grounds of reasonableness as there are different circumstances

735

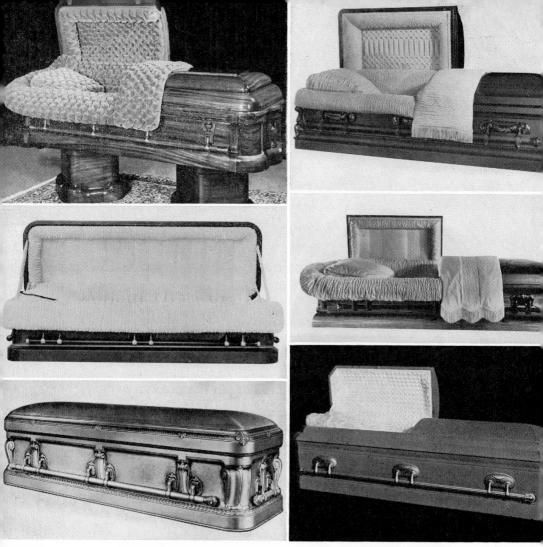

Typical American caskets. *Upper left,* Half-couch mahogany;
upper right, half-couch, metal; *center left,* full-couch, metal;
center right, half-couch, oak; *lower left,* seamless solid copper deposit;
lower right, hinge-cap, cloth-covered wood

surrounding individual families. Probate courts vary as to what
constitutes a proper and reasonable standard, while municipal,
county, state and federal agencies may hold different ideas,
and social reformers still others.

Age makes for a difference of opinion also. Youth is more
likely to consider as excessive the amount of money spent by

adults on a funeral. Young adults likewise are prone to counsel their elders to moderation in funeral spending. Funeral directors agree that racial, ethnic, and social class factors all exercise some influence upon spending. A small minority of people in the middle and upper socio-economic classes attempt to restrain and even conceal their emotions at death. This attempt has resulted in efforts to minimize or even abolish the funeral ceremony. On the other hand in the lower socio-economic classes and among certain ethnic groups, it is customary for all members to have a part in the funeral. The satisfaction derived from this participation results in more money being spent on the service.

In addition to these cultural factors which help to set prices and standards of quality in funeral services, several controls operate more or less perfectly to determine the business conduct of a funeral director. Thus it is poor business for him to provide a service for which a family cannot or will not pay. Most funeral directors write off only about two per cent of their income to bad debt losses. Part of the reason for this modest figure may be their awareness that funerals beyond a family's means are bad investments for funeral directors.

Two types of burial vaults used in the United States.
Metal left, concrete right.

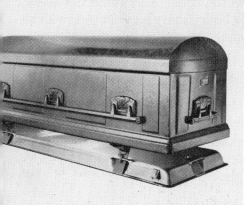 

Another important control is community pressure. Community opinion becomes a strong factor in determining the costs of services. State laws supply a further control. These generally prohibit funeral directors from soliciting, taking advantage of a family, misrepresenting merchandise and services, and false advertising. Selection of the funeral service is not only an important phase in itself, but should be understood in terms of the way the funeral director relates himself to his clients, to his community, and to his professional and business world.

Most funeral directors have casket selection rooms; some do not. If a member of the latter group is located in or close to a city where showrooms are maintained by casket manufacturers, he will either bring his client to their display rooms or he will use photographs of caskets, and samples of materials used in the coverings and in the interiors, as well as various finishes to show what is available. Recently three-dimensional color slides have been utilized for this purpose.

According to the Casket Manufacturers' Association, metal caskets are most used in the Carolinas, Virginia, the big cities of Pennsylvania, the Middle West, and Kentucky. In New England and New York hardwoods are selected extensively. Cloth covered wooden caskets are preferred on the West Coast, South, and Southwest.

American caskets can be grouped into three general types: the full-couch, which permits the entire body to be viewed; the half-couch, which shows the body from the waist up, with the panel and moulding lifting on hinges, so as to be at right angle with the casket proper; and the hinge-cap, which is the same as half-couch, differing only in the fact that the panel, not the moulding, is on hinges. The half-couch is the variety most used today, although in parts of New Jersey, New York and Pennsylvania, and in central and northern Ohio full-couch caskets are the preferred style. The hinge-cap casket is most used in some Southeastern states.

Except in the South the deceased is usually buried in clothing taken from his or her wardrobe. In the South a person is

738

generally buried in clothing purchased from the funeral director. Over the country as a whole, more women's than men's burial clothing is purchased from the funeral director.

The Funeral

The typical funeral, originating in an urban funeral home, covers a period of about three days, beginning with the removal of the remains and ending with the journey to the grave. The preparation for viewing is made by a licensed embalmer, trained in a school of mortuary science. In addition to embalming he will seek to restore facial skin tones in such manner that the features appear lifelike.

Once the body is placed in state, relatives and friends may call. In most instances this is done the afternoon and evening prior to the funeral service. However, in some sections, especially in areas in the East, the Midwest and the South this period may be extended to several days. Many more friends of the deceased pay their respects while the body is in state than attend the funeral services and burial. Exceptions to this general practice are to be found in the mountain states and the Pacific Coast areas. There more people attend the funeral service and go to the cemetery for the committal than visit the funeral home. In some parts of the country viewing is limited to established visiting hours. This is especially true in New England, the Eastern cities, and in scattered sections elsewhere.

In addition to personal contacts with the bereaved at the family residence, the funeral home, and at the cemetery, friends and relatives have other modes of expressing sympathy. These include the sending of flowers, cards, letters and telegrams of condolence, offering Mass cards, or making donations in the name of the deceased to various causes and charities.

On the third day following death the funeral service ceremony generally takes place. For this service custom today sanctions for most people the use of the funeral home, the church, or

On pages 740 through 745 in this chapter are pictures showing funeral homes located in various sections of the United States.

NEW ENGLAND

MIDDLE ATLANTIC

both. For Catholics, except in cases of infants, the church ceremony is required. Jews may or may not bury their dead from the synagogue or temple; and most Protestants likewise have free choice in the matter. In the Southern states the greatest percentage of Protestant funeral services are held in church. Probably less than one per cent of all funerals are conducted with no religious services.

The funeral ceremony marks a dramatic high point in the modern funeral. If it is conducted in a funeral home the room used is so arranged that attention focuses on the casket, which, open or closed, is placed on a catafalque in the center of a floral arrangement. Mourners gather along certain lines of protocol, and are seated in the room with the casketed body of the deceased, while the family and immediate relatives often are withdrawn in a wing. The privacy thus afforded them is in strong contrast to the older custom of putting them on display.

In the church, family members generally occupy the front seats, nearest to the casket. Although ritual of the Catholic funeral Mass is universal, in other matters there may be minor variations. The officiating Jewish rabbi is permitted some latitude in the services which he provides. Least constrained by formula is the Protestant minister. Nevertheless, the general pattern for the Protestant funeral service comprises four segments: the ritual, consisting of the reading of the Scripture and prayers; the funeral sermon; music; and the committal service.

For the most part in Protestant services prayers are intercessory, designed to bring comfort, consolation, and strength to the bereaved. While some clergymen still regard funeral sermons as offering opportunities to evangelize and make converts—as was frequently the case in the last century—more recently they give increasing recognition to the utility of the funeral service and sermon in expediting the mourning process. Backgrounds for this approach are supplied by mid-century pastoral counsellors, psychologists and psychiatrists who have turned their attention to the problems of bereavement. Although they are sometimes dispensed with along with all music, hymns are seen as a mode of reinforcing the sense of sharing which the

746

Hearse

Flower car

Ambulance

clergyman instills in the course of the funeral service. Protestant funeral services usually last between one half and three quarters of an hour.

Until a few years ago Sunday funerals were to be found in most parts of the United States. Today, however, the trend is away from them. Generally speaking, Catholic services are held in the morning, and Protestant and Jewish in the afternoon. However, in some areas throughout the United States Protestant services also are being held in the morning and there are places where the funeral services are held at night.

From reports of funeral directors in all parts of the country it would seem that there is a small trend away from having

747

United States
repatriates
her war dead.
Scene from funeral
of repatriated
soldier, casualty of
World War II

the family select friends and relatives as pallbearers and toward having the funeral director make these arrangements.

Today the average funeral procession to the cemetery for the committal contains fewer persons than formerly. Most of them ride in privately owned automobiles. In all instances the funeral director must be prepared to furnish transportation for the mourners and the clergyman. He will provide the hearse or casket coach, and many times a limousine for the immediate family. However, the custom of providing a limousine for the pallbearers shows some decline. At most services the funeral director supplies the car, stationwagon, or truck which carries the flowers to the cemetery. In some areas a special flower car is used with the vehicle a part of the cortege.

At the cemetery the traditional committal service is held, much the same as a century ago. Changes reflect, by and large, an increasing concern with the feelings and physical well-being of the bereaved. The harsh realities of the grave tend to be softened by the skills of the funeral director and cemetery personnel. Usually graves are lined with artificial grass to cover the upturned earth, canopies are raised in inclement weather, and the casket in most cases is not lowered until the bereaved have departed. As a general rule committal services are short, however, they are no less trying. In the words of Reverend Paul E. Irion, "The committal service provides, as nothing else . . . does so graphically, a symbolic demonstration that the kind of relationship which has existed between

748

the mourner and the deceased is now at an end."[5]

The close of the committal service marks the end of the funeral, although not necessarily the end of the relationship of the funeral director to the bereaved. The grave is filled by cemetery workmen after the participants in the ceremony have left.

Following some services, a funeral luncheon or dinner awaits the returning mourners. Following others, the group which has been held together by the bonds of ritual and ceremony becomes only a crowd, a dispersing aggregate of individuals and small groups, some still caught up with the mood or sorrow, some in mourning, and others already easing out from under the strain of sustaining the harmony and discipline necessary to the conduct of the funeral.

In a very few instances, memorial services replace the typical funeral service and ceremonies described in this chapter. Memorialization most generally means the honoring or remembering the dead by services held days, months and even years after the funeral.

On Memorial Day, May 30, the Nation's war dead have been honored traditionally by civic and military ceremonies. Confederate Memorial Day is variously April 26, May 10, May 30, June 3. In more recent times the visits to the cemetery to decorate the soldiers' graves have been expanded to include the decoration of all graves. Memorialization of the dead among Catholics also occurs on All Souls' Day, November 2. Although for these services Requiem Masses are ordinarily conducted in the churches, in some parts of the country rites sometimes include a cemetery service. A few ethnic groups participate in more elaborate celebrations. Some individuals use "In Memoriam" cards or newspaper notices to mark death day anniversaries.

Elements of the Mortuary Complex

Funeral Directing

In 1960 there were about 24,000 funeral establishments in the United States, for a ratio of about one funeral home for

749

every 7,400 people, and about 70 deaths per establishment. Combination establishments in which the funeral director engages in another business, such as a furniture store, include about one sixth of all funeral firms.

Due primarily to consolidations the number of funeral *firms* in recent times has remained static, while the number of funeral *homes* has increased. Meanwhile certain firms have added a second, and sometimes a third funeral home—or even have gone beyond this number to serve suburban families or to extend operations into nearby communities. With the volume of business per firm increasing, a general trend away from the very small and the combination business is noticeable. Changes for the most part are not rapid, and the average funeral firm today has been in business for over 35 years.[6]

Of the three basic legal forms of organization for funeral establishments the sole proprietorship form predominates, followed in rank order by partnerships and corporations. By and large the distribution of funeral homes reflects the distribution of the population. The major variations are in the East, with the largest ratio of funeral homes to the population; and on the Pacific Coast where the opposite is true.

About 75 per cent of all persons licensed in the funeral service field hold both funeral director and embalmer licenses, or a single license covering both functions. Six states, Michigan, Minnesota, New Mexico, New Jersey, New York and Pennsylvania, issue such combination licenses. For the rest of funeral service personnel, embalmers as such are licensed in all the remaining states, and funeral directors likewise except in Alabama, California, Mississippi, Missouri, Nevada, North Dakota, and South Carolina where only embalmers are licensed.

Licensing boards are usually composed of funeral directors and embalmers, although in at least twelve states the director of the state department of health serves as an ex officio member of the board. In about fourteen states board members must be selected from nominations submitted by the state funeral director associations.

The training of funeral service personnel is of course affected

750

by state requirements. These vary from a minimum of high school graduation plus a period usually of nine to twelve months at a school of mortuary education, to a three-year course involving one or two years of college work plus training in mortuary science. Sixteen states now have the latter requirement. In addition, apprenticeship training, mostly from one- to two-years' duration, is a requirement in most states. Recently the American Board of Funeral Service Education[7] has increased the length of mortuary science training to a 44-week course, and all schools accredited through an agency of the board now have adopted this length as the standard term of instruction.

Funeral directors have been organized into a variety of associations. The representative group is the National Funeral Directors Association, an organization of 48 state groups and the District of Columbia—Hawaii and Alaska have members at large. In 1960 its membership was over 14,000. Other special types of associations include the National Selected Morticians, with limited membership; the National Funeral Directors and Morticians Association, representing Negro funeral directors; and the Jewish Funeral Directors of America. Nine trade journals currently service the field.[8]

Cemeteries and Crematoria

A variety of institutions for the care of human remains exists

Left, Picturesque, monument-type cemetery. *Right*, Memorial park cemetery

American Cemetery Assn. Photo   Del Ankers Photo for National Assn. of Cemeteries

in the United States. *Monument cemeteries,* the older, traditional type in which the purchasers can within specifications erect monuments of their own choosing, predominate. *Memorial parks* require all memorials, whether bronze or stone, to be level with the grass. Many of the traditional cemeteries also have non-monument sections. Many cemeteries erect statuary with a religious motif.

There are about 1,250 memorial park cemeteries in which only bronze memorials are permitted, and another 1,250 in which both bronze and stone memorials are used. Another 12,500 are conventional monument-type, business-managed; and a final 37,000 are of the traditional municipal, county, village or churchyard type without a telephone on the premises and not set up to operate along conventional business lines. All-told, they enclose about a million acres of land.[9]

Community mausolea divide into two types: (1) Those having crypts indoors, crypts in corridors or rooms to accommodate visitors. (2) Those having outside crypts facing lawns or gardens. These are called "Garden Mausolea." *Crematorium-columbaria* are buildings containing niches in which cremated remains are placed in urns. While all types of cemeteries may provide cremation, columbaria are often combined with mausolea.

According to the Cremation Association of America, most of the 231 crematoria in the United States are owned and operated by cemeteries. Others are owned by funeral directors, and a few solely as crematorium-columbaria.[10]

Cremation in the last fifty years has shown a slow growth. At the turn of the century less than one per cent of the nation's dead were cremated. By 1950 the figure had risen to about 3.8 per cent. Since then, although the number of cremations has increased, the proportion of cremations to the number of deaths has declined. Interestingly, about one half of all cremations in the United States take place in the Pacific Coast States of California, Oregon and Washington.[11]

Funeral Costs

Four separate and distinct categories of charges make up

752

the cost of a funeral: those of the funeral director which are determined largely by the casket selected, the cemetery or cremation charges, the cost of a monument or marker, and miscellaneous expenses.

The amount paid to the funeral director for the service he provides ranges from nothing to over $1,000 depending upon the wishes of those who survive and their ability to pay. A study made for the National Funeral Directors Association indicates that in 1959 of all services, 52 per cent were provided for less than the average fee not including vault or burial clothing. This less than average fee group was made up of funerals for children, indigents, other adults and service calls. The fee income from services in this category accounted for only 28 per cent of total fee income. The remaining 48 per cent of the services, all of which were adult funerals, contributed 72 per cent of fee income not including vault or burial clothing.[12] The conclusion seems to follow that persons better situated in life generally help pay a portion of the funeral costs of the less fortunate.

For an earth burial many people wish the casketed remains to be placed in another receptacle known as a vault. Also, many cemeteries require permanent containers to help prevent cave-ins. Vaults are generally made of concrete or metal, and are usually sold by funeral directors for from $75 to $2,000. Some cemeteries that require outside receptacles permit the use of concrete section outer boxes which sell for $25 or more. Some also permit wooden outer boxes which sell for about $25.

Interment or cremation charges are in addition to those paid to the funeral director for the goods and services he provides. In the business-managed cemetery the cost of an individual grave space ranges from $75 to $350. Opening and closing charges range from $45 to $150. Prices for individual crypts in indoor mausolea start at about $600, and for individual rooms, which provide for a number of crypts, at about $7,500. Most outside garden crypts range in cost from about $350 to $15,000.

The cost of an actual cremation ranges from $35 to $100. Urns to hold a single cremated remains range from $40 to $100, while urns intended for several or more cremated remains

753

range from $100 to $500. Columbaria niches to hold such urns range from $25 to $750, the price depending on the size, location and quality of the niche.

Although most markers or monuments are purchased from monument dealers, some are bought from cemeteries, or in certain parts of the country from funeral directors. Bronze markers vary in price from $75 to $300, and stone monuments start at about $60. The cost of either can run into thousands of dollars, depending upon the size, material, design and craftsmanship of the memorial.

The cost of flowers, burial clothing, transportation of the body—if burial or cremation is to be at a place other than where death occurred—additional limousines or flower cars, and newspaper death notices make up some of the miscellaneous items paid through the funeral director or directly by the family.

It is unwise to do anything other than generalize as to over-all or specific costs. The needs and desires and circumstances surrounding a family as well as customs and usages are important factors. Then too, the general economy of the nation and the particular economy of an area have their effects. The statistics, ranges and percentages given are as the authors found them to be in the United States in 1960.

United States, *Passim*

View in Italian cemetery,
Independence, Louisiana

Jack Delano Photo, Library of Congress

Burial vault in
New Orleans cemetery

F.P.G. Photo

A 40-piece brass band plays
and marches in funeral
cortege of W. C. Handy,
"Father of the Blues," Harlem

U.P.I. Photo

Above, country graveyard with
"soul house," Kentucky

Left, All Souls' Day decorations,
New Roads, Louisiana

Above, Modern memorial chapel

Left, Favorite horse at funeral
of well-known Indian

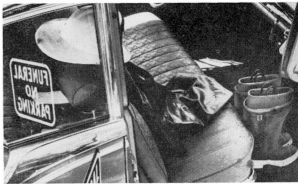

Left, Firemen stand honor guard as body of chief
leaves funeral home. *Above,* Chief's gear is carried
in his car as part of funeral cortege

Conclusion

There is no group, however primitive at the one extreme or civilized at the other, which left freely to itself and within its means does not dispose of the bodies of its members with ceremony. So true is this universal fact of ceremonial funeralization that it seems reasonable to conclude that it flows out of human nature. It is "natural," normal, reasonable. It satisfies deep universal urges. To carry it out seems "right," and not to carry it out, particularly for those who are closely connnected by family, feeling, shared living, common experience or other ties, seems "wrong," an unnatural omission, a matter to be apologized for or ashamed of. While the persons concerned may arrive at such conclusions by sound reasoning based on sound premises, even where the compulsions behind the desire to bury the dead with ceremony are not analyzed or reduced to language, they remain strong and operative. So true is this that to the various definitions of man there might be added another. He is a being that buries his dead with ceremony.

Funeral Ceremonies an Outgrowth of Necessary Actions

As students of ritual point out, much of the most sacred ceremony of even the more complex religions represents the commonest type of life. For many Christians the simple central vital processes of eating and drinking are wonderfully elevated into the Sacrifice of the Mass, the Holy Eucharist, the Lord's Supper.

Ceremony is born when a simple process becomes overlaid with secondary meanings, when it becomes not only a primary but a symbolic fact, when its performance is enriched to emphasize the symbolism, when it is enhanced with outward expression through words, actions and other adjuncts, so as to seize or hold the attention, and condition the mind and heart. Thus a sequence of action becomes a rite; the formula for its performance, a ritual; and the performers, whatever their titles, a group set apart. While a few funeral rituals may be ascribed to the authorship of a group of individuals, in most cases, like folk literature they have a folk or group origin, which is likely to be shrouded in antiquity. Among preliterate peoples they are handed down from generation to generation by verbal instructions and participation, and sometimes the forms persist long after the meanings are lost. Among literate cultural groups although verbal formulas are generally reduced to writing, certain unwritten elements may persist alongside the documents.

It is interesting to look across funerals the world over and to see how in specific cultures different parts of the simple sequence of acts between death and disposition have been ceremonialized into rites, particularly public rites, and what ritualistic treatment has been given to the formalized elements.

Funeralization a Conservative Social Process

While the viewpoint of this book is not historical—only in a few cases does it look back—it is clear everywhere that funeral beliefs, practices, customs have high survival powers, and are strongly resistant to change. Funerals lie at the very innermost

758

core of life's experiences. They represent grand and not trifling moments. They are social, solemn affairs. For each person there is only one funeralization, even though in a small minority of cases it may proceed through several or more stages. In addition, in every culture patterns of funeralization carry the enormous prestige of long and general acceptance, and to make substantial variation of these is to outrage the sense and conscience of the community. This is not to say that in any culture funeral customs do not change, because they do. In America, for instance, within the last three quarters of a century, among other changes, there has been a general movement away from the cult of sable pomp, with black drapes and crepe, liveried drivers, plumed horses and hearse, toward a funeral which lays emphasis upon meaning and beauty rather than upon stygian gloom. Change comes to funeralization, but it is slow, and there is much cautious clinging to old ways, with many a backward glance, and much compromise between the old and new.

Another point that scarcely needs elaboration is that funeralization tends to be a reflection of the whole viewpoint, the *Weltanschauung*, the world outlook, the basic philosophy of life of the culture in which it is found. A cultural group buries its dead partly in keeping with its economic dimensions, partly in keeping with its outlooks. Thus a classless society buries its dead in classless funerals. A society in which class distinctions are held extremely important buries its dead in ways that reflect the social stratification. The old order may have changed, so that classes or hereditary titles have no standing before the law, and democracy of some kind has been promulgated by decree; but as long as people recognize social classes based on title, position, or wealth among themselves, such a society is likely to provide funerals accordingly.

The Three Orientations of Funeralization

Funeralization obviously is a progression of activities leading from death to disposition—and having extensions beyond. It is clear that some of the activities involved in funeralization

759

center about the dead body—preparing it for disposition and disposing of it. It is also clear that another part of these activities is directed toward that portion of the person or personality which is conceived as having left the dead body. It is further clear that another part is directed toward the people who remain, the bereaved who are emotionally involved in the death through a sense of personal loss, and the larger social group or groups of which the deceased was a member.

(1) Funeralization and Disposition

Regarded only as a physical fact the dead body is a worthless, encumbering, corrupting, revolting and even menacing thing. It must be removed from the company of the living. Yet not even corruption can obscure the fact that once it bore the lineaments of an infant or a child, a man or woman, a person, a familiar friend, a member of a family, a loved one, an associate, and so for what it was rather than what it is, it is almost universally treated with reverence and sometimes affection, which may not be unmixed with fear and even horror, and it is disposed of with ceremony.

Men dispose of their dead in many ways: By burying them in the earth or beneath mounds of stones or bricks, by burying them in caves, or rock ledges, by exposing them in trees or on platforms, by feeding them to birds, by burning them, by exposing them to scavenging animals, by roasting them, by sinking them in water or allowing them to drift to seas or down rivers. The dead may be consumed by fire in crematories, native drums, their own houses, on burning ghats. The remains may be divided for burial with the head deposited in a box, and the body interred. Flesh may be removed from the bones and thrown away or buried, and the bones and teeth polished and kept. A body may be shut up in a house and the house abandoned.

The manner of disposition—and the foregoing list by no means exhausts its variety—will depend upon custom, law, religious beliefs, climate, condition of soil, availability of the goods of funeralization, and many other factors.

760

(2) Funeralization and the Persisting of Personality

People of most cultures believe that at death something which leaves the body has ongoing life. It may be called "soul," "ghost," "spirit," "shade," "shadow," or some other name, and it may have varying amounts of the "pure" spirit about it. Sometimes not one but several or more of these shades or spirits are believed to emerge from a single body. The image which the survivors have of them is derived from their religious concepts. In general, among primitive peoples these shadow beings are conceived as having many of the needs and faculties of human beings. An important faculty is that of memory, which grows out of and is continuous with the memory of the dead person. Another rather common characteristic is the fact such beings keep an interest in their former families and associates and are likely to interfere in their affairs. A third, is that they have counterparts of many human needs, and if these are not met, they will visit the negligent living ones with punishments. Such folk beliefs do not necessarily disappear with the acceptance of a higher form of religion, and sometimes persist side by side with it, or are swallowed up and become part of it.

(3) Funeralization and the Needs of the Bereaved

From the standpoint of the bereaved the need for the disposition of the body may be a *felix culpa*—the phrase comes out of the Latin liturgy—a happy fault, a fortunate misfortune. It creates the need for a physical act in successive stages— something must be done with the body—that can easily be made the central fact of a ceremony, that has significance and value reaching far beyond the remains and their disposition and affecting the living and their rehabilitation. The various factors which cause delay so that normally a day—or several days— intervenes between death and disposition and provide a period of transition which, while it would seem superficially to be given over to such matters as preparing the body, preparing the grave or other physical facility for disposition, or allowing

761

the mourning group to assemble, in reality has a deeper function, to provide therapy for the living. In this most critical period for them the living make the beginnings of the adjustments leading into a program by which they recover from the immediate and secondary effects of loss. The need for a program of this kind is so universal that it is safe to guess that if the body were to vanish at death, thus eliminating the need for disposition, there is strong evidence in the funeral customs of all cultures that some kind of ceremonies, perhaps prolonged, would still be held, the more to administer to the living than to honor the dead.

To understand this need it is necessary for us to ask, what does a death do to those who are allied by affection to the deceased? What is meant by that collective reaction which is frequently called the "sense of loss"? What reaction does the death of a loved one bring into the life of the bereaved? While overt and covert responses may, of course, differ from person to person in quantitative, qualitative and relative values, the general reaction is rather uniform.

A death produces grieving, a response which man shares with certain of the higher animals, but which is raised by his intelligence to a more complex level. Basically grieving is a sense of reaction with motor implications. It expresses itself in weeping, sighing, sometimes sobbing, screaming, or random activity disorientated from purpose.

A death produces a sense of unreality. The people we know are part of our world outlook. They "fit" us. When one of them goes the world outlook changes. Sometimes the change may seem as revolutionary as though we were transplanted suddenly into a distant unfamiliar place, or as though we were living in a dream. The saying is common "I can't believe it's true!"

A death produces a sense of loneliness and loss and a sense of disorder and confusion for those who are near to the deceased in physical fact or in affection or concern. A death smashes patterns that have grown to be part of an orderly way of life. Some of these patterns are set by personal habit, some by custom, with custom frequently crystallized into law. Death,

762

in disrupting intimate social units, deprives a wife of a husband, a husband of a wife, a parent of a child, a child of a parent. It disturbs stable living, income, property arrangements. It may change ownership so as to make the prosperous poor, or the poor prosperous. It changes support patterns. Sometimes it eliminates burdens, sometimes it adds to them.

A death immobilizes the bereaved. In varying degrees it tends to fix the attention of the bereaved on negative thoughts. It tends to "freeze" action. It creates a sense of the unworthwhileness of many of the normal routines of living. Sometimes it results in a desire not to live. A death creates panic, fear, insecurity and frustration and a sense of guilt in the living.

The simple fact is that for the bereaved death is a disturbing, disintegrating, hurtful experience. It is an injury to the personality. If the behavior patterns which it triggers should prove habitual or persist over a long time that personality is unhealthy, in the sense that it is partly out of its own control, it cannot handle successfully the day-to-day problems which it must face, and it is not getting as much of the positive values from life as it is entitled to get. Once we see this point it is not difficult to understand the therapeutic implications of funeralization for the bereaved.

The Therapeutic Values to be Found in Funeralization

By what device does funeralization restore a hurt or disintegrated personality to reintegrate itself, make itself well, wholesome, healthy, normal? How restore it to a condition in which it is capable of living a rich satisfactory life for itself, and of becoming a normal participating unit of the social organizations to which it belongs?

Out of many let us suggest eight therapies: 1. Direct expression; 2. Language; 3. Sharing; 4. Activity; 5. Aesthetics; 6. Viewing; 7. Ceremony; 8. Self-denial, suffering.

The distinctions as made below are neither radical nor exhaustive. As sorrow, grief, confusion, insecurity, loss, fear, anger, guilt, and all the other emotional responses made by

763

the living to a death blend the one into the other, so do the following remedial measures blend.

(1) The Therapy of Direct Expression

The period of funeralization provides a setting and an occasion—sometimes a provocation—for the direct physical expression by the bereaved of the emotional surcharges generated by death.

How much direct expression is enough depends partly on the individual, partly on the customs of the group to which he belongs. Among some groups steeled in self-restraint it is an expressive, satisfying, therapeutic experience to be permitted to weep silently. Among other groups, habitually less restrained, to be satisfying, direct expression must find a more violent outlet. To mention but a few there is self-mutilation, tearing of the garments, destruction of homes and goods.

(2) The Therapy of Language

Whether language is considered purely as self-expression, as when a person "talks to himself," or an expression resulting in communication, or as a substitute for action, or as action itself, or as any combination or all of these it is clear that for the emotionally surcharged speech has a therapeutic value.

So widespread is the use of language for this purpose that this generalization seems safe: for the bereaved there are no silent funerals. Shakespeare puts the universal need and the means of satisfying it well: "Give sorrow words. The grief that will not speak utters the o'erfraught heart and bids it break." Literature is replete with instances of the tragedy of silent grief.

The effect of language is easy to see; easy to describe. Purely as activity talking—even to one's self—provides release. Talking extroverts, and these functions are in addition to the deepened understandings, the social values, that develop out of conversation. Shakespeare further calls words "windy attorneys for their client woes." In any culture much of the

764

language of the bereaved will be repetition. The core experiences of life are simple and can be tersely expressed in the simplest of words. The statements that a man is dead, that he will be much missed, that he was a good husband and father, lose rather than gain by gilding. Most funeralization involves considerable conversational interchange between those who are deeply affected and a stream of less deeply concerned friends and relatives. What both parties say is less important than the fact that the surcharged speak, and thus find vent for their feelings. Here is another shaping up of the bereaved to reality, another sharing of grief; another means of reestablishing security through support. But not to be slighted is the fact that in such conversation the bereaved find relief through finding an outlet in speech.

(3) The Therapy of Sharing

Especially to be noted in all cultures is the manner in which the kinship group draws together to give emotional, physical, and frequently financial support to the bereaved when death occurs. In social and economic organizations with a low division of labor, relatives and friends frequently perform the necessary funeral tasks. Frequently, too, they make contributions of goods or money for the funeral. Generally they take measures to share the emotional burdens of the bereaved. In Western cultures the injunction, "Share ye one another's burdens," is supported by the recognition, universally accepted, that burying the dead is one of the corporal works of mercy. Equal recognition is given to the fact that visiting the bereaved is a meritorious phase of burying the dead. It is a truism that "joy shared is joy increased, while grief shared is grief diminished." The funeral practices of all peoples seem to bear out the accuracy of this statement.

(4) The Therapy of Activity

Among some primitive peoples one of the first effects of a death upon the bereaved may be a series of random bodily actions. These may include contortion of the limbs, jumping, running, rolling the eyes, and making of inarticulate sounds such as moaning, sobbing, screaming, keening, shouting. Sometimes men brandish weapons. Panic, anger, fear, confusion, expressing themselves in extreme measures soon exhaust those who indulge in them. Such behavior is judged infantile by peoples "higher" in the scale of civilization.

Civilized cultures recognize that while in some circumstances injury to limb or destruction of life may provide some kind of therapeutic outlet for the bereaved, such action is disruptive of the social order and may lead to great difficulties, feuding and warfare. In higher cultures, of course, social and legal pressures forbid direct, violent reaction, and the pressure resulting from loss must find outlet in some other fashion.

Funeralization for many persons provides routines by which they are aroused from immobility. "You must be at the funeral home. You must speak to those who come to offer sympathy. You must put on your best clothes, polish your shoes, comb your hair. You cannot withdraw; you must keep busy."

While the first responses may be listless, mechanical, the performance has therapeutic value because it prevents withdrawal from reality and activity, and provides an individually helpful and socially non-objectionable outlet for emotions.

(5) The Therapy of Aesthetics

Not all cultures take equal advantage of the opportunities given by funeralization for the transformation of the images of the bereaved from the unloveliness of the preliminaries of death, and of death itself to imagery that is more agreeable for the bereaved to remember and to live with.

Embalming in many countries is used solely as a sanitary measure for bodies that are to be shipped for burial elsewhere. Where it is generally used, together with the arts of cosmetology and restoration, it permits the bereaved to view the remains and thereby regain and reinforce the sense of reality.

Also to be recognized in the type of funeral increasingly provided in Western culture is the effort made to improve the aesthetic quality of the funeralization, to surround the ceremony with comfort, quiet, beauty. Such surroundings condition the mood of the bereaved and thereby supply therapy for grief and loss.

(6) The Therapy of Viewing

To some death is so disturbing that they find it difficult to accept it as reality or to view it in its proper perspective against the whole of their lives. The healthy personality sees life wholly and steadily, accepts it for what it is and adjusts to it. Another function of funeralization is to reorientate the living to the dead and to death.

Funeralization is antidote against the inability to make such reorientation. During the whole of the period, again and again, the point is made that a person has died. The relatives make this statement or those who participate in the ceremony make it. The presence of the body emphasizes it. If the remains are "in state," the eyes of the bereaved supply incontrovertible evidence of the fact of death.

Viewing has a deeper function than satisfying the curious, it establishes for the viewers the fact of death. Funeralization is to a healthy personality a definite closing of the door.

More than this, though, it creates a final and corrected image of the dead, which image is likely to crowd out the images formed during the final illness and at the time of death itself. The substitution of this corrected and more pleasing image, conforming more closely to the image of the deceased in life, is likely to have therapeutic value.

(7) The Therapy of Ceremony

Funeral ceremony is so universal at all levels of culture that, as stated above, man might well be described as a being who "buries his dead ceremoniously." Ceremony is, of course, important because it is a graphic, dramatic presentation of a content. Usually it appeals to several senses, and hence its mnemonic value is high. Again, it offers the various appeal that is

767

produced by such adjuncts as chanting in solo or chorus or both, dancing, dramatization, parading, the use of special vestments and masks, dialogue, monologue, ritualistic actions, symbolism, fighting, the use of special background properties. In a word, it has high attention value, and is likely to render the audience highly suggestible, particularly in moments of emotion when their critical faculties tend to be suspended.

Sociologists have long regarded ceremony as a powerful force in social control—in some cases a more powerful force than statutory law itself. For the bereaved the routines of ceremony in themselves represent discipline. Because most ceremony is of ancient origin its routine also represents the stability not only of the folkway but of the folk. New faces may come, old faces go, but the old order renews itself—a concept particularly important to those made insecure by death.

Ceremony has the power of ennobling and glorifying. Most funeral ceremonies represent an effort to bring death and burial within the framework of religious belief in the fact of a life hereafter, even though the nature of that life, and the relationship of the departed to it, may sometimes be vague or uncertain. When the doctrine that life persists after death is ceremoniously presented to the bereaved in moments of high suggestibility, and when it coincides with the hopes and wishes of the bereaved, then the acceptability of this belief is enhanced. The greater part of the human race finds consolation in this doctrine, and, to the extent to which ceremony increases its acceptance, another contribution to the therapy of the bereaved is indicated.

(8) The Therapy of Self-Denial, Suffering

It is interesting to see running through the funeral beliefs and practices of many cultures the thread of guilt. "That which I should not have done, I did; that which I should have done, I failed to do. Therefore I am guilty of this death and must pay the penalty and make some kind of reparation to the dead. Feelings such as these though perhaps largely subconscious will not allow the person burdened with real or imagined guilt

768

to rest easy until the debt has been paid. The length to which persons in some cultures will go to punish themselves so that they may be loosed of their guilt sometimes surpasses understanding and belief.

Funeralization is also a final summing up of accounts. It is an opportunity to say what has been left unsaid. "Expression," Emerson comments shrewdly, "is half the man." He might well have added that the unexpressed subtracts from the full man. "Did I forget to say thank you? Here is my chance to make public amends by spending of my accumulated hoard to provide funeral meats and sweetmeats. Was I less than faithful in the performance of my duties toward the loved one? Hand me sackcloth and ashes. Did rebellion sometimes rise in me? Behold the stumps of my fingers and hatchet wherewith I severed the missing joints." Certainly some part of grief and mourning and the rituals and customs by which these are formalized and expressed are egocentric in their origins.

Funeralization and the Satisfaction of Needs Unrelated to Death and Burial

On an individual basis, funeralization not only serves as therapy for the bereaved but it becomes a channel for draining off side-streams of emotion. In other cultures certain funeral customs make little sense when measured only in terms of the function of honoring the dead or restoring the bereaved. It seems worlds apart from the main purpose that mourning ceremonies should sometimes degenerate into eating and drinking bouts, or sports tournaments; or should be marked by dancing and gay music, drinking, carousing and story telling. But one must remember that social instinct, too, is powerful, and that mourners can be divided roughly into two groups, those whose grief for the dead prevents them from enjoying themselves, and those whose grief does not so prevent them. For the latter, to come together is to provide the first essential for sociability, a potentially festive group. And what more natural than that this group would become festive?

Funeralization and the Group

The process of ceremonial funeralization has rich implications not only for the individually bereaved or for the immediate family group who are emotionally involved in it. It is an important matter for the larger social groups to which the deceased belonged as well. Among primitive peoples these groups are few, simple, easily identifiable, usually confined to a small area, and largely based on blood lines. In a great nation this simplicity vanishes. But in either—or even in an intermediate condition—it is important to recognize that the death of a member of a group is a loss. Consequently, each group must take action to heal its hurt. In a small military society the death of a warrior means a weakening of the group's ability to wage warfare. In a political society facing hostile neighbors, or threatened with internal revolt, the death of a top man may produce a temporary weakening of the whole structure so that it may be necessary to conceal the loss, hold a private burial, select a successor and thus restore the political organization. When such restoration has been made the public funeralization is likely to serve the dual function of honoring the dead and presenting his successor. The equivalent of the old formula, "The king is dead; long live the king," has not passed out of use with the coming of twilight to many European monarchies, and can still be found in out-of-the-way corners of other continents today.

Conclusion

Much more, of course, could have been written descriptively about funeral customs, beliefs, and practices the world over, for the distinctive cultures of all peoples everywhere number literally into the thousands. In like fashion other generalizations, beyond those herein presented, might be drawn by those working within different frames of reference. Again the historical growth of funeral service as a vocation, profession, or set of institutionalized procedures might well be traced for any established society. In this respect the authors have chronicled the history of American funeral directing in an earlier volume.[1]

770

The picture has also been rounded out to some extent by analytical studies of death rites[2] and by explorations into the dynamics of death beliefs and responses to death by contemporary workers in the field of psychotherapy.[3]

In retrospect, the purpose of the book, as initially stated, was "to present a variety of profiles of funeral customs and procedures drawn from cultures, peoples, and nationality groups the world over." In following out this self-imposed task the authors have attempted to describe for each group, within the limitations of materials available, the routines or programs of funeral care of the dead from the moment of death to the final mourning ceremonies of the bereaved. In this, the conclusion, the descriptive efforts have been given over to an attempt to draw together, synthetically, a few common strands of funeral practice, and to state, interpretatively, some of the possible functions of funeralization as a universal feature of human existence.

For the convenience of those who would prefer a summary statement of such generalizations the authors state them as follows: Nowhere is there a lack of concern in the matter of death, care of the dead, or readjustment of the individuals and groups involved. The conceptions of body, soul, spirit, afterlife, and afterworld may and do vary greatly in different societies, in different religious beliefs, and on different continents. Yet the crisis of death is universally recognized wherever there is human society and culture. Consequently, ceremony and ritual give meaning to death and funerary behavior. The social chaos occasioned by the death of a family or community member is never brought to order by activities based solely upon rational or utilitarian considerations. Funeral customs develop as part of the social process; and, although their variety is legend, their growth is the consequence of such impinging factors as physical environment and social, economic, and religious conditions. From within man alone, as an aspect of human nature, comes the desire to care for the dead in the best of all possible ways. Funeralization in its optimum form permits the expression of such desire through a variety of socially approved patterns of behavior. The context of funeralization is dramatic, and its function, basically, is therapeutic. In brief, for all people everywhere, funerals and funeral ceremonies satisfy basic needs, allay suffering, and help to rescue death from the horror of meaninglessness.

Notes

PART ONE: Asia

Chapter 1

[1] J. J. M. de Groot, *Religion in China* (New York: G. P. Putnam's Sons, 1912), p. 12, *seq.*

[2] Wolfram Eberhard, *Chinese Festivals* (New York: Henry Schuman, Inc., 1952), p. 136, *seq.*

[3] Francis L. K. Hsu, "Chinese Religion and Ancestor Worship" in *Societies Around the World*, edited by Irwin I. Sanders, *et al.* (New York: Dryden Press, 1953), p. 91. Adapted from *Most of The World*, Ralph Linton, ed., (New York: Columbia University Press, 1949). By permission of Columbia University Press.

[4] *Ibid.*, p. 91, *seq.*

[5] Hsiao-Tung Fei, *Chinese Gentry: Essays in Rural-Urban Relations* (Chicago: University of Chicago Press, 1953), p. 30. By permission of the University of Chicago Press.

[6] Olga Lang, *Chinese Family and Society* (New Haven: Yale University Press, 1946), p. 19, *seq.*

[7] *Ibid.*, p. 163.

[8] Francis L. K. Hsu, *Under the Ancestor's Shadow* (New York: Columbia University Press, 1948), p. 31.

[9] Lang, *op. cit.*, p. 180.

[10] Hsu, *Under the Ancestor's Shadow*, p. 158.

[11] Mrs. J. G. Cormack, *Everyday Customs in China* (Edinburgh: The Moray Press, 1935), p. 112, *seq.*

[12] *Ibid.*, p. 91.

[13] V. R. Burkhardt, *Chinese Creeds and Customs* (Hong Kong: The South China Morning Post, Ltd., 1954), p. 177, *passim.*

[14] Sigmund Sameth, "Pompous Chinese Funerals," *Casket and Sunnyside*, April, 1943, p. 26.

[15] Cormack, *op. cit.*, p. 93, *passim.*

[16] *Ibid.*, p. 94.

[17] *Ibid.*, p. 94, *seq.*

[18] *Ibid.*, p. 95; also, Vernon Hill, in correspondence with Robert W. Habenstein, January 3, 1959.

[19] Hsu, *Under the Ancestor's Shadow*, p. 160. By permission of Columbia University Press.

[20] Vernon Hill, *op. cit.*

[21] Cormack, *op. cit.*, p. 95, *seq.*

[22] *Ibid.*, p. 103, *passim.*

[23] *Ibid.*, p. 97.

[24] *Ibid.*, p. 104, *seq.*

[25] Hsu, *Under the Ancestor's Shadow*, pp. 161-162.

[26] Cormack, *op. cit.*, pp. 106-111.

[27] Martin C. Yang, *A Chinese Village: Taitou Shantung Province* (New York: Columbia University Press, 1945), p. 86.

[28] Hsu, *Under the Ancestor's Shadow*, p. 158.

[29] Cormack, *op. cit.*, p. 107, *seq.*

[30] *Ibid.*

[31] *Ibid.*, pp. 109-110.

[32] De Groot, *op. cit.*, p. 309.

[33] *Ibid.*, p. 306.

[34] Cormack, *op. cit.*, p. 111.

[35] *Ibid.*, p. 112.

[36] *Ibid.*, p. 91.

[37] Vernon Hill, *op. cit.*

[38] Kenneth S. Latourette, *The Chinese* (New York: The Macmillan Co., 1934), Vol. II, p. 146.

[39] Hsu, *Under the Ancestor's Shadow*, p. 161.

[40] Cormack, *op. cit.*, p. 119.

[41] Hsu, *Under the Ancestor's Shadow*, p. 160.

[42] Vernon Hill, *op. cit.*

[43] Hsu, *Under the Ancestor's Shadow*, p. 160.

[44] *Ibid.*, pp. 159-160.

[45] Yang, *op. cit.*, p. 39.

[46] Vernon Hill, *op. cit.*

[47] Cormack, *op. cit.*, p. 122.

[48] *Ibid.*, p. 123.

[49] *Ibid.*, p. 126.

[50] *Ibid.*, p. 124.

[51] *Ibid.*, p. 125, *seq.*

[52] *Ibid.*, p. 90.

[53] Eberhard, *op. cit.*, p. 116.

[54] Burkhardt, *op. cit.*, p. 62.

[55] *Ibid.*, p. 61.

[56] Yang, *op. cit.*, p. 86.

[57] Cormack, *op. cit.*, p. 98.

[58] Hsu, *Under the Ancestor's Shadow*, pp. 46-48.

[59] *Ibid.*, pp. 49-52, *passim.*

[60] Hsein Chin Hu, *The Common Descent Group in China and Its Functions* (New York: Viking Publications in Anthropology No. 12, 1948), p. 36.

[61] *Ibid.*, pp. 38-40, 60.

[62] Hsu, *Under the Ancestor's Shadow*, p. 52.

63 *Ibid.*, p. 132.
64 *Ibid.*, p. 51.
65 *Ibid.*, p. 155.
66 *Ibid.*, p. 34.
67 Burkhardt, *op. cit.*, p. 176.
68 Hsiao-Tung Fei and Chih-i Chang, *Earthbound China: A Study of Rural Economy in Yunnam* (Chicago: University of Chicago Press, 1945), pp. 101-102.
69 *Ibid.*, pp. 261-263.
70 Fei, *op. cit.*, p. 133.
71 Burkhardt, *op. cit.*, p. 177.
72 Vernon Hill, *op. cit.*
73 *Ibid.*
74 Edward C. and Gail R. Johnson, "Funeral Customs, Hong Kong," *Funeral Directors' Review,* to be published in October, 1960 issue.
75 Marion J. Levy, *The Family Revolution in Modern China* (Cambridge: Harvard University Press, 1949), p. 341. *See also* Morton H. Fried, "The Family in China—the People's Republic," in *The Family: Its Function and Destiny* edited by Ruth Anshen (New York: Harper and Brothers, 1959), pp. 146-166.
76 Yang, *op. cit.*, pp. 70, 336, 337.
77 Sripati Chandrasekhar, "Chinese in Commune Give Up Freedom for Sixteen Guarantees," *St. Louis Post Dispatch,* February 20, 1959. Copyright 1959 by Associated Press.
78 As related by Paul Cheng, Hong Kong funeral director, to Edward C. Johnson.

Chapter 2

1 John F. Embree, *The Japanese* (Washington, D. C.: Smithsonian Institution, 1943), p. 27.
2 *Ibid.*
3 *Ibid.*, p. 28.
4 *Ibid.*, pp. 29-30, *passim.*
5 John F. Embree, *Suye Mura: A Japanese Village* (Chicago: University of Chicago Press, 1939). The authors have made liberal use of this monograph. Cf, particularly, pp. 130-133, 215-220, 261-263.
6 *Ibid.*, p. 216, *seq.*
7 *Ibid.*
8 *Ibid.*, p. 131.
9 *Ibid.*, p. 218.
10 *Ibid.*, p. 220.
11 *Ibid.*, p. 284.
12 *Ibid.*, p. 284.
13 *Ibid.*, p. 285.
14 Correspondence to Edward C. Johnson. Mr. Miyazaki also sent the authors several score of photographs, some of which are included in this work. The assistance of Francis B. Tenny, Field Supervisor, USIS American Embassy, Tokyo, is also recognized.
15 Composite of two letters, July 10, 1959, and August 11, 1959, written by Hidehisa Miyazaki to Edward Johnson.
16 William H. Erskine, *Japanese Customs* (Tokyo: Kyo Bun Kwan, 1925), p. 92. The description of the traditional death customs of non-rural Japanese follows Chapters 7, 8, 9, and 10 of this work.
17 *Ibid.*, pp. 98-99.
18 Arthur Lloyd, *Everyday Japan* (London: Cassell and Company, Ltd., 1911), p. 327.
19 Erskine, *op. cit.*, p. 104.
20 Alma O. Taylor, "The Funeral Rites of Japan," *The Embalmers' Monthly,* March, 1903.
21 Frank G. Carpenter, *Japan and Korea* (Garden City, New York: Doubleday, Page & Company, 1925), pp. 180-181.

Chapter 3

1 Information supplied by Gregory Henderson, Cultural Attaché, American Embassy, Seoul, Korea, and by Sang Beck Lee, Ph.D., Seoul National University Museum.
2 Charles A. Clark, *Religions of Old Korea* (New York: Fleming H. Revel Co., 1932), p. 114.
3 Cornelius Osgood, *The Koreans and Their Culture* (New York: The Ronald Press, 1951), p. 115 ff. Chapter 7, "Death and Religion," presents the most comprehensive, up-to-date account of village funerals in Korea.
4 Clark, *op. cit.*, p. 310.
5 Sten Bergman, *In Korean Wilds and Villages* (London: Travel Book Club, 1938), p. 93.
6 Osgood, *op. cit.*, p. 116.
7 Homer B. Hulbert, *The Passing of Korea* (New York: Doubleday, Page and Co., 1906), p. 442, *seq.*
8 Osgood, *op. cit.*, p. 117.
9 Tae Hung Ha, "Folk Customs and Family Life" quoted in *The Korean Republic,* Seoul, August 30, 1958, p. 3.
10 Bergman, *op. cit.*, p. 94.
11 Hulbert, *op. cit.*, p. 455.
12 William E. Griffis, *Corea: The Hermit Nation* (New York: Charles Scribner's Sons, 1882), p. 279.
13 Hulbert, *op. cit.*, p. 454, *seq.*
14 M. Heydrich, "Koreanische Landwirtschaft: Beitraege zur Voelkerkunde von Korea I," *Abhandlungen und Berichte der Mussen fuer Tierkunde und Voelkerkunde zu Dresden,* Vol. XIX (Leipzig: Druck

und Kommissionsverlag von B. G. Tuebner, 1931), p. 3.
[15] *Ibid.*, p. 4.
[16] Osgood, *op. cit.*, p. 32.

Chapter 4

[1] Tsung-lien Shen, and Shen-chi Liu, *Tibet and the Tibetans* (Stanford, Calif.: Stanford University Press, 1953), p. 147.
[2] Adapted from Bell's bald translation by William M. Lamers. Cf. Sir Charles Bell, *The People of Tibet* (Oxford: Clarendon Press, 1928), p. 298.
[3] *Ibid.*, p. 299.
[4] *Ibid.*
[5] David MacDonald, *The Land of the Lama* (London: Seeley, Service & Co., Ltd., 1929), p. 149.
[6] L. Austine Waddell, *The Buddhism of Tibet or Lamaism* (London: W. H. Allen & Co., Ltd., 1895), p. 498.
[7] Sarat Chandra Das, *Journey to Lhasa and Central Tibet*, Ed. W. W. Rockhill (London: John Murray, 1902), p. 252, *passim*.
[8] MacDonald, *op. cit.*, p. 149, *seq.*
[9] Waddell, *op. cit.*, p. 490.
[10] Shen and Liu, *op. cit.*, p. 150.
[11] Albert Tafel, *Meine Tibetreise (My Tibetan Trip)*, Vol. II (Stuttgart: Union Deutsche Verlagagesellschaft, 1914), p. 381. Translated for Human Relations Area Files from the German by Carole Cerf.
[12] Waddell, *op. cit.*, p. 493.
[13] MacDonald, *op. cit.*, p. 151.
[14] Ekai Kawaguchi, *Three Years in Tibet* (Adyar, Madras: The Theosophist Office, 1909), p. 388.
[15] Bell, *op. cit.*, p. 290.
[16] Shen and Liu, *op. cit.*, p. 150.
[17] Tafel, *op. cit.*, p. 383.
[18] Bell, *op. cit.*, p. 289.
[19] Das, *op. cit.*, p. 255.
[20] Kawaguchi. *op. cit.*, p. 389.
[21] Tafel, *op. cit.*, p. 382.
[22] *Ibid.*
[23] Shen and Liu, *op. cit.*, p. 150. By permission of Stanford University Press.
[24] Kawaguchi, *op. cit.*, p. 391.
[25] Shen and Liu, *op. cit.*, pp. 150-151. By permission of Stanford University Press.
[26] Kawaguchi, *op. cit.*, p. 392.
[27] Bell, *op. cit.*, p. 290.
[28] Heinrich Herrer, *Seven Years in Tibet.* Translated by Richard Graves (London: Rupert Hart-Davis, 1957), p. 81.
[29] Bell, *op. cit.*, p. 295.
[30] Kawaguchi, *op. cit.*, p. 393.
[31] MacDonald, *op. cit.*, p. 152.
[32] *Ibid.*, p. 153.

[33] *Ibid.*, p. 147.
[34] Das, *op. cit.*, p. 255.
[35] G. A. Combs, *A Tibetan on Tibet* (London: T. Fisher Unwin, Ltd., 1926), pp. 50-51.

Chapter 5

[1] Shigeru Hikage, "Eisei" in *Mocodaikan*, part III (Tokyo: Kaizosha, 1938), p. 5.
[2] Joseph Kler, "Sickness, Death, and Burial among the Mongols of the Ordon Desert," *Primitive Man*, Catholic Anthropological Conference, 1936.
[3] *Ibid.*, p. 29.
[4] *Ibid.*
[5] Owen Lattimore, *Mongol Journeys* (New York: Doubleday, Doran & Co., 1941), p. 184, *seq.*
[6] Kler, *op. cit.*, p. 30.
[7] *Ibid.*, p. 31.
[8] Lattimore, *op. cit.*, p. 184.
[9] Kler, *op. cit.*, pp. 31, 61.
[10] Lattimore, *op. cit.*, pp. 183-184.
[11] Kler, *op. cit.*, p. 31.
[12] Lattimore, *op. cit.*, pp. 184-185.
[13] Kler, *op. cit.*, p. 30.
[14] Herbert H. Vreeland, *Mongol Community and Kinship Structures* (New Haven: Human Relations Area Files, 1953), p. 224.

Chapter 6

[1] Thao Nhouy Abhay, Ministre du Gouvernment Royal, *Aspects du Pays Lao* (Vientiane: Editions Comite Litteraire Lao, 1956), p. 25. Translation, Jane Habenstein. The material in this chapter leans heavily on Abhay's monograph.
[2] *Ibid.*, p. 26.
[3] *Ibid.*
[4] *Ibid.*, p. 27.
[5] *Ibid.*, p. 28.
[6] *Ibid.*
[7] *Ibid.*, p. 29.
[8] *Ibid.*
[9] Karl Gustav Izikowitz, *Lamet: Hill Peasants in French Indochina* (Goteborg, Sweden: Goteborgs Etnografiska Mus., 1951), pp. 103-109. Izikowitz's account is partly paraphrased by the authors.
[10] *Ibid.*, p. 104.
[11] *Ibid.*, p. 104, *seq.*
[12] *Ibid.*, p. 105.
[13] *Ibid.*
[14] *Ibid.*, p. 106.
[15] *Ibid.*, pp. 106-107, *passim.*
[16] *Ibid.*, pp. 106-108.
[17] "Contrasts in Indo-Chinese Rituals," *Casket and Sunnyside*, November, 1943,

p. 25.
[18] Information supplied by Edward Johnson, from correspondence with George D. Webb, Singapore, Singapore Casket Co., Ltd. Mr. Webb is a member of the British Institute of Embalming.

Chapter 7

[1] *India,* Cornell University Sub-Contractor's Monograph S-4, 5. (New Haven: Human Relations Area Files, 1956), p. 406.
[2] *Ibid.,* p. 405.
[3] *Ibid.,* p. 409, *passim.*
[4] *Ibid.,* p. 410.
[5] *Ibid.,* p. 411.
[6] Drawn from a paper prepared especially for this work by the Ministry of Scientific Research and Cultural Affairs of the Government of India. Verse re-rendered by William M. Lamers.
[7] *Ibid.,* rephrased in part.
[8] In response to the request of Arthur S. Funk, Cultural Officer, U. S. Information Service, Madras, C. J. Jayadev prepared this detailed account of Hindu burial procedure for use by the authors. His and the report of the Indian Ministry of Scientific Research and Cultural Affairs provide the substance of this chapter.
[9] Margaret Cormack, *The Hindu Woman* (New York: Bureau of Publications, Teachers College, Columbia University, 1953), p. 93.
[10] *Time,* Vol. 64, November 1, 1954, p. 36.
[11] *Ibid.,* December 20, 1954, p. 29.

Chapter 8

[1] W. Crooke, *Natives of Northern India* (London: Archibald Constable & Co., Ltd. 1907).
[2] *Ibid.,* p. 276.
[3] *Ibid.,* p. 220.
[4] *Ibid.,* p. 220, *seq.*
[5] *Ibid.,* p. 212.
[6] W.H.R. Rivers, *The Todas* (London: Macmillan and Co., Ltd., 1906), p. 337. Rivers' study remains the most definitive, and is used as a basic source for this section.
[7] *Ibid.,* p. 338.
[8] Vitold de Golish, *Primitive India.* Translated by Nadine Peppard (London: George G. Harrap & Co., Ltd., 1953), pp. 10-20.
[9] Rivers, *op. cit.,* p. 343.
[10] *Ibid.,* pp. 345-346.
[11] De Golish, *op. cit.*
[12] Rivers, *op. cit.,* p. 351.
[13] *Ibid.,* pp. 351, 355, *seq.*

[14] *Ibid.,* p. 361, *seq.*
[15] *Ibid.,* p. 365.
[16] *Ibid.,* p. 367, *seq.*
[17] *Ibid.,* p. 374, *seq.*
[18] *Ibid.,* pp. 379-381.
[19] *Ibid.,* p. 383.
[20] *Ibid.,* p. 389.
[21] *Ibid.,* p. 397, *seq.*
[22] George P. Murdock, *Our Primitive Contemporaries* (New York: The Macmillan Co., 1934), p. 126.
[23] De Golish in 1951 witnessed the funeral of a Toda woman who was reputed to have been gifted with magical powers. Eight buffalos were sacrificed in the course of the ceremonies. De Golish, *op. cit.,* pp. 17 ff.
[24] Rivers, *op. cit.,* p. 402.
[25] This material has been adapted from a paper prepared especially for this work by C. M. Austin de Silva (B.A. London), Ethnologist, National Museum, Colombo, Ceylon. Diana Captain, Cultural Affairs Assistant, American Embassy, Colombo, also provided useful information to the authors.

PART TWO: Middle East

Chapter 9

[1] This section on Turkish burial customs is adapted from a document prepared specifically for this study by Miss Sevil Erel, assisted by Mr. Tulgar Can, both of Istanbul.

Chapter 10

[1] The basic source for this chapter is Henri Massé, *Persian Beliefs and Customs* (New Haven: Human Relations Area Files, 1954). This book, written originally in French in 1923, supplies a wealth of information on mortuary customs of the Persians, especially rural and village beliefs and folkways.
[2] *Ibid.,* p. 97, *seq.*
[3] *Ibid.,* p. 98.
[4] *Ibid.,* pp. 80-82.
[5] *Ibid.,* pp. 82-84.
[6] *Ibid.,* p. 84-100.
[7] *Ibid.,* p. 82.
[8] *Ibid.,* p. 86.
[9] *Ibid.,* p. 84.
[10] *Ibid.,* p. 102.
[11] *Ibid.,* p. 99.
[12] *Ibid.,* p. 92.
[13] *Ibid.,* p. 89.

[14] *Ibid.*, p. 101.
[15] *Ibid.*, p. 96.
[16] *India: Sociological Background—An Area Handbook* (New Haven: Human Relations Area Files, 1956), prepared as a sub-contractor's monograph, pp. 469-470.
[17] Wilton Wynn, "Zoroastrian Funeral Customs in the Middle East," *Director*, February, 1953, p. 4. This report by Wynn has been adapted by the authors for this section.
[18] *Ibid.*
[19] *Ibid.*, p. 5.
[20] *India: Sociological Background—An Area Handbook, op. cit.* p. 472.

Chapter 11

[1] Funeral customs in Lebanon described here are adapted from articles written for the National Funeral Directors Association's journal *The Director* by Mr. Wilton Wynn, Associated Press correspondent. Cf. *The Director*, December, 1952, and February, 1953.
[2] Wilton Wynn, "Christian Funeral Customs in the Middle East," *The Director*, February, 1953. The remainder of this section is an adaptation of this report.

Chapter 12

[1] C. J. Polson, R. P. Brittain, T. K. Marshall, *The Disposal of the Dead* (London: English Universities Press Ltd., 1953), pp. 119-182.
[2] Personal correspondence from Werner Braun, Jerusalem, Israel, to Robert W. Habenstein, July 23, 1960.
[3] Authors' thanks are extended to Samuel Bar-Shalom, Hebrew University, Jerusalem, for research performed specifically for them; to Maxwell W. Passerman, New York for his suggestions and additions; and to the Ministry for Religious Affairs, Department for Contact with the Diaspora, for its careful review and criticism of this chapter.

Chapter 13

[1] Tessema, Negga, "The Death Customs in the Province of Tigre," in *Bulletin No. 5*, the University College of Addis Ababa Ethnological Society, Addis Ababa, Ethiopia, June, 1956, pp. 13-23. This section on Ethiopian funeral customs is based in considerable degree on Tessema's definitive study.

[2] *Ibid.*, p. 14.
[3] *Ibid.*, p. 15, *seq.*
[4] *Ibid.*, p. 16.
[5] *Ibid.*, pp. 16-17.
[6] *Ibid.*
[7] *Ibid.*
[8] *Ibid.*, p. 18.
[9] *Ibid.*, p. 18, *seq.*
[10] *Ibid.*, p. 19.
[11] *Ibid.*, p. 20.
[12] *Ibid.*, p. 20, *seq.*
[13] *Ibid.*, p. 21, *seq.*
[14] *Ibid.*, p. 22.
[15] *Ibid.*
[16] *Ibid.*, p. 13.

PART THREE: Africa

Chapter 14

[1] An up-to-date summary description of the Ashanti of West Africa is found in *A Profile of Primitive Culture* by Elman R. Service (New York: Harper & Brothers, 1958), Chap. 16, pp. 338-357.
[2] R. S. Rattray, *Religion and Art in Ashanti* (Oxford: At the Clarendon Press, 1927). Rattray is the outstanding authority on the Ashanti. This section leans heavily on Chapters 15 and 16 of his study.
[3] *Ibid.*, p. 149.
[4] *Ibid.*, p. 152, *seq.*
[5] *Ibid.*, pp. 156-158.
[6] *Ibid.*, p. 158, *seq.*
[7] *Ibid.*, p. 160.
[8] *Ibid.*, p. 160.
[9] *Ibid.*, p. 162, *seq.*
[10] *Ibid.*, pp. 164-166.
[11] James B. Christensen, *Double Descent Among the Fanti* (New Haven: Human Relations Area Files, 1954). This doctoral thesis, presented to Northwestern University is based on field work carried out during a period of eleven months in the Fanti states of Anomabu, Abura and Esiam. Detailed data are presented on funerary rites as well as other Fanti-social relationships.
[12] *Ibid.*, p. 68.
[13] *Ibid.*, p. 68, *seq.*
[14] *Ibid.*, p. 71.
[15] *Ibid.*, p. 69.
[16] *Ibid.*, p. 70.
[17] *Ibid.*, p. 73.
[18] *Ibid.*, p. 74.

Chapter 15

[1] J. O. Opakunle, Nigerian student at the University of Missouri kindly prepared the materials upon which this account of

777

Yoruban funeral customs is based.
[2] Materials upon which this section is based were graciously supplied by Mr. Atta O. Nkere, Nigerian student attending the University of Missouri.
[3] Dr. Müller's account of the Nigerian tribal burial accompanied photographs made available from "Photo Freytag" of Zurich, Switzerland, through the courtesy of "Pictures International Publicity," New York. Translation by George Zollschan, University of Missouri.
[4] Communication from David Nwadiolu, Otolokpo, Benin Province, Nigeria, to Robert W. Habenstein, May 23, 1960.

Chapter 16

[1] Melville J. Herskovitz, *Dahomey: An Ancient West African Kingdom* (New York: J. J. Augustin, 1938), Vol. I. For a summary of Dahomean culture *see* George P. Murdock's: *Our Primitive Contemporaries* (New York: The Macmillan Co., 1934). Chapter XVIII, pp. 551-595.
[2] Herskovitz, *Ibid.*, pp. 157-193.
[3] *Ibid.*, p. 197.
[4] *Ibid.*, p. 238. By permission of J. J. Augustin Publishers.
[5] *Ibid., see* especially pages 352-390.
[6] *Ibid.*, pp. 352-354.
[7] *Ibid.*, pp. 353-355.
[8] *Ibid.*, p. 356.
[9] *Ibid.*, pp. 356-357.
[10] *Ibid.*, p. 358.
[11] *Ibid.*, p. 359.
[12] *Ibid.*, pp. 374-375.
[13] *Ibid.*, pp. 380-387.
[14] *Ibid.*, pp. 387-390.

Chapter 17

[1] Many ethnographic studies have been made of this large segment of the Bantus. *See,* for a modern analysis Merran McCulloch, *The Ovimbundu of Angola* (London: International African Institute, 1952).
[2] *Ibid.*, p. 35.
[3] Gladwyn M. Childs, *Umbundu Kinship and Character* (London: Oxford University Press, 1949), p. 57.
[4] Wilfrid D. Hambly, *The Ovimbundu of Angola* (Chicago: Field Museum of Natural History, 1934), p. 264-270.
[5] *Ibid.*, p. 278.
[6] Childs, *op. cit.*, p. 57.
[7] Hambly, *op. cit.*, p. 266.
[8] Childs, *op. cit.*, p. 88.

[9] Hambly, *op. cit.*, p. 270.
[10] *Ibid.*, p. 271. For a chief's burial in which the head is removed, *see* McCulloch, *op. cit.*, pp. 46-47.
[11] McCulloch, *op. cit.*, p. 33.
[12] Hambly, *op. cit.*, p. 199, *seq.*

Chapter 18

[1] The Rev. John Roscoe, *The Baganda: An Account of Their Native Customs and Beliefs* (London: Macmillan and Co., 1911), *see* especially Chap. IV.
[2] L. P. Mair, *An African People in the Twentieth Century* (London: George Routledge & Sons, Ltd., 1934); *also*, "Totemism among the Baganda," *Man: a Monthly Record of Anthropological Science,* Vol. 35, 1935. For a brief introduction to the culture see Chap. XVII, "The Ganda of Uganda" in George P. Murdock's *Our Primitive Contemporaries* (New York: The Macmillan Co., 1934).
[3] Roscoe, *op. cit.*, p. 98.
[4] Mair, *An African People in the Twentieth Century, op. cit.*, p. 205, *seq.*
[5] Roscoe, *op. cit.*, pp. 99-101.
[6] *Ibid.*, pp. 101-105.
[7] Mair, *op. cit.*, p. 205, *seq.*
[8] *Ibid.*, pp. 207-208.
[9] *Ibid.*, p. 206.
[10] *Ibid.*, p. 207, *seq.*
[11] *Ibid.*, p. 208.
[12] Roscoe, *op. cit.*, p. 103, *seq.*
[13] *Ibid.*, pp. 107, 109.
[14] *Ibid.*, pp. 106, *seq.*
[15] *Ibid.*
[16] *Ibid.*, p. 110, *seq.*
[17] Mair, *op. cit.*, p. 208, *seq.*
[18] *Ibid.*, p. 210, *seq.*
[19] *Ibid.*, p. 211.
[20] *Ibid.*, p. 213.
[21] *Ibid.*, pp. 214-219.

Chapter 19

[1] C. R. Lagae, "Les Azande ou Niam-Niam: L'organization Zande, croyances religieuses et magiques, coutumes familiales," Bibliotheque-Congo, Vol. 18 (Bruxelles: Vromant and Co., 1926), p. 206, *seq.*
[2] Edward E. Evans-Pritchard, "Zande Theology," *Sudan Notes and Records* (London: McCorquodale and Co., Ltd., 1936), Vol. 19, p. 38, *seq.*
[3] Jan Czekanowski, "Forschungen im Nil-Kongo Zwischengebiet." *Wissenschaftlicht Ergebnisse der Deutschen Zentral Afrika*

Expedition, 1907-1908, *unter Führung Adoph Friedrichs, Herzogs ze Mecklenburg* (Leipzig: Klinkhardt und Biermann, 1924), Vol. 6, Part 2, p. 68.

[4] Edward E. Evans-Pritchard, *Witchcraft, Oracles and Magic among the Azande* (Oxford: Clarendon Press, 1937), p. 380.

[5] Czekanowski, *op. cit.*, p. 69.

[6] R. G. Anderson, "Some Tribal Customs in Their Relation to Medicine and Morals of the Nyam-nyam and Gour People Inhabiting the Eastern Bahr-El-Ghazal," *Fourth Report of Wellcome Tropical Research Laboratories at the Gordon Memorial College of Khartoum* (London: Ballière, Tindall and Cox, 1911), Vol. B, p. 242.

[7] P. M. Larken, "An Account of the Zande," *Sudan Notes and Records* (Khartoum: McCorquodale and Co., Ltd., 1926-27), Vol. 10, pp. 85-134, and Vol. 19, pp. 1-55.

[8] Gaetano Casati, *Ten Years in Equatoria and the Return with Emin Pasha* (London and New York: Frederick Warne and Co., 1891), Vol. 1, p. 219.

[9] Enrico Graffen and Edoardo Columbo, "Les Niam-Niam," *Revue Internationale de Sociologie* (Paris: International Institute of Sociology and Society of Sociology of Paris, 1906), Vol. 19, pp. 787-789. 1932), pp. 534 ff.

[10] Charles G. and Brenda Z. Seligman, *Pagan Tribes of the Nilotic Sudan* (London: George Routledge and Sons, Ltd., 1932), pp. 534 ff.

[11] Czekanowski, *op. cit.*, p. 64.

[12] Lagae, *op. cit.*, p. 211.

[13] *Ibid.*

[14] Czekanowski, *op. cit.*, p. 66.

[15] Lagae, *op. cit.*, p. 220, *seq.*

[16] Anderson, *op. cit.*, p. 225.

[17] Lagae, *op. cit.*, pp. 61-64.

[18] Seligman, *op. cit.*, p. 521, *seq.*

[19] Edward E. Evans-Pritchard, "The Dance," *Africa* (London: International Institute of African Languages and Cultures, 1928), Vol. 1, p. 462.

[20] Edward E. Evans-Pritchard, "Some Collective Expressions of Obscenity in Africa," *The Journal of the Royal Anthropological Institute of Great Britain and Ireland* (London: 1929), Vol. 59, pp. 318-320.

[21] Evans-Pritchard, *Witchcraft, Oracles and Magic Among the Azande, op. cit.*, p. 462.

[22] *Ibid.*

Chapter 20

[1] Hugh A. Stayt, *The Ba Venda* (London: The Oxford University Press, 1931).

[2] *Ibid.*, pp. 236-238.

[3] *Ibid.*, pp. 240-241.

[4] *Ibid.*, pp. 249-252.

[5] *Ibid.*, pp. 279-283.

[6] The forms of burial follow descriptions by Stayt, *Ibid.*, pp. 162-164, also p. 84, and pp. 90-91.

[7] See also, *Ibid.*, pp. 164-165.

[8] *Ibid.*, pp. 210, 280-283, 211-213.

Chapter 21

[1] A brief summary treatment of the Nama Hottentots, one of the three large Hottentot groupings, is found in Peter Murdocks' *Our Primitive Contemporaries* (New York: The Macmillan Co., 1934), pp. 475-507.

[2] I. Schapera, *The Khoisan Peoples of South Africa: Bushmen and Hottentots* (London: George Routledge & Sons, Ltd., 1930). Additional materials on this group are found in the Human Relations Area Files.

[3] *Ibid.*, pp. 366-367.

[4] *Ibid.*, p. 369.

[5] *Ibid.*, p. 361.

[6] *Ibid.*, pp. 363-364.

[7] *Ibid.*, p. 365.

[8] *Ibid.*, pp. 365-366.

[9] *Ibid.*, p. 372.

Chapter 22

[1] Ralph Linton, *The Tanala, A Hill Tribe of Madagascar* (Chicago: Field Museum of National History, 1933).

[2] *Ibid.*, p. 169, *seq.*

[3] *Ibid.*, pp. 173-174.

[4] *Ibid.*, p. 179, *seq.*

[5] *Ibid.*, p. 180.

[6] *Ibid.*, p. 177.

[7] *Ibid.*, p. 78, *seq.*

[8] *Ibid.*, p. 172.

[9] *Ibid.*, pp. 180-181.

[10] *Ibid.*, p. 176.

[11] *Ibid.*, p. 182.

Chapter 23

[1] C. Douglas Pitt, Hunan and Pitt Funeral Services, Ltd., Cape Town. Personal correspondence with Howard C. Raether, December 23, 1959.

[2] C. D. Cook and David T. Cook, Funeral Directors, Johannesburg. Personal corre-

spondence with Robert W. Habenstein, December 8, 1960.
[3] *Ibid.*
[4] Ray H. Rogers and J. G. Jones, Funeral Directors, East London. Personal correspondence with Robert W. Habenstein, February 4, 1960.
[5] Pitt, *op. cit.*
[6] Cook, *op. cit.*
[7] *Ibid.*
[8] *Ibid.*
[9] *Ibid.*
[10] Rogers, *op. cit.*
[11] *Ibid.*
[12] Cook, *op. cit.*
[13] C. Oelofsen, C. Oelofsen, Ltd., Funeral Directors, Embalmers, and Monumentalists, Kitwe, N. Rhodesia. Personal correspondence with Robert W. Habenstein, July 5, 1960.
[14] *Ibid.*
[15] W. L. Maree, Information Officer, Information Bureau of the Dutch Reformed Church, Johannesburg. Personal correspondence with Robert W. Habenstein, July 6, 1960.
[16] Oelofsen, *op. cit.*
[17] *Ibid.*
[18] *Ibid.*
[19] *Ibid.*
[20] Maree, *op. cit.*
[21] *Ibid.*
[22] Oelofsen, *op. cit.*
[23] Maree, *op. cit.*

PART FOUR: Oceania

Chapter 24

[1] P. L. Chan, "Bali Cremation," a document prepared for the authors through the courtesy of Photographs-International Publicity, New York.
[2] Miguel Covarrubias, *Island of Bali* (New York: Alfred A. Knopf, 1937). This work, especially in Chapter XI, "Death and Cremation," provides the major reference source on Balinese funeral customs.
[3] *Ibid.*, pp. 362-363.
[4] *Ibid.*, p. 44.
[5] *Ibid.*, p. 366.
[6] "The Burning Biers of Bali," *True*, May, 1958, p. 76.
[7] Covarrubias, *op. cit.*, pp. 381 ff.
[8] *Ibid.*, p. 386.

Chapter 25

[1] Joseph T. Howard, "Funeral and Burial Customs in the Philippines," report was

prepared by Dr. Howard, rural sociologist and student of Philippine community development, for the authors March, 1959. Most of the materials presented on village funeral customs were adapted from this report.
[2] *Ibid.*
[3] Edward C. Johnson, personal report based on a survey of funeral establishment operations in some of the Pacific Islands, and in portions of Asia, February-March, 1960.
[4] Howard, *op. cit.*
[5] *Ibid.*
[6] "Embalmers Corps United States Army," *The Embalmers' Monthly*, January, 1905, pp. 1-3.
[7] Johnson, *op. cit.*
[8] M. C. Icasiano, "Procedure for the Disposal of the Dead in Manila," report for the authors prepared by the City Health Officer, Manila, August 6, 1959.
[9] *Ibid.* Supporting information supplied by Rufino Padillak, Funeraria Central, Novotas, Rizal, Philippines, in a personal communication to Robert W. Habenstein, July 30, 1959.
[10] Howard, *op. cit.*
[11] *Ibid.*
[12] *Ibid.*
[13] *Ibid.*
[14] *Ibid.*
[15] *Ibid.*
[16] Nicasio G. Valderrama, Cultural Assistant, Embassy of the Philippines, Washington, D. C. Personal communication to William M. Lamers, July 21, 1958.
[17] *Ibid.*
[18] Howard, *op. cit.*
[19] *Ibid.*
[20] *Ibid.*
[21] *Ibid.*
[22] Icasiano, *op. cit.*
[23] Howard, *op. cit.*
[24] *Ibid.*
[25] Valderrama, *op. cit.*
[26] Howard, *op. cit.*
[27] Valderrama, *op. cit.*
[28] *Ibid.*

Chapter 26

[1] This section, edited very slightly by the authors, was prepared expressly for this book by Dr. Jane C. Goodale, staff member of the University Museum of the University of Pennsylvania. Dr. Goodale spent the Fall and Winter of 1954 among the Tiwi gathering data for her PhD dissertation. For further references on this aborigine tribe *see:*

Jane C. Goodale, *The Tiwi Women of Melville Island, Australia,* Unpublished PhD Dissertation, University of Penn. 1959; "The Tiwi Dance for the Dead," EXPEDITION, Vol. 2, No. 1, Fall, 1959, pp. 3-13, Philadelphia.

C. W. N. Hart and Arnold Pilling, *The Tiwi of North Australia* (New York: Henry Holt & Co., 1960).

C. P. Mountford, *The Tiwi, Their Art, Myth and Ceremony* (London: Phoenix House, 1958).

Chapter 27

[1] The authors wish to extend thanks for the many courtesies shown them in gathering materials on funeral customs in Australia and for information supplied by: John Allison, Richmond, Victoria; S. M. Backe, American Consulate, Perth; Donald W. Born, The American Embassy, Canberra, A. C. T.; Donald J. Chipper and Son, Perth; Guy B. Gresford, Research Secretary, Commonwealth Scientific and Research Organization, East Melbourne, Victoria; Graham R. Hall, American Consul General, Melbourne; W. H. Robinson, Secretary, Victorian Funeral Directors' Association, East Malvern. The authors are also indebted to Edward C. Johnson, Chicago, for his additional information and research assistance.

Chapter 28

[1] E. Lloyd Sibun, "Funeral Service and Customs in New Zealand," an address, reprinted, given at the 38th Annual Meeting of the National Selected Morticians, September 27, 1955, pp. 42-44. Mr. Sibun is a funeral director in Auckland, New Zealand.

[2] G. W. Clark, Personal communication to Robert W. Habenstein, September 16, 1958. Mr. Clark is the Editor of the *New Zealand Funeral Directors' Journal.*

[3] A. H. Marker, Personal correspondence to Robert W. Habenstein, September 4, 1959. Mr. Marker is a Christ Church funeral director and a member of the British Institute of Embalming.

[4] *Ibid.*

[5] Clark, *op. cit.*

[6] Sibun, *op. cit.*

[7] Marker, *op. cit.*

[8] *Ibid.*

[9] *Ibid.*

[10] Sibun, *op. cit.*

[11] Clark, *op. cit.*

[12] Marker, *op. cit.*

[13] Clark, *op. cit.*

[14] Sibun, *op. cit.*

[15] Marker, *op. cit.*

[16] *Ibid.*

[17] Clark, *op. cit.*

[18] Sibun, *op. cit.*

[19] Clark, *op. cit.*

[20] *Ibid.*

[21] The gratitude of the authors is extended to Messrs. H. P. Jeffery and N. V. Lough, First Secretaries of the New Zealand Embassy, Washington, D. C., for help in providing both personnel and official forms and copies of rules and regulations of burial and cremation.

[22] Sibun, *op. cit.* For a comprehensive account of early Maori burial customs *see* Elsdon Best, *The Maori: Memoirs of the Polynesian Society,* Vol. V, II, New Zealand, 1924.

[23] *Ibid.*

[24] *Ibid.*

PART FIVE: Europe

Chapter 29

[1] Willmer G. Schmidt, Milwaukee, Wisconsin; unpublished report based on a personal survey of funeral service in Europe and Russia conducted in 1958.

[2] Etienne J. Guerin, "Funeral Customs in Sweden," *Embalmers' Monthly,* Vol. 71, No. 12, December, 1957, p. 17. Mr. Guerin was kind enough to read the chapter in its finished form and to bring up-to-date the statistics of Swedish Burial.

[3] Schmidt, *op. cit.*

[4] Guerin, *op. cit.,* p. 18.

[5] *Ibid.,* Reprinted with permission of *Embalmers' Monthly,* now *National Funeral Service Journal.*

[6] *Ibid.,* See also Willmer Schmidt, *op. cit.*

[7] *Ibid.,* p. 19.

[8] Mrs. Gunnar Holgersson, Holgersson's Press Service, Stockholm, "Funerals and Customs in Sweden," text accompanying 13 pictures of Swedish funerary behavior.

[9] *Ibid.*

[10] *Ibid.*

[11] Guerin, *op. cit.,* p. 19.

[12] Holgersson, *op. cit.*

[13] Guerin, *op. cit.,* p. 18.

[14] Holgersson, *op. cit.*

[15] *Ibid.*

[16] In 1958 there were 24.0 per cent of all burials in Sweden which ended in cremation. The rate of growth has been about

one per cent a year over the past five years. *See* "International Cremation Survey" in the *Funeral Service Journal*, Vol. 74, No. 10, October 15, 1959, p. 459.

[17] Guerin, *op. cit.* p. 18.

[18] *Ibid.*

[19] *Ibid.*, p. 19.

[20] The authors wish also to recognize assistance in securing material for this chapter from Dr. Anna-Maja Nylen, Fil. dr, Keeper, Nordiska museet.

Chapter 30

[1] This account closely follows information supplied to W. M. Lamers by Henrick Muller of Copenhagen, August 24, 1959.

[2] "International Cremation Survey," *Funeral Service Journal*, October 15, 1959, p. 457.

[3] Carlo Christensen, Cultural Attaché, Danish Embassy, Washington, D. C. to William M. Lamers, December 3, 1958.

Chapter 31

[1] Thomas B. Lesure, *The Grand Tour of Europe* (Greenlawn, N. Y.: Harian Publications, 1960), p. 13.

[2] Robert D. Cross, Cultural Officer, American Consulate General, Stuttgart, Germany, personal communication to Robert W. Habenstein, September 11, 1958. *See also* Dr. Jürgen Gaedke's *Handbuch des Friedhofs - und Bestattungsrechts* (Gottingen: Verlag Otto Schwarz & Co., n.d.).

[3] John Plank, "West Berlin Funeral Firm Operates Fifteen Branches," *The American Funeral Director*, December 1959, pp. 39-40.

[4] Willmer Schmidt, unpublished report based on personal survey of funeral procedures in Europe and Russia, 1958.

[5] John Plank, *op. cit.*, p. 40.

[6] John Plank, "West Berlin Funeral Prices Range from $50. to $375." *The American Funeral Director*, January, 1960, p. 56.

[7] John Plank, "West Berlin Funeral Firm Operates Fifteen Branches," *op. cit.*, p. 40.

[8] "Was kann eine Bestattung kosten?" A leaflet listing eight classes of funerals offered by a prominent West Berlin establishment. Courtesy of Hans Neff.

[9] Eldon G. Wolff, "Funeral and Burial Customs of Modern Germany," *The Director*, July, 1950, p. 4. Mr. Wolff is Curator of History, Milwaukee Public Museum.

[10] John Plank, "West Berlin Firm Operates

Fifteen Branches" *op. cit.*, p. 40.

[11] Edward C. Johnson, "Funeral Customs in Europe," a report prepared for the National Funeral Directors Association, 1959.

[12] Charles A. Johnson, *op. cit.*

[13] Wolff, *op. cit.*, p. 4.

[14] Willmer Schmidt, *op. cit.*

[15] Waldemar A. Nitz, Personal communication to Robert W. Habenstein, November 20, 1958.

[16] Wolff, *op. cit.*, p. 4.

[17] Nitz, *op. cit.*

[18] Charles A. Johnson, *op. cit.*

[19] Wolff, *op. cit.*, p. 4.

[20] Charles A. Johnson, *op. cit.*

[21] Nitz, *op. cit.*

[22] Charles A. Johnson, *op. cit.*

[23] *Ibid.*

[24] Wolff, *op. cit.*, p. 4.

[25] Nitz, *op. cit.*

[26] Wolff, *op. cit.*, p. 5.

[27] John Plank, "West Berlin Funeral Firm Operates Fifteen Branches," *op. cit.*, p. 40.

[28] "International Cremation Survey," *Funeral Service Journal*, Vol. 74, October 15, 1959, p. 458.

[29] Robert D. Cross, *op. cit.*

[30] Wolff, *op. cit.*, pp. 4-5.

Chapter 32

[1] Iurii M. Sokolov, *Russian Folklore*, translated by Catherine R. Smith, (New York: The Macmillan Company, 1950), pp. 164 ff.

[2] *Ibid.*, p. 167, *seq.*

[3] *Ibid.*

[4] *Ibid.*, p. 169.

[5] Nevin O. Winter, *The Russian Empire of To-Day and Yesterday* (Boston: L. C. Page & Company, 1913), p. 275.

[6] *Ibid.*, p. 276.

[7] Harry A. Franck, *A Vagabond in Sovietland* (New York: Frederick A. Stokes, 1935), pp. 160 ff.

[8] William L. White, *Land of Milk and Honey* (New York: Harcourt, Brace & Company, 1949). See Chapter 5, "Death," pp. 46-53, of which the present account is an abbreviated version.

[9] Close of White's account.

[10] Personal correspondence from D. Nosov, Manager of the Moscow City Funeral Trust, to Robert W. Habenstein, received April 25, 1960.

[11] *Ibid.*

[12] *Ibid.*

[13] *Ibid.*

[14] *Ibid.*

[15] *Ibid.*

[16] *Ibid.*
[17] *Ibid.*
[18] As reported to the authors by F. W. Patterson, Atlanta, Georgia, and Willmer Schmidt, Milwaukee.
[19] This release appeared in the *Southern Funeral Director*, May, 1959.
[20] Associated Press, December 9, 1958, dateline, Moscow.
[21] Marshall MacDuffie, *The Red Carpet* (New York: W. W. Norton & Co., 1955), p. 152.

Chapter 33

[1] Louise L. Jarecka, *Made in Poland* (New York: Alfred A. Knopf, 1949), p. 38. By permission of the publishers.
[2] Sula Benet, *Song, Dance and Custom of Peasant Poland* (New York: Roy Publishers, 1951), p. 83. This excellent source is used as the basis for the following presentation of Polish peasant funeral customs.
[3] *Ibid.*, p. 84.
[4] *Ibid.*, p. 85, 102, 103.
[5] *Ibid.*, p. 54.
[6] *Ibid.*, p. 234.
[7] *Ibid.*, p. 235.
[8] *Ibid.*, p. 236.
[9] Jarecka, *op. cit.*, p. 29.
[10] Benet, *op. cit.*, pp. 235 ff. Includes all quotations up to previous footnote.
[11] *Ibid.*, p. 238.
[12] *Ibid.*, pp. 238-239.
[13] *Ibid.*, p. 239, *seq.*
[14] Jarecka, *op. cit.*, p. 40.
[15] Benet, *op. cit.*, p. 242.
[16] William John Rose, *Poland: Old and New* (London: G. Bell and Sons, Ltd., 1948), p. 162.
[17] Benet, *op. cit.*, p. 243.
[18] *Ibid.*, p. 244.
[19] Jarecka, *op. cit.*, p. 40.
[20] Benet, *op. cit.*, p. 246.
[21] *Ibid.*, p. 247. By permission of Sula Benet.
[22] The authors are indebted to Mr. Walter S. Dydal, Chicago, for a personal account of funeral procedures in Urban Poland.

Chapter 34

[1] Indiana University, *The Hungarians.* Subcontractor's Monograph, HRAF-5, Indiana-19, prepared for HRAF in 1955. In typescript, p. 115.
[2] Akos Szendrey, "Hungarian Beliefs Concerning Death and Funeral Customs," a manuscript prepared for the authors through the courtesy of the Hungarian Ethnographical Museum at the request of G. Takacs, Jr., Cultural Secretary of the Legation of the Hungarian People's Republic, Washington, D. C. This document provides the basis for the present chapter.
[3] Károly Viski, *Hungarian Peasant Customs* (Budapest: Dr. George Vajna & Co., 1932), p. 174.
[4] *Ibid.*, p. 175; Indiana, *op. cit.*, p. 82, *seq.*
[5] Indiana, *supra.*
[6] Viski, *op. cit.*, p. 176.
[7] *Ibid.*, p. 175; Indiana, *op. cit.*, p. 82.
[8] *Ibid.*, pp. 176-181.

Chapter 35

[1] This account of Rumanian peasant funeral beliefs and practices follows closely material prepared for this work in 1958 and 1959 by Professor Adrian Fochi, Scientific Researcher on the staff of the Rumanian Folklore Institute, Bucharest, Rumania.
[2] Professor Fochi lists the following as supplemental readings and references:
S. Fl. Marian, "Inmormintare la romini" (Rumanian funerary rites), Bucharest, 1892.
T. T. Burada, "Datinile poporului romin la inmormintari" (Burial customs of the Rumanian people) in *Convorbiri Literare*, 15 (1882).
C. Brailoiu, "Despre bocetul de la Dragus (Fagaras)" (On the dirges of the village of Dragus, district of Fagaras). Note sur la plainte funebre du village de Dragus (District de Fagaras, Roumanie), Bucharest, 1932.
C. Brailoiu, "Bocete din Oas" (Dirges from the district of Oas) in *Grai si suflet*, 7 (1937).

Chapter 36

[1] This section is based primarily upon materials prepared specifically for this work by Ing Veda Zagorac, *Director of Information Service*, Belgrade, Yugoslavia.
[2] Dinko A. Tomasic, *Personality and Culture in Eastern European Politics* (New York: George W. Stewart, 1948), p. 29.
[3] Lovett F. Edwards, *Introducing Yugoslavia*, (London: Metheun & Co., Ltd., 1954), 95, *seq.*, 120.
[4] *Ibid.*, p. 225, *seq.*

Chapter 37

[1] Information supplied by Dr. Hans Jerusalem, Secretary General, Staedtische Bestattung, Vienna, Austria in personal com-

munication to Robert W. Habenstein, September 23, 1958.
[2] Information supplied by Willmer Schmidt, American funeral director, in unpublished report to the authors.
[3] Jerusalem, *op. cit.*
[4] *Ibid.*
[5] *Ibid.*
[6] Clarence E. Giese, "Funeral in Vienna," *Our Sunday Visitor*, June 19, 1960.
[7] *Ibid.*
[8] *Ibid.*
[9] *Ibid.*
[10] "International Cremation Survey," *Funeral Service Journal*, October 15, 1959, p. 457.
[11] Jerusalem, *op. cit.*
[12] "Festschrift zur 50-jahr-feier der stadtischen bestattung, Wien," 1952. Translation by Eldon Wolff, Milwaukee Public Museum.

Chapter 38

[1] P. Klingler, official of le Prefecture de la Seine, representing le Directeur du Service des Pompes Funèbres, et des Cemetières Paris, in a document prepared especially for the authors writes "Le service Municipal des Pompes Funèbres de la Ville de Paris, dont la création remonte au 1er Janvier 1906, est organisé conformément à la Loi du 28 Décembre 1904 qui a conféré aux Communes, à titre de service public, le monopole du service extérieur des Pompes funèbres comprenant la fourniture des cercueils et de leurs accessoires: poignées, vis, frettes, ainsi que des corbillards, voitures de deuil, tentures extérieures des maisons mortuaires et tout le personnel nécessaire aux inhumation, exhumations et crémations.

"Antérieurement à cette Loi, le monopole des inhumations appartenait, dans son intégralité, aux Fabriques des Eglises et aux Consistoires, en vertu du décret du 23 Prairial an XLL (13 Juin 1804) qui leur avait attribué le droit, exclusif de faire toutes les fournitures quelconques nécessaires pour les enterrements et pour la décence et la pompe des funérailles. Un décret du 30 Décembre 1809 avait mis, en outre, l'entretien des lieux d'inhumation à la charge des Fabriques."
[2] Frank H. Mason, "Burial System of the French," *The Embalmers Monthly*, Vol. 21, March, 1908, p. 59. Mr. Mason at the time he prepared this article was the American Consul in Paris.
[3] *Ibid.*

[4] Bernard J. Lane, "Funeral Customs in Europe," a talk delivered at the National Selected Morticians 36th Annual Meeting, October 27, 1953, pp. 41-42.
[5] *Ibid.*, p. 38, *seq.*
[6] Edward Jeanmonod, personal correspondence to Robert W. Habenstein, October, 1958. Mr. Jeanmonod is a prominent Parisian funeral director selected by the U. S. Information Service to provide the authors with information on funeral procedures in France. *See also* Lane, *op. cit.*, p. 37, *seq.*
[7] *Ibid.*
[8] *Ibid.*
[9] *Ibid.* *See also* Lane, *op. cit.*, p. 36, *seq.*
[10] Lane, *op. cit.*, p. 46.
[11] Jeanmonod, *op. cit.*
[12] *Tarifs:* Service Municipal des Pompes Funèbres (Paris: Impremerie Administrative Centrale, 1952). A price list for all funeral paraphernalia provided for the various classes of funerals by the municipal mortuary.
[13] Lane, *op. cit.*, p. 46 ff.
[14] *Ibid*, p. 40.
[15] *Tarifs:* Service Municipal des Pompes Funèbres, *op. cit.* The sixth class hardly comprises a funeral. Only transportation from house to a cemetery in Paris or in a commune of the Department of the Seine is provided.
[16] Lane, *op. cit.*, p. 39.
[17] Recognition is here given to Miss Anne-Marie Degory, Special Assistant to Cultural Attache, U. S. Information Service, Centre Cultural Américain, Paris, for her painstaking efforts to gather a variety of information on French customs for the authors.

Chapter 39

[1] Communication of John H. Scanlon, U. S. Information Service, Trieste, Italy, to Robert W. Habenstein, October 14, 1958.
[2] Communication of Charles M. Gerrity, American Consul, American Consulate, Venice, Italy, to Robert W. Habenstein, November 6, 1958.
[3] Cf A. O. Spriggs, "Embalming and Funerals in Italy," *Champion Expanding Encyclopedia of Mortuary Practice*, No. 296, April, 1959.
[4] Vera Gianini, Institute Italiano di Culture, New York, in a communication to Robert W. Habenstein, August 28, 1958.
[5] Gerrity, *op. cit.*
[6] Gianini, *op. cit.*
[7] Gerrity, *op. cit.*
[8] *Ibid.*

[9] *Ibid.*
[10] "International Cremation Survey," *Funeral Service Journal,* October 14, 1959, p. 459.
[11] Sir Henry Thompson, *Modern Cremation, Its History and Practice* (London, 1901).
[12] Gianini, *op. cit.*
[13] The information on "La Misericordia," including the quotation, is from material supplied by the Instituto Italiano di Cultura, 686 Park Avenue, New York City, New York.

Chapter 40

[1] Fernando Alcaniz, proprietor of the Manresa (Barcelona) Empresa de Pompas, personal communication to Robert W. Habenstein, July 7, 1959.
[2] *Ibid.*
[3] Angel M. Varela, Administrative offices of the American Consulate General, Barcelona, Spain, personal communication to Robert W. Habenstein November, 1958.
[4] John Plank, "Funeral Services in Old Madrid," *The American Funeral Director,* June, 1959, p. 40.
[5] Varela, *op. cit.*
[6] *Ibid.*
[7] Alcaniz, *op. cit.*
[8] Plank, *op. cit.,* p. 40.
[9] Varela, *op. cit.*
[10] *Ibid.*
[11] *Ibid.*
[12] Edward C. Johnson, personal report prepared for the National Funeral Directors Association, 1959.
[13] Alcaniz, *op. cit.*
[14] *Ibid.*
[15] *Time,* November 2, 1953, p. 76.
[16] Alcaniz, *op. cit.*
[17] Varela, *op. cit.*
[18] *Ibid.*
[19] John Plank, "Modern Funeral Service in European Countries," *The American Funeral Director,* February, 1959, p. 35.
[20] *Ibid.,* p. 36.
[21] *Ibid.*
[22] *Ibid.*
[23] Edward C. Johnson, *op. cit.*
[24] *Ibid.*
[25] John Plank, "Ornate Funeral Coaches Popular in Portugal," *The American Funeral Director,* April, 1959, p. 46.
[26] *Ibid.*

Chapter 41

[1] Communication of Mr. Sam E. Lesher, Vice Consul, U. S. Consulate General, the Netherlands, Rotterdam, to Robert W. Habenstein, August, 1958.
[2] *Ibid.*
[3] *Ibid.*
[4] Communication of Miss Rita Shea, Chief, European Branch, U. S. Information Center Service, to Robert W. Habenstein, October 20, 1958. Information supplied by Mr. Earle H. Balch, U. S. Cultural Affairs Officer in The Hague, the Netherlands.
[5] *Ibid.*
[6] Lesher, *op. cit.*
[7] *Ibid.*
[8] Balch, *op. cit.*
[9] *Ibid.*
[10] From information supplied by Leland A. Attaffer, American Consul, Antwerp, Belgium. Communication to Robert W. Habenstein, October 1, 1958.
[11] From information supplied September 15, 1958, to Robert W. Habenstein by Miss Rita Shea, *op. cit.*

Chapter 42

[1] J. Kirwan, esq., 21 a Fairview Strand, Dublin, N.E. 5., to W. M. Lamers, Nov. 5, 1958. The information concerning Southern Irish funerals is drawn from the account given by Mr. Kirwan in his correspondence.
[2] The information on Northern Ireland is based on a communication from N. Lancaster, Jr., American Consul General in Belfast, to Robert W. Habenstein, September 10, 1958.

Chapter 43

[1] For a brief orientation to the physical, economic and social characteristics of the English, *see,* for example, *Focus,* American Geographical Society, March 15, 1952.
[2] A. C. A. Hall, English funeral director and embalmer, in personal correspondence to Robert W. Habenstein, July 9, 1959. Mr. Hall's letters form a basis for much of the technical information presented in this chapter.
[3] *Ibid.*
[4] *Ibid.*
[5] *Ibid.*
[6] Leonard Fearnley, "Funeral Procedure in England," *The Director,* Milwaukee, August, 1950, pp. 6-8.
[7] *Ibid.,* p. 6.
[8] Morlais J. Summers, "The Influence of American Funeral Service in the United Kingdom," an address to the National Se-

lected Morticians, September 28, 1954.
[9] Hall, *op. cit.*, July 9, 1959.
[10] *Ibid.*
[11] *Ibid.*
[12] William Scales, "The British Funeral Service," *Mid-Continent Mortician*, March, 1960, p. 9.
[13] "A Statement on the Status of Embalming in Britain," *Funeral Service Journal*, August 15, 1959, p. 359.
[14] *Ibid.*
[15] *Ibid.*
[16] Scales, *op. cit.*, p. 37.
[17] Hall, *op. cit.*, August 23, 1959.
[18] Hall, *op. cit.*, July 9, 1959.
[19] Scales, *op. cit.*, p. 37.
[20] Hall, *op. cit.*, August 23, 1959.
[21] *Ibid.*
[22] Hall, *op. cit.*, August 23, 1959.
[23] *Ibid.*
[24] *Ibid.*
[25] *The Economist*, April 5, 1958, p. 10.
[26] Hall, *op. cit.*, July 9, 1959.
[27] *Ibid.*
[28] *The Economist*, *op. cit.*, p. 9 ff.
[29] Hall, *op. cit.*, July 9, 1959.
[30] *Ibid.*
[31] "International Cremation Survey," *Funeral Service Journal*, October 15, 1959, pp. 457-458.
[32] Ivor Leverton, "The Funeral Director Point of View," *Funeral Service Journal*, August 15, 1959, p. 348.
[33] Scales, *op. cit.*, p. 9.

PART SIX: Latin America

Chapter 44

[1] R. J. Bloomfield, American Consul, Monterrey, personal correspondence to Robert W. Habenstein, October, 1958.
[2] Manuel Barredo, Consular Assistant, American Consulate, Merida, Yucatan, personal correspondence to Robert W. Habenstein, October, 1958.
[3] W. E. Carson, *Mexico, the Wonderland of the South* (New York: The Macmillan Co., 1940), p. 154.
[4] Sr. Benito M. Flores, Funerales Modernos, Monterrey, Mexico, personal correspondence to Robert W. Habenstein, June 13, 1960. Sr. Flores is Secretario de la Association Nacional de Propietarios de Funerarias de la Republica Mexicana, A.C.
[5] Frank G. Carpenter, *Mexico* (New York: Doubleday, Page & Co., 1940), p. 57.
[6] Flores, *op. cit.*
[7] Barredo, *op. cit.*
[8] Flores, *op. cit.*
[9] *Ibid.*
[10] *Ibid.*
[11] W. B. Raymond, "An Experience in Mexico," *Embalmers' Monthly*, April, 1900.
[12] Carpenter, *op. cit.*, p. 58.
[13] Flores, *op. cit.*
[14] *Ibid.*
[15] Wallace Thompson, *The People of Mexico* (New York: Harper & Brothers, 1921), p. 311.
[16] Barredo, *op. cit.*
[17] Carpenter, *op. cit.*, p. 56.
[18] *Ibid.*
[19] As observed by one of the authors in Quetetaro, December 30, 1959. Local informants indicated this was by no means unusual.
[20] Barredo, *op. cit.*
[21] David St. Clair, "South of the Border," *Hobbies*, September, 1957, p. 25.
[22] *Ibid.*
[23] Gertrude Diamant, *The Days of Ofelia* (Boston: Houghton-Mifflin Co., 1942), p. 13.
[24] John W. Wagner, "Undertaking in Mexico," *Embalmers' Monthly*, November, 1900.
[25] Bloomfield, *op. cit.*
[26] Barredo, *op. cit.*
[27] Bloomfield, *op. cit.*
[28] Barredo, *op. cit.*
[29] Robert Redfield and Alfonso Villa, *Chan Kom, A Maya Village* (Washington, D. C.: Carnegie Institution of Washington, 1934). The description of the Chan Kom funeral is taken from this ethnographical study, pp. 198-204.
[30] *Ibid.*, pp. 198-199.
[31] *Ibid.*
[32] *Ibid.*, p. 199.
[33] *Ibid.*
[34] *Ibid.*, p. 160.
[35] *Ibid.*
[36] *Ibid.*
[37] *Preview*, Nov., 1959, p. 1. Editor's Comment.
[38] *Ibid.*
[39] Arthemise Goertz, *South of the Border* (New York: The Macmillan Company, 1940).
[40] *Ibid.*, pp. 421-422.
[41] *Ibid.*

Chapter 45

[1] Information supplied by Alfonzo Alcazar, Jr., Guatemalan funeral director, and Paul

T. Chase, Assistant Cultural Affairs Officer, U. S. Information Service, American Embassy, Guatemala City.

2 *Ibid.*

3 *Ibid.*

4 Charles Wagley, "The Social and Religious Life of a Guatemalan Village," *American Anthropologist, Memoirs,* Vol. 71, No. 4, Part 2. Much of the following description of rural Guatemalan funerals is taken from this monograph.

5 Additional information to this section supplied by Stephan Borhegyi, Director, Milwaukee Public Museum, in personal correspondence to William M. Lamers, June 6, 1960.

6 Wagley, *op. cit.,* p. 47.

7 *Ibid.*

8 *Ibid.*

9 *Ibid.,* p. 48.

10 *Ibid.*

11 *Ibid.*

12 *Ibid.*

13 *Ibid.,* p. 49.

14 *Ibid.*

16 Stephan Borhegyi to William M. Lamers, *op. cit.*

17 Charles M. Wilson, *Central America: Challenge and Opportunity* (New York: Henry Holt and Company, 1941), pp. 44-45.

18 The author's gratitude is extended to Oscar Reyes Duran, "Seisa," San Salvador, who provided them with most of the information on funeral procedures in that city; and to Alvaro L. Sanchez, Salvadorean student at the University of Missouri, for added assistance.

Chapter 46

1 John and Mavis Biesanz, *The People of Panama* (New York: The Columbia University Press, 1955), p. 283. This excellent work, the major author a sociologist, is the primary source for the authors in writing the present chapter.

2 *Ibid.,* p. 284.

3 *Ibid.*

4 *Ibid.*

5 *Ibid.,* p. 285.

6 *Ibid.,* p. 305.

7 Personal communication from Pastor Alvarado to Robert W. Habenstein, December Robert W. Habenstein, July 6, 1959.

10 John and Mavis Biesanz, *op. cit.,* pp. 306-308.

9 Personal communication from Pastor Alvarado, to Robert W. Habenstein, December

ber 7, 1959.

10 John and Mavis Biesanz, *op. cit.,* p. 301-308.

11 *Ibid.,* quoted on page 307.

12 *Ibid.*

13 *Ibid.,* p. 308.

14 *Ibid.*

15 *Ibid.*

16 *Ibid.,* p. 307.

17 John and Mavis Biesanz, *The People of Panama* (New York; Columbia University Press, 1955), p. 7. A substantial body of literature on the Cunas exists. A good introduction is found in Leon S. DeSmidt's *Among the San Blas Indians of Panama,* Troy, 1948.

18 Fred McKim, "San Blas: An account of the Cuna Indians of Panama," Etnologiska Studies, Vol. 15, Goteborg, 1947, p. 94.

19 *Ibid.,* p. 94.

20 DeSmidt, p. 7.

21 Herbert W. Krieger, "Material Culture of the People of Southeastern Panama," Smithsonian Institution, Bulletin 134. Washington, 1926, p. 88.

22 *Ibid.*

23 Eleanor T. Bell, "The Republic of Panama and its People, with Special Reference to the Indians." Annual Report of the Board of Regents of the Smithsonian Institution for 1909, Washington, 1910, p. 630.

24 McKim, *op. cit.,* p. 94.

25 Frances Densmore, "Music of Tule Indians of Panama." Smithsonian Miscellaneous Collections, Vol. 77, No. 11. Washington, 1926, p. 3.

26 McKim, *op. cit.,* p. 94.

27 DeSmidt, *op. cit.,* pp. 85-87.

28 Donald S. Marshall, *Cuna Folk,* unpublished m.s. presented to Dept. of Anthropology of Harvard University, 1950, p. 225.

29 David B. Stout, "San Blas Cuna Acculturation: An Introduction." Viking Fund Publications in Anthropology, No. IX, New York, 1947, p. 39.

30 McKim, *op. cit.,* p. 95.

31 *Ibid.,* p. 95, *seq.,* 155.

32 Stout, *op. cit.,* p. 39, *seq.*

33 McKim, *op. cit.,* p. 97.

34 *Ibid.*

35 DeSmidt, *op. cit.,* p. 89

36 Henry Wassén, "Contributions to Cuna Ethnography: Results of Expedition to Panama and Colombia in 1947." Etnologiska Studies, Vol. 16, pp. 38-40.

37 Marshall, *op. cit.,* p. 253.

38 Krieger, *op. cit.,* p. 89.

39 Stout, *op. cit.,* p. 98.

Chapter 47

[1] Elman R. Service, *A Profile of Primitive Culture* (New York: Harper & Brothers, 1958), pp. 182-185, *passim*.
[2] Rafael Karsten, *Headhunters of Western Amazonas: The Life and Culture of the Jivaro Indians of Eastern Ecuador and Peru* (Helsinki: Societas Scientiarum Fennica, Commontationes Humanarum Litterarum, Vol. 8, No. 1, 1935).
[3] George M. Dyott, *On the Trail of the Unknown in the Wilds of Ecuador and the Amazon* (London: Thornton Butterworth, Ltd. 1926), p. 175, *seq.*
[4] Karsten, *op. cit.*, p. 457, *seq.*
[5] *Ibid.*, p. 466.
[6] Juan Vigna, "Bosquejo Sobre los Indios Shuaras and Jivaros." *American Indigena*, Vol. 5, 1945, p. 48. Translator Elinor Stewart.
[7] Karsten, *op. cit.*, p. 469.
[8] *Ibid.*, p. 474.
[9] *Ibid.*, p. 468.
[10] Matthew W. Stirling, Bureau of American Ethnology, Bulletin 117: *Historical and Ethnographical material on the Jivaro Indians.* (Washington: Smithsonian Institution, 1938), p. 175.
[11] Karsten, *op. cit.*, p. 474, *seq.*
[12] *Ibid.*, pp. 474-476.
[13] *Ibid.*, p. 459.
[14] Stirling, *op. cit.*, p. 112, *seq.*
[15] Vigna, *op. cit.*, p. 48, *seq.*
[16] Paul Rivet, "Les Indians Jivaro: Etude Géographique, historique et ethnographique." *L'Anthropologie* (Paris: Masson et Cie, 1907), Vol. 18, p. 610, *seq.* Translator: Matthew Stirling.
[17] Stirling, *op. cit.*, p. 113.
[18] Karsten, *op. cit.*, p. 456.
[19] *Ibid.*, p. 460.
[20] Stirling, *op. cit.*, p. 114, *seq.*
[21] Karsten, *op. cit.*, p. 292.
[22] *Ibid.*, p. 292, *seq.*
[23] Rivet, *op. cit.*, p. 73.
[24] Karsten, *op. cit.*, p. 458, *seq.*
[25] Günter Tessman, *Die Indianer Nordost-Perus.* (Hamburg: Friederechsen, de Oruyter und. Co. 1930), p. 362.
[26] Karsten, *op. cit.*, pp. 461-463.

Chapter 48

[1] Elsie Worthington (Clews) Parsons, *Peguche, Canton of Otavalo, Province of Imbabura, Ecuador: A Study of Andean Indians* (Chicago: The University of Chicago Press, 1945), pp. 1, 77 ff.
[2] *Ibid.*, p. 78.

[3] *Ibid.*, p. 79.
[4] *Ibid.*, p. 80.
[5] *Ibid.*
[6] *Ibid.*, pp. 199 ff.
[7] *Ibid.*, p. 200, *seq.*
[8] *Ibid.*, p. 202, 203, *seq.*
[9] *Ibid.*, pp. 96-97.
[10] *Ibid.*

Chapter 49

[1] Jules Henry, *Jungle People:* A. Kaingáng Tribe of the Highlands of Brazil (New York: J. J. Augustin Publishers, 1941), p. xv. Henry spent the period from December, 1932 to January, 1934 among the Kaingáng, and his work is the most definitive on the tribe. This section as subsequent footnotes indicate is based almost *in toto* on his account.
[2] Ruth Benedict makes this assessment in her foreword to Henry's book, p. xi.
[3] *Ibid.*, p. 181.
[4] *Ibid.*, p. 85.
[5] *Ibid.*, p. 65.
[6] *Ibid.*, p. 181, *seq.*
[7] *Ibid.*, p. 182.
[8] *Ibid.*, p. 185, *seq.*
[9] *Ibid.*, p. 186.
[10] *Ibid.*, p. 189. Quoted with permission of the author and J. J. Augustin Publishers.
[11] *Ibid.*, p. 183, *seq.*
[12] *Ibid.*, p. 184.
[13] Alfred Métraux, *"The Kaingáng"* in Handbook of South American Indians, Julian H. Steward, ed. Vol. 1, p. 465.

Chapter 50

[1] Authors' thanks for information on funeral procedures in Brazil are extended to Angelo Osorio, Brazilian Consulate, Chicago; and to Wilson Velloso, Press Attaché, Brazilian Embassy, Washington, D. C.
[2] Thomas Lynn Smith, *Brazil: People and Institutions* (Baton Rouge: Louisiana State University Press, 1954), p. 161.
[3] *Ibid.*
[4] Harry W. Hutchinson, *Village and Plantation Life in Northwestern Brazil* (Seattle: The University of Washington Press, 1957).
[5] Julian H. Steward and Louis Faron, *Native Peoples of South America* (New York: McGraw-Hill Book Co., 1959), p. 333.
[6] Material for this section on Paraguayan funeral procedures was kindly forwarded by Francisco Crichigno, "La Moderna,"

Asunción, in personal correspondence to Robert W. Habenstein, December 21, 1959.

PART SEVEN: Canada and the United States

Chapter 51

[1] Primary sources for the materials presented in this section on the Copper Eskimos are: Diamond Jenness, *The Life of the Copper Eskimos,* Report of the Canadian Arctic Expedition, 1913-18, Vol. 12, (Ottawa: F. A. Acland, 1922) and Knud Rasmussen, *Intellectual Culture of the Eskimos,* Report of the Fifth Thule Expedition, 1921-24, Vol. 9 (Copenhagen, 1932). Authors' thanks are extended to H. J. Gilligan for editorial assistance in manuscript preparation.

Chapter 52

[1] Materials in this chapter were organized and written in manuscript by Paul R. Keenan, Director, Department of Mortuary Science, University of Kansas Medical Center, and appear in substantially the same form as originally written. Authors' thanks are tendered to the following who rendered either information or valuable criticism: Ruth S. Anderson, U. S. Vice Consul, Vancouver, B. C.; Keith A. Campbell, Ottawa, Ont.; Loren Carroll, U. S. Consul General, Quebec, P. Q.; Robert L. Fulton; A. G. Heltberg, U. S. Consul, St. John, New Brunswick; P. C. Hutton, U. S. Consul General, Winnipeg, Manitoba; Murray L. Jacques; Jean L. King, Office of the U. S. Consul General, St. John's, Newfoundland; P. Wesley Kriebel, Second Secretary of the U. S. Embassy, Ottawa, Ont.; Paul T. Meyer, U. S. Consul General, Halifax, Nova Scotia; James O'Hagan; John Snow; and Donald B. Steenson.

Chapter 53

Santee Sioux

[1] Field work in Manitoba was done at Sioux Village Reserve, Portage la Prairie and Oak River Reserve, Griswold by Wilson D. Wallis in 1914, and in 1951 and 1952 with Ruth S. Wallis. Short studies were also made at Morton, Granite Falls, and Prairie Island, Minnesota. *See* Wilson D. Wallis, *The Canadian Dakota,* Ameri-

can Museum of Natural History, Anthropological Papers, 41, Part I, pp. 1-225, 1947; *also* H. C. Yarrow, "A Further Contribution to the Study of the Mortuary Customs of the American Indians," *Annual Report* of the Bureau of American Ethnology, Vol. I, pp. 87-203, 1879-1880.

Salish

[1] Harry E. Stafford, *The Early Inhabitants of the Americas* (New York: Vantage Press, Inc., 1959), p. 252.
[2] James A. Teit, "The Salishan Tribes of the Western Plateau," *Forty-fifth Annual Report of the Bureau of American Ethnology to the Smithsonian Institution,* 1927-1928 (Washington, D. C.: U. S. Government Printing Office, 1930), p. 176.
[3] *Ibid.,* p. 383.
[4] Verne F. Ray, *The Sanpoil and Nespelem: Salishan Peoples of Northeastern Washington,* University of Washington Publications in Anthropology. Vol. 5, December 1932 (Seattle: University of Washington Press, 1935), p. 174.
[5] *Ibid.,* pp. 148-150.
[6] *Ibid.*
[7] *Ibid.*
[8] Teit, *op. cit.,* pp. 174-175.
[9] Ray, *op. cit.,* p. 150.
[10] Teit, *op. cit.,* p. 382, *seq.*
[11] *Ibid.,* p. 127.
[12] *Ibid.,* p. 174.
[13] *Ibid.,* p. 382, *seq.*
[14] Ray, *op. cit.,* p. 151.
[15] Teit, *op. cit.,* p. 175.
[16] Ray, *op. cit.,* p. 152.
[17] Teit, *op. cit.,* p. 175.
[18] Ray, *op. cit.,* p. 153.
[19] *Ibid.,* p. 154.
[20] Teit, *op. cit.,* p. 175.

Navaho

[1] Harry E. Stafford, *The Early Inhabitants of the Americas* (New York: Vantage Press, Inc., 1959), p. 234 ff.
[2] Irwin T. Sanders, ed., *Societies Around the World,* 2 Vols. (New York: The Dryden Press, 1953), Vol. I, p. 197.
[3] Clyde K. Kluckhohn, "Conceptions of Death Among the Southwestern Indians," Ingersoll Lecture on the Immortality of Man, delivered in Andover Chapel, April 6, 1948. Reproduced as a Divinity School Bulletin, Harvard University, Cambridge, Massachusetts, p. 8.
[4] Berard Haile, *Origin Legend of the Navaho Enemy Way* (New Haven: Yale Uni-

versity Press, 1938), p. 49.
[5] Gladys A. Reichard, *Social Life of the Navajo Indians* (New York: Columbia University Press, 1928), p. 151.
[6] *Ibid.*, pp. 142-143.
[7] *Ibid.*
[8] Leland C. Wyman, W. W. Hill, and Iva Osanai, *Navajo Eschatology*. University of New Mexico Bulletin, Vol. 4, No. 1. New Mexico, 1942, pp. 30-31.
[9] *Ibid.*
[10] Kluckhohn, *op. cit.*, p. 11.
[11] *Ibid.*

Chapter 54

Latter-Day Saints

[1] Gratitude of the authors is extended to the following for their help in the preparation of the materials on funeral procedures of the Latter-Day Saints: J. C. and Grace Sandberg, Vernon C. Soffee, Ralph Wing, and Joseph Fielding Smith, President-elect of the Church of Jesus Christ of Latter-Day Saints.

Amish

[1] John A. Hostetler, *Mennonite Life* (Scottdale, Pennsylvania: Herald Press, 1959), p. 5.
[2] *Ibid.*, pp. 9-10.
[3] John A. Hostetler, *Amish Life* (Scottdale, Pennsylvania: Herald Press, 1959), p. 5.
[4] *Ibid.*, pp. 5-7.
[5] *American Funeral Director*, August, 1957, p. 30.
[6] Hostetler, *Amish Life*, pp. 27-30.
[7] Elmer Smith, *The Amish People* (Exposition Press, 1958), p. 118, *seq.*
[8] *Ibid.*, p. 116.
[9] Charles S. Rice and Roland C. Steinmetz, *The Amish Year* (New Brunswick, New Jersey: Rutgers University Press, 1956), p. 77.
[10] Smith, *op. cit.*, p. 118.
[11] *American Funeral Director*, *op. cit.*, p. 31.
[12] *Ibid.*, p. 30.
[13] *Ibid.*
[14] Hostetler, *Amish Life*, p. 26.
[15] Rice and Steinmetz, *op. cit.*, p. 82.
[16] *American Funeral Director*, *op. cit.*, p. 30, *seq.*
[17] Rice and Steinmetz, *op. cit.*, p. 87.
[18] Smith, *op. cit.*, pp. 118, 119.
[19] Rhodona Long, "A Wisconsin Amish Farm Community," *Thirtieth Star*, May, 1959, p. 4.

Gypsies

[1] Joseph Mitchell, "The Beautiful Flower," *The New Yorker*, June 3, 1955, pp. 39-89. In this lengthy article the author reports the observations of former New York City Police Captain, Pickpocket and Confidence Squad, Daniel J. Campion, an outstanding police authority on the gypsies in the United States. *See also* Charles G. Leland, *The Gypsies* (New York: Houghton-Mifflin Company, 1924) and Konrad Bercovici, *The Story of the Gypsies* (New York: Cosmopolitan Book Corporation, 1928).
[2] Mitchell, *op. cit.*, p. 60, *seq.*
[3] *Ibid.*, p. 54, *seq.*
[4] *Ibid.*, p. 75.
[5] *Ibid.*, p. 72.
[6] A considerable amount of information on the burial customs of American gypsies was given to one of the authors by Floyd Hallowell, Chicago funeral director who has handled well over fifty gypsy funerals.
[7] "Funeral of Gypsy Princess Held in Rapid City," Walnut, Illinois, *Leader*, August 20, 1954.
[8] *Ibid.*
[9] Mitchell, *op. cit.*, p. 75.
[10] *Ibid.*, p. 76.
[11] *Ibid.*, p. 72.

Chapter 55

[1] Some examination of the roots of American funeral practices is made in *The History of American Funeral Directing* by Robert W. Habenstein and William M. Lamers (Milwaukee: Bulfin Printers, 1955).
[2] William Caudill, "Cultural Perspectives on Stress," *Symposium on Stress* (Washington, D. C., Army Medical Service Graduate School, Walter Reed Medical Center, March 17, 1953), p. 195 ff.
[3] *Ibid. See also* Chapter 5, "American Colonial Funeral Behavior" in Habenstein and Lamers, *op. cit.*, pp. 195-223.
[4] Robert W. Habenstein, "The American Funeral Director: A Study in the Sociology of Work." Unpublished dissertation, Department of Sociology, University of Chicago, 1954.
[5] Paul E. Irion, *The Funeral and the Mourners* (New York: Abingdon Press, 1954), p. 111.
[6] Information supplied by the National Funeral Directors Association, Milwaukee, August 6, 1960.
[7] The composition of the Board includes three representatives from the Conference

of Funeral Service Examining Boards, the National Funeral Directors Association, and one each from the three associations representing the mortuary schools and colleges.

[8] The journals servicing the funeral service field are: *The American Funeral Director, Casket and Sunnyside, Funeral Director's Review, The Mid-Continent Mortician, Morticians of the Southwest, Mortuary Management, National Funeral Service Journal, Northeast Funeral Director,* and *The Southern Funeral Director.*

[9] Information supplied by the American Cemetery Association and the National Association of Cemeteries, August, 1960.

[10] Information supplied by the Cremation Association of America, August, 1960.

[11] *Ibid.*

[12] Eugene F. Foran, "Funeral Service Facts and Figures," National Funeral Directors Association, Milwaukee, 1960.

Conclusion

[1] Robert W. Habenstein and William M. Lamers, *The History of American Funeral Directing* (Milwaukee: Bulfin Printers, 1955).

[2] For example, Effie Bendann, *Death Customs: An Analytical Study of Burial Rites* (New York: Alfred A. Knopf, 1930).

[3] Herman Feifel, Editor, *The Meaning of Death* (New York: McGraw-Hill Book Company, Inc., 1959). *See also, Explorations in Psychiatry,* edited by Alexander H. Leighton, John A. Clausen, and Robert N. Wilson (New York: Basic Books, Inc., 1957).

Historical Sketches of State
Funeral Director Associations

ALABAMA

The first meeting of the funeral directors of Alabama was called by ten men of the profession. The meeting was held in May, 1885 and delegates from all over the state were present along with several men from the state of Florida. The assembly was addressed by Mayor Lane of Birmingham, the host city, after which J. W. Diamond of Birmingham was elected honorary member, a committee was chosen to draft a constitution, and Dr. Rush of the *Christian Advocate* addressed the group. The following men served the new association as its first officers: *President*, E. Erswell, Birmingham; *Vice Presidents*, S. B. Hutchinson, Pensacola, Florida, J. S. Hanley, Tuscaloosa, C. H. Chandler, Montgomery; *Secretary*, W. S. Standifer, Gadsden; and *Treasurer*, James McKibbin, Oxford.

The new association worked hard at organization, and through members of the group was successful in getting the state legislature in 1894 to enact a law regulating the practice of embalming in Alabama, the second such law in the nation. At the end of its first five years of existence the association was able to report at the NFDA convention in Omaha, Neb. (1890): "We now have every legitimate undertaker in the state on our roll, and in good standing."

In 1892 Alabama funeral directors presented a bill to the legislature "for the protection of funeral directors." Although this bill failed of passage the first few times it was presented, a similar bill was finally enacted and made law in 1895. Percy B. Dixon reported this success to the convention of the National Funeral Directors Association at its convention in Atlanta in 1895 when he made the following speech: ". . . I am pleased to tell you that what Col. Roche then promised you he would do he has done and most well—he has placed upon the statute books of Alabama a law which recognizes us as a profession, one that has given us an equal recognition with the M.D.'s, he has placed us before the public at large where we rightly belong. And as President of this board I have had a most pleasant duty to perform in examining for license two M.D.'s, one of which is Prof. of Anatomy in our State Medical College and who today is a licensed embalmer." By this law a State Board of Examiners consisting of five licensed embalmers was to be appointed by the governor.

In the same year the Alabama association disbanded and almost

793

immediately reorganized. Each application for membership in the new association, called The Alabama Funeral Directors and Embalmers Association, had from that time to be accompanied by the applicant's license. There were 22 charter members of the reorganized group.

The chief interests of the association near the turn of the century were education, improvement of the existing law, adoption of a uniform transit permit, and means of increasing membership.

Many men of the Alabama association have been honored by their local governments, but one man, Percy B. Dixon, was singularly honored as a funeral director by being elected president of the National Funeral Directors Association in 1900 and of the state association in 1904.

Growth of the association was slow and rather unsteady. Alabama did not report to the NFDA conventions after 1914 and presumably was not so active an organization as it had been before this date.

In 1924 once more 28 funeral directors met in Birmingham and reorganized the Alabama Funeral Directors Association, thus supplanting the old state body, remnants of which had met from time to time in the state since 1914. The organization voted unanimously to apply to NFDA for a charter. Officers elected at this time were: *President,* E. J. Duncan, Alexander City; *First Vice President,* O. L. McLaughlin, Carbon Hill; *Second Vice President,* Thomas Roche, Mobile; *Secretary-Treasurer,* F. H. Sorrow, Atlanta.

In 1926 the Alabama association inaugurated a program of holding joint meetings with two sister states, Georgia and Tennessee. Each state held its separate meeting in a morning session for purposes of enacting purely state business and electing officers. Following these meetings, joint sessions were held, and educational lectures and demonstrations were given the combined groups.

Subsequently, the association has enjoyed growth and maturity. Membership over the past years has risen steadily, and in 1960 the number of members reached the all-time high of 85.

ASSOCIATION PRESIDENTS: 1885-86, Edward Erswell, *Birmingham;* 1887-94, Thomas T. Roche, *Mobile;* 1895-97, L. W. Kobb, *Ozark;* 1898-99, Edward Erswell, *Birmingham;* 1900, Geo. A. Thomas, *Montgomery;* 1901, Sam Foley, *Pratt City;* 1902, L. M. Cooper, *Opelika;* 1903, R. V. Taylor, *Birmingham;* 1904, Percy B. Dixon, *Mobile;* 1905, E. T. Shaw, *Birmingham;* 1906, J. M. Rogers, *Tuscaloosa;* 1907, James H. Hutchinson, *Mobile;* 1908, Oscar A. DuPree, *Attalla;* 1909, T. F. Leake, Jr., *Montgomery;* 1910 D. A. Echols, *Ensley;* 1911, W. C. Johns, *Birmingham;* 1912, A. W. Woodlif, *Gadsden;* 1913, T. F. Proctor, *Tuskegee;* 1914, A. B. Legg, *Jasper;* 1915, Horace E. Shaw, *Birmingham;* 1916, Fred O. Moore, *Montgomery;* 1917, W. L. Howard, *Syacauga;* 1918, J. W. Grossley, *Opelika;* 1919, A. G. Godwin, *Dothan;* 1921, Peter Burke, *Mobile;* 1924-25, E. J. Duncan, *Alexander City;* 1926, O. L. McLaughlin, *Carbon Hill;* 1927, T. S. Roche, *Mobile;* 1928-30, W. C. Vice, *Birmingham;* 1931-32, James J. Duffy, *Mobile;* 1933, J. Lee Bradley, *Gadsden;* 1934, R. W. Williams, *Opelika;* 1935-36, M. S. Brislin, *Selma;* 1937, Lee Headley, *Gadsden;* 1938, R. W. Williams, *Opelika;*

1939, Herbert Farish, *Huntsville;* 1940, K. L. Forrester, *Dothan;* 1941, R. W. Williamson, *Opelika;* 1942-43, W. T. Boyd, *Gadsden;* 1944-45, W. F. Leak, *Montgomery;* 1946-47, James J. Duffy, *Mobile;* 1948, W. Taylor Boyd, *Gadsden;* 1949, T. Flint Gray, *Anniston;* 1950, Joe W. Kilgore, *Pell City;* 1951, Homer E. McGraw, *Russellville;* 1952, James L. Mays, *Tuscumbia;* 1953, William L. Radney, *Alexander City;* 1954, Clinton G. Mann, *Tallassee;* 1955, Julian Lackey, *Birmingham;* 1956, Robert Collier, *Gadsden;* 1957, Clyde Blakely, *Lanett;* 1958, Oscar L. Pitman, *Geneva;* 1959, Bill R. Brooks, *Montgomery;* 1960, Marshall P. Craver, Jr., *Brewton.*

ARIZONA
Informant: Verna E. Yocum

The Arizona Funeral Directors' Association was organized November 15, 1904—eight years before the territory was admitted to statehood. More than half the funeral directors in the area attended the organizational meeting at which time a constitution and by-laws were adopted and officers elected including: *President,* H. M. Maus, Prescott; *Vice President,* J. T. Whitney, Phoenix; *Secretary,* S. L. Easterling, Phoenix. No treasurer was reported for the first year. Perhaps no dues had as yet been established and there seemed to be no immediate need for one.

Legislation was, from the early years, of great interest to the members of the association in Arizona. As early as 1905 an attempt was made by the association to bring about the passage of legislation regulating the practice of funeral directing and embalming in the territory. Although the various associa-

tion committees worked hard, it was not until 1945 that any legislation was passed governing the profession of funeral directing in the state. Until this time, the profession, through the state organization, directed and attempted to regulate itself by setting down rules and regulations which funeral directors and embalmers agreed to abide by. On January 8, 1945, the association presented a bill, which incorporated the most workable of the then existent rules of the organization, to the convening state legislature. At this time the legislative body considered the proposals and enacted the first law in the state governing funeral directing and embalming. This law set up "The Arizona State Board of Funeral Directors and Embalmers" —a body whose primary duty was to license and control the profession in Arizona.

Because in the early days the territory was not heavily populated, the organization remained a small group, hindered by poor transportation, remoteness of location, and economic difficulties. Many years— especially early in the century—the association did not even send a delegate to the national convention. In recent times these difficulties have been overcome and presently the Arizona Funeral Directors' Association is a growing association in a rapidly growing, progressive state.

As late as 1921 there were only 38 funeral directors in the entire state, 29 of whom had already joined the association. This number probably represents one of the better membership rosters, percentagewise, of any state in the union, and Arizona continues as an organization to be quite representative of

795

the profession within its boundaries.

In 1956 the statutes of the state governing the practice of funeral directing and embalming were revised. Currently the association is concerned with the "Pre-need Law." The recent opinion delivered by the Attorney General of the state concerning the pre-need contract has created great interest and controversey in the state among the members of the profession.

The Arizona Funeral Directors Association has attempted to keep members informed on the issue by sending explanatory releases from the office of the secretary to the membership. In 1958 the organization incorporated for the first time and is presently known as The Arizona Funeral Directors Association, Inc. The present executive secretary of the Arizona association is Verna E. Yocum.

Association Presidents: 1905-06, H. M. Maus, *Prescott;* 1907-08, J. I. Reilly, *Tucson;* 1909-10, J. T. Whitney, *Phoenix;* 1912-13, John I. Reilly, *Tucson;* 1914-15, Peter L. Hutton, *Winkleman;* 1916, Edgar Whipple, *Flagstaff;* 1917-20, D. O. Martin, *Florence;* 1921, C. R. Van Marter, *Kingman;* 1922-23, F. T. Whitney, *Phoenix;* 1924-25, John I. Reilly, *Tucson;* 1926-29, M. L. Gibbons, *Mesa;* 1930, J. T. Whitney, *Phoenix;* 1931, J. T. Whitney, *Phoenix;* 1932, A. Lee Moore, *Phoenix;* 1933-34, Lester Ruffner, *Prescott;* 1935, Mrs. H. M. Parker, *Tucson;* 1936-37, George McMillan, *Jerome;* 1938-40, J. S. Brazill, *Glendale;* 1942-45, W. L. Murphy, *Phoenix;* 1946-47, Chris Reilly, *Tucson;* 1948, Mrs. Rita G. Miles, *Miami;* 1949-50, Frank B. Carroon, *Nogales;* 1951,

C. Stanley Clegg, *Phoenix;* 1952, Lester Ruffner, Jr., *Prescott;* 1953, Oliver Maud, *Casa Grande;* 1954, Charles Whitney, *Glendale;* 1955-56, Hugh Dugan, Jr., *Bisbee;* 1957, Dalton Cole, *Coolidge;* 1958, Chester L. Hansen, *Sunnyslope;* 1959-60, Frank S. Bueler, *Chandler.*

ARKANSAS

Informant: James A. Henry

After two years of planning and discussion in meetings throughout the state, the Arkansas Funeral Directors Association came into being in the year 1900. The organization was later incorporated in the State of Arkansas. Signers of the articles of incorporation included: A. L. Stevens, Forest City; Harry Holderness, Pine Bluff; Ralph Robinson, Pine Bluff; C. A. Roth, Little Rock; R. T. Owens, North Little Rock; John Healey, Little Rock; R. F. Drummond, Little Rock; J. A. Pence, Conway; Paul Carruth, Hot Springs; A. L. Crouch, Sr., Batesville.

The Arkansas association began work early in its history on a strong legislative program. All the early reports to the meetings of the National Funeral Directors Association indicate that the pioneers in Arkansas worked hard to establish a State Board of Examiners for the licensing of embalmers. In 1910 the Arkansas association was instrumental in getting legislation passed which set up a Bureau of Vital Statistics in the State Board of Health. This bureau established a complete file by counties of the state for the keeping of records and adopted the standard rules then in effect in other progressive states for the shipping of bodies. It was in this year too that a bill, passed in 1909, to set up a board for the licensing of embalmers became law in the state. At the 1914 convention of the National Funeral Directors Association, Arkansas reported on the success of this bill in practice. "There are 157 undertakers who have complied with the Embalmers' Law of the state, 64 of whom are affiliated with this national body." Before the passage of this law the funeral directors themselves, with the help of the State Board of Health, had carried out the licensing function. However, it was not until 1953 that the state association sponsored and aided in passing through the legislature a law requiring funeral directors and their apprentices to be licensed.

The association has held meetings through the years in Hot Springs, Rogers, Fort Smith, Harrison, Texarkana, Pine Bluff, and Little Rock. Since 1927, the annual meetings have had exhibits of funeral merchandise as well as automobiles and ambulances displayed during these sessions. Because of this phase of the conventions, the committee has found it necessary to schedule the meetings regularly in Little Rock, a centrally located city where there is sufficient hotel and exhibit space for a convention of this magnitude. At convention time the election and installation of officers takes place, the installation ceremony usually occurring at a banquet the second night of the convention.

From the time of the very first meetings of the association a great interest in educational matters has been exhibited by the membership. A regular feature of the early conventions was a speaker of note who gave instructional and educational lectures and demonstrations to the assembled membership. The convention report of 1910 also stated that the association had been successful in " . . . the establishment of a school of embalming at Little Rock, under the able supervision of Dr. Hoffman. . . . " The course for embalmers in this school was of six weeks' duration and marked a start in the direction of more advanced education now required in the state by law.

Prior to World War II, the state was divided into four districts each having its own officers and sending delegates to report at state meetings. Membership now comprises about 90 per cent of the funeral directors active in the state, and for this reason the re-division of the state into four districts is again being considered.

Arkansas has been interested in civic and patriotic projects throughout the state and recently has sponsored both blood and skin banks. The association also has representatives on the state civil defense board. As late as 1959 the membership helped sponsor a bill in the legislature which permitted unclaimed bodies to be turned over to medical and anatomical classes for educational purposes. This same law also permitted persons to will usable sections of their own anatomies to institutions for grafting purposes.

Recent educational programs of the Arkansas association include a clinic every two years with outstanding leaders of the field as speakers. Both embalmers and funeral directors are required to attend these clinics at least every other year. The clinics which have been held in Little Rock are of two day duration at which time every phase of funeral service is discussed and the most modern methods and techniques are demonstrated.

797

Arkansas has sent its share of members to office in national organizations. Richard A. Jones of Crosett was a district governor of NFDA from 1945 to 1948. In 1959 Rufus Herndon of Hope was elected president of the National Conference of Funeral Service Examining Boards, of which he had been secretary in 1958. Another name important in state association work is that of Clarence A. Roth of Little Rock who was elected president of NFDA in 1921 and for 30 consecutive years prior to 1956 was state association secretary.

ASSOCIATION PRESIDENTS: 1900, A. L. Stevens, *Forrest City;* 1901, B. Gross, *Hot Springs;* 1902, Frank J. Cook, *Little Rock;* 1903-04, Harry I. Holderness, *Pine Bluff;* 1905, Dennis Keeshan, *Helena;* 1906, Ralph Robinson, *Pine Bluff;* 1907, Jesse G. Putman, Sr., *Fort Smith;* 1908-09, W. F. Meisner, *Texarkana;* 1910, R. F. Drummond, *Little Rock;* 1911, E. B. McCullough, *Monticello;* 1912-13, M. Lee Yount, *Lonoke;* 1914-15, Alva C. Harris, *Arkadelphia;* 1916, C. Albert Roth, *Little Rock;* 1917, Oscar E. Fentress, *Fort Smith;* 1918, Hugh B. Benton, *Fordyce;* 1919, John J. Healey, *Little Rock;* 1920, George R. Brenner, *Hot Springs;* 1921, Ben V. Hunter, *Oklahoma City;* 1922, Walter E. Stevens, Jr., *Forrest City;* 1923, W. B. Langford, *Jonesboro;* 1924, W. Grover Johnson, *Walnut Ridge;* 1925, A. D. Callison, *Rogers;* 1926-27, Samuel A. Roberts, *Booneville;* 1928, Miles D. Prator, *Texarkana;* 1929, Rufus V. Herndon, *Hope;* 1930, Jesse G. Putman, Jr., *Fort Smith;* 1931, C. B. Murry, *Arkadelphia;* 1932, Wm. H. Stovall, *Blytheville;* 1933, Allie L. Crouch, Jr., *Batesville;* 1934, Murphy Jones,

Hamburg; 1935, W. H. Irby, *Rector;* 1936, B. C. McConnell, *Hartford;* 1937, A. C. Christeson, *Harrison;* 1938, William M. Hardwicke, *Clarksville;* 1939, Delmar D. Edwards, *Fort Smith;* 1940, Herman G. McNabb, *Pocahontas;* 1941, C. Frank Leach, *Newport;* 1942, Pat Keeshan, *Helena;* 1943-45, Turner T. Doolin, *Conway;* 1946, Jesse B. Gregg, *Jonesboro;* 1947, James P. Sims, *Benton;* 1948, E. M. Holt, *Blytheville;* 1949, Avery Shinn, *Russellville;* 1950, Rufus V. Herndon, Jr., *Hope;* 1951, Lloyd L. Langford, *Jonesboro;* 1952, Raymond E. Stephenson, *Monticello;* 1953, Verlyn Heath, *Paragould;* 1954, William Y. Crane, *Fort Smith;* 1955, Paul Y. Griffin, Sr., *Little Rock;* 1956, J. D. Edwards, *Fort Smith;* 1957, Clifford McNabb, *Pocahontas;* 1958, Robert D. Harris, *Morrilton;* 1959, John Malaby, *Texarkana;* 1960, Charles Nelson, *Berryville.*

CALIFORNIA
Informant: George Williams

The history of the California Funeral Directors Association is as full of up's and down's as the history of the State itself. About 1880 the funeral directors of the Golden State were attempting to organize and, in 1882, 24 firms signed the Constitution and By-Laws and met at their first convention.

This was only one of many starts of the association. In October of 1886 the California group was strong enough to send C. S. Wright of San Francisco to the National Funeral Directors Association convention in Cleveland, Ohio, to give a report on the association in California.

At this stage of development we find that many of the problems fac-

798

ing the funeral directors of California in the 1880's were parallel to those confronting the profession in 1960.

In 1890 it appeared that the association's strength in California was beginning to form, and 130 firms were represented at that year's convention.

In 1891, J. L. Halsted of San Francisco reported that the California association had 150 members in good standing. This year saw the start of the first legislative work by the funeral directors in California. This was to be a long uphill pull, and direct results would not be seen for another 24 years.

The turn of the century marks the beginning of the California Funeral Directors Association, and the first portion of its history that has not been lost in the memories of those individuals who fought so hard to have an association.

Under the leadership of H. C. Bunker, who is known as the father of the "modern" California association, the group held its first annual convention in 1903 and elected the following officers: *President,* S. A. White, San Francisco; *First Vice President,* M. A. Breese, M.D., Los Angeles; *Second Vice President,* W. L. Woodrow, San Jose; *Secretary-Treasurer,* J. E. Henderson, Oakland; and *Sergeant-at-Arms,* H. J. McAvoy, San Francisco.

Ever since that initial convention, the organization has met regularly each year with a single exception. There were two conventions held in 1905, the second one at Los Angeles, October 18 to 21, and none held in 1906. At the second 1905 meeting it was voted to hold a convention in Oakland the second week of August, 1906. However, this meeting was never held due to the effects of the earthquake and fire in April. With that exception, meetings have been held annually since 1905.

By 1907, when Kenyon Warren of Pasadena gave his report to the National Funeral Directors Association convention in Norfolk, Virginia, the state association was a thriving, well-organized group which was able to hold a successful state convention, attended by members from all parts of the state.

At first the organization was known as the State Funeral Directors Association of California but the name was changed to the present one in 1908.

Almost as soon as the organization was formed, proposals to join the National Funeral Directors were considered. However, it was not until 1907 that the California Funeral Directors Association became a part of NFDA.

When the present-day California association came into being the membership at the end of the first year was 162. In two years it had increased to 200, and for a number of years the number of memberships fluctuated around that figure.

In reviewing the history of C. F. D. A., many names figure prominently. Among these are: George Lunt, Fred E. Pierce, B. C. Wallace, E. E. Place, John M. Brunner, Julius Godeau, Bessie Wood, S. A. White, Charles H. J. Truman, C. R. Vesper, Henry Maas, Frank Monahan and a host of others.

The problems in those days were in a great many respects no different from some of those that exist today. The one which predominated at the time of the launching of the association was the non-existence of laws governing the practice of embalming. Besides failing to protect the public and the funeral directors from the dangers of disease and infections and failing to encourage or demand a better quality of embalming, the absence of proper laws resulted in action by the Baggage Men's Association, an organization of national scope, when its members threatened to refuse to handle bodies shipped from California. That threat hovered over the heads of funeral directors in California for a period of several years. Efforts to secure passage of proper legislation were very disappointing. During every legislative year for a period of ten years, the California association faithfully sponsored a bill. But just as often, it was defeated. Several times a bill passed both the assembly and senate but the Governor's veto followed.

Price cutting was another matter always up for discussion. The secretary stated during the October, 1905, meeting, "I would venture a little criticism. In some places I find that competition has reached such unreasonable proportions that prices are being slaughtered and business thereby greatly injured. General Sherman says that 'War is Hell.' That is true whether it be industrial, commercial, or competitive. Competitive war in our profession is just what General Sherman meant. It will leave a path of ruin and failure behind it."

Another matter which came up for endless discussion at every convention was the matter of Sunday funerals. At each session one or more members would describe the condition in his community and what progress had been made toward discontinuing Sunday funerals. The record shows that at each convention this problem was becoming less and less acute.

About 1905-06, the funeral directors were strongly opposed to advertising in any form. The by-laws in effect in 1908 provided the following penalties for those who mentioned price in their advertising: For the first offense a fine of $10; for the second offense $25; third offense, $50; and expulsion from the association thereafter. The record does not indicate whether or not there were any convictions under the clause.

The competition of burial associations and its possible adverse effects came to the attention of the California association as early as 1905. A resolution voicing opposition to burial associations was presented and adopted at the convention that year, and the association went on record as favoring the abolition of all burial contract work by members of the profession.

From the beginning the members of the association were very much interested in education in embalming and sanitation. Nearly every year a demonstrator was engaged to conduct demonstrations.

During the last 40 years, overlooking minor up's and down's, the path of the California association has been fairly smooth, with the possible exception of 1933. That saw feverish activity in the legislature aimed at barring the operation of mortuaries within the confines of cemeteries. Bruce Payne, president at that time, proved equal to the task in hand and while the legislative fight waged by the association was unsuccessful, the organization by no means disgraced itself.

The California association today

is perhaps in the most promising stage of its entire history. It is now organized and administered in a business-like and efficient way by an experienced, full-time executive secretary, working under a conservative, impartial, businesslike board of directors.

The present administration has backed up the State Board and urged that its members stiffen the spine and toss off any easy-going manner which winks at law violations. The result is that without fear or favor, law violators have been punished. The books and records have been audited, disbursements are made on a budget basis, and the association knows exactly where it stands.

After such a shaky and insignificant start in 1880, the California Funeral Directors Association faces the year of 1960 with almost 500 active members interested in guaranteeing the future of the funeral service profession.

ASSOCIATION PRESIDENTS: 1903, H. C. Bunker, *San Francisco;* 1905, S. A. White, *San Francisco;* 1906, M. A. Breese, *Los Angeles;* 1907, George W. Lunt, *San Francisco;* 1908, W. L. Woodrow, *San Jose;* 1909, Fred E. Pierce, *Los Angeles;* 1910, B. C. Wallace, *Stockton;* 1911, P. J. O'Connor, *Los Angeles;* 1912, F. J. Monahan, *San Francisco;* 1913, C. H. Burden, *Sonora;* 1914, Kenyon Warren, *Pasadena;* 1915, C. H. Wever, *Alameda;* 1916, J. K. Kelly, *Marysville;* 1917, C. H. J. Truman, *San Francisco;* 1918, C. N. Cooper, *Oakland;* 1919, Frank Welti, *Santa Rosa;* 1920, T. Frank Bevan, *Marysville;* 1921, Chas. McDermott, *Santa Barbara;* 1922, J. D. Stephens, *Fresno;* 1923, J. M. Brunner, *Los Angeles;* 1924, J. H. Lowman, *Ala-*

meda; 1925, Dan W. Gray, *San Jose;* 1926, C. F. Lamb, *Pasadena;* 1927, Eugene L. Webber, *Napa;* 1928, Lawson F. Utter, *Los Angeles;* 1929, Lester W. Wessendorf, *Santa Cruz;* 1930, Arthur Cresse, *Los Angeles;* 1931, Frank M. Dickey, *Vallejo;* 1932, J. Bruce Payne, *Bakersfield;* 1933, Archie O'Leary, *Sebastopol;* 1934, John W. Eberle, *Pasadena;* 1935, Walter M. Flieri, *Haywood;* 1936, C. C. DeYoung, *Stockton;* 1937, Leon S. Utter, *Alhambra;* 1938, Louis Felder, *San Francisco;* 1939, Roy Brooks, *Visalia;* 1940, T. Clyde Drennan, *Oakland;* 1941, Maynard Turner, *Pasadena;* 1942, Donald B. Welch, *Santa Barbara;* 1943, Warren C. Tinkler, *Fresno;* 1944, Julius H. Kraft, *Woodland;* 1945, B. W. Bonham, *San Diego;* 1946, Ben E. H. Warren, *Stockton;* 1947, W. Wylie Brown, *Los Angeles;* 1948, Frank J. Keaton, *San Rafael;* 1949, Hamilton J. Stevens, *Pasadena;* 1950, Daniel J. O'Hara, Jr., *San Francisco;* 1951, A. D. Bennett, *Bakersfield;* 1952, Lloyd H. Truman, *Oakland;* 1953, Harry Groman, *Los Angeles;* 1954, Burwell Ullrey, *Yuba City;* 1955, Clarence C. Pierce, *Santa Monica;* 1956, Dan O'Connell, *San Mateo;* 1957, Lewis E. Franklin, *Modesto;* 1958, George T. Callanan, *Hollywood;* 1959, Stanley L. Lance, *Santa Rosa;* 1960, George B. Honold, *Garden Grove.*

COLORADO

Informant: Arthur J. Alcorn

As a consequence of two pre-organizational meetings, one at Denver on May 29, 1897, the other at Pueblo some three months later, the Colorado Funeral Directors Association was formally organized, October 7, 1897.

This organization during part of its early life comprised the states and territories of Wyoming, New Mexico, Utah, and Colorado and was then known as the Western Funeral Directors Association.

Due to the large territory and the difficulties of travel from distant states to Colorado (where all of the meetings were eventually held) membership from other states was never really representative of the funeral directors from these areas. As the other states, especially Utah, sought organization within their own boundaries, memberships dwindled in the Western Funeral Directors Association, and Colorado tended to dominate the organization, until in 1905, of the fifty members of the entire association, forty-five were from the state of Colorado. At this time the name was officially changed to The Colorado Funeral Directors Association.

Again in 1909 the name of the association was changed, this time to include the embalmers of the state. The name then chosen was The Colorado Funeral Directors and Embalmers Association.

Although no one person can be singled out as the father of the Colorado association, there are many pioneers who should get equal mention. The men who organized the first association and were present at its first meeting were: F. B. Waters, William D. Nash, William P. Horan, F. J. Buchheit, T. G. McCarthy, H. C. Howell, J. H. Hunt, T. N. Chapman, H. M. Balmer, B. B. Sipe, J. D. Mulligan, C. A. Rogers, W. H. Farnum.

Throughout the years there have been many other outstanding men in the Colorado association. George W. Olinger, founder of the National Selected Morticians; Edward A. Martin, the first person from Colorado to serve as President of the National Funeral Directors Association; Rex B. Yeager, President of the National Conference of Funeral Service Examining Boards; Henry McCarthy; Arthur Jackson; B. B. Sipe; M. G. Rice; J. G. Trezise; Hattie G. Pierson; I. L. Glenn; E. R. O'Malia, and others who have worked for the advancement of the funeral profession in Colorado.

Early in the history of the association the members appointed a legislative committee and began work on the legal aspects of funeral directing in Colorado. At the report to the National Convention in Denver, Colorado, October 4 and 5, 1900, the Western Association listed 150 embalmers licensed by the association. Again in 1901 in Charleston, South Carolina, the representative to the NFDA made a further report that the license system, administered jointly by the Western Association and the Colorado Board of Health, had been declared a success in the state. It appears then, that the association lost no time in working toward the enactment of an actual licensing law in the state of Colorado. Further progress is reported in 1903 and again in 1908 when the drafting of an embalming bill was noted, and finally in 1914 when the enactment of a state law establishing an Embalmers' Examining Board was made known in the state's report to NFDA.

By the time of this report (1914) two examinations had already been given, sixteen men had been examined under the new statute, and a reciprocity program encompassing states having similar laws was in the making.

By 1923 the embalmers' law was declared a huge success; membership in the association had grown so that four districts had been established, and meetings were held in different parts of the state in order to serve the interests of the entire membership. The association as a whole seemed ready to work toward a strong national organization, and in 1923 went on record as favoring the National's *per capita* tax.

The association has always been interested in the professional advancement of its members, and during the sixty-three years of its history has seen much done in this field. The Colorado Association has continued to work for educational advancement and for a strong legislative program both to protect and to govern the people of Colorado and to uplift the funeral directing profession in the state.

ASSOCIATION PRESIDENTS: 1897, W. D. Nash, *Denver;* 1898, F. B. Waters, *Denver;* 1899, J. G. Trezise, *Boulder;* 1900, T. F. Dunn, *Victor;* 1901, C. A. Rogers, *Denver;* 1902, Charles A. Rogers, *Denver;* 1903, T. G. McCarthy, *Pueblo;* 1904, George S. Thompson, *La Junta;* 1905, Fred B. Waters, *Denver;* 1906, James E. Collier, *Pueblo;* 1907, F. J. Bucheit, *Boulder;* 1908, I. L. Glenn, *Telluride;* 1909, H. M. Balmer, *Fort Collins;* 1910-11, E. R. O'Malia, *Leadville;* 1912, Milo G. Rice, *Longmont;* 1913, Arthur D. Jackson, *Sterling;* 1914, T. N. Chapman, *Colorado Springs;* 1915, W. P. Horan, *Denver;* 1916, C. C. White, *Pueblo;* 1917, E. T. Beyle, *Colorado Springs;* 1918, B. B. Sipe, *Trinidad;* 1919, F. J. Allnutt, *Greeley;* 1920, S. D. Church, *Lamar;* 1921, A. E. Howe, *Boulder;* 1922, A. L. Springer, *Alamosa;* 1923, W. T. Hollowell, *Fort Collins;* 1924, Rex B. Yeager, *Denver;* 1925, Henry M. McCarthy, *Pueblo;* 1926, W. D. Nash, Jr., *Denver;* 1927, Roy Campbell, *Trinidad;* 1928, Geo. I. Richards, *Windsor;* 1929, W. P. Horan, Jr., *Denver;* 1930, Wm. H. Farnum, *Glenwood Springs;* 1931, Gabe N. Furphy, *Walsenburg;* 1932, Carl M. Ustick, *Rocky Ford;* 1933, George R. Henning, *Louisville;* 1934, George W. Powell, *Los Animas;* 1935-36, O. A. Saunders, *Golden;* 1937, Carl W. Kibbey, *Loveland;* 1938, Edward A. Martin, *Grand Junction;* 1939, William J. Quinn, *Denver;* 1940, Curtis R. Green, *La Junta;* 1941, Bernard Vessey, *Colorado Springs;* 1942, Kendall Hammond, *Loveland;* 1943, George Lorton, *Alamosa;* 1944, A. R. McCormick, *Delta;* 1945, Glen Kirkpatrick, *Lamar;* 1946, George W. Howe, *Longmont;* 1947, Robert E. Long, *Denver;* 1948, W. Edward Sharp, *Monte Vista;* 1949, Ralph E. Peacock, *La Junta;* 1950, Thomas J. Sardy, *Aspen;* 1951, Lloyd B. Allnut, *Greeley;* 1952, C. Harry Blunt, *Colorado Springs;* 1953, R. Paul Horan, *Denver;* 1954, Bert Frezieres, *Brush;* 1955, Robert W. Burnam, *Colorado Springs;* 1956, Carl M. Ustick, Jr., *Rocky Ford;* 1957, W. Sidney Phelps, *Denver;* 1958, Jack Farnum, *Glenwood Springs;* 1959, John Allnutt, *Greeley;* 1960, James W. Buchanan, *Limon.*

CONNECTICUT
Informant: Raymond E. Donovan

A meeting of funeral directors in Connecticut was held in Hartford on May 8, 1889 for the purpose of organizing an "undertakers association."

803

The 20 persons present voted to organize "for mutual protection and interest" the Undertakers Association of Connecticut. Charter subscribers were: W. F. Bishop, Bridgeport; F. W. Crum, Unionville; H. J. Church, Meriden; H. W. Crawford, New Haven; Charles A. Cadwell, Southington; William F. Dillon, Waterbury; Ralph Foster, Hartford; D. W. Fox, Plainville; C. L. Fillmore, Willimantic; Charles W. Hills, Hartford; Edwin S. Hunt, Clinton; James D. Jenning, Norwalk; Theodore Keiller, New Haven; A. R. Leete, Thompsonville; Edward Muller, Stonington; W. R. Morgan, Hartford; B. C. Porter, New Britain; Edward C. Root, Thomaston; George H. Swan, Essex; John Sarsfield, Portland; G. H. Alford, Winsted; W. S. Gould, Plantsville; D. S. Ramsey, Moodus; E. B. Pratt, Chester; L. J. Johnson, Winsted; L. Hoyt & Son, Stamford; William H. Pease, North Bloomfield; John M. Blair, New Haven; E. L. Cooke, Hartford; William Mulligan, Thompsonville; H. B. Hunter, Madison; John W. Fitzgerald, Wallingford; William F. Stahl, New Haven; S. B. Miller, Branford; George W. Scoville, Norfolk; George H. Woolley, Hartford; and W. G. Spencer, Portland. Of these men mentioned the first 20 were actually present at the organizational meeting called by Mr. C. W. Hills; the others joined the new organization within the first year and are listed as charter members.

At the second annual meeting in 1890 it was voted to join the International Funeral Directors Association (now NFDA) and to pay the per capita tax on all members in good standing.

At the fifth annual meeting in 1893, a new classification of membership was created, the "honorable membership" status. Ralph Houghton of Randolph, Massachusetts, one of the oldest "undertakers" in the country, was chosen to receive this honor.

By 1894 the association had a regularly appointed legislative committee whose duty it was to promote the interests of the profession at the state capital and elsewhere.

By 1897 the legislative committee had met with the state legislature to urge the creation of a State Board of Examiners. Despite strong opposition at the state governmental level, this board was set up in 1903. Board membership was restricted to practical arterial embalmers, and surplus fees collected were used for educational purposes. By 1907, legislation brought about the restriction that only licensed embalmers or someone working under a licensed embalmer could practice embalming in the state of Connecticut. This law was finally amended in 1923, and from this time on, all funeral directors or embalmers were required to be licensed by the State Board of Health.

Legislative interest in Connecticut has continued to run high. From the mid-20's until the present, legal counsel has been retained by the association for the purpose of overseeing this part of the associational activity.

Legislation has not, however, been the only interest of the association. Education and professionalization have interested the membership since the inception of the organization. As early as 1902, the name of the association was changed from The Connecticut Undertakers Association to The Connecticut Funeral Directors Association. And in 1925, the association voted to urge the use of the term funeral director to replace that of undertaker at the national level. Early in the association's history, liaison with Yale University was sought and a course for aspiring funeral directors was urged by the association. The Connecticut Funeral Directors association has further supported all the major educational experiments of the national association.

In 1937, working with the Embalmers' Board, the association was instrumental in securing passage of a mandatory funeral home inspection law.

A need for a formal program of public relations within and outside the organization culminated in 1957 with employment of a year-round consultant to develop and carry out this program with association members.

In 1958 a formal membership oath and code of ethics were developed and a seal for the state association was created.

Connecticut has furnished three presidents to the national organization: Charles Dillon, Hartford; J. Leo Redgate, Bridgeport; and H. Fremont Alderson, New London.

As of 1959 the membership totals 250—a very large proportion of the funeral directors of the state.

ASSOCIATION PRESIDENTS: 1889, Charles W. Hills, *Hartford;* 1890, F. W. Crum, *Unionville;* 1891-92, H. J. Church, *Meriden;* 1893, George H. Alford, *Winsted;* 1894, George H. Hawley, *Bridgeport;* 1895, Isaac L. Mead, *Greenwich;* 1896, W. S. Gould, *Southington;* 1897, W. T. Marchant, *Hartford;* 1898, C. E. Lewis, *Derby;* 1899-1900, Charles H. Martin, *Stamford;* 1901, B. J. Porter, *New Britain;* 1902, Henry W. Beecher, *New Haven;* 1903, Howard M. Hickox, *Watertown;* 1904, Charles Fable, *Westport;* 1905, Edward C. Root, *Thomaston;* 1906, M. F. Walker, *New Haven;* 1907, W. F. Tomlinson, *Danbury;* 1908, William A. Gleeson, *Torrington;* 1909, James M. Bennett, *New Haven;* 1910-11, Albert A. May, *Meriden;* 1912-13, William Henry Allen, *Norwich;* 1914, William G. LaPlace, *Deep River;* 1915-16, Hugh A. Keenan, *New Haven;* 1917-18, George J. Smith, *Milford;* 1919-20, Charles J. Dillon, *Hartford;* 1921-23, Alfred Camerlin, *New Haven;* 1924, George W. Keeler, *Cheshire;* 1925, Frank J. Smith, *New Haven;* 1926, Idris Alderson, *Waterbury;* 1927, Willard J. Gould, *Southington;* 1928, James C. E. Dillon, *Hartford;* 1929-30, Edward H. Bishop, *Bridgeport;* 1931-33, James T. Pratt, Jr., *Hartford;* 1934-36, J. Leo Redgate, *Bridgeport;* 1937-38, Robert H. Byles, *New London;* 1939-40, William C. Celentano, *New Haven;* 1941, Fred L. Avery, *Willimantic;* 1942, Arthur M. Coughlin, *Middletown;* 1943, John H. Hull, *Danbury;* 1944, William P. Quish, *Manchester;* 1945, H. Fremont Alderson, *New London;* 1946, Cyril F. Mullins, *Bridgeport;* 1947, Raymond E. Snyder, *Waterbury;* 1948, M. Joseph Lillis, *New Milford;* 1949, Merrill G. Scott, *Terryville;* 1950, Edward P. Neilan, *New London;* 1951, Edward G. Hotchkiss, *Thomaston;* 1952, Leo J. Redgate, *Bridgeport;* 1953, Samuel B. Guiney, *Hartford;* 1954, E. Fenton Burke, *Rockville;* 1955, John T. MacDougall, *New London;* 1956, William F. Farrell, *New Britain;* 1957, Robert J. Burwell, *New Haven;* 1958-59, Joseph E. Biega, *Middletown;* 1960, Howard L. Holmes, *Manchester.*

DELAWARE
Informant: John F. Yasik

As long ago as June, 1888, funeral directors in Delaware were interested in organizing a state association. From 1889 until 1895 this state reported each year to the National Association, but from that time on the state association met with increasing organizational difficulties and was not officially reorganized until 1919.

On Tuesday, May 13, 1919, the first gathering of the Delaware State Funeral Directors took place. The following were elected: *President*, William H. Robinson, Jr., Wilmington; *Vice President*, Michael A. Mealey, Wilmington; and *Secretary*, Albert J. McCrery, Wilmington. Other members present at the meeting were Edward L. Hanna, H. Herbert Hirzel, Robert T. Jones, Daniel T. Killroy, Harvey E. Nichols, and Marshall H. Yeatman.

On August 11, 1919, the first official association meeting was held, with 44 members in attendance. At this meeting the constitution and by-laws were adopted, and James T. Chandler, Charles L. Clewell, Daniel Killroy and John B. Martin were elected delegates to the national convention.

On May 18, 1924, the charter of the National Funeral Directors' Association of the United States, signed by Fred P. Schoedinger, *President* and H. M. Kilpatrick, *Secretary-Treasurer*, was granted the Delaware State Funeral Directors Association.

In 1931 and 1932 conventions were held in Wilmington, Delaware, with some success. The association set one evening aside for the general public of Wilmington and vicinity to attend. Although this feature proved to be a successful public relations venture, due to increasing costs of holding conventions, the annual meetings as such had to be forsaken. The two exhibits held by the association did benefit the funeral profession in this state and created very favorable public opinion.

In 1959 Delaware had a small, compact 44 member association. Neither formal annual meetings nor exhibits are held but outings, to which are invited the supply house representatives and their salesmen, are featured instead. Ordinarily there is a dinner meeting followed by dancing.

In October of 1950, at the convention held in Philadelphia, John F. Yasik was elected to the National Funeral Directors Association Board of Governors as the Governor of District 2.

Association Presidents: 1911-13, John B. Martin, *Wilmington;* 1914, James T. Chandler, *Wilmington;* 1915, Charles H. Clewell, *New Castle;* 1916, William T. Atkins, *Lewes;* 1917, Daniel T. Killroy, *Wilmington;* 1918, Harvey E. Nichols, *Wilmington;* 1919, William Robinson, Jr., *Wilmington;* 1920, Michael A. Mealey, *Wilmington;* 1921, Wm. F. Lynn, *Wilmington;* 1922, Frank Kilroy, *Wilmington;* 1923, James J. Fox, *Wilmington;* 1924, Carl H. Krenien, *Wilmington;* 1925, Robert Cloud, *Marcus Hook, Pennsylvania;* 1926, Marshall H. Yeatman, *Wilmington;* 1927, Chandler H. Gebhart, *New Castle;* 1928, William J. Krienen, *New Castle;* 1929, J. T. Chandler, Jr., *Wilmington;* 1930,

Wm. G. Powders, *Milford;* 1931, Wm. A. Torbert, *Dover;* 1932, James F. Hearn, *Wilmington;* 1933, Lester G. Daniel, *Townsend;* 1934, John F. Yasik, *Wilmington;* 1935, John T. Carey, *Georgetown;* 1936, Wm. E. Haines, *Wilmington;* 1937, Raymond R. Atkins, *Lewes;* 1938, John W. Spicer, Jr., *Delaware City;* 1939, J. Ralph Carey, *Georgetown;* 1940, Nicholas J. Corleto, *Wilmington;* 1941, Winfred B. Dahling, *Elsmere;* 1942-43, Clinton H. Watson, *Frankford;* 1944-45, John J. Mealey, *Wilmington;* 1946, William E. Matthews, *Smyrna;* 1947, Winfred B. Dahling, *Elsmere;* 1948, John R. Rogers, *Frederica;* 1949, Russell O. Griffith, *Wilmington;* 1950, Daniel A. Mealey, *Wilmington;* 1951, G. Lester Daniels, *Middletown;* 1952, Frank R. Hayes, *Dover;* 1953, William F. Jones, *Claymount;* 1954, Wells A. Faries, *Smyrna;* 1955, James Mullikin, *Wilmington;* 1956, Wm. Fleischauer, Jr., *Greenwood;* 1957, John F. J. Yasik, *Wilmington;* 1958, William A. Berry, Jr., *Milford;* 1959, John M. Yeatman, *Wilmington;* 1960, Harry E. Darby, *Seaford.*

FLORIDA

Informant: S. A. Kyle

Pursuant to a call issued, a meeting of the funeral directors of Florida was held in Jacksonville on December 16, 1895. J. M. Tucker, Tampa, presided.

The officers elected to conduct the affairs of the association for the first year were: *President,* D. C. McIver, Ocala; *Vice Presidents,* E. O. Kane, Jacksonville; H. A. Wilson, St. Augustine; R. McClelland, Gainesville; H. A. Hanson, Leesburg; J. L. Wirt, Bartow; and *Secretary-Treasurer,* T. M. Tucker, Tampa.

It was decided at the first meeting to call the new association "The Undertakers' and Embalmers' Association of Florida" and to adopt, with a few unimportant changes, the by-laws of the Virginia Association. A communication was received by the members from the state health department soliciting the aid of the association in two important features of the work of the board of health—disinterment and the reporting of deaths.

In the first year of the association's history, there was only one home on the East Coast between Jacksonville and Key West—the Fee-Stewart Home at Fort Pierce, and among the farthest west was J. M. Cotter of Apalachicola, who had to make part of his convention trip on a river boat.

Through the years other Florida funeral directors also experienced travel difficulties. Notable among them was Benjamin Lopez of Key West who before the railroad was extended to the southern tip of the state, had to travel to Tampa by Peninsular & Occidental Steam Ship line and from Tampa to Jacksonville by railroad. This trip required ten days including the time at the convention. There were only two ships a week between Tampa, Key West, and Havana, Cuba.

One of the earlier concerns of the organization was proper licensing regulation. Success in this field was soon reported when state licensing legislation was passed in 1903. In May, 1904, at Jacksonville, the State Board of Health held its first examination for the licensing of embalmers. Approximately 40 took the examination. Embalmer's license #1 was issued to Chas. A. Clark, Jacksonville.

In 1917, a State Board of Examiners was created through the state legislature. These two events were certainly among the early aims and desires of the association and helped raise the standards of funeral directing in Florida.

In 1930 the by-laws of the association were changed to dissolve the four vice-presidential offices and in their places to establish four districts each having its own director and each empowered to hold meetings, transact business, and report to the state at the time of convention. Today there are five such district directors who are elected for two-year terms.

In 1932, the name of the association became "Florida Funeral Directors and Embalmers Association." On January 29, 1952, the name of the association was again changed to "Florida Funeral Directors Association, Inc."

In May, 1932, Charles S. McIntosh, who served as association secretary for 10 years and as president for 2 terms, published the first issue of *The Florida Funeral Director,* a small, four page, bulletin-type folder, released monthly without advertisements. The magazine is now a 9 x 12 "slick paper" publication, issued bi-monthly, with both local and national advertising, and is the official publication of "The Florida Funeral Directors Association."

Significant legislative developments (in addition to the creation of the State Board of Examiners and Embalmers in 1917) were: (1) In 1932 a legislative committee was appointed, with S. A. Kyle as chairman. (2) In 1933 House Bills #1518 and 1535 were passed. These bills exempted ambulances and hearses from being classed as "cars for hire." It was also arranged to have the Railroad Commission withdraw its position of placing ambulances under their jurisdiction. (3) In 1935 the Insurance Laws were amended in favor of the funeral director. In this year, too, the Funeral Director License Law was passed. (4) The association was successful in getting an opinion from the Attorney General which removed the funeral profession from a new gross receipts tax law, and all taxes paid by funeral directors under this law were refunded by the state. (5) The association was successful in preventing the passage of a law which would have permitted the issuing of a funeral director's license to anyone who had been engaged in the business at any time within the 30 years previous to 1941. (6) In 1942 the office of Executive Secretary was set up, and Mr. J. H. Dyer of Jacksonville was selected to fill the newly created position. (7) The State Board of Funeral Directors and Embalmers for Florida, in cooperation with the Florida Funeral Directors Association, published a hardbound text, *Funeral Direction and Management,* written by Mrs. Anne Hamilton Franz, and later issued a revised edition of 1000 copies. This book has been useful to many taking the funeral directors' examination in Florida as well as to students in many mortuary schools.

In 1947 the wives of the members present voted to organize an auxiliary and adopted the title: "Ladies Auxiliary to the Florida Funeral Directors and Embalmers Association." Mrs. W. Ray Highsmith of Jacksonville was elected

808

the auxiliary's first president.

In April of 1949 the University of Florida, General Extension Division, in cooperation with the association, presented a "Short Course of Training for Funeral Personnel" at the University of Florida in Gainesville. The sessions were designed for the employee or trainee who has not yet attended a mortuary college as well as for the embalmer who has been out of school for several years. These clinics continue to be held periodically.

In July, 1950, Miss Lida Lee Hunt was named Executive Secretary, and Robert V. Weeber was named Editor of *The Florida Funeral Director*.

In 1951 the office of Director-at-Large in the association was eliminated and that of Vice President was re-established in order to give this officer a year of associational experience before his probable succession to the presidency.

In the March-April 1952 issue of *The Florida Funeral Director*, a special section was devoted to the interests of the mortuary colleges—the first special "mortuary education" issue—and a copy of this issue was sent to the principal of every high school in the state for inclusion in the school library as a reference work for students seeking occupational information.

In 1953 a special meeting was held in Jacksonville to combat the invasion of the state by the so-called "package deal" cemetery-funeral promotion operators. At the legislative session the same year, through the alertness of association officials and the cooperation of the State Board of Funeral Directors and Embalmers and other public officials, a bill entitled "Pre-Need Burial Contracts" was passed which, as a protection to both the public and the funeral directors, placed severe limitations and restrictions on the burial insurance "package deal" type of operation. There have since been no significant attempts to re-establish this type of service.

In 1955 a short course for funeral directors and embalmers was presented in Tampa by Dr. Charles Nichols, Educational Director of the National Foundation of Funeral Service.

In 1955 many Miami funeral directors abandoned their ambulance service and turned over this portion of their business to Eastern Ambulance Service, Inc. Since this time funeral directors in other Florida cities have taken similar action.

The Florida association won the National Membership Award in Group II for 1955, with an 18.5 per cent membership increase, giving Florida a total of 222 paid-up members at that time.

The September-October 1957 issue of *The Florida Funeral Director* was a special "Salute to NFDA" issue in honor of the 76th Annual NFDA Convention in Atlanta.

In September, 1958 an important bill pertaining to the licensing of funeral homes was discussed, amended, and approved by the convention for presentation to the 1959 Florida State Legislature by the Association's Legislative Committee. This was a most significant bill, as it represented an earnest attempt by Florida's funeral directors to strike a blow at the unlicensed operation of funeral homes in the state.

Florida has had many public spirited and outstanding members in its association. Along with the

809

names already mentioned should stand the names: John S. Rhodes, state association President for three terms and national President for one term; Marcus Conant, the first in the state to adopt motorized equipment; C. M. (Neil) Franklin, Orlando, elected Governor of District 4 of the NFDA Board of Governors at the 76th Annual NFDA Convention in Atlanta, Ga.; Augustus H. Craig, St. Augustine, elected in 1958 to the Florida House of Representatives from St. Johns County; Frank L. Miller, Sanford served as association Secretary for 22 years; S. A. Kyle, President in 1934 and active in important work on the legislative committee; T. M. Lloyd, President in 1937, was recently voted an Honorary Life Membership in the association.

ASSOCIATION PRESIDENTS: 1896-1900, D. E. McIver, *Ocala;* 1900-06, Charles A. Clark, *Jacksonville;* 1907, John G. Wood, *Pensacola;* 1908-10, C. M. Bingham, *Daytona;* 1911, H. M. King, *Miami;* 1912-13, Wm. C. Cooper, Jr., *Jacksonville;* 1914-15, S. D. Harris, *St. Petersburg;* 1916-17, H. S. Moulton, *Jacksonville;* 1918-19, Carey Hand, *Orlando;* 1920-21, Benjamin Lopez, *Key West;* 1922, J. A. Allen, *DeLand;* 1923, W. H. Combs, Sr., *Miami;* 1924, John J. Skillman, *Miami;* 1925, Frazier T. Blount, *Tampa;* 1926, E. S. Ferguson, *West Palm Beach;* 1927, James R. Weeks, *Plant City;* 1928, J. W. Wilhelm, *St. Petersburg;* 1929, J. A. Smith, *Winter Haven;* 1930, W. H. Combs, Jr., *Miami;* 1931, J. M. Endicott, *St. Petersburg;* 1931-32, John S. Rhodes, *St. Petersburg;* 1933, B. Marion Reed, *Tampa;* 1934, S. A. Kyle, *Jacksonville;* 1935-36, H. G.

Van Orsdel, *Miami;* 1937, Tom Lloyd, *Pensacola;* 1938, Amos Griffith, *DeLand;* 1939, John S. Rhodes, *St. Petersburg;* 1940-42, Charles S. McIntosh, *Daytona Beach;* 1943, Jack B. Fannin, *Fort Lauderdale;* 1944, L. W. Baynard, *St. Petersburg;* 1945, W. L. Philbrick, *Miami;* 1946-47, DeWitt C. Jones, *Gainesville;* 1948, Cornelius M. Franklin, *Orlando;* 1949, Ivan E. Beyers, Sr., *Leesburg;* 1950, R. Gordon Brisson, *Sanford;* 1951, W. A. Maddox, *Marianna;* 1952, M. W. Gerhardt, *Miami;* 1953, J. E. Summerhill, *DeLand;* 1954, R. M. Naugle, *Jacksonville;* 1955, Maynard A. Duryea, *St. Petersburg;* 1956, Augustus H. Craig, *St. Augustine;* 1957, W. T. Robarts, *Sarasota;* 1958, C. James Mathews, *St. Petersburg;* 1959, George H. Hewell, *Jacksonville;* 1960, Brody C. Harris, *Live Oak.*

GEORGIA

Informants: James I. Robertson and Ralph S. Turner

In the March, 1881, issue of *The Casket* can be found the following announcement: "We, the undersigned, do call for a convention of professional funeral directors of Georgia to be held in the City of Atlanta, Ga., on Wednesday, May 4, 1881, and would most cordially invite every undertaker in the state to meet with us and give us their influence by being present."

Evidently the funeral directors of Georgia were not ready to organize at this particular time, because in 1882 it was reported in a letter to the editor of *The Casket* that the writer had gone to Atlanta on the date selected for a meeting and had been unable to find evidence of any meeting in progress!

An organization was finally

810

formed in May, 1886. This first meeting was held in Atlanta, in the reception rooms of Kimball House and the organization was formally named "The Georgia Funeral Directors' Association." Professor H. H. Clarke of Springfield, Ohio, was present and spoke to the members assembled. W. E. Platt of Augusta was elected president and Charles Henderson was elected secretary.

In 1888 the Georgia Funeral Directors' Association formally affiliated with NFDA and reported to the national convention in the year 1889. This association, composed of both funeral directors and manufacturers, was disbanded because of a legal decision brought about by a court suit which accused the organization of restraint of trade.

The first call for what is presently the GFDA was issued by I. B. Wilson of Augusta, and the first meeting was held in Atlanta on June 17, 1902. The charter members were C. M. Ferguson, Winder; G. H. Brandon, Atlanta; Jesse B. Hart, Macon; H. M. Patterson, Atlanta; W. E. (Boss) Platt, Augusta; R. E. Elliott, Augusta; E. L. Almand, Monroe; S. C. Kytle, Carrollton; and W. M. Yeagin, Cartersville. During this first meeting the ground work was laid for the associational interests of the future—education of the embalmer and funeral director, establishment of a state board (which was later headed by W. E. Platt who received the first embalmer's license issued by the state), and the effecting of legislation to better qualify members in their work.

Public reaction to the new association was very good—especially from the ministers, who seemed to endorse the idea with as much en-thusiasm as the members themselves.

Little is printed about the exact time or the composition and passage of the constitution and by-laws of the association. Speculation persists that they were brought up, discussed, and probably passed on at the 1903 meeting in Macon. At any rate, they were in effect by the year 1908 in written form.

One of the problems facing the Georgia embalmer in the early days was the use of chemicals in embalming. All the earlier chemicals were arsenic-based. In 1906 the use of such embalming fluid was declared illegal and the embalmers had to resort to the then little-known formaldehydes. These, of course, proved better in the long run, but at first presented problems to the profession.

An additional problem was the convincing of families of the advantages of embalming at all. At the turn of the century, the body of a loved one rarely left the house after death until it made the short trip to the family graveyard—often simply a fenced-in section of the family farm. Even as late as the 1930's in rural Georgia (and until recently rural Georgia has been more populous than urban) bodies were embalmed at home. By this time, however, church funerals were becoming more common than home funerals and the body was more frequently buried in a church cemetery than on the farm graveyard. The practice of embalming everyone was still not universal.

Other problems included recognition of the business as a profession, the elevation of standards for embalmers, better laws to govern the shipment of bodies dead of contagious diseases, and the problem of better cooperation between fellow funeral directors within as well as outside the state.

The development of the funeral home itself in Georgia, particularly in the past three decades, has been rapid. Because funeral directing was formerly practiced as a sideline or adjunct to another business, such names as The Fitzgerald Furniture Co. of Fitzgerald, Almand Hardware of Monroe, The Statesboro Buggy and Wagon Co. of Statesboro, and the Stephens Auto Co. of Thomaston were found on the early lists of funeral directors in the state. Georgia also has its list of unusual names for funeral establishments: The Planters Hardware Co. of Camilla, Ga., and the Traveler's Rest (an old hotel bought and converted to a funeral home by a funeral director in 1919). The oldest funeral home still in operation is Henderson Brothers, established in October of 1842.

The development of standards for the profession in Georgia went hand in hand with the State Board of Embalming. Members of the Board are also members of the association. In the early days all that was required for an embalmer's license was two years of apprenticeship to an accredited establishment, a reasonable ability to practice the art, and a halfway knowledge of anatomy and the use of chemicals. A favorite portion of the program at the early conventions was a panel discussion on embalming with state board members acting as panelists.

However, cooperation between the association and the state board brought about more rigid license requirements: first, by the board's making the examination hard enough to make some schooling necessary (whether it was required or not); and second, by their eventually passing a law which made mandatory the six months of schooling necessary to pass the examination. This requirement of six months of school was, of course, in addition to the already required apprenticeship period. By 1950, all laws were codified, a funeral director's license was required and standards were finally set up in their present form. Requirements for an embalmer's license included a full 12 months course in an accredited mortuary college.

In 1928, at the convention held in Atlanta, the first nationwide radio broadcast pertaining to the funeral profession took place. At this same meeting GFDA was awarded the cup presented annually by NFDA to the member association achieving the highest percentage increase in membership over the past year.

In 1937 GFDA set up districts corresponding to the ten congressional districts in the state. District chairmen and co-chairmen are appointed by the president of the association each year. At least one yearly meeting is required and a secretary and a legislative committeeman are elected by each group. The legislative committeeman from each district and the association officers form the Legislative Committee for the association, and these men meet to consider any future changes in the laws. Educational type programs have been used at the district meetings which are comprised of no more than 35 members in the largest district. However, 1959 brings three regional meetings scheduled over the state

812

in order to furnish advanced type of educational program.

If being elected to public office is any criterion of esteem, then funeral directors of Georgia are highly thought of by the general public. In town after town funeral directors are on councils and city commissions, and numbers even occupy the mayor's chair. In addition, there are state senators and legislators in each General Assembly who are funeral directors. At least thirty funeral directors are known to be coroners in their own counties. The list is too long for enumeration.

The funeral profession in Georgia furnished its share of men to the armed forces during the period of World War II and the Korean conflict. Many funeral homes found themselves severely handicapped for able help during this period. The war's end has also had its effect on the funeral homes of Georgia. The resultant free schooling under the G. I. Bill and the general movement from rural to urban areas has posed problems in distribution of facilities and personnel for Georgia funeral directors.

Georgia is proud of its leaders who have served the National Association with distinction. W. Bruce Donaldson, Jr. of Tifton, went through the chairs and then was elected President at the Minneapolis Convention in 1952. James W. Jennings of Rome, served on the Exhibit Committee.

ASSOCIATION PRESIDENTS: 1887-89, W. Edward Plann, *Augusta;* 1890-92, H. M. Patterson, *Atlanta;* 1902, W. I. Wilson, *Augusta;* 1903-04, G. H. Brandon, *Augusta;* 1905, C. M. Ferguson, *Winder;* 1906-07, Jessie B. Hart, *Macon;* 1908, J. E. Henderson, *Savannah;* 1909, E. F. Bond, *Atlanta;* 1910, H. M. Patterson, *Atlanta;* 1911, S. C. Kytle, *Carrollton;* 1912, Sam R. Greenberg, *Atlanta;* 1913, C. L. Stevenson, *Moultrie;* 1914-15, Joseph A. Moore, *Milledgeville;* 1916, W. V. Almand, *Monroe;* 1917, J. Freeman Hart, *Macon;* 1918, Nat LeMaster, *Americus;* 1919, W. W. Redwine, *Fayetteville;* 1920, F. Q. Sammon, *Lawrenceville;* 1921-22, E. L. Almand, Sr., *Monroe;* 1923, A. D. Wiseman, *Adel;* 1924, F. B. Lowndes, *Atlanta;* 1925, S. G. McGowan, 1926-27, John D. Custis, *Augusta;* 1928, L. E. Jackson, *Cartersville;* 1929, E. E. Brannon, *Statesboro;* 1930, S. R. Greenberg, *Atlanta;* 1931, Clyde McDorman, *Athens;* 1932, Harry White, *Conyers;* 1933, F. G. Sammon, *Lawrenceville;* 1934, R. C. Connally, *Macon;* 1935, Clyde Z. Harden, *Ashburn;* 1936, Raymond B. Nelson, *Atlanta;* 1937, Claude Peacock, *Canton;* 1938, Charles V. Curtis, *Thomson* (died soon after taking office); and was succeeded by Lester F. Elliott, *Augusta;* 1939, R. S. Newsome, *Thomaston;* 1940, W. Tom Bond, *Atlanta;* 1941, Carlos Hemperly, *East Point;* 1942, Cleve Mincey, *Waycross;* 1943, T. A. McCord, *Fort Valley;* 1944, Cecil Poe, *Fairburn;* 1945, W. Bruce Donaldson, *Tifton;* 1946, J. W. Jennings, *Rome;* 1947, Ed. L. Almand, Jr., *Monroe;* 1948, James F. Paulk, *Fitzgerald;* 1949, Dan C. Flinn, *Atlanta;* 1950, C. Freeman Harris, *Rockmart;* 1951, John P. Kelley, *Winder;* 1952, Brannon B. Lesesne, *Atlanta;* 1953, Elmer E. Barnette, *LaGrange;* 1954, Ed. Forsyth, *Cairo;* 1955, Millard R. Finch, *McCaysville;* 1956, S. Elmo Weeks, *Savannah;* 1957, W. Warren Haisten, *Griffin;* 1958, T. A. Hamby, *Columbus;* 1959, Howard E. Baker, *Canton;* 1960, Robert L. Harrison, *Jesup.*

IDAHO

Informant: A. B. Eckersell

In October, 1909, at the National Funeral Directors Association meeting in Portland, Oregon, H. E. Hunt of Idaho reported as follows: "In November last, fourteen Idaho funeral directors convened in Pocatello and organized the Idaho Association. We did what business was necessary and had our next meeting in Boise on August 11 of this year; there we met in convention and added to our number thirty-six members in good standing. Those of you who do not know the geographical 'lay' of Idaho will not recognize at once the impossibility of getting all the undertakers to unite with the organization. We have a state 522 miles long and over 400 miles wide. There are seventy-five undertakers in the state, thirty-six of whom are members of our new organization. I believe we hold the distinction of being the baby of the National Association."

Unfortunately the "baby of the National Association" did not survive, and it was not until 1936, after the brief existence of an association from 1921 to 1926, that the present Idaho State Association was organized. At that time H. L. McHan and Clyde Summers sent out the first call for a meeting in Boise. Approximately 25 funeral directors attended and elected officers for the year: *President,* C. V. Peckham, Caldwell; *Vice President,* H. R. Short, Moscow; *Secretary-Treasurer,* A. B. Eckersell, Rigby; and a board of directors consisting of C. V. Peckham, A. E. Thompson, E. T. Peck, C. E. Clovis, L. V.

Worstell, and A. B. Eckersell. These men, along with Don Reynolds, Executive Secretary of the Washington State Association, immediately set about canvassing the state for members, and within a few months a majority of the funeral directors in the state became members. It was not until December, 1938, however, that a constitution and by-laws were created and adopted by the association. It was at this time that the association became incorporated as the Idaho Funeral Service Association, Inc.

One of the pressing problems facing the association was the revision and up-dating of a state license law which had come into effect in 1904. In 1937 and 1939 substantial changes in the law were effected. Funeral directors were henceforth licensed and a three-man board of examiners was created, membership in which consisted of persons recommended by the state association. Educational standards were also increased.

In 1940, through the encouragement of John W. Eberle, president of the National Funeral Directors Association, the state association became a constituent member of the national association. Although growth in the funeral service field in Idaho has not been outstanding, and numerically the membership is relatively small, nevertheless about 94 per cent of those eligible have become members in the association. Nationwide this proportion is one of the highest.

Some of the more outstanding leaders in the state association, in addition to H. L. McHan, were Glenn Ailor, Byron B. Downard, Clyde Clovis, Clyde Summers, C. V. Peckham, Howard R. Short, A. W.

Davis, A. B. Eckersell and Henry Merchant.

Both A. W. Davis and A. B. Eckersell served in the State Senate, and were state presidents. Additionally A. B. Eckersell, the first secretary of the group, has been the only Idaho funeral director to go on to hold a National office. In 1954, after occupying a series of offices, he was elected President of the National Funeral Directors Association. A special recognition for her prominence in writing articles on various aspects of funeral service must be given to Mrs. Marie L. Green of Grangeville, Idaho. Lastly the association retains warm memories for the National Funeral Directors Association's Past President John E. Drummey whose influence through personal visits, speeches, and informal encouragement gave the association a clearer sense of purpose and direction.

ASSOCIATION PRESIDENTS: 1924, E. T. Peck, *Blackfoot;* 1925-26, Mrs. C. J. Vassar, *Lewiston;* 1936, C. V. Peckham, *Caldwell;* 1937, H. R. Short, *Moscow;* 1938, A. W. Davis, *American Falls;* 1939, Glen W. Ailor, *Grangeville;* 1940, Byron B. Downard, *Pocatello;* 1941, C. E. Clovis, *Craigmont;* 1942, A. E. Thompson, *Gooding;* 1943, Frank Williams, *Montpelier;* 1944, A. B. Eckersell, *Rigby;* 1945, Frank Morse, *Bonner Ferry;* 1946, J. C. Sandberg, *Blackfoot;* 1947, Bernard T. Albertson, *Buhl;* 1948, Vincent Vassar, *Lewiston;* 1949, John Alsip, *Nampa;* 1950, Howard Packham, *Blackfoot;* 1951, Grant McGlade, *Kellogg;* 1952, Ray McGoldrick, *Hailey;* 1953, Kermit Malcom, *Lewiston;* 1954, T. Wilbur Dakan, *Caldwell;* 1955, M. D. Hansen, *St.*

Anthony; 1956, Don English, *Coeur d' Alene;* 1957, James C. Reynolds, *Twin Falls;* 1958, A. S. Jones, *Weiser;* 1959, E. Russell Short, *Moscow;* 1960, John P. Grossman, *Pocatello.*

ILLINOIS
Informant: Roger B. Ytterberg

The history of the Illinois Funeral Directors Association reflects the characteristic growth of the state. Basically, Illinois is an agrarian area and during the early years, farming was the principal business. However, the tremendous growth of the city of Chicago as one of the largest metropolitan centers in the nation, particularly in the years following the Civil War, created a downstate versus Chicago division.

The Illinois Undertaking Association, founded in December, 1881, was comprised at the outset mostly of practitioners residing in the Chicago area and whose Chicago Undertakers' Association sponsored the organizational meeting for the state association. Later as the trend toward organizations grew apace, the persons residing in the rural sections joined the association and gradually laid the ground work for a truly state-wide group. Earliest concerns of the newly founded association were license legislation, interchange of ideas on the methods of professional funeral directing, and "protection of the members against manufacturers and jobbers in undertakers' materials."

Most records of the old organization, particularly the list of charter members, have been lost. The original officers were: *President,* Joseph Rogerson, Chicago; *Vice President,* George Murphy, Quincy;

815

Secretary, M. W. Bonfield, Chicago; and *Treasurer,* John Thompson, Peoria.

Minutes of the association and newspaper accounts contain this statement: "Something is needed to give new life to association work in Illinois and the convention meeting at the election of one of its members to a mayoral position should be in good favor." B. F. Knox, a funeral director, was elected mayor of Rock Island. The new wave of enthusiasm was reflected by the members following attendance at a meeting of the Iowa organization in May, 1895.

Apparently, the annual meeting held at Rock Island in October of that year set the stage for development of a full-scale organization. More than 40 persons attended the gathering and 20 new members joined. A correspondent for the *Embalmer's Monthly* in writing about the meeting said, "the state organization starts a new era of usefulness." The 1895 meeting was typical of many of the beginning conventions which featured demonstrations by early day experts in the field of mortuary science.

Throughout the entire early history it was evident the fledgling organization had to overcome some severe handicaps, one being the tendency of suppliers and casket makers to dominate the association and its affairs. As time went on, however, the association proceeded through many changes and gradually acquired a full degree of independence. Working relations were established with the national association and a delegation attended the national association conventions beginning in 1886.

In 1898 the association gathered in Chicago and President F. C. Vaughn, of Amboy, proudly proclaimed the association "one of the most flourishing state associations." "This meeting," he pointed out, "is trying to promote harmony between city and country mortuaries and to make operable a set of rules which were adopted by the railroad Baggage Association." Since the railroads were the principal means of transportation between cities in the years preceeding and following the turn of the century, discussion about transportation occurred frequently in convention meetings.

By 1899 when the convention was held in Peoria, the members reached an agreement on a "Check system" of baggage and bodies, but the privilege was limited only to licensed embalmers. Actually, this was a significant step taken by the association in a continuing effort to gain recognition of qualified practitioners. Incidentally, attendance at the Peoria meeting reached 200 including a number of new members. In 1898 delegates attending the state convention in Chicago laid the ground work for the creation of a state examining committee. It was believed the best approach was through the state board of health because such agencies would be in a position to give impartial and official sanction to successful applicants. Illinois gave strong support to the national association during this period for such a proposal, i.e., that such state boards should examine and license embalmers.

As a result of this activity the first state examination for an embalmers' license was held December 9, 1898, in Chicago. Illinois thus became the third state in our nation following Minnesota and Iowa to

816

establish such examination procedure. Out of a total of 300 initial applicants 263 successfully passed the first examination. Later tests were given in East St. Louis to accommodate 88 downstate applicants.

By 1901 when the members assembled at the annual convention in Rockford, President W. O. Kenney of Piper City reported: "The association has attained its majority." He was referring to the fact that the association was entering its twenty-first year as a working statewide organization. By that time 772 state licenses had been issued and this number later increased to 834 by the end of the year.

A bill regulating the profession for the first time was passed by the General Assembly and signed into law by Governor Charles S. Dineen in 1905. From this date the association gradually made its influence felt in legislative circles. For instance, other laws passed in the 1905 and 1907 sessions authorized railroads not to accept bodies unless embalmed by accredited licensees, and another measure prohibiting the embalming of bodies subject to an inquest without authorization from a coroner.

Another pioneer law approved at that time banned the use of arsenic in embalming. Records of early day meetings of the association also disclosed a trend away from Sunday funerals, and as early as 1908 the Ministerial Alliance at Alton proposed night funerals to accommodate workers in industrial plants in the area. In 1910 there is a notation in the minutes which stated, "there are too many undertakers—the supply is overtaking the demand." And in Chicago a proposal was made to charge a $100 fee

merely for the privilege of doing business. This was a very high price for the times.

By 1914 the association had attained real stature and had two "firsts" to its credit—a paid full-time organizer was sent to all sections of the state to increase interest in the association. In addition, a schedule of "booster meetings" was planned in various communities. The association also strengthened the state licensing act in 1915 to require applicants to have two years practical experience.

Relationships with the Chicago association varied at different times. In 1918 at the Alton convention President John Yehling, of Du-Quoin, reported the Chicago group had reaffiliated with the state association, boosting the state membership well over the 800 mark, but five years later in 1923 the Chicago association resigned from the state organization. This occurred at a joint Illinois—Missouri convention held at St. Louis in June. The meeting also marked another milestone in the history of the organization when the name was officially changed to the Illinois Funeral Directors and Embalmers Association. It was not until 1938 that the name again was changed to the present title—Illinois Funeral Directors Association. From the standpoint of over-all organization a significant move was made in 1929 when district organizations were created. The first district meetings were held at Canton, Kankakee and Oregon. In the following year the state was divided into nine districts and a full schedule of meetings was arranged.

The association observed its Golden Anniversary at the Peoria convention on June 12, 1930. This was at the outset of the great economic depression and in the early and middle 30's association records contain many references to the trials and financial hardships of the members. The association tackled many problems in that period, chief among them being price controls imposed following the creation of the National Recovery Administration (NRA).

Now in its eightieth year the association is a smoothly working organization with a full-time staff. Several landmarks contributed to our present position of strength. In 1936 an Officer's Advisory Board was created and two years later the membership approved establishment of a central office in Decatur. At the same time the officers set up a firm expense budget so that all administrative operation was placed on a business-like foundation. In 1941 the district plan was encouraged and carried through by the association.

Credit for progressive growth during this period belongs not only to vigorous leadership and member interest, but also to the stewardship of Eugene F. Foran, of Decatur, who acted as executive secretary and directed association affairs for many eventful years.

In 1956 state headquarters were transferred to Springfield. In 1958 the association retained the services of Roger B. Ytterberg as the first full-time executive secretary. For a short period, the association affairs had been handled on a part time basis by Attorney Harlington Wood, Jr. At the present time the organization has 692 members on the active list.

ASSOCIATION PRESIDENTS: 1881, Joseph Rogerson, *Chicago;* 1882, Geo. W. Murphy, *Quincy;* 1885, J. R. Ziegler, *Peoria;* 1886-87, H. T. Howland, *Streator;* 1888, J. Howell, *Alton;* 1889, J. M. Sweeney, *Geneseo;* 1890, C. E. Windom, *Sterling;* 1891, C. E. Windom, *Sterling;* 1892-94, Edwin P. Knox, *Moline;* 1895, W. V. McKinstry, *Delavan;* 1896, W. S. Lamb, *Gibson City;* 1897-98, F. C. Vaughan, *Amboy;* 1899, J. A. Beck, *Bloomington;* 1900, W. O. McKinney, *Piper City;* 1901, D. B. Quinlan, *Chicago;* 1902, J. W. Birney, *Bloomington;* 1903, F. H. Ketcham, *Chicago;* 1904, John B. Wilton, *Peoria;* 1905, R. K. Sloan, *Chicago;* 1906, James S. Hainline, *Macomb;* 1907, J. K. Platner, *Chicago;* 1908, P. W. Coleman, *Bloomington;* 1909, M. M. Goodale, *Chicago;* 1910, J. P. Foley, *Galesburg;* 1911, J. R. Willard, *Warrensburg;* 1912, E. H. Renner, *Urbana;* 1913, W. C. Wunderlich, *Joliet;* 1914, R. G. Fuller, *Savanna;* 1915, A. Swenson, *Bement;* 1916, B. F. Hertz, *Kankakee;* 1917, John Yehling, *Du Quoin;* 1918, J. B. Thorsen, *Leland;* 1919, A. E. Danielson, *Moline;* 1920, Wm. H. Bauer, *Alton;* 1921, Otto H. Riefenberg, *Carlinville;* 1922, W. R. Sebree, *Canton;* 1923, Anton E. Sundquist, *Toulon;* 1924, A. G. Zelle, *Murphysboro;* 1925, Albert G. Storme, *Herrin;* 1926, M. E. Wright, *Eureka;* 1927, Anthony A. Solon, *Streator;* 1928, P. J. Cummings, *Chicago;* 1929, Raligh J. Harris, *Pontiac;* 1930, J. H. Shirk, *Milledgeville;* 1931, John T. Downs, *Aurora;* 1932, W. B. Myers, *Mt. Vernon;* 1933, Roy M. Baker, *Dwight;* 1934, J. B. McHugh, *Kewaunee;* 1935, E. L. Bass, *Greenville;* 1936, J. Willard Jones, *Dixon;* 1937, Forest G. Wikoff, *Decatur;* 1938, Otis Stone, *West Frankfort;* 1939, Wm. J.

818

Wheelan, *Rock Island;* 1940, Harry F. Kelly, *Highland Park;* 1941, H. A. Williamson, *Jacksonville;* 1942-43, Llewellyn Fay, *Fulton;* 1944-45, Marvin C. Hutchcraft, *Lincoln;* 1946, Ralph E. Wilton, *Peoria;* 1947, B. Leo Schwarz, *Freeport;* 1948, James L. Woodruff, *Mt. Vernon;* 1949, Robert H. Streeper, *Alton;* 1950, Marshall B. Wood, *Rockford;* 1951, Warren R. First, *Galesburg;* 1952, Raymond E. Houghton, *Georgetown;* 1953, Walter C. Oehler, *Des Plaine;* 1954, John Barry, *Lincoln;* 1955, Raymond A. Crawshaw, *Murphysboro;* 1956, Harold C. Johnson, *Moline;* 1957, Walter D. Hansen, *Quincy;* 1958, George H. Krauspe, *Chicago;* 1959, William E. Froelrich, Jr., *Gridley;* 1960, Ralph Gent, *Alton.*

INDIANA
Informant: Herbert R. Wald

In April, 1881, *The Casket* printed a short letter from S. R. Lippincott of Richmond, Indiana, stating that a call issued previously for the formation of a new organization had been discussed by the funeral directors of the state of Indiana and "nearly all are in favor of Indianapolis as the place and some time in May as the time" for the meeting. Accordingly in the next issue of the same magazine the meeting was scheduled for "Wednesday morning, May 18, 1881, at 11 o'clock A.M., at the Bates House parlors in the City of Indianapolis." The constitution and by-laws were discussed and passed by the convention. The name chosen for the new organization was The Indiana Funeral Directors Association. Thus began the fourth funeral directors' association in the nation.

Officers for the first year were:

President, Isaac Ball, Terre Haute; and *Secretary,* Samuel R. Lippincott, Richmond.

Membership in the new organization grew rapidly at first, so that by 1886 there were 150 funeral directors in Indiana who claimed membership in the association. This number held fairly constant until 1889 when the organization experienced a notable increase in membership following an agreement entered into between the Indiana Funeral Directors and the National Burial Case associations, stipulating that funeral merchandise from members of the latter group would be sold only to members of the state association. The association claimed 225 members by 1907, 265 in 1908, 316 in 1910 and 634 in 1960.

The earliest problem to come before the Indiana Funeral Directors Association was that of setting an equitable fee among the counties for the burial of the pauper dead.

The Indiana association was one of the first to recognize the threat posed by burial associations organized as promotion ventures. In 1900 the state association formally disapproved such ventures, and in 1901 a committee was authorized to suggest revisions to the constitution and by-laws so that the proprietor of a burial association would be excluded from membership in the Indiana Funeral Directors Association. And in 1906 a final blow was dealt the burial associations by the Auditor and the Attorney General of the state who held them to be operating in violation of insurance laws.

In-service training in embalming, consisting chiefly of institutes held at the state conventions, was an early contribution of the association to its members. So successful were the demonstrations and lectures that in 1896 the education program was commended by the National Funeral Directors Association. The education program was then expanded to include the sponsorship of "schools" of embalming. Early in the present century the importance of an extended period of training for the embalmer was recognized, and the state association pressed for a twelve months' actual training course either under a practicing licensed embalmer or at any college prescribing a twelve-month course in embalming.

With respect to license legislation, the drive to bring embalmers under state jurisdiction was preceded by a program of certification through examination given by a committee of funeral directors representing the state association. In 1899 the State Board of Health took over supervision of this program, and in 1901 a law licensing embalmers was passed by the state legislature. An important amendment to the first law was added in 1917 making it necessary for a funeral director either to be a licensed embalmer or to keep a licensed embalmer constantly in his employ. Until 1931 the State Board of Embalmers created by this act functioned under that name, but by an act of 1931 it assumed the name "State Board of Embalmers and Funeral Directors."

A few of the more outstanding leaders of the association, especially in its formative years, need mention. Isaac Ball of Terre Haute, was the first president and served two terms of office. Samuel R. Lippincott of Richmond helped organize the association and went on to serve for many years as secretary of the National Funeral Directors Association. O. G. Davis of Williamsburg also helped found the association and later became its fifth president. J. H. McCully of Idaville served two terms as president of the association (1898-1900) and was later honored by election to the national presidency. Likewise, Bert S. Gadd of Indianapolis served as state president for three consecutive terms (1931-1933) and in October, 1933, was elected national president. At the national convention held in St. Louis in October, 1959, past president Bernard A. Dziadowicz of Hammond was elected governor of the third district. He had also served as state president in 1958-1959.

ASSOCIATION PRESIDENTS: 1881-82, Isaac Ball, *Terre Haute;* 1883, Charles Kregelo, *Indianapolis;* 1884, Charles T. Whitsett, *Indianapolis;* 1885, C. L. Woll, *Logansport;* 1886, O. G. Davis, *Williamsburg;* 1887, Frank W. Flanner, *Indianapolis;* 1888, M. L. Meeks, *Muncie;* 1889, Dexter Gardner, *Vincennes;* 1890, J. G. Chambers, *Madison;* 1891, H. R. Downing, *Richmond;* 1892, Rodney Strain, *Logansport;* 1893, James W. Buchanan, *Marion;* 1894, D. C. Barnhill, *Crawfordsville;* 1895, J. H. Fetter, *Peru;* 1896, Frank Munchoff, *Anderson;* 1897, Miss Fannie Gardner, *Vincennes;* 1898-99, J. H. McCully, *Idaville;* 1900, J. N. Frist, *Clinton;* 1901, M. F. Parsons, *Greensburg;* 1902, A. V. Weisinger, *Mount Vernon;* 1903, E. E. Davis, *Alexandria;* 1904, W. H. Hiss, *Plainfield;* 1905, M. B. Stults, *Huntington;* 1906, George C. Wyatt, *Rushville;* 1907, George J. Watson, *Cayuga;* 1908, H. M. Purviance, *Huntington;* 1909, Edwin R. Hisey, *Indianapolis;* 1910, J. D. Emmons, *Columbus;* 1911, W. A. Rushton, *Plainfield;* 1912, Mont Boord, *Covington;* 1913, B. K. Adams, *Peru;* 1914, Ivory C. Tolle, *Lebanon;* 1915, Folger P. Wilson, *Richmond;* 1916, W. F. Evans, *Brownsburg;* 1917, C. R. Wilson, *Mooresville;* 1918, H. P. Martin, *Terre Haute;* 1919, Charles C. La Follette, *Thorntown;* 1920, James M. Chappell, *Kendallville;* 1921, Clyde E. Titus, *Indianapolis;* 1922, J. Frank Hamilton, *Westport;* 1923, Harley E. Hickman, *Terre Haute;* 1924, Floyd E. Williams, *Gary;* 1925, Harry M. Allen, *Peru;* 1926, Paul H. Buchanan, *Indianapolis;* 1927, Floyd S. Culp, *Goshen;* 1928, Frank A. LePell, *Valparaiso;* 1929, Charles Herrlich, *New Palestine;* 1930, James A. Coffing, *Attica;* 1931-33, Bert S. Gadd, *Indianapolis;* 1934, Hallard A. Flynn, *Chesterton;* 1935, Jesse F. Phillippi, *Zionsville;* 1936-37, Dwight R. Baker, *Dayton;* 1938, Herbert R. Wald, *Indianapolis;* 1939, Morris H. Sleeth, *Shelbyville;* 1940, Frank M. McNeeley, *Indianapolis;* 1941, Frank J. Evans, *Noblesville;* 1942, Clarence G. Piepho, *Muncie;* 1943, John H. Blackwell, *Indianapolis;* 1944, Harold E. Rozelle, *Anderson;* 1945-46, Ralph McMullan, *Kempton;* 1947, Donald C. Ulrich, *Dillsboro;* 1948, Verlan L. Poindexter, *Washington;* 1949, J. Harold Fife, *East Chicago;* 1950, Raymond E. Needham, *Marion;* 1951, Harry W. Moore, *Indianapolis;* 1952, Kenneth G. Alexander, *Evansville;* 1953, Harry E. Danielson, *Plymouth;* 1954, Earl C. Hollis, *South Bend;* 1955, Frank W. Moore, *Rushville;* 1956, Gene E. Laird, *Amboy;* 1957, Earl K. Parson, *Muncie;* 1958, F. Walter Voss, *Seymour;* 1959, Bernard A. Dziadowicz, *Hammond;* 1960, Charles W. Pemberton, *Lynnville;* President-elect 1960, P. L. Myers, *Lebanon.*

IOWA

Informant: Louis E. Wilson

While there was no organized endeavor on the part of the Iowa undertakers before the year of 1881, we find some interested enough in the new art of embalming bodies to go East and see this work actually done; also, in the year 1881, Professor Renouard of New York, published his *Undertakers Manual.* This publication was received well throughout the country and served as a great stimulus for study. In January, 1881, W. P. Hohenschuh and A. B. Cree, a salesman of undertaking supplies, both of Iowa City, issued an invitation to the undertakers of Iowa to come to Iowa City on February 23 and 24 for the purpose of organizing a state association for undertakers. On those dates at the St. James Hotel in Iowa City, 20 men met and organized the third specific state funeral directors' association in the United States.

At this meeting a set of by-laws and a constitution were adopted, the preamble being: "The object of this association is to advance the interests of the profession by mutual interchange of thought, and the study of various phases of the profession in which its members are engaged."

The following were elected: *President,* Aaron Park, Wilton Junction; *Vice President,* C. B. Osborn, Atlantic; and *Secretary Treasurer,* W. P. Hohenschuh, Iowa City.

It was found that among the first problems were those of embalming and creating a more gen-

821

eral interest among the many who were rendering a service as "Undertaker." There were few laws governing the care of the dead human body and few general customs followed.

It was during the third convention held in June, 1883, at Ottumwa that the name of the association was changed from the Iowa Undertakers Association to the Iowa Funeral Directors Association.

As early as 1885, under the leadership of Professor Hohenschuh, there was introduced the subject of required educational standards and a required examination for embalmers. These subjects were the prime matters for discussion at each meeting for a number of years. In 1891, at the 11th meeting of the Iowa association held in Iowa City there were 250 in attendance. A great interest was shown in the state association. At this time, a yearly demand was being made before the State Board of Health that embalming be required and the "Undertaker" be recognized. It was not until 1898 that the first class was examined and the first "Embalmer's Permit" issued to Professor William Hohenschuh. Soon after the group was recognized new laws were passed by the legislature, and certain practices were required and enforced under the "Embalmer's Department" in the Iowa State Department of Health.

To the credit of the state association, it fostered a licensing program which first required an eighth grade, then high school, and lastly a two year college program as a basic education; and at the same time demanded first at least a six-week correspondence course, then a six month course, and last a full college

year of nine months in an accredited school of mortuary science. These progressive steps were taken in the support of the program proposed by the Board of Embalmer Examiners.

At first applicants for embalming were examined by a State Board of Health member, all of whom were physicians. In 1907, the composition of the board was changed by law to be two licensed physicians, two licensed embalmers, and the secretary of the Board of Health. In 1924, in a special session of the legislature, the law was changed; the General Practice Act was adopted, and a Board of Embalmer Examiners of three members was set up. The members of this board were to be appointed by the governor to serve a term of three years and were required to have held embalmer's licenses in the state for at least five years. In 1953, this act was amended to read "Embalmer and Funeral Director Examiners." The state association has always promoted legislative changes to improve the standards of the profession.

Within the organization two important changes have taken place within the last 30 years. The most important was in 1933 when the association became incorporated and changed its name to "The Iowa Funeral Directors and Embalmers Association," the other in 1952, with the adoption of the Amended and Substituted Articles of Incorporation.

The membership of the association represents about 70 per cent of all funeral establishments in Iowa who conduct about 90 per cent of all funeral services.

Iowa has had a minimum of price advertising. At one time quite a few co-operative funeral establishments

822

flourished, but as of 1960 few are left.

Among the leaders of the association the name of W. P. Hohenschuh belongs at the top. Known throughout the nation, as well as in his home state, he must be credited with playing a major role in the reformation of crude early embalming practices. Without his inspiration and guidance the fortunes of the state association in its early years might have been much the worse. Aaron Park, first president of the association was a man of dignity and foresight, and, in 1900 he wrote the first history of the association—a 20-year summary of the "up's and down's" of the organization. Another "historian," Louis E. Wilson, one of the earlier presidents, edited the *History of Seventy-five Years of Funeral Service in Iowa*, one of the first substantial state association histories ever written.

Iowa has been highly honored by the Conference of Funeral Service Examining Boards. During the years four Iowa funeral directors have held the office as president: Dr. Jesse A. West, Sioux City; Al M. Didesch, Dubuque; Paul D. McAuley, Mason City; and August Brandt, Jr., Dallas Center. Mr. Brandt also held the office of secretary.

Active in the affairs of the National Funeral Directors Association during the years were Professor William P. Hohenschuh, Dr. Jesse A. West, and Frank W. Alexander. At the present time Thomas Glidden of Des Moines is serving in the dual capacity of First Vice President and Chairman of the Exhibit Committee. Many other members have held responsible positions in government and, as in all states, members of the association are found among the leading citizens of their communities.

ASSOCIATION PRESIDENTS: 1881-82, Aaron Park, *Wilton Junction;* 1883-84, O. P. Arnold, 1885-86, J. B. McCurdy, *Oskaloosa;* 1887, Will Hohenschuh, *Iowa City;* 1888, J. L. Krebs, *Cedar Rapids;* 1889, M. H. Miller, *Tipton;* 1890, Ackley Hubbard, *Spencer;* 1891, H. K. Burket, *Creston;* 1892, J. B. Turner, *Cedar Rapids;* 1893, M. M. Hoffman, *Dubuque;* 1894, S. V. R. Slade, *Waterloo;* 1895-96, C. S. Hopkins, *Lake City;* 1897, F. W. Alexander, *Conrad Grove;* 1898, J. M. Brunner, *Mt. Pleasant;* 1899, F. L. Underkircher, *Burlington;* 1900, A. H. Duncan, *Humboldt;* 1901, Fred M. Stowell, *Boone;* 1902, Chas. Emerson, *Creston;* 1903, J. H. Hadley, *Eldora;* 1904, Aaron Park, *Wilton Junction;* 1905, C. M. Woods, *Waterloo;* 1906, Henry Gray, *Des Moines;* 1907, Leo V. Myers, *Red Oak;* 1908, J. E. Wescott, *Sioux City;* 1909, Frank L. Daggett, *Ottumwa;* 1910, R. R. McBride, *Des Moines;* 1911, J. A. Buchner, *Maquoketa;* 1912, C. H. Gregoire, *Dubuque;* 1913, A. A. Taylor, *Stuart;* 1914, F. D. Kerrick, *Fairfield;* 1915, Edd. H. Young, *Carlisle;* 1916, S. L. McIntire, *Pocahontas;* 1917, B. H. Wilder, *Humboldt;* 1918, Peter A. Koob, *Cascade;* 1919, E. M. Cheeseman, *Oskaloosa;* 1920, O. O. Greenlee, *Lineville;* 1921, T. R. Osborne, *New Sharon;* 1922, A. E. McAuley, *Mason City;* 1923, B. H. Wilder, *Humboldt;* 1924, H. G. Page, *Farmington;* 1925, E. F. Kistner, *Waterloo;* 1926, W. H. Gleim, *Arlington;* 1927-28, L. E. Wilson, *Eagle Grove;* 1929, E. Carl White, *Des Moines;* 1930, Chas. Beckman,

Iowa City; 1931-32, L. A. Jones, Washington; 1933, Charles Bartcher, Denison; 1934-35, Walter Sellergren, Red Oak; 1936, Vernon Barta, Cedar Rapids; 1937, Iver Newlen, Des Moines; 1938, Lester Jay, Ottumwa; 1939, A. Earl Ross, Hawarden; 1940, Harry L. Orr, Indianola; 1941, Burdette L. Roland, Atlantic; 1942, C. S. Wagler, Griswold; 1943, Clyde L. Slininger, Jefferson; 1944, Arthur S. Mason, Tama; 1945-46, Frank J. Monahan, Cedar Rapids; 1947, George J. Kaiser, Waverly; 1948, L. D. Fisher, Van Meter; 1949, Harley J. Wood, Iowa Falls; 1950, R. W. Hooker, Woodward; 1951-52, Al M. Didesch, Dubuque; 1953, John A. Christensen, Ida Grove; 1954, Elmer F. Baumgarten, Sutherland; 1955, O. Dale Smith, Grinnell; 1956, Cecil Goettsch, Monticello; 1957, Chris Wagler, Bloomfield; 1958, H. Clay Pauley, Harlan; 1959, Ken Murdock, Marion; 1960, Keith Steffy, Montezuma.

KANSAS

Informant: Harry E. Jolley

The first record of associational activity in Kansas appears in a report in *The Casket* that the Kansas Funeral Directors Association had met in Topeka, September 11, 1884, to carry on the organizational work started there by funeral directors some time earlier. President J. W. Stokes, it is reported, conducted the business meeting and received into membership six new members.

Again in 1887 *The Casket* makes note of a state organization: "a new association called The Kansas Embalming Association," with W. H. Kendle as President. The objective of the group was to issue stock and

create a school of embalming. In the year following *The Embalmers Monthly* reports the meeting of this group, and again, in 1889 it met to reorganize as the "Kansas University of Embalming and Undertaker's Association."

In 1890 Kansas made its first report to the annual meeting of NFDA under the above name. W. A. Repp was the organization president at that time. In 1891 under the leadership of H. Whitely, who had been an officer in the first aborted association, the group changed its name to the Kansas Undertakers' Association, and it was reported to National at this time that there were 200 members. In 1892 a lawsuit ending in a $5000 judgment against the association seems to have wrecked it, for no further reports from this group are to be found.

In 1897 fifteen of the leading funeral directors of the State of Kansas met in convention and decided to form an association of funeral directors. The meeting was quite informal and after discussion the group elected: *President,* W. B. Raymond, Kansas City; and *Secretary,* W. H. Gates, Rosedale. There being no need of a Treasurer at this time, this office was left vacant. The meeting for 1898 was held at Emporia, where the members elected: *President,* J. A. Harouff, Atchison; *Secretary,* L. M. Penwell, Topeka; and *Treasurer,* A. R. Hall. At this early date, they operated under rules and regulations under authority of the State Board of Health, whose offices were in Topeka. L. N. Penwell was re-elected Secretary, to continue in this office for fifteen years. The annual convention was held in Kansas City in

824

1899, at which W. Gates of Rosedale was elected President; L. M. Penwell of Topeka, Secretary; and Mary L. Gates of Rosedale, Treasurer. In passing, it is of interest that Mrs. Gates was reelected treasurer through the years until the 1939 convention. In the early years, the Association relied very much on the State Board of Health, in which Dr. J. S. Crumbine was the efficient Secretary for many years.

In 1907 the Association formulated a law which was introduced into the state legislature; with its passage, the first Embalmer's law was put upon the statutes. L. M. Penwell was a member of the legislature and sponsored the bill through. Dr. Crumbine aided very materially formulating the provisions in this law and stress was placed upon such items as: sanitation, disinfection, transportation of the dead, shipping rules, ethical conduct, and qualifications of would-be embalmers. The first embalming board was made up of Joe. S. Johnson, Osawatomie; George Southern, Manhattan; and W. H. Johnson, Hutchinson.

One of the contributing factors in the progressive development of funeral directors of Kansas must be credited to the frequent employment of such lecturers and demonstrators as Barnes, Hohenschuh, Eckels, Carpenter, and Williams. As time went on, frequent changes in the law were made to meet the improvement in theory and techniques. A very pronounced advance was made in 1935 when the law was made much more inclusive.

Formerly, the law related to embalmers only, but the legislators, realizing the funeral director is primarily responsible for the acts done in his establishment as owner, proposed and enacted a law to license the funeral director as well as the embalmer.

A provision of the law also defined the qualification of those desiring licenses as funeral directors and gave authority of the Board to enforce the laws and regulations of the Board and to assess penalties for violations. As time went on the weaknesses of some of the sections of the law became apparent and the association, with the assistance of the association's attorney, Mr. Ralph Glenn, proceeded to revamp the entire law relating to the burial and care of the human dead, in compliance with the latest and best thought regarding safety, public health and welfare of the state. After much counselling, the proposed law was ready in 1941 to be brought before the legislature. Senator Ernest McKensie and Representative C. W. Porterfield sponsored the bill, first through the Senate and then in the House. Much opposition was encountered in the House, and some twenty amendments to the bill were offered throughout the debate, but most of these were defeated. The end result was the passage of what Kansas funeral directors feel to be one of the best funeral laws in the land. Moreover, changes since 1941 have been added to keep abreast of the best in funeral practices. The Kansas association established a trade publication in the late thirties under the direction of Secretary Paul Cooms. At first it was a mimeographed publication and later was developed into one of the fine funeral trade papers of the country and is now under the supervision of Executive Secretary, Harry E. Jolley.

In this year, 1960, there still re-

825

mains on the scene of activity one of the original group, M. G. (Stevy) Stevenson of Ashland, Kansas, who is in his nineties and still active. Two Kansas members have been honored by election to the presidency of the National Association; L. M. Penwell of Topeka in 1904 and C. W. Porterfield in 1938. I. W. Gill was elected Vice President of the National Association in 1908.

ASSOCIATION PRESIDENTS: 1884, J. W. Stokes, 1887, W. H. Kendle, *Wichita;* 1890, W. A. Repp, *Arkansas City;* 1891, H. Whitley, *Solomon City;* 1897, W. B. Raymond, *Kansas City;* 1898, J. A. Harouff, *Atchison;* 1899, H. W. Gates, *Rosedale;* 1900, J. M. Doyle, *Wichita;* 1901, Joe S. Johnson, *Osawatomie;* 1902, James W. Sexton, *Leavenworth;* 1903, W. S. Twist, *Bonner Springs;* 1904, I. W. Gill, *Wichita;* 1905, C. W. Goodlander, *Fort Scott;* 1906, D. R. Maltby, *McPherson;* 1907, W. E. Samuels, *Emporia;* 1908, B. F. Bracken, *Beloit;* 1909, C. H. McDuffie, *Waverly;* 1910, W. H. Johnson, *Hutchinson;* 1911, A. G. Mueller, *Wichita;* 1912, W. J. Bowser, *Norton;* 1913, A. L. Harvey, *Baxter Springs;* 1914, Herb K. Eicholtz, *Abilene;* 1915, George W. Southern, *Manhattan;* 1916, L. M. Penwell, *Topeka;* 1917, P. P. Friesen, *Hutchinson;* 1918, M. E. Cheatum, *Halstead;* 1919, Ira Wilson, *Fredonia;* 1920, Rush V. Smith, *Salina;* 1921, R. M. Johnson, *Topeka;* 1922-23, C. W. Porterfield, *Holton;* 1924, Edwin Potts, *Independence;* 1925, S. T. Bostion, *McPherson;* 1926, John Fairweather, *Kansas City;* 1927, Harold J. Lamb, *Ottawa;* 1928, C. A. Hulpieu, *Dodge City;* 1929, J. Q. Ragan, *Hoisington;* 1930, H. E. Julien, *Olathe;*

1931, J. S. Meek, *Hiawatha;* 1932, Dale DeWeese, *Wellington;* 1933, V. L. Gordon, *Mulvane;* 1934, H. E. Livingston, *Kingman;* 1935, J. H. Downing, *Wichita;* 1936, Frank J. Conwell, *Topeka;* 1937, A. R. Sleeper, *Iola;* 1938, John B. Smith, *Stockton;* 1939, Glenn A. Stewart, *Wamego;* 1940, Fred Simmons, *Smith Center;* 1941, Clarence G. Wilke, *El Dorado;* 1942, Clyde E. Reinhart, *Sabetha;* 1943, Ernest McKenzie, *Cottonwood Falls;* 1944, Ferrol Cowan, *Manhattan;* 1945, Arel Olliff, *Kensington;* 1946, Ralph A. Fulton, *Kansas City;* 1947, A. Lee Soice, *Stafford;* 1948, Harold L. Swaim, *Dodge City;* 1949, Ward B. Runyan, *Louisburg;* 1950, Tom O. Waugh, *Iola;* 1951, William F. Cochran, *Wichita;* 1952, Clare S. Ford, *Coffeyville;* 1953, Richard W. Farris, *Garnett;* 1954, S. F. Peacock, *Stafford;* 1955, J. Glenn Hilyard, *Douglas;* 1956, P. H. Phillips, *Garden City;* 1957, Willis W. Birchard, *Osawatomie;* 1958, Otis A. Rogers, *Hugoton;* 1959, Oscar B. Rumsey, *Lawrence;* 1960, Clarence Webb, *Independence.*

KENTUCKY
Informant: John H. Kerr, Jr.

As early as 1861 persons engaged in undertaking or funeral directing in the cities of Louisville, Kentucky; New Albany, Indiana; and other neighboring towns had formed and kept active an organization known as The Funeral Directors Association of the Falls Cities. This organization met annually to conduct its business and at monthly meetings discussed practical educational topics.

This type of organization was extended state-wide in Kentucky beginning with the year 1882 when

826

in a Lexington, Kentucky newspaper of August 21, 1882, the following information was given: For a year past Mr. T. J. Danahy, of this city, has been in correspondence with the undertakers of the various towns and cities in Kentucky, with a view to organizing a convention or association of the craft in the state, for the purpose of mutual assistance, information, and so forth. His efforts culminated yesterday in the organization, in this city, of the Kentucky Undertakers' Association.

The first officers of the association were: *President*, T. J. Danahy, Lexington; *Vice President*, E. Whitesides, Frankfort; *Secretary*, F. H. Dudley, Winchester; *Treasurer* W. R. Milward, Lexington; and *Executive Committeemen*, Charles Donnelly, Covington; and William Taafe, Warsaw. Another leader of the profession of that period was Lee E. Cralle of Louisville who served the new association as its secretary for ten years, 1885 to 1895.

During this time there was much discussion on the achievement of legislation which would license embalmers and undertakers and raise the standards of the trade. However, these attempts seemed to have been lost in the events of the day particularly because of the efforts of the Kentucky legislature to call a constitutional convention to write a new constitution for the state. By the time of the 15th annual meeting, held in Louisville in 1896, many new members were discouraged and attendance was poor.

In 1900 after the organization was revitalized, John J. Barrett of Louisville was elected president and on September 24 and 25 a reorganization meeting was conducted, attended by about fifty funeral directors from various parts of the state. As noted in the minutes of that year, "A keen desire for legislation and higher education seemed to be the general sentiment of everybody." It is interesting to note that this reorganization was born somewhat out of adversity, for in the year 1901 the Funeral Directors Association was attacked in the courts and an indictment was obtained before a grand jury in Louisville against the association. Because of lack of any supporting evidence the case was thrown out of court on the motion of the Commonwealth's Attorney.

The organization grew from 101 members in 1903 to over 200 members in 1904 and in that year the state convention in Lexington "had one of the largest attendances in the history of the organization." In this same year the first embalmer's license bill was passed by the Kentucky legislature. Licenses were issued by the new board to about four hundred embalmers, numbers 1 and 1-A going to two of the leading funeral directors of the day, John Maas of Louisville, who later became President of the National Funeral Directors Association and R. Lee Shannon of Shelbyville, affectionately known as "Uncle Lee," who served the Funeral Directors of Kentucky in various capacities of leadership for many years.

The early years of the century were busy years for association work. In 1907 the organization was successful in securing the abolition of toll road charges for funerals. In 1915 the question of automobile funerals was discussed. In 1916 the association successfully sponsored legislation requiring burial associa-

827

tions to comply with insurance laws and also legislation providing a license for undertakers as well as embalmers. In 1918 and 1919 the sign of the times reflected itself in the activities of the association, "The stern work of war was foremost in Kentucky, and the ravages of disease and epidemic occupied our ceaseless attention. . . ."

At the annual meeting in 1917 the incorporation of the association was ratified and a set of comprehensive by-laws adopted. It was noted at that time that the Kentucky association was the first state funeral directors' association in the United States to incorporate.

The decade of the 1920's was an interesting one from an organizational standpoint for the Kentucky association. Early in the decade Kentucky withdrew from the national association. However, following incorporation and reorganization of the national association at Pittsburgh in 1924, the Kentuckians voted to reaffiliate with National Funeral Directors Association in October 1924 at the national convention in St. Paul, Minnesota, and the parent group graciously accepted this return. By 1928 Kentucky was honored to have one of its past presidents, Henry J. Bosse of Louisville, installed as President of the National Funeral Directors' Association. Other activity in this decade was pointed toward improvement of laws governing the profession. An amendment to the license law was passed in 1924 and other legislation was attempted in the legislatures of 1926 and 1928. In 1927, 1928 and 1929 the association moved toward the establishment and strengthening of district organizations, voting in 1927 to

establish five districts and in 1929 to increase the number to six.

The 1930's found the association back at the doors of the legislature but this time with more success. In 1932 after a bill had been passed regulating burial associations and strengthening the embalmer's license law, R. Lee Shannon was presented at the state convention with a life membership for his legislative activities. Recognition was given to Elizabeth Lyon of Benton, Kentucky, who assisted the legislative committee in its activities and lobbied for the bills in the legislature. In 1934 Mrs. Lyon was employed as Field Representative to help promote the Kentucky association. She still maintains this position as she continues to work in this capacity for the association, helping build membership, steering the state through another crisis with the national organization, and being instrumental in getting the national convention at Louisville in 1936. She was ably assisted early in this endeavor by the secretary-treasurer of the association, Henry W. Bradley. Eventually the position of Field Representative held by Mrs. Lyon was changed to that of Field Counsel, and the position was controlled jointly by the State Board of Embalmers and the Funeral Directors Association of Kentucky. In 1959 Mrs. Lyon was presented a gift in recognition of her twenty-five years of service as Field Counsel.

In 1944 the state legislature passed a bill requiring all burial associations to pay off proceeds in cash and to allow the beneficiary a complete choice of funeral director called to service any policy. In March 1947 this law was held unconstitutional by the Court of Appeals of Kentucky. The state now turned to the proposal of establishing a legitimate, fiscally sound and legally operated burial insurance plan which would be in the public interest and meet the desire for funeral insurance. The results of this activity were the establishment in 1948 of the Kentucky Funeral Directors' Burial Association. The funeral insurance plan of this association offered to the public a sound insurance program underwritten by an old line legal reserve life insurance company under contract with the burial association.

Efforts of the state association during the last decade have been pointed mainly toward education along with continued building of the organization. Most efforts have been pointed toward the strengthening of district associations, with the feeling that at these small local meetings many practical matters regarding mutual associations and conduct of the profession can best be solved and unity and harmony best engendered. A series of midwinter conferences on a state-wide basis has been sponsored by the association for the past six years, providing outstanding speakers and educational clinics for the advancement of the profession. The association in 1959 had a membership of 317 out of a total of 387 eligible firms in the state. This is the highest membership in the annals of the association.

Throughout the many years of existence of the Kentucky association its activities are best described in light of the objects and principles of its constitution: "To cultivate and promote the art and science of funeral directing and embalming;

to elevate and sustain the professional character and education of funeral directors and embalmers; to encourage among them mutual improvement, social intercourse, and good will; to enlighten and direct public opinion in relation to the advantages of enacting and enforcing proper and just laws on funeral directing and embalming in Kentucky; to publish reports and treatises; and collectively, to represent, have cognizance of, and safe-guard the common interests of its members; and to foster and maintain among them high professional ideals and public service."

ASSOCIATION PRESIDENTS: 1882, T. J. Danahy, *Lexington;* 1891, W. Hollis, *Pembroke;* 1892-93, J. J. Barrett, *Louisville;* 1894-96, W. S. Taylor, *Versailles;* 1898-1900, J. J. Barrett, *Louisville;* 1901, H. W. Miller, *Owensboro;* 1902, J. K. Woodruff, *Eminence;* 1903, Lyman Graham, *Frankfort;* 1904, John Maas, Jr., *Louisville;* 1905, R. H. Elliston, *Williamstown;* 1906, M. J. Costican, *Newport;* 1907, John C. Schildt, *Louisville;* 1908, R. L. Johnson, *Clinton;* 1909, John Allison, *Covington;* 1910, James Gillison, *Owensboro;* 1911, Stanley Milward, *Lexington;* 1912, C. H. Boden, *Louisville;* 1913, B. W. Slaton, *Madisonville;* 1914, G. W. Peak, *LaGrange;* 1915, Henry Bosse, *Louisville;* 1916, V. N. Booker, *Franklin;* 1917, W. O. Hinton, *Paris;* 1918, Fred Koth, *Paducah;* 1919, W. G. Dunlap, *Louisville;* 1921, Ernest Ashurst, *Georgetown;* 1922, Lee Sims, *Harrodsburg;* 1923, J. Raymond Barrett, *Louisville;* 1924, Fred Myers, *Jeffersontown;* 1925, James Rowland, *Henderson;* 1926, Walter L. Proctor, *Russellville;*

1927, T. A. Minish, *Carrollton;* 1928, C. L. Carlton, *Warsaw;* 1929-30, O. S. Clark, *Ashland;* 1931, John C. Schildt, *Louisville;* 1932, Kean Ashurst, *Georgetown;* 1933, Russell C. Swetnam, *Covington;* 1934, E. B. McCain, *Beford;* 1935, Kirk P. Byrn, *Mayfield;* 1936, C. G. O'Neil, *Corbin;* 1937, A. G. Spillman, *Bedford;* 1938, W. C. Tharp, *Dayton;* 1939, H. Clay Smith, *Cynthiana;* 1940, L. Porter Ray, *Jackson;* 1941, A. L. Mitchell, *Mt. Sterling;* 1942, A. W. Rawlings, *London;* 1943, J. Vernon Kemper, *Danville;* 1944-45, Roy Lowe, *Lowes;* 1946, W. H. Franklin, *Marion;* 1947, W. G. McDaniel, *Louisville;* 1948, Henry H. Curtright, *Louisa;* 1949, Jerome H. Harris, *Paducah;* 1950, H. E. Pruitt, *Jamestown;* 1951, J. Fred Miller, *Ashland;* 1952, W. G. Hardy, Jr., *Louisville;* 1953, Hubert Reid, *Earlington;* 1954, Edward Laws, *Harlon;* 1955, A. B. Fendley, *Paducah;* 1956, William Engle, *Hazard;* 1957, J. Harold Connley, *Covington;* 1958, Jack B. Stith, *Danville;* 1959, Oscar M. Plummer, *Vanceburg;* 1960, Lewis Boyd, *Salem.*

LOUISIANA

As early as 1892 the funeral directors of Louisiana were meeting in various cities of the state attempting to organize all interested funeral directors in a state association. One of the early meetings was held at Alexandria on May 10, 1892, at which time *The Embalmers' Monthly* reported that 20 new members had been added to the list of the 33 men already enrolled in the organization. At this meeting the following officers were elected: *President,* B. F. Morris, Clinton; *Vice-President,* H. L. Frantz, New Orleans; *Treasurer,* J. E. Peters, Monroe; and *Secretary,* Charles Fitche, Rayville.

This early association reported at meetings of the National Funeral Directors Association in the years 1892, 1893 and 1894, but apparently did not continue long as an organization after this date. However, *The Embalmers' Monthly* for June, 1900, reported a new organization in Louisiana organized May 10, 1900, in New Orleans, at which temporary officers were elected and a discussion of the need for an embalmers' law headed the business calendar. Professor J. H. Clarke was present and spoke on his experience in association work. After the signatures of 32 men were obtained, the formal organization began with the election of officers: *President,* Thomas Lynch, New Orleans; *Vice Presidents,* Frank E. Thomas, Hammond; C. Peters, Monroe; and John A. Barrett, Algiers; *Secretary,* Samuel D. Norwood, New Orleans; *Treasurer,* A. F. Bultman, New Orleans; and *Guard,* J. H. Kiblinger, Jackson.

Records at the national level do not reveal any further word from the Louisiana association until at the National Funeral Directors Association's annual meeting in 1913. Mr. B. F. Markey of Louisiana reported the reformation of the association informally in 1912, and formally at New Orleans, July 16-17, 1913.

There were 47 members and guests registered for this "annual" meeting. Such men as John Barrett, Henry Tharp, Albert Briede, Sr., and Philip J. Schoen, Sr., all of New Orleans; Frank Thomas of Hammond, and Roll Osborne of Shreveport were responsible for the formation of the organization at this time. So successful was the first year of the organization that the membership list grew in 1914 to a total of 66 members in good standing.

During the second year of its "re-existence" the Funeral Directors Association of Louisiana succeeded in having passed by its state legislature a bill regulating embalming and undertaking in the state by means of the establishment of a State Board of Embalmers and Undertakers appointed by the Governor of the state. The board, composed of funeral directors of the state, was empowered to issue licenses after examination of applicants. Licenses were required for both undertakers and embalmers.

The Louisiana association has been fortunate in its choice of officers, especially the office of secretary. In 1913 Benjamin Markey was elected secretary and filled this office until his death in 1918. At this time Philip J. Schoen, Jr., of New Orleans was given the position and held it for the next 23 years. In 1941 Charles Eagan of New Orleans was elected and served the organization for several years. Until his recent death Robert L. Laudumiey of New Orleans served the organization as secretary.

The State of Louisiana feels particularly honored in having sent one of its members on to the highest national office. Merle M. Welsh of Baton Rouge held the office of president of the National Funeral Directors Association for the year 1958-59 and was presiding officer at the 1959 St. Louis Convention. Louisiana has also been honored by being host to the NFDA Convention held in New Orleans in 1934.

ASSOCIATION PRESIDENTS: 1913, John A. Barrett, *New Orleans;* 1914, F. B. Thomas, *Hammond;* 1915, Henry Tharp, *New Orleans;* 1916, Roll Osborn, *Shreveport;* 1917-18, P. J. Schoen, Sr., *New Orleans;* 1919, C. P. Kramer, *Alexandria;* 1920, Roy C. Clark, *Oakdale;* 1921, P. J. Donegan, *New Orleans;* 1922, R. H. Grant, Jr., *Boyce;* 1923, Charles Schopp, *New Orleans;* 1924, G. C. Butler, *Minden;* 1925, James M. Fallo, *New Orleans;* 1926, P. S. Mulhearn, *Monroe;* 1927, Jas. M. Leitz, *New Orleans;* 1928, A. F. McGee, *Eunice;* 1929, A. S. Tharp, *New Orleans;* 1930-31, Kenneth E. Thomas, *Hammond;* 1932, Albert E. Briede, Jr., *New Orleans;* 1933, Cyprian J. Schoen, *Covington;* 1934, L. E. Bankson, *Shreveport;* 1935, E. H. Prescott, *New Orleans;* 1936, T. E. Williams, *Tallulah;* 1937, Adam A. Muhleisen, *New Orleans;* 1938, Harris J. Pellerin, *Breaux Springs;* 1939, Leonard Falgout, Sr., *Raceland;* 1940, Charles J. Eagan, *New Orleans;* 1941, Louis Peters, *Monroe;* 1942-43, Walter J. Ranson, *New Orleans;* 1944-45, Lloyd P. Geesey, *Crowley;* 1946, Phillip J. Schoen, Jr., *New Orleans;* 1947, Clifford Chauvin, *Houma;* 1948, Charles J. Eagan, *New Orleans;* 1949, Francis Felix Delhomme, *Lafayette;* 1950, Charles Jefferson Daniels Gerrets, *Algiers;* 1951-52, Dalton Lawrence Babineaux, *New Iberia;* 1953, Philip Joseph Schoen, III, *New Orleans;* 1954, Casper Philip Kramer, Jr., *Alexandria;* 1955, Lloyd Edwin Eagan, *New Orleans;* 1956, Edward James Segura, *Jennings;* 1957, Julius Bert McMahon, *New Orleans;* 1958, Thomas

H. Mulhearn, *Monroe;* 1959, Leonard Falgout, Jr., *Raceland;* 1960, Norman E. Tharp, *New Orleans.*

MAINE
Informant: John F. Farnham

An announcement of the formation of an association in the state of Maine was carried in the *Embalmers' Monthly* for November, 1900. According to the article, the meeting occurred in the State House in Augusta on October 24, 1900, and the name adopted for the new association was "The Maine Undertakers' Association." Forty-one men were present.

One of the major concerns of the day was the number of hack drivers and dealers in undertaking supplies who were listed in the Maine Register as undertakers. The newly founded association was to consist "of men who had studied the work of an undertaker in the present meaning of the term and who made the care of the bodies of the dead their work." It was suggested also that only those who held a diploma from some embalmers' school be eligible but the suggestion was rejected. The points at issue were all settled by the adoption of a constitution and by-laws admitting to membership all those at present engaged in the work.

After the adoption of a constitution, the following officers were elected and are recognized as the first "official family": *President,* J. F. Jefferds, Livermore Falls; *Vice President,* C. R. Foster, Ellsworth; *Secretary,* R. J. Duddy, Portland; and *Treasurer,* Frank B. Wood, Hallowell.

The following are charter members of the organization and were present at the first meeting in 1900:

F. B. Adams, Freeport; Amesbury and Wakefield, Gardiner; G. S. Bacon, Millinocket; A. S. Banks, Bangor; H. E. Bates, Augusta; A. D. Bryant, Freeport; H. D. Bryant, Portland; A. W. Brown, Bar Harbor; E. G. Cole, Buckfield; Jason Denslow, Dexter; W. B. Connell, Bowdoinham; G. G. Downing, Dover; R. J. Duddy, Portland; J. S. Flagg, Richmond; M. W. Fogg, Freeport; C. R. Foster, Ellsworth; W. H. Gould, Bowdoinham; Groder and Poulin, Waterville; F. W. Haley, Winterport; L. H. Hanscom, Machias; J. H. Jefferds, Livermore Falls; A. H. Kenniston, Boothbay Harbor; Gov. Charles Knowlton, Augusta; J. L. Martin, Milo; A. C. McDonnough, Lewiston, H. W. McKinney, Bridgeton; Onesime Nadeau, Biddeford; W. H. Plummer, Augusta; Wm. G. Preble, Gardiner; C. E. Rackliff, Old Town; Frank Redington, Waterville; H. W. Rich, Portland; Roak and Plummer, Auburn; W. P. Roberts, Readfield; E. P. Sampson, Lewiston; H. C. Sinclair, Winthrop; H. B. Snell, Waterville; F. E. Sherman, Bar Harbor; A. H. Teague, Lewiston; V. E. Trouant, Augusta; W. S. Varney, Bangor; W. H. Webster, Limestone; Frank B. Wood, Hallowell; S. D. Wyman, Newcastle.

Meetings in the 1900's were given over partly to demonstrations by a "professor" of embalming; partly to association business, with emphasis on the formulation of license legislation; and partly to interaction with salesmen of the supply houses.

After several years of persistent attempts to get a license law enacted, the association was pleased to report that on September 1, 1903 the law it had sponsored had gone into effect. It provided for an examination board consisting of two members of the State Board of Health, and two practical embalmers. Later the composition was changed to three undertakers and one member from the State Board of Health. A notable feature of the law was that it went beyond the mere licensing of embalmers and licensed undertakers as well.

The association prospered through the years, occasionally holding an annual meeting with adjoining states. In the early twenties a Tri-State Association consisting of the States of Maine, New Hampshire, and Vermont was organized. In 1926 the newly-named "Maine Funeral Directors Association" held its "first" annual convention in Lewiston. This meeting carried in its minutes the following notation: "The business taken up at this time was the motion to join the National Funeral Directors Association." That action became operative in 1927.

Over the past 60 years of its existence, the Maine Association in its various forms has successfully grappled with a variety of problems affecting the field of funeral directing. The more noteworthy have been the getting of progressive legislative enactments in keeping with a desire to upgrade the occupation; the effecting of harmonious relations with funeral directors and state agencies in adjoining states; and the bringing of a majority of men in the funeral service field in Maine under the influence of the ethics of good professional practice. Interestingly, in these 60 years the association has had only nine secretaries, one of whom, Harry C. Quinby served for 18 years.

ASSOCIATION PRESIDENTS: 1900-01, J. F. Jefferds, *Livermore Falls;* 1902-04, C. R. Foster, *Ellsworth;* 1905, J. C. Flagg, *Richmond;* 1906-07, George M. Phoenix, *Alfred;* 1908-09, Frank B. Wood, *Hallowell;* 1910-11, Herbert W. Rich, *Portland;* 1912, Albert S. Plummer, *Auburn;* 1913-14, Frank Redington, *Waterville;* 1915-16, James E. Warren, *Buckfield;* 1917-18, Frank E. Dillingham, *Auburn;* 1919-20, Bryce K. Edwards, *Madison;* 1921, Frank Hewins, *Augusta;* 1922, Ralph B. White, *Bangor;* 1925, Walter G. Hay, *Portland;* 1927, Marcellus Cain, *Clinton;* 1928-29, G. Ray Lewis, *Auburn;* 1930-31, Percy W. Lyon, *Danforth;* 1932-33, W. Raymond Davis, *Farmington;* 1934-35, Bradford H. White, *Gardiner;* 1936-37, William M. Mitchell, *Bangor;* 1938-39, Frederick J. Flaherty, *Portland;* 1940, Malcolm S. Hayes, *Bangor;* 1941, Irving L. Rich, *Portland;* 1942, T. H. Branch, *Waterville;* 1943, Harry Dillingham, *Auburn;* 1944-45, Fernando Potter, *Bridgeton;* 1946, Edmund F. Longley, *Waterville;* 1947, Joseph W. Brackett, *Brunswick;* 1948, Elwood A. Neal, *Gorham;* 1949, Howard W. Mayo, *Bath;* 1950, Horace F. Staples, *Gardiner;* 1951, Leah Davis Brooks, *Thomaston;* 1952, Harold L. Lary, *Dover-Foxcroft;* 1953, Donald A. Jordan, *Ellsworth;* 1954, Earl V. Bibber, *Kennebunkport;* 1955, Elwin L. Crosby, *Dexter;* 1956, Donald H. Shorey, *Pittsfield;* 1957, David B. Dunn, *Houlton;* 1958, Edward C. Jones, *Portland;* 1959, G. Stanton Giberson, *Bingham;* 1960, Philip S. Annis, *Dover-Foxcroft.*

MARYLAND

On September 23, 1884 a group of undertakers met in Baltimore for the purpose of forming a state association. C. C. Carty of Frederick City acted as temporary secretary and Henry W. Mears of Baltimore City was acting chairman. A resolution was presented requesting all funeral directors interested in forming an association to sign the roll. Fifty men signed, and the membership decided to name the new association "The Undertakers' Association of Maryland." Officers elected for the first year were: *President,* Henry W. Mears, Baltimore; *Secretary,* John M. Mason, Centerville; *Treasurer,* George Schilling, Baltimore; and *Executive Committee Members:* John Mason, W. H. H. Whiteford, C. C. Carty, Joseph B. Cook, and M. A. Daiger.

At a later meeting in Baltimore on October 27, 1884 the committee on laws and constitution presented a report and the first constitution and by-laws were adopted for the association.

Maryland first reported to the National Funeral Directors Association in 1886. Early reports indicate that the new association was having difficulty in gaining membership from the already existing city associations, but by 1888 the report to national indicated that "ninety out of every hundred undertakers in the state belong to the association." However, again in 1890, 1891, 1892, 1893, the report indicates that membership was not gaining. By 1896 membership had fallen off to 20; and although there was no further report to the national meetings until October, 1921, news items from *Embalmers' Monthly* indicate that an attempt was made to revive the association in 1902 when a meeting was held in Baltimore at which time John B. Spence was elected

president. The same source also indicated that a meeting was held in Baltimore in 1903 at which Pliny M. Hough was elected president.

An old letter indicates that Mr. John B. Martin, President of NFDA, came from New Jersey to Baltimore "on Friday and Saturday, February 13-14, 1920" to discuss with a group of local men the matter of forming an association in Maryland. From his visit the now existing Maryland State Funeral Directors Association was formed and later chartered. Approximately fifty-eight men, later called charter members, joined the association this year and held a meeting in Baltimore. The name chosen for the new association was "The Maryland State Funeral Directors' Association." Trade journals also reported the reorganization of the group and its new slate of officers headed by William E. Tickner of Baltimore. A constitution and by-laws were adopted for the new association soon after formation.

At the time of the organization of the association Maryland already had a State Board of Licensing. This same board then, as now, grants licenses to both funeral directors and embalmers. Originally the state had only the embalmer's license.

In 1939 the old coroners system passed out of existence and was supplanted by a modern system known as the Medical Examiners of Maryland.

The Maryland Association subscribes to a Code of Ethics similar to that of NFDA. However, the situation in Maryland is most unique in that a provision in the by-laws of the state association prohibits any member from doing any advertising containing "price."

834

Maryland contains no regional associations. By holding the state meeting in different locations in the state, this need seems to be filled. The state association has held meetings with and has consulted with representatives of local hospital groups, medical examiners' offices, cemetery associations, and even the traffic departments of various cities. Some legislative changes from time to time have become effective and a number of educational programs have been advanced.

Because our state is small and funds are limited elaborate state meetings are out of the question. However, our state meetings are devoted to business and the betterment of the profession and compare favorably with the meetings of most small states. The Association now has progressed to the status of a modern group with a new headquarters building to better serve its members.

ASSOCIATION PRESIDENTS: 1884-86, Henry W. Mears, *Baltimore;* 1887-88, M. A. Daiger, *Baltimore;* 1889, John B. Spence, *Baltimore;* 1890-93, Thomas W. Jenkins, *Baltimore;* 1894, J. E. Hough, *Baltimore;* 1895-99, C. N. Dodd, *Chestertown;* 1904, P. M. Hough, *Baltimore;* 1907-08, Henry C. Weidefield, *Baltimore;* 1920, I. S. Lawson, *Crisfield;* 1921-22, Wm. E. Tickner, *Baltimore;* 1923, C. C. Carty, *Frederick;* 1924, Philip Herwig, *Baltimore;* 1925, Jack Lewis, *Baltimore;* 1926, S. J. R. Holloway, *Salisbury;* 1927, Horace F. Burgee, *Baltimore;* 1928, W. R. Pumphrey, Jr., *Rockville;* 1929-30, Wm. F. Wooden, *Baltimore;* 1931, George L. Schwab, *Baltimore;* 1932, Milton H. Easton, *Ellicott City;* 1933, Bertram W. Gore, *Bal-*

timore; 1934, Harry N. Armacost, *Baltimore;* 1935, John G. Tarring, *Aberdeen;* 1936, Geo. A. Farley, *Baltimore;* 1937, Harry W. Fanning, *Baltimore;* 1938, Irving S. Albaugh, *Libertytown;* 1939, Robert S. Little, *Baltimore;* 1940, Chas. E. Delosier, *Ellicott City;* 1941, Theodore Ullrich, *Baltimore;* 1942, Warner E. Pumphrey, *Silver Spring;* 1943, Fred A. Cole, *Baltimore;* 1944, C. Richard Fleming, *Baltimore;* 1945, Elmer M. Quade, *Hughesville;* 1946, E. B. Harle, *Baltimore;* 1947, C. Vernon Lemmon, *Baltimore;* 1948, Clinton M. Easton, *Catonsville;* 1949, Paul A. Heemann, *Baltimore;* 1950, Martin J. Dippel, *Baltimore;* 1951, Thomas A. Singleton, *Glen Burnie;* 1952, Sol Levinson, *Baltimore;* 1953, L. P. Wiedefeld, *Baltimore;* 1954, B. Lee Feete, *Brunswick;* 1955, G. Howard Strong, *Baltimore;* 1956, Charles E. Shimunek, *Baltimore;* 1957, Frank H. Newell, *Pikesville;* 1958, J. Edwin Eline, *Reisterstown;* 1959, Sylvan S. Lewis, *Baltimore;* 1960, Richard A. Coleman, *Upper Marlboro.*

MASSACHUSETTS
Informant: L. Sheldon Daly

The History of the Massachusetts Funeral Directors' Association in its early days, is interwoven with that of the previously organized New England Undertakers' Association. In 1896 the New England Undertakers' Association had its 17th Annual Convention. This would indicate that the New England Undertakers' Association, made up of funeral directors from all New England States, was organized in 1878 which was only 14 years after the oldest funeral directors association of United States was formed in Philadelphia in 1864.

In 1899 the Massachusetts Funeral Directors Association, then known as the Massachusetts Undertakers' Association took over the older New England Undertakers' Association so it thereby traces back the origin of the Massachusetts Association to the formation of the New England Undertakers' Association in 1878. This is especially true in view of the fact that most of the men responsible for the formal organization of the Massachusetts Association in 1891 were the active members of the New England Undertakers' Association.

Records of the activities of the New England Undertakers' Association prior to its assimilation by the Massachusetts Association are scant except for two directories of members published in 1888 and 1898.

The directories of the New England Undertakers' Association were published as a result of a great effort on the part of Lewis L. Jones, as evidenced by his statement appearing in the 1888 directory: "In its preparation (the New England Undertakers' Directory) I have sent out five thousand letters and circulars to undertakers, manufacturers, and town clerks and no name appears that is not vouched for by one or more persons."

Not only did Mr. Jones serve as president of the Massachusetts Undertakers' Association and the New England Undertakers' Association, but he also served for many years on the executive committee of the Massachusetts Undertakers' Association, and he was one of the founders of the National Funeral Directors Association, attending the first ten annual meetings of the national association.

Dickinson, who was Mayor of Springfield as well as a Senator from Springfield, served as president of the Massachusetts association, the New England association and the national association.

There were many reasons in those days for joining together in an association. In the 1870's, '80's, '90's the shipping of bodies was a very difficult procedure because they were subject to the hybrid rules and regulations of the boards of health of the community to, from, and through which the bodies were shipped. Massachusetts did not have an embalming law so the baggage masters were not willing to accept certification of embalming from unlicensed embalmers and undertakers of Massachusetts. This made it very difficult for shipment of bodies. This was one of the major problems of the times.

In addition, there were a number of others such as Sunday burials, which apparently were growing in favor much to the dismay of the funeral directors, the churches, and the cemeteries. There were no standard death certificates or burial permits. Each city or town had its own forms and quite often would not recognize or honor that from another city or town. Numerous so called "burial-alive" bills were filed in the legislature as well as anti-embalming bills. Some of these bills proposed legislation which would have been very harmful to the interest of the public and the funeral profession such as one that was proposed that in each city and town all bodies would be transferred to some central point in the city or town, taken over by the town or city for examination and disposal.

Some facets of the early years of the association's history were given by an active association member in 1909. He said, in part, "Ever since 1890 a strict watch has been kept on all legislation, the proper committee has investigated every matter affecting undertakers, wiping out all laws governing us passed since the settlement of the state, and replacing them by a few which are easily understood. The law licensing the embalmers of the state and enabling us to legally ship bodies to and through more than forty other States was also an association matter, and has proved beneficial, and in a few years is going to be much more valuable to us. For the past eight years the committee has appeared each year and opposed, successfully, the so-called Burial Alive Bills—which would have been very costly to the State and very troublesome to us."

The first legislation supported by the association which became law was passed in 1892. This legislation provided "no embalming fluid or substitutes are or shall be injected into the dead body of any person who is supposed to have come to his or her death by violence, until that permit therefore in writing signed by the medical examiner has been first obtained. Legislation passed in 1905, effective January 1, 1906, made it necessary for embalmers to pass an examination. This legislation also set up a State Board of Embalming. A number of amendments to the law were successfully supported by the association over the years and finally the last major legislation affecting the licensing and registration of funeral directors, embalmers, and establishments was passed in 1954.

The association has been fortunate over practically all of its history to have had outstanding men interested enough in the profession and the association as presidents and officers who unselfishly devoted a great amount of time and effort towards the good of the association and the profession.

ASSOCIATION PRESIDENTS: 1891-92, George H. Waterman, *Boston;* 1893, Chency D. Washburn, *Springfield;* 1894, M. M. Cumming, *Fitchburg;* 1895-96, Oliver Walton, *Wakefield;* 1897, William T. Rice, *East Weymouth;* 1898, George M. Hopkins, *Pittsfield;* 1899-1900, Francke W. Dickinson, *Springfield;* 1901, Lewis L. Jones, *Boston;* 1902, Lawrence Reade, *Woburn;* 1903-04, Alman L. Eastman, *Boston;* 1905-07, Horace D. Litchfield, *Cambridge;* 1908, William H. McManus, *Brookline;* 1909, Thomas H. Reilly, *Westboro;* 1910, James P. Cleary, *Boston;* 1911, William T. Bulger, *South Boston;* 1912, George A. Clark, *Waltham;* 1913, Daniel W. Long, *Brockton;* 1914-16, Michael J. Dockray, *Canton;* 1917-19, Patrick J. McArdle, *Charlestown;* 1920, William H. Thomas, *Newton;* 1921-22, George W. Streeter, *Springfield;* 1923, Michael Porcella, *Boston;* 1924, Jeffrey E. Sullivan, *Fall River;* 1925, Arthur H. Chandler, *Brockton;* 1926, John L. McDonough, *Lowell;* 1927, Waldo E. Sessions, *Worcester;* 1928, Joseph Dee, *Concord;* 1929, Frank Lee Edgerly, *Reading;* 1930-32, William L. Spencer, *South Boston;* 1933, Herbert L. Shepherd, *Whitman;* 1934, James J. Hurley, *Randolph;* 1935, Leslie J. Williamson, *Allston;* 1936, George L. Doherty, *Somerville;* 1937, W. Everett King, *Clinton;* 1938, Michael J. Coughlin, *Fall River;* 1939, J. Frances Loftus, *Palmer;* 1940, Percy J. L. Peardon,

Boston; 1941, P. Edward Murray, Boston; 1942, Laurence Eaton, Needham; 1943, Edwin A. McCrea, Worcester; 1944, Robert H. Messer, Stoneham; 1945, Daniel F. O'Brien, Cambridge; 1946, Kenneth Sampson, Brockton; 1947, Thomas B. Gleason, Springfield; 1948, Frederick E. Allen, Lawrence; 1949, John T. Stringer, Wakefield; 1950, Robert T. Morse, Lowell; 1951, J. Alden Wentworth, Spencer; 1952, Edward W. Rhodes, Lynn; 1953, Arthur S. Porcella, Boston; 1954, George Sessions, Worcester; 1955, William J. Hickey, Hudson; 1956, Fred E. Sprague, Malden; 1957, Cornelius V. Keohane, Quincy; 1958, John H. Granstrom, Boston; 1959, George H. Reynolds, Northampton; 1960, Richard W. Holmes, Danvers.

MICHIGAN
Informant: J. R. MacDonald

In 1879 Allen Durfee, Grand Rapids undertaker and chemist, encouraged by A. H. Nirdlinger and Thomas Gliddon, editors of *The Casket*, made the first active attempt to weld the undertakers of Michigan into a working organization. The idea of a state association had been discussed locally and through the columns of *The Casket* for months, but in that year Mr. Durfee published a letter asking Michigan undertakers for their opinions on the possibility of holding a "State Convention of Undertakers at some central point, say Grand Rapids, Jackson, or Lansing, for the purpose of forming an Undertakers' State Association which the rapid advance in the science of undertaking seems to demand."

On January 1, 1880 then, the following call was printed in *The Casket:* "Having received most favorable and encouraging replies to the circular sent out on the 24th of November in regard to holding a State Convention of Undertakers, therefore, we the undersigned, make this call for said meeting to be held at the City of Jackson on the 14th day of January, 1880 at eleven o'clock a.m. for the purpose of forming an Undertakers Association of the State of Michigan, and for such business as may be deemed proper by said meeting."

The announcement carried the signatures of six most prominent funeral directors: Allen Durfee; E. A. Tompkins, Pontiac; C. A. Conklin, Adrian; Sammons and Quivey, Jackson; Charles L. Benjamin, Saginaw; and T. J. Roberts, Detroit. On January 14, 1880, 26 men from all over Michigan met in Jackson's Hibbard House. Business at hand: Organization of a state association. The preamble adopted by this group who adopted the name "the Undertakers Association of the State of Michigan" reads: "We the undersigned undertakers doing business in the State of Michigan, do hereby form ourselves into an association for the purpose of mutually disseminating the most correct principles of business management, the best methods of protecting our own interests in professional practice, and the general good of all recognized legitimate undertakers."

The following were named officers of the new Undertakers Association of Michigan: *President*, Allen Durfee, Grand Rapids; *Vice Presidents*, Joseph F. Sammis, Jackson, C. A. Conklin, Adrian, E. A. Thompkins, Pontiac; *Secretary*, T. J. Roberts, Detroit; *Treasurer*, Charles L. Benjamin, Saginaw. A. H. Nirdlinger and Thomas Gliddon were elected honorary members.

At this first Convention, Mr. Gliddon offered a bit of sound advice to the founders, advice which would apply today as well as 80 years ago. He urged those present to appoint committees on organization and resolution; to provide for publishing the proceedings of the convention; to provide for giving information to each other on professional duties; to agree upon some satisfactory method of advertising; to indicate a policy of distributing price lists, and to appoint committees to approach the legislature.

He was something of a prophet. At this first meeting he also outlined the possibilities of the gathering and "the arguments which it is hoped will convert this Convention into a State Association and in due time cause to be born of this humble beginning a general National Association, as broad as the United States and as imperishable as our National Union."

At the second annual meeting of the Michigan association in 1881, the name was changed to the Michigan Funeral Directors Association. At this meeting attendance jumped from the original 26 to 55. At the third Convention in Detroit, January 11-12, 1882, President Allen Durfee appealed for a National Funeral Exposition. It was decided such a Convention should be held at Rochester, New York in June of that year.

"Since our first meeting was called," President Durfee said, "Associations similar in plan to ours have been formed in many of the northern states and in one city, at least, in the south; and the undertakers association is now in existence. A National Association will be in order as soon as the State Organizations all get fairly to work and exhibit signs of permanent good."

The National Funeral Directors Association was born of the Rochester, New York meeting. Charles L. Benjamin of Saginaw was its first president. Mr. Durfee was assistant secretary (temporary). Also attending was Charles A. Conklin of Adrian. In 1908 another Michigan man, W. D. Farley of Battle Creek, was selected to head the national association.

During the 20 to 25 years following the formation of the Michigan Funeral Directors Association, other related organizations continued to rise, most of which failed of inertia or were merged with the growing MFDA. Among the more prominent of these was the Michigan Association of Embalmers.

At this first meeting it should be noted that as a part of the program one Charles Hathaway, secretary of the Detroit Board of Health, spoke on rules and regulations for transportation of bodies of persons who died of a contagious or infectious disease.

The organizations, then, were fulfilling the third goal set for them in the early precepts of occupational associations. They were making continuing education an integral part of the professional societies. And they already had begun establishing rules of conduct as well as ethical and professional standards.

Minutes of this organization cover only two conventions and the organizational meeting. But the Michigan Corporation and Securities Commission indicates that on September 13, 1900, a charter was filed for the Michigan Funeral Directors and Embalmers Association, which would indicate a merger of the two organizations. The name was again changed in 1955 to Michigan Funeral Directors Association, Inc.

No history of MFDA would be complete without mention of the "flying squadron" of 1922. By that year most of the major cities of Michigan and many of the counties and regional areas had formed loose associations which existed in various degrees of organization and independence. The state association acquired a Reo bus and sponsored a membership tour of the state. A group of funeral directors led by Charles Whitcomb of Oxford, Roy Shattuck of Coldwater, Fred Schrader of Plymouth and Roy Jennings of Flint, chugged all over Michigan, contacting each of these local organizations. Most of them consolidated into the state association. The tour was successful; by the end of 1922 the Michigan Funeral Directors Association was solid in every corner of the State.

Until 1901 requirements for licensing as an embalmer just did not exist, beyond the apprenticeship level. In that year the state began requiring examination. Anyone already practicing embalming was accepted and licensed automatically. Since that time MFDA has led the way in elevating the educational standards leading to state licensing. By 1907 a two-year apprenticeship was required, along with a common school education and a short course —two days to two weeks—in mortuary science. These courses were available by mail or through traveling schools which regularly visited the larger communities.

In 1923 academic requirements were raised to high school level. Registration of apprenticeship became mandatory. By 1935 the training course was lengthened to six months instruction at an embalming college. This specialized study was again lengthened in 1939 to nine months. In 1943, less than 20 years ago, the law required one academic year of instruction in a recognized college or university and two academic years of study in a prescribed course in mortuary science. The law, effective in 1943, included only embalming. Funeral direction training prerequisites were two years apprenticeship, a year of college and nine months of instruction in a prescribed course in funeral directing.

But in 1949 the requirements were dovetailed and the mortuary science license was created to include both embalming and funeral direction. Wayne State University School of Mortuary Science now is being petitioned by MFDA to provide an optional fourth year of study which would qualify mortuary science students for baccalaureate degrees.

Wayne State University since 1939 has been the hub of Michigan's mortuary science education program, for the most part under the guidance of Walter D. Pool, M.D.

In 1951 the Michigan Mortuary Science Foundation was created by the funeral directors of the State as an instrument of trust for handling contributions to this educational program. The Foundation was designed to publish textbooks, underwrite education surveys and research, sponsor educational conferences and administer scholarships. The Foundation has purchased a

$150,000 building on the Wayne State campus which now serves as the home of the School of Mortuary Science.

Through the efforts of the Michigan Funeral Directors Association and those other early organizational attempts the profession has more than kept pace with the changing times. Its members have labored diligently to raise the standards of performance and service, to bring educational requirements to a high level, to maintain a stable and steady rise in the standing of the profession in the occupational world.

ASSOCIATION PRESIDENTS: 1880-82, Allen Durfee, *Grand Rapids;* 1883, Chas. L. Benjamin, *Saginaw;* 1884, Joseph S. Sammons, *Jackson;* 1885, T. H. Roberts, *Detroit;* 1886, J. Wiseman, *Big Rapids;* 1887-89, Thos. J. Banfield, *Portland;* 1890, M. J. Buck, *Lansing;* 1891-92, John A. Dick, *Detroit;* 1893-94, P. H. O'Brien, *Grand Rapids;* 1895-96, C. M. Ranger, *Battle Creek;* 1897, C. W. Harrington, *Kalamazoo;* 1898, W. W. Bennett, *Jackson;* 1899, M. H. Knapp, *Owosso;* 1900, H. T. Lewis, *Hersey;* 1901, W. D. Farley, *Battle Creek;* 1902, Wm. J. Otter, *Detroit;* 1903, C. K. Wetherby, *Jackson;* 1904, A. C. Haight, *Springport;* 1905, C. D. Dunham, *Cadillac;* 1906, J. O. Rowe, *Benton Harbor;* 1907, C. S. Harrington, *Kalamazoo;* 1908, J. Schmalzriedt, *Detroit;* 1909, C. E. Singer, *Hillsdale;* 1910, E. L. Hughes, *Traverse City;* 1911, W. G. Wisner, *Charlotte;* 1912, E. S. Marsh, *Cambria;* 1913, J. B. Mc-Innes, *Grand Rapids;* 1914-15, James P. Mohler, *South Haven;* 1916, C. E. Bird, *Detroit;* 1917, R. A. Brown, *Greenville;* 1918, F. G. Marshall, *Detroit;* 1919, J.

J. Fisher, *Cassopolis;* 1920-21, R. Jennings, *Flint;* 1922, C. Whitcomb, *Oxford;* 1923, R. Shattuck, *Coldwater;* 1924, F. Schrader, *Plymouth;* 1925, A. Alt, *Grand Rapids;* 1926, H. I. Drescher, *Big Rapids;* 1927, V. Johnson, *Bellevue;* 1928-29, A. E. Crosby, *Detroit;* 1930-31, S. Wallace, *Saginaw;* 1932, G. D. Farley, *Battle Creek;* 1933-34, C. Metcalf, *Grand Rapids;* 1935, H. L. Baird, *Lapeer;* 1936, G. Huber, *Monroe;* 1937, H. Hibbard, *Traverse City;* 1938, L. A. Bates, *Jackson;* 1939, A. E. Swanson, *Marquette;* 1940, Orlo Roberts, *Belleville;* 1941, L. B. Lee, *Muskegon;* 1942-43, Wm. G. Cavanagh, *Detroit;* 1944-45, A. B. Ball, *Mason;* 1946, F. W. Estes, *Lansing;* 1947, E. W. Schmalzriedt, *Detroit;* 1948, J. R. MacDonald, *Howell;* 1949, M. B. Martin, *Mt. Morris;* 1950, W. P. Kershner, *Ironwood;* 1951, Wm. D. Clyne, Sr., *E. Detroit;* 1952-53, F. W. Staffan, *Ann Arbor;* 1954, K. N. King, *Albion;* 1955, G. H. Griffin, *Pontiac;* 1956, R. J. DeMeester, *Grand Rapids;* 1957, H. A. Cederberg, *Saginaw;* 1958, Glen Dunn, *Mason;* 1959, John Santeiu, *Dearborn;* 1960, Wynne J. Steuernol, *West Branch.*

MINNESOTA
Informant: F. Phil Iacovino

In 1890 the infant state of Minnesota was only 32 years old. During this same year a small group of funeral directors met in Minneapolis to attend an embalming clinic, and it was at this gathering that the associational movement which led to the formation of the Minnesota Funeral Directors Association had its origin.

The clinic of 1890 and similar clinics of the three ensuing years convinced the attending funeral di-

841

rectors of the great need for exchanging ideas in the hope of elevating the standards of their calling. The Minnesota associational movement was finally formalized in Minneapolis in 1894 with the election of officers. It was the thinking then that this new group should encompass members from Minnesota and the two Dakotas. This prompted the formation of the "Tri-State Funeral Directors Association," led by two Minneapolis men, N. J. Warner, *President,* and John M. Gleason, *Secretary-Treasurer.*

During the formative years of the association, the new art of embalming was causing much discussion among funeral directors. At the beginning, many practicing funeral directors opposed this innovation. Others saw it as a means of better serving the public through restorative methods made possible by this new science. Also injected into the debate was the realization that proper embalming could be a great preventive measure in protecting the public health from deaths caused by contagious diseases. The inquisitive interest in this new science by Minnesota funeral men led to the formation of the goals which, simply stated, were: scientific research, higher educational standards, and licensure.

With the high germicidal effects of the newly-marketed embalming fluids in mind, the association adopted plans to induce the state public health officials to prepare shipping regulations, enabling transportation of the dead. During this same period the association moved to conduct clinical education for its membership, hoping to qualify them in meeting the proposed shipping requirements when and if they were

evolved. However, association officers' plans were met with a wide divergency of opinions from local and state health officials, university authorities, the Railroad Baggage Men's Association, and from within the association.

The task of settling these differences rested on the shoulders of the association president, George R. Crosby, St. Cloud, who during his term in office (1897-1898) helped remove many of the roadblocks to association programming.

The year 1898 marked a milestone in association history. Dr. H. M. Bracken, after several meetings with association officials, saw fit to recommend creation of the first funeral service examining committee, working directly under the state Board of Health. The committee's responsibility was to prepare and administer examinations for embalmers' licenses. In September, 1898, at the state convention, the first embalmer's examination was administered to 134 association members, 84 of whom passed.

To acquaint embalmers with necessary basic knowledge in embalming and public health, President Lohse in 1899 prevailed upon Dr. Bracken to enlist the aid of doctors and university professors for instructions, and in that year a clinic embodying lectures in chemistry, anatomy and bacteriology was presented by the association to its members.

At this clinic Dr. L. B. Wilson, who was employed in the research laboratories of the State Department of Health, stated that unless more information was made available about the chemicals used in commercial embalming fluids, the task of preparing a set of safe shipping regulations by health officials

842

would be greatly impaired, if not impossible. The association immediately appointed a fluid research committee whose members eventually went on to open new avenues for the embalmers and set off "the great fluid investigation" of the early 1900's. The committee was instructed to work under the direction of the State Board of Health and the University of Minnesota.

The committee's quest to discover an acceptable fluid was aided not only by the direction of the State Board of Health and the cooperation of University of Minnesota professors, but through action of the legislature which in 1902 appropriated $1000 to continue embalming fluid research over the next two years.

The year 1902 also held an interesting sidelight in the history of the Association. It was the year the Minnesota delegation to the National Convention in Niagara Falls was instructed to invite the National to the twin cities in 1903. The invitation was accepted and Minnesota played host to its first National Convention the next year.

The following several years were productive ones. The membership was, at last, reaping the harvest of their many years of work. In 1905 the state legislature passed the embalmer's licensing law. Prior to this law, licensing was authorized by Department of Health regulation. Shipping regulations were adopted in 1906, permitting the safe transportation of the dead, and a new era was to unfold, giving swift rise to standards of the funeral profession in Minnesota. At the state convention of 1907, Dr. Bracken was given a standing ovation when he announced that Formula #3 was ac-

cepted as the approved fluid for use in shipping bodies of contagious disease within Minnesota.

Flushed with victory, the convention instructed President W. B. Marr of Aitkin to advise the Committee on Advanced Classes to consult with university officials as to the possibility of establishing a regular course of embalming within the university system. Thus was laid the groundwork that was later to lead to the establishment of the first program of mortuary science within the halls of a state university.

After many consultations with the university administrators, the association committee met with success on March 4, 1908, when the Board of Regents authorized an embalming school to be organized under the Medical College. In giving approval the Board of Regents set the condition obligating the association to guarantee the expenses entailed in administering the school. The association agreed to this condition, and the first regular session of five and a half weeks commenced later that year. Entrance to the school carried no educational prerequisites. Small attendance at the second session caused the cancellation of the program. However, in 1913, after four years of groundwork, including an agreement from the association to guarantee expenses up to $1200 for administrative costs, approval for reopening the school came from the university faculty. Thus the school was officially revived with the first session in 1914 covering a six week period. The length of the second session of January, 1915, was increased to eight weeks and carried an entrance requirement of one year of high school work. Attendance was so encouraging that the university agreed to absolve the association from its guarantee of financing the school.

Under the direction of Reuel P. Lee, Minneapolis, Chairman of the MFDA Education Committees, University officials were persuaded in 1926 to expand the curriculum of the Embalming School; and shortly afterwards, the administration of the school passed from the Medical School to the General Extension Division, and offered a curriculum of its own standing. Mr. Lee was also responsible in helping establish the first National accreditation procedures for the schools of mortuary science.

Recognizing his efforts, the profession voted Reuel P. Lee President of MFDA at the 1929 convention, and he later went on to become president of the National Funeral Directors Association. During the 50th Anniversary Program of the University's Department of Mortuary Science, on March 27, 1958, Lee received one of his greatest honors when he was presented with the Board of Regents' Citation by University President J. L. Morrill.

Association pressure to increase educational standards and requirements has been maintained through the present day. As early as 1932 the state convention voted a resolution urging the University of Minnesota to plan immediately for a two-year course in embalming and funeral directing with a matriculation prerequisite of two years of college work. This ambitious resolution was aimed at the granting of a Baccalaureate degree upon completion of the course.

In 1955 the Association joined with the Department of Health and the University to seek a new licens-ing law creating a single license in Mortuary Science, calling for a three-year college curriculum at an accredited university. Passing of the new law automatically eliminated the further issuance of Funeral Directors licenses which had been previously awarded to candidates serving only an apprenticeship and requiring no standard of formal education. Henceforth, the holders of the embalming license were issued the single license. The new law with its advanced standards recognized the funeral service practitioner as a complete entity in himself, having a total responsibility to the public for the conduct of the funeral service. The legislators were convinced that it was not in the public interest to divide this total responsibility among separate classes holding different licenses and requiring varying degrees of education.

In 1944 the Association created an Award of Merit to be presented each year to a worthy student of the University's Department of Mortuary Science's graduating class. And, in 1956, the Association voted to establish a scholarship fund, paying a full year's tuition for a select student entering his senior year in the Department of Mortuary Science.

Several failures to get a legislative enactment establishing a licensing law occurred around the turn of the century. It was not until 1905 that such a law won approval. Essentially it licensed embalmers through the State Board of Health. This law was enforced without alteration until 1927 when the association joined forces with the State Board of Health to increase standards. Still it concerned itself only with embalming, and funeral directing was left unregulated.

844

In 1931 an attempt to divert authority to regulate the field from the State Board of Health failed in the legislature; however, the principle of licensing funeral directors was established as desirable; and in 1933 and again in 1935, unsuccessful attempts were made to remedy the one-sidedness of the prevailing statute.

Through 1936 and 1937 attempts were made to formulate a bill which would give funeral directors a more direct and substantial control over the licensing procedures which would be acceptable to the State Board of Health. Failing to get agreement the association proceeded with a legislative proposal that would set up an examining committee predominantly consisting of funeral directors who would conduct examinations and give separate funeral director and embalming licenses.

Although the act, despite formidable opposition, was passed in 1937, a series of adverse Attorney General rulings vitiated much of its intended strength; but funeral directors were now licensed, and a better climate for the practice of the vocation developed in the years following its enactment.

In 1953 the association joined with the Department of Health and the Committee of Examiners to propose an entirely new approach to the licensing question. The proposal called for one license for the field, with qualifications increased to three years of college and one year of residence training. As already indicated in the section above dealing with educational programs, the bill was passed in 1955 and Minnesota joined the ranks of the more progressive states who conceive of the practice of funeral directing as indivisible as that of the general practitioner of medicine.

ASSOCIATION PRESIDENTS: 1895, N. F. Warner, *Minneapolis;* 1896-98, Geo. R. Crosby, *St. Cloud;* 1899-1900, A. E. Losey, *Brainerd;* 1901-02, G. F. Baird, *Austin;* 1903, W. L. Grapp, *Waseca;* 1904, W. H. Davies, *Minneapolis;* 1905, M. J. Gill, *Minneapolis;* 1906, Thos. Davidson, *Mankato;* 1907, W. B. Marr, *Aitkin;* 1908, Orlando Simons, *Glencoe;* 1909, J. A. Willwerscheid, *St. Paul;* 1910, M. J. Filiatrault, *Duluth;* 1911, Fred Gee, *Monticello;* 1912-13, Geo. J. Hillyer, *Winona;* 1914, E. T. Barnard, *Fergus Falls;* 1915, W. R. Earl, *Austin;* 1916, L. W. Andrist, *Mankato;* 1917, Martin Benson, *Fergus Falls;* 1918, E. C. Schroeder, *St. Paul;* 1919, V. M. Brady, *Duluth;* 1920, L. E. Willwerscheid, *St. Paul;* 1921-22, R. E. Dare, *Elk River;* 1923-24, A. P. Knaeble, *Minneapolis;* 1925, Burd P. Johnson, *Minneapolis;* 1926, Geo. Berggreen, *Sauk Centre;* 1927-28, A. C. Larson, *Zumbrota;* 1929-30, R. P. Lee, *Minneapolis;* 1931, W. C. H. Gordon, *Mankato;* 1932-33, Thos. G. Bell, *Duluth;* 1934, Leo M. Thompson, *Little Falls;* 1935, J. F. Willwersheid, *St. Paul;* 1936, Oscar C. Sathe, *Jackson;* 1937, W. L. Landkamer, *Mankato;* 1938, Fred F. Palen, *Rochester;* 1939-40, Walter H. Quast, *Hutchinson;* 1941, Leo E. Rainville, *Minneapolis;* 1942, Wayne B. Conings, *Blue Earth;* 1943-44, John L. Werness, *Minneapolis;* 1945-46, Bernard S. Boman, *Mankato;* 1947, Fred Johnston, *St. Paul;* 1948, O. L. Johnson, *McGregor;* 1949, V. E. Hansen, *Wells;* 1950, Raymond Gleason, *Minneapolis;* 1951, Norman L. Hanson, *Worth-*

ington; 1952, Gene Willwerscheid, *St. Paul;* 1953, Dwight West, *Detroit Lakes;* 1954, Peter Daniel, *St. Cloud;* 1955, Harry B. Hanson, *Minneapolis;* 1956, Jens J. Bonner-up, *Albert Lea;* 1957, Owen V. Wulff, *St. Paul;* 1958, Henry O. Filiatrault, *Duluth;* 1959, John W. Hoepner, *Redwood Falls;* 1960, N. L. Enger, *Minneapolis.*

MISSISSIPPI

Some obscurity surrounds the origin of the present Mississippi Funeral Directors Association, and its extant sources of information are in disagreement. However, it appears from the reports of the state association to the National Funeral Directors Association that a feeble attempt at organization was made in June, 1884. Six funeral directors adopted a constitution and by-laws, but this society existed as a paper organization until 1889 when another meeting was held with 15 or 16 members attending. This may be considered the first annual meeting of the association. *President,* W. H. Patton, Shubuta; and *Secretary,* A. B. Wagner, Meridian; were the officers chosen by the group.

By the following state convention the group had expanded to about 50 members and seemed on firm footing. However, the following year the Mississippi Funeral Directors Association joined with the older Georgia and Alabama groups to form the Tri-State Association of Funeral Directors. Quoting the July, 1945, *Southern Funeral Director:* "Though the purpose of the Tri-State group was to elevate the educational and moral standards of the profession, their manner of accomplishing these aims bordered on restraint of trade and later met with firm opposition from the Federal Government."

Mississippi's first secretary, A. B. Wagner, was president of the Tri-State Association. As a delegate to NFDA he reported for the Mississippi group as an entity in itself. Regular meetings were reported for 1890, 1891 and 1892. The Tri-State Association folded rather suddenly and nothing was heard of it nor of the Mississippi Association until some 15 years later when in July, 1900, the present-day association was organized and a constitution and by-laws were adopted.

In 1914 a brief report to NFDA's annual convention indicated that there were 28 members in good standing and six new members, and that the association had drafted a bill to go before the legislature to establish an embalmers' examining board. Three years later another report showed that the fight for licensing legislation had not yet been won. In 1921 the association was reported as flourishing, and in 1923 the last report given to NFDA indicated a state board of examiners was in existence. The words of delegate Harrie L. Wells sum up the feeling of the organization about this board, " . . . we are justly proud of its achievements and the standing it has with our Board of Health."

ASSOCIATION PRESIDENTS: 1906-10, Thomas E. Taylor, *Jackson;* 1911, W. W. Garner, *Grenada;* 1912, Allison H. Foster, *Natchez;* 1913, Frank Fisher, *Vicksburg;* 1914, Horace C. Smith, *Meridian;* 1915, Lyman Bradford, *Biloxi;* 1916, J. B. Wilson, *Greenwood;* 1917, W. B. Carter, *Water Valley;* 1918, B. T. Ethridge, *Jackson;* 1919, E. W.

Wright, *Columbia;* 1920, James F. Webb, *Meridian;* 1921, H. L. Wells, *Greenville;* 1922, W. H. Berry, *Tupelo;* 1923, W. J. Patton, *Shubuta;* 1924, T. A. Fisher, *Vicksburg;* 1925, C. O. Houghton, *Aberdeen;* 1926, L. F. Kitchen, *Laurel;* 1927-28, A. J. Foster, *Natchez;* 1929, J. O. Stricklin, Jr., *Yazoo City;* 1930, H. G. Rogers, *Indianola;* 1931, J. T. Biggs, Jr., *Crystal Springs;* 1932, J. W. Smith, *Columbia;* 1933, Ellis W. Wright, *Jackson;* 1934-35, W. D. Trewalla, *Winona;* 1936, C. C. Tweatt, *Cleveland;* 1937-38, Mrs. H. L. Wells, *Greenville;* 1939, Leon Pryor, *Calhoun City;* 1940, Louis Boyd, *Meridian;* 1941, Will Owens, *Pickens;* 1942, Mims Mitchell, *Magee;* 1943, J. R. McPeters, *Corinth;* 1944-45, Charles H. Thompson, *Laurel;* 1946, Douglas Terrell, *Collins;* 1947, J. Cliff Watts, *Meridian;* 1948, Jack McLain, *Philadelphia;* 1949, N. J. Brantley, *Olive Branch;* 1950, William Baldwin, *Jackson;* 1951, Arthur Lang, Jr., *Gulfport;* 1952, Hugh Lee, *Forest;* 1953, Jerry J. O'Keefe, *Biloxi;* 1954, Homer C. Dunn, *Water Valley;* 1955, James M. Spell, *Jackson;* 1956, Alex Daws, *Philadelphia;* 1957, John L. Maxey, *New Albany;* 1958, Albert C. Hulett, *Hattiesburg;* 1959, George Wilcox, *Carthage;* 1960, Andrew C. Puckett, *Columbus.*

MISSOURI
Informant: John D. Evans

In a letter dated March 14, 1882, to the editor of *The Casket,* Fred Hanley, secretary of The Undertakers' Association of The State of Missouri, reported a meeting had been held on February 28 and March 1 in St. Louis, Missouri. The meeting had been called at the request of a group of Missouri funeral directors for the purpose of forming an association of Missouri funeral directors.

At 4:00 P.M., February 28, 1888, Mr. E. Fritz, temporary chairman, announced the purpose of the meeting: to form an organization "for the mutual benefit and protection, to elevate the calling of an undertaker to its proper place in the social scale, *viz,* in the same grade with other professions, and to cultivate a more refined and aesthetic taste among its members, not only in the management and conduct of funerals, but in every other department of the undertaker's varied avocation."

Some discussion arose over the wording of the title of the association, whether "funeral directors" or "undertakers" should be used. Finally, the report of the Committee on Permanent Organization was accepted, and the name of the new organization became "The Undertakers' Association of The State of Missouri."

At this session an attempt was made to elect officers of the new association, but after nominating several men for president, all of whom declined the nomination, a motion to postpone the election of officers until the next day carried.

On Wednesday, March 1, 1882, the convention adopted the recommendations of the Constitution and By-Laws Committee, and thus the first organization of "undertakers" in Missouri came into being. The men chosen to lead the organization through its first year were: *President,* George N. Lynch, St. Louis; *Vice Presidents,* E. Fritz, Hannibal, J. Stampfli, Jefferson City, A. E. Cheatham, Warrensburg, S. A. Stone, Chillicothe, J. Albert, Ironton; *Secretary,* Fred Hanley, St.

Louis; and *Treasurer,* J. C. Bensick, St. Louis. A notice was placed in *The Casket,* March 1883, stating the first annual meeting of the association would be held in St. Louis, Missouri, Monday April 2, 1883.

Evidently, this Association did not continue its annual meetings for long, for an item appeared in *The Casket,* 1888, stating that a large number of funeral directors had assembled in Kansas City on April 3, 1888, "in obedience to the call for a convention to organize a State Association." Information, given in an article by John W. Wagner, President Emeritus, The Missouri Funeral Directors and Embalmers Association, in *The Southern Funeral Director,* May, 1956, verifies the article in *The Casket.* At the 1888 meeting the name of the organization was changed to The Missouri Funeral Directors Association.

Earlier in 1888, a new Committee on Constitution and By-Laws was appointed and requested to report their recommendations at the convention. At the conclusion of the convention, G. B. Hickman, president, took the newly adopted Constitution and By-Laws home with him to prepare them for the printer. But before he could do so and get them to the printer, his place of business burned along with the only copy of these documents. It was not until the annual convention of 1890 that this loss was rectified.

According to Mr. Wagner, as a result of his attendance at the Omaha convention, he came home fired with the realization of the need for legislation to regulate the practice of embalming in the state of Missouri. Starting in 1891, he inspired

concentrated effort to achieve his goal; however, it was not until 1895 that a license law was passed by the state legislature.

Governor William J. Stone appointed the following men to serve on the newly created State Board of Embalming: G. B. Hickman, Butler; Hoyt Humphrey, Lamar; M. N. Alexander, Marshall; J. C. Herms, Neosho; and John W. Wagner, Kansas City.

At the national convention, Chicago, 1906, in a report by the Missouri delegation, there appears for the first time mention of burial associations in Missouri. For many years the problem of burial associations occupied the program of annual state conventions, with a lot of bitterness resulting therefrom.

Most of these burial associations, with but few exceptions, were based on the Constitution of Missouri, 1875, Section 21, Article 10, which provided "No corporation, company, or association, other than those formed for benevolent, religious, scientific or educational purposes, shall be created or organized under the laws of this state, unless the taxes therein are paid."

The legislature in 1917 enacted into law certain statutes setting up burial associations.

The additional sections in substance authorized incorporation as benevolent corporations certain burial associations which were actually business corporations to operate upon an insurance basis.

When the 1945 Constitution was adopted, former Article 10, Section 21 of the 1875 Constitution was omitted. In 1949 the Legislature repealed the statutes on burial associations (Section 5451-56, RSMo. 1939) because the statutes had been held unconstitutional.

There is no record of The Missouri Funeral Directors Association being incorporated prior to 1933. In April, 1933, a *pro forma* decree of incorporation was issued in Monroe County, Missouri, to The Missouri Funeral Directors Association. It was organized under Article 10, Chapter 32, RSMo., 1929. In 1944, the name of the Association was changed to The Missouri Funeral Directors and Embalmers Association, with new Constitution and By-Laws.

During the administration of President Herman Lohmeyer, 1934, the state was divided into 12 districts in order to promote the organization of local associations of funeral directors.

For several years the association had felt the need of employing an executive secretary. In 1946, at the annual convention, President Clifford W. Austin, Tina and his Board of Directors sponsored an amendment to the Constitution and By-Laws which would permit the employment of an executive secretary. At this 1946 Convention, John D. Evans, St. Clair, Missouri, was employed as executive secretary and has been retained since that date.

As has been mentioned above, the funeral directors, led by John W. Wagner, were successful, in 1895, after three attempts, in securing legislation to regulate the practice of embalming in the State of Missouri. Since that time many more attempts have been made to secure the passage of a funeral director's licensing law, however, all to no avail.

In the 1959 session of the legislature, through the co-operation of the funeral directors and embalmers of the state, amendments were secured correcting the weakness of the original law. Missouri is one of the few remaining states which does not have a funeral director's licensing law, or a pre-need trust law. Interest in both pieces of legislature has not as yet reached the point where it is possible to secure passage of either.

The association, trying to follow the pattern established since its beginning, has always attempted to provide service to its members through educational programs at annual conventions. Early in 1950, and for several years thereafter, regional meetings were held at which outstanding men in the funeral service field were employed to meet with the funeral directors. However, it has been established that better results can be obtained by holding a single meeting in November of each year in the center of the State. The association is now sponsoring a Group Insurance Policy, with life, hospitalization, and surgical expense coverages.

ASSOCIATION PRESIDENTS: 1888-92, G. B. Hickman, *Butler;* 1893, George J. Eberle, *St. Louis;* 1894-95, J. C. Herms, *Neosho;* 1896, Joseph Martin, *Lees Summit;* 1897, J. W. Wagner, *Kansas City;* 1898, M. H. Alexander, *St. Louis;* 1899, Ely Paxon, *Springfield;* 1900, H. R. Brassfield, *Unionville;* 1901, F. R. James, *Higbee;* 1902, R. Meierhoffer, *St. Joseph;* 1903, M. Haughey, *St. Louis;* 1904, J. L. Hughes, *Savannah;* 1905, M. P. Parker, *Columbia;* 1906, E. H. Day, *Fredericktown;* 1907, J. M. White, *Springfield;* 1908, Thos. O'Donnell, *Hannibal;* 1909, F. C. Haley, Jr., *Louisiana;* 1910, Wm. E. Landvogt, *St. Louis;* 1911,

S. C. Davidson, *Grant City;* 1912, Harry R. McCaw, *Rolla;* 1913, C. R. Lupton, *St. Louis;* 1914, Irl T. Oliver, *Jefferson City;* 1915, W. M. McClure, *Kansas City;* 1916, Ed. A. Wengler, *Glasgow;* 1917, J. C. Goodding, *La Plata;* 1918, M. S. Bush, *Centralia;* 1919, Geo. E. Cobb, *St. Louis;* 1920, D. A. Robnett, *Columbia;* 1921, James E. Willis, *Carrollton;* 1922, John P. Collins, *St. Louis;* 1923, E. A. Keithley, *O'Fallon;* 1924, Albert Skinner, *Macon;* 1925, Charles C. Meek, *St. Louis;* 1926, C. A. Schoene, *Milan;* 1927, Allen W. Mansur, *Richmond;* 1928, Leon T. Wahl, *Kansas City;* 1929, Wm. Schumacher, *St. Louis;* 1930, J. T. Williams, *Sullivan;* 1931, Glenn E. Henderson, *Kansas City;* 1932, Fred A. Thompson, *Madison;* 1933, William A. Stock, *St. Louis;* 1934, Herman H. Lohmeyer, *Springfield;* 1935, Roy P. Schwartz, *Hannibal;* 1936, S. R. Sweeney, *Warrensburg;* 1937-38, Frank H. Niehaus, *St. Louis;* 1939, R. E. Buechel, *Kansas City;* 1940, Gus Baumann, *Overland;* 1941, Carl Konantz, *Lamar;* 1942, Ralph Suedmeyer, *St. Louis;* 1943, Jewell Windle, *Springfield;* 1944-45, Clifford W. Austin, *Tina;* 1946, C. M. Price, *Maryville;* 1947, Joseph Howard, *St. Louis;* 1948, A. C. Nieburg, *Washington;* 1949, Joseph W. Clark, *St. Louis;* 1950, Randolph Davis, *Kirksville;* 1951, John P. Sheil, *Kansas City;* 1952, Corley Thompson, *Neosha;* 1953, August Kron, Jr., *St. Louis;* 1954, Leland H. Francis, *Parkville;* 1955, John F. Nunnelee, Jr., *Charleston;* 1956, Hugo H. Blumer, *Hermann;* 1957, Frank W. Knell, *Carthage;* 1958, J. O. Mudd, *Bowling Green;* 1959, Joe R. Duncan, *Mountain View;* 1960, Robert Williams, *St. Louis.*

850

MONTANA

Informant: G. L. Banks

The Montana Funeral Directors Association traces its roots to the older Northwestern Association which included the states of Montana and Washington. From the very beginning of the Northwestern group men from Montana predominated and seemed to be leaders in the association so that often reports both to the National Funeral Directors and to the trade journals of the day were labeled "Montana Funeral Directors."

At any rate, in the year 1899 W. P. Hohenschuh was invited to attend a meeting of a group of funeral directors in Missoula, Montana, to give a series of instructional lectures. As an outgrowth of this meeting an association was formed which at the time was variously called The Montana Funeral Directors Association and the Northwestern Association. The first officers of this group, all men from the State of Montana, except one who is listed as living in both Spokane and Helena, are as follows: *President,* Joseph Richards, Butte; *Vice President,* S. M. Smith, Spokane and Helena; *2nd Vice President,* John M. Lucy, Missoula; *Secretary,* E. L. Flaherty, Helena; *Treasurer,* George Seltzer, Billings.

The following year this organization reported to NFDA as the Northwestern Association. The association was also termed the Northwestern Association in *Embalmers' Monthly* for 1900. Perhaps by this time several funeral directors from Washington had joined. Almost immediately the organization started work on an enabling bill to have a State Board of Health "compelled to examine us and pass on our competency." Presumably this was done simultaneously in both Washington and Montana.

At any rate by 1903 the Montana Funeral Directors Association was a recognized entity, new members were being added to the roll, and the meeting that year was called the "fifth annual meeting."

The first record of a Licensing Board appeared in 1915. Members of this board were appointed by the State Board of Health and included E. L. Flaherty of Helena and Dr. W. F. Cogswell also of Helena. In 1940 a bill was passed by the legislature which created a Board of Embalmers and Funeral Directors independent of the State Board of Health. Appointed to this board by Governor Sam Ford were Ralph Bray of Miles City; F. H. Campbell of Kalispell; H. H. Dokken of Bozeman; Frank Meyers of Great Falls, and Sam White, Jr., of Butte. This same bill also created a separate Funeral Directors License.

The problems of shipping also occupied a great deal of time in the early years and meetings with the baggage men were held from time to time in an attempt to arrive at a solution at least locally.

It is interesting to note that the first recorded constitution and by-laws were adopted at Great Falls in June, 1925 at which time a lengthy code of ethics was also appended to the document. The association had until this time been run on "understanding" arrived at by the founding fathers, signed by them at the first meeting, and lost in the interim.

The association has been actively behind all legislative changes, and has worked tirelessly to raise educational standards. All men appointed to the Examining Board have been members of MFDA.

The constitution has been so successful that few changes have been made in the organization since its adoption, the only change of note being the admission of associate members in 1958.

ASSOCIATION PRESIDENTS: 1901-02, E. L. Flaherty, *Helena;* 1903, John McAllister, *Great Falls;* 1904, Jacob Opp, *Helena;* 1905, George Safley, *Bozeman;* 1906, Wade H. George, *Great Falls;* 1907, Charles H. Connor, *Choteau;* 1908-09, J. S. Cook, *Belt;* 1910, Charles H. Marsh, *Missoula;* 1912, Albert Bien, *Deer Lodge;* 1913, T. F. O'Connor, *Great Falls;* 1914, James W. Whitfield, *Livingston;* 1915, T. F. O'Connor, *Great Falls;* 1916, James Cassidy, *Butte;* 1917, H. F. West, *Bozeman;* 1918, J. V. Kohler, *Helena;* 1919, N. M. Kvalnes, *Three Forks;* 1920, Charles E. Peterson, *Glasgow;* 1921, J. Victor Kohler, *Helena;* 1922, F. M. Smith, *Billings;* 1923, G. Walter Selby, *Livingston;* 1924, W. D. Kendrich, *Anaconda;* 1925, H. M. Grompf, *Libby;* 1926, Lawrence Opp, *Helena;* 1927, A. C. Retz, *Polson;* 1928, J. E. Graves, *Miles City;* 1929-30, R. W. Ross, *Deer Lodge;* 1931, W. G. O'Connor, *Great Falls;* 1932, H. H. Campbell, *Kalispell;* 1933, Herman H. Dokken, *Bozeman;* 1934, Arthur Opp, *Helena;* 1935, E. F. Wyse, *Conrad;* 1936, Fred I. Root, *Butte;* 1937, F. M. Smith, *Billings;* 1938, Ralph Bray, *Miles City;* 1939, Lawrence E. Opp, *Helena;* 1940, W. D. Kendrick, *Anaconda;* 1941, H. M. Brundage, *Dillon;* 1942-43, Sam R. White, Jr., *Butte;* 1944, James G. Holland, *Havre;* 1945, William F. Burns;

851

1946, Edward Olcott, Jr., *Red Lodge;* 1947, Kenneth Rudolph, *Miles City;* 1948, Howard C. Smith, *Billings;* 1949, Forest V. Retz, *Helena;* 1950, Thomas E. Connor, *Townsend;* 1951, Roderick Kippen, *Bozeman;* 1952, Lyman Clayton, *Wolf Point;* 1953, Ralph Beck, *Deer Lodge;* 1954, Mel M. Boice, *Billings;* 1955, Thomas Savage, *Anaconda;* 1956, Wayland E. Beals, *Forsyth;* 1957, Peter Hartman, *Great Falls;* 1958, Emil Dahl, *Bozeman;* 1959, Walter Brundage, *Dillon;* 1960, C. Ernest Retz, *Helena.*

NEBRASKA

Informant: Nebraska Associated History Committee, R. Luhrs, Chairman

Early in 1882 James T. Bonner, Jr., a man interested in spreading the good work of organization, prompted by a desire for learning more of funeral directing requested *The Casket* to publish the following announcement:

Osceola, Neb., March 24th, 1882 Dear Sir: Can you make it convenient to go to Lincoln, Neb. on Wednesday, April 26th, 1882 at 2 P.M. to form a State Undertakers' Association, for our improvement and benefit? Please let me know by return mail, so arrangements can be made.

On the given date and with Mr. Bonner as temporary chairman the undertakers of Nebraska met, established a constitution and by-laws, and elected the following officers: *President,* H. W. Hardy, Lincoln; *Vice President,* S. J. Faris, Nebraska City; *Secretary,* James T. Bonner, Jr., Osceola; *Treasurer,* W. J. Sutherland, Schuyler; *Executive Committee:* F. J. Switz, Kearney; E. C. Usher, Fremont; Thomas Smith, Tekama.

The group met each year through 1884, but apparently was not active in 1885. In June, 1886 again a call was made to the funeral directors of Nebraska, this time by E. T. Roberts, and at a meeting held in Lincoln the Nebraska Undertakers' and Embalmers' Association was born. The membership of this organization grew to 77 by 1887, and in this year a new constitution and by-laws were adopted.

The Nebraska association from the first has been interested in securing legislation and started work immediately on an embalmers' bill. This bill was presented to the state legislature at every session from 1891 until 1899 when the late J. W. Armstrong with the assistance of W. G. Roberts succeeded in getting a law enacted which provided for the registration and licensing of embalmers, and which authorized the State Board of Health to appoint a Board of Examiners in Embalming. P. C. Heafy of Omaha, Joseph Sonderman of Grand Island, and E. L. Troyer of Lincoln were appointed by the Governor to act on the new board. At the first meeting in Lincoln on July 19, 1899 the above named men were elected President, Secretary, and Treasurer respectively of the new board.

The first examinations were given in Omaha August 15-17, in Lincoln September 12-13, and in Grand Island on October 10-11 in the year 1899. Everyone engaged in embalming was required to register with the board and to pay a fee of $5.00. Those wishing license were required to appear before the board for examination and after paying a $10 fee and passing the required examination were given a license.

852

In 1919 the Embalmers' Law was changed to make it obligatory for the man seeking a license to apply to the Department of Health in writing for examination. Again in 1927 a more comprehensive law was passed which defined embalming and raised the educational requirements of an applicant to four years of high school and 26 weeks in an accredited school of embalming plus the completion of one year in apprenticeship under a licensed embalmer or two years' training, ten weeks' course, and the embalming of 25 bodies. In 1937 the law was again amended to require two years of college consisting of 16 hours each of chemistry and biological science, ten hours each of English and accounting. Again in 1955 changes were made in the law raising the educational requirements, this time to 60 hours of college credit which should include two semesters each of English and accounting and three semesters each of chemistry and biological science.

Further legal enactments were brought about from time to time, the most important being in 1931 when the law licensing funeral directors went into effect. This law defined "funeral director," made provision for his obtaining a license, and formulated rules to follow in cases of contagious disease, and set penalties for violations of rules and ethical practices. The original law was amended in 1937 when it defined funeral director, undertaker, and mortician; stated requirements for examination of applicants and establishments, and gave power to a Board of Examiners to appoint an inspector and an attorney. In 1957 new laws were passed governing the licensing of "funeral directors and establish-ments" in which the requirement of a written examination on the subjects of mortuary management, sanitary science, mortuary jurisprudence and related matters were added. Funeral Directors were also required under the new law to have two years or 60 semester hours in an accredited college or university and one school year in an accredited college of mortuary science. The new law also gave broad powers to the Board of Examiners to adopt such rules as are necessary to carry out the provisions of the act.

In 1925 when a new constitution was adopted for the association the name was changed to the Nebraska Funeral Directors and Embalmers Association, and the object of the association was restated at this time to be the advancement of the science of embalming and funeral directing. At this time, too, a new code of ethics was adopted. Five years later, 1930, the association was incorporated.

As the membership grew the need for more meetings in various parts of the state became apparent. To meet this need in 1931 the group was divided into eight districts so that necessary meetings could be held during the year at which funeral directors could be present who might not have found attendance at yearly meetings possible.

The Nebraska Association has several times been honored in that some of its members have achieved special recognition. Kenneth Wherry was elected to the United States Senate where he compiled a distinguished record. Jack Marshall was elected Governor of District Five of NFDA serving in this capacity for four years before becoming President of the national organization. W. H. Dorrance served one term as Governor of District Five and was elected President of the National Conference of Funeral Service Examining Boards. George M. Reynolds was also President of the National Conference of Funeral Service Examining Boards. A number of members have served their state and local governments in various ways by special interests in civic affairs. The association in Nebraska is proud to have in its membership men of this calibre who reflect honor on the entire association.

Association Presidents: 1885, S. J. Faris, *Nebraska City;* 1886-87, H. K. Burket, *Omaha;* 1888, M. Reed, *Hastings;* 1889-90, George Brown, *Superior;* 1891, M. Reed, *Hastings;* 1892, E. B. Warner, *North Platte;* 1893-94, G. R. Fouke, *Liberty;* 1895, Henry Boyle, *Ravenna;* 1896-97, James Heaton, *Lincoln;* 1898, J. C. McElheny, *Lyons;* 1899, Walton G. Roberts, *Lincoln;* 1900, P. F. Bell, *Norfolk;* 1901, Harry B. Davis, *Omaha;* 1902, Joseph Sanderman, *Grand Island;* 1903, J. W. Armstrong, *South Auburn;* 1904, J. W. Butt, *Nebraska City;* 1905, George Darling, *Alliance;* 1906, N. P. Swanson, *Omaha;* 1907, A. H. Fellers, *Humboldt;* 1908, W. N. Dorrance, *Omaha;* 1909, O. L. Shumann, *Fairbury;* 1910, Esburn Wheeler, *Stella;* 1911, Geo. H. Brewer, *South Omaha;* 1912, H. G. Karstens, *Nebraska City;* 1913, R. O. Castle, *Lincoln;* 1914, C. A. Baker, *Holdrege;* 1915, R. B. Skinner, *Neligh;* 1916, E. C. Cartensen, *Curtis;* 1917, W. M. Hill, *Hebron;* 1918, A. H. Hastings, *Arcadia;* 1919, E. F. Brailey, *Omaha;* 1920, A. A. Metz, *Yonk;* 1921, E. D. Lundak,

Pierce; 1922, Walter Livingston, *Hastings;* 1923, Fred D. Woll, *Norfolk;* 1924, W. R. Maloney, *North Platte;* 1925, C. E. Hopping, *Beaver City;* 1926, G. A. Volland, *Hastings;* 1937, C. C. Haynes, *Omaha;* 1938, Cecil E. Wadlow, *Lincoln;* 1939-40, William Beckenhauer, *Wayne;* 1941-43, Jack Marshall, *Tilden;* 1944-45, Roosevelt Luhrs, *Imperial;* 1946, J. B. Stockham, *Broken Bow;* 1947, Amos Brand, *Hastings;* 1948, E. E. McVay, *David City;* 1949, Vernon Kuhns, *North Platte;* 1950, Walter Canaday, *Bridgeport;* 1951, Jack Godberson, *Gibbon;* 1952, Walter Korisko, *Omaha;* 1953, Don Chaney, *Falls City;* 1954, Walton B. Roberts, *Lincoln;* 1955, William Hengstler, *Creighton;* 1956-57, Don Butler, *Hastings;* 1958, Stewart Dennis, *Gering;* 1959, William T. Adams, *North Platte;* 1960, Heath Griffiths, *Beatrice.*

NEVADA
Informant: Silas Ross

In 1907 a meeting to organize the funeral directors of Nevada was called by George W. Perkins of Reno, George Kitzmeyer of Carson City, Thomas Dunn of Goldfield, and J. L. Keyser of Elko. The meeting, held in Reno, was not well attended. Although there was some objection to the formation of an association, the more important reasons for the poor attendance were: poor transportation facilities, expense to a small business man, and the fact that many operations were one-man businesses. This group elected George W. Perkins as its first president and George E. Kitzmeyer, secretary. A second meeting, held in 1908, was attended by only a few members. In this year Nevada

854

paid a per capita fee for seventeen members to N.F.D.A. J. L. Keyser of Elko was elected president. The association held no more meetings until August 8, 1930 when the association was re-organized. Only the Ross-Burke Company of Reno held a membership-at-large in the National Funeral Directors Association from 1927 until the re-organization.

In the interim the statute governing the practice of embalming and its attendant State Board of Embalmers and examinations served as a unifying force for the profession in the state. J. L. Kaiser, Thomas Dunn and George Kitzmeyer, the men instrumental in organizing the early association were appointed to the original examiners' board which first met formally on April 20, 1909.

In August, 1909 Professor Hohenschuh was brought to Nevada to lecture to the first applicants for license. Of the 32 who attended the lectures and took the examination given September 1, 1909, 28 passed and were given licenses. Men taking the examination came not only from Nevada but from bordering areas east of the Sierra Range in California.

Changes in the Embalmer's Law were made in 1931, 1949 and in 1959. The first two amendments increased the educational requirements for licensing and the 1959 amendment extended the law to include funeral directors and apprentices under the licensing system.

The formation of the present Nevada Funeral Service Association was effected August 8, 1930. All funeral service operations in the state except two are presently members of this association.

The funeral directors of this state have always been interested in establishing standards of ethics, continuing service to the public, standardizing and training and educational criteria. In this connection, it should be reported that past-president Silas E. Ross, distinguished in the field of higher education, served on the Education Committee of NFDA.

ASSOCIATION PRESIDENTS: 1907, Geo. W. Perkins, *Reno;* 1908, J. L. Keyser, *Elks;* 1909, T. F. Dunn, *Goldfield;* 1924, J. B. Kenny, *Virginia City;* 1930-31, Silas E. Ross, *Reno;* 1932, Earl Marriott, *Ely;* 1933, H. E. Roe, *Fallon;* 1934, S. Gene Parks, *Las Vegas;* 1935, E. T. Butler, *Elko;* 1936, L. L. Burt, *Caliente;* 1937, J. P. O'Brien, *Reno;* 1938, Wm. F. Logan, *Tonopah;* 1939, Howell G. Garrison, *Las Vegas;* 1940, Cyrus Wyckoff, *Reno;* 1941-42, J. J. Noone, *Goldfield;* 1943-45, Hallie Eddy, *Winnemucca;* 1946-47, Chas. J. McGuigan, *Carson City;* 1948, H. Harmer Holloway, *Reno;* 1949, G. Alfred Rogers, *Reno;* 1950, Jerry Woodbury, *Las Vegas;* 1951, Robley E. Burns, *Elko;* 1952, Erb Austin, *Fallon;* 1953, Don DeVoe, *Las Vegas;* 1954, Jack LaGrange, *Carson City;* 1955, Berkeley Bunker, *Las Vegas;* 1956, Edgar Walton, *Reno;* 1957, Allen Bunker, *Las Vegas;* 1958, Beverly Thomas, *Carson City;* 1959, Hallie Eddy, *Winnemucca;* 1960, Howard Freitas, *Yerington.*

NEW HAMPSHIRE
Informant: Elmer D. Goodwin

On November 14, 1899 in accordance with an act of the legislature a meeting to be held in the state house in Concord was called by the New Hampshire State Board of

Health for the purpose of examining undertakers. At its conclusion a number adjourned to the rooms of Louis A. Lane where the subject of forming an association was discussed. A subsequent meeting was planned for January 10, 1900 to which all the embalmers of the state were invited. Again convening at the Lane apartments on the appointed date, these men formed the New Hampshire Licensed Embalmers Association. The following were elected officers: *President,* John A. Glidden, Dover; *First Vice President,* H. W. Nickerson, Portsmouth; *Second Vice President,* J. H. Wetherbee, Hinsdale; *Treasurer,* Elmer D. Goodwin, Manchester; *Secretary,* Louis A. Lane, Concord. A committee on by-laws was also established, and the following men were chosen to serve on this committee: Harry B. Tasker, Dover; Willis N. Bailey, Bradford; and Frank A. Doane, Concord.

The charter list contains the names of thirty men and one woman (Mrs. Sarah Robie of Bristol). The initiation fee was set at three dollars and the dues established at two dollars a year.

The new organization first reported to the National Funeral Directors Association as an affiliated member in 1901. At this time B. F. Foster expressed an interest in having a member of national visit the state of New Hampshire and reported that the association was interested in the further education of its members in the new processes and techniques of embalming.

In 1911 the state reported passage of a new license law. Examinations had already been given by the State Board of Health under the new law and a representative from the association was now empowered to act on the examining committee.

At every report to the national convention New Hampshire mentioned the great interest expressed by its members in educational matters. In 1920 the state decided to hold two state meetings, one to be devoted completely to educational matters. At these annual meetings held in various cities throughout the state, well-known instructors spoke before the assembly. Among those most often selected as demonstrators were the two professors, Auguste and Charles Renouard and Professor Charles Genung of Waterloo, New York.

After twenty-five years of existence the name of the association was changed to the New Hampshire Funeral Directors and Embalmers Association.

During the early years of the association the processes of embalming and its attendant alliances with embalming goods manufacturers and holders of patents for special gadgets held the attention of the membership. The travelling salesman did not always confine his sales to embalming fluids, but often left in his wake some wonderful gadgets such as the "flexible trocar" and the "suction leecher." In 1909 the fraternity was stirred by the coming of the "Mico Process," a discovery by Professor Barnes. One hundred dollars entitled an embalmer to its use and five hundred dollars prevented any competitor from using it. There were a few monopolies in New Hampshire, but most of these were soon suppressed legally.

At the time of the formation of the association the undertaker, laden with his layout board and embalming equipment, went by horse and buggy to the home where death had occurred and prepared the deceased. The next day the service took place in the home of the deceased. Today even the small town has its funeral home and the service is only rarely held at the family home.

When the licensing law was first in effect, there were many long-established undertakers who had no knowledge of arterial embalming. In order to differentiate and at the same time to protect the business of the older men and the reputations of the better educated undertakers, the Board of Health had printed two kinds of tickets which were to be attached to the outside case when a body was shipped by rail. A yellow ticket indicated that the body had been embalmed by a person skilled in arterial embalming; a white ticket indicated that the body had been prepared by an undertaker who had no knowledge of arterial embalming and that the body had instead been swathed with two inches of cotton batten and a winding sheet.

For several years in the early 1920's New Hampshire withdrew from the National Funeral Directors Association and instead held meetings jointly with the members of the state associations of Vermont and Maine. However, in 1926 differences with the national body were resolved and New Hampshire once more joined the ranks of NFDA. During the years the funeral directors of the state of New Hampshire have also held meetings with other related professional groups, in 1940 with the New Hampshire Florists' Association, and on several occasions with state health groups.

The New Hampshire Funeral Directors Association remains dedicated to the advancement of the field, and stands behind all efforts to educate the profession.

ASSOCIATION PRESIDENTS: 1900-01, John A. Glidden, *Dover;* 1902, Hiram W. McKinnon, *Portsmouth;* 1903, Benjamin Foster, *Milford;* 1904-05, Frank A. Dame, *Concord;* 1906, H. N. Aldrich, *Keene;* 1907-08, H. B. Tasker, *Dover;* 1909, Charles D. Fox, *Milton Mills;* 1910, C. H. Foster, *Concord;* 1911, John M. Lamb, *Hinsdale;* 1912, Charles W. Jellison, *Peterboro;* 1913, Elmer D. Goodwin, *Manchester;* 1914, Hiram B. Currier, *Hillsboro;* 1915, Charles O. Hopkins, *Lakeport;* 1916, Hiram G. Kilkenney, *Concord;* 1917, Homer C. Lowe, *Derry;* 1918-19, Ellis G. Gammons, *Ashland;* 1920-21, Lindley F. Wyman, *Amherst;* 1922-23, Willis N. Bailey, *Bradford;* 1924, Joseph N. Boufford, *Manchester;* 1925, Geo. P. Wallace, *Manchester;* 1926, Lewis W. Wilkinson, *Laconia;* 1927, Henry H. Croteau, *Marlborough;* 1928, George H. Stoughton, *Clarement;* 1929, Joel W. Steward, *Northwood;* 1930, John H. Perkins, *Pittsfield;* 1931, Leon C. Tucker, *Milford;* 1932, Myron S. Calkin, *Concord;* 1933, Philip J. Woodbury, *Hillsboro;* 1934, Thomas Brewitt, *Epping;* 1935, Harry L. Holmes, *Henniker;* 1936, Ben C. Lambert, *Manchester;* 1937, Ralph E. Wiggins, *Dover;* 1938, Chas. H. Farwell, *Nashua;* 1939, Paul T. McNamara, *Lebanon;* 1940, Lee H. Tasker, *Dover;* 1941, Edmond G. Hebert, *Somersworth;* 1942, Bertram E. Peabody, *Derry;* 1943-44, Alvin R. Hussey, *Concord;* 1945,

Lawrence Hale, *Franklin;* 1946-47, Marshall French, *Goffstown;* 1948, Bradford Butler, *Franklin;* 1949, Edward J. Kelley, *Concord;* 1950, Richard Rand, *Hanover;* 1951, William Cain, *Manchester;* 1952, Fred C. Nelson, *Wilton;* 1953, David P. Goodwin, *Manchester;* 1954, F. Harold Shepherd, *Tilton;* 1955, James L. Heald, *Littleton;* 1956, Paul B. Maxham, *Concord;* 1957, Roger H. Beane, *Laconia;* 1958, L. Keeley Smith, *Milford;* 1959, Edmund F. Sweeney, *Nashua;* 1960, George B. Ward, *Portsmouth.*

NEW JERSEY

Informant: S. J. Failla

The New Jersey State Funeral Directors' Association was organized in Masonic Hall, Trenton, May 9, 1902. Seventeen of twenty-one counties of the state were represented. The meeting was called to order by Fred Hulberg, of New York, president of the National Funeral Directors' Association. The charter members elected the following officers to guide the new association: *President,* George Stevens, Jersey City; *Vice Presidents:* Joseph A. Logan, Newark; W. H. Crawford, Trenton; *Secretary,* William N. Gray, Cranford; and *Treasurer,* C. W. Springer, Englewood. Fifty-nine funeral directors were enrolled and an assessment of one dollar for each member was voted. The first annual meeting was held Sept. 9, 1903 in Atlantic City.

The major and immediate objective of drafting and securing the passage of legislation licensing funeral directors and embalmers, and regulating the conduct of the undertaking business was reached within four years with the passage of the 1906 Act establishing the New Jersey Board, with power to license and control.

The New Jersey Association has grown from a small nucleus to a membership of 586 funeral directors, the highest membership in the history of the association, while her treasury has increased from an original balance of $45 to a comfortable figure, adequate for carrying on the business of such a substantial group. This same group is led by a Board of Directors which includes the officers, presidents of local associations, and three members-at-large.

The Embalmer Law, originally passed in 1906, was revised in 1927 and again in 1952. The New Jersey association has further improved the qualifications for membership in the profession from no educational requirements to a minimum of graduation from an accredited high school plus one year of training at a recognized mortuary school and three years apprenticeship. The association has recently introduced legislation which will increase the educational requirements to a two-year college education followed by one of embalming college.

New Jersey funeral directors have also cooperated with the Department of Health in the revision of the Sanitary Code of the state of New Jersey. Perhaps the most important thing for the profession in general is the step taken when the New Jersey Association gained legislative recognition of the funeral director as a professional man in this state, and the association is now a member of the New Jersey Council of Professions.

The association throughout the years has also contributed to the growth and strength of the profession generally by helping defeat legislation which would class funeral directors with barbers and beauticians by the State Department of Health; by succeeding in having a municipality recind an ordinance to tax funerals entering its local cemetery; and by defeating a bill which would have permitted cemeteries to engage in the funeral directing business. In this case the New Jersey State Funeral Directors Association was successful in obtaining a permanent injunction restraining a cemetery corporation from owning and operating a funeral home.

The association has had further success in defeating an ordinance adopted by a municipality whereby a mercantile tax was imposed on every funeral home in the community. The tax was at a minimum of $25 per year and up. This court decision in favor of the funeral directors of New Jersey prevented a similar mercantile tax in other communities.

The state association was also successful in amending the state statute so that the welfare boards would pay $255 per welfare funeral, the maximum for which could be $350, $95 of which would be permissible for the next of kin to contribute.

The New Jersey Association is proud of its part in aiding the National Foundation of Funeral Service. It is the only state association which donated a room to the foundation.

New Jersey has many outstanding members and as an association is proud of all of its members. The following perhaps deserve to receive special mention because of specific work they have done for the group. Bert A. Waters, founder of the Hudson County Funeral Directors' Association publication, *The Forum*, a very well-known funeral director in the state, played a prominent part as secretary of the State Board of Embalmers where he served until the time of his death.

John H. Broemel served the association as Corresponding Secretary and as Secretary for forty years. He aided in formulating the 1927 Mortuary Science Act, and acted as advisor to the committee in drafting the act of 1952, almost singlehandedly seeing it through both houses of the legislature and even to the governor's office. Mr Broemel was also instrumental in the adoption of several insurance plans for funeral directors: Funeral Directors' Comprehensive Liability Insurance, Health and Accident Insurance, and Term Group Insurance. Mr. Broemel bent his efforts toward increases in welfare burial allowances, the establishment of the Embalmers' Emergency Corps and of *The Forum*, the official publication of the N.J.S.F.D.A. Mr. Broemel was also an outstanding civic leader and in his own community, Newark, where he helped initiate a plan for purchasing Rupper Stadium as an athletic field for use by the high schools of the city.

Peter J. Mitchell, editor of *The Forum*, a practicing funeral director for many years also contributed his talents as member of the staff of *Casket and Sunnyside* and as representative in the eastern area for *Embalmer's Monthly*. Mr. Mitchell also did extensive research on the education of the public to the funeral profession. James P. Mitchell, present Secretary of Labor, is his son and has gone several times to

859

conventions of NJSFDA.

Frank J. Codey served as Secretary of the State Board of Mortuary Sciences for 21 years before his death in 1953. Prior to his selection as secretary, he served as president of the State Board. At the time of his death he was the oldest living past president of the state association. John F. Martin was elected President of the National Funeral Directors Association in 1919 and served one term.

ASSOCIATION PRESIDENTS: 1889, F. S. Simmons, *Camden;* 1890-91, W. N. Parslow, *Hoboken;* 1892-93, A. W. Grobler, *Pemberton;* 1894-95, Wm. Delaney, *Jersey City;* 1902, George Stevens, *Jersey City;* 1903, W. Nelson Knapp, *East Orange;* 1904, Charles S. Lawson, *Salem;* 1905-06, John F. Mathews, *Newark;* 1907-08, W. B. M. Burrell, *Camden;* 1909, George H. Bunnell, *Jersey City;* 1910, William M. Dufford, *Paterson;* 1911, Frank S. Bolles, *Newark;* 1912, James J. Higgins, *Elizabeth;* 1913, George H. Paulson, *Trenton;* 1914, Frank B. Potter, *Vineland;* 1915, William D. Kingsland, *Hackensack;* 1916, Ivans D. Applegate, *Hoboken;* 1917, James H. Sexton, *Asbury Park;* 1918, Clark B. Rogers, *Bordentown;* 1919-20, Frank J. Codey, *Orange;* 1921, August F. Schmidt, *Elizabeth;* 1922, John Iliff, *Newton;* 1923, Michael J. Corrigan, *Jersey City;* 1924, J. Preston Potter, *Clayton;* 1925-26, William C. Collins, *Lyndhurst;* 1927, John J. Engel, *Elizabeth;* 1928, G. Franklin Guiney, *Newark;* 1929, J. M. Houghton, *Jersey City;* 1930, Claude A. Hill, *Hackensack;* 1931, J. Prescott Cadman, *Ocean City;* 1932-35, Ralph E. Kimble, *Princeton;* 1936, Lloyd B. Cochran,

Hackettstown; 1937, Nelson H. Collins, *Rutherford;* 1938, William B. Mathis, *Pitman;* 1939, Jonas A. Meyer, *Newark;* 1940, William S. Heer, *Hightstown;* 1941, William P. Rush, *Bloomsbury;* 1942, John M. Corrigan, *Jersey City;* 1943, Lawrence A. Kenny, Jr. *South Amboy;* 1944-45, C. Ensley Clayton, *Adelphia;* 1946, James F. Caffrey, Jr., *Newark;* 1947, Clarence J. Eichel, *Camden;* 1948, Robert C. Moore, Jr., *Paterson;* 1949, Floyd W. Smith, *Newton;* 1950, M. A. Maliszewski, *South River;* 1951, Lawrence G. Fallon, *Jersey City;* 1952, George F. Kierman, *Belleville;* 1953, Harold J. Stout, *Trenton;* 1954, Ralph J. Damiano, *Long Branch;* 1955, Thomas A. Lewsi, *Boonton;* 1956, John Paolerico, *Newark;* 1957, Daniel H. Conroy, *Bound Brook;* 1958, C. Calvin Rone, *Vineland;* 1959, H. Lawrence Scott, *Atlantic City;* 1960, Brar V. Riewerts, *Bergenfield.*

NEW MEXICO
Informant: A. J. Exter

A complete history of the New Mexico Funeral Directors' and Embalmers' Association would be very difficult to assemble. However, it is known that the present state association is the off-shoot of the old Western Funeral Directors' Association which was organized in Denver, Colorado, in 1897. Two New Mexico men were members of this organization. They were O. W. Strong, of Albuquerque, and J. C. Johnsen of Las Vegas, New Mexico. Mr. Johnsen was at that time a resident of Aspen, Colorado.

It was not until 1906 that a group of fourteen men met in Albuquerque and organized the New Mexico Funeral Directors' and Embalmers' Association.

The first man to be licensed in New Mexico was Alphonse Simpier. The license was signed by the then Territorial Governor in 1888, and an error was made in the date which read: "1988."

These fourteen men had vision. They began work immediately and were successful in getting New Mexico's first Embalmers' Law passed in 1908. Funeral directors operated under this law until 1947. These pioneers also wrote a code of ethics, one clause of which provided that "When two funeral directors were called in the same case, both should retire while the family made up their minds which should take charge."

The old law, which took effect on March 17th, 1909, established a State Board of Embalmers, required that applicants have a High School education or its equivalent, as well as a year of apprenticeship under a licensed embalmer. It also provided that an embalmer holding a valid license in another state should be given a temporary license effective until the next meeting of the Board, at which time he would be required to take the New Mexico State Board examination. In July 1933, the old law was amended requiring applicants to have two years practical experience and a completed course of 26 weeks in a conference graded school of embalming.

The record, or history, is completely lost from 1908 to 1919, except for personal records kept by the now secretary-treasurer. His own certificate shows that T. E. Kelley was President of the association in 1919, and C. A. Rising was Secretary; and his embalmer's certificate shows that C. A. Rising was Vice President of the Board; O. G. Reeder was secretary.

In 1933, there was organized the Tri-State Association, consisting of New Mexico, Colorado and Wyoming. Tri-State conventions were held in 1934 and 1935.

The year A. J. Exter became president of the association (1933), he and Carl Russell decided that since the records were so incomplete they should be set up in the form of a permanent Secretary's Record Minute Book. After spending many hours going through old records written on envelopes, paper sacks, wrapping paper and such, they established the present minute book for the secretary.

It was that year that the association was notified by the Corporation Commission that it should comply with the Transportation Act of 1929 or cease operating ambulances; but the association leaders were successful in convincing the Commission that it was the intention of the legislature that ambulances were to be exempt, just as were hearses. Funeral directors in New Mexico continued operating without interference until the first term of Allen Rollie as President, when the matter came up a second time; and he and the late A. L. Zinn were successful in attaching an amendment to the "Share The Ride Bill," exempting Ambulances from the Transportation Act. This bill was later declared unconstitutional by the State Supreme Court, so funeral directors were back where they started.

Finally, a bill *was* passed exempting ambulances. Under the leadership of Allen Rollie, a committee headed by Robert M. Fitzgerald,

861

with the able assistance of the late A. L. Zinn, prepared our present state law which became effective in 1947.

The State Association has constantly fought for the things that are good for the field of funeral service. Through the years, beginning as far back as 1933, it has been successful in preventing nearly all of the so-called Burial Insurance Companies from entering New Mexico.

In the last two sessions of the State Legislature, the association has been successful in helping passage of relevant laws, such as the minimum for trust funds for perpetual care cemeteries, and having ambulances operated by funeral directors declared emergency vehicles. The association feels it imperative that constant vigilance be observed in the matter of the so-called funeral "package deals."

At the last session of the State Legislature the association was successful in helping get passed legislation raising the burial allowance for indigents.

Even though New Mexico is numerically a small association, it is in favor of any policy which will promote the general well being of all funeral directors, and it hopes that some day the funeral directors of this state can again hold joint meetings with members of associations in surrounding states.

ASSOCIATION PRESIDENTS: 1906-07, Clarence Ullery, *Rosewell;* 1908, A. Borders, *Albuquerque;* 1909, J. A. Mahoney, *Demig;* 1910, Frank H. Strong, *Albuquerque;* 1911, R. M. Thorne, *Carlsbad;* 1912, Thomas A. Johnson, *Las Vegas;* 1913, Clark Dilley, *Rosewell;* 1914-15, H. O.

Strong, *Albuquerque;* 1916-17, M. H. Koch, *Tucumcari;* 1918-19, T. E. Kelley, *Carrizozo;* 1920, Ed. J. Neer, *Portales;* 1921-22, D. Rollie, *Gallup;* 1923, C. A. Rising, *Santa Fe;* 1924, G. T. Hinman, *Silver City;* 1925, Thomas Blakemore, *Albuquerque;* 1926, C. G. Mason, *Hagerman;* 1927, O. W. Strong, *Albuquerque;* 1928, Frank Talmage, *Roswell;* 1929, C. G. Bero, *Farmington;* 1930, E. F. Dunn, *Tucumcari;* 1931, L. E. Hanlon, *Williard;* 1932-34, A. J. Exter, *Albuquerque;* 1935-36, R. M. Fitzgerald, *Las Vegas;* 1937-38, Foster Sayre, *Santa Fe;* 1939, L. W. Leadinghaus, *Alamogordo;* 1940, O. L. Parker, *Hot Springs;* 1941-43, Dayton M. Talmadge, *Roswell;* 1944-45, Allen Rollie, *Gallup;* 1946, J. H. Hanlon, *Toos;* 1947, Ernest Wheeler, Jr., *Portales;* 1948, Clifton E. Dunn, *Tucumcari;* 1949, Lawrence E. Hanlon, *Albuquerque;* 1950, Richard W. Thorne, *Albuquerque;* 1951, Llyle M. Westrum, *Rosewell;* 1952, Sidney H. Curtis, *Silver City;* 1953, Thomas A. Johnsen, *Las Vegas;* 1954, Jack Cope, *Farmington;* 1955, J. H. Nelson, *Las Cruces;* 1956, Lester E. Salazar, *Albuquerque;* 1957, Walter Julian, *Fort Sumner;* 1958, Carl Wolf, *Clovis;* 1959, Manuel Stern, *Albuquerque;* 1960, Lloyd E. Roberts, *Clovis.*

NEW YORK

New York funeral directors have always been among the nation's leaders in organizing the profession. In July, 1879, Sylvanus Hawley of Wyoming, wrote a letter to the editor of *The Casket* urging funeral directors to join together in groups for mutual aid. He urged organization not only on a local scale but even on a national basis.

The first call to a state organizational meeting appeared in *The Casket* on June 1, 1880. "The undersigned hereby unite in urging the profession doing business in the State of New York to assemble in convention at Utica on Wednesday, June 16, 1880, at two o'clock, for the purpose of consulting on the present status of our business, and, if thought best, to organize an Association for the general good of the undertakers. You are therefore personally requested to be present, and assist in the deliberations."

This first meeting, held at Bagg's Hotel in Utica, on Wednesday, June 16, 1880, was highly successful. The 40 men present wrote a constitution and by-laws, in which the organization was called "The Undertakers' Association of the State of New York," and then selected a group of officers to serve for the first year: *President,* Oscar N. Crane, Canandaigua; *Vice Presidents:* John H. Douglass, Utica; Robert F. Atkins, Buffalo; James W. Morange, Albany; *Secretary,* Thomas Gliddon, an editor of *Casket,* Rochester; *Treasurer,* William Madden, Troy; and an *Executive Committee:* Michael Ryan, Syracuse; William B. Dean, Auburn; and G. T. Davis, New Rochelle. Thus, following Michigan by only a few months, New York became the second state to organize an association of funeral directors.

Within the first two years the membership of the association more than doubled, and the secretary reported to the assembled members in 1882 the further growth of professional organization in the United States in these words: ". . . You will also be requested by your acting president to elect delegates to

attend what, a year ago, we never dreamed of—a National Convention of Funeral Directors." At this meeting New York elected delegates to represent her association at the first meeting of the national association held in Rochester in June, 1882.

New York was one of the first states to attempt to regulate the conduct of its membership through the by-laws of the association itself. In 1882 O. N. Crane suggested that a certificate of membership be given each member of the association as he was received into the group, and that the certificate be revoked and taken back by the association if the member "does not behave himself, or disgraces himself."

New York also in many other ways has been interested in the members of her group, and, from the very first days of the association, has attempted to bring to the membership the best in educational materials and lectures, the best in legal advice, and the best spiritual and ethical opinions. At every meeting the lectures to the membership were on timely subjects and were given by recognized experts in the field.

The greatest felt need by funeral directors in the early days was knowledge of the new art of embalming.

Along with the education of the membership came the idea that for the protection of the knowledgeable members should come a law granting them rights and privileges and placing upon them the obligation of upholding the profession. After more than a decade of legislative set-backs success was achieved, and the first law of New York to recognize the embalmer as a professional person with special talents and knowledge was passed in 1898. This law required all persons practicing embalming after January 1, 1899 to pass an examination given by a board of five undertakers who had "Had at least five years of practical experience." All undertakers who were already established in business were exempt from the examination but were permitted to receive a certificate upon payment of a five dollar fee.

The law had not been passed without a battle and in years that followed, only the vision, foresight, vigilance, and hard work of the funeral directors of the state kept a whole series of "anti" legislation from being enacted. Among these was a proposal labeled as the "anti-embalming bill."

In 1910 the revised undertakers' law passed the previous year was declared unconstitutional by the state supreme court, and the association's legal committee immediately set about formulating a new law. Twice the new law was passed by both houses of the state legislature only to have the governor veto the bill. A bill, not completely satisfactory to the profession, was passed in 1911, and in 1913 the licensing of undertakers was made obligatory. The latter bill established educational standards and examination subjects to be passed by those wishing the license. New York now had a dual system—an embalmers' license and a funeral directors' license, and thus became one of the handful of states to license funeral directors as well as embalmers before World War I.

The first major enactment was brought about again in 1917. This law made it obligatory for board members to have had five years of experience as undertaker and embalmer and to be licensed in each capacity, but it also gave the board power to investigate and revoke existing undertakers' and embalmers' licenses for good cause. The new requirements set up by the law included those suggested by other states: that the candidate be at least 21 years old, and that he pass an examination in sanitation, disinfection, and preparation of bodies for burial or transport.

A 1920 amendment gave broad power to "revoke or *suspend* licenses." Until this time the board had had power only to revoke a license.

As part of Governor Alfred E. Smith's general reassignment of most state governmental functions in 1926 the Board of Embalming Examiners was abolished and all its powers and duties transferred to the Department and Commissioner of Health. The new statute created a Supervisor of Undertaking and Embalming to be appointed by the State Commissioner of Health. Requirements for both the embalmers' and undertakers' licenses remained substantially the same except that the apprenticeship requirement was added. Under the new arrangement a system of reciprocity with other states who licensed embalmers and undertakers was developed.

In 1929, legislation proposed by the funeral directors and adopted by the Legislature, established the high school requirement in this state, starting with a one-year requirement for 1930 and increasing progressively to four years by 1933. To make the change more acceptable the "equivalent" of high school

864

was made sufficient for qualifying for license, and on the basis that the new law had resulted in a few hardship cases, the Association was urged in 1932 to concur in legislation providing a "grandfather" provision.

These two—the "high school equivalency" and the "grandfather clauses," veritably opened the flood gates and only the herculean efforts of the association eventually stopped the field from being overrun by thousands of untrained and unqualified.

Despite the heroic efforts of Committees on Character and Fitness appointed by the Health Commissioner when the full effects of the grandfather law began to show, over eight hundred were licensed within eight months under this special statute. It took years of effort to obtain the later amendment, which finally limited the high school equivalency to "educational equivalents."

The New York State Association was among the first to advocate factors other than public health for justifying license laws in the public interest, by urging that the funeral director's fiduciary relationship to his client should be the principal concern of the Legislature and the licensing authorities.

In 1944, the association proposed and the Legislature adopted the single funeral director license and the license qualifications as they presently prevail—two years of practical training or an approved course in a funeral director school and one year of practical training.

Since 1950, the Association has been engaged in a constant campaign to obtain an adequate system of funeral director license and law enforcement, similar to the systems of licensing and administration of the other eighteen professions in New York State. A pilot bill was introduced for study in 1957. A 1959 bill, introduced late in the session, got lost in the log jam of its closing days. The 1960 Legislature passed a bill to transfer the function of funeral director licensing to the Department of State and create a seven-man board of funeral director examiners. On the very last day to act on bills before him, the Governor vetoed the measure.

The story of the growth of the Association in New York at a time when similar groups both in New York and in other states were experiencing a loss in membership is an interesting one. For many years, there were two separate associations in the state of New York, the New York State Undertakers' Association and the New York State Embalmers' Association, each holding its own annual meeting and exhibit, and with a great deal of overlapping of memberships. In 1929 they formed a Joint Law Committee, financed by the generous contributions from members of both groups after they heard the committee's plans at a series of regional meetings held for that special purpose in various parts of the state.

By 1933 the members of both associations were convinced of the value of solidarity, and they worked out a plan for consolidating the two groups into the New York State Undertakers' and Embalmers' Association. After the single license law was adopted in 1944, the name was changed to the New York State Funeral Directors Association, Inc.

This joining of forces was the

beginning of a new era for the funeral profession in New York State. With the accelerated tempo and greater strength and vigor which came with the formation of the consolidated association, the members set about their tasks of making their association into the potent force and effective influence which it since has become.

In 1934 the association was one of the first to set up a full-time office and staff and to retain a lawyer-association executive to give full time and attention to the problems and needs of the association and the profession in the state.

In all its determinations and efforts, the association has steadfastly been guided by this principle: "What serves the interests of the public best, serves the interests of the profession most." In this regard a three-point program has continued as the blueprint of its activities: the protection against adverse and unnecessarily oppressive legislation and the promotion of legislation in keeping with the needs of the public, the profession, and changing times; the assurance of a healthy professional and economic climate; and the deserved acquisition of public confidence and good will.

It is the responsibility of the Committee on Legislation and Law Reform and the Association Counsel to check carefully, on the morning after they are introduced, each of the over 8,000 bills presented annually to the New York legislature to be sure that nothing slips by which might even remotely affect funeral directors and their clients. The bill "titles" do not always reveal the full purposes and effects of the bill, and frequently through the years, this careful screening has repaid the association by resulting in the detection of undesirable provisions before they could be enacted into law.

In 1934, and long before anyone began to think about introducing into New York any of the burial schemes and promotion plans which were already plaguing other states, the New Yorkers decided to apply "the ounce of prevention" rule and sponsored legislation to outlaw schemes and plans which did not afford families all the benefits of unrestricted selection and free competition. To implement this legislation, they obtained at different times, the aid and assistance of the Attorney General, the Insurance Superintendent, the Banking Department, the Consumers Department, the Better Business Bureau, and a host of quasi-public and private organizations, interested in the protection of the public.

Over the years, the New York State Association has been successful in obtaining the aid of the authorities to enjoin and drive from the state a long list of burial schemes, funeral-insurance plans, extended credit plans, pre-need funeral contracts offered to individuals and sold *en masse* through unions and other organizations, pre-need sales of caskets and vaults, and a variety of other promotions.

During World War II and in the years that followed, New York was in the forefront of the fight against unnecessary restrictions and limitations. Its representatives were constantly in the nation's Capitol with N.F.D.A., and took on all-comers in debating the futility and the unnecessary oppressions of many of the restrictions and regulations proposed under O.P.A., O.P.S., and the

866

other wartime agencies.

To supplement the state administrative rules, regulations, and enforcement, the New York Association several years ago adopted an amplified and extensive code of ethics and rules of professional conduct, restating the responsibilities of the funeral director and pledging the highest professional standards and practices. A nine-member grievance committee, whose procedures were patterned after those of the state bar associations and medical societies, was appointed with comprehensive and unlimited powers to hear complaints and initiate investigations of their own. It is the committee's purpose always to assure enforcement of the laws, the rules, and the code while at the same time guaranteeing the funeral director against unjust complaint or annoyance.

It is especially noteworthy that the local Better Business Bureau refers any complaints and inquiries about funeral service to the Association Headquarters.

1934 was an auspicious year for New Yorkers also because in that year, the New York Association introduced its policy of plain talk. Encouraged by its success in winning over such "doubters" as Dr. Lee K. Frankel, the Vice President of the Metropolitan Life Insurance Company, who initiated the survey which culminated in John C. Gebhart's volume on Funeral Costs and Dr. John Haynes Holmes, the principal proponent of municipal mortuaries, the association decided to experiment with a new type of luncheon club talk.

The first few appearances could have disheartened less courageous and determined men. Even those who initially were concerned about the new "no secrets, no holds barred" type of talk, soon began to express a new-found satisfaction, comfort and pride from the public understanding and appreciation which was expressed by the luncheon club members after each talk. The value of the program was amplified by press releases to the newspapers in each locality.

Simultaneously, the Association adopted a funeral contract form with adequate emphasis upon the funeral directors' professional services and its part in the total funeral bills. In a series of special meetings the members were alerted to their potent opportunities when making arrangements and when billing for the funeral, for improving their clients' understanding of funeral service generally and for developing their greater appreciation of them personally.

The three-way effort gained national recognition in 1938 when NFDA featured this public relations blueprint as "A Practical Program of Public Relations" on its Convention Program in New York City.

More recent developments in the field of public relations in New York State include the introduction of a number of programs and devices which have also been adopted by many associations and included in other NFDA programs. Each of them has been designed to present the funeral director to the public in the proper perspective, to dispel existing doubts and suspicions, and to develop greater understanding. Among the more important later developments are a number of dramatic presentations, "Secrets—What Secrets," "What's Your Answer," "There is No Unimportant

Corpse," and "The Exkiliro Club." A highlight of recent years was the Association's participation in an unrehearsed TV panel discussion, "The High Cost of Dying" which, as a kinescope recording, has been shown to funeral director audiences all over the country. The association is now engaged in developing other programs designed especially for members' home-town use.

The New York Association with its unique location in the heart of "writer land" is well suited to keeping a lookout for stories which unjustifiably present the funeral director in a bad light. Many stories originally planned as "exposés" have never come to print after the facts have been presented to their planners by the New York representatives. In this capacity, the New York Association office has also been instrumental in alerting NFDA a number of times to public relations opportunities, thus serving the interest of the funeral directing profession at large.

Other pioneering efforts of the association in New York have resulted in improved funeral director-clergy relations; better relations with hospitals and the medical profession; greater understanding through cost surveys; improved relations with social welfare authorities resulting in more liberal welfare regulations and allowances than prevail in most other places.

Great efforts have also been made to help members with their own professional and economic problems through the Annual Junior Conference, a two-day school for sons and daughters of funeral directors, their junior executives and all funeral directors still young enough to learn. This is now replaced by a three-day Post Graduate Review. The association also conducts an annual Conference of Local Presidents, Secretaries, and State Directors, which is principally a school for the officers of its 26 local groups, but is also used to review statewide policies and programs.

The association is presently engaged in three major projects: to encourage and aid in the establishment of a two-year community college course for funeral directors in the State University of New York; to obtain legislation establishing a Board of Funeral Director Examiners and an adequate system of license law administration and enforcement; and to further highlight and publicize its Code of Ethics and Principles of Professional Practice, in order to encourage strict compliance by all members and their associates to their vocational obligations and to gain greater public recognition and appreciation of the functions and responsibilities of the professionals who display the Code.

New York has been honored on several occasions in having its members designated to high places in NFDA. The following men from New York have served the National as President: Oscar N. Crane, Canandaigua; S. Merrit Hook, New York City; Fred Hulberg, New York City; August Eickelberg, New York City; James H. McLarney, New York City; John W. Mattle, Rochester; Samuel J. Waters, New York City; John N. Gennerich, New York City; and Roy T. Merrill, Albion. New York is justly proud of the contribution made by these outstanding men and by her state association as a whole to the profession of funeral directing in

New York State and in the United States.

ASSOCIATION PRESIDENTS: 1880-81, Oscar N. Crane, *Canandaigna;* 1882, John H. Douglass, *Utica;* 1885-86, John B. Sackett, *Buffalo;* 1887, Jacob M. Hopper, *Brooklyn;* 1888-90, S. Merritt Hook, *New York;* 1891, P. J. O'Reilly, *Utica;* 1892, W. L. Earle, *Tully;* 1893-94, W. J. Phillips, *Albany;* 1895-96, A. Eickleberg, *New York;* 1897-1901, William J. Phillips, *Albany;* 1902-03, James E. McLarney, *New York;* 1904-05, William H. Newlan, *Brooklyn;* 1906, W. I. Timeson, *Schenectady;* 1907-08, William Boardman, *Brooklyn;* 1909-10, George Fairchild, *Syracuse;* 1911-13, James McLarney, *New York;* 1914, Howard F. Smith, *Buffalo;* 1915-17, Lester W. Hill, *Brooklyn;* 1918-19, Charles F. Moadinger, *Brooklyn;* 1920, Fred Hulberg, *New York;* 1921-22, Harry T. Pyle, *Brooklyn;* 1923-24, Frank W. Traugott, *Syracuse;* 1925-28, Fred L. Dascher, *Albany;* 1929-30, John W. Mattle, *Rochester;* 1931-32, I. Jay Bookhout, *Oneonta;* 1933, T. Wm. O'Neill, *Syracuse;* 1934-35, Samuel J. Waters, *New York;* 1936, Frank C. Lankton, *Utica;* 1937-38, A. D. MacAffer, *Cohoes;* 1939, Harry B. Cornelius, *Rhinebeck;* 1940-41, John Gennerich, *New York;* 1942-43, Roy T. Merrill, *Albion;* 1944-45, Joseph M. Kennedy, *Lockport;* 1946-47, William M. Weigand, *Brooklyn;* 1948-49, Leland P. Pulling, *Ellenville;* 1950-51, Harold B. Crandall, *Hornell;* 1952-53, Jeremiah D. Buckley, *New York;* 1954, Charles R. Loomis, *Buffalo;* 1955-56, Marcus H. Millspaugh, *Walden;* 1957-58, Burr Davis, *Mt.*

Vernon; 1959-60, Fred R. Sears, *North Syracuse.*

NORTH CAROLINA
Informant: Clyde Robinson

On Tuesday, August 23, 1887 representatives of eight firms in the state of North Carolina met in Goldsboro to consider the organization of a state funeral directors' association. The following were represented: D. P. Haskitt & Son, Goldsboro; Moore and Robinson, Goldsboro; J. W. Woolvin & Son, Wilmington; Wooten & Stevens, Wilson; John W. Brown, Raleigh; L. C. Bagwell, Raleigh; G. B. Webb & Co., Kinston; and C. W. Jogner, La Grange. Temporary officers were chosen to serve until a call could be sent out to all the funeral directors of the state to meet in Raleigh in October. Mr. J. W. Woolvin was chosen temporary chairman and J. J. Robinson temporary secretary of the group of planners. A Committee of three men to write a constitution and by-laws was also chosen at this time. John W. Brown headed the committee and was assisted by the two temporary officers.

Formal organization of the North Carolina Funeral Directors and Embalmers Association was effected on October 19, 1887 at Raleigh. Although John W. Brown is usually given credit as the father of the organization, actually four men signed the original letter requesting the meeting: John W. Brown; Frank H. Vogler, Winston-Salem; John M. Barnes, Henderson; and A. C. Vogler, Winston-Salem.

Fifteen men attended the first meeting, six from the western section of the state and nine from the east. The following officers were elected to serve the organization during the first year: *President,* John W. Brown, Raleigh; *Secretary,* Frank H. Vogler, Winston-Salem; and *Treasurer,* John M. Barnes, Henderson.

The organization itself sponsored a school for the education of its own members. It was held in the Brown Funeral Home in Raleigh and was conducted by Dr. Charles A. Renouard of New York. Although classes were held only every three years and the course extended for a mere three weeks, many funeral directors who wished to learn more about the new science of embalming attended the lectures. Fees for the course were $25.

In 1893 the word "undertaker" first appeared on the statutes of North Carolina in a new law which "exempted all undertakers from jury duty." On July 1, 1901 the state established its first State Board of Embalming, a five man commission consisting of three doctors and two licensed funeral directors. By 1905 the state had passed its first law setting requirements for embalmers and funeral directors as well as establishing certain requisites for funeral homes.

Early in the history of the organization in North Carolina a code of ethics was given consideration, and in 1893 Frank H. Vogler submitted to the assembled membership a code which was deemed suitable by the group and thus became the first code to which the organization subscribed.

Shortly after the code of ethics was adopted the organization suffered internal disorders and was forced to disband for a period of about two years. In April of 1900 the group reorganized and again affiliated and began to report to

NFDA. At this time there were only about 20 members in the association, but the group reported passage of a law regulating the profession in the state and termed it "one of the best laws regulating the practice of embalming of any state in the Union." Under this law "no one not holding a license is allowed to use embalming fluid in any way."

From its inception until 1944 the group was known as The North Carolina Funeral Directors and Embalmers. At this time the organization consolidated with the North Carolina Burial Association, and since then has been known as the North Carolina Funeral Directors and Burial Association, Inc.

Five years after the amalgamation a state office was established in Raleigh, capital of the state. This office houses all business of the funeral industry, examining board, and funeral homes. The North Carolina Burial Association is controlled by the legislature of the State of North Carolina. A separate office, controlled by a commissioner who is appointed by the governor, known as the Commissioner of Burial Associations is maintained in Raleigh for carrying on the business relating to all Burial Associations in the State.

On June 15, 1949, the North Carolina Funeral Directors and Burial Association, Inc., and the North Carolina State Board of Embalmers and Funeral Directors Examiners opened a joint office in Raleigh and employed an executive secretary to supervise both the association and the licensing board. The office is today operating to the satisfaction of both agencies.

ASSOCIATION PRESIDENTS: 1887,

870

John W. Brown, *Raleigh;* 1888-89, W. P. Wooten, *Wilson;* 1890-92, J. Robert Parker, *High Point;* 1893-94, Frank H. Volger, *Salem;* 1895, John M. Harry, *Charlotte;* 1896, Frank H. Volger, *Salem;* 1897-1900, John M. Harry, *Charlotte;* 1901, Charles W. Brown, *Asheville;* 1902, Frank H. Vogler, *Salem;* 1903, A. T. Barnes, *Henderson;* 1904, James F. Woolvin, *Wilmington;* 1905-06, J. Frank Morris, *Winston;* 1907-08, D. W. Hardee, *Henderson;* 1909, F. G. Flannagan, *Greenville;* 1910, W. T. Nicholson, *Statesville;* 1911, H. G. Rowe, *Weldon;* 1912, J. W. Laney, *Monroe;* 1913, J. K. Willis, *New Bern;* 1914, L. F. Siegler, *Edenton;* 1915, E. Poole, *Greensboro;* 1916-18, F. E. Vogler, *Winston-Salem;* 1919, P. J. Honeycutt, *Albemarle;* 1920, J. H. Blue, *Greensboro;* 1921, J. Robert Wood, *Oxford;* 1922, Frank Hovis, *Charlotte;* 1923, W. H. Wilkinson, *Reidsville;* 1924, T. W. Summersett, *Salisbury;* 1925, W. N. Vogler, *Winston-Salem;* 1926, H. T. Fulton, *Kings Mountain;* 1927, R. H. Sechrest, *High Point;* 1928, D. G. Smaw, *New Bern;* 1929-30, Ben E. Dauglas, *Charlotte;* 1931, Henry Hanes, *Greensboro;* 1932, David T. Yow, *High Point;* 1933, Paul Yelverton, *Wilson;* 1934, Fab Brown, *Raleigh;* 1935, Albert T. Willis, *New Bern;* 1936, Fenner Paul, *Kings Mountain;* 1937, Oscas P. Breece, *Fayetteville;* 1938, W. Edward Yopp, *Wilmington;* 1939, W. Earnest Thompson, *Burlington;* 1940, Charles P. Rogers, *Sanford;* 1941, Dennis Biggs, *Lumberton;* 1942, Arnold Koonce, 1943, Harlow Mims, *Raleigh;* 1944-45, W. D. Hardin, *Scotland Neck;* 1946, John L. Rusher, *Salisbury;* 1947, O. C. Pennington, *Raleigh;* 1948, A. Lee Forbis, *Greensboro;* 1949,

W. D. Townson, *Murphy;* 1950, Fred Kesler, *Henderson;* 1951, W. N. Hovis, *Charlotte;* 1952, Joel Cook Holland, *Murfreesboro;* 1953, Dennis W. Moody, *Mount Airy;* 1954, Robert W. Wynn, Jr., *Raleigh;* 1955, William M. Shepherd, *Hendersonville;* 1956, Charles P. Rogers, *Sanford;* 1957, Karl C. Miller, *Charlotte;* 1958, Paul L. Hofler, *Gatesville;* 1959, J. Ollie Harris, *Kings Mountain;* 1960, Hiram Rose, *Benson.*

NORTH DAKOTA
Informant: Neal Bradburn

For several years preceding the first attempts to organize a separate state association, funeral directors of North Dakota were joined with Minnesota and South Dakota in an organization known as the Tri-State Assn. When attempts were made shortly before the turn of the century to effect such an independent group, they were unsuccessful. However, in 1901 the *Embalmers' Monthly* reported "A meeting of the funeral directors of North Dakota was held at Fargo on the 2nd of October, at which there was organized the North Dakota Funeral Directors' Association." After adopting a constitution and by-laws, officers were elected. These included *President,* Don McDonald, Grand Forks; *Vice Presidents,* J. D. VanFleet, Larimore; R. M. Bushee, Jamestown; *Secretary,* George W. Wasem, Fargo; *Treasurer,* M. M. Borman, Abercrombie. Although a meeting was scheduled to be held between January 1, and April 1, 1902, no further word is heard of this group until 1904, when under the banner "New Association in North Dakota," the *Embalmers' Monthly* reported that although the earlier attempt of three years previous had not succeeded, the officers of the group had continued to press informally for an independent association. In this year, 1904, the ten or eleven members who met elected the same officers as had been elected in 1901, but considered that the North Dakota Funeral Directors Association was now officially "organized." History shows that this organizational attempt did indeed "take," and that the association has enjoyed continued existence.

The first meetings were alternated between Fargo and Grand Forks. Shortly after the organization most of the meetings were held at the State University at Grand Forks. One of the first lectures and demonstrations was given by Professor W. P. Hohenschuh, and the second by Professor Howard S. Eckles.

In 1913 the ninth annual convention was held in Jamestown in February. Program highlight was a talk by Reverend G. W. Simon on clergy-funeral director relations. The association at this time consisted of 100 members, both honorary and active. Forty-nine were present at the convention.

The tenth annual convention, held in 1914, was at the University at Grand Forks. The state was at that time divided into four districts, Northwest, Southwest, Northeast, and Southeast. It was reported in the minutes that the temperature was twenty-five degrees below zero, and that a majority of the members voted to have the convention henceforth held in May instead of the winter months.

In 1917, the annual convention highlight was a film on new caskets shown through the courtesy of J.

W. Maxwell. Also at this convention, President G. C. Jensen of Edinburgh presented a handmade gavel to incoming President J. W. Calnan. Every president since has used this gavel in conducting the annual meetings.

In 1918 no convention was held because of the war and flu epidemic. It was about this time that the North Dakota Funeral Directors Association became affiliated with the National Funeral Directors Association.

In 1920, during the fifteenth annual convention at Grand Forks, the dues were $5 per membership, with 60 cents going to National for National membership.

In 1922 at the seventeenth annual convention in Minot, the funeral directors and hardware dealers had a joint convention. A resolution favoring the establishment of an embalming school similar to that in operation at the University of Minnesota was passed.

During these early years the association would sponsor a two-week embalming course at the University at Grand Forks. The cost was $40, and those passing the examination at the conclusion of the course received an embalmer's license.

At the twenty-second annual convention held in Bismarck in 1927, the association recommended to the Board of Health that a twenty-five mile limit be imposed as the distance that a funeral director could transport remains that were not embalmed.

The Association withdrew from the National Association in 1926, but reaffiliated a year later.

The silver anniversary convention was held in Grand Forks in June of 1930. J. W. Calnan of Ber-

872

thold gave the anniversary address and paid tribute to the past presidents and secretaries. Other old timers giving reports were: T. G. C. Kennelly of Mandan, George Thomas of Williston, J. W. Rowan of Minot, A. H. Johnson of Mayville, Andy Nelson of the St. Paul Casket Company, and M. Norman of Grand Forks. After one of the sessions in the afternoon, the members held a memorial service at Memorial Cemetery for the late Don McDonald. G. L. Anderson was the convention chairman. O. J. Hanson of Fargo presented a bill on behalf of the Legislative Committee, that would prevent the burial associations from coming into the state of North Dakota. G. L. Anderson was elected President.

During the twenty-sixth annual convention in 1931, at Mandan, prizes were awarded to the salesmen who signed up the most members in that year. During this twenty-sixth annual convention, the association took in thirty-seven new members, the largest number of memberships in one year, in the association's history. Many of these members are active in the association at the present time. During this meeting a Code of Ethics Committee was appointed and instructed to draft a code and report at the next annual convention.

The twenty-eighth annual convention was held in Jamestown in 1933. The Association at this time consisted of 96 members. Speakers at this convention were Grant Williams and Walter Quist of Minneapolis.

The twenty-ninth annual convention was held in Bismarck in 1934. At this convention interest was shown in the Funeral Industry Code

drafted for the N.R.A. Business matters, this being the middle of the great depression, also were taken up and discussed. It is noted that at this time the North Dakota Funeral Directors Association unanimously voted to give whole-hearted support to the National Recovery Act.

The thirtieth annual convention was held in Valley City in 1935. One of the speakers in this year's convention was the State Tax Commissioner who notified the delegation that rules and regulations concerning the State Sales Tax would be in the mail soon.

At the thirty-second annual convention in 1937, held in Mandan, a side trip was again taken to old Fort McKean. The tour was made very interesting and educational by Col. Welch, adopted son of the Sioux Indians. The Association also went on record as recommending to the State Health Board that due to the good roads and fine automobiles that the 25 mile limit for transportation of unembalmed bodies be changed to 75 miles.

The thirty-third annual convention was held in Grand Forks in 1938. Lloyd P. Everson of Williston presided as President. One of the main speakers, Perry O. Powell, Secretary from Minnesota, discussed funeral costs, noting that 57 per cent of all funerals in the United States came between $200 and $500, 32 per cent were less than $200, and only 11 per cent were above $500.

Regular conventions were held all through the depression and the early years of the war. However, there was no convention in 1943, and only an abbreviated meeting was held in 1944. It is noted in the minutes that bad weather upset the convention schedule in 1945 and that the banquet had to be postponed from the first to the second night.

Jamestown was again the site for the 1946 convention. G. Lee Anderson, President of the Embalming Board, welcomed back the funeral director war veterans.

Grand Forks was the site of the 1947 convention. One feature was a talk on the government's repatriation program given by Lt. Colonel Carl R. Yost, representing the Graves Registration Service. President Willet was instructed to appoint four district chairmen and have each chairman schedule two meetings in each district for the coming year.

At the 1950 convention, held in Bismarck, the following twenty-five year buttons were presented: G. L. Anderson, W. E. Perry, C. W. Kyle, and R. C. Lindsey. Paul W. Eddy, President of the Embalming Board, stated that at the time there were approximately 270 embalmers licensed in North Dakota and 204 of these were living in the state.

At the 1953 convention, held in Bismarck, one of the featured speakers was Mr. A. R. Aslekson of the Social Security Administration office. Mr. Aslekson spoke on how the social security affects the funeral director. In this year's convention, Paul W. Eddy took charge of the memorial service. For many, many years the memorial service had been in charge of Jim Maxwell, a charter member. At this time, the Funeral Directors Association paid reverence in the memory of Jim Maxwell, long-time and faithful supporter of the North Dakota Funeral Directors Association. The

newly revised constitution and by-laws were presented for the adoption at this convention. The Board of Governors was changed from three members to four members, and were termed Board of Trustees.

The 1955 convention was the fiftieth for the North Dakota Funeral Directors Association. The exhibits were held in the University field house, and in one portion of the field house a space was set aside for many different types of items that funeral directors have used in the past fifty years. There were several horse-drawn hearses, early motorized hearses, older types of caskets, and many other items that were common equipment in the funeral home of years gone by.

At the 1958 convention, one of the major items of business was the report of the Insurance Committee which recommended that the North Dakota Funeral Directors Association adopt a group policy plan presented by the Blue Cross-Blue Shield Insurance.

ASSOCIATION PRESIDENTS: 1901-07, Don McDonald, *Grand Forks;* 1908-11, William M. Chandler, *Grafton;* 1912, George J. Bonine, *Balfour;* 1913, M. M. Borman, *Abercrombie;* 1914, John Challey, *Lisbon;* 1915, T. G. C. Kennelly, *Mandan;* 1916-17, G. C. Jensen, *Edinburg;* 1918, J. W. Calnan, *Berthold;* 1919, C. V. Ferguson, *Glenburn;* 1920, W. M. Edwards, *Larimore;* 1921, E. W. Gilbertson, *Devils Lake;* 1922, J. W. Rowan, *Minot;* 1923, Henry C. Hanson, *Harvey;* 1924, O. C. Olson, *Kenmore;* 1925, David Johnson, *Park River;* 1926, G. M. Thomas, *Williston;* 1927, G. D. Challey, *Lisbon;* 1928, B. J. Thomas, *Minot;* 1930-31, G. L. Anderson, *Grand*

Forks; 1932, Leo Finnegan, *Minot;* 1933, Carl Jacobson, *Crosby;* 1934, J. W. Murray, *Cando;* 1935, A. W. Bethke; 1936, Dave Price; 1937, Lloyd P. Everson, *Williston;* 1938, Charles Kyle, *Northwood;* 1939, L. S. Jensen, *Edinburgh;* 1940, Paul W. Eddy, *Jamestown;* 1941, K. P. Egge, *Mayville;* 1942-43, Oliver Peterson, *Valley City;* 1944, Ralph Ivers, *Fargo;* 1945, Harry Knott, *Charrington;* 1946, Elmer Willet, *Jamestown;* 1947, Hub Peterson, *Valley City;* 1948, Ed Bolter, *Bismarck;* 1949, Harold Anderson, *Rugby;* 1950, A. B. Strong, *Devils Lake;* 1951, Truman Dahle, *Mohall;* 1952, Alvin Berg, *McClusky;* 1953, Marlin V. Olson, *Dickinson;* 1954, Maynard Lindsay, *Page;* 1955, Don M. Scramstad, *Grand Forks;* 1956, James Bolger, *Fargo;* 1957, T. A. Wonder, *McVille;* 1958, Bernhard Aarthun, *Hazen;* 1959, W. C. Adams, *Grafton;* 1960, Selmer Walby, *Lidgewood.*

OHIO

Informant: Austin Richards

In the fall of 1880, preliminary plans were drafted to establish an organization of funeral directors and embalmers. In February, 1881, J. H. Sharer of Alliance arranged a meeting to convene in Mansfield on March 15. There were 21 persons in attendance and a temporary association was effected with the appointment of a committee to plan a meeting to be held in Columbus on June 8, 1881. At this meeting the 72 firms registered officially organized what was then known as the Ohio State Association of Funeral Directors and Embalmers with E. Hatcher of Zanesville elected to serve as the first president.

The first ten years of the Association showed the usual growing pains of a beginning organization with an annual meeting being held each year. On the tenth anniversary of the association, discussion developed on consideration of a code or what was termed "The Ten Commandments" of the Association to govern the practice of funeral directing in Ohio. It is significant to note that "The Ten Commandments," originally offered by George Wickens of Lorain in 1891, who became president of the association in 1892, were not finally adopted until 1913. Many of these original "commandments" later found their way into other associations' codes of ethics.

At the turn of the century, OFDA adopted the first Constitution and By-Laws of the Funeral Directors and Embalmers Association of Ohio, dated June 5, 1900. It is significant to note that this preamble has stood as a prototype for many subsequent preambles to other state constitutions.

On July 5, 1902 the first State Board of Embalming Examiners came into existence after the legislature had passed a law setting up a state board made up of funeral directors and physicians from the state board of health. The first President was W. M. Bateman of Zanesville, and the first Secretary was J. H. Sharer of Alliance. The first embalmer's license was issued in this state in the year 1902.

The first printed bulletin in the State of Ohio was called the "Buckeye Funeral Director" and was published by Edward E. Fisher of Columbus. Volume One, Number 1, appeared in October, 1903 when James A. Lynn of New Philadelphia was serving as president. This 27 page bulletin set out the purpose of the new publication: cooperation with the funeral directors, embalmers, and sanitarians. It was in 1904 that A. C. Walter of Toledo became President of the Ohio Association. We mention this because he probably holds the record for attending the highest number of national association conventions—45 consecutive conventions.

In 1905 the 25 year old association boasted a membership of 250. In 1906 an amendment to the association's constitution was passed which provided that no funeral firm nor a member of a firm could be elected to a membership in the association if the firm or any member of a firm was engaged in promoting a burial association. In 1908 the legislature brought burial associations under the scrutiny of the Superintendent of Insurance. Also in this year the validity of the new burial insurance law was upheld. The law was designed to prohibit embalmers and funeral directors from being named as beneficiaries on insurance policies for burial of other persons. This decision had the effect of outlawing burial insurance in Ohio.

In 1910 the funeral directors began to move another step forward by seeking to attain higher educational standards for apprentices. In 1917 an amendment was made to the Embalming Law to the effect that only a person licensed by the State Board of Examiners could embalm a dead human body.

In 1922, the famous case of Mosier vs. B. G. Jones, funeral director in Columbus, was filed by a neighbor of the Jones Funeral Home to enjoin the operation of a funeral home in a strictly residential district. The court held that a funeral establishment is not a nuisance *per se,* and therefore dissolved the injunction and dismissed the petition. This case was significant in that the Ohio Association played a very important role in assisting the Jones Funeral Home. Litigation on this famous case ended on October 1, 1925, when the Ohio Supreme Court decided in favor of the defendant funeral director when the plaintiffs failed to file a motion for a re-hearing.

In the years of 1923, 1924, and 1925 the Association was reorganized, revising the Constitution, changing the name to "The Ohio Funeral Directors Association," and making provision for the hiring of a Field Secretary. In 1925 the embalmer's law was changed to require a mortuary college course of at least 26 weeks in addition to two years of practical training under the guidance of a licensed embalmer. This law also created a state board of three members, consisting of embalmers with at least five years experience in embalming, and made the state board independent of the health department by dropping the physicians from the board.

In 1927 the constitution of the association was changed to give the executive committee the authority to hire an executive secretary. They then retained Professor Deming in the capacity of Executive Secretary; and from 1927 to 1929 the association grew considerably in numbers, published a bulletin, reorganized dormant districts, and became an active association typical of the boom era.

In 1928 Harry J. Gilligan of Cincinnati was elected to the Presidency of the National Funeral Directors Association, serving for two years. He later became Secretary-treasurer of the National organization. When this office was separated, Mr. Gilligan was elected Treasurer of NFDA, an office he has held for many years.

In 1929 the crash came and the bottom seemed to drop out of all association activities for a few years. Also in that year the Ohio Embalmers Association was formed after a rift in the State Association.

In 1933 the law was again changed when the funeral director's license was inaugurated. The State Board was also changed from three to five members and a state inspector was employed to police the profession.

In 1936 the right of the Board of Embalmers and Funeral Directors to adopt rules governing the professional conduct of funeral directors in Ohio was upheld by the courts.

In 1937 the Association hired an executive secretary, Russell Knight, a newspaperman of Wilmington, Ohio, as a full time executive to manage the association office. This was a year of disastrous floods when many funeral directors of the southern and western part of the state suffered great losses in funeral homes and equipment.

In 1942, World War II was underway and the association was faced with the loss of Executive Secretary Knight, whose untimely death occurred during a meeting of over 1,000 funeral directors in Columbus who were discussing OPA rulings and funeral pricing. On January 1, 1943, Jerame (Jerry) Z. Gordon, of Columbus, formerly of the Ohio State Bar Association was hired as Executive Secretary and Counsel. In 1943 the association conducted the first series of regional meetings held for the purpose of discussing war problems involving shortages of materials, manpower, and general inflation; and in 1944 OFDA conducted a follow-up series of regional meetings to cover the subjects of education, public relations, merchandising and advertising, news from Washington and problems relating to G. I. Joe.

It was in the 1946-47 fiscal year that the educational program was advanced to include two years of academic college training, 12 months of mortuary college and 12 months of internship. Profession-wise this was the greatest advancement in setting up educational requirements for embalmers and funeral directors in the history of the association.

In 1947 the association built the largest convention in its history with over 3,000 in attendance under the theme of "Memory Lane."

The Year of 1949 was historic in that OFDA President J. A. Shaidnagel of Massillon, was appointed by the War Department to visit cemeteries overseas as a part of an official governmental inspection tour and to help formulate the repatriation program. It was in this year also that OFDA started what is now known as the Mid-Winter Institute, an educational program designed mainly to consider funeral management problems.

In 1949 and 1950 the association continued to grow under the leadership of Jerry G. Spears, Sr., who later became President of the National Funeral Directors Association. For the first time the membership reached 1,000.

The Code of Ethics and Manual of Professional Practice for funeral directors was adopted at the 70th Annual Convention June 20, 1950.

After many years of quiet on the subject, the year of 1952 marked the year of controversy involving burial and funeral insurance. The birth of Memorial Gardens and the need of legislation to curtail such activities gave rise to a series of meetings throughout the state followed by the enactment of legislation on pre-arrangement contracts, October 14, 1953; also enacted was a bill to prohibit cemeteries from discriminating against vault companies. It was in this year too that the association met with representatives from the Ohio Medical Association, the Ohio Hospital Association, the Ohio Embalmers Association and the Ohio Society of Pathologists to formulate and draft a Code of Autopsy Procedure. It is significant that a funeral director, Austin Richards, Springfield, was selected chairman of the joint committee.

In 1953 and 1954 a survey was conducted, and it was determined that over 100 local and district meetings were held throughout the State. At this time the Reverend Alvin Kershaw, a minister in Oxford, Ohio, and a hot jazz enthusiast, received wide recognition for an article which appeared in his church paper and later in *Time* magazine, criticizing elaborate funerals.

In 1955 the Association celebrated its 75th Diamond Jubilee Convention and Exhibition. The Convention session was highlighted by "This Is Your Heritage," at which time a complete review of Association history was presented with blown-up pictures of all past presidents spotlighted during the performance.

The Association successfully assisted in defending the funeral director's position in the case of Baltes vs. Johnson in which a next door neighbor attempted to secure an injunction against the operation of a funeral home as a nuisance. The Supreme Court of Ohio ruled that the local zoning board had authority to re-zone a district and permit the operation of a funeral home in a semi-residential zone and holding further that a funeral home was not a nuisance *per se*.

In 1956 President Ted Siferd of Lima traveled throughout the state presenting charts and figures on Memorial Gardens' operations and how it was enveloping funeral service operations throughout the country.

In 1957 the state association supported a bill in the legislature to prohibit picketing one hour before and during a funeral service and the funeral procession, and, during services at the cemetery. This bill passed and is now law in Ohio.

During the fiscal year 1957-58, the association conducted a series of 10 regional meetings throughout the state. It was during these meetings that the new hospital and medical coverage program and the health and accident plan were presented to the membership and adopted.

In 1958 the association reverted from regional meetings to district meetings throughout Ohio. This year also marked the 10th anniversary of the Mid-Winter Institute. The NFDA exhibit at the Cleveland Convention was the largest display of funeral merchandise, supplies and

878

services ever known with 127 exhibitors and a registration of almost 5,000.

The 1959-60 fiscal year marked the 80th anniversary of the Ohio Funeral Directors Association. The Association's legislative program was introduced during the previous administration to include such matters as: granting five-day delay period to funeral directors in filing death certificates; increasing the preferred claim allowance under the Probate Code from $350 to $500 and increasing the aid for the aged burial allowance in cases involving recipients with insurance from $300 to $500.

ASSOCIATION PRESIDENTS: 1881, Edmund Hatcher, *Zanesville;* 1882, John Epply, *Cincinnati;* 1883, I. N. Thompson, *Perrysburg;* 1884-85, Charles Miller, *Cincinnati;* 1886, Charles W. Gath, *Hamilton;* 1887, George Billow, *Akron;* 1888-89, John W. Sharer, *Alliance;* 1890, A. T. Wilson, *Middletown;* 1891, John I. Nunn, *Cleveland;* 1892, George Wickens, *Lorain;* 1893, Charles J. Krupp, *Sandusky;* 1894, H. D. McCrea, *Canton;* 1895, W. M. Bateman, *Zanesville;* 1896-97, R. E. Jones, *Columbus;* 1898, George J. Schoedinger, *Columbus;* 1899, H. W. Morey, *Marysville;* 1900, W. M. Bateman, *Zanesville;* 1901, George H. High, *Cincinnati;* 1902, Louis Grim, *Hamilton;* 1903, James A. Linn, *New Philadelphia;* 1904, A. C. Walter, *Toledo;* 1905, H. W. Bennett, *Lima;* 1906, W. W. Wagner, *Piqua;* 1907-08, B. G. Jones, *Columbus;* 1909, Joseph Gilligan, *Cincinnati;* 1910, Charles E. Eckert, *Lima;* 1911, H. A. Mohler, *Middlepoint;* 1912, E. A. Klever, *Washington Court House;* 1913,

Edward E. Fisher, *Columbus;* 1914, C. E. Fisher, *McConnelsville;* 1915, C. A. Morrison, *Delaware;* 1916, W. I. Winegarner, *Columbus;* 1917, Fred M. Branch, *Lakewood;* 1918, Walter N. McCoy, *Middletown;* 1919, J. E. Sullivan, *Cincinnati;* 1920, Ferd Schoedinger, *Columbus;* 1921, R. R. Whitmer, *Dayton;* 1922, Joseph I. Acker, *Toledo;* 1923, Paul Huth, *Cincinnati;* 1924, Roscoe Sharer, *Alliance;* 1925, Yaro Nosek, *Cleveland;* 1926, C. E. Shriver, *Youngstown;* 1927, E. T. Snyder, *Mt. Sterling;* 1928, H. T. Maher, *Cleveland;* 1929, B. F. Linville, *Bremen;* 1930, Harry A. Mangold, *Zanesville;* 1931-32, Burch D. E. Arthur, *Wilmington;* 1933, Ira I. Garner, *Toledo;* 1934, George W. Eckert, *Lima;* 1935, Harry Shaw, *Columbus;* 1936, John H. Finefrock, *Mansfield;* 1937, R. W. Kirkpatrick, *Ripley;* 1938, Ralph S. Millard, *Cleveland;* 1939, Ben L. Jauman, *Delphos;* 1940, J. L. Richards, *Portsmouth;* 1941, John N. Orebaugh, *Norwalk;* 1942, John W. Toland, *Dover;* 1943, George Schoedinger, Jr., *Columbus;* 1944, Paul E. Billow, *Akron;* 1945, Leo F. Walter, *Dayton;* 1946, Garrett P. Trostel, *New Carlisle;* 1947, Walter M. Barnes, *Eaton;* 1948, Loren A. Vaughan, *Akron;* 1949, J. A. Shaidnagle, Jr., *Massillon;* 1950, Jerry G. Spears, Sr., *Columbus;* 1951, Wendell P. Grisier, *Stryker;* 1952, Austin Richards, *Springfield;* 1953, Robert L. Mock, *New Concord;* 1954, Charles Malone, *Metamora;* 1955, Ted Siferd, *Lima;* 1956, Walter Edwards, *Toledo;* 1957, Ward R. Halteman, *Lancaster;* 1958, Warren Pim, *Wooster;* 1959, Charles L. Zabor, *Parma;* 1960, Leonard D. Gerber, *Wakeman.*

OKLAHOMA

The funeral directors in Oklahoma and Indian Teritory made their first attempt at organization in 1899 at a gathering in Oklahoma City on December 27 and 28. Invitations had been previously issued by a group of men from Oklahoma City to all the funeral directors of the state. After J. G. Street explained the object of the proposed association to the men present, R. E. Wade of Perry was chosen temporary chairman of the meeting. During the course of the meeting the decision was made to admit to membership men from both Oklahoma and Indian Territories, and a committee was chosen to draft a constitution and by-laws. The following men were elected to office after the constitution and by-laws were adopted: *President,* J. G. Street, Oklahoma City; *Vice President,* Charles Binding, Hennessy; *Secretary Treasurer,* W. C. Pine; *Executive Committee:* R. E. Wade, Perry; W. Rhodes, Guthrie; J. M. Draper, Shawnee.

The Oklahoma association first reported to a meeting of the National Funeral Directors Association in 1903 at which time the delegate stated that "the association had been organized in June, 1903 with a membership of twenty-four." What had happened to the original association is not known. The re-organization was accomplished through the efforts of I. W. Gill of Kansas who had visited the territory and promised aid in organization work. At this time Oklahoma reported that there existed in the territory an embalmer's law, but that this particular law had not been working very satisfactorily. Officers chosen

to head the reformed group were: *President,* T. S. Robinson, Oklahoma City; *Vice Presidents:* L. E. Prall, Oklahoma City; W. K. Patterson, Guthrie; *Secretary,* J. M. Dolde, Stillwater; *Treasurer,* T. E. Smith, Shawnee; *Delegate to National Convention,* T. S. Robinson, Oklahoma City; and *Sergeant-at-arms,* S. Fowler, Perry.

By 1906 the original 24 members had grown to 166, and by 1907 to 197 members. The embalmer's law which had been changed in 1905 was working to the benefit of the association, although the examination was still not compulsory for the men in Indian Territory. The Board of Embalmers of Oklahoma was at this time composed of three members of the association, and it received the cooperation of the State Department of Health.

In the year 1924 Oklahoma funeral directors voted in favor of a plan then in force in Texas, namely, to require members of the profession to attend a course of lectures every three years. In 1926 Oklahoma again went on record as favoring higher standards and a more liberal education for members of the profession in their state. At this time the suggestion was made by Dr. Bradford Knapp, president of Oklahoma A. &. M. College, that a department of embalming be established as part of the curriculum at the college. After consultation by Dr. Bradford Knapp and the State Board of Embalmers the agreement was made that plans be drawn toward establishing a course either at Stillwater or Oklahoma City later in the year. Apparently, the program envisioned did not get beyond the planning stage for there is no record of such course ever materializing.

From the first, Oklahoma men were interested in furthering the education of their membership. One of the main features of each meeting was a speaker who demonstrated the latest embalming techniques. An attempt was also made at each meeting to employ a man to give an inspirational lecture to the membership on such subjects as ethics, professional behavior, service to the public, or bereavement. It is interesting to note that the interests of the profession in Oklahoma earlier in the century were not dissimilar to those of the profession-at-large today. More than thirty years ago, one of the main speakers chose as his subject, "As the Minister Sees Us."

ASSOCIATION PRESIDENTS: 1903, T. S. Robinson, *Oklahoma City;* 1904, W. E. Harper, *Oklahoma City;* 1905, C. M. Chayey, *South McAllister (In. Ter.);* 1906, W. H. Ryan, *Enid;* 1907, R. J. McCune, *Norman;* 1908, C. J. Crocker, *Stilwell;* 1909, D. H. Buffington, *Sapula;* 1910, J. L. Burke, *Hobart;* 1911, T. C. Bridgeman, *Ardmore;* 1912, F. T. Wentworth, *Carmen;* 1913, A. C. Strong, *Wilburton;* 1914, George McLellan, *Frederick;* 1915, Geo. B. Stanley, *Tulsa;* 1916, J. D. Humphrey, *McAlester;* 1917, W. H. Hamilton, *Portland;* 1918, J. I. Johnson, *Pawhuska;* 1919, Allen M. Street, *Oklahoma City;* 1920, J. G. Price, *Lone Wolf;* 1921, E. L. Hahn, *Oklahoma City;* 1922, John St. Clair, *Lawton;* 1923, W. E. Gaskill, *Shawnee;* 1924, George Hodge, *Cherokee;* 1925, E. E. Vincent, *Stillwater;* 1926, W. E. Gill, *Ponea City;* 1927, Wm. Fowitz, *Alva;* 1928, C. F. Pe-

tering, *Muskogee;* 1929, Beeson Grantham, *Duncan;* 1930-31, C. F. Harvey, *Ardmore;* 1932, Oren Landrith, *Sapulpa;* 1933, W. P. Brown, *Chickasha;* 1934, Harry Chaney, *McAlester;* 1935, Jack Jones, *Oklahoma City;* 1936, Eugene L. Greer, *Mangum;* 1937, Jack Powers, *Checotah;* 1938, James Stufflebean, *Pauls Valley;* 1939, Henry P. Meyer, *Norman;* 1940, Julius Cook, *Oklahoma City;* 1941, R. J. Evans, *Hartshorne;* 1942-43, Gerald Brown, *Enid;* 1944, Frank Tims, *Altus;* 1945-46, George W. Roesch, *Shawnee;* 1947, J. F. Owens, *Guthrie;* 1948, Robert L. Speece, *Fairview;* 1949, Wm. F. Bernhardt, *Stillwater;* 1950, Russell Chapman, *Tishomingo;* 1951, Ted Newton, *Perry;* 1952, Ben V. Hunter, *Oklahoma City;* 1953, Alfred Martin, *Elk City;* 1954, L. A. Smith, *Cherokee;* 1955, Jodie Sevier, *Chickasha;* 1956, Amos Dunn, *Sulphur;* 1957, Warren Fossett, *Enid;* 1958, Robert J. Stanley, *Tulsa;* 1959, Byron Mason, *Woodward;* 1960, Jack Keeley, *Bartlesville.*

OREGON
Informant: Edith I. A. Dailey

The first funeral directors' association in the northwestern area of the United States of which there is record was established on October 13, 1887 at a meeting of funeral directors in Portland, Oregon, at which time a Constitution and By-Laws were adopted by the Northwest Funeral Directors' Association. Its members were "Funeral Directors, Manufacturers, and Jobbers in Undertakers' supplies in Oregon, Washington Territory, Western Idaho, and Southwestern British Columbia."

Its roster contained names of

881

thirty-eight members from Oregon, fourteen from Washington Territory, and one each from Idaho and British Columbia—a total of fifty-four members. Among the first officers elected were: *President,* A. P. DeLin, Portland; *Secretary of the Board,* Edward Holman, Portland; and *Treasurer,* J. P. Finley, Portland.

Records quickly run out on the Northwest Funeral Directors Association. Although they reported to NFDA for several years, it is almost a certainty that by 1900 the association was no longer in existence.

The history of the present Oregon Funeral Directors Association actually begins in 1904 when a call was issued to the funeral directors of the state inviting them to be present at an organizational meeting.

Twenty-nine funeral directors of the state answered the call and met in Portland on September 19, 1904 and there formed the Oregon Funeral Directors' Association. W. P. Hohenschuh, a member of the committee on legislation of the National Funeral Directors Association, and the featured speaker, addressed the group on legislative matters and the importance of organizing as the first step in achieving proper professional legislation. The following officers were elected: *President,* J. P. Finley, Portland; *Vice Presidents:* W. M. Shank, Oregon City; and J. S. Buxton, Forest Grove; *Secretary,* William C. A. Pohl, Astoria; *Treasurer,* H. H. Butler, Medford; *Board of Directors:* Walter J. Holman, Portland; W. T. Macy, McMinville; James Henry, La Grande; V. C. Dunning, Portland; M. A. Miller, Portland.

At this meeting the association agreed to affiliate with the National Funeral Directors Association, and Arthur Finley of Portland was appointed as delegate to the national convention to invite the national body to hold its meeting in Oregon during the Lewis and Clark Exposition celebration.

A bill to establish the licensing of embalmers was submitted to every legislature from 1907 until 1921 when a law was finally enacted "creating a state embalmers' examining board, defining its duties, providing for expense of same, regulating and licensing the practice and art of embalming and disposing of dead human bodies in the state of Oregon in the interest of public health." A grandfather clause protected those who already held embalmers' licenses issued by the old Board of Health. The new law also established licenses, created a three-member board, set standards and requirements for licensees and established membership on the board.

In 1925 educational requirements of the applicant for license were increased from common school to four years of high school. Also late in the decade the new Funeral Directors' and Embalmers' law was passed. This new law set qualifications, educational standards and period of apprenticeship for licensing funeral directors, embalmers, and apprentices; increased board membership to five; and clarified powers of the board to grant, renew, suspend, or revoke licenses after hearings; and provided penalties and recourse.

From time to time increases have been secured in the amounts available for the burial of needy persons, and other enactments have been secured such as the increased workman's compensation burial allowance, and the "Anatomy Act." The association also favored passage of a bill which permitted "expense of last sickness" to share equally with the "funeral charge" as the first claim against estates. In this decade also a shipping agreement was put into effect and a bill creating a "hearse tax" was defeated.

All these legislative enactments were not accomplished without funds. In 1929 a legislative fund was created by assessing each member one dollar for each case handled. The first bill sponsored by the profession under the legislative fund regulated "the selling, offering for sale, or disposing of any share, certificate, right or interest, granting or purporting to grant any fight for funeral services and burial services, and providing a bond and a deposit, and providing a penalty for violation thereof."

The acceptance of the insurance plan now in effect in Oregon is a story in itself. After several outside companies had attempted through the years to gain a firm hold in the state by one means or other, a few companies attempted to secure individual endorsement of their funeral plans by approaching funeral directors separately and offering them exclusive handling of their plan in a particular area. These attempts were of special concern to the association, and in the 1930's legislation was secured prohibiting the selling of "funeral certificates" by some groups.

A decision was finally reached by the association to ban from membership anyone participating in an insurance plan. Two members were consequently dropped from the association. Seeing the threat to the group as a whole and to the general public of the state if such insurance plans were to gain foothold, the Oregon association conducted a survey to determine the feeling of the membership. Although the results of this survey showed that there was still some doubt about the action a member might take if his competitor were to accept one of the insurance plans offered him on an exclusive basis, the great majority of those answering the questionnaire were not in favor of endorsing such a plan at this time.

Finally, at a special meeting held August 23, 1958 in Portland, with a large representation from every district in the state, the Oregon Funeral Plan was presented. Members approved the plan unanimously and procedures were followed for incorporating and stock subscriptions signed.

The Oregon Funeral Plan has created a common interest among the members. The Agency is separate and apart from the association. Members serve on the board of directors and can control the type of salesmen who represent the funeral directors as well as their selling and advertising policies. Thus, the men selling the Oregon Funeral Plan are creating good public relations for all funeral directors. The motto of the association in this regard is "Let insurance men sell insurance." In this way the membership is not being subjected to competitive pressures, but can continue to compete in the funeral profession on a friendly basis while as a group they present a united front on problems that confront them from time to time. The interests of the public are also protected in that the insured has free

883

choice in selecting a funeral director.

Through the years the dues on a case load basis have been increased two times, in 1951 to one dollar per case and seven years later, to $1.50, the present rate.

Other legal matters have come up for discussion and support by the association. In 1944 at the annual convention delegates voted in support of an amendment to the Oregon funeral director and embalmers' law permitting the state board to approve embalming schools other than those rated by the conference of embalmers examining boards. This legislation eventually was passed. In 1951 a law was passed amending the existing statute and as a result licensing fees were increased. The appointment of an additional member was also added. In 1953 the legislature passed a law making it legally necessary for monies received for prearranged funerals to be placed in trust until such time as the monies were released to pay for a funeral service. This protected not only the funeral directors but the people of the state.

The office of coroner has long been a matter of legislation. On several occasions bills to abolish it have been defeated. However, on the last day of the 1959 session of the legislature Senate Bills 258 and 259, with no provision for appropriation of enabling funds, were passed. They created a Medical Investigator System, under the State Board of Health with county or district health officers the medical investigator for that county or district. This medical investigator replaces the former county coroner but has more authority. These provisions do not apply to Multnomah County, the populous county, but only to counties of under 400,000 population. The initial request to the Emergency Board for funds for $56,000 was not granted. The exact amount for the establishment of the provisions of the new law is not known. It is pertinent, however, to state that under the County Coroner system the survey of 1955 operation by funeral directors exclusive of the most populous county, was approximately $25,000. That amount is said to be the required annual salary of the chief medical investigator. The new provisions become effective January 1, 1961, or on the date of expiration of the term of office of any county coroner whose term of office expires beyond that date.

Throughout the years Oregon has successfully engaged in a number of "professional projects." Among these are the hiring of an executive secretary for the organization. Oregon has had four executive secretaries to date. The first, George Ryan, saw the organization through some of the early battles in the legislature; the second, J. King Bryon, who was also secretary to the Retail Furniture Association and Gas Appliance Society saw service during the hectic days of World War II; Beatrice Lauritsen served as temporary executive secretary after the untimely death of J. King Bryon; and Edith I. A. Dailey succeeded Miss Lauritsen as secretary and has held the position since September of 1950. Developments within the profession and association growth have emphasized the importance of the headquarters office and a full time executive secretary

884

both in the field and in the office.

In 1925 the name was changed from the original "Oregon Funeral Directors and Embalmers Association" to Oregon Funeral Directors Association. In 1930 a new constitution and by-laws were adopted by the group and articles of incorporation were signed for the organization by the officers of the group for that year: E. B. Hughes, Glen S. Macy, and G. W. Henkle. During this period the NFDA Code of Ethics was also adopted by the Oregon association.

Also through the years other problems which now seem of a more minor nature were acted upon by the association: an appointment of a committee to secure cooperation between the medical profession and funeral directors concerning autopsy problems; the effecting of a shipping agreement; the acceptance of a request from florists to discourage the use of "please omit" in the obituary notices; the defeat of a bill creating a "Hearse Tax"; the discussion of needed improvements in the embalmers' law. This period, too, saw the beginning of a long and pleasant relationship with the Social Security Office in Portland.

A practice which has resulted in a continued service to members of the profession is the establishment in 1940 of a clearing house for employment in the association offices where records of available employees both licensed and unlicensed are kept.

The Oregon association has been organized into six districts which hold meetings during the year to discuss local and state problems. Membership bulletins mailed from the central office further create an informed membership.

Oregon has on several occasions been honored on a national basis in having her members elected or selected for high office in the national body. In 1941 Kenneth Holman was elected governor of the sixth district (which during his term of office was changed to the seventh district of NFDA) and in 1951, Lot Snodgrass was elected governor of the same district.

The Oregon association has engaged in a number of enterprises for the better education of the public at large regarding funeral directors. The educational committee has sent copies of the NFDA booklet "Funeral Service as a Profession" and the Better Business Bureau Bulletin, "Facts Every Family Should Know About Funerals" to the vocational guidance counsellors in all of the Oregon highschools. Again, when the *History of American Funeral Directing* was first published, copies of it were bought for resale to Oregon members, and in 1958 the association bought sufficient copies to present to libraries, bible schools, members of the clergy, and colleges throughout the state.

The Oregon association has in the past faced problems and solved them to the benefit of the membership. Oregon looks forward with the knowledge that whatever comes the association which began as the Northwest Funeral Directors Association will survive.

ASSOCIATION PRESIDENTS: 1904, J. P. Finley, *Portland;* 1905, W. T. Macy, *McMinnville;* 1906, S. N. Wilkins, *Corvallis;* 1907, M. A. Rader, *Pendleton;* 1908, E. E. Erickson, *Portland;* 1909, W. T. Gordon, *Eugene;* 1910, R. L. Holman, *Oregon City;* 1911, W. T. Rigdon, *Salem;* 1912, W. F. Walker, *Spring-*

field; 1913, Ray Richardson, *Salem;* 1914, L. B. Hall, *Grants Pass;* 1915-16, F. E. Roth, *Amity;* 1917, W. H. Hamilton, *Portland;* 1919, W. W. Branstetter, *Eugene;* 1920, A. J. Rose, *Portland;* 1921, W. A. Weddle, *Stayton;* 1922-23, Glen Macy, *McMinnville;* 1924, Lloyd T. Rigdon, *Salem;* 1925, E. G. Swink, *Portland;* 1926, Earl Whittock, *Klamath Falls;* 1927, C. B. Webb, *Salem;* 1928, Leo Goetsch, *Portland;* 1929, E. B. Hughes, *Astoria;* 1930, C. E. Wilson, *Portland;* 1931, E. R. Ekman, *Silverton;* 1932, C. P. Niswonger, *Bend;* 1933, H. W. Conger, *Medford;* 1934, Arthur Pearson, *Portland;* 1935, Clarence V. Simon, *Eugene;* 1936, Philip Zeller, *Portland;* 1937, Karl K. Mills, *Cottage Grove;* 1938, Kenneth W. Holman, *Portland;* 1939, E. F. Fortmiller, *Albany;* 1940, H. K. Lounsbury, *Portland;* 1941, J. B. Hollingsworth, *Corvallis;* 1942, R. Morris Holman, *Oregon City;* 1943, Charles N. Rogers, *St. Helena;* 1944, Thomas H. Grice, *Portland;* 1945, Arthur C. Lundberg, *Tillamook;* 1946, William L. Finley, Jr., *Portland;* 1947, G. W. Winslow, *Bend;* 1948, Charles A. Lundberg, *Portland;* 1949, Charles W. Claggett, *Salem;* 1950, Horace C. McGinnis, *Portland;* 1951, Walter Kropp, *Albany;* 1952, Lot L. Snodgrass, *La Grande;* 1953, A. Craig Finley, *Portland;* 1954, Willard W. Ward, *Klamath Falls;* 1955, Edward C. White, *Portland;* 1956, Fred S. Buell, *Springfield;* 1957, Charles J. Burns, *Pendleton;* 1958, J. Paul Bollman, *Dallas;* 1959, Howard B. Holman, *Portland;* 1960, Glen Macy, *McMinnville.*

PENNSYLVANIA

Informant: Lewis W. Price

When Acting Secretary George E. Distelhurst of Lewistown sent the following call for a meeting of Pennsylvania funeral directors, he started what was destined to become the largest organization of its kind in the United States:

"Having received many letters from professionals throughout the state sanctioning the movement set forth in the circular of June 27, 1882; namely, of forming a state organization of funeral directors, the undersigned funeral directors of Pennsylvania make the following call:

"That you are hereby cordially requested to meet in Shakespeare Hall, Harrisburg, on the third Wednesday of September, 1882, at 10:00 A.M. for the above-mentioned purpose. Funeral directors will please report at Bolton's Hotel, where reduced rates have been secured."

The circular of June 27, 1882, mentioned by Mr. Distelhurst in his communication had been sent to many funeral directors in the state five days after several of them had attended the meeting in New York City at which time the National Funeral Directors Association was founded.

Agreeable to the call, some fifty Pennsylvania funeral directors assembled in Harrisburg and formed the Funeral Directors Association of the State of Pennsylvania.

The following officers were elected at this first meeting: *President,* E. S. Earley, Philadelphia; *Vice Presidents:* A. P. Burton, Erie; E. J. Phillips, Wilkes-Barre; W. P. Roberts, Sunbury; J. Lewis Good, Philadelphia; Aaron Ball, Quakertown; *Secretary,* George E. Distelhurst, Lewistown; *Treasurer,* J. B. Boyd, Harrisburg.

Following election of officers the By-Laws Committee made its report and By-Laws were adopted, an interesting sidelight being an extended debate regarding the use of "funeral director" instead of "undertaker." It will be noted that while the organizers referred to themselves as "undertakers" they called their newly formed organization a "funeral directors" association.

As a consequence of the adoption of a resolution to establish county associations, a number of such associations were founded throughout the state, with membership in the state and national associations being first dependent upon membership in one of these locals, there being, in other words, no direct state membership or membership-at-large.

According to available records, the first local association organized in Pennsylvania was in Philadelphia, its organizational meeting being held about two weeks prior to the meeting at which the state association was formed. The Funeral Directors Association of Philadelphia was actually a merger of three existing organizations, one of them, possibly the first in the country, Undertakers Mutual Protective Association, having been formed in 1864. This group, along with the Philadelphia Undertakers Association and the Undertakers Protective Association became one on September 7, 1882.

While it has been impractical, for various reasons, to have an association in each of Pennsylvania's 67 counties, there are presently 32 local groups, composed of one or more counties, which cover the entire state. Two of them, the Allegheny and Philadelphia County Associations, have memberships larger than a number of state associations, and the Allegheny County association has a headquarters office under the direction of a full time executive secretary.

For the first several years following its organization the members of the Pennsylvania association were interested in three major items: expansion of membership, development of the art and science of embalming, and recognition by the legislature as a professional group entitled to licensure.

The sights were set on this last goal at the eleventh annual convention held in 1892. A month following this convention President Attwood reported the reorganization and expansion of the Committee on Legislation.

The Committee on Legislation did its work well. On June 7, 1895 an Act of Assembly created a State Board of Undertakers and provided for the registration and licensure of "any person, persons or corporation engaged in the business of undertaking, care, preparation, disposition and burial of the dead." This first act, however, covered only cities of the first, second and third classes, there being opposition to a licensing act among the rural sections of the state.

The act was later amended to cover the entire state, to provide for an annual registration fee and the registration of funeral directors' assistants; and in 1927 the first step toward higher educational requirements was taken when the act was amended to provide that after 1931 all applicants for licensure must have a high school education or its equivalent.

Later amendments followed in

1929, and then in 1931 an entirely new licensing act was passed and approved by the governor, it being amended in 1935, incidentally, to provide that corporations could no longer be licensed as funeral directors in Pennsylvania. The 1931 act had already prohibited the issuance of branch licenses, and it had also continued Pennsylvania as a single-license state—only an "undertaker's" license being issued.

As time went on there became an increasing awareness on the part of the members that entrants into the field of funeral service must be better trained and educated. As a result, the association in conjunction with the State Board of Undertakers and the Pennsylvania schools of mortuary science succeeded during the 1951 session of the General Assembly in having a new licensing law adopted which maintained the single (combined) license (now called a funeral director's license), prohibited the issuance of branch and corporation licenses, and provided that applicants for licensure must have completed two years of general college and at least one year of mortuary science. The act also provided that educational work could be integrated and, under the law and at the discretion of the State Board of Funeral Directors, a four-year integrated college course be developed. It is significant that, following the adoption of the act, Temple University in Philadelphia instituted a three-year course leading to a degree in mortuary science.

While the association has been interested through the years in keeping the state's licensing law abreast of changing conditions, it has likewise amended its own By-Laws on several occasions to keep its organ-izational structure up-to-date, and in 1908 it became a non-profit corporation.

At the annual meeting in 1941, revised By-Laws were presented and adopted unanimously. It is under these By-Laws that the Pennsylvania association has made considerable progress in membership standing, services, and achievements. A distinctive feature of the By-Laws is that the association cannot accept any money or gratuities from manufacturers or suppliers in the funeral service field. There is no sale of advertising, nor requests for donations; the association stands on its own financial feet.

In its own headquarters building two blocks from the state capitol in Harrisburg, the association is served by a full time executive secretary, two staff members, and a general counsel. A complete program of services and activities is provided, constant representation is afforded before the various state agencies and the legislature. The present membership is over 1700.

Throughout the years Pennsylvania has been fortunate in the calibre of men who have been its leaders. Prior to the establishment of the headquarters office in Harrisburg in 1942, the elected association secretary carried on the affairs of the organization from his own establishment. It is interesting to note that during this period—a total of 60 years—only five men served in this capacity. They were George E. Distelhurst, Lewiston, 1882-1884; George C. Paul, Philadelphia, 1884 to 1911 when he was elected president; Albert E. Miller, Kingston, 1911-1913; W. Scott Newcomer, Pittsburgh, 1913-1932 and Benjamin L. Herr, Lampeter, 1932-1942.

888

Since 1942 a secretary-treasurer is elected from the Board of Governors each year, and he cannot succeed himself.

In reviewing the history of the National Funeral Directors Association it becomes apparent that Pennsylvania has had a great deal to do with the growth and success of this national organization. Not only is Pennsylvania the largest constituent member of the national body, but its members have taken active part in the organization's leadership since its founding. The third and fourth presidents of NFDA were from Pennsylvania—Hudson Samson of Pittsburgh who served two terms, and Robert R. Bringhurst of Philadelphia who served four terms. Other Pennsylvanians who are past presidents of NFDA are: Josiah H. Pearce, Ardmore, elected in 1899; George C. Paul, Philadelphia, elected in 1912; Charles C. Reel, Pittsburgh, elected in 1917; Joseph L. Galen, Philadelphia, elected in 1934 and 1935; Ronald C. Jones, Scranton, elected in 1948; William E. Lutz, Warren, elected in 1956.

Throughout the years members of the Pennsylvania association have been active in community affairs, many of them serving as mayors and burgesses, while others have been active in state political circles. Two members served with distinction in the State Senate— Herman P. Brandt of Perrysville and Alonzo S. Batchelor of Monaca—and many others have served in the House of Representatives. It is of interest that one of these, Clifford S. Patterson of Monongahela, was the sponsor of the bill that created the Pennsylvania Turnpike, the first of the express toll roads; and another member, John R. Bebout, served as a member of the first Turnpike Commission.

In looking ahead, it seems clear that the Pennsylvania association will continue to serve the needs of the profession, by disseminating the most correct principles of business management, by promoting proper professional practices, and by serving the public in its own interests.

ASSOCIATION PRESIDENTS: 1882, Edward S. Earley, *Philadelphia;* 1883, Hudson Samson, *Pittsburgh;* 1884, A. P. Burton, *Erie;* 1885-86, Robt. R. Bringhurst, *Philadelphia;* 1887-88, Wm. H. Maxwell, *Pottstown;* 1889-90, Josiah S. Pearce, *Ardmore;* 1891-92, W. James Atwood, *Philadelphia;* 1893-94, B. F. Kirk, *Germantown;* 1895-96, James Lowrie, *Pittsburgh;* 1897, B. T. Lyle, *Philadelphia;* 1898-99, J. H. Ostertag, *Columbia;* 1900-01, Charles W. Naulty, *Philadelphia;* 1902, D. B. Widmyer, *Lancaster;* 1903, James M. Fullerton, *Pittsburgh;* 1904, F. C. Beinhauer, *Pittsburgh;* 1905, R. R. Bringhurst, *Philadelphia;* 1906, M. F. Leslie, *Pittsburgh;* 1907, Charles H. Cutler, *Pittston;* 1908, John A. Kress, *Pittsburgh;* 1909, H. F. Mooney, *Wilkes-Barre;* 1910, Fred F. Groff, *Lancaster;* 1911, Geo. Chandler Paul, *Philadelphia;* 1912, Harry A. Wray, *Pittsburgh;* 1913, John M. Armstrong, *Leechburg;* 1914, E. S. Lowrie, *Pittsburgh;* 1915, Allen E. Keim, *Downingtown;* 1916, Harry McCunney, *Philadelphia;* 1917, Merle W. Coulter, *Homestead;* 1918, W. L. Dowler, *Braddock;* 1919, J. Fred Fisher, *Lancaster;* 1920, E. D. Steelman, *Philadelphia;* 1921, J. K. Kimes, *Spring City;* 1922-23, Ramsay Burton, *Erie;* 1924, Her-

889

bert W. Lowrie, *Pittsburgh;* 1925, Harry G. Davis, *Plymouth;* 1926, J. C. Henninger, *New Holland;* 1927, James T. Anderson, *Beaver;* 1928, Joseph L. Galen, *Philadelphia;* 1929, Wendell Richards, *Wilkes-Barre;* 1930, George W. Karmany, *Hummelstown;* 1931, J. Howard Lanterman, *E. Stroudsburg;* 1932, John R. Dougherty, *Reading;* 1933-34, Frank A. Hornstein, *Aliquippa;* 1935, M. A. Hoff, *New Cumberland;* 1936, J. Elmer Lutz, *Reading;* 1937, Paul D. Miller, *Conshohocken;* 1938, George A. Baker, *Pittsburgh;* 1939-40, T. J. Kenny, *Archbald;* 1941, Miles B. Zimmerman, *Lingleston;* 1942, Vincent D. Curron died in office in 1942 and was replaced by Louis Beinhauer, Jr., *Pittsburgh;* 1943, Ronald C. Jones, *Scranton;* 1944, Earle K. Angstadt, *Reading;* 1945, Donald C. Burton, *Erie;* 1946, Charles D. R. Kinot, *Shillington;* 1947, Wm. Rowen Grant, *Philadelphia;* 1948, Richard S. Brandt, *Perrysville;* 1949, Willard L. Gruver, *Coopersburg;* 1950, John R. Donohue, *Philadelphia;* 1951, William Varcoe, *Wycombe;* 1952, William E. Lutz, *Warren;* 1953, I. Parker Miller, *Reading;* 1954, James W. Staman, *Columbia;* 1955, Ralph E. Piatt, *Washington;* 1956, Stanley Stephens, *Allentown;* 1957, J. Lester Laughlin, *Altoona;* 1958, Howard N. Deeter, *Philadelphia;* 1959, George Binner, *Auburn;* 1960, John D. O'Connor, *Pittsburgh.*

RHODE ISLAND
Informants: A. Raymond Pearson and Frank Trainor

On October 21, 1885 a group of funeral directors of Providence met in an attempt to form a state association. After writing a short constitution and necessary by-laws, they chose the name The Undertakers' Association of the State of Rhode Island. The following men, all from Providence, were elected officers of the new organization: *President,* H. B. Knowles; *Vice President,* Thomas McMurrough; *Secretary,* J. P. Luther; and *Treasurer,* T. F. Monahan. In all, twelve men signed the constitution and became charter members. It was not until 1903, however, that the organization counted among its members men from the outlying districts of the state, and in that year some trade journals recognized the association as a permanent state association when it met in Providence with a membership of seventy-five.

In the same year 13 new members were added and steps were taken to introduce into the legislature and to secure passage of a bill to license embalmers. But it was only in 1908 that the General assembly of Rhode Island passed an act requiring the licensing of embalmers. The first Board of Registration in Embalming appointed by the governor under the new bill was comprised of three funeral directors, all members of the association: Robert C. Cottrell, Newport; Charles E. Barber, Providence; John J. McKenna, Woonsocket.

This original association being rather limited in its aims was unable to continue as a group for very long and shortly before World War I began gradually to cease its activities. In the early 1920's another small group of Providence funeral directors met to talk about reorganization and called upon other funeral directors to join in starting some kind of organization to improve social and neighborly relations as well as to promote better ethical and professional standards. After several such small meetings, arrangements for a large organizational meeting were made. The Brennan House was selected for the place of meeting. Through the efforts of Thomas F. Monahan, Sr. and Charles Dillon of Hartford, Connecticut, a past president of the National Funeral Directors Association, the funeral directors of the state were encouraged to begin once more an association in Providence with the hope of later expanding to include the rest of the funeral directors in the state.

Again new officers were chosen: *President,* Frank P. Trainor; *Vice President,* Charles H. Page; *Recorder,* Joseph Harlow; *Financial Secretary,* Valentine H. Marian; and *Treasurer,* Thomas A. Toye. Also present at this meeting were many of the pioneers of the earlier association who gave helpful advice and encouragement to the new membership.

This new group held monthly meetings and soon made application to the National Funeral Directors Association for membership in that body.

The old Embalmers' law was extensively modified through a series of amendments in 1932. Included was the requirement that all funeral directors be licensed embalmers. There was a grandfather clause which permitted funeral directors who were in business prior to that time and who were not embalmers to continue in business. Many of the major provisions of the present law were adopted in the 1932 amendment. In 1933 the law was further amended to make the operators of

cemeteries ineligible as funeral directors.

An important Rhode Island Supreme Court decision was handed down in 1936. This decision upheld the constitutionality of certain sections of the embalming and funeral directing law and declared other provisions to be unconstitutional. The decision also upheld the constitutionality of the section providing for revocation and suspension of licenses as well as the section on prohibiting the making of payments to secure business. The court declared as unconstitutional the provisions that were effective at that time prohibiting participation in burial plans.

In 1935 a reorganization of the state government placed all examining boards for occupational licensing under the jurisdiction of an administrative subdivision of the State Department of Health which is now titled Division of Professional Regulation. At that time the Board of Registration in Embalming became the Board of Examiners in Embalming.

After four or five years of the new association's existence, a lull in interest followed and the association met only occasionally until Thomas F. Monahan, Jr. became president. Under Mr. Monahan a new effort was made to include the funeral directors of the entire state, and the association has made great progress since that time.

In 1939 and again in 1942 the organization helped defeat a bill authorizing burial insurance in the state of Rhode Island. This was not done without incurring considerable expense, and the treasurer's office of the association requested at this time a contribution of $10.00 from each member to help meet these additional organizational expenses.

In December of 1946 the association adopted a new constitution and by-laws which admitted to membership individuals rather than firms. This was a big step for the organization to take at this time. Since then membership has increased, dues revenues are larger, and the group is on a firmer financial footing.

Rhode Island is proud of all its members, but especially proud of those who have been honored by their fellow funeral directors from other states. Most recently A. Raymond Pearson has been chosen second vice-president of the National Funeral Directors Association.

ASSOCIATION PRESIDENTS: 1885-87, H. B. Knowles, *Providence;* 1904-05, Charles E. Barber, *Providence;* 1906, Charles G. Hill, *East Greenwich;* 1907, Robert F. Carroll, *Providence;* 1908, H. B. Knowles, *Providence;* 1909, Irving H. Drabble, *Providence;* 1910, Frank M. Whipple, *Pascoag;* 1911, John H. Walsh, *Providence;* 1912, John E. Keefe, *Providence;* 1913, Robert F. Jones, *Providence;* 1914, John F. Harlow, *Providence;* 1915, L. W. Patterson, *Phenix;* 1916, Vincent J. McAloon, *Pawtucket;* 1917-18, John J. Cauntanche, *Providence;* 1919-20, Charles H. Page, *Providence;* 1921, Eugene F. Carroll, *Providence;* 1922-23, Ernon Holdredge, *Providence;* 1925-26, Frank P. Trainor, *Providence;* 1931-36, Thomas F. Monahan, Jr., *Providence;* 1937-38, James M. Heffern, *Pawtucket;* 1939, Ira M. McKenzie, *Providence;* 1940-41, George A. Brouilette, *Central Falls;* 1942-44, John J. Moynihan, *Providence;*

1945-46, A. Raymond Pearson, *Providence;* 1947-49, Frank P. Trainor, *Providence;* 1950, Newell C. Shipper, *Providence;* 1951, John E. Rebello, *East Providence;* 1952-54, John M. Skeffington, *Providence;* 1955, Valentine Mariani, *Providence;* 1956-57, Cleveland M. Judson, *Pawtucket;* 1958-60, Francis King, *Providence.*

SOUTH CAROLINA
Informant: J. Anderson Bass

The South Carolina Funeral Directors' Association was organized September 15th and 16th, 1899 at Charleston, South Carolina with thirty-seven members electing the following men to serve for the year: *President,* J. M. Connelley, Charleston; *Vice Presidents;* James F. Mackey, Greenville; W. W. Moore; *Secretary,* G. W. Bolger, Charleston; and *Treasurer,* Wade Hampton Dukes, Orangeburg.

At the time of the organization there were 105 men engaged in the funeral business or the selling of caskets.

It was in the same year, 1899, that the State Board of Health prepared a bill to be introduced in the next state legislature requiring everyone in the funeral business pass an examination before he could prepare or ship dead bodies.

On February 19, 1900, the state legislature passed a bill requiring an examination before shipment of bodies. An embalming board of examiners was established within the State Board of Health, and the first embalmer's examination was held in Columbia in July 1900. Fifteen men took and passed the examination, receiving certificates entitling them to embalm.

James F. Mackey and W. W.

892

Moore, delegates to the national association meeting held in Charleston, South Carolina on October 9th, 10th, and 11th, 1901, reported 40 paid members and progress being made in the educating of the funeral directors.

The years from 1901 through 1911 are marked with constructive progress. The educational program was expanded and the association increased in number and began to take its place in the professional life of South Carolina.

The legislative committee was also exceedingly active between 1901 and 1911. A movement was begun to exempt licensed embalmers from jury duty and to have two members of the association, selected by the association and appointed by the governor, to serve with the State Board of Health in examining embalming applicants.

In 1907 embalmers were exempt from jury duty and the legislative committee began composing a bill to have the laws regulating the Embalming Board changed so that the State Board of Health might be relieved of this duty, and merge the same into a Board of Embalmers, to examine all applications for the embalmer's license.

South Carolina Funeral Directors Association was recognized nationally when, in 1903, J. M. Connelley of Charleston, South Carolina was elevated to the presidency of the National Funeral Directors Association.

The period from 1911 through 1921 marked another era of progress. The legislative committee was busy . . . the first embalming board, composed of expert embalmers selected by the state association and appointed by the governor, was organized in 1912. A new law, carrying a severe penalty, prohibited a non-licensed embalmer from embalming or pretending to embalm a body and took effect on January 1, 1913. Also, in 1921, the law was changed requiring a diploma from an embalming school, recognized by the State Board, from an applicant for the examination.

By 1921 there were 123 men in the funeral profession or engaged in the selling of caskets, 87 of which had joined the association.

In the early twenties, the state was divided into four groups, The Coastal, The Central, The "Pee Dee," and The Piedmont.

On October 14, 1938 a State Charter was issued to the South Carolina Funeral Directors and Embalmers Association. The trustees securing this charter were J. B. Hatcher of Gaffney, Arthur H. Mackey of Greenville, and Thomas F. McAfee of Greenville.

In 1945 the services of W. B. Love, Jr. were secured as executive secretary.

On January 14, 1958, the name of the Association was changed to the South Carolina Funeral Directors Association, Inc.

In 1958, the first Funeral Service Board was organized, composed of seven members including J. T. Pennington of Bennettsville, President; Harry Hooker of Charleston; Edward George of Aiken; Douglas MacDougald of Anderson; Fletcher L. Kirkland of Greenville; J. Anderson Bass of Rock Hill; and Jim Rogers of McCall.

A Ladies Auxiliary was organized at Myrtle Beach, South Carolina May 25, 1950. The first officers were Mrs. Robert Mayer of Georgetown, President; Mrs. Rube Hatcher of Charlotte, Vice-President; and Mrs. Leon Pennington of Hartsville, Secretary-Treasurer.

Four men have served in national offices: J. M. Connelley, president of the National Funeral Directors Association in 1907; A. C. Connelley, president of the National Selected Morticians in 1940. Douglas McDougald of Anderson served as secretary to the National Conference of Funeral Service Examining Boards, and also District Governor, District Four of the National Funeral Directors Association. He was elected secretary of the National Funeral Directors Association in 1957-1958. Fletcher L. Kirkland of Greenville was elected in 1958 to the National Conference of Funeral Service Examining Boards to serve two years.

ASSOCIATION PRESIDENTS: 1899, J. M. Connelley, *Charleston;* 1900, James F. Mackey, *Greenville;* 1901, W. W. Moore, *Barnwell;* 1902, W. M. Waters, *Florence;* 1903, John F. Floyd, *Spartanburg;* 1904, George M. Tolly, *Anderson;* 1905, William C. Chandler, *Sumter;* 1906, J. W. McCormick, *Columbia;* 1907, W. Hampton Dukes, *Orangeburg;* 1908, J. M. VanMetre, *Columbia;* 1909, T. J. McCarty, *Charleston;* 1910, W. V. Blyth, *Greenwood;* 1911, R. Y. Leavell, *Newbury;* 1912, W. C. Wise, *Sumter;* 1913, Frank Hodges, *Spartanburg;* 1914, C. E. Kennedy, *Laurens;* 1915, J. D. Wood, *Greer;* 1916, C. L. Pace, *Marion;* 1917, C. E. Taylor, *Lexington;* 1918, A. J. White, *Manning;* 1919-20, A. C. Connelley, *Charleston;* 1921, E. H. Peeples, *Hampton;* 1922, A. C. Connelley, *Charleston;* 1923-24, Arthur H. Mackey, *Greenville;* 1925, J. S. Dunbar, *Columbia;* 1926, James A. McAlister, *Charles-*

ton; 1927, W. M. Goldfinch, *Conway;* 1928, Thos. F. McAfee, *Greenville;* 1929, J. B. Hatcher, *Gaffney;* 1930, J. A. Bass, *Rock Hill;* 1931, J. S. Andrews, *Greenwood;* 1932, W. T. Cox, *Belton;* 1933, A. D. Cannon, *Fountain Inn;* 1934, Charles E. Mackey, *Greenville;* 1935, C. L. Boyter, *Woodruff;* 1936, J. Gordon Floyd, *Spartanburg;* 1937, W. L. Oulla, *Florence;* 1938, J. G. Duckett, *Central;* 1939, William W. King, *Anderson;* 1940, D. Fred Parker, *Walterboro;* 1941, Heyward D. Brown, *Hartsville;* 1942, John McAlister, *Charleston;* 1943, Geo. E. Hurst, *Sumter;* 1944, F. Van Clayton, *Pickens;* 1945, Robt. Mayer, *Georgetown;* 1946, John Kendrick, *Greer;* 1947, Albert Stuhr, *Charleston;* 1948, Harold Sale, *Lexington;* 1949, Neal Folk, *Williston;* 1950, Joe Waters, *Florence;* 1951, Luther Pruitt, *Honea Path;* 1952, Leon Pennington, *Hartsville;* 1953, Dick Wood, *Greer;* 1954, Heyward Goldfinch, *Conway;* 1955, Chas. M. Cox, *Belton;* 1956, Harry Stuhr, *Charleston;* 1957, L. R. Redfearn, *Cheraw;* 1958, Douglas McDougald, *Anderson;* 1959, J. L. Petty, *Landrum;* 1960, J. T. Pennington, *Bennettsville.*

SOUTH DAKOTA
Informant: Leslie E. Mathiesen

Although the South Dakota funeral directors had been active members of a tri-state group comprising the areas of Minnesota, North Dakota, and South Dakota, they did not form an association of their own until 1898. In that year H. Billion of Sioux Falls sent invitations to all practicing funeral directors in the state inviting them to attend a meeting to be held September 28 of that year.

After appointing a committee on constitution and by-laws, discussing the necessity for a state association, and determining the purpose of this group to be the furtherance of education and the enactment of legislation for funeral directors, the men from South Dakota signed the roll as charter members. Later the proposed constitution was adopted and election of officers was held. The first officers of the state association of South Dakota were as follows: *President*, H. Billion, Sioux Falls; *Vice President*, Frank Kirby, Parker; *Secretary*, W. E . Jones, Hudson; and *Treasurer*, J. N. Wass, Beresford.

Mr. Elab Myers of the Champion College of Embalming delivered a series of lectures to this first group.

The editor of the *Embalmers' Monthly* also addressed the assembly and made a few remarks about the work of organizations in other states. Representatives of other associations who were present gave advice on organization.

The association in South Dakota started out at some advantage in that even before the funeral directors met for the first time a law had already been presented in 1895 to the state legislature for its approval. Although the law failed of passage, some of the original hard work and planning had already been done by the time the association was formed. The new association lost no time in furthering the work already begun. Before the year 1900, South Dakota had an embalmers' law on the statute books.

At every early meeting a lecturer was hired to demonstrate to the assembled membership. From year to year the number of men joining the association steadily increased. By 1902, the sixteen-member infant association had grown to 47; by 1903 to 117—even though there were only 180 funeral directors in the state at this time. Except for a set-back in membership in 1904, this growth continued through the first quarter century of the group's existence.

From time to time changes were made in the old embalmers' law and additional bills regulating the practice of funeral directing introduced and passed by the legislature. One new law of interest to the profession at this time outlined the procedures for disposal of unclaimed bodies. A court decision having great interest to the profession involved the acceptance in a murder trial (S. Dakota vs. Lora E. Cook) of a funeral director as an expert witness on the same basis as a physician.

South Dakota is proud of and grateful to many of its members who served long and faithfully for the betterment of the association. Outstanding among these is John Hermanson of Dell Rapids who held the office of secretary-treasurer for 35 years and who is presently first vice president and assistant to the secretary. The state association has also been honored in having A. L. Coleman of Redfield elected as Governor for District Five of the National Funeral Directors Association. Five families have supplied the South Dakota organization with eleven presidents—a father and a son from each family. These men are Ray and Ellis D. Gates, H. E. and O. H. Frost, Adolph and Floyd Schenk, and C. O. and Allen Lee and D. J. Noble and sons Darwin and Harvard. South Dakota also boasts having had a woman as its president in 1934, Mrs. Cora Campbell, a funeral director and embalmer in her own right. There are eight members of the South Dakota Funeral Directors' Association who have held licenses in the state for fifty years or more: Fred Boller, Faulkton; Mrs. Myrta Hallenbeck, Madison; Albert F. Hofmeister, Chancellor; J. L. Huebl, Aberdeen; L. J. Lewis, Lake Preston; Samuel A. Spratt, Mellette; Albert Williamson, Redfield; Conrad Lee, Volga.

The members of the South Dakota Funeral Directors Association are proud of its growth and the members who have made it large. They also point proudly to the accomplishments in line with its original purpose, the educational advantages attained for its membership and the legislation obtained not only for its members but for the protection of the people of the state.

ASSOCIATION PRESIDENTS: 1898, Henry Billion, *Sioux Falls;* 1899, Frank Kirby, *Parker;* 1900, S. R. Smith, *Lead;* 1901-02, M. F. Cummings, *Wilmot;* 1903, Edmund Wilson, *Parker;* 1904, George A. West, *Brookings;* 1905, S. L. Brown, *Centerville;* 1906, W. F. Lumbard, *Chamberlain;* 1907, A. A. Snashall, *Sioux Falls;* 1908, W. J. Byrnes, *Canton;* 1909, C. T. Liddle, *Iroquois;* 1910, D. J. Noble, *Mitchell;* 1911, August Tamms, *Huron;* 1912, J. J. Mead, *Lead;* 1913-14, W. H. Wilson, *Aberdeen;* 1915, J. E. Hamaker, *Spencer;* 1916, H. E. Frost, *Belle Fourche;* 1917, L. J. Lewis, *Lake Preston;* 1918, L. D. Miller, *Sioux Falls;* 1919-20, Ray A. Gates, *Bradley;* 1921, Archie Odell, *Montrose;* 1922, C. H. Lindekugel, *Spencer;* 1923, E. A. Tilgner, *Humboldt;*

1924, I. M. Dotson, *Pierre;* 1925, Conrad O. Lee, *Volga;* 1926, A. C. Hallenbeck, *Madison;* 1927, W. H. Davis, *Flandreau;* 1928, Melvin Eggers, *Tyndal;* 1929-30, Robt. de Malignon, *Bowdle;* 1931, Frank Mohs, *Webster;* 1932, Norman Hanson, *Garretson;* 1933, A. E. Mason, *Winner;* 1934, Cora Campbell, *Madison;* 1935, Albert Williamson, *Redfield;* 1936, W. H. Broadbent, *Mitchell;* 1937, W. R. Montgomery, *Alexandria;* 1938, A. G. Schenk, *Yankton;* 1939, Glen Minor, *Sioux Falls;* 1940, George Kohnke, *Clear Lake;* 1941, J. J. Anderson, *Canton;* 1942-43, Duane L. Anderson, *Plankinton;* 1944-45, William Welter, *Huron;* 1946, Darwin J. Noble, *Mitchell;* 1947, Albert Clements, *Armour;* 1948, Paul Wagner, *Vermillion;* 1949, Alfred Paetznick, *Groton;* 1950, Victor J. Hirsch, *Scotland;* 1951, Allen Lee, *Wessington-Springs;* 1952, Harvard Noble, *Mitchell;* 1953, Harry C. Behrens, *Rapid City;* 1954, A. L. Coleman, *Redfield;* 1955, Clayton Crosby, *Avon;* 1956, Floyd Schenk, *Yankton;* 1957, Leslie E. Mathiesen, *Watertown;* 1958, O. H. Frost, *Belle Fourche;* 1959, Ellis D. Gates, *Aberdeen;* 1960, Hardy M. Langslet, *Gettysburg.*

TENNESSEE

Informant: R. Fentress Casey

The original call to organization in Tennessee was sent to the funeral directors of the state by 26 firms of the state whose operators were interested in the work being done by other states toward the betterment of the men in the profession. The following text of the call was printed in the leading journals of the day:

"A state Convention of all re-

896

spectable funeral men of Tennessee will be held in this City on Wednesday, May 23, 1883, for the purpose of organizing a State Association and otherwise adopting measures for the promotion of the interest of our profession. Your presence is expected as a full representation is desired. Matters of the greatest importance to us will be considered. Half-fare rates, no doubt, can be obtained as it will be Military week. You are cordially invited to participate in the proceedings."

This group, although doomed to failure as a continuing entity, laid the ground work for later attempts at successful organization. Again in 1887 a group of Tennessee undertakers convened to hold its first annual meeting in Nashville. Most of the men who had attempted the earlier organization were present and elected the following officers: *President*, A. Barr, Columbia; *First Vice President*, J. C. Wells, Franklin; *Second Vice President*, L. C. Umphlette, Jackson; *Secretary*, F. M. Dorris, Nashville; and *Treasurer*, W. E. Cole, Goodletsville. Tennessee Funeral Directors' Association was the name chosen for the new organization. Dues were set at two dollars and the next meeting scheduled for August, 1887 in Nashville. At this point formal associational activities seem to have been suspended.

"Schools" of embalming, usually of less than a week's duration, were held several times in the ensuing years, and the leading funeral directors in the state were brought together by attendance at these schools rather than by attendance at any formal meetings of the association. It was not then, until December 29, 1903 at a meeting in Nashville of the funeral directors who were attending a school of embalming conducted by Professor Barnes under the auspices of the National Casket Company, that sentiment was expressed favorable to the formation of an association. At the meeting held later, on December 29, W. S. Cook of Nashville, who had done some of the pioneer work in the formulation of a proposed embalmer's law, announced to the assembled profession that there would be a meeting next day of all men interested in the reorganization of the Tennessee association. On December 30, 1903 then, with Professor Barnes as chairman *pro-tem*, and W. S. Cook as secretary, the meeting took place. A committee of five to draft a constitution and by-laws was appointed. After adopting the report of the committee next day and choosing the name Tennessee Funeral Directors Association, officers were elected to serve until June 14, 1904, the date chosen for the first annual meeting. The following men elected by the 87 charter members present served the organization as its first official family: *President*, T. E. McReynolds, Clarksville; *First Vice President*, Joseph Henry, Springfield; *Second Vice President*, L. R. Jacobs, Murfreesboro; *Secretary*, W. S. Cook, Nashville; and *Treasurer*, F. M. Dorris, Nashville.

At the time of organization Tennessee had no law governing either embalming or funeral directing. Through the untiring efforts of the association in its repeated rounds with the state legislature, an embalmer's law was passed by an act of the Fifty-sixth General Assembly of Tennessee on February 4, 1909, just five years after the reorganization of the group. By this act a State Board of Embalmers was created and established, its duties defined, and the compensation of its members fixed. The issuance of licenses to embalmers was legalized, and the board was given the authority to impose penalties for the violation of the provisions of the act.

In 1916 the new name, "Tennessee Funeral Directors and Embalmers Association," was adopted and in May, 1936, the association was incorporated under the name "Tennessee Funeral Directors and Embalmers Association, Inc."

It was also in the year 1916 that the secretary of the State Board of Embalmers, a member of the Tennessee association, helped to organize the Negroes of the profession in Tennessee into The Tennessee Negro Funeral Directors Association. There were 25 charter members of this group.

Tennessee has always been interested in anything which would improve the educational status of its members. Aside from the usual lecture on embalming given at the state meetings, in 1917 other types of demonstrations were tried as an experiment. Different members of the association gave demonstrations of certain religious and fraternal funeral rituals familiar to them.

In 1921 Tennessee decided to join with her neighbor states of Mississippi and Arkansas in a tri-state meeting. These meetings proved satisfactory to all the states involved and were scheduled to be held in several different years, although the states retained their separate associational entities. The chief purpose of the tri-state meetings was the scheduling of a program better

than any one state could have produced alone and the exchange of ideas between men of similar though different territories. In 1955 the group attracted over 1200 persons to its convention.

In 1951 the Tennessee Funeral Directors and Embalmers Association, Inc. was successful in encouraging the state legislature to pass a law governing funeral directing, and in February of that year the Tennessee State Board of Funeral Directors and Embalmers was established to take the place of the old State Board of Embalmers.

The Tennessee Funeral Directors & Embalmers Association, Inc. continues its efforts for a more enlightened and a better educated group of professionals in funeral service. The association's membership in 1959-60 stands at 182 working members.

ASSOCIATION PRESIDENTS: 1885, M. S. Combs, *Nashville;* 1887, A. Barr, *Columbia;* 1888, E. B. Mann, *Knoxville;* 1904, T. E. McReynolds, *Clarksville;* 1905, J. W. Norris, *Memphis;* 1906, J. R. Spicer, *Paris;* 1907, A. G. Mann, *Knoxville;* 1908, A. B. Rollow, *Clarksville;* 1909, William Martin, *Nashville;* 1910, E. C. Nowell, *Tracy City;* 1911, J. W. Doyle, *Bolivar;* 1912, J. W. Carroll, *Chattanooga;* 1913, B. F. Cornelius, *Nashville;* 1914, Frank Thompson, *Memphis;* 1915-16, J. C. D'Armond, *Harriman;* 1917, Finley M. Dorris, *Nashville;* 1918, J. T. Woodfin, *Murfreesboro;* 1919, W. G. Jones, *Nashville;* 1920, J. Q. Alexander, *Martin;* 1921, R. D. Martin, *Brownsville;* 1922, G. C. Collins, Jr., *Dickson;* 1923, L. H. Bodkin, *Humboldt;* 1924, R. J. Coulter, *Chattanooga;* 1925, Joe Curry, *Dy-*

898

ersburg; 1926, C. L. Moffatt, *Tulla-homa;* 1927, O. L. McLain, *Cleve-land;* 1928, C. M. Thompson, *Shel-byville;* 1929-30, W. A. McDowell, *Memphis;* 1931, H. C. Moore, *Mur-freesboro;* 1932, J. B. Rogers, *S. Pittsburg;* 1933, Frank J. Sturla, *Memphis;* 1934, M. R. Bracey, *Nash-ville;* 1935, Bryan Wilson, *Memphis,* 1936, Hiram Higgins, *Fayetteville;* 1937, J. L. Thomas, *Lenoir City;* 1938, Vernon Peters, *Ripley;* 1939, John W. High, *McMinnville;* 1940, Jos. Curry, Jr., *Dyersburg;* 1941, Gilbert Marshall, *Nashville;* 1942, J. Avery Bryan, *Chattanooga;* 1943, Gus White, Jr., *Union City;* 1944, J. S. Bowen, *Waverly;* 1945, A. X. Hunt, *Humboldt;* 1946, Frank Rose, *Knoxville;* 1947, W. H. Wiseman, *Erin;* 1948, Douglas Murphy, *Mar-tin;* 1949, Paul Cook, *Bristol;* 1950, Elmer Buckner, *Dickson;* 1951, Wm. J. Lanier, Jr., *Jackson;* 1952, Fred O. Berry, *Knoxville;* 1953, Thomas L. Austin, *Springfield;* 1954, Ed-ward Johnson, *Newbern;* 1955, Wil-liam Miller, *Maryville;* 1956, Manus R. Bracey, Jr., *Nashville;* 1957, Robert L. Dilday, *Huntingdon;* 1958, Ray P. Weaver, *Knoxville;* 1959, Charles Gallant, *Fayetteville;* 1960, Thomas Curry, *Dyersburg.*

TEXAS
Informant: Ralph A. Wooster

"Among other things it is the in-tention of this meeting to organize a state association." So read the *Dallas Morning News* for April 27, 1886, in describing the first con-vention of the Texas Funeral Di-rectors and Embalmers Associa-tion (then named the Undertakers' Association of Texas) at that time meeting in Ft. Worth. Although some organizational work was done previously, the Ft. Worth conven-

tion may be said to make the for-mal beginning of the Texas Asso-ciation.

This first meeting was devoted largely to organizational matters. Officers elected were: *President,* and delegate to National, Edward C. Smith, Dallas; *Vice Presidents:* I. T. Martin, Waco; G. W. Sage, Terrell; *Secretary,* Abe Flenner, Ft. Worth; *Treasurer,* J. R. Wil-liams, Weatherford, Alternate *Dele-gate to National,* Frank Steiner, Waco. Upon recommendation of a committee headed by Steiner, the convention adopted a constitution and by-laws based on those of the New York Association of Under-takers. Copies of the constitution and by-laws were to be mailed to all funeral directors and embalm-ers in Texas, together with blanks for membership in the new organ-ization.

Growth of the new association was rather steady in the first years, but actually no greater than the in-crease in the number of directors and embalmers in the state. By the second meeting in Dallas in 1887, the membership had increased from 11 to 41, and by 1893 had soared to 82 members.

Efforts at increased professionali-zation of members were made in the early annual conventions. The lack of any state laws regulating embalming practices formed an ob-vious handicap and a committee on legislation was instructed to request aid from the state legislature in this direction. Too, the association stressed education of its own mem-bers from the very first meeting; and by 1892 this seemed to be the chief objective of the organization. The record of each convention dur-ing the period 1886-1894 shows that various lecturers, including Professors Renouard of Kansas City, Lutz of New York City, and Clarke of Springfield, Ohio, appeared before the association to speak on the art of embalming.

The progress of the early years was not without some discouragements. The failure of the legislature to pass an embalming bill, the fact that most members were interested in other branches of business and considered funeral directing and embalming a secondary matter, and the lack of understanding by the general public were having an effect.

So discouraging was the future that there was no meeting in 1895. Business conditions were poor throughout the state, partly due to a nationwide depression occasioned by the Panic of 1893. Members began dropping their associational affiliation, and the organization seemed doomed to failure.

Led by President A. Harrington, the association fought back, however, and in 1896 the annual convention was held in Tyler, Texas, and steps in reorganization were made. The association, whose name had been changed from the Texas Undertakers' Association to the Texas Funeral Directors Association in 1889, now had only 18 members. The rebuilding process was slow but continuous and by 1903 the total membership had exceeded 200.

These years, 1896-1903, constitute the second phase of associational growth and represent some of the most formative years in the 75 year history of the Texas Association. Edward C. Smith, one of the original founders of the organization, was elected president in 1896, and in his annual address in

1897 expressed clearly the objectives of the association: "Not to regulate prices or create methods to keep others out of business, but to educate members and prepare them to intelligently care for those whose loved ones die; and to assist boards of health in stamping out contagious diseases. At this same 1897 convention, the organization changed its name from Funeral Directors Association of Texas to the Funeral Directors and Embalmers Association of Texas.

From 1896 to 1903 the chief concern of the association was the securing of legislation to regulate embalming practices throughout the state. The legislature considered an embalming bill in 1901, but by a narrow margin failed to pass it. However, in March, 1903, the state legislature passed the bill, creating the Texas State Board of Embalming, which would prescribe an examination before a required embalmer's license would be issued.

The pre-World War I years witnessed sporadic growth of the Association. The new law requiring examination for an embalmer's license resulted in larger attendance at the annual conventions as one day was devoted to administration of such an examination by the State Board. Membership in 1905 reached 226 and went up to 325 in 1907. However, poor business conditions in 1908-09 (again a nationwide business recession) resulted in a membership drop down to 254. This decline continued for several years, and by 1915 only 214 members were enrolled. A new membership drive led by Secretary Porter Loring of San Antonio was pushed in 1916-17 and enrollment figures began moving upward again. By 1918

900

the Association listed 396 members.

Throughout this period the association strove to add further educational and professional requirements. A series of additional laws which required embalmers to attend annual lectures and demonstrations held by the State Board of Embalming were secured from the legislature in 1915.

The 1920's and early 1930's marked some innovations for association membership. In 1926 the holding of district conventions was tried; in 1927 the first joint convention of the Texas, New Mexico and Arizona associations was held; and in 1928 a code of ethics was adopted by the association. Formal incorporation of the association was attained in 1932 when a charter was secured from the Secretary of State. Finally, in 1935 the passage by the state legislature of a law establishing and creating the licensing of funeral directors in Texas made a legal distinction for the first time between the embalmer and funeral director.

Celebration of the Golden Anniversary at Houston in 1936 found the association in the strongest position in its fifty year existence. The adoption of a strong code of ethics at the Houston meeting seemed further to illustrate the strength of the association.

New problems soon appeared on the horizon. The code of ethics proved to be unworkable and in 1938 a more moderate code along with new rules of competition were adopted.

An even greater menace to legitimate funeral operations in Texas appeared during this same period in the form of unethical burial association operators. These operators, who wrote and sold cheap burial insurance policies binding the purchaser to one particular funeral firm, were not new and not all unethical; but the Association felt they should be regulated for the protection not only of legitimate funeral directors but also the innocent public. In 1939 the legislature passed laws regulating operations of burial associations within the state.

The employment of Hugo Swan of Dallas as Executive Secretary of the association in 1941 was a recognition of the increased role that the state organization was playing.

In 1944-45 during Pete Elliott's administration, regional associations were created with considerable success, and today the state is divided into seven clearly defined regions, each with its own organization.

The return of peace following World War II brought new challenges to the funeral industry (for example, the return and reinterment of thousands of veterans who were killed overseas). In 1948 a comprehensive revision of the constitution and by-laws was made which more clearly defined the organization's purpose, responsibilities, and procedures. Although amended four times since, this is still the constitution of the Texas Association.

The Texas City disaster of April, 1947, shocked the entire state, and association members took a direct part in the relief operations. A disaster commission supervised the work and brought some order out of chaos, handling 536 bodies in thirteen days. For its part the funeral profession received praise and commendation from Governor Bu-

901

ford Jester, and the Texas Funeral Directors and Embalmers Association was asked to participate in setting up a permanent emergency relief program for the state.

A full time Executive Secretary was appointed for the first time in 1950, Bob W. Taylor of Brownwood being selected for the post to replace Hugo Swan of Dallas.

The year 1953 was especially bright for the Texas association. In this year the association received notification from the State Insurance Commission that Texas funeral homes had been placed under their own fire insurance rating schedule, effective December 30, 1952. Also in this year the legislature passed a new law creating the State Board of Morticians in place of the old Embalming Board. In these achievements the Association played an active part; both were the result of several years planning and working on the part of Association membership. The new Morticians law, sponsored jointly by the Texas association and the Embalming Board, not only changed the name of the state board but provided it with sufficient power to be able to supervise adequately the practice of funeral directing and embalming in the state. Too, educational requirements for funeral directors were raised in this legislation.

In May, 1954, Executive Secretary Bob W. Taylor resigned, and the Board of Directors selected Edward McGuire of Beaumont as his successor. A personal campaign to recruit new members resulted in the first rapid rise in membership figures in years. For four years 1951-1954 membership had ranged constantly from 320-350 members; but by spring, 1956, the Association had

513 members enrolled.

A new threat to the profession appeared in the early 1950's in the form of out-of-state cemetery organizations, and to meet this threat an all out campaign was launched through the association's legislative committee. In June, 1955, Senate Bill N. 52, providing that all sellers of pre-need funeral contracts had to be licensed by the State Banking Department and that all funds collected had to be placed in trust in the state until time of need, was passed. Operating under this new law, the Attorney-General of Texas obtained an injunction against the operations of violators, and the injunction has been upheld by the State Supreme Court. This decision of the courts to sustain the injunction is important not only to Texas but to the twenty-odd states that have adopted similar legislation.

In 1960 the Texas Association enters into its seventy-fifth year of existence, and while conscious of and proud of its heritage, the Association looks to the future, seeking in new and better ways to serve the public and the profession. Plans to establish a school of mortuary science on the college level in Texas have borne fruit with the creation of a two year course of instruction in San Antonio College leading to an Associate in Arts Degree. This development is in keeping with the Association's time-honored goal of increased education and professionalization of the Texas funeral directors and embalmers.

ASSOCIATION PRESIDENTS: 1886, Edward C. Smith, *Dallas;* 1887, R. R. Dulin, *Sherman;* 1888, J. P. Crouch, *McKinney;* 1889-90, A. Harrington, *Sherman;* 1891-92, E. C. Smith, *Dallas;* 1893, J. A. McCormick, *Galveston;* 1894, J. B. Crouch, *McKinney;* 1895, A. Harrington, *Sherman;* 1896, Edward C. Smith, *Dallas;* 1897, C. B. Sutherland, *Corsicana;* 1898, Tom Hillier, *Franklin;* 1899, G. W. Sage, *Terrell;* 1900, J. T. Cotten, *Weatherford;* 1901-02, J. W. Wright, *Temple;* 1903, W. L. Norwood, *Galveston;* 1904, S. R. Spaulding, *Waxahachie;* 1905, Hood F. Smith, *Dallas;* 1906, L. W. Crouch, *McKinney;* 1907, J. H. McCullum, *Smithville;* 1908, Jos. Shelley, *San Antonio;* 1909, W. B. Carson, *Pilot Point;* 1910, J. H. McCollum, *Smithville;* 1911, J. L. McCartney, *Waxahachie;* 1912, George M. Williamson, *Jacksonville;* 1913, J. L. McCarty, *Houston;* 1914, S. E. Rosengreen, *Austin;* 1915, George A. Brewer, *Dallas;* 1916, Colby E. Smith, *Dallas;* 1917, J. V. Taylor, *Beaumont;* 1918, N. S. Griggs, *Amarillo;* 1919, Tom S. Wright, *Temple;* 1920, Dan Laughter, *Abilene;* 1921, R. B. Leatherwood, *Hillsboro;* 1922, Philip P. Wise, *Bonham;* 1923, Porter F. Loring, *San Antonio;* 1924, W. T. Orr, *Ferres;* 1925, C. B. Cook, *Austin;* 1926, F. M. Compton, *Waco;* 1927, John G. Dannel, *Sherman;* 1928, J. C. Keever, *Ennes;* 1929, L. A. Morse, *Houston;* 1930, Geo. F. Weiland, *Dallas;* 1931, R. H. Beetham, *Mineral Wells;* 1932, O. W. Hines, *Wichita Falls;* 1933-34, Wm. G. Vollus, *Houston;* 1935-36, George A. Brewer, Jr., *Dallas;* 1937, Maynard Kreidler, *McAllen;* 1938, George Kearns, *San Antonio;* 1939, Roy Crowder, *Fort Worth;* 1940, J. B. Earthman, *Houston;* 1941, Pete Murray, *San Antonio;* 1942, Fred R. Cotten, *Weatherford;* 1943, J. V. Cossaboom, *Houston;* 1944-45, Pete Elliott, *Abilene;*

1946, Gilbert Koenig, *LaGrange;* 1947, Jerry Crane, *Dallas;* 1948, Harold Brand, *Dallas;* 1949, Romney Rudolph, *Waxahachie*—resigned, 1949, Dale Broussard, *Beaumont;* 1950, LeRoy Rader, *Kilgore;* 1951, Howard Maxon, *El Paso;* 1952, W. O. Stringer, *Jasper;* 1953, Boyd C. Dillon, *Cleburne;* 1954, George H. Lewis, Jr., *Houston;* 1955, Ben. E. Hamner, *Eastland;* 1956, Harold J. Zeigler, *Fort Worth;* 1957, Ira G. Broughton, *Wharton;* 1958, E. C. Harper, Jr., *Fort Worth;* 1959, Alton B. Boxwell, *Perryton;* 1960, Harold C. Saunders, *San Antonio.*

UTAH

It is reported that the funeral history in Utah dates back to the time when Brigham Young, President of the Church of Jesus Christ of Latter Day Saints (commonly known as the Mormon Church) in the year 1860, requested Jos. E. Taylor, a cabinet maker, to act as undertaker in the burial of early settlers in Utah, many of whom died from the hardships suffered and experienced in the early days. Joseph Wm. Taylor, son of Joseph E. Taylor, started assisting his father in this work at the age of 15 years.

Records show that the first embalmer's license in the State of Utah was issued September 1, 1898 to Lorenzo Stohl. At the same time licenses were issued to J. H. Richardson, E. L. Jones, M. Wedekind, and Geo. W. Larkin. Also the same year licenses were issued to R. W. Wall, S. D. Evans, S. T. Ricketts, Thomas L. Allen, Geo. W. Lindquist. A. M. Wallace received his license September 1, 1899. Elijah A. Larkin was licensed on May 19, 1903. Mr. Larkin has been very active in the association's work and was at one time District Governor of the National Funeral Directors Association. Although he is now past 80 years of age, he is still active in the field. Alma J. Larkin, a brother of Elijah A. Larkin, was licensed July 1, 1905. Geo. W. Larkin, their father, the first to study outside the State was graduated from the United States College of Embalmers in New York.

The first mention of an association in Utah is found in the report of the Western Association at the meetings of the National Funeral Directors Association in the year 1902. Although at this time the Western association was still in existence, the decision had already been made by the group to hold all future meetings in the State of Colorado, and the reporting delegate from Utah stated: "I think possibly when we meet with you again our territory may be divided. There is a movement in Utah, headed by that grand old Mormon, Joseph E. Taylor, to organize a separate association there. They are a long distance from us, and we feel that it would be a great thing for them, especially as our association (Western), which met in Colorado Springs on September 16th to 19th last, decided that they would meet permanently in Denver."

As a member of the Western association, Utah was helpful in carrying association work into the states of Colorado, Idaho, Montana and Washington by helping to establish the Northwestern Funeral Directors Association.

An announcement of the formation of a separate state association in Utah was published in *Embalmers' Monthly* in 1906. The first formal meeting of the funeral directors of the state was held in Provo on July 3, 1906 and an association was organized with the following officers elected: *President,* E. W. Hall, Salt Lake; *First Vice President,* O. H. Berg, Provo; *Second Vice President,* G. W. Lindquist, Logan; *Secretary,* E. L. Jones, Provo; *Assistant Secretary,* Wyman Berg, Provo; and *Treasurer,* J. P. Sorrington, Manti.

The first regulatory statute, providing for an embalmers' examination board, was enacted by the 1921 Utah Legislature. Amendments to this statute were made in 1929 and continued to be the law until 1937, when additional amendments were made thereto and a Funeral Directors' License Law was enacted. During this time S. T. Ricketts, Elmer M. Qualtrough, Geo. W. Darling, Geo. A. Jenkins and other association members worked diligently through the years 1931, '33 and '35 in the Legislature for amendments to the state law to elevate the standards and requirements for funeral directors. In 1937, W. Douglas Allen of Murray, Utah, a practicing attorney and also a licensed embalmer and funeral director, drafted the Funeral Directors' License Law and several amendments to the statute regarding embalming. Mr. Allen was a member of the 1937 state legislature and sponsored these bills, which were finally passed and enacted into law during that session.

Through the years the Utah association has been interested in getting legislation for the betterment of the profession and for the protection of the public welfare. In 1929 the association gave notice to the State Securities Commission that it would protest the granting of a permit to the Deseret Mortuary

Company to sell its burial certificates. Again in 1940 it cheered the decision of C. Clarence Nelson, Utah's state insurance commissioner, when he declared it illegal for the Guardian Benefit Association of Salt Lake to issue a policy which provides one amount as a cash benefit and a different amount where funeral services are furnished. After this decision the company was instructed to issue non-discriminatory policies in the future and to prepare and submit for approval to the insurance department a rider to be added to all outstanding policies.

In 1948, after a fact-finding committee studied for about one year, the association organized the Sentinel Insurance Company, later to be known as Sentinel Security Life Insurance Company. It was financed by the association members and continued to operate and grow as a mutual company until January 1, 1957, on which date the company was converted to an old line legal reserve stock organization. It now is owned and operated by funeral directors of Utah, Arizona, and other western states.

In 1955 the association reported its continued interest in legislation, when at its annual convention in Salt Lake City, LaVar Tate, retiring president, "recommended that a coroner's law acceptable to doctors, law enforcement officers, and other officials should be readied for the annual session of the legislature, and observed that a faultily prepared and unworkable medical examiner's bill had failed to pass the previous session of the state legislature."

Within the state at various times local organizations have been established and have been an aid to the state association in bringing news of importance to the profession to many who would not otherwise be able to attend the regular state meetings.

ASSOCIATION PRESIDENTS: 1926, Alma J. Larkin, Sr., *Salt Lake City;* 1927, S. T. Rickets, *Salt Lake City;* 1929, George A. Jenkins, *Murray;* 1930-31, E. A. Larkin, *Ogden;* 1932, Anson Hatch, *Provo;* 1933, George A. Jenkins, *Murray;* 1934-35, Wyman Berg, *Provo;* 1936-37, Carl A. Lindquist, *Ogden;* 1938-39, Lee R. Fry, *Salt Lake;* 1940, W. L. Warner, *Richfield;* 1941, Neil O'Donnell, Sr., *Salt Lake;* 1942, Joseph R. Kingdon, *Salt Lake;* 1943-44, Leo W. Goates, *Salt Lake;* 1945, W. Loyal Hall, *Logan;* 1946-47, W. Douglas Allen, *Murray;* 1948, Harold B. Felt, *Brigham City;* 1950-51, Clyde A. Lindquist, *Ogden;* 1952-53, Richard T. Mitchell, *Price;* 1954, LaVar Tate, *Tooele;* 1955-56, Alva R. Wing, *Lehi;* 1957, Merrill R. Holbrook, *Bountiful;* 1958-59, Vaughn C. Soffe, *Murray;* 1960, Max W. Berg, *Provo.*

VERMONT

On October 24, 1900 the funeral directors of Vermont met at Montpelier and formed an organization to be known as The Vermont Funeral Directors and Embalmers Association. This group gave as its purpose the forwarding of legislation which would provide a license system for the profession in that state. The officers elected to guide the association through its first year were: *President,* H. E. Bond, Brattleboro; *Vice Presidents:* B. W. Hooke, Barre; J. Warren Roberts, Burlington; *Secretary,* C. G. Roakes, Montpelier; and *Treasurer,* W. B.

905

Hudson, Montpelier. After adopting a constitution and by-laws the membership adjourned to hold its first annual meeting in Burlington on June 25, 26 and 27, 1901.

The association first reported to the national body in the year 1902 and at that time expressed regret that no law had been passed in the state, that the membership was progressing slowly, and also added that the education of its membership was considered of prime importance.

By 1903 membership had increased so much that there were 40 members present at the third annual convention to hear Professor Eckels lecture on embalming techniques and to hear Mrs. M. C. Brigham, one of the first women ever to be chosen secretary of an association, read the minutes of the preceding year's business meeting. At this time it was also reported to the members present that the legislative committee had succeeded in getting a bill through the legislature, and that plans were already in the making to amend the law to make it an even better one.

After securing the aid of the Vermont Health Officers' Association and meeting jointly with them in 1904, work continued toward the establishment of suitable legislation for the advancement of the profession and the protection of the people of the state. After several set-backs and false starts a better law was put through the legislature in 1909. According to the delegate who reported on the new law to National, "All undertakers, at the inception of our new law, were by that act made registered embalmers; since then seventy-one have taken state examinations and are denominated

licensed embalmers. Our State Board of Health conducts the examinations, and many capable embalmers are finding the technical questions of these most excellent physicians very difficult."

Meanwhile, educational matters were still important to the men of Vermont. Speakers of note and demonstrators respected in the profession were on hand at every convention to conduct schools for the membership, bringing to them the latest in both technical advances and general educational matters of the times. The membership had grown from 50 to nearly three times that number by the year 1917. Meetings were well attended and the work of the national body was taken seriously, discussed, and acted upon.

In the year 1921 the association favored the increase in per capita tax to National and during its biggest and most successful convention to date went on record as opposing Sunday funerals.

In 1935 Vermont Funeral Directors' Association amended their by-laws to give their executive committee power to recommend expulsion of members from the association ranks for unethical practices or conduct. They also considered at this time the acceptance of the National Diploma suggested by Chairman Jones of the Conference Grading Committee at New Orleans earlier in the year.

In 1940, in line with the desires of the membership to broaden their service to their respective communities and motivated by the humanitarian activities characteristic of the funeral profession, the Vermont Funeral Directors Association in annual convention at Lyndonville, June 19 and 20, adopted resolutions

906

providing for the organization of a Purple Cross Emergency Squadron of funeral directors and embalmers to be affiliated with the state association.

ASSOCIATION PRESIDENTS: 1900-02, H. E. Bond, *Brattleboro;* 1903-04, C. W. Spencer, *Rutland;* 1905, M. J. Moran, *Brattleboro;* 1906, J. B. Carrigan, *Poultney;* 1907, C. M. Edson, *Williamstown;* 1908-09, C. H. Hayden, *Riverside;* 1910, J. E. Keefe, *Bellows Falls;* 1911, John R. Kelly, *Burlington;* 1912, A. C. Hale, *Bradford;* 1913, C. A. Calderwood, *St. Johnsbury;* 1914, John B. Stearns, *Rutland;* 1915, Marshall S. Rounds, *Barre;* 1916, J. A. Gibson, *Enosburg Falls;* 1917, Frank J. Dwyer, *Burlington;* 1918, C. H. Stanley, *St. Johnsbury;* 1919, E. J. Seamans, *Fair Haven;* 1920, T. W. Gurney, *Burlington;* 1921-29, J. C. Hennessey, *Bellows Falls;* 1930, Harris H. Metcalf, *Waterbury;* 1931, Paul Adams, *Chester;* 1932, Elmer Sturk, *Bethel;* 1933-34, S. M. Driscoll, *St. Albans;* 1935, Carl A. Mitchell, *Brattleboro;* 1936, W. D. Cabot, *Woodstock;* 1937, Morris B. White, *Morrisville;* 1938, H. E. Converse, *Orleans;* 1939, W. A. Wood, *Lyndonville;* 1940, Elbert Davis, *Springfield;* 1941, L. F. Palmer, *Burlington;* 1942, Fletcher Kenyon, *Barre;* 1943, Arthur L. Rhode, *Brattleboro;* 1944, George Ready, *Burlington;* 1945, A. J. Messier, *Barre;* 1946, Arthur J. Blackmer, *Middlebury;* 1947, John C. Hennessey, Jr., *Bellows Falls;* 1948, Myron Eastman, *Barton;* 1949, George H. Bryce, *Springfield;* 1950-51, Robert H. Gadue, *Swanton;* 1952, Robert W. Judd, *Bradford;* 1953, Gordon H. Brown, *Bristol;* 1954, Rudolph Day, *Randolph;* 1955, C. C. Staf-

ford, *Stowe;* 1956, Ralph M. Knight, Jr., *Windsor;* 1957, Raymond W. Heald, *St. Albans;* 1958, Albert W. Rich, *Fairfax;* 1959, Dean Hanson, *Bennington;* 1960, Mack B. Converse, *Newport.*

VIRGINIA

At a meeting of funeral directors held at the Atlantic Hotel in Norfolk on August 6, 1887 four men were appointed a committee to issue a call to every funeral director in the state of Virginia to attend a meeting to be held in Richmond, September 20, 1887. They stated in their letter to the directors of the state the benefits of such an organization to be limitless not only to the profession but to the public in general. The notice was signed by A. E. Hall, H. D. Oliver, S. H. Hines, H. C. Smith, and L. T. Christian.

A group of 50 funeral directors assembled at the appointed time, Mr. A. E. Hall of Norfolk acting as temporary chairman and Mr. L. T. Christian acting as temporary secretary. The committee previously appointed for the purpose reported the following declaration as a basis for the association:

"We, the undertakers of Virginia, this day organize into an association, the object of which shall be the mutual advancement and elevation of our calling; the attainment of a higher standard of excellence, that we may the better be enabled to serve the public who entrust their dead to our care. Our aim is to place our profession on a basis which will ensure the respect and esteem of the community."

After the assembly subscribed to the report of the committee, election of officers for the ensuing year followed. *President,* Joseph W. Laube, Richmond; *Vice Presidents:* J. T. Morriss, Petersburg; W. D. Diuguid, Lynchburg; Thomas Scott, Portsmouth; S. H. Hines, Norfolk; and James Perley, Charlottesville; *Treasurer,* A. E. Hall, Norfolk; *Secretary,* L. T. Christian, Richmond.

On the second day of the convention the committee on constitution and by-laws suggested the name The Virginia Funeral Directors Association. This name, after some deliberation was adopted along with the complete report of the committee. Further, the assembled membership decided to affiliate with the National Funeral Directors Association, and chose at this time delegates to attend the annual national convention soon to be held.

By the time of the second meeting of the funeral directors of Virginia it could be reported to the group that already the state legislature had recognized them and that they as professionals were exempt from jury duty. After reporting growth, progress and interest in associational activities over a period of years, in 1894 Virginia announced at the annual convention of NFDA success in putting on the statute books of the old commonwealth a law licensing embalmers, the first such enactment of any state in the union. The new law went into effect January 1, 1895, but before the end of the 1894 fiscal year many funeral directors had already taken the embalmers' examination and were qualified under the law. Mr. L. T. Christian, one of the founders of the Virginia association was the first secretary of the Virginia Board of Embalmers.

The original law covered embalmers in cities of over 5,000 population. In March of 1901 the law was extended to cover all embalmers in the state. All those practicing embalming in Virginia prior to January 1, 1902 could either continue to embalm without license or take the examination and receive a license, but men who wished to begin the practice of embalming after that date were required to take the examination for license before setting up a practice in any city of any size in the state. An amendment in 1910 gave the board the power to revoke a license for incompetence. From time to time since that date, the law has been amended to add either educational requirements or experience, to establish reciprocity with other states, or to bring the statute of the state up to date.

In 1897 a resolution was adopted requesting the colored funeral directors in the state to meet with the association for advice in order to enable them to form an association of their own.

The state of Virginia was fortunate in its selection of early officers, some of whom served many terms and gave the association a sense of continuity. Even the delegates to the national convention were frequently the same men. Among these early workers for the state were L. T. Christian who served as delegate to national and secretary of the Virginia association for thirty-three years and James Perley Treasurer of the group for many years.

Virginia received honors from the profession nationally in that many of her members have been elected to office in NFDA, two of them elected to the high office of president of the national body are L. T. Christian and Joseph W. Laube both of

908

Richmond.

Through the years the problems of the profession nationally were also the problems of Virginia, agreement with the national baggage association on transportation problems, legislation helpful to the profession, education of its membership, relations with the public at large. By selecting its members carefully and by educating the new members, the association grew not only numerically but ethically and spiritually to take its place among the number of outstanding state associations in the United States, backing the national body and the funeral directing profession generally in any movement for the good of all.

ASSOCIATION PRESIDENTS: 1887-90, Joseph W. Laube, *Richmond;* 1891, John W. Brown, *Hampton;* 1892-93, W. D. Diuguid, *Lynchburg;* 1894-95, C. W. C. Woolwine, *Roanoke;* 1896-97, W. B. Johnson, *Portsmouth;* 1898, W. M. Bucher, *Harrisonburg;* 1899, H. C. Smith, *Norfolk;* 1900-01, John M. Oakey, *Salem;* 1902-03, G. W. Kurtz, *Winchester;* 1904, R. W. Baker, *Suffolk;* 1905, F. W. Townes, Sr., *Danville;* 1906, H. D. Oliver, *Norfolk;* 1907-08, M. W. Stevens, *Pulaski;* 1909, W. J. Morrissett, *Richmond;* 1910, C. W. Alexander, *Waynesboro;* 1911, J. R. Williams, *Norfolk;* 1912, R. W. Thompson, *Culpeper;* 1913-14, A. B. Woodward, *Louisa;* 1915-16, John S. Owen, *South Boston;* 1917, M. M. Price, *Ivanhoe;* 1918, M. M. Seaver, *Marion;* 1919-20, Henry W. Woody, *Richmond;* 1921, C. Edward Forrest, *Mathews;* 1922-23, J. C. Hudgins, *Lynchburg;* 1924-25, T. A. Bell, *Staunton;* 1926-27, Samuel G. Oakey, *Roanoke;* 1928, Walter M. Clark, *Chincoteaque;*

1929-30, George H. Vermilya, *Clifton Forge;* 1931-32, W. R. Preddy, *Orange;* 1933, Fred H. King, *Norton;* 1934-35, F. W. Townes, Jr., *Danville;* 1936, Paul S. Bliley, *Richmond;* 1937, C. N. Loving, *Hot Springs;* 1938, B. O. Hill, *Suffolk;* 1939, F. C. Stover, *Strasburg;* 1940, L. T. Christian, *Richmond;* 1941, John A. Williams, *Chihowie;* 1942, D. H. Reames, *Petersburg;* 1943, E. H. McConnell, *Gate City;* 1944-45, Frank A. Bliley, *Richmond;* 1946, A. Raymond Thacker, *Scottsville;* 1947, W. L. Crawford Oakey, *Roanoke;* 1948, Thomas H. Jennings, *Crewe;* 1949, R. Marshall Loving, *Covington;* 1950, William R. Hill, *Charlottesville;* 1951, J. T. Morriss IV, *Petersburg;* 1952, Laurens P. Jones, *Winchester;* 1953, James P. Farmer, *Richlands;* 1954, John M. Oakey, *Roanoke;* 1955, Robert N. Baker, Jr., *Suffolk;* 1956, O. Kenneth Updike, *Staunton;* 1957, William L. Hoy, *Bowling Green;* 1958, John C. McKee, *Lynchburg;* 1959, Mark Farris, *Abingdon;* 1960, W. J. Smith, Jr., *Newport News.*

WASHINGTON
Informant: C. G. Hoerling

The Washington State Funeral Directors' Association has its historical roots in the old Northwestern Association. From the very first, interest among the members was high and the association prospered financially. The year 1902 may be regarded as the organizational year, although there had been one or two preliminary meetings.

The first meeting was called by the State Board of Health for the purpose of administering the Board's own examination to the funeral directors of the state who wished to obtain the embalmer's license. This meeting was held in Tacoma in 1902, and from it the present association was formed. Committees were appointed to draft a constitution and by-laws and the following officers were elected: *President*, E. R. Butterworth, Seattle; *Vice Presidents:* Alex Turnbull, Spokane; J. F. Jerread, Everett; *Secretary*, H. L. Mead, Centralia; and *Treasurer*, C. L. Hoska, Tacoma. The first annual meeting was held a few months later in October, 1902 in Spokane at which time the proposed constitution and by-laws were adopted.

Shortly after the first annual convention, the association requested admission to the national association, and in 1903 a report read at the meetings of NFDA by Mr. Kilpatrick, National Secretary, indicated that the association in the state of Washington, "the only state association on the West Coast," was already attempting to secure better licensing legislation, and was growing rapidly.

Reports to NFDA in the years 1907 and 1908 again indicate dissatisfaction with the licensing setup in the state. At this time a license was not required to practice embalming, but the Board of Health was empowered to give an examination to those who wished to take it in order to become licensed. The funeral directors of the state were able by late 1908 to secure the passage of the first license law which made the embalmer's license obligatory in the state of Washington. The Washington State Board of Embalming consisted of the secretary of the State Board of Health and two licensed embalmers who were appointed by the governor, and in 1909 the law was reported working

successfully in the state.

Year after year the association in Washington reported growth both financially and numerically and expressed satisfaction with the way in which the new law was working. The prosperity of the Washington association spread, and in 1910 it tried something new in state association meetings, a convention held on board a steamship which sailed from Seattle to Vancouver. The Washington funeral directors were at this time instrumental in founding an association in British Columbia by giving advice and encouragement to the funeral directors there.

Washington has always had good relations with surrounding territories and has worked in many ways to further the aims of the national association. In 1913 the state of Oregon invited the Washington funeral directors to a joint meeting which was held in Portland, and in 1914 another successful joint meeting was held in Walla Walla. The first man honored by the mother association was J. W. Cookerly who was elected to serve the NFDA as president in 1911. In 1945 the Washington State Association was again honored by having J. E. Drummey of Seattle elected to serve as President of NFDA.

Perhaps the most important step by the Washington Association was taken at the Thirty-third Annual Convention in Tacoma August 8-9, 1934, when definite plans for an Executive Office were proposed and a Board of five Trustees elected to serve in the interest of establishing a permanent business executive office. After investigating costs of such a venture, the board reported and proposed a plan by which the

910

state organization could be reorganized. An Initiation fee of five dollars was set and dues of fifty cents per case, payable monthly were established. In September, 1934, George S. Ryan was employed by the board as the first executive secretary. He helped in the further reorganization of the association and was successful in bringing into the group many new firms as well as reinstating many old ones. Mr. Ryan helped organize the Oregon Association on a similar basis. Other executive secretaries followed him to continue the work in Washington. Among these were: Don Reynolds who aided in the establishment of an association in Idaho; Eli L. Duncan who guided the association through the trying days of World War II, Beatrice E. Duncan who served until November, 1945; C. A. Erickson under whose direction a plan for pre-paid funeral service was established; and the present executive Mrs. Olive Halvorsen who succeeded Mr. Erickson in 1948 and is carrying on the work of the association and its funeral service plan.

Perhaps the boldest step taken by the association was the organization in 1947 of the Funeral Service Association, an association formed following the vote of the members of the Washington State Funeral Directors' Association for the purpose of selling pre-paid funeral insurance. "The Purple Cross Plan" is the name given to the program.

From the members who started the Washington association it has grown until there are now 160 firms which are members, four which are honorary members, 19 associate members in Alaska, Idaho, Montana and Canada. Only 17 firms in the entire state claim no affiliation with the organization.

Much credit for the success of the Washington State Association is due to such men as C. O. Lynn, Emmett Hennessey, L. L. Bruning, J. E. Drummey as well as all those who have ever served on the Board of Trustees and in all the various other offices and committees throughout the existence of the Washington State Funeral Directors' Association.

ASSOCIATION PRESIDENTS: 1902, E. R. Butterworth, *Seattle;* 1903, W. H. Mock, *Bellingham;* 1904, J. W. Cookerly, *Walla Walla;* 1905, C. C. Mellinger, *Tacoma;* 1906, S. M. Smith, *Spokane;* 1907, D. J. Jerue, *Medical Lake;* 1908, Conrad L. Hoska, *Tacoma;* 1909, O. W. Stone, *Davenport;* 1910, W. R. Whiteside, *Aberdeen;* 1911, J. F. Jones, *Buckley;* 1912, Geo. MacMartin, *Walla Walla;* 1913, L. S. Mellinger, *Spokane;* 1914, J. E. Turner, *Harrington;* 1915, L. M. Gaffney, *Tacoma;* 1916, C. G. Chittenden, *Kent;* 1917, W. E. Stoddard, *Gifford;* 1918, T. Frank Koepfle, *Seattle;* 1919, L. L. Bruning, *Colfax;* 1920, N. B. Challacombe, *Everett;* 1921, Claude M. Vassar, *Pomeroy;* 1922, A. A. Collins, *Seattle;* 1923, D. W. Jones, *Wenatchee;* 1924, C. O. Lynn, *Tacoma;* 1925, J. B. Hazen, *Spokane;* 1926, W. J. Knapp, *Vancouver;* 1927, Ray B. Lee, *Pasco;* 1928, E. B. King, *Tacoma;* 1929, C. M. Phillips, *Wilbur;* 1930, J. E. Drummey, *Seattle;* 1931, E. S. Hennessey, *Spokane;* 1932, C. C. Pinnick, *Hoquiam;* 1933, C. E. Smith, *Spokane;* 1934, Gene Whiteside, *Aberdeen;* 1935, H. A. Shaw, *Yakima;* 1936, E. R. Warnica, *Olympia;* 1937, Frank Hennessey, *Seattle;* 1938, Martin L.

911

Dawson, *Elma;* 1939, Merle W. Chapman, *Yakima;* 1940, L. C. Howden, *Seattle;* 1941, Irwin H. Jones, *Wenatchee;* 1942, J. A. Knapp, *Vancouver;* 1942, Earl S. Coleman, *Hoquiam;* 1943, W. S. Tinsley, *Spokane;* 1944, Beryl Wells, *Seattle;* 1945, W. R. Goodrich, *Colfax;* 1946, D. L. Reynolds, *Bremerton;* 1947, Robert Groseclose, *Walla Walla;* 1948, Frank T. Walters, *Tacoma;* 1949, Dan. J. Hennessey, *Spokane;* 1950, Walter J. Precht, *Everett;* 1951, C. G. Hoerling, *Centralia;* 1952, John C. Gilchrist, *Port Orchard;* 1953, Paul H. Pugsley, *Spokane;* 1954, Emmett Drummey, *Seattle;* 1955, Donald C Keith, *Yakima;* 1956, W. C. Merchant, *Clarkston;* 1957, Oliver W. Jacobson, *Seattle;* 1958, Theo. B. Gaffney, *Tacoma;* 1959, John Westford, *Bellingham;* 1960, Stuart N. Adams, *Seattle.*

WEST VIRGINIA
Informant: H. Eugene Merrill

The records of the formative period of the West Virginia Funeral Directors Association were destroyed many years ago, and in 1921 the burning of our State Capitol destroyed many other records. From the few records available, it would appear that the individuals then engaged in funeral directing and embalming were realizing the significance of contagious diseases and protection of the public from them as well as the requirements for a professional service and the need for some form of regulation for these services. In the late 1800's after the experiences of the Civil War, contagious diseases, epidemics, and shipment of bodies were being given serious consideration in many states and this included West Virginia. Records mention that four funeral directors met in Wheeling, West Virginia, during January of 1895 and discussed the advisability of organizing a state association. It was decided to request the funeral directors throughout the state to meet in Wheeling, in the establishment of Alexander Frew on February 8, 1895 for the purpose of forming a State Funeral Directors Association. All 16 of the funeral directors attending are not identifiable, but it is known that Alexander Frew was made Temporary Chairman and G. Ed. Mendel, Temporary Secretary. After discussing the feasibility and methods of organizing a state association, a motion was made and passed that a permanent organization be formed. Subsequent elections were conducted with Alexander Frew being elected President and D. M. Thornburg of Elm Grove being elected Secretary.

The meeting was called to order on June 24, 1895 and opened with a prayer by Rev. C. E. Wilbur. Following this an address of welcome was made by State Senator C. E. Smith, in the absence of the Mayor of Fairmont, and President Frew of Wheeling responded on behalf of the assembled convention. The following business of electing officers was then conducted and the initial officers of the organized association are as follows: *President,* Alexander Frew, Wheeling; *First Vice President,* R. L. Cunningham, Fairmont; *Second Vice President,* J. H. Markwood, Keyser; *Secretary,* D. M. Thornburg, Elm Grove; and *Treasurer,* T. E. Cole, Grafton.

From the early reports made by this new association at the national conventions, it is obvious that the purposes and goals of the new or-

912

ganization were to develop ethical practices and regulatory legislative measures that would govern the practice of embalming and funeral directing as necessities for the public protection. This is evidenced by the fact that the West Virginia Association quickly adopted the Code of Ethics of the national association, the language of which clearly demonstrates the feeling of responsibility that these individuals felt as a part of professional relationship to the persons in their community. This is further evidenced by the urgency to develop legislation that would be regulatory in measure and would be an added feature of public protection. At their 1896 convention they discussed legislature and studied the features of a law in the state of Pennsylvania; and at the June convention of 1897, a Legislative Committee was appointed and was directed to prepare a bill for presentation at the annual meeting for 1898. The Committee did draft a bill, which was presented and approved at the 1898 convention at which time the membership decided to present it to the State Legislature. The bill was passed by the legislature on February 24, 1899, and became a law 90 days later.

In accordance with the provisions of this new law, the Governor made the appointments and the original State Board was established. It then held its first meeting on September 8, 1899 in Parkersburg. West Virginia, at which time 127 certificates were issued under Section 5, and 19 were granted licenses under Section 6. Thus, the first efforts to license those engaged in embalming became a reality. As could be expected, practical experiences and improved techniques in the chemical industries, caused modifications of existing practices, and related amendments were presented to the legislature from time to time. The board soon realized that the licensing and regulation of the embalmer was not sufficient regulation to cover all of those becoming engaged in funeral service. It at first appeared that funeral directing and embalming were two distinct and separate occupations, but it soon became apparent that the functions and duties of the person performing the acts of a funeral director were also of such nature as to be in the need of regulatory measures. This line of reasoning culminated in the 1931 legislation to license the occupation of funeral director. By amendment, the existing law was changed and the existing State Board was given the added duties and responsibilities of regulating and issuing licenses for both embalmers and funeral directors. Its new name became the West Virginia State Board of Embalmers and Funeral Directors.

During these years, the association was constantly endeavoring to build membership and to formulate policies and programs for self-improvement. An important feature at the state convention was a demonstration of new embalming chemicals and new techniques in the preservation of human bodies. Automotive equipment was progressively improved, and the occupation of funeral director soon outgrew the confines of a sideline occupation and began to manifest itself in special structures that were developed as funeral homes. As these progressive achievements were accomplished, new attitudes developed and a new awareness of their responsibilities

913

became apparent. It was realized that additional education requirements and professional abilities would be needed. It also became apparent that the operation of an association could best be accomplished by securing the services of an Executive Secretary, and in 1948 the association engaged the services of H. Eugene Merrill as its first Executive Secretary.

Through the efforts of various committees and a renewed interest in the association, the annual dues were increased and extensive campaigns for membership were conducted. In 1951 legislative amendments were submitted and passed by the legislature effective July 1, 1951. The new law required two years of college plus 12 months of embalming college, plus 12 months of apprenticeship for a license in the state of West Virginia.

Concurrent with the increase in membership and the revised legislation, other problems were being met. The delays and conditions of bodies which had been subjected to post mortem examinations presented grave difficulties to the embalmer; and the relationships between the funeral homes, the pathologists and the hospitals were at a very critical stage. This condition was brought to the attention of the Medical association, and through joint committee representation of the four associations concerned, the first state-wide Standard Code of Autopsy Procedure was developed and placed in effect in April, 1951. At about the same time, the State Legislature authorized the building of a Medical Center at the State University, and the association made a presentation to the Board of Governors requesting that time and

space in the new facilities be allocated for the establishment of a four year college course leading to the issuance of a Bachelor of Science Degree in Mortuary Science. This request received favorable consideration, and plans have been started toward the realization of such a goal.

Due to the origins of funeral service, as affiliated with retail establishments, it was only natural that many practitioners considered their activities as a part of a retail trade and thus were inclined to advertise in the same vein as they had previously done with their furniture store or livery stable. The Codes of Ethics and the principles of many practitioners, to some extent restricted the tone of advertising; but as large amounts of capital became invested in rolling stock and funeral home structures, economic necessity tended for many to make false, misleading and unprofessional ads in the various mediums of advertising. In this state, this condition reached a critical stage between late 1940's and the early 1950's. The West Virginia State Board made repeated efforts to discipline several of these offenders, but due to lack of Rules and Regulations, such persons evaded the proper applications of the law. This frustrating situation caused the State Board to issue stringent rules relating to advertising, and this action was immediately challenged. Rules and Regulations were effective May 15, 1954; but it was not until December 22, 1956, that the legal proceedings in this controversy were settled by the West Virginia Supreme Court, which was unanimous in upholding the Rules and Regulations of the State Board and the police power of the state,

914

as delegated by the State Legislature.

Since the early meeting of a few funeral directors in 1895, through their original organization on June 24, 1895, to the present time, the association has been blessed with good quality leadership, as is evidenced by the list of the presidents of this association.

ASSOCIATION PRESIDENTS: 1895, Alexander Frew, *Wheeling;* 1896, R. L. Cunningham, *Fairmont;* 1897, H. D. Wells, *Spencer;* 1898, W. H. Fredlock, *Piedmont;* 1899-1902, R. L. Cunningham, *Fairmont;* 1903-04, W. G. Osborne, *Clarksburg;* 1905, M. A. Kendall, *Elkins;* 1906, S. C. Furbee, *Wheeling;* 1907-08, H. S. Thompson, *Keyser;* 1909, L. E. Kramer, *Ronceverte;* 1910, W. R. Cooey, *Wheeling;* 1911-12, John A. McCabe, *Grafton;* 1913, O. C. Ogdin, *St. Marys;* 1914, George M. Cokeley, *Harrisville;* 1915, L. H. Mott, *Davis;* 1916, W. Lawrence Noble, *Martins Ferry;* 1917, G. T. Barlet, *Grafton;* 1918, Chas. Jenkins, *Morgantown;* 1919, M. J. Lynch, *Clarksburg;* 1920, Frank E. Foster, *Wellsburg;* 1921, P. A. Simpson, *Charleston;* 1922, R. R. Steele, *Huntington;* 1923, Edward Cooey, *Wheeling;* 1924, F. E. Vandale, *Spencer;* 1925, Virgil A. Brown, *Morgantown;* 1926, O. T. Davis, *Clarksburg;* 1927, J. W. Luther, *Welch;* 1928, D. B. Klingel, *Huntington;* 1929, P. D. Bratton, *Bluefield;* 1930, L. A. Harper, *Point Pleasant;* 1931, Wade H. Kepner, *Wheeling;* 1932, R. G. Coffman, *Martinsburg;* 1933, J. D. Thomas, *Clendenin;* 1934, C. J. Bertschy, *Wheeling;* 1935-36, Edgar J. Harmer, *Shinnston;* 1937, C. A. Ruttencutter, *St. Mary's;* 1938, Bruce Spindler, *Kingswood;* 1939-40, R. C. Jones, *Fairmont;* 1941, Howard Brown, *Martinsburg;* 1942, N. Howard Rogers, *Keyser;* 1943, Joseph Ford, *Fairmont;* 1944-45, Joseph H. Bosnall, *Charleston;* 1946, Prentiss Watson, *Terra Alta;* 1947, V. S. Carpenter, *Huntington;* 1948, C. O. Phillips, *Philippi;* 1949, John D. Altmeyer, *Wheeling;* 1950, Dayle Fidler, *Belle;* 1951, E. E. Allen, *Hurricane;* 1952, Harry Weaver, *Clarksburg;* 1953, J. Donald Eackles, *Harpers Ferry;* 1954, John V. Iams, *New Martinsville;* 1955, Charles E. Dodd, *Webster Springs;* 1956, J. P. Fanning, *Iaeger;* 1957, Marshall A. Shanklin, *White Sulphur Springs;* 1958, M. Tabor Ball, *Williamson;* 1959, C. Harold Beard, *Huntington;* 1960, William H. Ford, *Fairmont.*

WISCONSIN

Informants: Robert F. Scheible
George E. Johnson
C. W. Laemmrich

"Wide-awake Wisconsin" is the caption in a trade journal article reporting the tenth annual convention of the Wisconsin State Funeral Directors Association in Milwaukee. President H. M. Lowry's prophesy at this 1891 meeting is quoted as follows: "And in these discussions and labors for to-day, we should not lose sight of the possibilities of the future and the coming of that day when our vocation shall be lawfully and in every other possible way, recognized as a profession." Thus did he keynote an educational program for the funeral service profession in Wisconsin that has continued for the past 69 years.

The beginning of the association was inauspicious. John P. Schumacher, Green Bay, in later years describes its founding as follows: "In the latter part of February, 1881, I sent out notices to Wisconsin undertakers requesting them to attend a meeting at the Newhall House, Milwaukee, for the purpose of perfecting a working organization. . . . A big snowstorm occurred on March 2nd; all railroads were tied up for ten days and prevented a meeting. Accordingly, a second notice was sent out to meet at the same place in the latter part of March. I arrived at the Newhall House at 10:00 A.M., but finding suitable accommodations not available, I transferred the meeting to the Kirby House. However, no one appeared for the meeting, so I began the work of rounding up the Milwaukee undertakers. I went to see Mr. Sam Peacock on Broadway who promised me his hearty cooperation in bringing together the Milwaukee undertakers to meet at the Kirby House at 2:00 P.M. and undertake an organization meeting. Ten or twelve Milwaukee embalmers appeared, and an informal meeting was held at which arrangements were made to call a formal meeting on May 10th, at which time those attending would perfect an organization. This meeting was held and the organization came into being."

The first *president* elected at this 1881 meeting was William Spikes, Oshkosh; other officers were S. F. Peacock, *vice-president*, R. D. Johnson, *secretary*, J. P. Schumacher, *treasurer*, and J. F. Smith, H. J. Smith and C. S. Warren, *executive committee*. The earliest function of the association appears primarily to have been education through the sponsorship of clinics; the first such demonstration in Wisconsin was in 1883 according to the recollection of

Charles L. Truesdell a number of years later.

Four hundred seventy-four undertakers were reported in Wisconsin in 1887, only 40 of whom were association members. The growth of the organization and of funeral service the next seven years are reflected in the comments of Thomas Hansen in his president's address at the seventh annual convention, October 3, 1888.

S. F. Peacock and O. F. Renning, both of Milwaukee, were unsuccessful in introducing a bill at Madison in 1890 "to require undertakers to pass a regular examination before being admitted to our ranks." Fifty members attended the 1895 convention at which W. P. Hohenschuh was present in a two-fold capacity: president of the National Funeral Directors Association and demonstrator of the Chicago College of Embalming.

President after president urged legislation to initiate a license system in Wisconsin; legislative committees reported continued failures in 1891, 1893 and 1895. During this period the City of Milwaukee considered but did not enact an ordinance to require funeral directors to pass examinations before beginning practice. Meanwhile S. F. Peacock urged members at the 1897 convention to "educate yourselves and make yourselves worthy in every town and hamlet . . . and I dare say that the undertaker will not be unwelcome." The education program is reflected in the following excerpt from Secretary George L. Thomas' 1898 convention announcement: "For the purpose of putting the proper information within the reach of all, we will hold a school of instruction during the meeting of the state association, presided over by Prof. J. H. Clarke." Later, in 1899 "Briggs, the Tropical Man," a "drummer" (salesman) in his dispatch to *The Casket* wrote: "President Wittig seems very confident that the bill now before the legislature licensing undertakers will pass, and his idea of giving a man a graded license according to his ability seems to meet with general approval throughout the state." However, the bill did not pass.

The optimism of F. H. Pratt, president of the association which had since changed its name to the Funeral Directors and Embalmers Association of the State of Wisconsin, is reflected at the nineteenth annual convention, September 1900, at the Milwaukee Medical College and School of Dentistry in his following observations: "To attain the position the profession now occupies has been a struggle, but to-day no apology is necessary for the position it holds in the professional world."

Subsequently, in 1901 Chapter 401 authorized the State Board of Health to adopt rules concerning the transportation of the dead, which was done effective June 25, 1901. Two years later the Wisconsin salesmen organized as the Traveling Mens' Auxiliary to the W.F.D.A.; Edward Ihrig, Oshkosh, was elected its first president.

1905 was an historic year for the association. The reversals of previous years culminated in the first license law in Wisconsin for embalmers. The new law, Chapter 420, became effective June 24, 1905. Its major feature was the provision for licensing embalmers requiring that no person shall be granted a license under this act who has not practiced embalming dead human bodies for at least six months, or shall have had at least six months practical instruction in embalming and disinfecting under a licensed embalmer. Dr. C. A. Harper, state health officer, was awarded honorary membership for his assistance in the enactment of Wisconsin's first licensing bill. The members of the legislative committee were F. H. Pratt, S. F. Peacock and A. H. Schram. Retiring president George W. White echoes the pride of accomplishment and optimism of 1905: "The law pertaining to embalming as it now reads places us on an equality with many other states, giving us privileges that place us in the eye of public as well as professional men, as a profession worthy of its name." The membership roster this year totaled 263, including the following family names still active in funeral service: Brett, Boston, Bauer, Borgwardt, Brettschneider, Beebe, Bruns, Boyle, Candlish, Dobratz, Dahl, Eckstein, Eberhardt, Feerick, Franzen, Froemming, Fennig, Frautschi, Heuer, Heiden, Helke, Hansen, Holly, Harper, Kondrad, Kaufmann, LeSage, Luecher, Lins, McLain, Meiselwitz, MacQueen, Mc Candless & Zobel, Nick, Nowack & Kohl, Nelson, Pratt, Prasser, Ritter, Randall, Ritter & Deutsch, Rhode, Rozga, Saether, Smith, Schmidt, Schram, Schmutzler, Sauer, Stenberg, Stohr, Schramka, Tellefson, Voss, Wendler, Weiss, Weiand, Wichmann, Zuengler and Zacherl.

The State Board of Health reports 707 embalmers in Wisconsin in 1907, the year in which the Bureau of Vital Statistics was established. In 1909 George L. Thomas, Milwaukee, was elected the first

917

president of NFDA from Wisconsin. In 1911 Chapter 242 was enacted requiring two years of practical instruction in embalming. The next attempt at increasing educational quirements to one year high school in the 1913 session failed. President J. N. O'Boyle gave a strong address at his 1914 convention on the importance of education. He was the first to urge a chair of embalming at the University of Wisconsin or Marquette. The next year the convention approved a recommendation guaranteeing $1,200 tuition to Marquette University to inaugurate a College of Embalming and Funeral Technique. The University of Wisconsin Medical School previously had rejected the program due to a lack of facilities. Seventeen students attended the first course at Marquette University, June 1 to July 27, 1916, the tuition for which was $50.00, and the association paid $475 to Marquette in accordance with its guarantee agreement.

Bill 850-A which provided that no person engaged in the business of embalming would be eligible to hold the office of coroner or deputy coroner was not passed by the 1915 legislature. The July 1917 convention at Oshkosh adopted a resolution urging the U. S. Government to use skilled embalmers and to discontinue the practice of returning repatriated veterans in "zinc-lined caskets filled with quick lime or other antiquated methods."

In 1921 a comprehensive change in the law was enacted as Chapter 464 establishing what was intended to be a funeral director's license in addition to the embalmer's license which had now been in existence sixteen years. The Attorney General held, however, that the law was not clear and did not distinguish between the work of a funeral director and embalmer; the law was later held unconstitutional. C. R. Fiss, Oshkosh, in giving the legislative committee report, urged members to use the term "funeral director" instead of "undertaker." President Jack Wendler, Milwaukee, presided at the 1923 Wisconsin Rapids convention where there was vehement disagreement with the State Board of Health on the establishment of a Board of Embalmers, legislation for which was introduced and then withdrawn. Because of continuing losses, the association also voted in 1923 to withdraw the financial support it had given the mortuary school at Marquette University the past nine years, and the program was consequently terminated.

Convention programming in the 1920's, in addition to the customary clinical demonstrations, began to include an awareness of operating costs, accounting procedures, and merchandising. In 1925, at Eau Claire, President A. S. Kingsford, Baraboo, again stressed the importance of increasing the educational requirements of the embalmer. Secretary Kroos, Sheboygan, reported the interest of the University of Wisconsin Medical School, Madison, to initiate a course in mortuary science. The State Board of Health adopted minimum mortuary school requirements. At a time when the state of Wisconsin contained only one organized county association, Milwaukee County, A. T. Hansen, Kenosha, in his 1926 presidential message at Superior recommended local meetings throughout the state. This speech sparked the eventual formation of the present twelve district associations.

918

In 1929 Harry B. Goodman chairmaned the legislative committee to a long sought-after goal with the enactment of increased qualifications, effective July 31, 1930, requiring a high school education and (a) six months mortuary school and six months apprenticeship, or (b) two years apprenticeship. The association successfully opposed Bill 242-S sponsored by an American Mortuaries Company which would have permitted the sale of promotional burial contracts in advance of need. At the 1930 convention in LaCrosse, Secretary James A. Crossin, Kenosha, reported 338 members, and recommended greater attention to convention location. He also noted the decreased significance of practical demonstrations. One hundred seventeen of the 142 applicants passed the embalmers examination prior to July 31, 1930, effective date of the new law.

1931, the golden anniversary year of the Wisconsin Funeral Directors & Embalmers Association, and the year of the second term of Frank D. Candlish, Fond du Lac, as president, saw another eventful legislative session. The six month apprenticeship requirement was increased to one year, and Chapter 256, which had the effect of prohibiting burial insurance in Wisconsin, was enacted. T. L. Pendergast was employed by the State Board of Health as the first field educator. License examinations were no longer held at the same time as the annual convention. President Coad A. LeSage, Superior, reported increasing membership to a high of 383 in 1932. In accordance with a resolution adopted at this year's convention Perry T. Powell, Milwaukee attorney, was retained as legislative counsel and soon thereafter was employed by the National Funeral Directors Association as field counsel. In 1933 comprehensive legislative changes were enacted, initiating the long discussed and desired separate funeral director's license as well as a requirement based on the so-called Texas Plan, making it compulsory for each licensee to attend the annual school of instruction sponsored by the State Board of Health a minimum of once every three years. The first issue of the association bulletin called "The Wisconsin Funeral Director," planned for quarterly distribution, was published in December 1933, according to President Thomas O. Sletten's report at the 1934 convention. Compulsory three-way membership (state-national-district) was discussed at length; Milwaukee County already had this mandatory provision a part of its organization. These 53rd convention proceedings were the first printed for distribution to each member; previously proceedings were printed by the various trade journals. The first school of instruction conducted by the State Board of Health followed this convention on June 21, 1934. Dr. W. G. Henika, assistant state health office, reported approximately 600 funeral establishments in Wisconsin with 990 funeral director licenses issued and 1411 embalmer licenses.

In 1935, the year of George E. Johnson's presidency, association by-laws were completely revamped, including a compulsory three-way membership within the discretion of each district association. Insurance rating of funeral homes, public relations, welfare funerals, and the NRA were the principal subjects of convention consideration. A. A. Frautschi, Madison, completed 26 years as treasurer. Dues were increased from $10 annually to a schedule ranging from $10 to $25, based on volume. Membership certificates as well as a Code of Ethics were initiated. George Johnson, Appleton, was elected secretary in 1936 and in October of that year inaugurated a new bulletin called the *Spotlight,* which continues to be the name of the association's monthly mimeographed publication. Attorney A. W. Kopp, Platteville, was retained as legal counsel for the association in 1938. Cooperative funeral homes continued to be a problem, especially in central Wisconsin. Attendance at convention exhibits was limited to members, their families and employees; membership totaled 598 out of 765 establishments. The maximum statutory welfare funeral allowance was $100. The 1939 convention, presided over by C. W. Laemmrich, Menasha, approved retaining an executive secretary and increased dues to a schedule ranging from $12 to $60. At the State Board of Health school following, Dr. Carl Neupert, assistant state health officer, explained the new law, Chapter 93, effective May 25, 1939, relating to the qualifications necessary for licensing: funeral director, two years apprenticeship, or one year apprenticeship and graduation from a recognized school of funeral directing; embalming after July 1, 1940, three years apprenticeship, or eighteen months apprenticeship and graduation from nine months embalming school. The license fee for the combined funeral director and embalmer license was $6; a funeral establishment was required to have a preparation room.

At the 1940 convention President Willmer G. Schmidt, Milwaukee, introduced Howard C. Raether, Milwaukee attorney, who was retained as executive secretary and counsel of the association on January 2, 1940. The public relations program sponsored by the association was broadened considerably. C. W. Laemmrich succeeded Carroll Downing as treasurer in 1941. President in 1941 was Arthur E. Taylor, Merrill, who in 1959 became the second Wisconsin president of the National Funeral Directors Association. E. R. Dobbert was appointed as a field educator of the State Board of Health this same year. World War II that year brought with it familiar regulations such as price ceilings, standardization of merchandise and shortages. Milwaukee County funeral directors developed a pooling agreement. In the spring of 1943 Howard Raether was commissioned as a naval officer; the office secretary, Geraldine L. Doehler, maintained the office with Eugene F. Foran, executive secretary of the Illinois Funeral Directors Association, retained on a part-time basis. John Schumacher, association founder, died this year. A major legislative change occurred in 1943 with the licensing of funeral establishments in Wisconsin. Convention exhibits were omitted during 1943-44-45.

Following World War II association members adopted a policy of making no charge for their professional service or the use of their funeral home for the funeral services of repatriated veterans, a policy which earned the commendation of the Wisconsin Military District, Fifth Army. The post-war era included such activities as apprentice

920

training under the GI bill, regional meetings, and a renewed interest in increasing educational requirements. Charles Truesdell was accorded a standing tribute at the 1946 65th annual convention; he attended 60 of the 65 conventions in the history of the association. Howard Raether reported 514 of the 699 establishments were members as of April 1, 1946. This same year the University of Wisconsin approved the recommendation of the association establishing a two year college mortuary training program at the University of Wisconsin-Milwaukee. Bill 246-A, which would have made two years of college a compulsory requirement, was defeated in the 1947 legislature, cancelling the anticipated college program.

When Howard C. Raether was retained as the executive secretary of the National Funeral Directors Association, Harold J. Ruidl succeeded him on June 15, 1948 as executive secretary and counsel. In 1950 the association name was changed to the Wisconsin Funeral Directors Association. Effective August 3, 1951 the educational requirements for both licenses were increased by legislative enactment to one year of college, nine months of mortuary school, and twelve months apprenticeship. The one year college requirement was further increased by the legislature over the objections of the governor to two years of college, effective October 2, 1959. Other legislative activities in the past decade have included the enactment of the prearranged trust law in 1953, limitation against a funeral director providing the funeral service for any individual whose death he was re-

quired to investigate as coroner, and increasing welfare funeral allowances to $200 and actual cemetery expenses. At the 1960 convention the by-laws were changed, effective January 1st following, granting membership without payment of additional dues, to all licensed employees in addition to the proprietors of each funeral establishment remitting dues.

The membership of the association as of July 1, 1960 totaled 735, representing 87.7% of all funerals conducted in Wisconsin annually. Wisconsin's 79 years of progress—as well as its future—is reflected in the title of a paper deliver at its 1960 convention, "The Technical and Economic Feasibility of Radiation Preservation of Human Remains."

ASSOCIATION PRESIDENTS: 1881, William Spikes, *Oshkosh;* 1885, S. F. Peacock, *Milwaukee;* 1886, George L. Thomas, *Milwaukee;* 1887-88, Thomas Hansen, *Kenosha;* 1889, Samuel Peacock, *Milwaukee;* 1890-91, H. M. Lowry, *Milwaukee;* 1892-93, Thomas Hansen, *Kenosha;* 1894, S. F. Peacock, *Milwaukee;* 1895-96, H. F. Thiele, *Whitewater;* 1897-98, Jacob H. Wittig, *Marinette;* 1899-1900, F. H. Pratt, *Richland Center;* 1901, J. J. Hanchett, *Sheboygan;* 1902, C. A. Bugdon, *Oconto;* 1903, George M. Deutsch, *West Bend;* 1904, George W. White, *Oakfield;* 1905, W. F. Saecker, *Appleton;* 1906, T. D. Phillips, *Menasha;* 1907, J. R. Ragan, *Grand Rapids;* 1908, J. R. McLain, *Marinette;* 1909, B. M. Hoppenyan, *Ashland;* 1910, W. H. Crandall, *Walworth;* 1911, C. L. Truesdell, *Milwaukee;* 1912, William W. Powers, *Madison;* 1913, J. A. Morris, *Chip-*

pewa Falls; 1914, J. N. O'Boyle, Milwaukee; 1915, Henry Fessler, Sheboygan; 1916, A. P. LeSage, Superior; 1917, Ole Elbertson, La Crosse; 1918, E. Voth, Milwaukee; 1919, Joseph L. Wattawa, Manitowoc; 1920, David Brettschneider, Appleton; 1921, Arthur J. Brett, Milwaukee; 1922, F. Grant, Lake Geneva; 1923, J. J. Wendler, Milwaukee; 1924, Robert H. Stokes, Eau Claire; 1925, A. S. Kingsford, Baraboo; 1926, Alwin T. Hansen, Kenosha; 1927, Philip J. Weiss, Milwaukee; 1928, Robert H. Kroos, Sheboygan; 1929, Carl F. Nowack, Watertown; 1930-31, Frank D. Candlish, Fond du Lac; 1932, Coad A. LeSage, Superior; 1933, Fred W. Krohn, Wisconsin Rapids; 1934, Thomas O. Sletten, La Crosse; 1935, George E. Johnson, Appleton; 1936, Gustav A. Hinterberg, Winthrop, Minn.; 1937, F. J. Peacock, Jr., Milwaukee; 1938, Clarke B. Habecker, Lake Geneva; 1939, Clem W. Laemmrich, Menasha; 1940, Willmer G. Schmidt, Milwaukee; 1941, Arthur E. Taylor, Merrill; 1942, George R. Kellermann, Cumberland 1943, Dennis R. Jones, Palmyra; 1944, Frank C. Ritter, Milwaukee; 1945, Fred B. Doudna, Richland Center; 1946, Donald L. Goodrich, Menomonie; 1947, E. F. Ramm, Sheboygan; 1948, G. H. Wartman, Ashland; 1949, August J. Abe, Milwaukee; 1950, E. J. Overton, Janesville; 1951, L. F. Thielen, Marinette; 1952, Raymond H. Raetz, Milwaukee; 1953, E. J. Crossin, Kenosha; 1954, Walter J. Karth, Shawano; 1955, Frederick S. Voegeli, Monticello; 1956, Frederick J. Bremer, Colfax; 1957, Alfred B. Kaufmann, Milwaukee; 1958, Robert S. Betzer, Delevan; 1959, Harold A. Lulloff, Dodgeville; 1960, C. W. Mittnacht,

Manitowoc; 1961, Robert F. Scheible, Baraboo.

WYOMING

The Wyoming Funeral Directors Association traces its ancestry back to the old Western Associaton which comprised the states of Colorado, New Mexico, Utah, and Wyoming. This association, founded in 1899, was the parent association for the four later state groups. When the Colorado association was formed from the older group, there was great difficulty in reorganizing the remaining states, and although Wyoming tried on several occasions to form its own state group, due to the difficulties of travel and the distances between cities in this sparsely settled region, these attempts ended in failure.

It is interesting to note that the funeral directors and embalmers of the state must not have been completely idle in these years during which they had no formal organization. From the earliest days of the Western Association licenses were granted to embalmers from Wyoming through the courtesy of the State Board of Health of Colorado; however in 1907 Wyoming began issuing embalmers' licenses through its own State Board of Health. By 1916, the organizational year, Wyoming could already boast 65 licensed embalmers within her territory.

In the same year a representative group of funeral directors met for the purpose of forming an organization. They elected a slate of officers consisting of: President, H. Rasmussen, Rawlings; Vice Presidents: C. H. Hoffman, Douglas; Clyde Early, Chezemi; Secretary, W. J. Chamberlin, Casper; and

Treasurer, Lew M. Gay, Casper. In 1917 the organization sent a written report to NFDA and paid dues to the national body of $13. These officers were truly the pioneers and the fathers of the present state organization. Both H. Rasmussen and Lew Gay served for several years on the Board of Embalmers Examiners with various physicians of the state, and both held more than one office in the early association.

Little is known of the organization from 1916 to 1924 except that it did exist and continued to report itself to NFDA and to pay dues to that organization, although no representative was actually sent from the group to the conventions of the national body.

On May 19, 1924 the state of Wyoming issued a charter to the Wyoming Funeral Directors Association. The first officers to serve under the chartered organization were: *President,* Lew M. Gay, Casper; *Vice Presidents:* P. H. Knight, and Charles A. Champion, Sheridan; *Secretary Treasurer,* John A. Benson, Lander.

Wyoming has always been a small association and has used various methods of encouraging funeral directors to affiliate with the group. In 1926 the slogan for the group was, "Every member get a member." Since at this time there were only 28 firms doing business in the state, the members of the organization did not find it an impossible task to contact a nonmember, and the group increased in number within the next few years.

By 1935 Wyoming funeral directors were holding meetings occasionally with funeral directors of Colorado and New Mexico groups in order to be able to furnish a better program for the members of all three groups.

In 1940, as a public relations gesture, the Wyoming Funeral Directors Association, Inc., donated a copy of T. J. Bonniwell's book *We Have to Die* to every library in the state. During that year the association also sponsored educational addresses before service clubs throughout the state and visitations were held at leading mortuaries to better acquaint the public with both the funeral directors and the profession in the state.

ASSOCIATION PRESIDENTS: 1917-18, H. Rasmussen, *Rawlings;* 1919, C. H. Hoffman, *Douglas;* 1920, J. A. Berson, *Lander;* 1922, Thomas Longhurst, *Casper;* 1923-24, Lewis X. Gay, *Casper;* 1925, Charles Champion, *Sheridan;* 1926, B. B. Reed, *Sheridan;* 1930, W. W. Fox, *Gillette;* 1931, Frank P. Rogan, *Rock Springs;* 1932, A. A. De Pau, *Kemmerer;* 1933, O. J. Colyer, *Torrington;* 1934, Paul H. Worland, *Cheyenne;* 1935, Leo Wildermuth, *Rock Springs;* 1936, George E. Peet, *Lusk;* 1937, Charles A. Champion, *Sheridan;* 1938, R. E. Bryan, *Evanston;* 1939, W. L. Bustard, *Casper;* 1940, J. C. Atwood, *Basin;* 1941, Paul McKelvey, *Rawlins;* 1942, J. Warden Opie, *Rock Springs;* 1944, Bertha Reed, *Sheridan;* 1945, Lewis Colyer, *Torrington;* 1946, Floyd C. Payne, *Lander;* 1947, Ted S. Schrader, *Wheatland;* 1948, Arnold Veile, *Worland;* 1949, Carl H. Horstman, *Casper;* 1950, Cecil M. Stark, *Douglas;* 1951, Marvin G. Schrader, *Cheyenne;* 1952, Max Mortimore, *Thermopolis;* 1953, T. E. Haskell, *Lovell;* 1954, J. W. Adams, *Buffalo;* 1955, Percy T. Davis, *Riverton;* 1956, Ray Easton, *Powell;* 1957, John Conroy, *Rawlins;* 1958, Daniel Ballard, *Cody;* 1959, Don McColley, *Newcastle;* 1960, Gilbert D. Bills, *Evanston.*

THE DISTRICT OF COLUMBIA
Informants: Don DeVol and Sigmund Danzansky

From 1913 until 1937 a series of attempts to organize a group of funeral directors in Washington, D.C., was made. Each one resulted in failure until on November 2, 1937 an organizational meeting was held at the Willard Hotel in Washington, D. C. Nineteen funeral directors attended this meeting and adopted the "Resolution of Organization." The men signing the document were Martin W. Hysong, James T. Ryan, Almas Speare, William F. Taylor, W. Reuben Pumphrey, William Sardo, Jr., Harry M. Padgett, Harold J. Taltavull, William J. Nalley, W. R. Frank Hines, Sigmund Danzansky, Francis J. Collins, Percy J. Saffell, Roy Perry, Charles Zurhorst, Archer L. Haycock, John R. Wright, William Gawler, Warner E. Pumphrey.

Temporary chairman, Martin W. Hysong, was succeeded by Archer L. Haycock as the first *president* of the Association in 1938.

In March, 1940, the District of Columbia Funeral Directors Association started on the road to affiliation with the NFDA, and was finally chartered with the national organization in October, 1951.

An interesting commentary gleaned from a perusal of the early minutes, shows that of a then-enumerated list of ten or more problems for consideration for this newly organized group, all but one are still present in varying forms. As listed at the early meetings and recorded in the minutes these are: burial societies or foundations; special auto tags; parking spaces at health department, taxation (including the two per cent District of Columbia tax and others); advertising, ethical and unethical; Federal Trade Commission (FTC); easy acquisition of removal and burial permits; labor unions; social security benefits; reciprocity (almost accomplished at this date); and a licensing law. (This licensing law was established in 1947).

One of the major reasons for the success of the District of Columbia's Funeral Directors Association has been the cooperation and participation of the affiliated funeral directors of the Washington Metropolitan area. Such cooperation also is extended to NFDA which, at times, looks to us for the last word on Congressional developments of interest to funeral directors. This was especially true during the last days of the 86th Congress when final action was being taken on the Social Security amendments of 1960.

The annual Installation of Officers affair has grown from a small dinner meeting to a large gathering consisting of a reception, dinner, and dance. These affairs are attended by well over two hundred people—funeral directors and their wives as well as representatives of both the District and National governments, officers of the associations in the nearby states of Maryland and Virginia, and even representatives of other state associations.

Our present membership is as follows: James E. Betts, Francis J. Collins, Sigmund Danzansky Robert E. Wilhelm, William Demaine, H. Don De Vol, Ernest Gart-

924

ner, William A. Gawler, Archer L. Haycock, Frank C. Higgenbotham, W. R. Frank Hines, Wilson Huntmann, Thomas M. Hysong, Ernest Lee, Robert A. Mattingly, William Nalley, Robert A. Pumphrey, Mrs. Warner E. Pumphrey, Michael Rinaldi, James T. Ryan, Percy J. Saffell, Leonard H. Simmons, J. Arthur Walters, William P. Gasch.

ASSOCIATION PRESIDENTS: 1906, W. P. Speare, *D. C.;* 1907-08, Charles J. Gawler, *D. C.;* 1909-10, George Zurhorst, *D. C.;* 1911-12, Isaac Birch, *D. C.;* 1913-16, Charles Zurhorst, *D. C.;* 1919-21, Isaac Birch, *D. C.;* 1938-40, Archer L. Haycock, *D. C.;* 1941, Percy J. Saffell, *D. C.;* 1942-46, William Gawler, *D. C.;* 1947-49, Warner E. Pumphrey, *D. C.;* 1950-51, J. William Lee, *D. C.;* 1952-53, Thomas M. Hysong, *D. C.;* 1954, Sigmund Danzansky, *D. C.;* 1955, Robert E. Wilhelm, *D. C.;* 1956, J. Arthur Walters, *Tacoma Park*, *D. C.;* 1957-58, H. Donald De Vol, *D. C.;* 1959-60, James E. Betts, *D. C.*

925

APPENDIX II

Funeral Procedure of Religious Groups and Fraternal Organizations*

PART ONE: Churches and Religious Groups

Advent Christian General Conference of America

Informant: LEE E. BAKER, *President Executive, National Headquarters*

While there is no church ruling in the matter of a clergy being present when death is imminent or sudden, they do feel it would be very much in order. The funeral director might notify the clergy.

The removal and embalming may be accomplished in the usual manner, since the church has no ritual or opinions on either. They have no expressed opinion on cremation, or mausoleum interment, but prefer an earth burial. The dressing and encasketing may be done in the usual manner. No special equipment is required on or about the encasketed remains.

Sometimes private, informal, services are held prior to the regular funeral services.

There is no opinion as to where a service must be held. The funerals of ministers should be from the church, otherwise local custom may prevail. If the services are held at the church, arrival may be handled according to local custom. The casket should be placed at the front of

the church prior to arrival of the congregation. Flowers may be handled according to local custom. They would prefer an open casket service. The family may select casket bearers without restriction.

On leaving the building in which the services have been held, the minister will lead the procession to the casket coach.

At the committal, the minister will lead from the casket coach to the lowering device, and take his place at the head of the grave.

It is preferred that only instrumental music be used during the service.

General Conference of Seventh Day Adventists

Informant: W. R. BEACH, *Secretary, National Headquarters*

There are no church rules that the clergy be present at the time of death or immediately thereafter, but it is desirable that the minister visit and pray with the family of the deceased.

*Originally published as *Manual of Funeral Procedure* by John Myers (Casper, Wyoming: Prairie Publishing Co., 1956). Reprinted with permission of the author.

926

The church has no ritual, procedure, or opinions on the removal, embalming, cremation, earth or mausoleum interment, dressing, or encasketing. All this may be taken care of and arranged in the usual manner.

There is no ritual or service to prepare for prior to the regular funeral service, and no special equipment is needed on or about the encasketed remains.

The place where the funeral service is held is left entirely up to the wishes of the family.

It is preferred that the casket be placed before arrival of the congregation.

The floral displays may be handled according to local custom.

Regarding the funeral music, it is sometimes felt that soft organ music is sufficient unless the family desires vocal music.

Local custom may determine a closed or open casket service. The family may select the casket bearers without restriction.

If the service is held in the church, the congregation will retire row by row under the direction of the funeral director.

On leaving the building in which the services have been held, the minister will lead the procession to the awaiting casket coach.

At the cemetery, the minister will again lead the procession to the grave from the casket coach and take the most convenient position facing the family.

The balance of the committal may be accomplished according to local custom.

The whole service should be brief and dignified.

American Unitarian Association
Informant: MASON F. McGINNESS,
Assistant to the President,
National Headquarters

The national association has no jurisdiction over the local church in the matters of funeral procedure.

The following is not contrary to the national headquarters.

The official church does not deem it a necessity that a member of their clergy be present when death is imminent or sudden. The individual local minister is free to do as he sees best under such circumstances.

There are no expressed opinions, rules, or ritual on the removal, embalming, dressing, encasketing, cremation, earth or mausoleum interment.

The family is free to select the casket bearers, place of service, and music, without restriction, as long as it is compatible with the local church. If the services are held in the church, local church custom may prevail in all aspects.

Local custom may govern the committal in all aspects.

Assemblies of God
Informant: J. ROSWELL FLOWER, *General Secretary, Springfield, Missouri*

This group does not require the presence of the clergy when death is imminent or sudden.

The church has no rules, opinions, or ritual regarding the removal, embalming, dressing, encasketing, cremation, earth or mausoleum interment. All this may be taken care of and arranged in the usual manner.

The family is free to select the place of service, music and casket bearers without restriction.

The Assemblies of God have the congregational form government, consequently there is great latitude in forms and practice. This latitude does not exist in the matter of the doctrines of the church.

If the services are held at the church, there are no specifications to follow as to how, when or where the casket shall be placed, other than the local church custom.

Flowers and floral displays may be handled in the usual manner.

Local church custom may determine whether the service shall be closed or open casket.

On leaving the place where the services have been held, the minister prefers to walk in front of the casket to the casket coach.

At the cemetery the minister again leads the procession from the casket coach to the grave.

The remainder of the committal will be governed by local custom.

American Baptist Association
Informant: Dr. A. L. Patterson, *Secretary, National Headquarters*

This group does not deem it a necessity that a minister be present when death is imminent or sudden.

The church has no rules, ritual, or opinions on the removal, embalming, dressing, encasketing, cremation, earth or mausoleum interment. All this may be taken care of and arranged in the usual manner.

If the services are held in the church, the arrival and handling of the encasketed remains will be according to local custom. They have no objection to opening the casket after the service if it is a closed casket service.

The family is free to select the place of service, casket bearers, and music, as long as the music is sacred.

The actions of the minister and funeral director on leaving the building where the services have been held, and en route from the casket coach to the lowering device, may be accomplished according to local custom. The minister will stand where it is most convenient.

The remaining portion of the committal will be accomplished according to local custom.

Conservative Baptist Association
Informant: Dr. B. Myron Cedarholm, *General Director, National Headquarters*

The Conservative Baptist Association of America is not an ecclesiastical church organization. It is a fellowship of free, self-governing churches, and the churches make all their own decisions in all matters.

Local custom may be the guiding factors in all arrangements with members of this group, and none will be contrary to any church rules.

American Baptist Convention
Informant: W. Hubert Porter, *Assistant General Secretary, National Headquarters*

This church does not demand the presence of the clergy when death is imminent or sudden from a ritualistic view. Frequently a minister is called from the standpoint of family comfort.

There is no overall definite church opinion, rules or ritual regarding the removal, embalming, dressing, encasketing, cremation (rare among American Baptist), earth or mausoleum interment. All this may be accomplished and arranged for in the usual manner.

The minister may have a private service with the family sometime prior to the regular funeral service. This will probably not involve the mortuary service.

No special equipment is needed on or about the encasketed remains.

It is a general feeling among the American Baptist to have the funeral service in the church. They continually try to encourage the use of the church in such matters. If the services are held at the church, local church custom may determine nearly all aspects of the service. Sometimes it is preferred that the casket be taken down the center aisle of the church in formal procedure with the minister leading and reciting Bible verses.

The family is free to select the music and casket bearers without restriction.

Local custom may determine the procedure in leaving the place where the services have been held, and same will hold true from the casket coach to the lowering device in the cemetery. The minister will usually take his place at the head of the grave.

The balance of the committal may be determined by local custom.

United States of America National Baptist Convention
Informant: REVEREND T. J. JEMISON, *Secretary, National Headquarters*

This church does not deem it a necessity that a member of the clergy be present when death is imminent or sudden, neither do they have any rules, ritual, or opinions on the removal, embalming, dressing, encasketing, cremation, earth or mausoleum interment. This may be accomplished in the usual manner.

There are no services to prepare for prior to the regular funeral services, and no special equipment is needed on or about the encasketed remains.

The family is free to select the place of service, music, and casket bearers without restriction.

If the services are held at the church, local church custom may determine all aspects of the service.

When leaving the place where the services have been held, the minister will lead the procession in front of the casket to the casket coach. The same will hold true from the casket coach to the lowering service, and the minister will take his place at the head of the grave.

Flowers may be handled according to local custom, as well as all other aspects of the committal.

The Southern Baptist Convention
Informant: JAMES W. MERRITT, *Senior Secretary, National Headquarters*

"Neither the Southern Baptist Convention, nor the various State Baptist Conventions exercise control over the pastors in the various churches." The foregoing is one of the paragraphs in a letter of information.

The following may be determined from the additional information.

They do not feel the need of the clergy when death is imminent or sudden, from a ritualistic view. The clergy would appreciate being called when a member of his congregation passes away so that he may contact the family.

They have no church opinion, ritual, or rules regarding the removal, embalming, dressing, encasketing, cremation, earth or mausoleum interment. All this may be accomplished and arranged for in the usual manner.

There are no specific services to prepare for prior to the regular funeral service.

The place of the service, selection of casket bearers and music, may generally be accomplished by the family without restriction.

If the services are held at the church the entire procedure may be determined by local church custom, as well as arranging the flowers.

929

The exit from the place where the services have been held to the awaiting casket coach, and from the coach to the lowering device, as well as the entire committal, may be determined by local custom.

Free Will Baptists
Informant: REVEREND W. S. MOONEYHAM, *Executive Secretary, National Headquarters*

This group does not feel it is necessary that a member of the clergy be present when death is imminent or sudden.

This church has no opinions, rules, or ritual regarding the removal, embalming, dressing, encasketing, cremation, earth or mausoleum interment. This may be taken care of and arranged in the usual manner.

There are no services to prepare for prior to the regular funeral service. No special equipment is needed on or about the encasketed remains.

For members of the church, they would prefer the services be held in the church, but for non-members they would prefer they be held in the mortuary.

If the services are held at the church there are no special procedures of arrival. The casket will be placed directly in front of the pulpit in the usual manner.

The family is free to select the casket bearers, and suitable music.

Local custom may be your guide in taking the casket down to the pulpit; the floral arrangements may be governed by local custom. They usually have a closed casket service, opening the casket after the service is over and escorting the people by the deceased.

On leaving the building in which the services have been held, the minister usually takes the lead. He does the same from the casket coach to the lowering device at the cemetery and takes his place at the head of the casket.

There are no special rules regarding the funeral music.

General Baptists
Informant: REVEREND OLLIE LATCH, *Clerk, National Headquarters*

It is desirable but not required that a minister be present when death is imminent or sudden.

Since there are no rules, ritual, or opinions on removal, embalming, earth or mausoleum interment, dressing, or encasketing, this may be accomplished and arranged for in the usual manner.

They do, however, frown on the practice of cremation, but no official opinions are expressed on it.

There is no special equipment needed on or about the encasketed remains. There are no pre-funeral services to prepare for. They would prefer that the funeral service be held in the church.

If the services are held at the church, procedure of arrival may be governed by local custom. The casket should be placed near the pulpit or altar rail prior to arrival of the congregation. The floral displays may be handled according to local custom.

Local custom may prevail whether the services will be a closed or open casket procedure.

The family is not restricted in any way as to selection of casket bearers. Funeral service music may be the usual selections.

On leaving the building where the services have been held, the minister will walk ahead of the casket. The minister would probably prefer to ride in a private car, or with the funeral director, to the

930

cemetery, rather than in the casket coach.

The minister will take the lead from the casket coach to the lowering device and stand at the head of the grave.

It is suggested that the funeral director work with the minister, ascertaining his personal choices. No set form is required in this church.

Baptist General Conference of America
Informant: WILLIAM C. TAPPER, *Executive Secretary, National Headquarters*

This church does not consider it a necessity that a member of their clergy be present when death is imminent or sudden.

They have no opinion, ritual, or rules regarding the removal, embalming, dressing, encasketing, cremation, earth or mausoleum interment. This may be taken care of and arranged in the usual manner.

There are no services to prepare for prior to the regular funeral service, and no special equipment is needed on or about the encasketed remains.

The family is free to select the casket bearers, music and place of service without restriction.

If the services are held at the church, local church custom will prevail. However, the casket will generally be placed in front of the pulpit before arrival of the congregation.

On leaving the place where the services have been held, the minister will take the lead in front of the casket to the awaiting casket coach. The same procedure will hold true in the cemetery en route to the lowering device from the casket coach, and the minister will take his place at the head of the grave.

The balance of the committal may be accomplished with local custom governing.

The North American Baptist General Conference
Informant: REVEREND FRANK H. WOYKE, *Executive Secretary, National Headquarters*

Since Baptist Churches are autonomous, local customs are prevalent and not dictated by the Conference.

The group does not deem it a necessity that a member of their clergy be present when death is imminent or sudden from a ritualistic standpoint. They would like to be called for the comfort of the family.

The church has no rules, opinions, or rituals regarding the removal, embalming, dressing, encasketing, earth or mausoleum interment. They have no official voice in the matter of cremation, but it is not generally practiced.

There are no specific services to prepare for prior to the regular funeral service. No special equipment is needed on or about the encasketed remains. The place of service may be determined by local custom and wishes of the family.

If the services are held at the church, the manner in which the casket is handled may be determined by local custom. It is usually placed in the church prior to arrival of the congregation, and usually is open during the service.

The family is free to select the casket bearers and music without restriction.

On leaving the place where the services have been held the minister will take the lead to the casket coach, and the same will hold true from the casket coach to the lowering device at the cemetery.

931

Lowering the casket is not required from a ritualistic standpoint, but is generally practiced as such.

General Conference of Seventh Day Baptists

Informant: A. BURDET CROFOOT, *Executive Secretary, National Headquarters*

This church does not deem it a necessity that a member of the clergy be present when death is imminent or sudden. They have no opinion, rules, or ritual regarding the removal, embalming, dressing, encasketing, cremation, earth or mausoleum interment.

There are no services to prepare for prior to the regular funeral service, and no special equipment is needed on or about the encasketed remains.

The family is free to select the music, casket bearers, and place of service without restriction. There is some preference for the church but nothing definite.

If the services are held at the church, local church custom may determine the method in which the casket is handled. It is usually placed in front of the pulpit before arrival of the congregation. Flowers may be handled according to local custom.

On leaving the place where the services have been held, the minister will take the lead to the awaiting casket coach.

Local custom may determine all aspects of the committal service.

Buddist Churches of America

Informant: REVEREND S. NAITO, *Executive Secretary, National Headquarters*

This church deems it a necessity that a minister give a short service immediately after death has taken place.

There is no opinion, rules, or ritual regarding the removal of the deceased to the mortuary, embalming, earth or mausoleum interment, but it is a custom to cremate their dead. Dressing and encasketing may be accomplished in the usual manner. Frequently there is a wake prior to the regular funeral service.

There is no special equipment needed on or about the encasketed remains.

The place of service may be determined by the family of the deceased.

If the services are at the church, local custom is to place the casket at the front of the church near the altar. The head of the deceased should be on the left. The casket is left open and usually a casket veil is used.

The casket should be taken down the center aisle of the church after the congregation has been seated as a matter of formality.

The floral offerings may be taken care of according to local custom, and the family is free to select the casket bearers without restriction.

The music is provided by the church.

On leaving the place where the services have been held, the minister will lead the procession to the awaiting casket coach with the family following immediately behind the casket.

The minister would prefer not to ride in the casket coach to the crematory. At the crematory another short service will take place very similar to the first service.

Bulgarian Eastern Orthodox Church

Informant: KALINA MIHAYLOVSKA, *Secretary, National Headquarters*

This church deems it a necessity that a member of the clergy be present when death is imminent or sudden.

They have no rules, ritual, or opinions on the removal, embalming, earth or mausoleum interment. Cremation is forbidden.

The deceased must be ritualistically washed and dressed before encasketing.

The Trisagio will be prayed prior to the regular funeral service.

While the deceased is lying in state, candles, a cross or icon will be placed about the encasketed remains.

All funeral services should be held from the church. The priest will lead the procession to the church. The encasketed remains will be taken into the church feet first toward the altar. The services are conducted with the casket open.

When leaving the place where the services have been held, the priest will precede the casket to the awaiting casket coach. The priest will probably prefer to ride in the casket coach next to the driver to offer prayers.

The priest will walk on the right side of the casket from the casket coach to the lowering device and take his place at the head of the grave. The casket is lowered as part of the committal ritual and all present will sprinkle dirt or flower petals thereon.

There is no music during the service and the family is free to select casket bearers without restriction. The flowers may be handled according to local custom.

Roman Catholic Church
Informant: REVEREND FATHER AUGUSTINE CORTEZ, *S.F., et al Del Norte, Colorado*

In case of sudden or imminent death a priest should always be called to administer the Sacrament of Extreme Unction.

If the individual has wilfully taken his own life, the church will not permit the funeral mass to be celebrated in the church.

They have no rules, opinions, or ritual regarding the removal, embalming, dressing (of laymen), earth or mausoleum interment. Cremation is forbidden. If the deceased is a priest or nun, the priest will be dressed in his Eucharistic Vestments; if a nun she will be vested in her usual habit.

In most cases, a Rosary will be recited at the church, mortuary, or home the evening prior to the regular funeral Mass. If the Rosary is recited at the home or mortuary, the floral arrangements may be taken care of according to local custom. In all probability, the floral arrangement will be curtailed in the church. Some churches will permit the floral displays as far as the altar rail, some will not permit them in the church door. Absolutely no flowers are to be on the casket while in the church.

In most cases, while the remains are lying in state, a crucifix is placed directly behind and higher than the casket. One burning taper is placed at the head of the casket and one at the foot. A prayer rail is placed in front and along the side of the casket toward the foot end. This equipment is not required, but customary.

The funeral Mass must be officiated in the church, and in most cases at some hour before noon.

Plan the cortege to arrive at the church just at the time set for the Mass. The priest will receive the encasketed remains at the front, or main entrance of the church. If the deceased is a layman or nun, the casket is taken into the church feet first; if a priest, head first. After the receiving priest blesses the casket and starts down the aisle toward the altar, the casket will follow, with the casket bearers immediately ahead or alongside of the casket. The casket bearers should be given their instructions as to where to sit. In most cases, they will take the first pew on the left side of the church, while the family sits in the first pew on the right side. The family will immediately follow the casket while the friends follow the family. If the deceased is a priest, the casket is frequently left open; if a layman or nun it is always closed. In many cases a pall is used over the casket.

Presuming the deceased is a layman, the casket is taken within a few feet of the altar rail and placed at a right angle with the altar rail, feet toward the altar rail. Be sure enough room is left around the casket for the priest to move about it.

There may be six candles at the church, three to be placed along each side of the casket.

After the funeral Mass, the priest will officiate the ritual of libera with the use of holy water and incense. He may do this immediately after the Mass or after the sermon following the Mass.

After the libera or sermon, whichever is last, the funeral director, with his assistant, will proceed toward the altar to retrieve the casket. In most cases, the casket bearers will precede the casket to the main exit, the family will immediately follow the casket with the friends making their exit from the pews after the casket has passed their pew going toward the main exit. Local church custom may determine if the casket should be opened at the door.

At the cemetery, the priest will take his place at the foot end of the grave. Among the Spanish of the Southwest, the casket is customarily lowered when the priest finishes the committal. Local custom may govern elsewhere.

The Christian and Missionary Alliance
Informant: H. E. NELSON, *Home Secretary*

This group has no rules, ritual, or opinions on the need of a member of the clergy to be present at the time of, or immediately after, a death occurs. Neither do they set forth opinions on embalming, cremation, mausoleum, or earth interment.

The place of service, selection of casket bearers, etc., may be made by the family without restriction.

There are no services to prepare for prior to the regular funeral service, and no special equipment is needed on or about the encasketed remains.

If the services are held at the church, local custom may determine the method of arrival, the way the casket is handled during and after the service, etc.

Local custom may determine the entire committal service.

Christian Reformed Church
Informant: DR. R. J. DANHOF, *Stated Clerk, National Headquarters*

From a ritualistic view, it is not necessary that a member of the clergy be present when death is imminent or sudden.

They have no rules, opinions, or ritual regarding the removal, embalming, dressing or encasketing. They do not believe that cremation is a biblical precept and prefer earth or mausoleum interment.

There are no services to prepare for prior to the regular funeral services, and no special equipment is

934

needed on or about the encasketed remains.

The place of service, selection of music and casket bearers may be left to the family without restriction.

If the services are held in the church, procedure of arrival and how the casket is handled before, during, and after the service may be governed by local church custom.

On leaving the place where the services have been held, the minister will take the lead to the awaiting casket coach. The same will hold true in the cemetery from the casket coach to the lowering device.

The committal may be governed in all aspects by local custom.

Church of Christ, Scientist
Informant: MRS. CATHERINE G. RUNNER, *Corresponding Secretary National Headquarters*

The manual of The Mother Church by Mary Baker Eddy, has made no provisions for funeral services, and any services held are of an unofficial nature. No rulings or procedures are given out by The Mother Church, and for this reason the matter is left to the judgment of those concerned. Frequently, the services are conducted by a Reader from a branch church, but any experienced Christian Scientist, man or woman, may be called upon to act in this capacity.

In view of the fact that there are no rules from the church, whatever is planned between the family, funeral director and persons officiating will not be contrary to the views of the church.

Church of God (Anderson, Indiana)
Informant: LAWRENCE E. BROOKS, *Secretary, National Headquarters*

The Church of God has never formulated any definite funeral procedure, but the following is generally accepted as church custom.

While it is not deemed necessary for a clergyman to be present when death is imminent or sudden, from a ritualistic view, the wise clergyman will be on hand at the earliest moment.

The church has no opinions, rules, or ritual regarding the removal, embalming, dressing, encasketing, cremation, earth or mausoleum interment. All this may be taken care of and arranged in the usual manner.

There are no services to prepare for prior to the regular funeral service, and no special equipment is needed on or about the encasketed remains.

In most cases they would prefer the funeral service to be held from the church.

If the services are held at the church, local church custom may determine the procedure. The casket is usually placed in front of the pulpit, closed. It may be opened after the service.

The family is free to select the casket bearers and music without restriction, as long as the music selected is compatible with the local church.

On leaving the place where the services have been held, the minister will take the lead in front of the casket to the awaiting casket coach. The same formation will hold true at the cemetery from the casket coach to the lowering device, where the minister will take his place at the head of the grave.

The balance of the committal may be governed by local custom.

Church of God (Cleveland, Tennessee)
Informant: H. D. WILLIAMS, *General Secretary, National Headquarters*

This church would like to have

their clergyman present when death is imminent or sudden.

They have no opinions, rules, or ritual, regarding the removal, embalming, dressing, encasketing, cremation, earth or mausoleum interment. These procedures may be accomplished in the usual manner.

No special equipment is needed on or about the encasketed remains. The only service prior to the regular service may be a prayer at the home of the family of the deceased.

They would prefer the service be held in the church, but no ruling is in force from the church.

Local custom may determine the procedure of arrival, how, when, and where the casket is handled in the church, as long as it is placed near the altar rail.

Flowers may be taken care of according to local custom.

When leaving the place where the services have been held, the clergyman prefers to lead the way to the casket coach in front of the casket.

The same processional formation will take place from the casket coach to the lowering device. Local custom may determine the balance of the procedure in the committal.

The Church of God
(Queensvillage, New York)
Informant: BISHOP HOMER A. TOMLINSON, *General Overseer, National Headquarters*

This church does not deem it a necessity that a clergyman be present when death is imminent or sudden.

They have no opinions, rules, or ritual regarding the removal, embalming, cremation, earth or mausoleum interment, dressing, or encasketing the deceased. This may be done in the usual manner.

There are no services to prepare for prior to the regular funeral service, and no special equipment is needed on or about the encasketed remains.

There are no rules to determine where the services must be held. If they are held at the church, the procedure of arrival, and how the casket is handled in the church may be governed by local custom.

The family may select the music and casket bearers without restriction.

Local custom may also determine the method used in the procession from the place the services are held to the casket coach and from the casket coach to the lowering device over the grave.

Local custom may determine the entire course of the committal.

Churches of God in North America
Informant: REVEREND C. C. GEORGE, *Clerk, National Headquarters*

This church usually has a member of the clergy present when death is imminent or sudden, but it is not necessary for any specified ritualistic procedure.

They express no official opinions, rules, or ritual in regard to the removal, embalming, dressing, encasketing, cremation, earth or mausoleum interment. This may be taken care of and arranged in the usual manner.

There are no services to prepare for prior to the regular funeral service, and no special equipment is needed on or about the encasketed remains.

The family is free to select the casket bearers, place of service and music without restriction.

The flowers may be handled according to local custom.

If the services are held at the church, local church custom may dictate the procedure in all aspects.

The procedure in leaving the place where the services have been held, arrival and procedure of the committal may be handled according to local custom.

Pentecostal Church of God

Informant: REVEREND R. DENNIS HEARD, *General Superintendent, National Headquarters*

This church does not deem it a necessity that a member of the clergy be present when death is imminent or sudden.

They have no rules, opinions, or ritual regarding the removal, embalming, dressing, or encasketing. Earth burial is preferred, but there is no objection to a full mausoleum crypt interment. Cremation is definitely objected to.

There are no services to prepare for prior to the regular funeral service, and no special equipment is needed on or about the encasketed remains.

The family is free to select the place of service, casket bearers, etc., without restriction. The music must be religious and not secular or purely sentimental.

If the services are held in the church the casket is placed between the pulpit and altar, opened, before arrival of the congregation. Flowers may be handled according to local custom.

On leaving the place where the services have been held, the minister will lead the procession to the awaiting casket coach. The same formation will hold true at the cemetery, and the minister will take his place at the head of the grave. Most ministers use flowers in the committal, in place of sand or dirt.

The remainder of the committal may be governed by local custom.

Church of Jesus Christ of Latter-Day Saints (Mormon)

Informant: A. WILLIAM LUND, *Assistant Church Historian, National Headquarters*

The bishopric of a ward or the presidency of a branch in which one of the members dies goes immediately to the family and offers their services and condolences. They try very hard to carry out all of the wishes of the family in respect to music, speakers, casket bearers, and place and time of the funeral service.

The Church of Jesus Christ of Latter Day Saints have no paid or employed ministers. The officiating is done in its entirety by local residents, who have official positions in the church.

They do not deem the presence of an official necessary when death is imminent or sudden.

They have no ritual as to removal of the deceased to the mortuary for embalming. They discourage cremation and state that "no prayer should be offered during or following a cremation ceremony." The church prefers an earth burial but has no objection to mausoleum interment.

If the deceased has had the Temple Ordinances, they are dressed by their own officials, usually in white. If they have not had Temple Ordinances, it may be handled in the usual manner.

There are no services to prepare for prior to the regular funeral service, and no special equipment is needed on or about the encasketed remains.

It is preferred that the funeral service be held at the church, but no objection is noted on having it at any other place.

If the services are held at the church, how and when the casket is taken down the aisle and placed in front of the pulpit may be determined by local custom. Local custom may determine the method of floral displays.

The casket must be closed during the funeral service and not opened afterward, if the services are held at the church. On leaving the church, the casket is first followed by the relatives, then friends.

There are no rituals or rules in regard to taking the remains from the casket coach to the lowering device. The official selected to perform the committal will stand at the head of the grave.

The Reorganized Church of Jesus Christ of Latter-Day Saints
Informant: ISRAEL A. SMITH, *President, National Headquarters*

This church does not deem it a necessity that a church official be present when death is imminent or sudden.

They have no opinions, rules, or ritual regarding the removal, embalming, dressing, encasketing, cremation, earth or mausoleum interment. This may be accomplished and arranged for in the usual manner.

There are no services to prepare for prior to the regular funeral service, and no special equipment is needed on or about the encasketed remains.

The family may select the casket bearers, place of service, and music without restriction.

If the services are held at the church, local church custom will prevail in all aspects.

The procedure of leaving the place where the services have been held, and interment at the cemetery, may be governed by local custom.

Church of the Nazarene
Informant: R. R. HODGES, *Assistant to General Secretary, National Headquarters*

This denomination does not require the presence of a minister when death is imminent or sudden.

This church has no ritual, rules or opinions on embalming, dressing, encasketing, cremation, earth or mausoleum interment. This may be handled and arranged for in the usual manner.

Sometimes the local minister would like to have some type of prefuneral service at the mortuary.

No special equipment is needed on or about the encasketed remains.

With this group there is no requirement that the service be held at the church or mortuary, however, most of the Nazarene services are held from the church.

The family is free to select the music and casket bearers without restriction.

If the services are held at the church, there are no specifications as to procedure of arrival. The casket is placed near the altar rail before arrival of the congregation. In most cases they like to have an open casket service, viewing the remains after completion of the service.

On leaving the church, the minister prefers to walk with the funeral director in front of the casket.

At the cemetery, the minister will lead the procession to the lowering device. Individual preference will determine whether the minister stands at the head or foot of the grave. The rest of the committal will be according to local custom.

The funeral music is usually furnished by the local church members. The policy of the Church of the Nazarene is to leave all minor details to the preference of the individual or local congregations.

General Council Congregational Christian Churches
Informant: FRED S. BUSCHMEYER, *Director, Department of Ministry*

This church does not demand the presence of the clergy when death is imminent or sudden, neither have they rules, ritual, or opinions on the removal, embalming, dressing, encasketing, cremation, earth or mausoleum interment.

There are no services to prepare for prior to the regular funeral service, and no special equipment is needed on or about the encasketed remains.

They prefer the services to be held at the church, but no rules exist regarding this.

The casket is usually placed in the church prior to the arrival of the congregation, but local custom may determine how it is otherwise handled. It is generally closed during the services.

Flowers may be taken care of according to local custom.

When leaving the place where the services have been held the minister will precede the casket to the casket coach. The same will hold true from the casket coach to the lowering device.

The family is free to select the music, casket bearers, etc., without restriction.

Disciples of Christ, International Convention
Informant: GAINES M. COOK, *Executive Secretary, National Headquarters*

This church does not deem it a necessity that a member of their clergy be present when death is imminent or sudden.

They have no opinions, ritual, or rules regarding the removal, embalming, dressing, encasketing, cremation, earth or mausoleum interment. All this may be taken care of and arranged in the usual manner.

There are no services to prepare for prior to the regular funeral service, and no special equipment is needed on or about the casket.

The place of service, casket bearers and music may be determined by the family without restriction, however, the music should be hymns of faith.

If the services are held at the church, local church custom may determine how the casket is handled in all aspects of the church service, except it is desired that the casket be closed during the service.

Flowers may be handled according to local custom.

On leaving the building where the services have been held, the minister will precede the casket to the awaiting casket coach. On arrival at the cemetery the same will hold true, and the minister will take his place at the head of the grave. The minister would probably not prefer to ride in the casket coach, but may wish to furnish his own car.

The balance of the committal may be governed by local custom.

The Protestant Episcopal Church
Informant:
RIGHT REV. JOSEPH S. MINNIS, D.D., *Bishop, Diocese Headquarters*

The Rector of the parish, or priest in charge of a mission has complete authority over all services in his church. He must be consulted before any arrangements for any services are made.

The church deems it a necessity that a priest be notified when death is imminent or sudden.

The church has no opinion, rules

939

or ritual on the removal, embalming, dressing (for laymen), encasketing, cremation, earth or mausoleum interment. This may be arranged in the usual manner.

The officiating priest should be consulted regarding any pre-funeral service, and the use of special equipment on or about the encasketed remains.

All services for Episcopalians should be held in the church. A family may request a Requiem Mass, as well as the burial office in the Book of Common Prayer. Sometimes the Requiem Mass is officiated in the morning, and the burial office from the Book of Common Prayer in the afternoon.

The family is free to select the casket bearers without restriction. The music should be from the church hymnal. For any other selections consult the local priest for sanction. (Example: Lord's Prayer.) The local priest should be consulted regarding floral displays in the church.

If the services are held at the church, the funeral cortege should arrive on the hour appointed for the service. The priest will meet the casket at the casket coach or door of the church and precede same down the center aisle of the church, feet first (priest head first) and place in the nave with feet toward the altar. In all probability a pall will be used over the casket. The casket is closed and not opened again.

When leaving the place where the funeral services have been held, the priest will lead the procession alone. He may be preceded by a processional cross. The same formation will hold true in the cemetery from the casket coach to the lowering device.

If possible the priest will stand at the head of the grave. The priest sprinkles sand (never flower petals) on the casket. Consult the local priest whether to lower the casket as part of ritualistic service.

The local Episcopal Church may be what is called High or Low Church. One church may differ from another in certain minor aspects regarding the service, that is why it is advisable to consult the local priest regarding most aspects of the service.

Reformed Episcopal Church
Informant:
REVEREND THEOPHILUS J. HERTER,
*Secretary, General Council,
National Headquarters*

Imminent or sudden death does not require the presence of the clergy as a necessity of "last rites," but his presence is appropriate.

The church has no opinions, rules, or ritual regarding the removal, embalming, dressing, encasketing, earth or mausoleum interment. Some pastors may not favor cremation.

There are no services to prepare for prior to the regular funeral service.

There is no official church decision as to where the funeral services may be held.

If the services are held in the church, the casket should be taken to the front of the church and placed on the congregation side of the altar rail, before arrival of the congregation. There is no opinion as to whether the casket should be open or closed during the service. Palls may be used over the casket which would necessitate that it be closed.

After the services, the minister will lead, alone, in front of the casket to the awaiting casket coach. The same formation will follow from the casket coach to the lowering device. The minister will take his place at the head of the grave. The funeral director may be asked to sprinkle sand on the casket as a ritualistic procedure.

Before the committal begins, the casket will be lowered until the top of the casket is on the same level as the ground.

Evangelical Covenant Church of America
Informant:
REVEREND JOSEPH C. DANIELSON, *Secretary, National Headquarters*

This church does not deem it a necessity from a ritualistic view that a clergyman be present when death is imminent or sudden. Frequently the family may call the clergy however.

They have no opinion, rules, or ritual regarding embalming, dressing, encasketing, cremation, earth or mausoleum interment. All this may be accomplished and arranged for in the usual manner.

The only service that may occur before the regular funeral service, may be a service with the family. It will probably not involve the mortuary service.

No special equipment is needed on or about the encasketed remains.

The family will have much latitude in determining the place of service. Selection of casket bearers and music may be made without restriction.

The method used in handling the casket in the church may be left in its entirety to local church custom.

In most cases, when leaving the building where the services have been held, the minister will take the lead to the awaiting casket coach. The same will probably hold true at the cemetery when en route to the lowering device from the casket coach.

The entire committal service may be conducted according to local custom.

Evangelical and Reformed Churches
Informant:
REVEREND W. SHERMAN KERSCHNER, *Secretary, National Headquarters*

Many of the church procedures in a funeral service are left to local clergyman. They have no stated opinion of the necessity of the clergyman's presence when death is imminent or sudden.

They have no rules, ritual, or opinions on the removal, embalming, dressing, encasketing, cremation, earth or mausoleum interment.

There is no set ritualistic service to prepare for prior to the regular funeral service. No special equipment is needed on or about the encasketed remains.

The place of service, music, and selection of casket bearers, may be determined by the family without church restriction.

If the services are held at the church, local custom in agreement with the local minister may prevail. The same holds true in leaving the church, arrival at the cemetery, and the committal service.

Evangelical United Brethren Churches
Informant: PAUL V. CHURCH, *Conference Superintendent, National Headquarters*

This church does not deem it a necessity for clergymen to be present when death is imminent or sudden.

They have no opinions, rules, or ritual regarding the removal, embalming, dressing, encasketing, cremation, earth or mausoleum interment. This may be accomplished and arranged for in the usual manner.

A service may be held in the

941

home prior to the regular service. No special equipment is needed on or about the encasketed remains.

The place of service, selection of casket bearers, and music may be determined by the family without restriction.

If the services are held in the church, the procedure of arrival and how the casket is handled therein may be determined by local church custom.

The minister will stand at the head of the grave during the committal service, otherwise the entire committal may be determined by local custom.

International Foursquare Gospel Evangelism
Informant: ROLF K. MCPHERSON, D.D., *President, National Headquarters*

This church does not deem it necessary that a member of the clergy be notified when death is imminent or sudden from any ritualistic view, but the minister may render comfort to the family at such a time.

They have no rules, ritual, or opinions on the removal, embalming, dressing, encasketing, earth or mausoleum interment. Cremation is frowned upon.

There are no services to prepare for prior to the regular funeral service, and no special equipment is needed on or about the encasketed remains.

In regards to the place of service, if the deceased has been prominent in the church, and an anticipated congregation would do justice to the seating capacity, then the church should be used; if not, the services may be held elsewhere. Consult the local clergyman as to the way the casket will be placed during the service.

The casket should be placed and opened before arrival of the congregation.

The family is generally free to select the casket bearers and music without restriction. The flowers may be handled according to local custom.

When leaving the place where the service has been held, the minister leads the procession from the door to the casket coach and will do the same from the casket coach to the lowering device, and take his place at the head of the grave.

The balance of the committal may be governed by local custom.

Religious Society of Friends, Five Year Meetings
Informant: RUSSEL E. REES, *Assistant Secretary, National Headquarters*

The presence of clergy is not necessary when death is imminent or sudden.

The removal, embalming, dressing, encasketing, etc., may be accomplished in the usual manner.

The church has no opinion as to cremation, earth or mausoleum interment. No special equipment is needed and there is no official preference whether the funeral services are held at the mortuary or church. If services are held at the church, the arrival, entry, placement of casket, etc., may be ruled by local custom. Flowers and floral display may be guided by local custom.

Having an open or closed casket service may be ruled by local custom, and the family is not restricted in any way regarding selection of casket bearers.

Local custom may govern the method in leaving the place where the services have been held, as well as procedure after arrival at the cemetery.

Friends generally use a very sim-

942

ple Protestant service. Occasionally, this Society will wish a meeting for worship based on silence to be part of the funeral service.

Greek Orthodox Church (Hellenic)
Informant: REVEREND GEORGE PAPADEAS, *Secretary, Mixed Council of the Greek Archdiocese of North and South America, National Headquarters*

This church does not deem it a necessity that a priest be called when death is imminent or sudden.

They have no rules, ritual, or opinions as to the removal, embalming, dressing, encasketing, earth or mausoleum interment. Cremation is forbidden.

The family is free to select the casket bearers without restriction.

The church custom is to have a short service at the mortuary prior to the regular funeral service. The church wishes candles at each end of the casket with a Holy Icon at the casket.

All funerals should be held from the church. The priest precedes the procession into the church. The casket will be taken down the aisle, feet first, and placed near the altar in special open area for ceremonials, with feet nearest the altar. The bereaved will follow the casket into the church and down the center aisle.

As for funeral music, only the Greek Orthodox will be read.

The church has no rules regarding flowers or floral displays. The casket must be open during the funeral services.

When leaving the church, the priest will precede the casket.

At the committal, the priest will stand at the side of the grave. There are no specifications or rules regarding taking the casket from the casket coach to the lowering device.

Union of American Hebrew Congregations
Informant: EUGENE J. LIPMAN, *Director of Synagogue Activities, National Headquarters*

When death is imminent or sudden, this group prefers that a member of their clergy be notified as soon as possible.

They have no ritual, rules, or opinions on the removal, embalming, dressing, encasketing, cremation, earth or mausoleum interment. They have a preference for earth burial but no official opinion has been voiced.

This denomination has no specification regarding the casket the family may prefer.

They prefer the funeral services be held at the mortuary, except for congregational leaders and clergy. If the deceased is a congregational leader or clergy, there are no regulations as to procedure of arrival at the synagogue.

There are no specifications, except local, as to how the casket should be placed in the synagogue, but the casket should be so placed before arrival of the congregation.

While there is no opinion as to whether the casket should be opened or closed during the service, it is preferred that it be closed, and not opened again at any time.

Floral arrangements are designed by local custom.

There are no restrictions as to whom the family may select as casket bearers.

There are no specifications other than local custom in taking the remains from the building in which the funeral services have been held to the awaiting casket coach.

The clergy would prefer to ride with the family from the place the services have been held to the ceme-

943

tery. On arrival at the cemetery, the clergy will take the lead to the lowering device, ahead of the casket, and the family will follow the casket. After the casket has been placed on the lowering device, the clergy will stand at the head. While this group does not prefer the casket to be lowered as part of the committal, local custom may prevail.

The foregoing applies only to Reform Jewish funerals; Conservative and Orthodox rituals vary considerably.

Holy Orthodox Church in America (Eastern Catholic and Apostolic)

Informant: MOST REVEREND ARCHBISHOP THEODOTIS S. DEWITOW, *National Headquarters*

This church deems it a necessity that a priest be present when death is imminent or sudden.

They have no ritual regarding the removal, embalming, dressing for the laity (Eucharistic vestments for priest), and encasketing. This may be accomplished in the usual manner.

Cremation and mausoleum interment are forbidden. Earth burial is mandatory.

There may be a short service held at the home of the deceased prior to the regular funeral Mass.

The usual special equipment will be used about the encasketed remains while the decedent is lying in state.

The funeral services must be held in the church.

Procedure of arrival at the church will be accomplished according to ritual. The casket will be taken in the church and down the center aisle to the altar rail and placed according to Catholic ritual.

Flowers may be handled according to local custom, and the casket is closed during the service except in the case of clergy. It is preferred that it not be opened again.

The family is free to select the casket bearers without restriction.

On leaving the church the priest will take the lead from the church to the casket coach followed by the funeral director. The same will hold true from the casket coach to the grave. The priest would prefer going to the cemetery in a car other than the casket coach.

After the casket has been placed on the lowering device, the priest will take his stand near the head of the grave. Immediately after conclusion of the committal ritual the casket will be lowered.

Suggest reference be made to the Roman Catholic procedure, as there is great similarity in most particulars.

Independent Fundamental Churches of America

Informant: JOSEPH W. HANCIOM, *Acting National Executive Secretary, National Headquarters*

It is not necessary that a member of the clergy be present when death is imminent or sudden.

There are no rules, ritual, or opinions as to removal, embalming, dressing, encasketing, earth or mausoleum interment. This may be accomplished and arranged for in the usual manner.

Cremation is forbidden. We quote their answer to this question on the original questionnaire: "We believe, according to the scriptures, that the body should not be destroyed."

There are no services to prepare for prior to the regular funeral service, and no special equipment is needed on or about the encasketed remains.

The church leaves the matter of where the services are to be held up to the relatives of the deceased.

944

If the services are held at the church, the procedure of arrival, how, when, or where the casket is handled is entirely according to local custom.

The music and selection of casket bearers is left up to relatives of the deceased.

The floral displays may be handled according to local custom.

The actions of the minister on departure from the place where the services have been held, and from the casket coach to the grave are a matter of local custom.

The entire committal may be governed by local custom.

Jehovah's Witnesses
(Watchtower Bible and Tract Society)
National Headquarters

This church has no opinions, ritual, or rules, regarding the necessity of the clergyman when death is imminent or sudden, removal, embalming, dressing, encasketing, cremation, earth or mausoleum interment. All this may be taken care of and arranged in the usual manner.

There are no services to prepare for prior to the regular funeral service, and no special equipment is needed on or about the encasketed remains.

The family is free to select the place of service, casket bearers, and music without restriction.

Flowers may be handled according to local custom.

The procedure when leaving the place where the services have been held, arrival at the cemetery, and entire committal may be governed by local custom.

American Lutheran Church
Informant: HENRY F. SCHUH, *President,*
National Headquarters

This church does not deem it a necessity that a member of the clergy be present when death is sudden or imminent, neither do they have any opinion, rules, or ritual on the removal, embalming, dressing, encasketing, cremation, earth or mausoleum interment. This may be arranged for in the usual manner.

There are no services to prepare for prior to the regular funeral service, and no special equipment is needed on or about the encasketed remains.

The family is free to select the casket bearers without restriction.

Flowers may be taken care of according to local custom.

The local pastor should be consulted regarding the music selected. It is preferred the services be held at the church.

If the services are held at the church, local church custom may govern all aspects of the procedure which is followed.

All aspects of the committal may be governed by the local pastor and custom.

Augustana Evangelical Lutheran Church
Informant: DR. D. VERNER SWANSON,
Secretary

This church does not deem it a necessity from a ritualistic view that a member of the clergy be present when death is imminent or sudden.

They express no opinion, rules, or ritual on the removal, embalming, dressing, encasketing, cremation, earth or mausoleum interment. This may be taken care of and arranged in the usual manner.

There are no services to prepare prior to the regular funeral service, and no special equipment is needed on or about the encasketed remains.

Some pastors prefer the church as the place for the funeral service, especially for members thereof. The

945

family is free to select the casket bearers and music without restriction, as long as the music is suitable.

The flowers may be handled according to local custom.

If the services are held at the church, local custom may rule the entire procedure.

On leaving the place where the services have been held, the minister will take the lead to the awaiting casket coach. The entire committal service is left to local custom.

Evangelical Lutheran Churches
Informant: REVEREND O. H .HOVE, *General Secretary, National Headquarters*

It is desirable that a clergyman be present when death is imminent but not required as church ritual.

There is no ritual, rules, or opinions, regarding the removal, embalming, dressing, encasketing, earth or mausoleum interment. This may be accomplished in the usual way.

Cremations are viewed with misgivings in some quarters, but no specific action is on record.

There may be a brief service with the family prior to the regular funeral service, but probably will not involve the mortuary service in any way.

They would like the service to be held from the church for its members, otherwise no opinions exist as to where the services should be held.

If the services are held at the church, the arrival, and how the casket is handled throughout the service may be determined by local custom, if agreeable with the pastor.

In most cases the casket is closed during the services. The casket may be opened after the service, but they would prefer the family and friends pay their last very personal respects at the mortuary while the remains are lying in state.

On leaving the place where the services have been held the minister will take the lead in front of the casket to the awaiting casket coach. The same will hold true at the cemetery. The minister probably will not wish to ride in the casket coach unless circumstances make it the sensible thing to do.

At the cemetery the minister will take his place at the head of the grave.

The funeral music should be hymns expressing Christian truth rather than sentimentality. The family is free to select the casket bearers without restriction. The flowers may be handled according to local custom.

A joint church service and a fraternal order service is frowned upon.

The United Lutheran Church in America
Informant: F. EPPLING REINARTZ, *Secretary, National Headquarters*

The information below is in no sense to be considered official church policy. It has been taken from information that was unofficial, and a personal reply for the requested information.

When death is imminent or sudden, church policy does not demand the presence of a clergyman, but the congregations are encouraged to give the clergyman an opportunity to minister to the dying. The service is an "Order for Commendation of the Dying." If no clergyman is present or available it may be used by the head of the family or any other Christian.

The church has no official opinion, rules, or ritual regarding embalming, dressing, encasketing, cremation (rare among members), earth or mausoleum interment. This may be

946

taken care of and arranged in the usual manner.

There is no pre-funeral service for the mortuary to prepare for, but when the remains are taken to the home prior to the funeral service, the clergyman frequently conducts a brief service of departure, just before the cortege moves to the church.

No special equipment is needed on or about the encasketed remains.

The church is advocated for the funeral services of members, otherwise there are no opinions as to where the services should be held.

If the services are held in the church, local church custom may determine the procedure used in entering the church, and how the casket is handled therein. The practice is increasing to have the foot of the casket toward the altar if the deceased is a layman, and the head of the casket toward the altar if the deceased is a clergyman.

In most cases, when the casket is taken into the church, it proceeds with the family following to the reserved pews. Only flowers of the immediate family should be taken into the chancel.

This church feels that all services should be of closed casket nature and the casket not to be opened again.

It is preferred that the family select Christians as casket bearers for the deceased. There are some congregations that use palls over the casket.

On leaving the place where the services have been held, the minister will lead the procession to the awaiting casket coach. The same formation will hold true from the casket coach to the lowering device. The minister will take his place about the casket where it is most convenient for the family to hear what is said.

If the funeral director takes part in an "earth to earth" committal, he should use earth or sand, not flower petals.

In regards to the lowering of the casket, the rubric says: "When the body has been committed to the grave, the minister may say . . . " If the committal is to be true in every sense, it would mean the lowering of the casket before the committal service begins. Local church custom may govern the procedure.

The music selected by the family should be historic hymns of Christian faith and hope.

Lutheran Church, Missouri Synod
Informant: Dr. M. F. Kretzmann,
Secretary, National Headquarters

While it is not mandatory that a clergyman be present when death is imminent or sudden, he is usually called.

The church has no opinion, rules, or ritual regarding the removal, embalming, dressing, encasketing, cremation, earth or mausoleum interment.

The church does provide a service prior to the regular funeral service, but does not require its execution.

No special equipment is needed on or about the encasketed remains.

The music must be sacred and devotional, but the family is free to select the place of service and casket bearers without restriction. The flowers may be handled according to local custom.

If the services are held at the church, the casket is usually taken down the center aisle as a matter of ritual and placed in front of the pulpit, after the congregation has arrived and been seated. Palls are rarely used.

947

On leaving the place where the services have been held, the minister will lead the procession to the awaiting casket coach. He may object to riding in the coach to the cemetery, and prefer to furnish his own car.

At the cemetery, the minister will again take the lead from the casket coach to the lowering device. There are no specifications as to where he should stand during the committal. The rest of the committal may be accomplished according to local custom.

The Norwegian Synod of the American Evangelical Lutheran Church
Informant:
Reverend Walther C. Gullixson,
Secretary, National Headquarters

The pastors of this church officiate only for professing Christians, and they wish to be called while there is time to counsel with the dying. There is no ritualistic reason to be called after time of death, except what comfort the family may need.

Gratuities should be decided by the family rather than the funeral director, and the church custodian should be included.

This church has no opinions, rules, or rituals regarding the removal, embalming, dressing, or encasketing. This may be accomplished and arranged for in the usual manner. There is no objection to mausoleum interment, but earth burial is preferred. Cremation is objected to.

At times a service is held in the home prior to the regular funeral service. Local inquiry may determine any action needed on the part of the funeral director.

There is no special equipment needed on or about the encasketed remains. All funeral services should be held from the church.

Local church custom may determine methods employed in arrival at the church and the way the casket is handled during the service. The casket is usually placed in the nave before the altar or chancel steps, closed.

There are no regulations regarding the casket bearers, except Christians are preferred.

The local pastor should be consulted regarding the selection of the music.

Local custom may determine the floral displays.

On leaving the place where the services have been held, the minister would prefer to lead the procession alone to the awaiting casket coach. The same will hold true at the cemetery from the casket coach to the lowering device. The minister will take his place at the head of the grave. The remainder of the committal will be governed by local custom.

In all probability, difficulty would be encountered if any lodge or organization had any part in the service or committal, especially if any lodge symbols were taken inside the church.

United Evangelical Lutheran Church
Informant: Reverend L. Siersbeck,
Secretary, National Headquarters

The church does not demand the presence of the clergy when death is imminent or sudden for any specific last rites, but if notified would come immediately for the family comfort.

The church has no opinions, ritual, or rules regarding the removal, embalming, dressing, encasketing, earth or mausoleum interment. They have no official opinion on cremation, but it is not widely accepted.

For the church members, it is

948

desirable that the services be held in the church.

There is a service provided prior to the regular service, but it is not mandatory. A check with the local pastor will indicate the procedure regarding this. No special equipment is needed on or about the encasketed remains.

If the services are held in the church, the casket will be placed in the center aisle at the front of the church, right angle to the altar. If a layman, the foot will be closest to the altar; if a pastor, the head will be closest to the altar. It should be so placed prior to the arrival of the congregation.

The casket will be closed during the service and a pall may be used.

The church chancel and furniture should not be covered with flowers, otherwise local custom may prevail.

It is preferred that the casket not be opened after the service.

When leaving the place where the services have been held, the minister will take the lead to the casket coach. The same will hold true from the casket coach to the lowering device, after which he will take his place in the most convenient position, usually at the head of the grave.

If secular organizations are involved in the committal, they must come after the benediction at the grave. They cannot be a part of the church ritual.

Lutheran Free Church
Informant:
REVEREND FORREST T. MONSON,
Secretary, National Headquarters

This church finds it desirable for a member of the clergy to be present when death is imminent or sudden, but it is not required.

They have no opinions, rules, or

ritual regarding the removal, embalming, dressing, encasketing, cremation, earth or mausoleum interment. This may be performed in the usual manner.

In some congregations, local custom calls for a service in the home prior to the regular funeral service.

There is no special equipment needed on or about the encasketed remains.

If the deceased is a member of the church, it is desirable that the funeral service be held in the church.

If the services are held in the church, a closed casket is taken to the front of the church and placed in the usual manner according to local church custom.

The remaining portion of the procedure in the church may be ruled by local church custom. The casket may be opened after the service.

On leaving the place where the services have been held, the minister will take the lead, alone, to the awaiting casket coach. The same procedure will hold true when en route to the lowering device from the casket coach. The minister will take his place at the head of the grave.

It is suggested that the funeral director have bottled sand on hand for the minister to use in the committal.

Music should consist of standard hymns.

Evangelical Lutheran Joint Synod of Wisconsin and Other States
Informant: THEODORE SAUER, *Secretary, National Headquarters*

This church does not deem it a necessity that a member of the clergy be present when death is imminent or sudden. They have no rules, ritual, or opinions on the removal, embalming, dressing, encas-

949

keting, earth or mausoleum interment. Cremation in general is avoided.

There is a service provided but not required prior to the regular funeral service. It is short and usually held for the benefit of the family on the same day, or perhaps, one hour before the regular service. It is usually held at the place where the remains are lying in state.

The family is free to select the place of service, and casket bearers without restriction, if agreeable to local custom. The local pastor should be consulted regarding the music selection.

If the services are held at the church, local custom may determine all aspects of it. Local custom may determine all aspects of the committal service.

Lutheran Synodical Conference of North America
Informant: WALTER A. BAEPLER, *President, National Headquarters*

This church does not deem it a necessity that a member of the clergy be called when death is imminent or sudden.

They have no rules, ritual, or opinions on the removal, embalming, encasketing, earth or mausoleum interment. Cremation will be tolerated only in an emergency.

Sometimes there is a private service prior to the regular funeral service. No special equipment is needed on or about the encasketed remains.

The church is preferred as the place for a funeral service. When the services are in the church, the casket may be placed near the altar rail, usually closed, in whatever method local church custom may dictate.

Music selected should have church approval.

It is preferred that the casket bearers be members of the church. Palls are optional.

After the service the minister will precede the procession to the casket coach. He would probably prefer not to ride in the casket coach.

The same procedure will hold true at the cemetery and the minister will take his place at the head of the grave.

The balance of the committal may be governed by local custom.

Mennonite Church
Informant: PAUL ERB, *Executive Secretary, National Headquarters*

This church does not deem it a necessity that a member of the clergy be present when death is sudden or imminent, neither have they rules, rituals, or opinions on the removal, embalming, dressing, encasketing, earth or mausoleum interment. Cremation is frowned upon.

There are no services to prepare for prior to the regular funeral service, and no special equipment is needed on or about the encasketed remains.

All services should be held at the church. If the services are held at the church, local church custom may govern the procedure followed throughout the service.

The family may select the casket bearers without restriction. The music will be provided by the church.

On leaving the place where the services have been held, the minister will lead the procession to the casket coach. At the cemetery the minister will take his station at the head of the grave.

The remainder of the committal may be governed by local custom.

950

The Methodist Church
(Washington, D. C.)
Informant: BISHOP G. BROMLEY OXNAM, *Secretary, National Headquarters*

It is not deemed necessary for a clergyman to be present at the time of imminent or sudden death. As a pastoral duty, they will call on the family immediately following death.

The church expresses no ritual, rules, or opinions on the removal, embalming, earth or mausoleum interment, dressing, or encasketing. This may be taken care of and arranged in the usual manner.

There are no services to prepare for prior to the regular funeral service. There is no special equipment needed on or about the encasketed remains.

There may be a preference that the funeral service be held in the church, but most pastors adjust to the present situation which increasingly involves the use of a chapel at the mortuary.

If the services are held at the church, the procedure of arrival may be governed by local custom. The casket is usually placed at the front of the chancel on the level of the main floor, but there is no requirement.

In regards to taking the casket down the center aisle, the Methodist ritual assumes that the minister will precede the casket as it is brought into the church. This would indicate the casket would be taken down the center aisle of the church as ritualistic procedure after the congregation had been seated.

Flowers may be handled according to local custom.

Whether the service is conducted with an open or closed casket may be governed by local custom.

The family may select the casket bearers and music without restriction as long as the music is considered suitable by the local minister.

On leaving the place where the services have been held, the minister will precede the casket to the casket coach. The same formation will hold true at the cemetery from the casket coach to the grave.

At the grave the minister may stand where most convenient. The remainder of the committal may be governed by local custom.

Wesleyan Methodist Church of America
Informant: REVEREND CARL BEAVER, *Secretary of the General Conference, National Headquarters*

This church does not consider it a necessity that a member of their clergy be present when death is imminent or sudden from any ritualistic view.

There are no official rules, ritual, or opinions on the removal, embalming, dressing, encasketing, earth or mausoleum interment. Cremation is not favored generally by the members of the church.

It is preferred that the services be held in the church for members, otherwise the family is free to select the music and casket bearers without restriction.

The floral arrangements may be taken care of according to local custom.

If the services are held at the church, local custom may determine the procedure of arrival and how the casket is placed in the church. Generally the casket is placed in front of the pulpit. Local custom may determine an open or closed casket service.

On leaving the place where the services have been held, the minister will lead the procession to the awaiting casket coach. The same formation will hold true at the cemetery from the casket coach to the lowering device. The minister will stand where most convenient to benefit the people.

The remainder of the committal may follow local custom.

Free Methodist Church of North America
Informant: L. R. MARSTON, *Chairman of Board of Bishops, National Headquarters*

This church has no defined policy, but it can be generally presumed the following will not be contrary to the church references.

The presence of a member of the clergy is not necessary from a ritualistic view, when death is imminent or sudden.

They have no opinions, rules, or ritual regarding the removal, embalming, dressing, encasketing, cremation, earth or mausoleum interment. All this may be arranged for in the usual manner.

There are no services for the mortuary to prepare for prior to the regular funeral service.

The family is generally free to select the casket bearers, place of service, and appropriate funeral music, without restriction.

If the services are held at the church, local church custom may prevail in all aspects.

The procedure when leaving the place where the services have been held may be governed by local custom, as well as the committal in all aspects.

African Methodist Episcopal Zion Church
Informant:
REVEREND F. CLAUDE SPURGEON, *General Secretary, National Headquarters*

The clergy attempts to see the family as soon as possible after a death of a member. They would appreciate being called and so notified. It is not necessary for a member of the clergy to be present when death is imminent or sudden.

The church has no ritual or rules regarding the removal and has no opinions on embalming, cremation, earth or mausoleum interment. They have no ritual to consider regarding the dressing or encasketing. There are no services to prepare for prior to the regular funeral service, and no special equipment is needed on or about the encasketed remains.

Whether the services are held in the church or mortuary is entirely up to the family, however, the minister would appreciate being called before a definite time and date of service has been set.

Casket bearers may be selected without restriction.

The funeral service music may be any suitable selections.

If the services are held in the church, local custom may govern the method of arrival and how the casket is placed at the altar rail. Local custom may also govern whether the casket is open or closed during the service, and whether it is opened after the service if it is a closed casket service. Palls are not regularly used over the casket.

On leaving the building in which a service has been held, the minister will walk in front of the casket with the funeral director to the casket coach. It might be well to ask the minister if he wishes to ride in the casket coach.

At the cemetery, the minister will again take the lead in front of the casket from the casket coach to the grave, and take his place at the head of the grave.

952

The casket is usually lowered in the grave as part of the committal ritual.

The Moravian Church in America (Northern Province)
Informant:
BISHOP KENNETH G. HAMILTON, *Secretary, National Headquarters*

This church does not deem it essential that a member of the clergy be present when death is imminent or sudden.

They have no opinions, rules or ritual regarding the removal, embalming, dressing, encasketing, cremation, earth or mausoleum interment. This may be accomplished and arranged for in the usual manner.

There are no services to prepare for prior to the regular funeral service, and no special equipment is needed on or about the encasketed remains.

It is preferred that the services be held at the church. The procedure of arrival at the church and method employed in handling the casket in all aspects of the church service may be governed by local church custom.

The flowers may be handled in the usual manner, and the family is free to select the casket bearers without restriction. The music usually consists of chorals.

When leaving the place where the services have been held, the minister will take the lead in front of the casket to the awaiting casket coach. The same procedure will hold true in the cemetery from the casket coach to the lowering device, and the minister will take his place at the head of the grave. The committal will follow according to local custom.

Southern Province Moravian Church
Informant:
REVEREND GEORGE C. HIGGINS, *Secretary of the Provincial Elder Conference, National Headquarters*

This church does not deem it a necessity that a member of the clergy be present when death is imminent or sudden.

They have no rules, ritual, or opinions on the removal, embalming, dressing, encasketing, cremation, earth or mausoleum interment. This may be taken care of and arranged in the usual manner.

The family is free to select the casket bearers and place of service without restriction. It is preferred the services be held in the church, and the family may select the music desired in consultation with the minister.

The methods employed in handling the casket during the church service may be governed by local church custom.

General Convention of New Jerusalem in the U. S. A.
Informant: HORACE B. BLACKMER, *Recording Secretary, National Headquarters*

This church does not demand the presence of the clergy when death is imminent or sudden.

They have no official opinions, rules, or ritual regarding the removal, embalming, dressing, encasketing, cremation, earth or mausoleum interment.

There are no services to prepare for prior to the regular funeral service, and no special equipment is needed on or about the encasketed remains.

The family may determine the casket bearers, and place of service without restriction. The present practice regarding the music is prelude and postlude music only.

953

The procedure on leaving the building where the services have been held may be left up to local custom.

If the services are held at the church, the casket should be so placed at least one-half hour before arrival of the congregation. The casket is usually left open for the service, however, if it is closed, individual tastes usually leave it closed.

In case of emergency, the minister would not object riding to the cemetery in the casket coach. Otherwise, he would prefer to furnish his own car.

Local cutom may determine the procedure from the casket coach to the lowering device. The minister will usually stand at the head of the grave. It is not required that the casket be lowered in the grave as ritual, but it is customary.

American Orthodox Church (Western Rite)
Informant: RT. REV. ALEXANDER TURNER, *Bishop Administrator, National Headquarters*

The ritual and procedure of the American Orthodox Church (Western Rite) are similar to those used in the Roman Catholic Church.

It is vital that a priest be called when death is imminent, or in case of sudden or unexpected death.

The church has no ritual or opinions regarding the removal, embalming, earth or mausoleum interment, but does oppose cremation.

In regard to dressing, all priests are vested in Eucharistic vestments. The usual procedure may govern the dressing and encasketing of all others.

The only service prior to the regular funeral service will be commendation of the soul at the time of death.

In regard to special equipment needed around the encasketed remains, the following is deemed necessary: Three long tapers should burn at the head and three at the foot. A crucifix should be nearby, and one may rest on the chest of the deceased. It is also desirable that the funeral director have Holy Water available at the mortuary and cemetery, and a black stole kept at the mortuary for the use of clergy who might visit during time of repose.

All funeral services are held at the church. Upon arrival at the church the priest will meet the casket coach, sprinkle the casket, and then it will be taken down the center aisle, near the altar rail, with feet toward the altar if a layman. If a priest the head will be closest to the altar. The candles will be placed at the head and foot of the casket, making sure there is enough room left all around the casket for the priest to move about.

Local custom may determine the display of flowers. It is always a closed casket service, and the casket is not opened again.

The family is free to select the casket bearers without restriction. In all probability, the church will have a pall to use over the casket.

On leaving the church, the priest will proceed first, followed by the casket, family and friends.

The music used during the service will be liturgical. Sentimental, seculars are not used.

On arrival at the cemetery the formation of the procession will be the same as entering and leaving the church. The priest will take his place at the foot of the grave.

In most cases, the priest and family will remain while the casket is lowered into the grave.

954

United Pentecostal Church

Informant: STANLEY W. CHAMBERS, *Secretary, National Headquarters*

This church does not deem it a necessity that a member of the clergy be called when death is imminent or sudden. They have no rules, ritual, opinions, etc., on the removal, embalming, dressing, encasketing, cremation, earth or mausoleum interment. All this may be arranged for, and taken care of in the usual manner.

There are no services to prepare for prior to the regular funeral service and no special equipment is needed on or about the encasketed remains. The family is free to select the casket bearers, music and place of service without restriction.

If the services are held at the church, local custom may determine how the casket is handled in all aspects.

Local customs may determine how the flowers are handled, procedure used in leaving the place the services have been held, and all aspects of the committal.

Pentecostal Holiness Church

Informant: REVEREND R. CORVIN, *General Secretary, National Headquarters*

This church does not deem it necessary that a member of their clergy be present when death is imminent or sudden. Neither do they have any opinions, rules, or ritual regarding the removal, embalming, cremation, dressing, encasketing, earth or mausoleum interment. There are no services to prepare for prior to the regular funeral service, and no special equipment is needed on or about the encasketed remains.

They prefer the funeral service be held in the church, but have no rule on this.

If the services are held in the church, local custom may dictate the procedure of arrival, how, when and where the casket may be handled in the church.

The family is free from restriction in their selection of casket bearers and music, as long as the music is sacred.

The flowers and entire committal service may be governed by local circumstances and custom.

Cumberland Presbyterian Church

Informant: H. S. SCATES, *Stated Clerk, National Headquarters*

This church does not feel it a necessity that a member of their clergy be present when death is imminent or sudden.

They have no ritual, rules, or opinions on the removal to the mortuary, embalming, dressing, encasketing, cremation, earth or mausoleum interment. These may be accomplished and arranged for in the usual manner.

The only service prior to the regular funeral service may be some simple prayers. No special equipment is needed on or about the encasketed remains.

The minister would prefer that the service be held in the church, but there is no official statement.

If the services are held in the church, the procedure of arrival and placement in the church may be ruled by local custom. The minister would prefer that the casket be placed prior to arrival of the congregation. Floral displays may be handled according to local custom.

Most services are held with the casket open.

The family may select the casket bearers and music without restriction.

On leaving the place where the services have been held, the minister will lead the procession to the casket coach.

The minister will take the lead from the casket coach to the lowering device and take his place at the head of the grave. The remaining portion of the committal may be governed by local custom.

Reformed Presbyterian Church in North America (General Synod)
Informant:
REVEREND ROBERT W. STEWART,
Stated Clerk, National Headquarters

This church does not deem it a necessity that a member of the clergy be present when death is imminent or sudden. They have no rules, opinions, or ritual regarding the removal, embalming, dressing, encasketing, cremation, earth or mausoleum interment. All this may be arranged and accomplished in the usual manner.

There are no services to prepare for prior to the regular funeral service, and no special equipment is needed on or about the encasketed remains.

The family may select the casket bearers, place of service, and music without restriction.

If the services are held in the church, the manner of arrival and how the casket is handled in the church before, during, and after services may be left to local church custom.

On leaving the place where the services have been held, the minister will probably precede the casket to the casket coach. The same will likely hold true at the cemetery from the casket coach to the lowering device.

The entire committal may be accomplished according to local custom.

Presbyterian Church in the U. S. (Southern Church)
Informant: ARCHIE C. SMITH, *Assistant to the Stated Clerk, National Headquarters*

The church does not deem it necessary for a member of their clergy to be present when death is imminent or sudden.

The church has no ritual, rules, or opinions regarding the removal, embalming, dressing, encasketing, earth or mausoleum interment, or cremation.

There are no services to prepare for prior to the regular funeral service, and no special equipment is needed on or about the encasketed remains.

The family is free to select the place of service, casket bearers, and music without restriction.

The flowers may be handled according to local custom.

If the services are held at the church, the procedure of arrival, how the casket is handled during the entire service, etc., may be left to local custom.

On leaving the place where the services have been held, the minister will take the lead to the casket coach. The same procedure will follow from the casket coach to the lowering device, and he will take his place at the head of the grave. The remainder of the committal will be governed by local custom.

Presbyterian Church in the U. S. A.
Informant: EUGENE C. BLAKE, *Stated Clerk, National Headquarters*

While there is no requirement for a clergyman to be present at the time of death, the Presbyterian clergyman always appreciates, as early as possible, notice, either in terms of immediate notification when death has occurred or in cases where there is a serious accident.

The removal, embalming, arrangements for burial or cremation, dressing, encasketing, etc., may be taken care of and arranged in the usual manner.

There are no services to prepare for prior to the regular funeral service, and no special equipment is needed on or about the encasketed remains.

This church official expressed the opinion that they would prefer to have the funeral service in the home or church, rather than the mortuary.

If the services are held in the church, arrangements should be made with the local pastor as to when the casket will be taken into the church and how it will be placed. Normally the casket is at the front of the church on the main floor of the auditorium, at the foot of chancel steps, or below the pulpit in central-pulpit churches.

Usually there is no ritual of taking the casket down the center aisle before the service, but after the service it is taken back up the aisle with the minister leading and the casket bearers following.

There are no church specifications in regard to music, but most ministers prefer hymns or sacred music and not various kinds of semi-popular or sentimental semi-sacred poetry.

The floral displays may be handled according to local custom.

It is preferred that the casket be closed during the service. They feel that the casket should not be opened after the service.

The family is not restricted regarding selection of casket bearers.

On leaving the building in which the services have been held, the minister will walk in front of the casket to the casket coach. The same procedure will follow true from the casket coach to the lowering device, and the minister will take his place at the head of the grave.

The minister should be consulted before the family has been allowed to make a decision as to the time the services will be held.

Reformed Presbyterian Church of North America
Informant: CHESTER B. FOX,
Stated Clerk, National Headquarters

This church does not deem it a necessity for the presence of the clergy when death is imminent or sudden.

They have no opinions, ritual, or rules regarding the removal to the mortuary, embalming, dressing, encasketing, cremation, earth or mausoleum interment. All this may be taken care of and arranged in the usual manner.

There are no services to prepare for prior to the regular funeral service, and no special equipment is needed on or about the encasketed remains.

The family is free to select the place of service and casket bearers without restriction. The music is Psalms, a Cappella. Flowers may be handled according to local custom.

If the services are held at the church, the procedure the way the casket is handled may be primarily governed by local custom. They do prefer an open casket service with casket toward the front, and want it so placed before arrival of the congregation.

On leaving the place where the services have been held, the minister will take the lead in front of the casket en route to the casket coach. The same formation will hold true en route from the casket coach to the lowering device, and he will take his place at the head of the grave. The remaining portion of the committal may be governed according to local custom.

United Presbyterian Church of North America
Informant: DR. S. W. SHANE, *Stated Clerk, National Headquarters*

This church does not feel it necessary for a member of their clergy to be present when death is imminent or sudden.

They have no opinions, ritual, or rules regarding the removal, embalming, dressing, encasketing, cremation, earth or mausoleum interment.

The minister may have prayer with the family prior to the regular service at either the home or mortuary.

There is no special equipment needed on or about the encasketed remains, and the choice of the place of service is left up to the family. They would prefer that no service be on Sunday, unless of necessity.

If the service is held in the church, the procedure of arrival and how the casket is handled in the church may be determined by local custom.

The family is free from restriction regarding the selection of casket bearers and music.

The entire committal service may be governed by local custom.

Rabbinical Council of America
Informant: ISRAEL KLAVAN, *Executive Secretary, National Headquarters*

This group of the Jewish religion does not deem it necessary that a Rabbi be present when death is imminent or sudden, but it is very desirable. They would appreciate being called as soon as possible.

They have no rules or ritual regarding the removal of the remains to the mortuary, but embalming is forbidden, as is cremation, and mausoleum interment. They require an earth burial, one person to a grave.

After the remains have been moved to the mortuary, it is prepared by restricted members of the faith, in accordance with a specific ritual. It is then dressed in a white shroud, and a prayer shawl, in case of men, and placed in the casket.

Candles are placed next to the encasketed remains, usually two tapers at the head.

Funerals in the synagogue are discouraged. They are usually held in the home or mortuary; it is felt that the home is most desirable.

In rare cases when the synagogue is used, the officers of the synagogue will decide on the procedure to be followed.

Very frequently after the funeral service, the funeral procession will go by the synagogue where the decedent worshipped and stop. The door of the casket coach and synagogue are opened and memorial prayers are given.

Flowers are not used and the casket is closed during the service. They would prefer it not be opened after the service. A special cloth covering is used as a pall over the casket. The Rabbi usually rides in the front seat of the family car to the cemetery.

From the casket coach to the grave, the Rabbi will precede and make seven stops en route to the grave. It is immaterial where he stands in relation to the grave.

The casket is lowered and the grave covered as part of the committal ritual. Prayers are said during this procedure.

958

It is desired that the casket be of plain wood without nails or metal trimmings. In all probability, an overcase or outside box will be forbidden.

Central Conference of American Rabbis
Informant: SOUEY E. REGNER, *Executive Vice-President, National Headquarters*

This group of the Jewish religion does not feel the necessity of a Rabbi when death is imminent or sudden, but it is advisable to notify the Rabbi, who is to officiate, as soon as possible.

They have no opinions, rules, or ritual as to the removal, embalming, dressing, encasketing, cremation, earth or mausoleum interment. This may be taken care of and arranged in the usual manner.

There are no services to prepare for prior to the regular funeral service. While the remains are lying in state, candles, or a candelabra are used. Consult the local officiating Rabbi in this regard.

The family is free to select the place of service and casket bearers without restriction.

If the services are held at the synagogue, the casket is placed in the synagogue closed, prior to arrival of the congregation and usually is not opened again. Consult the officiating Rabbi regarding any other aspects of the service.

Flowers may be handled according to local custom.

Consult the officiating Rabbi regarding the procession from the place where the services have been held to the casket coach, and from the casket coach to the lowering device over the grave. The Rabbi will stand at the head of the grave. The remainder of the committal may be governed by local custom.

Do not confuse the Reform Rabbis with Orthodox or Conservative groups.

Reformed Church in America
Informant: REVEREND JAMES E. HOFFMAN, *Stated Clerk, National Headquarters*

This church does not deem it a necessity that a member of the clergy be present when death is imminent or sudden.

They have no rules, opinions, or ritual regarding the removal, embalming, dressing, encasketing, cremation, earth or mausoleum interment. All this may be accomplished in the usual manner.

There are no services to prepare for prior to the regular funeral service, and no special equipment is needed on or about the encasketed remains.

The place of the funeral service, selection of music and casket bearers may be made without restriction.

If the services are held at the church, procedure of arrival and the method employed in handling the casket may be determined by local custom.

The flowers may be handled according to local custom.

On leaving the place where the services have been held, the minister will take the lead, ahead of the casket. The procedure will hold true from the casket coach to the lowering device.

The remaining portion of the committal may be handled according to local custom.

Romanian Orthodox Church
Informant: REVEREND EUGENE LAZAR, *Secretary, National Headquarters*

This church does not deem it a necessity that a priest be present when death is imminent or sudden.

They have no rules, ritual, or opinions regarding the removal, embalming, encasketing, earth or mausoleum interment. Cremation is forbidden. If the deceased is a priest the removal may vary from that of a layman and the dressing will be under the supervision of a priest.

There are evening prayers where the remains are lying in state prior to the day of the funeral service. Candles are usually placed at the head and foot of the encasketed remains.

The services may be held at the home or church, or perhaps the mortuary in some localities.

If the services are held at the church there will be a short service at the mortuary immediately prior to going to the church.

The music is determined by the church.

The casket will be taken into the church and down the center aisle, feet first, in formal procedure, and placed near the altar rail in this position, after which the casket is opened.

Selection of casket bearers may be left to the discretion of the family or organization of which the deceased may have been a member.

When leaving the place where the services have been held, the priest will precede the procession followed by a cantor and casket.

The same will hold true at the cemetery from the casket coach to the lowering device. Usually a short prayer is said when placing the casket into or taking the casket from the casket coach.

The priest will take his place at the head of the grave and customarily the casket is lowered as part of the committal ritual.

960

Russian Orthodox Greek Catholic Church of North America

Informant: REVEREND JOSEPH P. KRETA, *National Headquarters*

This church does not deem it a necessity that a member of the clergy be present when death is imminent or sudden. They have no rules, ritual, or opinions, regarding the removal, embalming, dressing, encasketing, earth or mausoleum interment. Cremation is forbidden.

A Requiem service is held on the evening preceding the funeral service. While the deceased is lying in state, a cross is placed nearby or fastened on the casket. All services are held at the church if possible.

When leaving the mortuary or home, for the church, arrangements should be made for the priest to escort the remains to the church. The casket will be taken into the church head first, and down the center aisle with the priest leading and the congregation following. The casket will be placed lengthwise with the aisle with head toward the altar, and open. Arrangement of flowers may be governed by local custom.

Only prescribed church music is used during the funeral.

The family may select the casket bearers without restriction.

On leaving the place where the services have been held, the priest, or church reader, will precede the casket alone to the casket coach. The same will hold true at the cemetery from the casket coach to the lowering device. The priest will take his place at the foot of the casket.

Custom teaches that all participating should sprinkle dirt or flower petals at the end of the committal. The priest will indicate when to lower the casket.

International General Assembly of Spiritualists

Informant: WILLIAM BLOUNT DARDEN, *Secretary, National Headquarters*

The church does not feel the necessity of the presence of a clergyman when death is imminent or sudden from a ritualistic point of view. They do, however, prefer to have prayer with the family soon after death has occurred.

No ritual, opinion, or rules are expressed in the removal to the mortuary, embalming, dressing, encasketing, cremation, earth or mausoleum interment. All this may be taken care of in the usual manner.

The only service prior to the regular funeral services are prayers with the family which in all probability would not affect the mortuary service.

The family is free to select the place of service, music and casket bearers without restriction.

If the services are held at the church, the casket is placed in front of the church near the altar rail with head to the left.

The casket is taken in the church after arrival of the congregation, but before the arrival of the family. It may either be opened or closed during the service. Local custom may determine. Flowers may be handled according to local custom.

The church feels that when the casket has been closed, it should remain closed, unless specifically requested by the immediate family to open it.

On leaving the place where the services have been held, the casket is first in the procession followed by the minister, family and congregation.

The minister would probably prefer to furnish his own car to travel to the cemetery rather than ride in the casket coach.

At the cemetery, the minister will go to the head of the grave and await the arrival of the casket and congregation.

The remainder of the committal may be handled according to local custom.

Syrian Antiochian Orthodox Church

Informant: FATHER ELIA, *Secretary, National Headquarters*

The presence of a priest when death is imminent or sudden is a necessity.

They have no ritual, opinions, or rules, regarding the removal, embalming, dressing, encasketing, cremation, earth or mausoleum interment. This may be taken care of in the usual manner.

They do have a service prior to the regular funeral service, which can be worked out with the local priest. No special equipment is needed on or about the encasketed remains.

The funeral services should be from the church.

The arrival at the church may be handled according to local church custom. There is no formal procedure in taking the casket in the church. This may be handled according to local custom.

The casket will be placed near the altar rail, facing east. Flowers are not permitted in the church, and the casket will remain closed and not be opened again. The church provides the music. The family is free to select the casket bearers without restriction.

At the cemetery, the priest will lead the procession and stand at the head of the grave. He will sprinkle sand on the casket. The funeral di-

961

rector might provide such for him.

All other aspects of the committal may be handled according to local custom.

Ukrainian Orthodox Church of U. S. A.
Informant:
VERY REVEREND D. D. LESCHISHIN,
Secretary of the Consistory,
National Headquarters

This church deems it necessary that a clergyman be present when death is imminent or sudden.

They have no rules, opinions, or ritual regarding the removal, embalming, dressing, encasketing, earth or mausoleum interment. Cremation is forbidden. They do have a service prior to the regular funeral service, which may be explained by the local clergyman.

While the remains are lying in state, the equipment needed about the encasketed remains are the cross and candles on each end.

All funeral services are held at the church.

The procedure of arrival at the church may be determined by local church custom. The casket may be taken down the center aisle of the church as a matter of formal procedure, and placed near the altar rail and remain closed during the service. It may be opened after the service is over.

There is no music in connection with the funeral service.

Palls are not used.

The family is free to select the casket bearers without restriction.

On leaving the place where the services have been held the clergyman will take the lead in front of the casket to the casket coach.

At the cemetery local custom may determine the procedure from the casket coach to the lowering device.

The clergyman will take his place at the foot of the grave. The rest of the committal may be determined by local custom.

Universalist Church of America
Informant: PHILIP RANDALL GILES,
Director, Department of Ministry,
National Headquarters

This church does not deem it necessary that a member of the clergy be present when death is imminent or sudden, from a ritualistic view, but it is highly desirable and recommended.

There are no official church opinions, rules, or ritual regarding the removal, embalming, dressing, encasketing, cremation, earth or mausoleum interment. This may be arranged for and accomplished in the usual manner. Any opinions individual ministers express regarding these things are purely personal.

There are no services to prepare for prior to the regular funeral service, and no special equipment is needed on or about the encasketed remains.

The family is free to select the casket bearers without restriction. Floral arrangements may be handled according to local custom. If the services are held in the church the music selected should have church sanction.

If the services are held from the church, they like the closed casket placed therein prior to the arrival of the congregation. The balance of the service may be governed by local church custom.

When leaving the place where the services have been held, the minister will take the lead in front of the casket to the awaiting casket coach. The same will hold true at the cemetery, from the casket coach to the lowering device. The minister will take his place at the head of the grave.

The remainder of the committal may be governed by local custom.

Volunteers of America
Informant: COLONEL JOHN F. McMAHON, National Secretary, National Headquarters

This church does not consider it necessary that a clergyman be present when death is imminent or sudden from a ritualistic view.

They have no opinions, rules, or ritual on the removal, embalming, dressing, encasketing, cremation, earth or mausoleum interment. This may be taken care of and arranged in the usual manner.

There are no services to prepare for prior to the regular funeral service, and no special equipment is needed on or about the encasketed remains.

The family may select the place of service, music and casket bearers without restriction.

If the services are held at the church, local church custom may dictate the procedure in all aspects.

The floral arrangements may be handled according to local custom.

Local custom may determine the procedure on leaving the place the services have been held, arrival and procedure of the committal service, in all aspects.

PART TWO : Fraternal Organizations

American Legion
Informant: American Legion Ritual, National Headquarters

The American Legion service is non-sectarian, therefore it may be varied in accordance with the religious belief of the deceased comrade. The wishes of the family of the deceased, and of the officiating pastor, should be respected.

The American Legion has both a regular funeral service to be officiated inside a building and committal service at the grave. They will officiate at either one or both, depending on the wishes of the family.

There is no necessity that an officer be present when death is imminent or sudden. They have no rules, ritual or opinions, regarding the removal, embalming, dressing, encasketing, cremation, earth or mausoleum interment. This may be taken care of in the usual manner.

There are no services to prepare for prior to the regular funeral service, and the only special equipment

needed will be the American Flag on the casket.

The family is free to select the place of service, music and casket bearers without restriction, unless it is an American Legion service. In that case, the casket bearers should be uniformed members.

Ranks will be formed on arrival at the place where the services are to be held and on leaving, with the chaplain leading the procession in front of the casket. The same formation holds true at the cemetery when ranks are formed from the casket coach to the lowering device. The chaplain will take his place at the head of the grave.

The casket bearers may prefer to walk three on each side of a slow moving casket coach, firing squad, family, American Legion members, distinguished persons, societies, and others.

If the Legion members walk any portion of the distance from the

963

place where the services have been held to the place of committal, the cortege will take the following formation: Band, colors, chaplain and bugler, followed by casket bearers. The casket will be entirely surrounded by members of the organization performing their official duties.

American Legion Auxiliary
Informant: JANE GOULD RITHWORTH, *National Secretary, National Headquarters*

This organization has both a funeral and committal service, and at the request of the family they will officiate at either or both.

In all matters, the wishes of the family and officiating minister will be respected.

They have no ritual, rules, or opinions regarding the removal, dressing, encasketing, cremation, earth or mausoleum interment. All this may be taken care of and arranged in the usual manner.

There are no services to prepare for prior to the regular funeral service, and no special equipment is needed on or about the encasketed remains.

The family is free to select the casket bearers, music and place of service without restriction.

If the organization officiates at the funeral service, just before the closing, the members will wish it to be convenient to go by the casket and deposit a flower in or on it.

At the committal, the unit president will stand where most convenient. The remainder of the committal may be governed by local custom.

B'nai B'rith
Informant: Ritual sent from National Headquarters

This is a Jewish organization. They do not presume to overshadow or interfere with any branch of the Jewish religion the deceased may have been a member of. (Conservative, Reform, or Orthodox.)

They have a memorial service which is officiated sometimes prior to the regular funeral service. The equipment needed is a seven-branch Menorah, the Tables of the Law, the Bible, and symbols of B'nai B'rith. An appropriate place is needed to place these symbols in regard to the position of the encasketed remains.

National Society of the Daughters of the American Revolution
Informant: MISS GERTRUDE CARRAWAY, *President General, National Headquarters*

This organization does not consider it necessary for the presence of an official when death is imminent or sudden.

They have no rules, opinions, ritual, etc., on the removal, embalming, dressing, encasketing, cremation, earth or mausoleum interment. This may be taken care of and arranged in the usual manner.

There is no special equipment needed on or about the encasketed remains and no services are necessary to prepare prior to the regular funeral service.

The family is free to select the place of service, casket bearers, and music without restriction.

If the services are held at the church, there is no procedure to consider as far as the D.A.R. is concerned.

Order of De Molay
Informant: CHARLES A. BOYCE, *Executive Assistant to the Secretary General, National Headquarters*

This order has no rules, ritual, or opinions regarding the removal, embalming, dressing, encasketing, cremation, earth or mausoleum inter-

964

ment. This may be taken care of, and arranged in the usual manner.

There is no special equipment needed on or about the encasketed remains. The family is free to select the place of service and casket bearers without restriction.

In some cases a choir sings after certain ritualistic parts.

Flowers may be taken care of according to local custom.

The De Molay service may be officiated at the home, church, mortuary, or cemetery. If not at the cemetery, it will usually follow the regular funeral service.

There are no rules regarding the formation of ranks to the casket coach, or from the casket coach to the lowering device. If the service is officiated at the cemetery, the officers will take stations around the grave with the presiding officer standing at the head.

The balance of the committal may be accomplished according to local custom.

Order of Eastern Star
Informant: Mrs. Mamie Lander, *Right Worthy Grand Secretary, National Headquarters*

This organization does not deem it a necessity that an official be present when death is imminent or sudden. They have no rules, opinions, or ritual regarding the removal, embalming, dressing, encasketing, cremation, earth or mausoleum interment. This may be arranged for in the usual manner.

There is no special equipment needed on or about the encasketed remains, and generally there are no services to prepare for prior to the regular funeral service.

Sometimes the Eastern Star service is officiated the evening before the regular funeral service, but generally is incorporated into the regular funeral service. It may be officiated at the place the services are held or at the cemetery.

No special equipment is needed on or about the encasketed remains, and the family is free to select the place of service, casket bearers and music without restriction.

Ranks are not formed from the place the services are held to the casket coach, or from the casket coach to the lowering device.

Benevolent and Protective Order of Elks
Informant: Wade H. Kepner, *Past Grand Exalted Ruler, et al, National Headquarters*

This organization does not deem it a necessity that an official be present when death is imminent or sudden.

They have no rules, ritual, or opinions on the removal, embalming, dressing, encasketing, cremation, earth or mausoleum interment. All this may be taken care of and arranged in the usual manner.

There is no special equipment needed on or about the encasketed remains and the family is free to select the place of service, casket bearers, and music without restriction.

The Elks have both a regular funeral service and committal service. At the request of the family they officiate with either or both. If the funeral service is strictly Elks, there is no need of a minister. The service may vary in length from ten minutes to thirty minutes, depending on music and poetry involved.

If such a service is held in an Elks Lodge hall or mortuary, the casket is usually placed at the front of the hall, well to one side of the center. During the service the Elks will place a small American flag on the casket and the members will file past the casket placing a small flower on top of same. The officers will file into the hall in formal procession and leave formally.

The officers will form themselves around the casket at the grave and the presiding officer will take his place at the head of the grave.

The balance of the committal may be governed by local custom.

The National Grange
Informant: HARRY A. CATON, *Secretary, National Headquarters*

This organization has no requirements that an official be present when death is imminent or sudden, neither do they have any opinion, rules, or ritual regarding the removal, embalming, dressing, encasketing, cremation, earth or mausoleum interment.

The family is free to select the casket bearers, place of service, and music without restriction. No special equipment is needed on or about the encasketed remains.

Local custom may determine the way the flowers are taken care of.

The Grange has both an optional grave and mortuary service. They are not designed to take the place of a regular Christian service. Local circumstances may determine the order of service.

The formation of the procession on leaving the place where the services have been held to the casket coach and from the casket coach to the lowering device may be determined by local custom.

At the cemetery, the ritual calls for the deposit of evergreen on the casket. They have no stipulation as to where the officers stand in relation to the casket.

The remainder of the committal may be determined by local custom.

Imperial Order of Dragon
Informant: ENOCH R. L. JONES, SR., *Grand Custodian Archives-Finance, National Headquarters*

This organization has no opinion, rules or ritual regarding the necessity of the presence of an official when death is imminent, removal, embalming, dressing, encasketing, cremation, earth or mausoleum interment.

There is no service to prepare for prior to the regular funeral service, and no special equipment is needed on or about the encasketed remains.

The family is free to select the place of service, casket bearers, and music without restriction.

All aspects of the service and committal may be taken care of according to local custom.

Knights of the Golden Eagle
Informant: FRED W. ANTON, *Supreme Master of Records, National Headquarters*

This Lodge has no rules, ritual, or opinions regarding the presence of an official when death is imminent or sudden, removal, embalming, dressing, encasketing, cremation, earth or mausoleum interment. This may be taken care of and arranged in the usual manner.

There are no services to prepare for prior to the regular service, and no special equipment is needed on or about the encasketed remains.

The family is free to select the casket bearers, music and place of service without restriction.

The Lodge has only one service. This service may be officiated either inside where the regular funeral service is held, or at the grave. In either case, the presiding officer will stand at the head of the casket, chaplain in the center, and other members at the side facing the casket.

This Lodge service is officiated after the regular funeral service.

There are no regulations regarding the formation of the ranks from the place where the services have been held to the casket coach, or from the casket coach to the lowering device.

The cars carrying the lodge members shall lead the automotive cortege preceded only by the casket coach.

After the lodge ceremony at the grave, local custom may govern the procedure.

Knights of Pythias
Informant: Pythian Service Book, et al.

This Lodge does not deem it a necessity that an official be present when death is imminent or sudden, neither do they have any opinion, ritual, or rules on the removal, embalming, dressing, encasketing, cremation, earth or mausoleum interment. This may be arranged in the usual manner.

They have both a service for inside a mortuary or other appropriate place and the graveside.

If the service for inside is officiated, the casket should be so placed that the Chancellor Commander may stand at the head and Vice-Chancellor and Prelate will stand on opposite sides of the casket near the foot end, forming a triangle.

Ranks are generally formed on all occasions when the casket is being formally moved, such as from the place the services have been held to the casket coach, and from the casket coach to the lowering device. The nights of Pythias will officiate for either or both services, depending on the wishes of the family.

At the grave, the Chancellor Commander will stand at the head and the Vice-Chancellor at the foot, with two other officials on opposite sides. After the Knights finish with the ritualistic work, the balance of committal may be governed by local custom.

The family is free to select the place of service, casket bearers, and music without restriction. Flowers may be governed by local custom.

Maccabees
Informant: D. A. TULUCCI, Director of Public Relations, National Headquarters

This organization has no rules, ritual, or opinions as to the need of the presence of an official, when death is imminent or sudden, the removal, embalming, dressing, encasketing, cremation, earth or mausoleum interment.

There are no services to prepare for prior to the regular funeral service, and no special equipment is needed on or about the encasketed remains.

The family is free to select the music and place of service without restriction. Casket bearers should be restricted to lodge members, if a lodge ceremony is requested.

The lodge has both a service to be officiated inside and a committal service. The ceremony used inside in no way serves to augment the regular church service. The Maccabee ritual does not state the necessity of an open or closed casket service.

The officiating officers will stand at the head of the casket both at the cemetery conducted inside and at the committal.

There are no requirements that ranks be formed from the place the services are held to the casket coach, or from the casket coach to the lowering device.

The remainder of the committal may be governed by local custom.

Masons (Ancient Free and Accepted Masons) A. F. & A. M.

Informant: HARRY W. BUNDY, *Grand Secretary and* GILES N. ALKIRE, *Grand Lecturer, State of Colorado, State Headquarters*

NOTE: There is no national headquarters for the Masons. Each state is supreme and independent. All masonic work is generally similar, but there are minor variations in various aspects of the work from state to state.

The Masons do not require the presence of an official when death is imminent or sudden. They have no rules, opinions, or ritual regarding the removal, embalming, encasketing, cremation, earth or mausoleum interment. The dressing may be accomplished in the usual manner, except it may be requested that a white square leather apron be placed on the deceased with the top of the apron at the belt line.

The Masonic service must be the last rite given the deceased. All other services must precede it.

There is no special equipment needed on or about the encasketed remains with the possible exception in clothing mentioned above, and there are no services to prepare for prior to the regular funeral service.

The family is free to select the music and place of service without restriction as far as the masonic aspects of the service are concerned.

Generally the casket bearers must be Masons, clothed as such. They will wear a square white apron, white gloves, a black band around the left arm and a sprig of evergreen in the left lapel. The sprig of evergreen is later deposited in the grave.

The way the casket is placed in the building where the services are held may be determined by local custom. The Masons generally take charge of the remains at the end of the regular funeral service, when the casket is moved to the casket coach. They will form ranks from the door of the building where the services have been held to the awaiting casket coach, and from the casket coach to the lowering device. The Master of the lodge will take his place at the head of the grave and members will form ranks around the casket, except the foot and should present a clear view for the family.

Technically, the casket bearers for the deceased need not be Masons until the Master of the lodge takes charge of the remains. If the Master does not take charge until the casket is placed on the lowering device (no ranks will be formed), the bearers need not be Masons. Such technicalities should be discussed with the local Master before any decisions are made.

Loyal Order of Moose

Informant: GEORGE EUBANK, *Supreme Secretary, National Headquarters*

This organization has no rules, ritual, or opinions regarding the necessity of an official when death is imminent or sudden, removal, embalming, dressing, encasketing, cremation, earth or mausoleum interment. This may be taken care of and arranged in the usual manner.

There are no services to prepare for prior to the time of the regular funeral service, and no special equipment is needed on or about the encasketed remains.

The family is free to select the place of service, casket bearers, and music without restriction.

968

The Moose funeral service consists of two parts: One part is specifically provided for the place where the service is held, and the second at the site of committal. The family and local officiating Moose Lodge may determine which part or parts are desired.

Forming ranks from the place the services have been held to the casket coach and from the casket coach to the lowering device is optional.

There are no specifications as to where the officers should stand in regards to the casket.

All other aspects of the service and committal may be governed by local custom.

Neighbors of Woodcraft
Informant: FAUN P. RUEDY, *Grand Clerk, National Headquarters*

This Order has no rules, opinions, or ritual regarding the presence of an official when death is imminent, embalming, removal, dressing, encasketing, cremation, earth or mausoleum interment. All this may be arranged for and taken care of in the usual manner.

There is a funeral ceremony which the local Lodge officers will officiate if requested. It may be accomplished prior to the regular funeral service. No special equipment is needed on or about the encasketed remains. If the services are in a church, it would be well to check with church policy regarding organizations.

If the local Circle is officiating at the mortuary, they would prefer the casket be placed before arrival of the congregation.

When leaving the place where the services have been held, they will wish to form ranks from the door to the casket coach.

At the committal, the Guardian Neighbor will stand at the head of the grave. After the Lodge is finished, the balance of the committal may be completed according to local custom.

Independent Order of Odd Fellows (I. O. O. F.)
Informant: EDWARD G. LUDVIGSEN, *Sovereign Grand Secretary*

This order has no national rules, rituals, or opinions regarding the necessity of the presence of an official when death is imminent, removal, embalming, dressing, encasketing, cremation, earth or mausoleum interment. This may be taken care of in the usual manner.

There are no services to prepare for prior to the regular funeral service, and no special equipment is needed on or about the encasketed remains.

The family may select the casket bearers, place of service, and music without restrictions.

All aspects of the service and committal may be governed by local custom.

P. E. O.
Informant: Personal Research

This organization does not deem it a necessity that an official be present when death is sudden or imminent, neither do they have any rules, ritual, or opinions on the removal, embalming, dressing, encasketing, cremation, earth or mausoleum interment.

As far as the P.E.O. is concerned, the family may select the casket bearers, place of service, and music without restriction.

Members may be interred with their P.E.O. star pin.

A P.E.O. guard should be present at the place of service to guide the members to correct seating. Each member carries a yellow or white flower. A floral star piece is furnished which should be on or near the casket. If the star is placed on the casket the treasurer should carry it to the cemetery. Prior to the service an official of the P.E.O. should consult with the funeral director to inform him of P.E.O. customs.

The officials will form a star around the casket during the interment ritual. The burial ritual is divided so that part of it may be officiated at the place of the funeral service and the remainder at the graveside, or it may all be officiated at the graveside.

The remainder of the committal may be governed by local custom.

The membership will file by the casket leaving their flower on the casket.

The regular officiating minister will be called for benediction.

Order of Pythian Sisters
Informant: Manual of Procedure in Funeral Service

This order does not deem it a necessity that an official be present when death is imminent or sudden, neither do they have any opinion, ritual, or rules on the removal, embalming, dressing, encasketing, cremation, earth or mausoleum interment. This may be arranged for in the usual manner.

The family is free to select the casket bearers, place of service, and music without restriction. Flowers may be taken care of according to local custom.

No special equipment is needed on or about the encasketed remains, and there are no services to prepare for prior to the regular funeral service.

There are no specifications calling for the formation ranks around or about the casket coach in the revised changes.

The ritual is designed to be officiated at the graveside after all religious ceremonies have been concluded. The officiating officer will take stations around the grave with the head officers standing at the head. The officers carry flowers and the Sisters sprigs of white pine.

During the committal service the Pythian Sisters will in turn place the flowers, sprigs of evergreen, etc., on the casket. The remainder of the committal may be governed by local custom.

Order of Rainbow Girls
Informant: LETA SEXSON, et al, National Headquarters

This Order does not feel it necessary for an official to be present when death is imminent or sudden. Neither have they any rules, ritual, or opinions regarding the removal, embalming, dressing, encasketing, cremation, earth or mausoleum interment.

There are no services to prepare for prior to the regular funeral service, and no special equipment is needed on or about the encasketed remains.

The family is free to select the place of service, casket bearers, and music without restriction.

The Rainbow Girls may officiate with the one ceremony either at the cemetery or inside the building where the services have been held. In most cases, the officiating will be done at the cemetery or place of interment.

It would be well to see that seats are reserved for the members who will form ranks from the chapel or church door to the casket coach, and the same will hold true from the casket coach to the grave. The presiding officer will take her place at the head of the grave.

The balance of the committal may take place according to local custom.

Rebekahs
Informant: MRS. ALICE SHIVELY, *and Personal Research, National Headquarters*

This Order does not feel it necessary that an official be present when death is imminent or sudden, neither do they have any rules, ritual, or opinions on the removal, embalming, dressing, encasketing, cremation, earth or mausoleum interment.

There are no services to prepare for prior to the regular funeral service, and no special equipment is needed on or about the encasketed remains. The family may delegate the selection of the casket bearers to the Order if they so wish.

The Rebekah service may be officiated at the home, mortuary, church, or graveside.

If the service is officiated inside a building, it may be requested that the casket be so placed that the membership may file by with locked fingers over the remains.

The Noble Grand will officiate from the head of the casket.

If the services are confined to the graveside the membership will form ranks from the casket coach to the lowering device, through which the casket and bearers will pass.

After the officiating minister finishes the members will take their stations around the casket with the Noble Grand at the head. The membership will file by the casket depositing a flower.

The balance of the committal will be governed by local custom.

Improved Order of Redmen
Informant: WALTER T. GROSS, *Great Chief of Records, National Headquarters*

This organization does not deem it necessary that an official be present when death is imminent or sudden. They have no rules, ritual, or opinions regarding the removal, embalming, dressing, encasketing, cremation, earth or mausoleum interment. This may be taken care of and arranged in the usual manner.

The family is free to select the place of service, music, and casket bearers without restriction.

No special equipment is needed on or about the encasketed remains.

The Redmen have a ritualistic service for both their regular funeral service and committal.

If the regular funeral service is used, it would be appropriate to have the casket placed so that the officiating officers may take their stations around it.

When the committal is used, the officiating officers will take their stations at the foot of the grave.

There are no regulations regarding the formation of ranks to pass through and the ritual does not require the casket be opened if a closed casket service is desired.

All other aspects of the service and committal may be taken care of in the usual manner.

Royal Neighbors of America
Informant: ANNA B. SPANGLER, *Supreme Oracle, National Headquarters*

The Royal Neighbor ritual is very flexible. They attempt to conform with any rules that the church may have regarding procedure.

They have no opinions, rules, or ritual regarding the need of an official when death is imminent, removal, embalming, dressing, encasketing, cremation, earth or mausoleum interment. All this may be taken care of and arranged in the usual manner.

There are no services to prepare for prior to the regular funeral services, and no special equipment is needed on or about the encasketed remains.

The family is free to select the place of service, casket bearers, and music without restriction.

All aspects of the funeral service may be handled according to local custom.

At the committal the presiding officer will stand at the head of the grave.

A Royal Neighbor service has nothing to do with final rites at the grave. The remainder of the committal may be governed by local custom.

National Society of the Sons of The American Revolution (S.A.R.)
Informant: Harold L. Putman, *Secretary, National Headquarters*

This organization sees no necessity that an official be present when death is imminent or sudden. They have no rules, ritual, or opinions regarding the removal, embalming, dressing, encasketing, cremation, earth or mausoleum interment. All this may be arranged in the usual manner.

The family is free to select the place of service and music without restriction. It is preferred that the casket bearers be members of the S.A.R.

The ritual of the S.A.R. has been designed to be used in conjunction with any religious ceremony. The membership represents all faiths.

The S.A.R. ritual is designed to be officiated inside the building where the funeral service is to be held. The casket must be opened as they place a symbol of the order and flower inside the casket and a small American flag on top. There should also be adequate room at the head and foot of the casket for the placement of the American flag and S.A.R. flags.

All other aspects of the service, including leaving the place where the services have been held, arrival at the cemetery and entire committal may be governed by local custom.

Veterans of Foreign Wars of the United States
Informant: E. L. Jenkins, *Assistant to Adjutant General and Ritual, National Headquarters*

This organization has no rules, ritual, or opinions regarding the presence of an official when death is imminent, or the removal, embalming, dressing, encasketing, cremation, earth or mausoleum interment.

In most every case the family is free to select casket bearers, place of service and music without restriction.

In some instances it may be suggested that all the casket bearers be uniformed members of the organization, and they might further suggest one of the music selections be "Sleep, Soldier Boy, Sleep."

The V.F.W. has both a regular funeral service and a committal service. Either one or both may be officiated.

If the funeral service is officiated by the V.F.W. the casket should be so placed that the flag may be raised to place floral articles beneath it.

The V.F.W. will form ranks to pass through both at the place where the services have been held, and at the cemetery.

972

The funeral director may or may not be given the flag to present to the family.

Ranks will be formed around the casket after it has been placed on the lowering device. Lowering the casket is not part of the V.F.W. ritual.

Veterans of Foreign Wars of the United States Ladies Auxiliary
Informant: Portions of Ritual

This organization does not deem it a necessity that an official be present when death is imminent or sudden, neither do they have any ritual, opinion, or rules regarding the removal, embalming, dressing, encasketing, cremation, earth or mausoleum interment. This may be arranged for in the usual manner.

They have one service which may be officiated in the building where the funeral services are held or at the graveside. Any portion of their ritual that may conflict with church dogma may be omitted. If the services are officiated inside the church or mortuary, the ritual is designed for the Auxiliary to officiate first, followed by the minister. The Auxiliary will sing "Abide With Me," and "Lead Kindly Light."

The casket should be so placed so the officers may stand around it. An emblematic flag will be placed on the casket, which is later removed, and the membership will file by the casket placing a flower thereon.

The remainder of the committal may be governed by local custom.

Modern Woodmen of America
Informant: HENRY R. FREITAG, *Director of Public Relations and Ritual, National Headquarters*

This organization does not deem it a necessity that an official be present when death is imminent or sudden, neither do they have any ritual, rules, or opinions on the removal, embalming, dressing, encasketing, cremation, earth or mausoleum interment. This may be arranged for in the usual manner.

Flowers may be handled according to local custom. The family is free to select the place of service, music and casket bearers without restriction.

There are no services to prepare for prior to the regular funeral service, and no special equipment is needed on or about the encasketed remains.

The Modern Woodmen have both a service to be officiated inside and at the grave. The entire service may be officiated at the grave if desired. If the service is officiated inside, the officiating officer will stand near the head of the casket.

At the cemetery, the membership will drop flowers or evergreen sprigs on the casket. If the service is confined to the cemetery, a minister may be used to offer some prayers.

The balance of the committal may be governed by local custom.